STRUCTURED PROGRAMMING USING PASCAL

J. WINSTON CRAWLEY

WILLIAM G. McARTHUR

Shippensburg University

PRENTICE HALL
ENGLEWOOD CLIFFS, NEW JERSEY 07632

Library of Congress Cataloging-in-Publication Data

CRAWLEY, J. WINSTON.
  Structured programming using PASCAL.

  Includes index.
  1. PASCAL (Computer program language)
2. Structured programming. I. McArthur, William G.,
1940-   . II. Title.
QA76.73.P2C73 1988   005.13′3   87-29068
ISBN 0-13-854035-7

Editorial/production supervision: Elena LePera
Interior design: Lorraine Mullaney
Cover design: Jayne Conte
Manufacturing buyer: Ed O'Dougherty

 © 1988, by Prentice-Hall, Inc.
A Division of Simon & Schuster
Englewood Cliffs, New Jersey 07632

Printed in the United States of America
10 9 8 7 6 5 4 3 2 1

ISBN 0-13-854035-7 025

Prentice-Hall International (UK) Limited, *London*
Prentice-Hall of Australia Pty. Limited, *Sydney*
Prentice-Hall Canada Inc., *Toronto*
Prentice-Hall Hispanoamericana, S.A., *Mexico*
Prentice-Hall of India Private Limited, *New Delhi*
Prentice-Hall of Japan, Inc., *Tokyo*
Simon & Schuster Southeast Asia Pte. Ltd., *Singapore*
Editora Prentice-Hall do Brasil, Ltda., *Rio de Janeiro*

To parents,

Winston and Margaret Crawley

wives,

Margaret Crawley
and
Cathy McArthur

and children,

Allyson and Winston Crawley
and
Alex, Bill, and Katie McArthur

USING
PASCAL

Input:	Length	Real	Length of rectangle
	Width	Real	Width of rectangle
Output:	Area	Real	Area of rectangle

Along with planning the data, we begin our plan for the program. If we were calculating the area of a single rectangle, we might list this sequence of steps:

ask the user to enter a length and a width
read values for Length and Width variables
calculate the value for the Area variable (Length times Width)
print the value of the Area variable

Because we are to write a program that handles many rectangles, we realize we will need a loop structure. The program must repeat the four steps listed above a number of times.

As with all the loops we will write, we must decide on how to terminate the loop. Although there are a number of possible ways to achieve this **loop control**, we will concentrate on one specific technique for the early part of this text. This technique consists of asking the person using the program (the user) to supply some special value as input, to signal that there are no more rectangles to be processed. For example, we might use a value of 0 for the Length variable as a signal that the repetition should cease. This special value is referred to by many names, including **sentinel**, **terminal value**, **dummy value**, **trailer value**, and **terminating value**. We will generally describe the value as a terminating value.

Unless the user is told that a length of 0 will terminate the process, he will not know. We will, therefore, print some instructions to notify the user of this fact. This step occurs once, at the very beginning of the program.

This discussion leads to the following refined variable list and algorithm (plan).

COMMENT We have added a constant named EndOfData to our list. This constant will be used as part of the loop control.

Strictly speaking, we now have a "Constant and Variable List." However, we will use the simple term "variable list" throughout the text.

Constant:	EndOfData		Value 0, used to terminate loop
Input:	Length	Real	Length of rectangle
	Width	Real	Width of rectangle
Output:	Area	Real	Area of rectangle

print instructions
repeat these steps until the user enters 0 for the Length:
    ask the user to enter a length and a width
    read Length, Width values
    calculate Area value (Length times Width)
    print Area value

As we will see in the next subsection, this algorithm, together with the variable list and some knowledge of Pascal looping mechanisms, is detailed enough to allow us to write the program.

□

WRITING THE LOOPING PROGRAM

The program whose plan we have just developed is typical of many programs. (For the early part of this textbook, all our programs will follow this pattern.) We may indicate the pattern as follows:

print instructions
repeat these steps until the user enters the terminating value:
    "prompt" the user to supply input
    read the input values
    perform calculations
    print answers

In this subsection, we will continue our example by writing the desired Pascal program. The methods we use will apply to any program that follows this pattern. There are other ways that this same general plan could be realized as a Pascal program. In Chapter 3, we will analyze all the possible looping structures in some detail. For now, however, we will concentrate on learning one possible way to write the program.

The complete program is given in Figure 1-3. As before, the line numbers to the left are for reference; they are not part of the program.

To write a program such as this, we need to know the following about Pascal:

1. The general program layout
2. How to declare constants and variables
3. How to print (messages, values of variables)
4. How to read values for variables
5. How to perform calculations
6. How to write loops, including loop control

The first five in the list were introduced in the last section. We will provide a quick review based on the program in Figure 1-3.

Lines 1, 14, and 31 form the basic program layout. Line 1 names the program and specifies that it will be reading and printing values. Between lines 1 and 14 are the declarations (and some comments), and between lines 14 and 31 are the statements to be performed by the program.

Lines 6 and 7 define the constant EndOfData, with a value of 0. Lines 9 to 12 declare (and comment on) the variables the program uses.

Lines 15 to 18 use Writeln to print a series of lines as instruction to the user. Lines 21 and 22 issue the "prompt," requesting input. Line 21 prints a blank line. This will separate the prompt from the previous answer. Line 22 prints the actual prompt, staying on the same line to wait for user input.[1]

```
 1)      program Rectangles(Input, Output);
 2)      {
 3)        Written by:   XXXXXXXX  XX/XX/XX
 4)           Purpose:  To calculate the areas of rectangles.
 5)      }
 6)      const
 7)        EndOfData = 0;                 {used to terminate loop}
 8)
 9)      var
10)        Length : real;                 {length of rectangle, input}
11)        Width  : real;                 {width of rectangle, input}
12)        Area   : real;                 {area of rectangle, calculated}
13)
14)      begin
15)        Writeln('   This program calculates areas of rectangles. You');
16)        Writeln('supply the length and width when asked, separated by');
17)        Writeln('a space. To stop the process, enter a length of 0,');
18)        Writeln('along with any value for the width.');
19)
20)        repeat
21)           Writeln;
22)           Write('Enter length and width: ');
23)           Readln(Length, Width);
24)           if Length <> EndOfData then
25)             begin
26)                Area := Length * Width;
27)                Writeln('The area is ', Area)
28)             end
29)        until Length = EndOfData
30)
31)      end.
```

Figure 1-3   A Looping Program

Line 23 reads the values entered by the user. The area is calculated in line 26 and printed in line 27. Line 27 is worth examining a little closer. As we described in the last section, a Writeln can be used to print any constants, expressions, or variables. The message enclosed in apostrophes will be printed verbatim, and the current value of the Area variable will be printed. Another possibility would have been to write

```
    Writeln (Area, ' is the area of the rectangle.')
```

printing first the value and then the message of explanation.

COMMENT   We generally include a blank space within a message to separate it from any variable value being printed. For example, consider the blank just before the word "is" in the example above and the one just after the word "is" in line 27 of the sample program.

Another example appears in line 22, where the blank space provides a separation between the colon and the data the user will enter.

The remaining lines, which are shaded in the figure, provide the looping and the loop control. Lines 20 and 29 form the skeleton of a **repeat until loop**. The form is

```
repeat
    list of steps to be repeated
until condition
```

In our example, we want to repeat lines 21 to 28 until the user inputs a length of 0 (that is, EndOfData).

There is a slight subtlety here, however. When we wrote the plan, we surely did not intend the program to calculate and print the area after the user indicated he was done (by entering a length of 0). Although we did not say so explicitly, it was clear that those two steps should only be done when the user inputs an actual rectangle's length and width. In a program, however, we must explicitly make sure that this is what happens. This is what lines 24 to 28 accomplish. They say, in essence,

"If the user entered an actual length and width value, then calculate and print the area of that rectangle."

More precisely, they say,

"If the Length variable's value is not equal to 0 (EndOfData), then do these two steps: calculate the area, print the area."

The if statement's form is

```
if condition then
    begin
        steps to be done if condition is true
    end
```

Notice (line 24) that "<>" means "not equal to" in a condition. As with ":=" this is a double symbol, so no blank is allowed between the < and the >.

This completes our description of the sample program. In the next section, we will discuss what happens when the program is run. Before we quit, however, we want to discuss two topics briefly: indentation and semicolons.

Pascal programs are free-form. Any division into individual lines, and any indentation or spacing patterns, are optional. However, a judicious use of blank space and indentation can improve a program's readability. The sample program illustrates a few general rules we will follow:

1. We will indent the body of the program (lines 15 to 30).

2. We will indent the steps that are repeated in a loop (lines 21 to 28).

3. We will indent the steps involved in an if statement (lines 25 to 28).

4. We will use blank spaces to improve readability (around the "<>" in line 24, the ":=" and "*" in line 26, and the "=" in line 29).

5. We will use blank lines to improve readability. In particular, we will place blank lines before and after loops (lines 19 and 30).

One thing that frequently bothers beginning Pascal programmers is the placement of semicolons. Within the declarations, the rules are fairly rigid and not too difficult. Within the body of the program, they can cause more difficulty. We will have more to say about this later. For now, notice that semicolons are used between steps. For example, consider the if statement form:

```
if condition then
   begin
      steps to be done if the condition is true
   end
```

Semicolons are used between the steps to be done if the condition is true. If there are 10 steps, there will be 9 semicolons; if 2 steps, then 1 semicolon. In the sample program, a semicolon separates the two steps on lines 26 and 27 within the if statement.

Likewise, in the sample program, the steps within the repeat until loop are separated by semicolons. There are four steps—the two Writeln's, the Readln, and the if. (The entire if is considered to be one step of the loop body.) Thus there are three semicolons, at the ends of lines 21, 22, and 23.

Similarly, the entire body of the program contains five steps—four Writeln's and the repeat until loop. There are, therefore, four semicolons (lines 15, 16, 17, and 18).

This will take some getting used to. Keep in mind that semicolons go *between* statements and that such words as repeat, if, begin, and end are not (by themselves) statements.

□

DPT Two possible pitfalls are suggested by the sample program. The first relates to the use of the if statement in the program. As indicated in the discussion earlier, we do not want to do the calculations and print the answer for the user's terminating entry. The purpose of the dummy entry is to say, "I'm finished." In the type of program illustrated by the example, we will always have an if statement whose meaning is, "If the user did not enter the dummy value, then perform the calculations and print the answers."

What will happen if we forget this? The program will calculate and print a meaningless answer for the terminating value. Although this is not as serious as some errors, we should try to write our programs to do exactly what they are supposed to do.

The second possible pitfall relates to the use of semicolons. This issue will be explored in much more detail later. For now, we simply advise you to be careful. In writing programs that use the sample program as a guide, use the placement of semicolons in the example to guide you.

▪▪▪▪▪▪
REVIEW

Terms and concepts

algorithm	procedure
syntax rules	program structure
refinement	loop control
sequence	sentinel

loop	terminal value
decision	dummy value
subprogram	trailer value
module	terminating value
submodule	prompt
function	repeat–until–loop

Four program structures

sequence

loop

decision

subprogram (module, submodule, function, procedure)

Pascal statements

```
repeat
   steps to be repeated
until condition

if condition then
   begin
      steps to be done if condition is true
   end
```

General plan for sample program (and similar programs)

print instructions
repeat these steps until the user enters a terminating value:
    "prompt" the user to supply input
    read the input values
    perform calculations
    print answers

General program form for sample program (and similar programs)

Italicized portions are those that depend on the specific program.

```
program name (Input, Output);
   declarations
begin
   Writeln(instructions);
   Writeln(more instructions);
         .
         .
   repeat
      Writeln;
      Writeln(prompt);
      Readln (input variables);
      if not the terminating value then
         begin
            calculate;
                .
                .
```

```
        Writeln(answers)
        end
    until terminating value
end.
```

■■■■■■
EXERCISES

1. By following the example given in this section and by using the typical algorithm and program form in the Review portion at the end of the section, write programs for the following. You should make a variable list, decide on an appropriate terminating value to terminate the loop, write an algorithm, and finally write the program.

   *a. The area of a square can be found by multiplying the length of a side by itself (side × side). Write a program to find the areas of squares.
   b. The perimeter of a square is four times the length of the side. Write a program to find the perimeters of squares.
   c. Write a program that repeatedly reads two real numbers. For each pair of real numbers it reads, it should calculate and print their sum.

*2. What changes would you make to the program in Exercise 1(c) in the order to find the difference rather than the sum?

3. What changes would you make to the program in Exercise 1(c) if the numbers were integers rather than real numbers?

□
**NOTES FOR
SECTION 1-3**

1. On some Pascal systems, the Write statement does not actually print anything until it is followed by a Writeln. On such a system, the prompt should be issued using a Writeln rather than a Write, and the user input will appear on the next line.

1-4
□□□□□□
**PLANNING
AND
WRITING
LOOPING
PROGRAMS
(PART 2)**

We will now discuss the execution of the program shown in Figure 1-3. In Figure 1-4 we show the results of running the program. (As we described in Section 1-1, we are using Turbo Pascal as an example throughout the text. If you have a different version of Pascal, you may see minor differences when you run the program.) The printout in the figure begins with the output caused by the program. There may be other messages printed by the compiler before your program begins running.

□
**RUNNING THE
PROGRAM**

In this figure the portions in red indicate what was typed by the user when the program ran. All other portions were generated by the program itself.

Throughout the text, when we illustrate a sample run of a program, we will do the same thing. Red will indicate user input.

The three Writeln statements in the program caused three lines of instructions to be printed. This was followed by the prompt (a blank line, then the message "Enter length and width: "). The computer then waited for the desired input to be supplied on the same line by the person running the program. When the user hit the "return" key (or a similar key) to indicate the end of the line of input, the two numbers 4.0 and 5.0 were read into the variables Length and Width, respectively.

```
        This program calculates areas of rectangles. You
supply the length and width when asked, separated by
a space. To stop the process, enter a length of 0,
along with any value for the width.

Enter length and width: 4.0 5.0
The area is    2.0000000000E+01

Enter length and width: 2.5 2.0
The area is    5.0000000000E+00

Enter length and width: 0.05 0.05
The area is    2.5000000000E-03

Enter length and width: 0.001 0.001
The area is    1.0000000000E-06

Enter length and width: 175.72 39.045
The area is    6.8609874000E+03

Enter length and width: 1000.0 1000.0
The area is    1.0000000000E+06

Enter length and width: -5.0 -4.0
The area is    2.0000000000E+01

Enter length and width: 10 15
The area is    1.5000000000E+02

Enter length and width: 4
5
The area is    2.0000000000E+01

Enter length and width: 7                          8
The area is    5.6000000000E+01

Enter length and width: 0 0
```

Figure 1-4 Sample Input and Output

The computer next checked the Length variable. Since its value was not 0, the Area value was calculated and printed. Notice that the answer is printed in the exponential notation 2.0000000000E+01. As was explained in Section 1-2, this means 2.0 times 10 to the power 1, or 20.0.

NOTE The exact form of the answer can vary with different computers. In any case, we will learn, in Section 2-4, how to exercise some control over the exact form in which the answers appear. This will allow us to obtain output in a more familiar form, rather than the exponential form shown in Figure 1-4.

The prompt, input, calculate, and print cycle was repeated a number of times, as illustrated in the figure. The last five input lines are of particular interest. They illustrate the following points:

1. The program was not designed to detect erroneous input, so the data line "−5.0 −4.0" was accepted. In future sections, we will become more sophisticated about not allowing bad data into the program.

2. We may supply whole-number values when the program is reading real variables.

3. We may put more than one blank space between the numbers.

4. If we only enter one number on a line when the program is reading two variables, it will continue to wait for further input.

5. The last data line contains the terminating value of 0. Because the program is reading two variables, we had to supply a value for both the Length and Width. Because the Length is 0, the calculation and print of the Area did not occur, the loop terminated, and the program was finished.

TURBO NOTE The behavior described in point 4 is what standard Pascal specifies. Turbo Pascal is set up to behave slightly differently. To get Turbo Pascal to follow the standard in this matter, you should include the "compiler directive" comment {$B−} before the *program* line of your program.

□
WHAT CAN GO WRONG

Unfortunately, any human endeavor is subject to errors. In computer programs, these errors are frequently called **bugs**. The programming process includes a number of techniques whose goal is to eliminate errors. The DPT (Defensive Programming Tips) sections throughout the text provide guidelines for avoiding common bugs (**antibugging**) and for removing those which do occur (**debugging**).

The compiler itself can be a useful tool in uncovering certain types of bugs. It is especially valuable for the type of error that is caused by a typing mistake, or by a lack of familiarity with the programming language. For example, the following list shows some possible errors in the rectangles program. For each, it shows the error message Turbo Pascal generated. (Other compilers might generate different messages.)

```
omit semicolon line 16              ';' expected
omit right parenthesis, end of line 27  ')' expected
write Area = Length * Width, line 26    ':=' expected
misspell "until," line 29           ';' expected
omit left parenthesis in line 27    ';' expected
< > rather than <> on line 24       Unknown identifier or syntax error
misspell "Area," line 26            Unknown identifier or syntax error
```

As you can see, sometimes the error message tells exactly what the error is, but sometimes it does not. To fix the error, we might see if the error message does correctly describe the problem. If not, we may need to review the Pascal rules to see what we did wrong. Sometimes, the error will have occurred earlier in the program. For example, misspelling "Area" in line 12 might cause an error message in line 26.

These errors are sometimes called **compile-time errors**. Another class of errors is known as **run-time errors**. They are not caused by violations of the syntax rules of the language, but by some problem occurring when the program is running. For example, here are some errors that could occur as the rectangles program is running

The user entering a number that is too large

The user entering an invalid character when a number is being read

The product of the two numbers entered is too large

Turbo Pascal will, when an error occurs, locate the portion of the program that was running at the time. Other systems provide similar types of aid. As for the compile-time errors, it may take some investigating to find the exact cause of the error.

Writing programs fully protected from errors in user input requires a sophistication generally beyond the scope of a first course. However, we can (and will) write programs that avoid other common run-time errors, such as division by zero.

A third type of error is sometimes called a **logic error**. The computer does not indicate that anything went wrong, but the program is nonetheless incorrect. As a simple example, replacing the ''*'' in line 26 with a ''+'' could not be detected by the compiler. It would be detected by us when we observed the incorrect answers produced. This will be explored further in the next subsection.

□ PROGRAM TESTING

Testing a program begins, at least informally, as soon as planning is begun. As we design the algorithm, we are probably thinking about how the algorithm will perform with some sample input. For complex programs, we may write down some input data to help guide our plans.

In addition, there are several types of more formal testing we may perform as we develop the program. First, we may **hand-trace** either the algorithm or the program, using some sample data. This involves ''playing computer,'' tracing the actions the computer will perform step by step. For example, we might step through the algorithm or program for the rectangles example using input data lines of ''2.5 4.0'' and ''0.0 0.0.'' This hand-tracing process can be done before running the program to detect errors in our planning process.

A second type of testing uses the compiler as a tool. This involves running the program and fixing the compile-time errors that may be present.

Eventually, we get all the syntax errors fixed and get a ''clean compile.'' If we are very careful typists, we might even get a clean compile the first time we run the program. In addition, we may not have any obvious run-time errors. At this point, we must avoid the tendency to think that we are done. We still need to test the program for any remaining bugs. There are two general types of bugs that we hope to detect by doing this testing. The first involves an error in thinking about the algorithm, and the second involves erroneous coding of the algorithm into Pascal. In an attempt to uncover these errors, we run the program with a variety of input data, and we examine the answers carefully to see if they are correct.

The only way to thoroughly test a program would be to run it with every possible combination of input. However, this is impossible in practice. We must be satisfied with a compromise—a carefully chosen sample of input data.

It is difficult to say what constitutes ''adequate'' testing, especially for a complex program. As evidence of this, we may point to the fact that bugs are sometimes discovered months or years after a program has been pronounced "correct." However, we can give some general guidelines. This section, and others like it throughout the text, will present some of these guidelines.

In testing the sample program, we used data that illustrates a few of the principles involved. First, we included some input for which the answers could easily be verified by doing the calculations in our head. If the program contained an error, such as adding the length and width rather than multiplying them, these input lines would have allowed us to detect the error quickly. However, not all the data was of this form. Some of the input included some more "realistic" values, such as 175.72 and 39.045. We did, however, use a calculator to make sure that the answers for these input lines were also correct.

A second principle illustrated by the sample test data concerns boundaries. The length and width could be any number from just greater than zero on up. We included data very close to the lower limit, or boundary, for the input. In fact, we included both 0.05 and 0.001 as test data. Although there was no stated upper limit for the length and width, we did also check with some relatively large numbers (1000.0 for each). Experience has shown that errors are more likely to occur for data near boundaries, so these tests may be among the most important that we do.

(However, not all our tests should be boundary tests. We should also include some data that is between the boundaries. In our sample test run, we had a number of values between the very small and the very large.)

A third principle concerns "bad" data. In this example, we entered negative numbers for the length and width. Since the program was not designed to detect negative values, we got a wrong answer. In later programs, where the program is supposed to detect such errors and print warning messages about them, this type of testing will become very important.

There are a number of other important testing principles that we will introduce later in the text when we write programs for which the principles become pertinent. For now, we can summarize the three ideas we have presented:

1. Check all answers. Include some data that is easy to check.

2. Test near boundaries; also test a random sampling away from the boundaries.

3. Include some erroneous input, especially if the program is designed to detect and warn about such errors.

CASE STUDY NO. 1

To conclude this section, we develop another example similar to the one developed in the previous section. This case study will be expanded in later sections.

Statement of problem. A class instructor needs a program to calculate the total of the scores on three tests for each of his students. The student's name should be printed along with the score.

Preliminary analysis. In order to output the student's name, the program will have to obtain the name from the instructor (the user) as he runs the program. The other input will consist of the three test scores. Output will contain the student's name and the total of the three scores. (Note: Having the name with the total on the output will be especially useful if the program is to be run on a terminal that generates a printed copy of the output.)

Algorithm and variable list. Based on the preliminary analysis, we can develop this list of variables (and one constant):

Constant:	EndOfData		Value ' ', indicates end of input
Input:	Name	string[20]	Student name, also printed
	Score1	integer	Test scores
	Score2	integer	
	Score3	integer	
Output:	Total	integer	Total of 3 scores

Recall that the string[20] variable type signifies a string of characters of maximum length 20. We are using a Turbo Pascal feature that is not present, or that may vary slightly, in other versions of Pascal. The EndOfData constant ' ' can be matched by the user by just hitting RETURN when prompted for a name.

The algorithm will involve a loop of the same general form as that in the previous example: obtain input, calculate answers, and print answers. We will choose to ask for the student's name first, then for the three test grades.

COMMENT In general, we will avoid entering character or string values on the same input line as numerical data. In the conversational programs we are writing, obtaining a few data at a time is a good idea. In addition, there are subtleties involved in mixing numerical and nonnumerical data on the same line. We choose not to get bogged down in these subtleties now.

To terminate the looping process, the user will be asked to enter an empty name. We will have the program print a message, "Grades program terminating," just before quitting. This planning leads to the following algorithm. (Steps marked (*) are not done if the user enters an empty name.)

```
print instructions
repeat the following until the user inputs an empty name:
      prompt asking for name
      read Name
      prompt asking for three scores (*)
      read Score1, Score2, Score3 (*)
      calculate Total (*)
      print Name and Total with a message (*)
print the termination message
```

Compare this to the algorithm for the areas of rectangles. You will see that it is almost identical in form. The only difference, besides the termination message, is that the reading of the name is separated from the reading of the scores. This general form of algorithm will frequently be appropriate for the types of programs written in the early chapters of the text.

Test plan. At this point, we might pause to plan our testing strategy. Recalling the discussion earlier in this section, we might include the following types of tests for the three scores (we are assuming that valid test scores are in the range from 0 to 100). It can be a good idea to jot down the expected result for each test, as shown here.

easy to check:	70, 70, 70	: 210
	50, 100, 50	: 200
more realistic:	87, 94, 78	: 259
	68, 92, 75	: 235
boundaries:	0, 0, 0	: 0
	100, 100, 100	: 300
bad data:	101, 103, 110	: 314 ⎫
	−1, −5, −10	: −16 ⎭ (program does not detect bad data)

As we gain more sophistication in our testing, we will discover some other tests that might be important here. Notice that we have, for instance, included some bad data (101 and −1) on the boundary between being good and being bad.

In addition to these specific tests, we would include some randomly chosen input lines.

Write program. We now write the program, which is shown in finished form in Figure 1-5. Again, we have numbered the program lines for reference.

The following paragraphs contain brief notes on how we translated our plan into Pascal.

a. Lines 2 to 6 form the **header comments** for the program, explaining what the program does and listing information about the authorship.
b. Lines 18, 32 to 33, and 48 also contain comments. This is the first instance of a program that uses this type of comment, sometimes called a **signpost comment**. Signpost comments explain what important portions of the program do. They act as "signposts," leading the reader to a quick understanding of the overall structure and contents of the program.

In this program, there are three major portions: the loop body, the steps performed before the loop, and the steps performed after the loop. We have, therefore, inserted brief comments before each of these three portions. The comments not only help someone reading our program to understand it, but help us understand it when we come back to it after a period of time. We feel that signpost comments, in addition to the header comments, provide a valuable piece of documentation for any program.

In order to make them stand out, we always surround signpost comments by blank lines. In general, judicious use of **white space** (blank lines) aids the program's readability.

In this text, we will consistently utilize signpost comments. Early in the text, they will be directed partially to the reader of the book. This means that they will sometimes explain some Pascal or programming features. Later, they will be directed primarily to the reader of the program and may become somewhat more terse.
c. Lines 1, 16, and 52 form the basic structure of the program. They are similar to the previous program.

```
 1)      program TestScores(Input, Output);
 2)      {
 3)        Written by:  XXXXXXXXX  XX/XX/XX
 4)           Purpose:  To calculate the total on three tests, and
 5)                     print that total with the student's name.
 6)      }
 7)      const
 8)        EndOfData = '';                    {empty string to terminate input}
 9)
10)      var
11)        Name   : string[20];              {student name, input}
12)        Score1, Score2, Score3
13)               : integer;                 {three test scores, input}
14)        Total  : integer;                 {total of test scores, calculated}
15)
16)      begin {TestScores}
17)
18)      {*** Before the loop print instructions.}
19)
20)        Writeln('   This program totals test scores. For each');
21)        Writeln('student you will be asked to enter the student''s');
22)        Writeln('name. You may use up to 20 characters for the');
23)        Writeln('name when you type it in. After that, you will');
24)        Writeln('be asked to type in the three test scores, in the');
25)        Writeln('range from 0 to 100. Enter these all on one line,');
26)        Writeln('separated by blank spaces.');
27)        Writeln('   The program will then print the name and the');
28)        Writeln('total score, and repeat the whole process. When');
29)        Writeln('you wish to terminate the program, just tap the');
30)        Writeln('return key when asked for the name.');
31)
32)      {*** In the loop, read name and scores; calculate and print total;
33)           quit when user enters empty name.}
34)
35)        repeat
36)          Writeln;
37)          Write('Enter the name (just tap return to quit): ');
38)          Readln(Name);
39)          if Name <> EndOfData then
40)            begin
41)              Write('Now enter the three scores: ');
42)              Readln(Score1, Score2, Score3);
43)              Total := Score1 + Score2 + Score3;
44)              Writeln('The total is ', Total, ' for ', Name)
45)            end
46)        until Name = EndOfData;
47)
48)      {*** After loop print message and stop the program.}
49)
50)        Writeln;
51)        Writeln('Scores program is terminating.')
52)      end.
```

Figure 1-5 A Looping Program with Instructions

d. Lines 7 to 15 contain the constant and variable declarations, based directly on the variable list. For each, we have provided a brief comment.

e. The algorithm step, "print instructions," generates lines 20 to 30. Notice that, in line 21, in order to print the word "student's," which includes an apostrophe, we must add a second apostrophe.

f. The "repeat" step in the algorithm leads to several things in the program. First, lines 35 and 46 form a Pascal repeat until loop, used to accomplish the repetition. In addition, we must remember that we do not want to do the steps following reading the name if the user has entered an empty name. Thus, we also include the if statement beginning in line 39. This if statement automatically includes the "begin" in line 40 and the "end" in line 45.

   In Turbo Pascal, a blank name would not be considered the same as an empty name; the user must hit return without typing any characters to terminate the loop.

g. The prompt asking for name causes lines 36 and 37. We include a Writeln to print a blank line before the prompt.

h. "Read Name" results in line 38.

i. The prompt asking for three scores is in line 41. Line 42 reads the three

```
     This program totals test scores. For each
student you will be asked to enter the student's
name. You may use up to 20 characters for the
name when you type it in. After that, you will
be asked to type in the three test scores, in the
range from 0 to 100. Enter these all on one line,
separated by blank spaces.
     The program will then print the name and the
total score, and repeat the whole process. When
you wish to terminate the program, just tap the
return key when asked for the name.

Enter the name (just tap return to quit): John Jones
Now enter the three scores: 70 70 70
The total is 210 for John Jones

Enter the name (just tap return to quit): Sue Smith
Now enter the three scores: 50 100 50
The total is 200 for Sue Smith

Enter the name (just tap return to quit): Ab Simpson
Now enter the three scores: 87 94 78
The total is 259 for Ab Simpson
                    .
                    .
                    .
Enter the name (just tap return to quit):

Scores program is terminating.
```

Figure 1-6 Sample Input and Output

scores, line 43 calculates the Total. The next section has more details on the assignment statement in Pascal.

j. "Print Name and Total with a message" generates line 44. Notice that we print a message, then the Total variable, then another brief message, then the Name variable. The resulting line printed will read like a sentence. Notice also the extra spaces around the word "for" to separate it from the total and from the name.

k. The termination message occurs in lines 50 and 51. Also, because there is a step following the repeat until loop in this program, line 46 ends with a semicolon.

Run program. The results of a short sample run are given in Figure 1-6. Only a portion of the actual run is shown. The total run tested all the planned test items (from step 4 above), along with some other randomly chosen input. Notice that the word "student's" is printed by the program with just the one apostrophe.

□
DPT
1. The entire section on Program Testing can be viewed as a defensive programming tip. In particular, hand tracing an algorithm or program can uncover a logic error in a fraction of the amount of time it takes to find it after running the program.

2. Comments aid in making a program understandable. They do, however, introduce a pitfall. If we forget the closing bracket ("}") to end the comment, the compiler will ignore parts of the program. This can cause error messages seemingly unrelated to the actual mistake.

3. The "begin" in line 40 and the "end" in line 45 of the Case Study program (Figure 1-5) are mandatory.

▪▪▪▪▪▪
REVIEW

Terms and concepts	bug	logic error
	antibugging	hand-trace
	debugging	header comment
	compile-time error	signpost comment
	run-time error	white space

Program testing   Three phases: 1. Hand-tracing algorithm
2. Removing syntax errors
3. Running program with test data

Test data: 1. Some easy to check (but all should be checked, perhaps using calculator)
2. Test near boundaries and away from boundaries
3. Test bad data

1. Using the procedures for your particular computer, type and run the first sample program (Figure 1-3).

2. Using the program from Exercise 1, experiment with compile-time and run-time errors.

    a. Make changes, such as misspellings, and notice the error messages generated. Include omitting "}" symbols at the close of some comments.
    b. Change the '*' to a '/' and enter a width of 0 to obtain a "division by 0" run-time error.
    c. Enter inappropriate data (for example, words) for the length or width.
    d. Enter extremely large numbers for length and width.

3. Using the procedures for your particular computer, type and run the second sample program (Figure 1-5).

4. Using the procedures for your particular computer, type and run the programs from Exercise 1 of Section 1-3.

*5. Determine an appropriate set of test data for each of the programs from Exercise 1 of Section 1-3. Be sure to include some that are easy to check, some that are near any boundaries, some that are not near the boundaries, and some bad data (if applicable).

6. By following the method used in the example in the subsection titled Case Study No. 1, write programs for the following.

    a. The perimeter of a triangle is the sum of its three sides. Write a program to find perimeters of triangles.
    b. The distance traveled in miles can be calculated as the product of the speed in miles per hour and the number of hours traveled. Write a program that reads appropriate input, and calculates the distance traveled, for a number of different inputs.
    *c. If we have a number that represents the number of inches, we can convert this to centimeters by multiplying by 2.54 (approximately). Write a program that does so for different values of inches read from the user.
    d. Write a program that, for each employee in a company, prints the name and the weekly pay. The weekly pay is calculated as the hours worked times the hourly pay rate. (No overtime is calculated by this program.)
    e. Write a program that updates the amount owed by each customer of a company, based on the following rule. The new amount owed should be calculated as 1.015 times the old amount owed. The program should, for each customer, print the customer name and the new amount owed.

*7. Tell how to modify the first example (Figure 1-3) so that, just before it stops, it prints a message, "Have a nice day," preceded by a blank line.

8. Tell how to modify the first example (Figure 1-3) to read the user's name at the beginning of the run, then print a message similar to the following at the end: "Have a nice day, John." Here we are assuming that John is the user's name.

9. Tell how to modify the second example (Figure 1-5) to read the date as a string of characters and print the date prior to obtaining the lists of names and grades. It should simply print the date exactly as the user inputs it.

2 FUNDAMENTALS OF PASCAL PROGRAM DESIGN

Chapter 1 introduced sufficient information about writing programs and the programming language Pascal to enable you to write some short programs (which, hopefully, you have done by now). In this chapter, we will build on this foundation by discussing program design and Pascal in more detail. By the end of this chapter, you will have seen examples of each of the four techniques of program design: sequencing, looping, decisions, and subprograms.

We begin our study by providing a more complete description of the assignment statement than that of the previous chapter.

Recall that the assignment statement assigns values to variables. The form of the statement is

$$variable := expression$$

where "variable" represents any Pascal variable name, and "expression" represents some combination of variables, constants, and operations. The two combined symbols ":=" are called the **assignment operator**. The expression on the right of the assignment operator can be simple or it can be very complicated. The purpose of an assignment statement is to give a new value to a variable. Each variable has a particular place in the computer memory where its value is stored. The overall effect of an assignment statement is to store a new value in that memory location. We say that the new value is "assigned to the variable."

When the assignment statement is executed, there are two major events that occur in specific order:

1. The expression on the right side of the assignment operator is evaluated. Because the expression can be complicated, the evaluation process can involve several variables and subexpressions. The current value of all variables is used in calculating the value represented by the expression.

2. The value obtained from the right side of the assignment operator is assigned to the variable on the left side of the assignment operator.

In the remainder of this section, we will first look at numeric assignment statements and then at a few simple character and string assignments.

□ **A numeric assignment statement** is one for which the value on the right side of the assignment operator is a number and the variable on the left side of the assignment operator is a numeric type (integer or real for now). For example, the following are numeric assignment statements (all variables are real):

```
TaxRate := 0.06
Balance := Balance + 345.68
X := Y
Price := 1.5 * Cost
```

The first example gives the variable "TaxRate" a value of 0.06. The second changes the variable "Balance" by adding 345.68 to the previous value of "Balance." The third copies the value of the variable "Y" to the variable "X", and the fourth gives the variable "Price" the product of the variable "Cost" multiplied by 1.5. The variable "Y" in the third example and the variable "Cost" in the fourth example are not changed by the execution of the assignment statements. Only the variables on the left side have their values changed.

NOTE   The assignment operator ":=" is suggestive of a left-facing arrow, which reminds us that values flow from the right to the left. There is *no* space between the colon and the equals sign.

□ As you may have noticed, the assignment statement appears somewhat similar to an algebraic formula. For example, the formula

PRECEDENCE

$$d = rt$$

tells us how to calculate the distance d for a given value of r (rate) and t (time). In a formula such as this, just as in an assignment statement, the quantity on the left is the quantity that we wish to calculate, using the formula or expression on the right. Our Pascal rendering of the above formula might be

```
D := R * T
```

or more clearly

```
Distance := Rate * Time
```

Formulas typically involve combinations of variables and constants using such operators as addition, subtraction, multiplication, and division. For example, the familiar formula

$$F = {}^9/_5C + 32$$

(for determining the Fahrenheit temperature corresponding to a given Celsius reading) involves division (9 divided by 5), multiplication, and addition. The inverse formula

$$C = {}^5/_9 (F - 32)$$

involves division, subtraction, and multiplication. The latter formula also introduces parentheses to control the order in which the operations are to be performed (in this case, they ensure that the quantity "F − 32" is evaluated before being multiplied by "⅝").

The following rules are commonly used as conventions in determining the order of operations in algebraic formulas.

1. A unary minus (as in "−5 + 6") is evaluated by acting upon the constant, variable, or parenthetical group that immediately follows to the right of the minus sign.

2. Multiplication and division are performed before addition and subtraction, unless parentheses force another sequence of evaluation. When multiplications or divisions occur in a row, they are evaluated from left to right.

3. Addition and subtraction are then performed, again from left to right.

4. Within a parenthetical expression, the evaluation occurs according to the above rules (including this one).

The following is a set of examples that illustrate these rules:

$$3 + 4 \cdot 7 \; is \; 31$$

(Multiplication takes precedence over addition.)

$$(3 + 4) \cdot 7 \; is \; 49$$

(Parentheses force evaluation of addition first.)

$$-5 + 9 \; is \; 4$$

(The unary minus acts first.)

$$8/4 \cdot 2 \; is \; 4$$

(Division and multiplication go from left to right.)

$$8/(4 \cdot 2) \; is \; 1$$

(Parentheses force evaluation of multiplication first.)

$$7 - 4 - 2 \; is \; 1$$

(Subtractions go from left to right.)

$$7 - (4 - 2) \; is \; 5$$

(Parentheses force evaluation of right subtraction first.)

$$6 \cdot (5 - (2 + 1)) \; is \; 12$$

(Innermost parentheses are evaluated first.)

The Pascal symbols for the arithmetic operators are:

```
+   addition
−   subtraction (and unary minus)
*   multiplication
/   division
```

NOTE   (For the curious.) There is no standard Pascal operator for exponentiation. We will discuss an alternative in Section 2-4.

In Algebra, you may recall, a dot indicates multiplication, as in the formula

$$y = a \cdot b$$

Later, you were allowed to drop the dot, writing

$$y = ab$$

Consider, however, the corresponding Pascal assignment statement

```
Y := AB
```

Because Pascal variable names can be (and are encouraged to be) more than one letter long, we cannot be sure whether the right side refers to a single variable "AB" or to the variable "A" multiplied by the variable "B". To clarify the situation, we must always include a symbol for multiplication. The asterisk symbol was chosen to represent the multiplication operator in Pascal for historical reasons.

In Algebra, we are accustomed to seeing fractions that have expressions for both numerator and denominator; for example,

$$z = \frac{a + 2b}{c - 3d}$$

In Pascal, we use the slash (/) symbol for the division operator. Note that a naive translation of the above formula into the Pascal assignment statement

```
Z := A + 2*B / C - 3*D
```

yields an erroneous result. The correct translation to Pascal is

```
Z := (A + 2*B) / (C - 3*D)
```

COMMENT The reason the first is incorrect is that, without the parentheses, the subexpression 2*B / C is calculated before the addition and subtraction. For example, suppose the variables A, B, C, and D contain the values 4, 6, 8, and 2 respectively. The correct value for z is

$$(4 + 2 * 6)/(8 - 3 * 2) =$$
$$(4 + 12)/(8 - 6) =$$
$$16/2 =$$
$$8$$

The incorrect assignment statement would yield

$$4 + 2 * 6/8 - 3 * 2 =$$
$$4 + 12/8 - 6 =$$
$$4 + 1.5 - 6 =$$
$$5.5 - 6 =$$
$$-0.5$$

The **precedence** rules for the arithmetic operators of Pascal coincide with the algebraic rules:

1. Unary minus (−) first
2. * and / next, left to right
3. + and − next, left to right
4. Parentheses can be used to group operations

Because the precedence rules in Pascal are the same as those for algebraic formulas, most algebraic formulas can be rewritten as Pascal assignment statements with little difficulty. We must, however, remember to use the asterisk (*) for multiplication and the slash (/) for division and to group numerator and denominator expressions with parentheses.

The following table illustrates the correspondence between algebraic formulas and Pascal assignment statements.

```
-------------------------------------------------------
Algebraic Formula       Pascal Assignment Statement
-------------------------------------------------------
  y = x + t              Y := X + T
  x = 2y                 X := 2 * Y
  x = y/z + r            X := Y/Z + R
  y = ax + b             Y := A*X + B
  a = x(t + w)           A := X * (T + W)
-------------------------------------------------------
```

NOTE It is permissible to add extra parentheses to an expression in order to emphasize the meaning of subexpressions. For example, we can write

$$Y := (B * A) / C$$

instead of the equivalent

$$Y := B * A / C$$

if we wish to emphasize that the multiplication comes before the division. Similarly, we can write

$$Y := (40 * R) + (1.5 * R * T)$$

if we wish, although no parentheses are required to obtain the desired precedence.

□ **REAL AND INTEGER EXPRESSIONS**

In the examples given above, we have usually been assuming that all variables are real. As we mentioned earlier, Pascal does make a distinction between integer and real quantities. Some implications of this are discussed in detail in Section 2-4. However, a brief discussion is in order here.

Fortunately, Pascal's way of handling expressions is what we would normally expect. For example:

2.5 + 7 *is* 9.5

(Adding a real to an integer is allowed.)

5 * 6.43 *is* 32.15

[Multiplication (and division or subtraction) is also allowed.]

5 / 2 *is* 2.5

(Dividing two integers gives just what we expect here.)

4 / 2 *is* 2.0

(The answer from the division operator "/" is always real.)

Only the last example may be somewhat of a surprise.

In general, then, we can write our assignment statements in a completely natural way. For example, if the Price of an item is a real and the Quantity purchased is an integer, an assignment

```
TotalCost := Price * Quantity
```

is acceptable (TotalCost is real).

There is one important restriction to note. We cannot assign a real expression to an integer variable. For a simple example, even if it is known that an integer number N is evenly divisible by 10, an assignment such as

```
N := N / 10
```

would fail because division using the slash (/) always yields a real number. Section 2.4 will address this issue further.

□
DPT For the most part, assignment statements in Pascal are straightforward. If we know what formula or expression is needed to calculate a new value for a variable, we place the expression to the right side of the assignment operator and the variable to the left. There are however, six points that deserve special emphasis.

1. The main point to remember is that the assignment operator is written as ":=". A common mistake made by those new to Pascal is to use the "=" incorrectly as the assignment operator. Another common mistake is to put space between the colon and the equals sign. Fortunately, the Pascal compiler will detect and report any such erroneous usage of symbols.

2. Multiplication cannot be implicit in an expression; it must always be made explicit by use of the symbol "*". The compiler will generally detect this error, but it might give a misleading error message. For example, if we write

```
Y := AB     instead of    Y := A*B
```

the error message will say that we forgot to declare the identifier AB.

3. Extra parentheses may be needed to group numerators and denominators when using the division symbol "/". Failure to do so will not be detected by the compiler; the program will yield incorrect results.

4. Using "/" to divide always yields a real value; and a real value cannot be assigned to an integer variable.

5. Although the assignment statement is similar to an algebraic formula, it is not at all similar to an algebraic equation. For example, an assignment statement similar to

```
K := K + 1
```

is seen commonly in Pascal programs. The meaning of the statement is

    a. Evaluate the right side by taking the current value of the variable K and adding it to 1.

    b. Change the value of the variable K to the value obtained on the right side.

If we translate the assignment statement into the algebraic equation

$$k = k + 1$$

we obtain an unsolvable equation and a surprising equality if we attempt to solve it $(0 = 1)$.

    6. A variable should never appear on the right side of an assignment statement until it has been given a value. For example, if the variable K has not yet been given a value in a Pascal program, then the statement

```
K := K + 1
```

will have an unpredictable result. The resulting value of K will not be under the control of the programmer or the program. When you are reading through your Pascal code to check it for correctness, ask for each instance of a variable that appears on the right side of an assignment statement: "How did this variable receive its value?"

□
CHAR ASSIGNMENT STATEMENTS

A variable of type "char" can have as its value any single character. Some of these characters correspond to the characters that can be generated on the keyboard and printed on a printer. The two most common ways to assign values to a char variable are by the use of a char literal or by use of the built-in function "Chr". If "X" and "Y" are char variables, we can also assign the value of "Y" to "X" by use of the statement

```
X := Y
```

    A char **literal** consists of exactly one character enclosed between apostrophes. For example, the statement

```
Letter := 'C'
```

assigns to the variable "Letter" the value of upper case "C". In similar fashion, but less obviously, the statement

```
Blank := ' '
```

assigns to the variable "Blank" a single blank space. Note that the statement

```
Blank := ''
```

does not have the desired effect because there is no blank space between apostrophes. In fact, this will generate an error when the program is run.

    If you want to represent the apostrophe as a char variable, type it twice in consecutive columns as in the statement

```
Apostrophe := ''''
```

    The standard Pascal function "**Chr**" generates a char value from any of the numbers from 0 to 255. (This range is typical.) The character set that is used on the computer determines the meaning of any particular instance of this function. If the character set is **ASCII** (most microcomputers), then the value of Chr(67) is the uppercase letter "C". The assignment statement

```
Letter := Chr(67)
```

assigns the character 'C' to the variable Letter. (Appendix F contains a list of ASCII values for characters.)

STRING ASSIGNMENT STATEMENTS

□ In Turbo Pascal, a variable of the type "string" has associated with it a maximum length that is declared with it in the "var" section of the program. The most common ways to assign values to a string variable are by using string literals or the concatenation operator. Other string operations are discussed in Chapter 8.[1]

A string literal consists of 0 or more characters enclosed between apostrophes. The **null string** is denoted by

```
' '
```

and means a string of no characters. This particular string is also referred to as the **empty string**. Note that the string literal consisting of one blank space, ' ', is not the same as the null string. Also note that a string literal consisting of a single character is indistinguishable from a char literal. For example, the expression

```
'C'
```

could represent either a string literal or a char literal. Another point to remember is that the following two strings are different:

```
'The lazy fox'
'The lazy fox '
```

The latter string contains one more character (a blank space) than does the former string.

Suppose that the string variable ShortWord has a maximum size set to 4 (declared as string[4]) and that the following statement is executed

```
ShortWord := 'longest'
```

The effect of the assignment is the same as if the statement

```
ShortWord := 'long'
```

had been executed instead. This process of trimming off unusable characters is called **truncation**. Notice the danger of assuming that the variable has the value "longest" when in fact it has the value "long." Suppose that for the same variable ShortWord, the following statement is executed

```
ShortWord := 'is'
```

This does not have the same effect as does the statement

```
ShortWord := 'is '
```

because the lengths of the two string literals in question are different. A string variable with a maximum length 4 can contain a string of length 0, 1, 2, 3, or 4.

As in the case of char variables, if you want to include the apostrophe within the string literal, use two consecutive apostrophes. For example, to assign the value "Wanda's" to the string variable Whose, we would use the statement

```
Whose := 'Wanda''s'
```

The **concatenation** operator used in Turbo Pascal is denoted by "+". We can think of concatenation as the "pasting" together of two strings. For example, if First, Second, and Third are strings of declared sizes 8, 6, and 7, respectively, then the execution of the statements

```
First := 'apple';
Second := 's';
Third := First + Second
```

would result in Third having the value 'apples'. Note that the declared sizes of the three variables does not matter as long as each is large enough to hold the desired value without truncation. Some other possible methods of placing the value 'apples' in the variable Third are:

Method One:
```
First := 'apple';
Third := First + 's'
```

Method Two:
```
First := 'apple';
Second := Chr(115);      {Assuming ASCII machine}
Third := First + Second
```

Method Three:
```
Third := 'apple' + 's'
```

Method Four:
```
Third := 'apples'
```

CAUTION

If concatenation yields a value with length greater than 255, a run-time error results.

NOTE The relationship between variables of type "char" and "string" with respect to the assignment statement can be summarized as follows: variables of type char and strings of length 1 behave similarly. Thus, we can assign a string to a char variable provided the length of the string is exactly 1.

□ **EXAMPLES** In Figures 2-1 and 2-2, we present complete Pascal programs that utilize numeric and string assignment statements. In each case, the program reads lines of input until the value chosen to denote end-of-data is read.

REVIEW

Terms and concepts

assignment operator (:=)	literal
numeric assignment statement	Chr
+	ASCII
−	null string
*	empty string
/	truncation
precedence	concatenation (+)

```
program Volume(Input, Output);
{
        Written by:   XXXXXXXX   XX/XX/XX
           Purpose:   To compute the volume of cones.
}
const
  EndOfData = 0;                      { Terminating value for Radius.}
  Pi = 3.14159;

var
  Radius  : real;                     { Radius of Base of the cone.}
  Height  : real;                     { Height of the cone.}
  Volume  : real;                     { Volume of the cone.}

begin {Volume}

{*** In loop, read Radius and Height.}

  repeat
    Writeln;
    Write('Enter the Radius: ');
    Readln(Radius);
    if  Radius <> EndOfData   then
      begin
        Write('Enter the Height: ');
        Readln(Height);
        Volume := Pi * (Radius*Radius) * Height;
        Writeln('The volume of the cone is: ', Volume)
      end
  until  Radius = EndOfData;

{*** Print terminating message and stop program.}

  Writeln;
  Writeln('Volume program is terminating.')
end.
```

SAMPLE INPUT AND OUTPUT

```
Enter the Radius: 3.7
Enter the Height: 10.85
The volume of the cone is:    4.6664078303E+02

Enter the Radius: 34.6
Enter the Height: 2.3
The volume of the cone is:    8.6502675341E+03

Enter the Radius: 0

Volume program is terminating.
```

Figure 2-1 Numeric Assignment

```
program Join(Input, Output);
{
        Written by:  XXXXXXXX  XX/XX/XX
            Purpose:  To concatenate two strings.
}
const
  EndOfData = '';                        { Terminating value for Prefix.}

var
  Prefix  : string[20];          { First string.}
  Suffix  : string[20];          { Second string.}
  Joined  : string[40];          { Joined strings.}

begin {Join}

{*** In loop, read Prefix and Suffix.}

    repeat
      Writeln;
      Write('Enter the first string: ');
      Readln(Prefix);
      if  Prefix <> EndOfData  then
        begin
          Write('Enter the second string: ');
          Readln(Suffix);
          Joined := Prefix + Suffix;
          Writeln('The joined string is: ',Joined)
        end
    until  Prefix = EndOfData;

  {*** Print terminating message and stop program.}

    Writeln;
    Writeln('Join program is terminating.')
  end.
```

SAMPLE INPUT AND OUTPUT

```
Enter the first string: GOOD
Enter the second string:  MORNING!
The joined string is: GOOD MORNING!

Enter the first string: Goodbye for
Enter the second string:  now.
The joined string is: Goodbye for now.

Enter the first string:
Join program is terminating.
```

Figure 2-2 String Assignment

NOTE In entering the strings in the example above, the user placed a blank prior to "MORNING!" and "now." If she had not done so, the output would have appeared as "GOODMORNING!" and "Goodbye fornow."

| *Pascal syntax* *(the assignment statement)* | `variable := expression` |

Pascal syntax (the assignment statement)

`variable := expression`

"expression" contains one or more variables or constants.

Possible operators:
1. For numbers +, −, *, /
2. For strings + (concatenation)

Action:
1. Evaluates expression using current values of variables
2. Assigns result to variable

Precedence:
1. Unary minus
2. * and /, left to right
3. + and −, left to right
4. Parentheses can group

Truncation:
1. String assignments can truncate the result to fit the maximum length of the string variable.

DPT

1. Use := for assignment.

2. Use * for multiplication.

3. May need parentheses to group numerators and denominators.

4. Using / (a slash) yields a real answer; real values cannot be assigned to integer variables.

5. Assignment is not an algebraic equation; it is more like an algebraic formula.

6. Make sure that a variable has been given a value *before* it is used on the right side of an assignment statement.

EXERCISES

*1. Give the value of the following Pascal expressions.

a. 3*2 + 7
b. 4 / 3
c. 6.5 / 2
d. 3 / 2 + 1
e. 3*(2 + 5)
f. 3 − 7 + 2
g. 3 − (7 + 2)
h. 'A' + 'B'
i. 4 * 3 / 2
j. 4 * (3/2)
k. 8 / 2 * 4
l. '4*6' + '5'

*2. Assume that A, B, and C are real and X, Y, and Z are integer. Also assume that at the time the assignment statement is executed, the variables have the values:

| A 3.2 | B 6.0 | C 1.5 |
| X 4 | Y 63 | Z 17 |

What value is given to the variable on the left side of each assignment statement?

a. A := 0.5 * A
b. X := X + 1
c. B := A / 2
d. A := 12.3
e. Y := X * Z
f. C := C − A − B

*3. Convert the following algebraic formulas to Pascal assignment statements. Assume that all variables are real.

a. $y = ax + b$
b. $t = \frac{1}{2} a + r$
c. $w = \frac{x + y}{2}$

d. $j = k + 5$
e. $s = 5t$
f. $r = \frac{x}{y + 3}$

g. $w = \frac{x + 3y}{r + a - 3}$
h. $j = (k + 3)j$

*4. For the following assignment statements, determine what value is assigned to the variable on the left. Assume that all variables are of a "string" type and that the declared size of Str3 is 3, Str5 is 5, and Str7 is 7. Suppose that the string variable Bees has the value 'bbb' and that Sees has the value 'cccc'.

a. Str3 := Bees
c. Str3 := Sees
e. Str7 := 'b' + Sees
g. Str3 := 'cBc'
i. Str7 := '''b'' + c'

b. Str5 := Bees
d. Str3 := 'b' + Bees + Sees
f. Str7 := 'b' + Bees + Sees
h. Str3 := 'Str3'
j. Str5 := '' + Bees

5. Write Pascal assignment statements to perform each of the following calculations. Use meaningful variable names and give declarations for your variables.

*a. Calculate the area of a rectangle given its length and width.
 b. Convert inches to centimeters (1 inch = 2.54 centimeters).
 c. Find the average of three real numbers.
*d. Find a person's age in months given his age in years and months (for example, 3 years, 4 months yields 40 months as the answer).
*e. Find the local tax given the income. The rule is: 5 percent of the portion of the income in excess of $1000. (Assume that the income is at least $1000.)
*f. Prefix a last name with "Professor".
 g. Calculate the batting average given the times at bat and the number of hits.
 h. Find the percentage of mutated ants in an ant colony given the number of mutated ants and the total number of ants in the colony.
 i. Convert a speed in kilometers per hour to meters per second.
 j. Convert a swimmer's time (seconds) for the 50-meter freestyle to an estimate of the time for the 50-yard freestyle by multiplying the time by 0.9.

6. Using the assignment statements you wrote in Exercise 5, plan and write complete programs that calculate the indicated values for a number of input lines.

7. Write a complete Pascal program to read a person's name and print the message:

```
Hi, <name read in>, how's it going?
```

For example, if the user enters the name "Howard," then the program will output

```
Hi, Howard, how's it going?
```

8. Write a program to allow experimentation with the Chr function. For each numeric value input by the user (in the range 0 to 255), it should print the corresponding character. Use the program to experiment. Is Chr(67) a "C" for your computer? What is Chr(68)? What happens if you enter a value not in the prescribed range?

*9. Using three separate Readln statements, write a program to read a person's last name, then the first name, and finally the middle initial. Use string variables for the first and last names and a char variable for the initial. Sample output might be

```
To the parents of Joan H. Smith
```

The program should "calculate" a variable AddressLine as indicated by the sample and print that variable.

10. Write a complete Pascal program to read a person's current weight, calories burned per day, goal weight, and calories intake per day. Calculate and print the number of days that it will take for the person to attain the goal weight by using the relationship

$$3500 \text{ calories} = 1 \text{ pound}$$

11. Listed below are two Pascal programs. Run the programs in the order

```
run program Trash
run program None
run program Trash
run program None
```

and note the results. You are not expected to understand the program Trash. However, you should remember that a variable should be given a value *before* it is used on the right side of an assignment statement. The program None violates this rule for the variable K.

```
program Trash(Input, Output);
var
  I   : integer;
  Can : array[1..100] of real;
begin {Trash}
  Randomize;
  for I := 1 to 100 do
    Can[I] := Random
end.

program None(Input, Output);
var
  K : integer;
begin {None}
  K := K + 1;
  Writeln('The value of K is: ', K);
  Writeln('Touch RETURN to quit.');
  Readln
end.
```

NOTES FOR SECTION 2-1

☐

1. Many versions of Pascal support string variables. For some, this discussion will apply directly. For others, there can be minor differences.

If your version of Pascal does not support string variables, you do not need to panic. For most of the text, we use strings primarily to allow us to, for example, read and print student names. By replacing names with identification numbers, you can work the problems without using string variables.

Standard Pascal does allow us to define our own string type as a "packed array of char." Appendix E contains a brief outline of how you may do this.

In any case, you should refer to your instructor or reference manual for more details.

2-2
☐☐☐☐☐☐
INTRODUC-
TION TO
PROCEDURES

Previously (in Section 1-3), we discussed the four building blocks used for developing programs:

1. Sequencing
2. Looping
3. Decisions
4. Subprograms

The examples discussed so far have used the first three techniques. Sequencing will appear in any program where we have a series of steps to perform, one after the other. We should expect to continue to find segments of all of our programs that fall into the sequencing category. Looping has been used in many of our examples to provide the structure in which we could repeatedly read values, make calculations, and print the results. Thus far, the loops have been terminated by the user inputting a terminal (dummy) value. Decisions have been used to ensure that the dummy value is not processed inside of our read, calculate, and print loops. Subprograms will be introduced in this section in one specific context. The variety of subprogram that we will discuss is known in Pascal as a **procedure**.

☐
AN EXAMPLE
PROCEDURE

The algorithm used to develop the program for the example (Case Study 1) from Section 1-4 is reproduced here as Figure 2-3 and the program as Figure 2-4. As we study the algorithm and then go on to read the program, we are struck by the fact that the printing of instructions has seemed to attain relatively more importance in the Pascal program than it had in the algorithm.

In the algorithm, the task of printing the instructions occupies one line out of a total of nine algorithm lines. However, in the program, the printing of instructions occupies 11 out of a total of the 25 lines of Pascal (ignoring blank and comment lines) that lie between the "begin" and "end" for the program. It seems that the proportion of lines dedicated to instructions in the algorithm is appropriate and that the program is harder to understand because of its inordinate emphasis on printing instructions. The process of refining the algorithm line "print instructions" into the details of the instructions themselves has hindered the readability of the resulting program. It would be nice if one could just say "print instructions" in the Pascal program and get the desired results when the program

---

```
print instructions
repeat the following until the user inputs an empty name
      prompt asking for name
      read Name
      prompt asking for three scores
      read Score1, Score2, Score3
      calculate Total
      print Name and Total with a message
print the termination message
```

Figure 2-3   Looping Algorithm

```pascal
program TestScores(Input, Output);
{
   Written by:   XXXXXXXX  XX/XX/XX
      Purpose:   To calculate the total on three tests, and
                 print that total with the student's name.
}
const
   EndOfData = '';              {empty string to terminate input}

var
   Name    : string[20];        {student name, input}
   Score1, Score2, Score3
           : integer;           {three test scores, input}
   Total   : integer;           {total of test scores, calculated}

begin {TestScores}

{*** Before the loop print instructions.}

   Writeln('    This program totals test scores. For each');
   Writeln('student you will be asked to enter the student''s');
   Writeln('name.  You may use up to 20 characters for the');
   Writeln('name when you type it in.  After that, you will');
   Writeln('be asked to type in the three test scores, in the');
   Writeln('range from 0 to 100.  Enter these all on one line,');
   Writeln('separated by blank spaces.');
   Writeln('    The program will then print the name and the');
   Writeln('total score, and repeat the whole process.  When');
   Writeln('you wish to terminate the program, just tap the');
   Writeln('return key when asked for the name.');

{*** In the loop, read name and scores; calculate and print total;
     quit when user enters empty name.}

   repeat
     Writeln;
     Write('Enter the name (just tap return to quit): ');
     Readln(Name);
     if Name <> EndOfData then
       begin
         Write('Now enter the three scores: ');
         Readln(Score1, Score2, Score3);
         Total := Score1 + Score2 + Score3;
         Writeln('The total is ', Total, ' for ', Name)
       end
   until Name = EndOfData;

{*** After loop print message and stop the program.}

   Writeln;
   Writeln('Scores program is terminating.')
end.
```

Figure 2-4 Instructions in Program

```
procedure Instructions;
{
   Written by:  XXXXXXXX  XX/XX/XX
      Purpose:  To print instructions.
}
begin {Instructions}
   Writeln('    This program totals test scores.  For each');
   Writeln('student you will be asked to enter the student''s');
   Writeln('name. You may use up to 20 characters for the');
   Writeln('name when you type it in. After that, you will');
   Writeln('be asked to type in the three test scores, in the');
   Writeln('range from 0 to 100.  Enter these all on one line,');
   Writeln('separated by blank spaces.');
   Writeln('    The program will then print the name and the');
   Writeln('total score, and repeat the whole process.  When');
   Writeln('you wish to terminate the program, just tap the');
   Writeln('return key when asked for the name.')
end; {Instructions}
```

Figure 2-5   Instructions Procedure

is executed. In fact, as we shall see, we can attain that goal by the use of procedures in Pascal.

The form of a Pascal procedure is similar to that of a Pascal program. This similarity lends itself well to the concept of subtasks of a task, which is what we will be using procedures to implement. When we remove the lines of the Pascal program of Figure 2-4 and place them within the confines of a Pascal procedure (named Instructions), we obtain the result shown as Figure 2-5.

Note that there are three essential details that differentiate the procedure from a program:

1. The keyword "procedure" appears instead of "program".
2. The files designator "(Input, Output)" does not appear.
3. The final "end" is followed by ";" and not ".".

A more significant difference is that a Pascal procedure cannot be run by itself, but must be "called" by another program unit to execute. In order to call our example procedure, the Pascal program just has to invoke its name:

```
Instructions;
```

When it does so, the statements in the Instructions procedure are executed. The

```
program TestScores(Input, Output);
{
   Written by:  XXXXXXXX  XX/XX/XX
      Purpose:  To calculate the total on three tests, and
                print that total with the student's name.
}
```

Figure 2-6   Procedure Placement and Use (Continued)

```
const
  EndOfData = '';                    {empty string to terminate input}

var
  Name    : string[20];              {student name, input}
  Score1, Score2, Score3
          : integer;                 {three test scores, input}
  Total   : integer;                 {total of test scores, calculated}

  procedure Instructions;
  {
    Written by:  XXXXXXXX  XX/XX/XX
       Purpose:  To print instructions.
  }
  begin {Instructions}
    Writeln('    This program totals test scores. For each');
    Writeln('student you will be asked to enter the student''s');
    Writeln('name. You may use up to 20 characters for the');
    Writeln('name when you type it in. After that, you will');
    Writeln('be asked to type in the three test scores, in the');
    Writeln('range from 0 to 100. Enter these all on one line,');
    Writeln('separated by blank spaces.');
    Writeln('    The program will then print the name and the');
    Writeln('total score, and repeat the whole process. When');
    Writeln('you wish to terminate the program, just tap the');
    Writeln('return key when asked for the name.')
  end; {Instructions}

begin {TestScores}

{*** Before the loop print instructions.}

  Instructions;

{*** In the loop, read name and scores; calculate and print total;
     quit when user enters empty name.}

  repeat
    Writeln;
    Write('Enter the name (just tap return to quit): ');
    Readln(Name);
    if Name <> EndOfData then
      begin
        Write('Now enter the three scores: ');
        Readln(Score1, Score2, Score3);
        Total := Score1 + Score2 + Score3;
        Writeln('The total is ', Total, ' for ', Name)
      end
  until Name = EndOfData;

{*** After loop print message and stop the program.}

  Writeln;
  Writeln('Scores program is terminating.')
end.
```

Figure 2-6 Procedure Placement and Use

program then continues with the statement following the invocation of the procedure.

For the Pascal program to invoke a procedure, it must have access to it. To achieve this, we simply include the procedure definition in the region of the program's code that immediately follows the "var" section and immediately precedes the "begin" of the program.

The program with procedure Instructions included appears as Figure 2-6. We have shaded the differences between this and the program in Figure 2-4.

□ **SOME CHARACTER-ISTICS OF PROCEDURES**

We note here some of the properties of Pascal procedures that are illustrated in our example procedure, Instructions.

Name: A Pascal procedure has a name that is formed according to the rules for Pascal identifiers. The name of a procedure should not conflict with any of the program variables or constants (there will be more specific details on this issue later).

Body: A Pascal procedure must have its lines of code contained between the "begin" and "end;" pair (note the mandatory semicolon after "end").

Use: A Pascal procedure is invoked by a program by specifying its name as an entire statement (including semicolon, if needed).

Place: A Pascal procedure must be completely contained (from "procedure" to "end;") in the area of the program that follows the "var" section and that precedes the "begin" of the program.

NOTE We are discussing the simplest form of a Pascal procedure in this section. In subsequent sections, other types of subprograms will be treated.

□ **STANDARD PROCEDURES**

From the beginning, we have been dealing with procedures that are supplied with the Pascal language. In particular, we have used the two procedures: "Readln" and "Writeln." When we used the statement

```
Writeln;
```

in our examples, we were using the procedure in the same manner that we have used the procedure "Instructions" in this section. We used Writeln to print a blank line in order to format our program's output in a more readable fashion. In our other uses of Writeln and Readln, we supplied some information for the procedures by enclosing that information within parentheses that followed the procedure name. For example, in the statement

```
Readln(Score1, Score2, Score3);
```

we communicated to the procedure Readln that we wished to receive keyboard input for the three specified variables. Later, we will encounter other **standard Pascal procedures** and we will also learn how we can communicate with our own procedures.

□ *Simplify*: By using the procedure Instructions, we were able to simplify the code of the main program so as to make it more understandable. Both the **main program** and the procedure are sometimes referred to as **modules** of the program.

Focus: By using the procedure "Instructions," we are able to take a closer look at the function of supplying directions without being distracted by the other details of the program. Some people call this kind of focus "divide and conquer." The activity of dividing a program into modules is called **modularization**.

Reuse: Some other program might have a similar set of directions. We will be able to reuse the idea of giving instructions, and, if we have a cooperative editor, we may be able to "cut and paste" the code of the procedure and make some minor textual changes. Some call this kind of reuse "not reinventing the wheel."

*****: We can assure you that there are many other advantages to the use of procedures, but we will discuss them when we have presented the ideas with examples later.

When we isolate the task of supplying instructions for a program, we may realize that there are at least two categories of users: novices and experts. A novice user is grateful for detailed explanation and, in fact, can hardly be satisfied in his quest for clarification. On the other hand, an expert user is put off by the condescending tone of directions and may be angered by the inconvenience and loss of valuable time resulting from having to view unnecessary and unwanted details. Although these ideas about users are obvious, the implications might not be considered during program design because "print instructions" is just one of many tasks that the program has to perform. However, when the only task under scrutiny is that of giving the user directions, we might more naturally consider the user's needs.

A simple solution to the novice versus expert user dilemma is to ask the user if directions are to be received. Thus, we may wish to refine the algorithm step

print instructions

into the rough steps

ask the user if directions are desired
if the answer is yes, then print instructions

These steps can be further refined into a smooth algorithm for the procedure "Instructions" as follows:

print 'Do you want directions (Y or N)'
read Answer
if Answer = 'Y' then
    print detailed instructions

In the algorithm above, we have introduced another use of the if–then decision structure. We will translate this use of the decision into Pascal in a manner similar to what we used to decide whether to execute the body of a repeat until loop in our previous examples.

We have introduced a more subtle idea in the use of the variable "Answer." This variable is not used by the main program and need not be known (declared) by the main program. Such a variable is said to be a **local variable** for the procedure in which it appears. As we shall see, the variable is declared and used exclusively within the procedure Instructions. Since the variable Answer is intended to hold a single character, we will use the type char in its declaration.

The program TestScores, including the modified procedure Instructions, appears as Figure 2-7. Changes have been shaded for emphasis.

```pascal
program TestScores(Input, Output);
{
   Written by:  XXXXXXXX  XX/XX/XX
      Purpose:  To calculate the total on three tests, and
                print that total with the student's name.
}
const
   EndOfData = '';             {empty string to terminate input}

var
   Name   : string[20];        {student name, input}
   Score1, Score2, Score3
          : integer;           {three test scores, input}
   Total  : integer;           {total of test scores, calculated}

procedure Instructions;
{
   Written by:  XXXXXXXX  XX/XX/XX
      Purpose:  To print instructions.
}
var
   Answer : char;              {user response to question, input}
begin {Instructions}
   Writeln;
   Writeln('Do you want directions (Y or N)?');
   Readln(Answer);
   if Answer = 'Y' then
      begin
         Writeln('    This program totals test scores. For each');
         Writeln('student you will be asked to enter the student''s');
         Writeln('name. You may use up to 20 characters for the');
         Writeln('name when you type it in. After that, you will');
         Writeln('be asked to type in the three test scores, in the');
         Writeln('range from 0 to 100. Enter these all on one line,');
         Writeln('separated by blank spaces.');
         Writeln('    The program will then print the name and the');
         Writeln('total score, and repeat the whole process. When');
         Writeln('you wish to terminate the program, just tap the');
```

Figure 2-7 Local Variable (Continued)

```
            Writeln('return key when asked for the name.')
        end
  end; {Instructions}

  begin {TestScores}

  {*** Before the loop print instructions.}

     Instructions;

  {*** In the loop, read name and scores; calculate and print total;
       quit when user enters empty name.}

     repeat
       Writeln;
       Write('Enter the name (just tap return to quit): ');
       Readln(Name);
       if Name <> EndOfData then
         begin
           Write('Now enter the three scores: ');
           Readln(Score1, Score2, Score3);
           Total := Score1 + Score2 + Score3;
           Writeln('The total is ', Total, ' for ', Name)
         end
     until Name = EndOfData;

  {*** After loop print message and stop the program.}

     Writeln;
     Writeln('Scores program is terminating.')
  end.
```

SAMPLE INPUT AND OUTPUT (RUN NO. 1)

```
Do you want directions (Y or N)?
Y
      This program totals test scores. For each
student you will be asked to enter the student's
name. You may use up to 20 characters for the
name when you type it in. After that, you will
be asked to type in the three test scores, in the
range from 0 to 100. Enter these all on one line,
separated by blank spaces.
      The program will then print the name and the
total score, and repeat the whole process. When
you wish to terminate the program, just tap the
return key when asked for the name.

Enter the name (just tap return to quit): Joan Smith
Now enter the three scores: 67 87 97
The total is 251 for Joan Smith

Enter the name (just tap return to quit): Tim Rae
Now enter the three scores: 45 65 23
The total is 133 for Tim Rae
```

Figure 2-7 Local Variable (Continued)

```
Enter the name (just tap return to quit):

Scores program is terminating.
```

SAMPLE INPUT AND OUTPUT (RUN NO. 2)

```
Do you want directions (Y or N)?
N

Enter the name (just tap return to quit): Joan Smith
Now enter the three scores: 67 87 97
The total is 251 for Joan Smith

Enter the name (just tap return to quit): Sally Tie
Now enter the three scores: 34 67 100
The total is 201 for Sally Tie

Enter the name (just tap return to quit):

Scores program is terminating.
```

Figure 2-7   Local Variable

Note that the modified procedure Instructions now contains a "var" section just as does the main program. In the "var" section of a procedure, all of the local variables of the procedure are declared. Remember that these are the variables, such as Answer, used within the procedure itself and not in the main program.

□
A REVIEW OF PROGRAM DESIGN

We show below the variable lists and algorithms for the main program and the procedure "Instructions" that led to the Pascal program of Figure 2-7.

For the TestScores main program:

Constant:	EndOfData	value "	Null string for dummy name
Input:	Name	string[20]	Student name, also printed
	Score1	integer	Test scores
	Score2	integer	
	Score3	integer	
Output:	Total	integer	Total of 3 scores

```
print instructions (using procedure Instructions)
repeat the following until the user inputs an empty name
    prompt asking for name
    read Name
    prompt asking for three scores
    read Score1, Score2, Score3
    calculate Total
    print Name and Total with a message
print the termination message
```

For the Instructions procedure:

Input: Answer   char   User response 'Y' or 'N'

```
print 'Do you want directions (Y or N)'
read Answer
if Answer = 'Y' then
    print detailed instructions
```

In this example, we have explicit use of the four building blocks that are used to erect the program structure: sequencing, looping, decisions, and subprograms.

SEQUENCING

We can find several instances of sequencing in our example. Recall that sequencing refers to programs steps that are performed one after another in the same order that we can read them from top to bottom. One instance of sequencing is seen in these steps of the main program

```
prompt asking for three scores
read Score1, Score2, Score3
calculate Total
print Name and Total with a message
```

LOOPING

We have a single loop in the main program of our example that has the form that we have been using throughout the previous portions of the book. This loop is of the form "repeat . . . until". In subsequent sections of the book, we will encounter other forms of looping that can be represented in Pascal. An important feature of the kind of loop that we are currently using is that the loop is terminated by the user when a terminating value is input (for Name, in this case).

DECISIONS

We have seen two instances of decision in our example. Both the decision structures are of the form "if . . . then". Our roster of decision structures will grow as we proceed through the book.

We have encountered two different kinds of procedures in our example. We have been using the standard Pascal procedures Readln and Writeln in previous sections, and we have introduced our first use of a defined procedure Instructions. Once again, Pascal has many variations on the subprogram theme, which we will study later.

□ DPT

The following are the most common pitfalls that threaten the Pascal programmer who is using procedures.

1. If the programmer doesn't declare the variable Answer as a local variable of the procedure Instructions, then the compiler will produce an error message indicating that a variable has been used without prior declaration.

2. The final "end" of the procedure body must be followed by a semicolon. If incorrect, the compiler should detect the absence of the semicolon.

3. The final "end" of the procedure body must *not* be followed by a period. The compiler should detect and report the inappropriate presence of a period.

4. The name of a procedure must not also be used as the name of a variable used by the main program or as the name of another procedure declared within the main program. If this error is made, the compiler should detect and report the presence of redundancy.

5. The programmer must be aware of the execution sequence of the program. A procedure executes only when "**called**". Execution of a program always starts with the first statement after the "begin" of the *main program*. When a procedure is called, execution continues with the first statement after the "begin" of the procedure body. When execution reaches the final "end" of the procedure, then it continues with the next statement *after* the procedure call.

REVIEW

Terms and concepts

procedure
standard Pascal procedures
main program

module, modularization
local variable
call, invoke

Procedures

Syntax

1. Heading line containing the name of the procedure.

2. Declarations similar to a main program.

3. The initial "begin".

4. The body of the procedure.

5. The final "end", followed by a semicolon.

Properties

Name: identifier for the procedure
Body: code between the "begin" and "end;"
Use: just mention the name to activate
Place: define after "var" section

DPT
1. Declare local variables.
2. Place ";" after "end" of procedure body.
3. Do not place "." after "end" of procedure body.
4. Do not also use the name of the procedure as a variable or constant.
5. Remember to activate the procedure in the main program.

EXERCISES

1. Rewrite the program of Figure 1-3 (Section 1-3) to utilize an instruction printing procedure.

2. Run the revised program from Exercise 1. Is there any difference in what appears on the screen as the program is running? Could a user tell whether or not the program uses a procedure?

*3. Choose one of the parts (a to e) of Exercise 6 in Section 1-4. Rewrite and run the program using an Instructions procedure that asks the user if the instructions are to be shown.

*4. Consider the enhanced version of the Instructions procedure (Figure 2-7). What will happen if the user accidently enters 'y' instead of 'Y' when asked if the instructions are to be shown? Suggest any possible solutions. (Note: At this point, you have not covered enough Pascal to code some of the possible solutions; however, you should be able to describe in words what you might do.)

*5. Suppose that there are 35 lines of instructions to print. (Note: Most display terminals have 24 lines available for printing.) Your enhanced Instructions procedure should print the first 20 lines, then pause until the user hits return, then print the remaining 15 lines.

6. Make the Instructions procedure in Figure 2-7 "fancier" by having it print a pattern similar to this prior to asking if the user wishes instructions:

```
 SS          CCC         000        RRRR      EEEEE       SS
S  S        CC  C       0    0      R   R     E          S  S
S           CC         00    00     R   R     E          S
  S         CC         00    00     R   RR    EEEE          S
    S       CC         00    00     RR        E              S
      S     CC         00    00     R R       E               S
S  S       CC  C       0    0      R   R     E          S  S
 SS          CCC         000        R    R    EEEEE       SS
```

7. (Challenge) What do you think would happen if the main program in our example of Figure 2-7 contained its own variable named "Answer"? Under those circumstances, what if we forgot to declare "Answer" in the procedure "Instructions"?

2-3
□□□□□□
DECISION STRUCTURES

In this section, we begin our formal study of decision structures. Recall that decisions are one of the four program structures described in Chapter 1. (The other three are sequences, loops, and subprograms.)

We can classify decisions in three general categories:

1. There are some steps to be done if some specific condition is true. (We have already seen examples of this type.)

2. There is one set of steps to be done if some condition is true and a different set of steps if the condition is not true.

3. There are a number of conditions, one of which could be true, and a set of steps corresponding to each condition.

We will examine "**multiple-way branches,**" this third category of decisions, in some detail in Section 2-5. In this section, we limit our attention to the first two categories.

In order to successfully use decision structures in a program, there are three steps to be followed. First, we recognize that we need a decision structure; that is, that the choice of steps to be performed depends upon some condition or conditions. Words such as "if," "depends upon," "whether or not," and so on, used in describing the task to be done, can indicate the need for a decision structure. Second, we should classify the structure as one of the three types listed above, identifying the conditions and the corresponding steps. Third, we must accurately reflect the decision structure using the appropriate Pascal code.

□
IF–THEN

The **if–then** is the first category of the decision structure described above. It is used when we have a set of steps to be performed, provided a condition is true, and nothing is to be done when the condition is false. We have already seen two uses of this structure. First, we have used it several times to perform calculations and print the answers, provided the user did not enter the terminating input value. Second, the instruction printing procedure in Section 2-2 used it to print instructions, provided the user specified that he wished to see the instructions.

To code this structure in Pascal, we use the if statement. We have used the if statement in this form:

```
if condition then
  begin
    list of steps to be performed if condition is true
  end
```

The individual steps in the list of steps are separated by semicolons. There is a second form of the if statement that is frequently convenient. If there is exactly one statement to be performed when the condition is true, we can use the form

```
if condition then
    one statement to be performed if condition is true
```

COMMENTS

1. To be precise, this is the only form of the if statement. However, the "one statement" can be a **compound statement**, which consists of a list of statements enclosed in a begin and end. This is the form we have seen before.

2. There are many ways to present the form of statements in a language. One choice, which we are using throughout, is a semiformal description with italics to indicate items that will be filled in based on the situation. Our descriptions of the if–then are of this form. In this form, the language descriptions look somewhat like a sample of the item they explain.

Two other popular ways to present the language are (a) by a more formal notation called the **Backus-Naur form (BNF)**; and (b) by means of **syntax diagrams**. For those who prefer this more diagrammatic presentation, Appendix D presents the language elements by means of syntax diagrams.

NOTE Although it is not a requirement of the language, we do indent the if statement as illustrated here and in the examples below. It is difficult to give a single rule which explains the particular indentation style we use. One might say that the indented statements in some sense "belong to" the statements they are indented from. For example, the statements within a repeat-until-loop are indented from the repeat and the until. The statements within a compound statement are indented from the begin and the end. The statement to be performed if the condition is true is indented from the if. Our advice is to follow the examples when you write your own programs. A good, consistent use of indentation helps anyone reading the program to understand the program's structure and, therefore, what it does and how.

As an example of the if statement, suppose we wish to write Pascal code to print a person's name if his blood is type O. We may use a decision structure in either of these forms:

```
if BloodType = 'O' then          if BloodType = 'O' then
  begin                            Writeln(Name)
    Writeln(Name)
  end
```

COMMENTS *1.* This is only a segment, or piece, of a program. The complete program would include declarations, among them those for BloodType and Name:

```
BloodType: char;
Name      : string[20];
```

It would also, more than likely, include various looping, input, output, and assignment statements. It might even include other decision structures. In order to concentrate our attention on the details of Pascal decisions, many of the examples in this section will present only segments of a program.

2. If the if statement given in this example were followed by another statement in the complete program, there would be a semicolon between the if statement and that next statement.

For our second example, let us write a Pascal segment that adds 1 to a variable named HighCount and adds the income to a variable named HighTotal, provided the income is greater than \$25,000. Assuming that among the declarations we have

```
HighCount: integer;
HighTotal: real;
Income    : real;
```

the solution can be given as

```
if Income > 25000.00 then
   begin
      HighCount := HighCount + 1;
      HighTotal := HighTotal + Income
   end
```

In this case, there are two statements, so we must use the begin and end to group them. Notice the semicolon separating the two statements. Notice also how we "add 1" to a variable. The assignment statement assigns a new value to HighCount. The new value is the old value of HighCount plus 1.

□
CONDITIONS IN PASCAL

These two examples illustrate the use of the if–then. To complete our discussion, we need to know the rules for writing a condition. Actually, the rules are fairly complex, so we will not tackle them all at this point.

Simple conditions can be written to compare any two expressions. The expressions must be "compatible." For example, we cannot compare integers to character strings. There are six possible relationships in the comparison, as listed:

Pascal notation	meaning
=	is equal to
>	is greater than
<	is less than
>=	is greater than or equal to
<=	is less than or equal to
<>	is not equal to

In performing the comparisons, the two expressions can be as simple or as complex as we require. For example, each of the following is a valid condition.

```
Sum = 15
R - C <= 0
0.05 * Nickels < 0.25 * Quarters
State = 'Virgina'
Name > 'Brown'
```

The last two examples involve string variables (State and Name). They might, therefore, behave differently for different computers. In fact, they might be illegal on some. For Turbo Pascal, two strings are equal if their values are identical (including having the same length). For example,

```
'Jerry' = 'Jerry'
```

is true, but

```
'Jerry   ' = 'Jerry'
```

is false.

When we compare two strings in Turbo Pascal to see if one is greater than the other, we get an alphabetical comparison. A blank space precedes any digit, which precedes any uppercase letter, which precedes any lowercase letter. Thus,

`' ' < '0' < '1' < . . . < '9' < 'A' < . . . < 'Z' < 'a' < . . . < 'z'`

In our example, Name > 'Brown', the condition will be true for any value beginning with C, D, and so on, or any lowercase letter. It will also be true for any value beginning with 'Brown' but longer than five characters. If we compare two strings in Turbo Pascal, the longer is considered greater if they match up through the last character of the shorter.

This set of rules is fairly complex, but it does ensure that, in most situations, a string comparison will have the results we would expect (except for lowercase, which is handled differently from a dictionary).

Some other verbal conditions, such as "is not greater than," can be seen to be equivalent to one of those listed earlier. In fact, we can give a list of **negations** for each of the six relationships, as shown in the table. (The negation of a condition is the result of using the word "not" with the condition.) The negation of "greater than" (>) is "not greater than," which is equivalent to "less than or equal to" (<=).

```
---------------------
Condition   Negation
---------------------
    =          <>
    >          <=
    <          >=
   >=           <
   <=           >
   <>           =
---------------------
```

The use of comparisons in conditions is illustrated by our earlier examples and will be further illustrated in the following subsection.

IF–THEN–ELSE   □   The second general category of a decision structure is commonly referred to as an **if–then–else structure**. It recognizes that sometimes there are two sets of steps to be performed: one if the condition is true and the other if it is not. Pascal has a statement that is specifically designed to handle this situation. Its form is summarized as follows:

```
if condition then
   statement to be performed if condition is true
else
   statement to be performed if condition is false
```

As for the if–then, the "statement to be performed" can be a compound statement (a list enclosed between a begin and an end). Thus, for example, if both branches are compound statements, we will have

```
if condition then
  begin
    list of steps to be performed if condition is true
  end
else
  begin
    list of steps to be performed if condition is false
  end
```

NOTE In each "list of steps", the steps are separated by semicolons. However, *there must be no semicolons before or after the "else"*. Again, the indentation pattern shown is optional but useful in conveying the structure to a reader.

In the English language, situations that require this type of decision structure frequently are described using the word "otherwise". Other possible indications that two branches are involved might include phrases such as "if not, . . .".

As an example, let us give a code segment for this situation. We wish to double the value of an integer variable J if its current value is less than 5, otherwise triple the value. In addition, we will print a message telling which occurred.

Notice that this does fall in the general category of decision we are discussing. There are two possible branches: J is less than 5 or it is not. The if–then–else is therefore appropriate, and we write

```
if J < 5 then
  begin
    J := 2 * J;
    Writeln('J was doubled to ',J)
  end
else
  begin
    J := 3 * J;
    Writeln('J was tripled to ',J)
  end
```

Notice that each branch includes two steps, so each branch uses a begin and end.

For our next example, we will find the smaller of two test scores, Score1 and Score2, placing the answer in the variable SmallScore. Assuming these declarations,

```
Score1, Score2 : integer;
SmallScore     : integer;
```

we can write:

```
if Score1 < Score2 then
  SmallScore := Score1
else
  SmallScore := Score2
```

At first glance, this example sometimes bothers students. They ask (reasonably), "What if the scores are equal?" The answer is that, for example, if the two scores are both 90, the answer should be 90. This program segment will take the else branch because the condition 90 < 90 is false. It will set SmallScore to Score2, which is 90. Thus, when they are equal the segment does in fact yield the correct answer.

For our final example in this subsection, we develop a short program that uses a decision structure. This common example occurs in companies that pay for overtime. In its simplest form, the rule might be that any hours in excess of 40 earn "time and a half." This means that the pay for those hours is 1.5 times the pay for the usual hours. We will write a program to calculate pay, given the hours worked and the hourly pay rate.

We begin, just as we did for the programs in Chapter 1, with a tentative variable list and a preliminary algorithm.

Constant:	EndOfData	value 0	Used to terminate loop
Input:	Hours	real	Hours worked
	HourlyRate	real	Pay per hour
Output:	Pay	real	Pay (before taxes, etc)

```
print instructions
repeat these steps until the user enters 0 for hourly rate
    prompt for hours and hourly rate
    read Hours, HourlyRate
    if HourlyRate is not 0 do these steps:
        calculate Pay
        print Pay
```

We have chosen an HourlyRate value of 0 for the terminating entry.

Since the pay is not calculated by a single formula, we need to refine this step. The rule described above indicates that the method to use depends on how many hours were worked. This leads us to an if–then–else decision structure, with the condition "Hours > 40" determining what steps to perform. If the condition is true, we pay overtime; if false, we do not. We obtain the following incomplete Pascal segment. (The italicized portion needs more refinement.)

```
if Hours > 40 then
    calculate Pay using overtime rule
else
    Pay := Hours * HourlyRate
```

To refine the first branch, we might do the calculations in three steps:

1. Calculate the regular pay for the first 40 hours.

2. Calculate the overtime pay for the remaining hours. This is the number of overtime hours (Hours − 40) times the overtime rate (HourlyRate * 1.5).

3. Add the two to get Pay.

If so, we would write

```
if Hours > 40 then
    begin
        RegularPay := 40 * HourlyRate;
        OvertimePay := (Hours - 40) * HourlyRate * 1.5;
```

```
                        Pay := RegularPay + OvertimePay
            end
          else
            Pay := Hours * HourlyRate
```

Notice that this adds two variables, RegularPay and OvertimePay, that were not in the plan for our original variables list. In addition, we *must* write the three steps enclosed in a begin and end. The complete program appears in Figure 2-8. We have shaded the decision structure for calculating the pay. Observe that it is placed precisely where the pay calculation would have gone if pay were calculated by a single assignment statement.

One other point to observe is the form of the output in the sample run. The default for printing a real number is the exponential notation. In the next section, we will learn some techniques for obtaining a more readable output for real numbers.

```
program Payroll(Input, Output);
{
      Written by:  XXXXXXXX   XX/XX/XX
         Purpose:  To calculate pay based on hours worked and hourly pay
                   rate, where the rule used depends on whether overtime
                   was earned (hours in excess of 40).
   Procedures used:  Instructions, to print instructions for user.
}
const
   EndOfData = 0;                          {used to terminate loop}

   var
      Hours        : real;                 {hours worked, input}
      HourlyRate   : real;                 {hourly pay rate, input}
      Pay          : real;                 {pay before taxes, output}
      RegularPay   : real;                 {pay for first 40 hours}
      OvertimePay  : real;                 {pay for overtime hours}

   procedure Instructions;
   begin
   {
       The details of this procedure are left as an exercise.
   }
   end; {Instructions}

   begin {Payroll}

   {*** Before the loop, print instructions for the user.}

      Instructions;

   {*** Process input: read hours and hourly rate; use an if-then-else
         structure to calculate pay; print answers. Quit when hourly rate
         of 0 is entered.}

      repeat
         Writeln;
```

Figure 2-8 If . . . then . . . else (Continued)

```
        Write('Enter hours and hourly rate (rate 0 to quit): ');
        Readln(Hours, HourlyRate);
        if HourlyRate <> EndOfData then
          begin

            if Hours > 40 then
              begin
                RegularPay := 40 * HourlyRate;
                OvertimePay := (Hours - 40) * HourlyRate * 1.5;
                Pay := RegularPay + OvertimePay
              end
            else
              Pay := Hours * HourlyRate;

            Writeln('The pay earned was ',Pay)
          end
    until HourlyRate = EndOfData

  {*** After loop, simply terminate program.}

  end.
```

SAMPLE INPUT AND OUTPUT

```
Enter hours and hourly rate (rate 0 to quit): 40 5.50
The pay earned was    2.2000000000E+02

Enter hours and hourly rate (rate 0 to quit): 34 23.45
The pay earned was    7.9730000000E+02

Enter hours and hourly rate (rate 0 to quit): 0 0
```

Figure 2-8 If . . . then . . . else

□
DPT There are a number of points to be observed in connection with decision structures in Pascal:

1. The negation of "greater than" is "less than or equal to." It is not "less than." Similar comments apply to other comparisons.

2. There is sometimes confusion concerning the use of ":=" and "=" in Pascal. Pascal uses "=" to mean "is equal to" and uses it in comparing two quantities or in identifying a named constant with its value. It can therefore be used in connection with an if statement, a repeat until loop, and some other situations we have not yet seen. The ":=" symbol, on the other hand, assigns a new value to a variable.

3. Due to the imprecision with which real values are stored in the computer, comparing two real quantities for equality can be misleading. For example, if we obtain a value for a variable X by adding ten 0.1's, the resulting value might not be exactly 1.0. Section 2-4 will discuss this issue further.

4. The issue of where to place semicolons and where not to can be confusing. Some incorrect placements can be caught by the compiler. Others cannot and simply lead to incorrect running of the program.

In general, semicolons separate statements in a list of statements. (Observe that the lists of statements are either set off by a begin and an end, or by a repeat and an until.) Based on what we have studied so far, we can formulate some guidelines.

Use a semicolon when the next step begins with:
    a "Readln" or "Writeln"
    a procedure name (e.g., Instructions)
    a variable for an assignment statement
    an "if" (there are exceptions to this)

Do not use a semicolon right before these words:
    end (marking the end of the list of steps)
    until (also marking the end of the list of steps)
    begin (exception—at the start of the procedure or the main program)
    else

Do not use a semicolon right after these words:
    begin
    if
    then
    else
    repeat

For the short term, you can refer to these concrete guidelines. For the long term, you will want to remember the general rule:

> Use semicolons to separate statements in a list of statements.

5. As described earlier, the rule for the if–then and if–then–else statements require a begin and end only when there is more than one statement in the branch. The fact that the compiler follows this rule can lead to some strange interpretations if we forget the begin or end. For example, consider

```
Written:                    Intended:
if X > Y then               if X > Y then
    T := 1;                     begin
    S := 3;                        T := 1;
                                   S := 3
                                end;
```

The compiler assumes that only the T:=1 goes with the if. The S:=3 assignment is executed whether or not X is greater than Y.

Similarly, consider

```
Written:                    Intended:
if X > Y then               if X > Y then
    S := 0;                     begin
    T := 0;                        S := 0;
else                               T := 0
```

```
      S := 1;                              end
      T := 2;                           else
                                          begin
                                            S := 1;
                                            T := 2
                                          end;
```

The compiler, when it sees the "else" will think that the if terminated with the assignment S:=0. It will therefore indicate an error on this line. However, it would not detect the error in the else branch.

Even experienced Pascal Programmers can fall into the trap of forgetting the begin and end. Leaving it off for the special case (1 statement in the branch) allowed by the compiler increases the likelihood of making this mistake.

One way to avoid this trap is to always use a begin and end, even if the branch contains only one statement. There are some tradeoffs involved in this. In addition to avoiding the pitfall, it makes the program easier to modify in the future. On the other hand, the extra, unneeded begins and ends can hinder program readability.

6. Finally, programmers sometimes view an if–then–else as equivalent to two if–then's. In fact, this is frequently true. For example, these two segments of code have identical meaning:

```
if Score1 < Score2 then              if Score1 > Score2 then
   SmallScore := Score1                 SmallScore := Score1;
else                                 if Score1 >= Score2 then
   SmallScore := Score2                 SmallScore := Score2
```

However, these do not:

```
    if J < 5 then                        if J < 5 then
       J := 2*J                             J := 2*J;
    else                                 if J >= 5 then
       J := 3*J                             J := 3*J
```

For example, suppose that J has a value of 4 when the segment is executed. In the left hand segment, since J < 5 is true, the first branch will be executed, causing J to become 8. The else branch will not be executed. In the right hand segment, since J < 5 is true, the first if statement will change J to 8. Now the condition J >= 5 in the second if statement is examined. Since it is true (8 >= 5 is true), the second if statement will change J to 24.

To avoid this type of pitfall, we should NOT code if–then–else structures with two consecutive if statements.

ADDING TO CASE STUDY No. 1

In this subsection, we consider further modifications to Case Study No. 1, begun in Section 1-4. The program is one which, for each student, calculates the total score on three tests. In Section 2-2, we added a procedure to handle the printing of instructions for the user. (The latest version of the program appears in Figure 2-7.)

We now consider two possible enhancements. First, we could modify the algorithm to also print an indication of whether the student is passing or failing. If we assume that a total score of 210 is a passing grade, then we might reason as follows:

If the Total is 210 or higher, then the student's result is "passing," otherwise it is "failing."

We may add a string[7] variable to our list of variables, which we will call Result. This variable will be assigned either the word "passing" or the word "failing" based on the total score. Thus, we have this segment of Pascal to add to our main program:

```
if Total >= 210 then
    Result := 'passing'
else
    Result := 'failing'
```

We will place this immediately after the step that calculates the Total variable, on which it is based, and modify the Writeln statement to include this variable in its list of items to print.

Our second modification will, in addition, print a message identifying those students who are exempted from the final exam (total score above 290). We would like the output to look something like this for such a student:

```
The total is 298 for John Smith - passing
********* EXEMPT FROM FINAL *********
```

Since the message appears after the line with the total, name, and result, we will place the steps to do this after the Writeln statement that prints these values.

Notice that this is an if–then situation; no message is desired for those who are not exempt. Thus, we will write

```
if Total > 290 then
    Writeln('********* EXEMPT FROM FINAL *********')
```

Figure 2-9 contains the modified program, with the changes shaded. Notice that these changes do not directly affect the Instructions procedure, although we should probably modify it to reflect the changes. This is left as an exercise. (The sample input and output was generated by running the program exactly as it appears, without inserting the body of the Instructions procedure in the program.)

□ **TESTING** In Section 1-4, we introduced some of the concepts involved in program testing. At this point, we are concerned with testing after we have obtained a "clean compile." By this we mean that the compiler has not listed any syntax errors. The program runs, and we want to see whether it is generating correct answers. In that section, we listed three principles:

1. Check all answers. Include some data that is easy to check.

2. Test near boundaries; also test a random sampling away from the boundaries.

3. Include some erroneous input, especially if the program is designed to detect and warn about such errors.

In this subsection, we will look at the second of these principles in more detail.

When a program includes branching, boundary testing becomes especially important. By a "boundary" we mean a point at which the rule for determining

```
program TestScores(Input, Output);
{
  Written by:   XXXXXXXX   XX/XX/XX
     Purpose:   To calculate the total on three tests, and
                print that total with the student's name.
}
const
  EndOfData = '';                    {empty string to terminate input}

var
  Name    : string[20];             {student name, input}
  Score1, Score2, Score3
          : integer;                {three test scores, input}
  Total   : integer;                {total of test scores, calculated}
  Result  : string[7];              {'passing' or 'failing' result}

procedure Instructions;
begin
{
```

The *Instructions procedure is placed here, exactly as it*
appears in Figure 2-7.

```
}
end; {Instructions}

begin {TestScores}

{*** Before the loop print instructions.}

  Instructions;

{*** In the loop, read name and scores; calculate and print total;
     determine whether passing or failing, and whether exempt from
     final; quit when user enters empty name.}

  repeat
    Writeln;
    Write('Enter the name (just tap return to quit): ');
    Readln(Name);
    if Name <> EndOfData then
      begin
        Write('Now enter the three scores: ');
        Readln(Score1, Score2, Score3);
        Total := Score1 + Score2 + Score3;
        if Total >= 210 then
          Result := 'passing'
        else
          Result := 'failing';
        Writeln('The total is ', Total, ' for ', Name, ' - ', Result);
        if Total > 290 then
          Writeln('********* EXEMPT FROM FINAL *********')
      end
```

Figure 2-9   If . . . then (Continued)

```
      until Name = EndOfData;

{*** After loop print message and stop the program.}

   Writeln;
   Writeln('Scores program is terminating.')
end.
```

SAMPLE INPUT AND OUTPUT

```
Enter the name (just tap return to quit): Joan Smith
Now enter the three scores: 78 67 87
The total is 232 for Joan Smith - passing

Enter the name (just tap return to quit): Tim Rae
Now enter the three scores: 34 99 71
The total is 204 for Tim Rae - failing

Enter the name (just tap return to quit): Sally Tie
Now enter the three scores: 60 61 59
The total is 180 for Sally Tie - failing

Enter the name (just tap return to quit): Alex Wilkins
Now enter the three scores: 100 95 96
The total is 291 for Alex Wilkens - passing
********* EXEMPT FROM FINAL *********

Enter the name (just tap return to quit):

Scores program is terminating.
```

Figure 2-9   If . . . then

the answer changes. Experience has shown that programs are more likely to contain errors at or near boundary points. As a result, we want to include special tests to make sure that the program works at and near the boundary points.

For example, consider our case study program. There are now a number of different boundary points. Of course, there are still the boundaries of 0 and 100 for each individual score, which we included in our original test plan in Section 1-4. In addition, we now have two more boundaries, based on the total score. They are 210 and 290. At 210, the rule for determining pass or fail changes, and at 290, the rule for telling whether or not the student is exempt from the final exam changes. It is a good idea to include test cases that result in values exactly on the boundary, just below the boundary, and just above the boundary. Hence, in our test plan, we might write

Boundary on passing:
    70, 69, 70—total 209, fail
    65, 76, 69—total 210, pass
    100, 50, 61—total 211, pass

Boundary on exempting final:
    100, 90, 99—total 289, not exempt
    95, 97, 98—total 290, not exempt
    99, 96, 96—total 291, exempt

In addition to these boundary values, we would also include other passing and failing grades chosen randomly and other exempting and nonexempting grades chosen randomly.

COMMENT   Of the three tests listed for the boundary on passing, the first two are the most vital: 209 is the highest failing grade and 210 is the lowest passing grade. For the second list, the second and third tests are the most vital.

In general, in testing a program involving branching, we will choose some test cases that exercise the boundary points, as well as others chosen more randomly within the different branches.

REVIEW

Terms and concepts

multiple-way branches
if-then structure
compound statement
Backus-Naur form (BNF)

syntax diagram
negation
if-then-else structure

Pascal syntax

Conditions

```
expression relationship expression
```

The relationship is one of =, >, <, >=, <=, and <>.

The expressions must be "compatible" (e.g., cannot compare integers to strings).

String comparisons (Turbo Pascal)

```
' '<'0'<...<'9'<'A'<...<'Z'<'a'<...<'z'
```

To be equal, the strings must be the same length. Examples:

```
'John' < 'Johnson'
'Joe' > 'Bill'
'An' < 'an'
'Sue   ' <> 'Sue'
```

Decisions (see also Appendix D)

```
if-then:  if condition then
             statement
```

The "statement" can be a compound statement, yielding:

```
            if condition then
                begin
                    list of statements separated by semicolons
                end
if-then-else:   if condition then
                    statement (can be compound statement)
                else
                    statement (can be compound statement)
```

EXERCISES

1. Run the payroll program exactly as it appears in Figure 2-8. Then add appropriate steps for the instructions procedure and run it again.

2. Give an appropriate decision structure (if–then–else or if–then) for each of these situations. Use appropriate variables, and give both the necessary declarations and the segment of Pascal for the decision.

   *a.

Income	Tax Rate (%)
Less than $8000.00	2
$8000.00 or higher	4.5

   *b. If the sex code is "M," add 1 to the variable Males, otherwise add 1 to the variable Females.

   c. The commission rate is 3 percent if the sales amount is less than $150. If the sales amount is $150 or more, the commission rate should be 5 percent.

   d. Sales tax is 6 percent on any purchase of $500 or less, but only 3.5 percent on a purchase over $500.

   *e. If the tax is greater than $550, a penalty of 6 percent should be added to the tax.

   f. If T is currently 0, do nothing, otherwise add 1 to the value of T.

   g. Calculate the bonus based on the current value of Years and Sales. If Years is 5 or less, then the bonus is nothing, otherwise it is 0.1 percent of the sales.

   h. If the average of the three test scores is greater than 59.5, print "passes".

   i. If the ratio of two integers I and J is above 4.7, then calculate K as the sum of I and J; if not, K is the difference.

   j. If Sex is 'female', then daily caloric need is 16 times body weight in pounds. If Sex is 'male', then daily caloric need is 18 times body weight in pounds. (Assume that Sex has one of the two listed values.)

   *k. Given variables representing hours and minutes in the range from 1:00 to 7:00, add 1 minute to the time. (For example, for Hours = 5 and Minutes = 59, the segment should change Hours to 6 and Minutes to 0).

   l. A variable Dice contains a value between 2 and 12. Your program segment should print a message "you lose $5" and subtract 5 from a Money variable if the value of Dice is 7 or less; for 8 or more, it should add 5 and print "you win $5".

*3. For each program segment of Exercise 2, determine all boundary values and come up with a minimum set of test cases for each branch at and near each boundary value.

*4. Add appropriate input, output, and looping steps to create an entire program built around the situations described in Exercise 2(a), (c), (d), and (g). Where it makes sense, add names to the list of data input by the user.

*5. Modify the case study example (Figure 2-9) to print "IMPROVING" for those students whose third grade is better than the average of the first two grades. What additions would be needed in the test plan?

For each of Exercises 6 to 10, (a) determine the input and output and give a variables list; (b) write and refine an algorithm; (c) create a test plan; (d) write the program in Pascal; and (e) run the program, utilizing your test plan to help locate errors.

6. Each line of data has three integers A, B, and C. These form a "Pythagorean triple" if A*A + B*B = C*C. Write an algorithm to read each input line; print the values of A, B, and C; and print a message: either "is a Pythagorean triple" or "is not a Pythagorean triple."

7. The amount of sales is quantity times price. The discount is 1 percent of the sales amount if the quantity is over 100, otherwise 0. The net price is the sales amount minus the discount. The commission is 3 percent of the net price if the net price is less than $250, 5 percent for $250 or more. The program should input quantity and price, then calculate and print the sales amount, discount, net price, commission rate, and commission.

8. The first input line contains the beginning balance of a savings account for a year. This is followed by a series of inputs, each representing one transaction for the account. Each consists of a transaction code ('W' = withdrawal, 'D' = deposit) and an amount. Write a program to determine the final balance at the end of the year by adding and subtracting from the running balance based on each transaction. (You can assume that the code is either a 'W' or a 'D'.)

   Revise the program to print a running account of the transactions for the account, including the beginning and ending balance for each transaction.

9. Each data set has an employee name, an incentive factor (in the range 0.01 to 0.15), a weekly base salary, and the number of units produced during the week. Write a program to calculate the payroll for the company. A person's actual salary is computed from the base salary as follows: If the number of units produced is less than 500, then 10 cents is deducted from the pay for each unit by which the quota of 500 was missed. If the units produced is 500 or more, then the base salary is increased by an amount consisting of the incentive factor times the number of units produced.

   Modify the program to also print a message "at or above quota" or "below quota" for each employee.

10. The data is the same as in Exercise 9. However, this time the salary is computed as follows: If the number of units produced is less than 750, the salary is merely the base salary. If 750 or more units were produced, the incentive factor is treated as a percentage; this percentage of the base salary is added to the base salary to obtain the actual salary.

11. Write a complete Pascal program to input sex, current weight in pounds, goal weight, and daily caloric intake. Use the calculation of Exercise 2(j) to calculate and print the projected number of days that are required to attain the weight loss. Use the relationship

$$3500 \text{ calories} = 1 \text{ pound}$$

and calculate the daily caloric need based on the average of the current weight and the goal weight.

2-4 ADDITIONAL PASCAL TOPICS

In this section, we will explain how to control the appearance of output from a Pascal program and introduce the use of the printer. We will also investigate some of the built-in features of Pascal that aid us in writing our programs. We will discuss integer and real numbers in more detail and show how we can convert numbers from real to integer and from integer to real.

FORMATTING OUTPUT

When we ran the programs from previous examples, we probably were not overjoyed by the form of the output of our real numbers. Instead of seeing an old friend such as "23.49," we may have seen scientific notation such as "2.34900000E+01." The two forms for the number are mathematically equivalent, but they are vastly different from the point of view of simplicity and understandability. Admittedly, there are certainly cases in which one would prefer scientific notation to the explicit presence of all the decimal positions; for example, we probably would prefer the scientific form "3.5E−12" to the explicit form "0.0000000000035". The best approach is for the programmer to decide on the form of the output as part of the program design process. We will now describe the **formatting** tools that Pascal provides for programmer control of the way numbers should look when printed by a program.

Output position

Whether we are outputting to a display screen or to a printer, we write the first character of the output to a particular location. This location has both vertical (row) and horizontal (column) attributes with respect to the top and left margin of the screen or sheet of paper. We will refer to this location as the **output position**. Also, to ease the discussion, let us assume that the top line of the screen or sheet is line 1 and the leftmost character position is column 1.

If we cause the output position to become line 1, column 1, then we will refer to this action as "going to **top-of-form**". In the case of output to a screen, top-of-form is usually accompanied by erasing all the information that may have been on the screen. Some versions of Pascal provide the standard procedure "Page" to accomplish top-of-form. Turbo Pascal has taken a nonstandard approach. The built-in procedure ClrScr can be used to clear the screen. To advance the paper in the printer to a new page, Turbo Pascal provides the capability of sending control characters to the printer. For many popular printers,

```
Write(Lst, Chr(12))
```

will generate a form feed, causing the printer to advance to what it thinks is the top of the page.[1]

For the rest of this discussion, we will assume that we are in some given print position and that we wish to control the output of the next item, including the setting of the print position of the beginning of the following output item.

Output of integers

Suppose that we wish to output the integer variable Area, starting at the current print position and within the next three output columns. In this case, we can use one of the two Pascal statements:

```
Writeln(Area:3)
```

or

```
Write(Area:3)
```

The effect of "Writeln(Area:3)" is to output the value of Area right-justified within the next three columns and to set the print position to column 1 of the next line. The effect of "Write(Area:3)" is to output the value of Area right-justified within the next three columns and to set the print position to the next column of the same line (that is, three columns from the original print position).

NOTE Right-justified means that the number is printed in the columns allotted as far to the right as possible. For example, if we print a two digit number right justified in five columns, it will be preceded by three blanks.

We illustrate the results for an Area that has a value of 12:

```
Writeln(Area:3)
                       current print position
                                 ↓
    current line  →            12
                          |#  ← marks next print position
            left margin   |
```

```
Write(Area:3)

                       current print position
                                 ↓
    current line  →            12#  ← marks next print position
                          |
            left margin   |
```

We are assuming that there are enough columns remaining on the current line to fit all of the output. If not, part of the output can **wrap** to the next line of the output device. Note that the **filler** character (to the left of "12") is a blank space. If the value to be output is larger than the number of columns specified, then the output will begin in the current print position and extend to the right for as many columns as are necessary to represent the number. We should also note that the "−" sign for a negative number will occupy an output column. We can use any reasonable number of columns in place of the "3" used in the above example. If "Writeln(Area)" or "Write(Area)" is used without specifying the number of columns, the resulting form of the output will be as if "Writeln(Area:1)" or "Write(Area:1)" were used.[2]

To provide maximum flexibility for the programmer, the number of columns can be expressed as an integer variable or expression. For example, if "Width" is an integer variable or constant, we can validly use the statement

```
Writeln(Area:Width+3)
```

Output of reals

In order to specify the format for a real number output, we can specify not only the number of columns (**fieldwidth**) to be used, but also the number of decimal places (**precision**). Suppose that "Number" has the value 34.567. We will show various possibilities for outputting "Number." In all cases, we assume that the current print position is in column 1.[3] (The ¦ symbol signifies the left margin of the output.)

Statement	Output	Comment
Writeln(Number:6:3)	¦34.567	Perfect fit!
Writeln(Number:6:2)	¦ 34.57	Blank on left, rounded
Writeln(Number:7:2)	¦ 34.57	Right-justified
Writeln(Number:7:0)	¦ 35	No decimal point!
Writeln(Number:2:2)	¦34.57	Takes all it needs, if you don't specify enough
Writeln(Number:7)	¦3.5E+01	Tight squeeze
Writeln(Number:8)	¦3.46E+01	Increasing precision
Writeln(Number:9)	¦3.457E+01	Ditto
Writeln(Number:10)	¦3.4567E+01	Ditto
Writeln(Number:11)	¦3.45670E+01	How far will it go?
Writeln(Number:18:10)	¦ 34.5670000000	
Writeln(Number:18)	¦ 3.4567000000E+01	Aarrrggh!
Writeln(Number)	¦ 3.4567000000E+01	Turbo's default
Writeln(Number:19)	¦ 3.4567000000E+01	Another space
Writeln(Number:0)	¦3.5E+01	Minimum configuration
Writeln(Number:0:10)	¦34.5670000000	Precision 10

As we can see from the table, the possibilities are almost endless. One principle that we note is that the desired precision is always printed, even if the fieldwidth must be violated in order to do it (the example with fieldwidth = 0 and precision = 10 provides an extreme situation). The next priority after precision is fieldwidth.

Again, to provide maximum flexibility for the programmer, the fieldwidth and precision can be expressed as integer variables or expressions. For example, if "Width" and "Places" are integer variables or constants, we can validly use the statement

```
Writeln(Number:Width+3:Places-1)
```

Character and string output

A fieldwidth value can also be used with a char variable or a string variable. The treatment of the two is identical, so we combine them in our discussion.[4]

Suppose that Name is a string[12] variable whose current value is 'Joe'. The following table indicates the output for various uses of fieldwidth. Observe that the current length of the string, not its maximum length, determines what is printed.

```
     Statement            Output              Comment
--------------------------------------------------------------
Writeln(Name)          | Joe
Writeln(Name:4)        |  Joe             Preceded by one blank
Writeln(Name:7)        |     Joe          Four blanks
Writeln(Name:2)        | Joe              Will print entire value
--------------------------------------------------------------
```

The output is right-justified in a field of the proper width. In any case, the entire value is printed.

A technique that can be useful is illustrated by the following example:

```
Writeln(Test1:5, ' ':7, Test2:5, ' ':7, Total:5)
```

This prints Test1, Test2, and Total. In between, the ' ':7 prints a blank space, right-justified in a field of width 7. This has the effect of printing seven blank spaces. For example, for values 95, 68, and 100 for the three tests, this would print the following. (The underscores on the line represent blank spaces printed.)

```
___95_____68_____100
```

This technique can be useful in creating tables of output.

Mixed output

To complete this discussion of formatting output, we show two ways to produce the output line

```
        The Weight of Player 85 is 211.6 pounds.
```

For this example, we suppose that the integer variable "Number" contains the value 85 and that the real variable "Weight" contains the value 211.6.

First method:

```
Writeln;
Writeln('     The Weight of Player ', Number:1,
   ' is ', Weight:1:1, ' pounds.')
```

Second method:

```
Writeln;
Write('     The Weight of Player ');
Write(Number:1);
Write(' is ');
Write(Weight:1:1);
Write(' pounds.');
Writeln
```

The running of the above two segments of code should produce identical results. In the first, the entire line is written with one Writeln. In the second, the Write is used to print each part of the line. The final Writeln moves the print position to the following line.

Which is preferable? It is a matter of choice. There are several exercises at the end of the section that will help to clarify this subject of formatting output.

□

OUTPUT TO THE PRINTER

For many programs, it is more appropriate to print output on the printer than on the terminal screen. Sending the output to the printer is accomplished by including the word **Lst** in the Write or Writeln statement as shown:[5]

```
Writeln(Lst, 'This will go to the printer.')
```

The appearance of output on a printed page is often quite different from the way it appears on a screen. A printed page is sometimes organized into a table consisting of columns of information, whereas the screen usually shows lines of interactive dialogue. The program shown in Figure 2-10 illustrates both of these points. The purpose of the program is to produce a small table of square roots. Note the way that the page and column headings are handled using the formatting techniques discussed earlier in this section. [The expression "Sqrt(Number)" in the Writeln calculates the square root of the number. It will be more fully explained in the next subsection.]

```
program RootTable(Input, Output);
{
        Written by:  XXXXXXXXX  XX/XX/XX
           Purpose:  To create a small table of square roots on
                     the printer.
}
const
  EndOfData  = -1;                     { terminating value }

var
  Number  : integer;                   { user input }

begin {RootTable}

{*** Print headings.}

  Writeln(Lst, ' ':29, 'TABLE OF SQUARE ROOTS');
  Writeln(Lst);
  Writeln(Lst, ' ':28, 'Number          Square Root');
  Writeln(Lst, ' ':27, '--------      --------------');
  Writeln(Lst);
```

Figure 2-10   Output to a Printer (Continued)

```
{*** Read numbers in a loop, calculate square roots and print.}

   repeat
     Write('Enter a number (-1 to terminate): ');
     Readln(Number);
     if  Number <> EndOfData then
       Writeln(Lst, ' ':29, Number:4, ' ':7, Sqrt(Number):10:4)
   until  Number = EndOfData;

{*** Print terminating message and stop program.}

   Writeln;
   Writeln('RootTable program is terminating.')
end.
```

SAMPLE INPUT AND OUTPUT

Screen display:

```
Enter a number (-1 to terminate): 2
Enter a number (-1 to terminate): 4
Enter a number (-1 to terminate): 6
Enter a number (-1 to terminate): 8
Enter a number (-1 to terminate): 10
Enter a number (-1 to terminate): 12
Enter a number (-1 to terminate): 14
Enter a number (-1 to terminate): 16
Enter a number (-1 to terminate): 18
Enter a number (-1 to terminate): 20
Enter a number (-1 to terminate): 22
Enter a number (-1 to terminate): 24
Enter a number (-1 to terminate): -1

RootTable program is terminating.
```

Printer:

```
             TABLE OF SQUARE ROOTS
          _____

          Number          Square Root
          _____        _____

             2              1.4142
             4              2.0000
             6              2.4495
             8              2.8284
            10              3.1623
            12              3.4641
            14              3.7417
            16              4.0000
            18              4.2426
            20              4.4721
            22              4.6904
            24              4.8990
```

Figure 2-10   Output to a Printer

COMMENT As illustrated by this example, in Turbo Pascal a program can send output to both the printer and the screen. Sometimes we display the answers on the screen and we print on paper to obtain a permanent record.

For example, we might modify the example to read

```
if Number <> EndOfData then
  begin
    Writeln('The square root is ', Sqrt(Number):1:4);
    Writeln(Lst, ' ':29, Number:4, ' ':7, Sqrt(Number):10:4)
  end
```

Observe that the form of the output for the printer can differ from that for the screen.

SQUARE ROOTS AND ABSOLUTE VALUE

There are several built-in library functions of Pascal that can help the programmer with numerical calculations. Among the most common and useful are those that take the **square root (Sqrt)** of a number or the **absolute value (Abs)** of a number.

In order to calculate a square root, the programmer can use the form

```
Sqrt(exp)
```

where "exp" is any real or integer variable or expression. The value of the square root function is always a real number and only makes sense when "exp" has a nonnegative value. Some example values of the square root function are listed.

Number	Sqrt(Number) to two places
25	5.00
10.3	3.21
0	0.00
−1	*** error, Number must be positive or zero
1	1.00
0.5	0.71

Some example Pascal statements that use the square root are

```
Deviation := Sqrt(Variance);
Range := 3 * Sqrt(Number + 5);
Writeln(Sqrt(Number):6:2)

Root := (-B + Sqrt(B*B - 4*A*C)) / (2*A)
```

In order to calculate an absolute value, the programmer can use the form

```
Abs(exp)
```

where "exp" is any real or integer variable or expression. The value of the absolute value function is an integer if "exp" is an integer and is real if "exp" is real. Some example values of the absolute value function are listed.

Number	Abs(Number)
25	25
−10.3	10.3
0	0
0.0	0.0
−1	1

Some example Pascal statements that use the absolute value are

```
Magnitude := Abs(Measurement);
Writeln(Abs(Number):5);
Distance := Abs(X - Y);
GeoMean := Sqrt(Abs(N*M));
if Abs(X - 1) < 0.00001 then
   Writeln('The number is close to 1');
```

Note that the square root and absolute value functions can be combined as in the expression "Sqrt(Abs(N*M))". (This expression means to take the square root of the absolute value of N*M. That is, first N*M is calculated, then its absolute value is determined, and finally the square root of that absolute value is obtained.)

In earlier sections, we observed that real arithmetic is not always precise. The reason for this has to do with the way real numbers are stored in the computer. For example, if we add 0.1 ten times, placing the answer in Sum, the if statement

```
if Sum = 1.0 then Writeln('Precisely 1.0')
```

might not print the message.

One approach to dealing with this difficulty uses the absolute value function. We would expect that Sum would be very close to 1.0. We might write

```
if Abs(Sum - 1.0) < 0.000001 then
   Writeln('Sum is "close to" 1.0')
```

(The expression "Abs(Sum − 1.0)" calculates the difference between X and 1.0.) If *absolute* precision is required, then real variables will not be appropriate.

□
FUNCTIONS

Sqrt and Abs are just two examples of standard Pascal functions. Others will be discussed later in this section. One (Chr) was introduced very briefly in Section 2-1.

The examples given above illustrate a number of important ideas associated with functions in general.

1. The **call** (or **invocation** or **use**) of the function takes the form

```
function-name(argument)
```

The **argument** is the value the function uses in doing its calculation. For example, in the expression

```
Sqrt(Variance)
```

the variable Variance is the argument. It represents the number whose square root is to be calculated.

(As we will see later, some functions have two or more arguments.)

2. The use of the function can take place almost anywhere that a variable or expression can be used. For example, it can appear on the right side of an assignment statement, in the condition for an if statement, or in the list of values to be written by a Writeln statement.

It may not appear in a call to Readln or on the left side of an assignment statement.

3. The precedence rules are expanded when a function appears in an expression. Function values are calculated first, prior to unary minus. This involves calculating the value of the argument with the usual precedence rules.

For example, consider the following expressions. The operations are done in the indicated order.

```
Sqrt(3*2+30)/5     First, evaluate the argument:
Sqrt(6+30)/5       * first
Sqrt(36)/5         + to finish the argument
6.0/5              Then, use the function
1.2                Finally, do the division.
```

□ **INTEGER OPERATIONS: MOD, DIV** In Section 2-1, on the assignment statement, we included a discussion of the "/" operator for division. This operator is sometimes called the "real division" operator because the result is always real. This is true even if the numbers being divided are integers. Some examples follow:

N	M	N / M
15	0.3	50.0
6.3	21	0.3
−32	5	−6.4
100	5	20.0
45	0.0	*** error, division by 0 is undefined ***

Pascal also allows for the concept of integer division, which is similar to the *long division* that is practiced by students in elementary school. In long division, we speak of a **quotient** and a **remainder** when we divide one integer into another. Similarly, in Pascal, we have two operations available: "**div**" to compute the quotient of two integers and "**mod**" to compute the remainder. The "div" and "mod" operations are used in the same way that the more familiar operations +, −, *, and / are used. Some examples of the operations of "div" and "mod" follow:

N	M	N div M	N mod M
5	2	2	1
−5	2	−2	−1
5	−2	−2	1
−5	−2	2	−1
23	23	1	0
−38	7	−5	−3
12	19	0	12
9	0	error	*** error, division by 0 is not allowed ***
5	2.0	error	*** error, both numbers must be integers ***

For two integers "N" and "M," the following relationship holds:

```
N = M*(N div M) + (N mod M)
```

as long as "M" is not equal to zero. The above statement is known as the **division algorithm** and is the basis for many other numerical algorithms.[6]

The operators div and mod have the same precedence as * and /. Thus, we can summarize the precedence rules so far as:

1. Function evaluation. This involves evaluating the arguments (using these rules), then invoking the function

2. Unary minus

3. *, /, div, and mod (left to right)

4. + and − (left to right)

5. Can use parentheses to group

□
INTRODUCING PREDEFINED IDENTIFIERS: MAXINT

The Pascal programming language supplies some assistance to the programmer in the form of **predefined identifiers**. As the term suggests, these identifiers can be used without the programmer declaring them, and, in addition, they have values that have already been established. One of the most useful of these identifiers is "**maxint**", which establishes the largest valid integer value that can be used for a specific implementation of Pascal. For Turbo Pascal (on a PC-compatible machine under MS-DOS), the value of maxint is 32767. This means that any integer values that are input, output, or calculated must lie in the range from −32767 to 32767 inclusive. The general rule is that all integer values must lie in the range from −maxint to maxint, inclusive. For some implementations, the value −maxint − 1 is also valid, but *defensive programming* suggests that the exception not be assumed or used. Another commonly seen value for maxint is 2147483647 (for some mainframe and minicomputer implementations of Pascal). The short Pascal program shown in Figure 2-11 can be used to discover the value of maxint for a particular implementation.

```
program CheckMax(Input, Output);
{
  Written by:  XXXXXXXXX  XX/XX/XX
     Purpose:  To discover the value of maxint.
}
begin {CheckMax}
  Writeln;
  Writeln('The value of maxint is ', maxint)
end.
```

Figure 2-11 Maxint

Note that the identifier "maxint" is not declared in the program. In fact, if "maxint" were declared as a constant or variable, it would no longer function as intended. For the curious, some experiments will be suggested in the exercises.

There are a number of standard predefined identifiers that will be introduced later. Implementations of Pascal often have their own special (nonstandard) predefined identifiers, but the use of these hinders **program portability** and should be avoided if possible.

□ **REAL-TO-INTEGER CONVERSIONS**

One of the most difficult aspects of numerical programming is the distinction between integers and real numbers that must be made by computer programs. We are accustomed in algebra to deal with integers as merely special cases of real numbers and not as an entirely different set of entities with their own rules and operators. However, as we have already seen, there are differences between the "worlds" of real numbers and integers in Pascal. Some of the differences are summarized in Figure 2-12.

One way to manage the differences between the two types of numbers might be to avoid mixing them; however, it is not always possible (or desirable) in practice.

For example, if we were attempting to calculate the average amount of rainfall per day for the month of June in a particular area, we would probably calculate the total amount of rain for the month (to tenths of an inch) and divide by 30. We see here that the total amount of rain is "naturally" a real number and the number 30 is "naturally" an integer (the number of days in the month). Therefore,

---

Real Numbers and Integer Numbers

Accuracy. Integer arithmetic is accurate. Real arithmetic can be inaccurate

Limits.   Integer numbers are limited to the range of −maxint to maxint inclusive. Real numbers also have limits of magnitude, but the range is immensely greater, so that the practical limit is more of precision than magnitude.

Operators. Integer numbers can use the "div" and "mod" operators. Real numbers cannot use these operators.

Figure 2-12 Real vs. Integer

our calculation of the average would involve a "**mixed-mode**" computation (a mix of a real and an integer). Suppose that the total is contained in the variable TotalRain and the number of days is contained in the variable Days. If the variable Average is to contain the answer, we have already seen that the statement

```
Average := TotalRain div Days
```

is illegal because TotalRain is a real variable. The alternative choice

```
Average := TotalRain / Days
```

is not only legal, but it will accomplish the purpose. The way that we know which division to select is our realization that the result Average is to be a real quantity. The rule that we must know about the operator "/" is

---

N / M is always real, regardless of the types of N and M.

There are other cases of mixing modes that are not so easily handled. For example, suppose that we have an amount of money in the real variable Allowance and we wish to calculate the number of video games that we can play at a quarter per game. The number of games should be expressed as an integer (it is not usually possible to purchase one half of a video game) and might be represented in the integer variable Games. We are naively led to the following mixed-mode Pascal statement

```
Games := Allowance / 0.25
```

Unfortunately, as we indicated in Section 2-1, this is *illegal* and leads to a run-time error. For this type of situation, Pascal provides the built-in function "**Trunc**" which converts a real number to an integer number by merely dropping the fractional part (that which follows the decimal point) of the real number. Thus, the Pascal statement that we should use is

```
Games := Trunc(Allowance / 0.25)
```

Some examples of the results of this conversion are

Allowance	Allowance/0.25	Games
10.34	41.36	41
5.20	20.8	20
1.99	7.96	7

As another example, suppose that a teacher grades on the basis of a final average according to the table:

$$90 - 100 = A$$
$$80 - 89 = B$$

$$70 - 79 = C$$
$$60 - 69 = D$$
$$\text{under } 60 = F$$

Suppose further that the final average is based on three 100-point examinations according to the computation

```
FinalAverage := (Exam1 + Exam2 + Exam3) / 3
```

where FinalAverage is a real variable and Exam1, Exam2, and Exam3 are integer variables. Consider the hypothetical student who has earned:

$$\text{Exam1} = 90$$
$$\text{Exam2} = 89$$
$$\text{Exam3} = 90$$
$$\text{FinalAverage} = 89.67$$

Should the student be awarded a grade of B for the course? Many teachers would handle this situation by treating FinalAverage as an integer variable instead of real. In this case, the value of FinalAverage would be 89 if we computed

```
FinalAverage := (Exam1 + Exam2 + Exam3) div 3
```

or if we computed

```
FinalAverage := Trunc((Exam1 + Exam2 +Exam3) / 3)
```

Pascal provides us with another possibility via the built-in function "**Round**". If we computed the final average for the student in question with the formula

```
FinalAverage := Round((Exam1 + Exam2 + Exam3) / 3)
```

then the value of FinalAverage would be 90 and the student would receive a grade of A for the course. The results of the function Round is illustrated as follows:

Exam1	Exam2	Exam3	(Exam1 + Exam2 + Exam3)/3	FinalAverage
90	89	90	89.67	90
89	90	89	89.33	89

To further illustrate the effect of the Round and Trunc functions, suppose that Number is a real variable and consider the table:

Number	Round(Number)	Trunc(Number)
12.1	12	12
11.99	12	11
−1.3	−1	−1
2.5	3	2
2.49	2	2
−2.5	−3	−2
−2.49	−2	−2
−0.5	−1	0

INTEGER-TO-REAL CONVERSIONS

Sometimes it is desirable to treat an integer number as a real number. For example, suppose that the integer variable Count represented the number of dollar bills that Jack has torn in trying to "stretch" his salary. If we wanted to output the value of the torn money, we might try the statement

```
Writeln('The value destroyed is $', Count:7:2)
```

However, the above statement is not allowed because "Count" is an integer variable. One remedy would be to use the statement

```
Writeln('The value destroyed is $', Count / 1:7:2)
```

Although the above statement has the desired result, its form is not readable programming. Pascal provides two possible solutions for this problem. For the first, suppose that Value is a real variable. Then, the job can be accomplished by the following statements

```
Value := Count;
Writeln('The value destroyed is $', Value:7:2)
```

The statement "Value := Count" is an **implicit conversion** from an integer value to a real value.

Turbo Pascal provides a second solution, not available in standard Pascal. This second solution involves the use of the built-in function "**Int**". The value of "Int(Count)" is a real number of the same magnitude as Count. Therefore, we can use the following statement

```
Writeln('The value destroyed is $', Int(Count):7 :2)
```

NOTE When Int is used on an integer argument, it performs an **explicit conversion** from integer to real. In the subsection below we shall see that Int may also be used for real arguments. (Its behavior for real arguments is somewhat different.)

REAL TO REAL CONVERSIONS

Often, when we are dealing with a real number, we want to know what number comes before the decimal point (the **integer part**) and what number comes after the decimal point (the **fractional part**). For example, if we are studying the distribution of our allowance into bills and change then

The integer part of the amount is the number of dollar bills that we could receive.

The fractional part of the amount represents change that we could receive.

Turbo Pascal provides the functions "Int" and "**Frac**" for the integer and fractional parts respectively.[7] Note that the values calculated by using Int and Frac are always real. The following table illustrates the behavior of the two functions

Number	Int(Number)	Frac(Number)
2.13	2.0	0.13
−5.67	−5.0	−0.67
17	17.0	0.0
−0.5	0.0	−0.5

To complete the discussion of the distribution of our allowance, suppose that the real variable Amount represents the money that we are to receive. The Pascal program of Figure 2-13 asks the user to input the amount of allowance to be received and distributes the allowance into $20, $10, $5, and $1 bills and quarters, dimes, nickels, and pennies for the change.

```
program Allowance(Input, Output);
{
    Written by:  XXXXXXXXXXXX  XX/XX/XX
        Purpose:  To distribute an allowance into $20, $10, $5 and $1 bills
                  and quarters, dimes, nickels, and pennies.
}
const
  EndOfData = 0;                          {Used to terminate loop}

var
  Amount     : real;                      {Value of allowance, input}
  Dollars    : integer;                   {Number of dollars to distribute}
  Twenties   : integer;                   {Number of twenty dollar bills}
  Tens       : integer;                   {Number of ten dollar bills}
  Fives      : integer;                   {Number of five dollar bills}
  Ones       : integer;                   {Number of one dollar bills}
  Cents      : integer;                   {Number of cents to distribute}
  Quarters   : integer;                   {Number of quarters}
  Dimes      : integer;                   {Number of dimes}
  Nickels    : integer;                   {Number of nickels}
  Pennies    : integer;                   {Number of pennies}

begin {Allowance}

{*** Print heading.}

  Writeln;
  Writeln('          A L L O W A N C E S');
  Writeln('          -------------------');
  Writeln;

{*** Read amount, calculate and print distribution.}

  repeat
    Writeln;
    Write('Enter the amount of the allowance (0 to quit): ');
    Readln(Amount);
    Writeln;
    if Amount <> EndOfData then
      begin
        Writeln('     DISTRIBUTION');
        Writeln;
        Dollars := Trunc(Int(Amount));
        Cents := Round(100 * Frac(Amount));
```

Figure 2-13   Mod and Div (Continued)

```
{*** Distribute the bills.}

Twenties := Dollars div 20;
Dollars := Dollars mod 20;
if Twenties > 0 then Writeln('$20 bills: ', Twenties:0);
Tens := Dollars div 10;
Dollars := Dollars mod 10;
if Tens > 0 then Writeln('$10 bills: ', Tens:0);
Fives := Dollars div 5;
Dollars := Dollars mod 5;
if Fives > 0 then Writeln('$5 bills: ', Fives:0);
Ones := Dollars;
if Ones > 0 then Writeln('$1 bills: ', Ones:0);

{*** Distribute the change.}

Quarters := Cents div 25;
Cents := Cents mod 25;
if Quarters > 0 then Writeln('Quarters: ', Quarters:0);
Dimes := Cents div 10;
Cents := Cents mod 10;
if Dimes > 0 then Writeln('Dimes: ', Dimes:0);
Nickels := Cents div 5;
Cents := Cents mod 5;
if Nickels > 0 then Writeln('Nickels: ', Nickels:0);
Pennies := Cents;
if Pennies > 0 then Writeln('Pennies: ', Pennies:0);
Writeln
end
until Amount = EndOfData;

{*** Print message and stop the program.}

Writeln;
Writeln('Allowance program is terminating.')
end.
```

SAMPLE INPUT AND OUTPUT

```
        A L L O W A N C E S
        -------------------

Enter the amount of the allowance (0 to quit): 234.56

        DISTRIBUTION

$20 bills: 11
$10 bills: 1
$1 bills: 4
Quarters: 2
Nickels: 1
Pennies: 1


Enter the amount of the allowance (0 to quit): 123
```

Figure 2-13 Mod and Div (Continued)

```
        DISTRIBUTION

$20 bills: 6
$1 bills: 3

Enter the amount of the allowance (0 to quit): 10.34

        DISTRIBUTION

$10 bills: 1
Quarters: 1
Nickels: 1
Pennies: 4

Enter the amount of the allowance (0 to quit): 0

Allowance program is terminating.
```

Figure 2-13 Mod and Div

COMMENTS

1. Consider the shaded step

```
        Cents := Round(100 * Frac(Amount));
```

near the top of the loop. If the amount is 17.23, we would expect Frac(Amount) to be 0.23 and 100 * Frac(Amount) to be 23.0. However, due to the imprecision of real numbers, it might be just below or just above 23.0. To be on the safe side, we use Round rather than Trunc to convert to an integer.

2. Consider the two shaded steps

```
        Twenties := Dollars div 20;
        Dollars := Dollars mod 20;
```

Suppose that Dollars has the value 114. The first step sees how many twenty dollar bills this represents. The second sees how much is left to be distributed as smaller bills (114 mod 20 is 14). The Dollars variable is changed to this value and the program continues.

□
OTHER STANDARD NUMERIC LIBRARY FUNCTIONS

There are several other standard Pascal functions that are available for numeric computation. Each of these is supplied with an **argument** (sometimes called a **parameter**) and returns a **value**. In the table on page 95, we list the functions that we have discussed along with the other standard numeric functions.

□
DPT

Defensive programming for the topics covered in this section consists primarily of remembering several key points.

1. Division by 0 is illegal. A good program will check the value, as in this example:

```
        if NumberOfTests = 0 then
          Writeln('No tests taken')
        else
```

Function	Argument	Value	Comment
ArcTan	Either	Real	Arctangent in radians
Abs	Either	Same	Absolute value
Cos	Either	Real	Cosine of angle given in radians
Exp	Either	Real	Exponential function
Frac	Either	Real	Fractional part
Int	Either	Real	Integer part
Ln	Either >0	Real	Natural logarithm
Round	Real	Integer	Rounds off
Sin	Either	Real	Sine of angle given in radians
Sqr	Either	Same	Square
Sqrt	Either >=0	Real	Square root
Trunc	Real	Integer	Truncates fractional part

```
begin
  Average := TestTotal / NumberOfTests;
  Writeln('The average is ', Average:6:2)
end
```

2. Both mod and div require integer operands and yield integer results.

3. Sqrt provides a real answer; Abs provides an answer of the same type as its argument.

4. The division operator (/) always yields a real result.

5. The trigonometric functions (Sin, Cos) require arguments in radians. (Recall that we can convert degrees to radians by multiplying by $\pi/180$.)

6. An assignment of the form

```
integer variable := real expression
```

is illegal. We must explicitly choose whether to round or truncate. (The existence of this rule in Pascal is itself an aid to defensive programming—it forces us to face the issue head on.)

■■■■■■ REVIEW

Terms and concepts

formatting	maxint
output position	program portability
top-of-form	mixed mode
wrap	Trunc
filler	Round
fieldwidth	implicit conversion
precision	explicit conversion
Lst	integer part
square root (Sqrt)	fractional part
absolute value (Abs)	Int
call	Frac
invocation	argument

use	parameter
argument	value
quotient	ArcTan
remainder	Cos
div	Exp
mod	Ln
division algorithm	Sin
predefined identifier	Sqr

Output in Pascal programs

Formatting

1. For integer, character, or string variables and expressions, we can use

```
Writeln(exp:fw) or Write(exp:fw)
```

where "exp" represents an integer, character, or string variable or expression to be output, and "fw" represents an integer variable or expression for the fieldwidth to be used. We can omit the fieldwidth.

2. For real variables and expressions, we can use

```
Writeln(exp:fw:prec) or Write(exp:fw:prec)
```

where "exp" represents a real variable or expression to be output, "fw" represents an integer variable or expression for the fieldwidth to be used, and "prec" represents an integer variable or expression for the precision (number of decimal places) to be used. We can omit the precision or both the fieldwidth and the precision.

Output to a printer (Turbo Pascal)

To direct output to a printer, add Lst to your Write and Writeln statements as in the following:

```
Writeln(Lst, X, Y, Z)
```

Page

1. Not incorporated in Turbo Pascal (but see Appendix E).

2. In Turbo Pascal, can accomplish new page on screen by procedure ClrScr.

3. Can accomplish (for many printers) new page on printer output by Writeln(Lst, Chr(12)).

Library functions

1. See the table on page 95 for a list.

2. Form to use (call or invoke) a function:

```
function-name (argument)
```

3. Can use:
(a) on the right side of an assignment statement

(b) in the condition of an if statement
(c) in a Writeln
(d) NOT on the left side of an assignment statement
(e) NOT in a Readln

DPT

1. Avoid division by 0.
2. Mod and div require integers and yield integer results.
3. Sqrt yields a real. Abs yields the same type as its argument.
4. Division (/) yields a real.
5. Sin and Cos require radian arguments.
6. Must use Trunc or Round for real to integer conversion.

■■■■■■
EXERCISES

1. Write a Pascal program to read an integer into the variable Number and write it using several variations of the statements "Writeln(Number:3)," "Writeln(Number:4)," . . . . Discover the number of columns that you have available for output on your terminal or printer.

2. What is the result of the following lines of Pascal code?

```
Writeln;
Write(3);
Write(4);
Write(5)
```

3. Write a Pascal program to read a real number into the variable Number and write it using several variations of the statements "Writeln(Number:7:2)," "Writeln(Number:7)", "Writeln(Number)", and so on (changing the "7" and "2" to other choices). Discover the number of columns and the precision used by "Writeln(Number)".

4. Suppose that player numbers range from 0 to 99 and that player weights range from 145.0 to 312.9 pounds. Write a Pascal program to read the numbers and weights of players and produce printed output similar to the following:

```
THE PLAYERS' BEEF
--------------------
Player Number   Weight
--------------------
      12        185.3
      89        298.8
      55        216.2
--------------------
```

```
**** Processing Terminated Normally ***
```

*5. Give Pascal expressions corresponding to the following algebraic expressions.

a. $1 + \sqrt{x}$ d. $|3 - 2x| + y$ g. $\sqrt{b^2 - 4ac}$

b. $\sqrt{1 + x}$ e. x^3 h. $\sqrt{\dfrac{|r + 5| - 5}{5 - y}}$

c. $|x - y|$ f. $\left|\dfrac{x + 2}{y + 3}\right|$ i. $\sqrt{\dfrac{x - y}{|z|}}$

*6. A variable Money contains a real number that is to represent a money figure. Give Pascal steps to round the value in Money to the nearest cent (e.g., if Money is 100.5372, the answer would be 100.54).

*7. Give the value of the following expressions (if they are illegal, give the reason):

a. 5 mod 2
b. 2 mod 5
c. 103 mod 7
d. 1900 mod 4
e. Abs(16-11)
f. Abs(15-23*2)
g. Trunc(23/4)
h. 23 div 4
i. 200 div 11 mod 4

j. 200 div (11 mod 4)
k. 5 * Sqrt(96/4+1)
l. Sqrt(4) div 2
m. Abs(-16) div 5
n. 100 div 4 div 5
o. 100 div (4 div 5)
p. 100 div (4/5)
q. 100/(4/5)
r. 5123 div 100 mod 10

*8. Write a Pascal program that in a loop reads a real number, calculates the square root and absolute value of the number, and prints the results. If the number input is negative, then print an appropriate message in place of the square root, which does not exist. After each number is processed, ask the user whether or not to continue.

9. Write a Pascal program that in a loop reads two integer numbers N and M; calculates the expressions "N div M", "N mod M", and "N / M"; and prints the results. If M is equal to 0, then print an appropriate message in place of the three expressions, which do not exist. After each number is processed, ask the user whether or not to continue.

10. Write a Pascal program that in a loop reads two integer numbers N and M; calculates the expressions "N div M", "N mod M", and "M*(N div M) + (N mod M)"; and prints the results. Is the division algorithm: "N = M*(N div M) + (N mod M)" true in all cases for which M does not have the value 0?

11. (For the curious) Try the following experiments with the predefined identifier "maxint":

a. Violate the range of valid integers established by maxint by input, output, and calculation. What happens?
b. Change the program of Figure 2-11 by declaring maxint as a variable of the integer type.
c. Write a program in which you declare maxint as a constant whose value is different from that used in your implementation. Does the range of valid integers change?

12. Suppose that you output the real variable Number with the statement "Writeln(Number:7:0)". Is the output statement equivalent to "Writeln(Trunc(Number):7)" or "Writeln(Round(Number):7)"? Write a Pascal program to discover which it is.

13. Does "Writeln(Trunc(100 * Frac(23.46)))" output the value 46? Think of a safer alternative and then try them both.

*14. a. Write a segment of Pascal code that, for a given four-digit positive integer, will calculate the second digit. (If the number is 3612, the answer is 6.) Hint: See Exercise 7(r).
b. Do the same for the third digit.
c. Do the same for the first digit. The fourth digit.

15. Using Exercise 14, write a program that reads a series of four-digit positive integers and calculates their value "reversed." (For input 3612, the answer is 2163.)

*16. "Hand trace" the program of Figure 2-13, that is, trace its calculations for several different values for the Amount variable. Record the values for the different variables. Try these input values: 37.62, 2.99, and 0.41. This should help you understand how the program works.

*17. A barrel will hold 11 monkeys, a crate will hold 7 monkeys, and a coconut will hold 1 monkey. Write a Pascal program that will ask the user for a quantity of monkeys and will distribute the monkeys to minimize the number of containers used.

18. A runner reports the number of minutes run daily in a diary with a running (no pun intended) total for the year. Write a Pascal program to ask the user for the total amount of minutes run for the year, and output the equivalent amount of time in months, weeks, days, hours, and minutes.

19. An electrical supplier sells wire in rolls of 500, 300, and 75 feet. Write a program to ask the user for the total number of feet of wire required, and output the number of 500-, 300-, and 75-foot rolls, and the number of feet left over. (For 1695, the answers would be 3, 0, 2, and 45.)

20. A familiar trigonometric identity translated into Pascal states that

```
Sqr(Sin(X)) + Sqr(Cos(X) = 1
```

Write a Pascal program to read values for X and print the left side of the identity rounded to two decimal places.

21. Another trigonometric identity translated into Pascal states that

```
ArcTan(Sin(X)/Cos(X)) = X
```

unless Cos(X) = 0. Write a Pascal program to read values of X and print the two sides of the above identity, both rounded to two decimal places.

22. Pascal does not come with a standard operator for raising one integer to another integer power. For two integers N and M, the value of "N raised to the Mth power" is expressible as

```
Round(Exp(M * Ln(N)))
```

Write a Pascal program that asks the user for two positive integer values and outputs the first raised to the power of the second by means of the above formula.

23. (Challenge) Write a Pascal program for computing "N raised to the Mth power" for positive integers N and M using a loop and only multiplication and the "Sqr" function. Try to write an efficient algorithm. Hint: To compute 2 to the 6th power, here are some possibilities:

Five multiplications:
```
2
2*2 = 4
2*4 = 8
2*8 = 16
2*16 = 32
2*32 = 64
```

Three multiplications:

```
2*2 = 4
4*4 = 16
4*16 = 64
```

1. One coding approach would be to use ClrScr and Write(Lst, Chr(12)) to achieve top-of-form. Another would be to include a Page procedure in the program. Appendix E contains a Page procedure that works with Turbo Pascal for several popular computers and printers.

The advantage of this second approach is transportability. If we transfer our program to a Pascal environment that does follow the standard, we could simply remove our own Page procedure and utilize the standard Page procedure.

We will use both approaches in our examples.

2. The whole general area of output formatting is one in which minor differences exist from computer to computer. For example, this statement is not necessarily true on all versions of Pascal. Experimentation and reference to authorities (manuals and/or instructors) are two ways to determine the exact situation in your own setting.

3. In allowing 0 for the fieldwidth and precision, Turbo Pascal is providing an extension to standard Pascal. Some versions of Pascal may require a value bigger than 0.

4. Reminder: String variables are not standard, but are frequently available. If your Pascal has strings, their output rules may differ slightly from those of Turbo Pascal.

5. Standard Pascal makes no provisions for sending output to a printer. As a result, the methods used vary greatly in different versions of Pascal. We present the Turbo Pascal approach here.

6. The examples where both numbers are positive are valid for any version of Pascal. Some versions do not allow M to be negative, and, for some versions, the division algorithm statement is not true if N is negative.

7. Int and Frac are provided by Turbo Pascal. They are not standard. In standard Pascal you could use Trunc and assign the result to a real variable to imitate the effect of Int for a real argument. If you then subtracted this from the original number, that would imitate the effect of Frac. (See also Exercise 17 of Section 2-7.)

2-5
MORE ON DECISION STRUCTURES

This section continues the discussion of Section 2-3. In that section, we examined decision structures with two important limitations:

1. The condition involved consisted of comparing two expressions.

2. There were only two branches (if–then–else), and one branch might be empty (if–then).

In this section, we will learn about some more complex forms the condition can take and about how to develop multiple-way branches. In addition, we will examine **nested decisions** (decisions within decisions).

BOOLEAN EXPRESSIONS

The technical term for the condition in the if statement is **Boolean expression**. A Boolean expression in Pascal is one whose value is either true or false. (Such an expression is sometimes called a **logical expression**, although that is not the official Pascal terminology.)

One simple way to obtain a Boolean expression, as we have seen, is to compare two quantities using one of the six **relational operators** (=, <>, >, <, <=, and >=). In addition, comparisons such as this can be combined, as illustrated in the following examples:

```
(X > 0) or (Y > 0)
(Sex = 'F') and (Age > 21)
(Grade = 'A') or (Grade ='B') or (Grade = 'C')
(State <> 'PA') and (State <> 'VA')
```

As you can see, we can combine one or more comparisons using an "and" or an "or". When we combine using "and", the resulting condition is true provided *all* of the individual conditions are true. When we use "or", the resulting condition is true if *any one (or more)* of the individual conditions is true.

We can therefore paraphrase the meaning of these four examples as

either X or Y (or both) is positive

female over age 21

Grade is either an A, B, or C

State is not Pennsylvania, and it is also not Virginia

NOTE The parentheses in these examples are mandatory. In general, when we combine individual comparisons, those comparisons must be placed in parentheses. This is true because the relational operators (<, =, etc.) have lower precedence than "and" and "or".

In these examples, the "and" and "or" used to combine the comparisons are called **Boolean operators** (or **logical operators**). They operate on Boolean expressions (the individual comparisons) to create new Boolean expressions. There is a third Boolean operator in Pascal: "not". This operator forms the **negation** (the logical "opposite") of a Boolean expression. For example,

```
not (X = 0)
```

means the same as

```
X <> 0
```

These operators, just as the arithmetic operators, have precedence rules. The order of precedence is

not: highest
and: next
or: lowest

This means that we sometimes have to include parentheses to obtain the desired order of operation. We will illustrate these ideas by a series of examples, each writing a Pascal Boolean expression corresponding to a particular English language condition. (We will make up variable names for quantities in the examples. In a complete program, of course, these variables must be declared.)

1. *Not a female over age 21.* We need the negation of the condition "female over age 21," which was one of our earlier examples. The easiest way to

negate a condition is simply to place the entire condition in parentheses and precede it by the not operator:

```
not( (Sex = 'F') and (Age > 21) )
```

Another way to negate the condition is to negate each individual comparison, and change the "and" to "or". To see why this works, we may reason as follows. If a person is not a female over age 21, there are two possibilities: The person either is not female or is not over 21 (or both). We write

```
(Sex <> 'F') or (Age <= 21)
```

2. *Operation code is one of '+', '−', '*', or '/'.* There are two possible approaches: The first uses "or" to link the possibilities:

```
(Operation = '+') or (Operation = '-') or
(Operation = '*') or (Operation = '/')
```

Pascal also provides an easier way to state this condition:

```
Operation in ['+', '-', '*', '/']
```

This condition says that Operation has one of the values listed between the square brackets. This list is called a **set**. We will study the general concept of sets in Pascal at a later time. For now, we simply note that it will be useful in conditions of this type:

```
variable in [list of values separated by commas]
```

The variable and the list of values must be of the same "ordinal" type. Of the types we have studied so far, they can be integer or char because these are "ordinal" types. They cannot be real or string. These are not "ordinal" types.

3. *Operation code is not one of '+', '−', '*', or '/'.* We can negate either solution from number 2 above:

```
not ((Operation = '+') or (Operation = '-') or
     (Operation = '*') or (Operation = '/'))
not ( Operation in ['+', '-', '*', '/'] )
```

Alternatively, we can negate each comparison and change each "or" to "and". We reason that the operation code is not a '+'; it is also not a '−'; and so on. This yields

```
(Operation <> '+') and (Operation <> '-') and
(Operation <> '*') and (Operation <> '/')
```

4. *The sum is between 25 and 35, inclusive.* To be between, the sum must satisfy two conditions: It must be at least 25, and it must be no more than 35. Since it must satisfy both, we use "and":

```
(Sum >= 25) and (Sum <= 35)
```

The word "inclusive" causes us to use $>=$ and $<=$ rather than $>$ and $<$.

5. *The answer is neither 'Y' nor 'N'.* When we use neither/nor in English, we mean that both conditions are false. Therefore, we use "and" to join the conditions:

```
(Answer <> 'Y') and (Answer <> 'N')
```

Alternatively, we can reason that the answer is not in the set consisting of 'Y' and 'N', and write

```
not ( Answer in ['Y', 'N'] )
```

6. *Data is good, meaning that the code is 'T' and the numerical value is either below 10 or above 500.* We write

```
(Code = 'T') and ((Value < 10) or (Value > 500))
```

The extra parentheses (shaded in the example) grouping the two conditions joined by "or" are necessary. Because "or" has lower precedence than "and," we need the parentheses to force the "or" to be performed first.

7. *Data is bad (see number 6).* We must negate the condition in number 6:

```
not ( (Code = 'T') and ((Value < 10) or (Value > 500)) )
```

Although there are other ways to negate an expression involving both and's and or's, we suggest using the not operator.

COMMENT In some of these examples we have used **DeMorgan's laws** for negating compound conditions. The negation of a compound condition consisting of several individual conditions joined by "and" may be formed by: 1. negating each individual condition; 2. changing each "and" to "or".

Likewise, to negate a compound condition consisting of several conditions joined by "or", we: 1. negate each individual condition; 2. change each "or" to "and".

If both "and" and "or" appear in a compound condition, properly applying DeMorgan's laws requires a great deal of care; hence our suggestion to simply use the "not" operator.

☐
MULTIPLE-WAY BRANCHES— GENERAL

In this subsection, we will learn how to write **multiple-way branches** in Pascal. These are a direct extension of the if–then and if–then–else decision structures.

Multiple-way branches occur when the steps to be performed depend on certain conditions in three or more different categories. As a simple example, suppose we have variables BobHeight and JimHeight, containing the heights of Bob and Jim in inches. We wish to print a message telling which is taller or stating that they are the same height. We identify three possibilities:

1. BobHeight > JimHeight
2. BobHeight = JimHeight
3. BobHeight < JimHeight

We will write, in Pascal,

```
if BobHeight > JimHeight then
   Writeln('Bob is taller')
else if BobHeight = JimHeight then
   Writeln('They are the same height')
else
   Writeln('Jim is taller')
```

In general, the form for this structure (which we will informally call an "if–elseif" structure) is the following:

```
if condition 1 then
   statement to be done if condition 1 is true
else if condition 2 then
   statement to be done if condition 2 is true
else if condition 3 then
   statement to be done if condition 3 is true
        .
        .
        .

else
   statement to be done if none of the listed conditions is true
```

As usual, any of the "statements" can be compound statements (lists of statements grouped using begin and end). For example, if each statement were a compound statement, we would have this form:

```
if condition 1 then
  begin
    steps to be done if condition 1 is true (separated by semicolons)
  end
else if condition 2 then
  begin
    steps to be done if condition 2 is true (separated by
       semicolons)
  end
else if condition 3 then
  begin
    steps to be done if condition 3 is true (separated by
       semicolons)
  end
        .
        .
        .
else
  begin
    steps to be done if none of the previous conditions are
       true (separated by semicolons)
  end
```

We simply deal with the branches one at a time by specifying

   1. A condition that identifies the branch
   2. The steps for the branch to be performed if the condition is true

A word about the "semantics" (that is, the meaning) of this structure may be in order. Because we have "else if *condition 2* then", condition 2 will not be examined if condition 1 is true. Likewise, condition 3 will not be examined if either of the first two conditions is true, and so on. The basic meaning of the structure is:

Examine the conditions in the order listed. For the first one (and only the first one) that is true, perform the indicated steps. If none are true, perform the steps in the final "else" branch.

COMMENTS

1. The final "else" is optional, just as it is in the if–then structure. If there are no steps to be done when none of the listed conditions is true, we simply omit the last branch.

2. As in Section 2-3 on the if–then and if–then–else, the "begin" and "end" statements indicate to the compiler that there is more than one step in the branch.

3. In the example given above, the three conditions are **exhaustive**. They "exhaust" all the possibilities. In the third branch, we were able to omit the condition, writing

```
else
    Writeln('Jim is taller')
```

We could, however, make the condition explicit if we wished:

```
else if JimHeight > BobHeight then
    Writeln('Jim is taller')
```

To further illustrate these ideas, we develop three more program segment examples.

In the first example, we utilize the following simple tax table, similar to the one used by the federal government:

Income	Tax
Below $10,000	0
$10,000 or more but less than 15,000	7% of income over $10,000
$15,000 or more	$700, plus 10% of income over $15,0000

We immediately identify three conditions, with the corresponding formulas for the tax:

1.   Condition: `Income < 10000`
         Formula: `0`

2.   Condition: `10000 <= Income < 15000`
         Formula: `0.07 * (Income - 10000)`

3.   Condition: `Income >= 15000`
         Formula: `700 + 0.10 * (Income - 15000)`

Before we begin coding in Pascal, it will be helpful to think about the conditions more carefully. Because of the semantics (meaning) of the if–elseif structure, we can simplify the second condition. We do not need to verify that Income $>=$ 10000. If it were not, the first condition would already have been true. Similarly, by the time the third branch is reached, we know the Income must be at least 15000. The three conditions are exhaustive, so we can omit the third condition. This discussion leads us to write

```
if Income < 10000 then
    Tax := 0
```

```
    else if Income < 15000 then
        Tax := 0.07 * (Income - 10000)
    else
        Tax := 700 + 0.10 * (Income - 15000)
```

In the second example, let us assume that a company has had a sales contest, with the eastern branch (code 'EA') winning and the northwestern branch (code 'NW') coming in second. Each employee in the winning branch is to have a bonus of $1000 added to her next check, with a $500 bonus for the second place employees. We could write

```
    if Branch = 'EA' then
        Pay := Pay + 1000
    else if Branch = 'NW' then
        Pay := Pay + 500
```

In this example, we definitely need the condition in our second branch. This is not an if–then–else structure. There is an implicit third branch ("none of the above") with no steps.

COMMENT We could make the third branch explicit, adding

```
    else
        Pay := Pay
```

to the code given above. However, assigning a variable's value to itself does not change the value, and these extra two lines seem pointless to us.

For our final example, assume we are given a variable Letter known to contain a valid letter grade (A, B, C, D, or F). We are to print an appropriate message ("excellent" for A, etc.) and also add 1 to an appropriate variable (ACount for A, etc.). We can write

```
    if Letter = 'A' then
        begin
            Writeln('excellent');
            ACount := ACount + 1
        end
    else if Letter = 'B' then
        begin
            Writeln('good');
            BCount := BCount + 1
        end
    else if Letter = 'C' then
        begin
            Writeln('average');
            CCount := CCount + 1
        end
    else if Letter = 'D' then
        begin
            Writeln('below average');
            DCount := DCount + 1
        end
    else
        begin
            Writeln('failing');
            FCount := FCount + 1
        end
```

Pascal offers an alternative approach to coding certain decision structures. This approach applies when the conditions on which the branches are based consist of seeing whether a variable has a certain value. For example, the last decision structure of the previous subsection is of this type. We present the structure by rewriting that example using the **case structure** of Pascal.

```
case Letter of
   'A': begin
            Writeln('excellent');
            ACount := ACount + 1
        end;
   'B': begin
            Writeln('good');
            BCount := BCount + 1
        end;
   'C': begin
            Writeln('average');
            CCount := CCount + 1
        end;
   'D': begin
            Writeln('below average');
            DCount := DCount + 1
        end;
   'F': begin
            Writeln('failing');
            FCount := FCount + 1
        end
end
```

The semantics for this example are simple: Based on the value of Letter, the list of statements given for that value is executed.

In its simplest form, the case statement has the structure below. Later, we will learn about some possible extensions.

```
case variable of
    value 1: statement for first value;
    value 2: statement for second value;
      .
      .
      .
    value n: statement for last value
end
```

Observe the shaded areas. Each branch except the last ends with a mandatory semicolon. The last branch need not have a semicolon. Also, there is an extra "end" with no matching begin to mark the completion of the case structure.

As usual, any of the statements can be a compound statement, as in our example. Notice that, in the example, there are two "ends" at completion: one for the final branch and the other for the entire case structure.

Consider the following example:

```
case NumberOfChildren of
   0: Writeln('Childless');
   1: Writeln('Have an only child');
   2: Writeln ('About Average')
end
```

What happens if the value of the variable NumberOfChildren is not one of those listed? The answer is "nothing."[1] We could modify the example:

```
case NumberOfChildren of
     0: Writeln('Childless');
     1: Writeln('Have an only child');
     2: Writeln ('About Average')
  else  Writeln('Larger than the average family')
end
```

The structure illustrated is the following.[2] There *can* be semicolons after the "value n" statement and the "else" statement. There *must* be semicolons after the "value 1" statement, etc.

```
case variable of
     value 1: statement 1;
     value 2: statement 2;
          .
          .
          .
     value n: statement for last value
  else
          statement for any value not listed
end
```

CAUTION

Just as for the "set" condition, "*variable* in [*list*]", the variable and the list of values in the case structure must be of the same type. Moreover, that type cannot be real or string. Among the types we have studied, only integer and char types can be used in the case structure (because they are "ordinal" types).

□
**NESTED
DECISIONS**
When we write any type of decision structure (if–then, if–then–else, if–elseif, or case), each branch of the structure can be either a single statement or a compound statement of this form:

```
begin
     list of steps for the branch, separated by semicolons
end
```

One or more of the steps can itself involve a decision structure. (In fact, we have been using this type of structure without calling attention to it; see, for example, Figure 2-9 in Section 2-3.)

We describe this situation by saying that we have *nested decisions*. One decision is contained totally within ("nested" within) a branch of another decision structure. Generally speaking, the need for this type of structure arises quite naturally as we refine our algorithm. For example, consider the following. We wish to calculate a bonus based on the years an employee has worked with the company and the number of sales made.

The bonus for people with 10 years or more at the company is calculated based on the number of sales for the year: less than 500 earns a bonus of $100, 500 to 1000 earns $150, and over 1000 earns $250. For those with less than 10 years, the rules are as follows: 0 to 4 years, $20; 5 to 7 years, $50; 8 to 9 years, $70 plus $1 for each unit sold in excess of 1000, if any.

This is a fairly complex problem made more so by the fact that the information has been presented in a somewhat disorganized fashion. Our first task is to organize the rules given above. As we attempt to organize the information, we may come up with four branches based on the number of years:

condition (years)	Bonus
0–4	$20
5–7	$50
8–9	Based on sales (rule 1)
10 or more	Based on sales (rule 2)

We begin to write:

```
if Years <= 4 then
   Bonus := 20
else if Years <= 7 then
   Bonus := 50
else if Years <= 9 then
   here we must place the code for rule 1
else
   here we must place the code for rule 2
```

To refine the algorithm (and the Pascal), we must determine the structure for rules 1 and 2. These are fairly simple:

```
rule1:
if NumberOfSales <= 1000 then
   Bonus := 70
else
   Bonus := 70 + (NumberOfSales - 1000)

rule2:
if NumberOfSales < 500 then
   Bonus := 100
else if NumberOfSales <= 1000 then
   Bonus := 150
else
   Bonus := 250
```

The entire decision structure simply consists of our original code with the appropriate code for rules 1 and 2 inserted.

```
if Years <= 4 then
   Bonus := 20
else if Years <= 7 then
```

```
      Bonus := 50
   else if Years <= 9 then
      begin
        if NumberOfSales <= 1000 then
          Bonus := 70
        else
          Bonus := 70 + (NumberOfSales - 1000)
      end
   else
      begin
        if NumberOfSales < 500 then
          Bonus := 100
        else if NumberOfSales <= 1000 then
          Bonus := 150
        else
          Bonus := 250
      end
```

The inserted steps are shaded. Notice that we have written each as a compound statement. Strictly speaking, this was not necessary because each if–then–else is a simple statement. However, we will generally follow this practice in writing nested decisions. One advantage is that it avoids the so-called "dangling else" pitfall, discussed in the next section.

COMMENT   Consider these two code segments, where we have exaggerated the indentation to emphasize the differences

```
if BobHeight > JimHeight then
    Writeln('Bob is taller')
else if BobHeight = JimHeight then
    Writeln('They are the same height')
else
    Writeln('Jim is taller')

if BobHeight > JimHeight then
    Writeln('Bob is taller')
else
    if BobHeight = JimHeight then
        Writeln('They are the same height')
    else
        Writeln('Jim is taller')
```

To the compiler, they are identical. The compiler does not concern itself with indentation patterns or new lines. To the reader, however, they suggest two ways of viewing the problem:

   1. As a "three-way branch". Bob's height is either greater than, equal to, or less than Jim's.
   2. As a nested decision. Either Bob is taller or he isn't. If he isn't, there are two possibilities: either he is the same height or he isn't.

Which is correct? Both are. Which is better? It depends on the specific problem. In this example, we like the first code better because we view the situation as a three-way branch (>, =, <). Sometimes the choice is not so clear. For example, a program used by a bank might contain a decision structure with three branches:

1. Deposits
2. Checks that are good (sufficient funds)
3. Checks that bounce (insufficient funds)

Another, equally valid way to structure this would be as two branches:

1. Deposits
2. Checks

with a decision structure in the second branch with two subbranches

2a. Good checks
2b. Checks that bounce

□ **TESTING** Two important testing strategies, introduced in Section 2-3, apply equally well here:

1. Test the boundaries for each branch.
2. Include other tests for each branch not at the boundary points.

For example, for the previous program segment that calculates a bonus, we might devise the following test plan:

Branches and boundaries for Years
Boundaries: Years = 0   Others: Years = 3
             Years = 4   Years = 6
             Years = 5   Years = 12
             Years = 7
             Years = 8
             Years = 9
             Years = 10
Branches and boundaries for NumberOfSales (for Years in 7–9 range)
Boundaries: NumberOfSales = 0   Others: NumberOfSales = 529
             NumberOfSales = 1000   NumberOfSales = 1325
             NumberOfSales = 1001
Branches and boundaries for NumberOfSales (for Years in 10 or over range)
Boundaries: NumberOfSales = 0   Others: NumberOfSales = 217
             NumberOfSales = 499   NumberOfSales = 632
             NumberOfSales = 500   NumberOfSales = 1107
             NumberOfSales = 1000
             NumberOfSales = 1001

A third strategy is a new one for this section:

3. When complex conditions are involved (with "and" or "or"), we should test all possible combinations of the individual parts. As an example, for the condition

<code>female over age 21</code>

we should include test cases covering these four possibilities

female	over age 21	sample test case	expected result
true	true	'F', 30	true
true	false	'F', 20	false
false	true	'M', 27	false
false	false	'M', 17	false

As another example, for the condition "valid data," where to be valid the code must be 'T' and the numerical value either below 10 or above 500, we would have

Code = 'T'	Value < 10	Value > 500	sample test case	expected result
true	true	true	Impossible	—
true	true	false	'T', 5	true
true	false	true	'T', 519	true
true	false	false	'T', 17	false
false	true	true	Impossible	—
false	true	false	'R', 9	false
false	false	true	'M', 1000	false
false	false	false	'Q', 490	false

□ **DPT** The first two tips are generally similar to some of those discussed in Section 2-3. The others are new.

1. We must take care in the placement of semicolons. In the if–elseif type of structure, the only semicolons are those occurring between the statements of the branches, within a begin/end series of steps. However, the case structure introduces special semicolons at the end of each branch but the last.

2. The begin and end delimiters on a branch are *required* when the branch contains more than one statement. They should be used, as a defensive programming measure, if the branch consists of another decision structure.

3. When we use *and*, *or*, or *not* with comparisons, the comparisons must be enclosed in parentheses.

4. The precedence order (in the absence of parentheses) is: *not*, then *and*, then *or*. Parentheses may be required to obtain the desired meaning when two or more of these occur in the same condition. In particular, one way (frequently, the easiest and best way) to negate a condition is to place the entire condition in parentheses preceded by *not*.

5. In mathematics and in everyday language, we take certain shortcuts in describing conditions. For example, we can write

$$5 < x < 10$$

to mean x is between 5 and 10, and we can say

$$x \text{ is less than } y \text{ and } z$$

to mean that x is less than both.

In Pascal, there are no such shortcuts. We must write the conditions explicitly:

```
(5 < X) and (X < 10)
(X < Y) and (X < Z)
```

6. Suppose we wish to write

```
if Y/X > 5 then . . .
```

To be safe, we ought to make sure that X is not 0. We might be tempted to combine the check that X is not 0 with the original condition, as shown here:

```
if (X <> 0) and (Y/X > 5) then . . .
```

However, this will not work. The difficulty occurs because both conditions are checked when the if statement is executed. If the first condition (X <> 0) is false, then the second condition (Y/X > 5) will cause the program to bomb, due to division by 0.

NOTE   There are languages in which the computer would not bother checking the second condition if the first were false. In fact, some versions of Pascal might behave this way. However, Turbo Pascal always checks all parts of a compound condition. Since the Pascal standard does not specify which interpretation is to be made, we should write code, as described below, that will work under either interpretation.

To avoid this pitfall, we must write something like

```
if X <> 0 then
   begin
      if Y/X > 5 then
         .
         .
         .
```

We will see some more common instances of this type of pitfall later.

7. The case statement has its own "end", which is in addition to any use within the individual branches. The compiler should detect the error of omitting this "end".

REVIEW

Terms and concepts

nested decisions	negation
Boolean expression	set
logical expression	multiple-way branch

relational operator	"exhaustive" conditions
Boolean operator	case structure
logical operator	

Pascal

Conditions

1. Can combine comparisons using relational operators *not*, *and*, and *or*.

2. The precedence is: *not*: highest
                        and: next
                        or: lowest

3. Can use this form (for integer or char variables and values):

```
variable in [list of values separated by commas]
```

4. Can negate any condition by:

```
not ( condition to be negated )
```

"if–elseif" structure (any branch can be a compound statement)

1. Form

```
if condition 1 then
  statement to be done if condition 1 is true
else if condition 2 then
  statement to be done if condition 2 is true
else if condition 3 then
  statement to be done if condition 3 is true
  .
  .
  .
else
  statement to be done if none of the previous conditions are true
```

2. Meaning: Examine the conditions in the order listed. For the first one (and only the first one) that is true, perform the indicated statement. If none are true, perform the statement in the final "else" branch, if present.

Note: The final else branch is optional.

Case structure (any branch can be a compound statement)

1. Form

```
case variable of
      value1: statement 1;
      value2: statement 2;
        .
        .
        .
      last value: statement for last value
      else statement for any value not listed
end
```

Note the following.

a. Semicolons after each branch but the last.

b. Final end means "end of the case structure".

c. Standard Pascal: Error if no branch applies, and no "else" branch allowed. (But many, including Turbo, relax this restriction.)

Testing
1. Test all boundaries of branches.
2. Test all branches away from boundaries.
3. Test all combinations of parts of complex conditions.

DPT
1. Semicolon placement must be watched, especially with a case statement.
2. Begin/end must be used for branches with more than one statement.
3. Comparisons are to be enclosed in parentheses in complex conditions.
4. Precedence (not, and, or) must be followed; use extra parentheses as necessary.
5. Final end is required for case statement.
6. All the parts of a compound condition are evaluated. Hence, for example,

```
if (X <>0) and (Y/X > 5) then . . .
```

will bomb if X is 0.

EXERCISES

*1. For each of the following, choose variable names and write Pascal Boolean expressions for the given condition:
   *a. Married male
   *b. Not a married male
   *c. Neither married nor male
   *d. Either a freshman ('FR') or a sophomore ('SO')
   *e. Neither a freshman nor a sophomore
   *f. Either a freshman with a QPA of 4.0, a sophomore with a QPA of 3.7 or higher, or a junior or senior with QPA of 3.5 or higher
    g. I divides evenly into both J and K
   *h. One of I, J, or K is even
    i. All of I, J, and K are multiples of 10
   *j. J is between 0 and 100, inclusive
    k. J is not between 0 and 100, inclusive
    l. Made a passing grade (A, B, C, or D)
   *m. x and y are both positive
    n. x and y are not both positive
   *o. Exactly one of x and y are positive
   *p. Neither x nor y are positive
    q. The pair (x,y) lies in the "unit box" in the plane, that is, both lie between 0 and 1, inclusive.
    r. Either z is negative or both x and y are greater than 5
   *s. y is greater than 5, and either z is negative or x is greater than 5

*2. Integer variables I, J, K, and L have values 4, 7, 12, and 19, respectively. What is the value of each of these logical expressions?
   a. `(I > J) and (K > L)`
   b. `(J < 10) or (K = 7) and (L > 10)`
   c. `((J < 10) or (K = 7)) and (L > 10)`
   d. `not(I < J) or (I <> K) and (K <> L)`
   e. `not((I < J) or (I <> K)) and (K <> L)`
   f. `(not(I < J) or (I <> K)) and (K <> L)`
   g. `I in [3, 4, 5]`
   h. `not(K in [10, 11, 15])`

3. Negate the following logical expressions:

*a. X = 45
b. I < J
c. Class <> 'SR'
*d. (Y < Z) or (Y >= Z + 4.0)
*e. (Class = 'FR') and (Sex = 'M') and (QPA < 3.2)
f. (I mod J = 0) or (I mod K = 0)
g. (Percent > 0.49) and (Years < 4) and (Bonus > 5.53)
*h. (Class = 'FR') or (Class ='SO') and (Hours < 35)
*i. ((Class = 'FR') or (Class ='SO')) and (Hours < 35)
*j. I in [3, 4, 5]
k. (I in [6, 7]) or (J in [6, 7])
*l. not(I in [3, 4, 5])

4. Choose variable names and write a Pascal *segment* for each of the following situations:

*a. Football players are marked on their performance in the preceding game. A grade above 93 percent is considered excellent, below 75 percent poor. Your segment should, given a grade, print the name, grade, and appropriate message ("excellent" or "poor").
b. Given three test grades, print "improving" if the third test score is greater than the average of the first two tests; print "declining" if it is 5 or more points less than the average.
c. For a quadratic equation $ax^2 + bx + c$, the value $b^2 - 4ac$ is called the "discriminant." This value determines how many real roots the equation has (none if it is less than 0, one if it is 0, and two if it is greater than 0). Write a segment that, given a, b, and c, prints a message telling the number of roots the equation has.
*d. Given a value representing a roll of the dice, print one of these messages based on the roll value:

'You win'   (7, 11)
'You lose'   (2, 12)
'Roll again'   (anything else)

e. (Simplified roulette) The following variables have assigned values, and you are to write a segment based on them: (1) a number indicating the result on a roulette wheel (0 to 32); (2) the amount of a bet; (3) a char variable telling the type of bet made (value 'E'—even, 'O'—odd, or 'N'—number); (4) the number bet on if the char variable is 'N' (1 to 32).

Your segment should calculate the winnings based on these rules. If the number on the wheel was 0, you lose. If you bet on a number and you matched it, you win 30 times the bet. If you bet 'E' (even) or 'O' (odd) and were correct, you win twice your bet.
*f. Given three numbers representing a date, the segment should print the date. The input numbers 11, 7, 85, for example, would cause the date "November 7, 1985" to be printed.
g. Revise part (f) to assign the date value to a string[20] variable rather than printing the date.

5. Follow the instructions of Exercise 4.

*a. Wage tax rate is based on city codes, as given in the table:

City code	Tax Rate
'MUR'	0.005
'MORR'	0.01
'JCY'	0.03
'BSTA'	0.005
Others	0.0

Compute the taxes for a given annual wage and city code.

b. Write a segment to calculate charges for a checking account. For "regular" accounts, the charge is $5.00 unless the lowest monthly balance is $500.00 or more, in which case there is no charge. For "special" accounts, the charge is 20 cents per check; and for "VIP" accounts, there is no charge. Note: Use a variable AccountType with value 'R', 'S', or 'V' to determine the type of account.

c. Taxes in a certain state are based on taxable income and are calculated differently depending on whether the person is single or married. The taxable income is either 0 or the weekly income minus $13 for each dependent, whichever is more. The taxes are given by the tables:

Taxable income	Tax (married)
Less than 145.00	1% of income
145.00–293.00	2% of income
Over 293.00	$50.00, plus 3% of amount over 293.00

Taxable income	Tax (single)
Less than 130.00	1% of income
130.00–250.00	2% of income
250.01–350.00	$60.00, plus 3% of amount over 250.00
Over 350.00	100.00

Write a Pascal segment to calculate taxable income and tax for a taxpayer given the needed information.

*d. A certain small company manufactures five items. The prices are given below. Write a Pascal segment that, given a valid item number, will calculate the price.

Item No.	Price
4927	100.50
2178	3000.00
2111	100.50
1137	143.50
1342	25505.00

e. Revise part (d) to print an error message if the item number is invalid.

6. Indicate some tests that should be in a test plan for each of the following exercises.

*a. Exercise 4(a)
  b. Exercise 4(b)
  c. Exercise 4(c)
*d. Exercise 4(d)
  e. Exercise 5(b)
  f. Exercise 5(c)
  g. Exercise 5(e)

*7. (a–s) For each of Exercises 1(a) through 1(s), create a test plan relating to the condition. Use a table format similar to that used in the testing subsection of this section.

□
NOTES FOR
SECTION 2-5

1. In standard Pascal, this is an error (the program "bombs"). However, many versions of Pascal use the same approach here as does Turbo Pascal.

2. Again, many versions of Pascal include an "else" option in the case structure, although it is not standard. For those versions of Pascal with no "else" option, an equivalent program segment can be written in this form:

```
if variable in [list of values for case structure]
   case
      value1: statement 1;
      value2: statement 2;
         .
         .
         .
      lastvalue: statement for last value
   end
else
   statement for any values not listed
```

If your Pascal supports the "else" within the case structure, that approach is preferable.

2-6
□□□□□□
YET MORE ON
DECISION
STRUCTURES

In this section, we complete our formal study of decision structures. We will introduce a few more ideas relating to decisions and conclude with a case study.

□
THE
"DANGLING
ELSE"
PITFALL

Consider these two segments of Pascal code, where we have exaggerated the indentation to emphasize the difference:

```
if X > 5 then                 if X > 5 then
   if Y > 0 then                 if Y > 0 then
      Z := 1                        Z := 1
   else                          else
      Z := 2;                       Z := 2;
```

Under exactly what conditions will the step "Z := 2" be performed?

The indentation patterns suggest what the author had in mind: for the left-hand code, when X > 5 and Y <= 0; for the right-hand code, when X <= 5.

However, the compiler pays no attention to indentation. To the compiler, these two segments are the same. Moreover, the interpretation the compiler takes is the one implied by the left-hand indentation pattern:

Each else is matched with the most recent unmatched if.
(within the same begin . . . end grouping)

To obtain the meaning desired by the right-hand example, we would use begin and end as illustrated below. In fact, in the interest of defensive programming, we might choose to use a begin and end for both program segments. This would make sure that we obtained the desired results. Here are the two examples rewritten in this fashion:

```
if X > 5 then                    if X > 5 then
    begin                            begin
        if Y > 0 then                    if Y > 0 then
            Z := 1                           Z := 1
        else                         end
            Z := 2               else
    end;                             Z := 2;
```

The problem illustrated by this example arises when the "then" branch of an if–then–else consists of another decision structure. It therefore pays to be especially careful when writing nested decisions. Our defensive programming tip is:

> When the "then" branch of a decision structure involves another decision structure, use a begin . . . end to surround the nested decision structure. (In fact, when we nest decisions, we frequently include all the nested decision structures within begin . . . end groupings.)

Some of the exercises give other examples illustrating this point.

☐
BOOLEAN
VARIABLES

In the preceding section, we discussed Boolean expressions. They are expressions whose values are either true or false. It should not surprise you to learn that Pascal has variables capable of holding such values. Just as integer variables store integer values and char variables store one-character values, Boolean variables store Boolean values.

These variables are declared as are other variables and used analogously to the ways in which real and integer variables are used. Remember that the only values they can contain are true and false. For example, we can declare

```
var
    X, Y          : integer;
    XBigger       : boolean;
    YZero         : boolean;
    BothPositive  : boolean;
```

and include steps such as these in our program:

```
XBigger := X > Y;
YZero := Y = 0;
BothPositive := (X > 0) and (Y > 0);
Writeln('Is X bigger? ', XBigger, ' Are both positive? ',
        BothPositive);
if XBigger and BothPositive then
  Writeln('Both are positive but X is larger');
```

This example illustrates several points about Boolean variables. These and other points are described in the following list:

1. The Boolean expressions that we assign to Boolean variables are of exactly the same form as those used in an if statement.

2. The assignment "YZero := Y = 0" assigns "true" to YZero if the condition "Y = 0" is true, false if not. To understand this step, you must realize that "Y = 0" is a comparison (Boolean expression) whose value is either true or false. This value is assigned to the boolean variable YZero.

Another way to accomplish the same thing would be

```
if Y = 0 then
  YZero := true
else
  YZero := false
```

3. The Boolean operators "and", "or", and "not" act with and yield Boolean values. Thus,

```
XBigger and BothPositive
```

is true if both XBigger and BothPositive are true, otherwise false. An equivalent way to write this is

```
(XBigger = true) and (BothPositive = true)
```

The "= true" is redundant, but it is allowed. When you first start working with Boolean variables, this second approach may seem clearer. However, you will soon become used to the first approach, especially because it reads "more like English."

4. Similarly, these two if statements are equivalent:

```
if not YZero then               if YZero = false then
  Writeln('Y is not 0');          Writeln('Y is not 0');
```

5. We can print Boolean values. The resulting output will be either the word "true" or the word "false."

6. We *cannot* read values for Boolean variables using the Readln procedure. (We can, if we wish, read a char variable and use it to assign a value to a Boolean variable, as in the code segment below.)

```
Readln(Ch);
if Ch in ['T', 't'] then
  BVar := true
else
  BVar := false
```

7. Boolean variables can be used in case statements and in the "variable in [list of values]" type of condition. For example, the following three segments are equivalent, although the first is most readable:

```
if X > Y then          XGreater := X > Y;            XGreater := X > Y;
   T := 0              if XGreater in [true] then    case XGreater of
else                      T := 0                        true : T := 0;
   T := 5;            else                              false : T := 5
                          T := 5;                    end;
```

8. Boolean variables are useful whenever we have a "yes or no" situation. They can make a program more readable. For example, the line

```
if UpperClassman and HighAverage then
```

is easier to follow than the line

```
if ( (Class = 'JR') or (Class = 'SR') ) and (QPA > 3.75) then
```

Of course, this is only true if we choose meaningful variable names. To be appropriate, a Boolean variable's name should be suggestive of what its "true" value denotes.

9. You may have noticed that we have used "boolean" and "Boolean" in our descriptions. The capital letter usage is based on the fact that the name "Boolean variable" is named after logician George Boole. The lowercase usage is consistent with our treatment of other standard types (integer, real, char, and string). The compiler, of course, does not care about uppercase or lowercase.

10. We can even use boolean constants that are declared using a declaration such as

```
const
   TestPhase = true;
```

The program might have steps such as these:

```
Readln(Number1, Number2);
if TestPhase then
   Writeln('Values entered: ', Number1, Number2);
```

This idea is frequently used to allow extra information to be printed during program development. When the program is turned over to the user, the declaration would be changed to

```
const
   TestPhase = false;
```

and the extra information would no longer be printed. (Later, if modifications were to be made, the extra prints could be reinserted simply by changing the constant's value back to true.)

□
ENHANCEMENTS OF THE CASE STATEMENT

There are some minor enhancements to the case statement, presented in earlier sections. To illustrate the first enhancement, consider this example:

```
case Letter of
   'A' : Writeln('Above average');
   'B' : Writeln('Above average');
   'C' : Writeln('Average');
   'D' : Writeln('Below average');
   'F' : Writeln('Below average')
end
```

This has the same meaning as the following, slightly shorter, version:

```
case Letter of
   'A', 'B' : Writeln('Above average');
         'C' : Writeln('Average');
   'D', 'F' : Writeln('Below average')
end
```

Instead of placing just a single value before the colon for each branch, we can place a list of values separated by commas.

In fact, many versions of Pascal, including Turbo Pascal, extend this idea a little further (although this extension is not standard). These versions allow a range of values to be entered. For example, consider this fragment that calculates a letter grade based on an integer average:

```
case Average of
   90 .. 100 : LetterGrade := 'A';
   80 ..  89 : LetterGrade := 'B';
   70 ..  79 : LetterGrade := 'C';
   60 ..  69 : LetterGrade := 'D';
    0 ..  59 : LetterGrade := 'F'
end
```

The first branch of the example is equivalent to either a branch written as

```
90, 91, 92, 93, 94, 95, 96, 97, 98, 99, 100 : Lettergrade := 'A'
```

or to a list of 11 separate branches for all possible grades.

The general form of one branch of the case statement would also allow a list of single values and ranges as in

```
10 .. 14, 17, 19 .. 21, 25 : statement for these values
```

The listed statement would be executed for any of the values 10, 11, 12, 13, 14, 17, 19, 20, 21, or 25. (The values and ranges in the case statement as a whole may not overlap.)

This feature is useful when applicable, but some care should be taken in using it. Values should be grouped only if they really belong together, not if they just happen to have the same statement to be executed. As a simple example, consider the code segment

```
case ItemNumber of
   10, 931 : Price := 0.98;
            .
            .
end
```

When the price for item number 931 changes, there is a danger that we will also change the price for item number 10. Even if we remember to avoid this, the program will be harder to modify than if we had separate branches for these two item numbers.

□ **CASE STUDY NO. 2**

This case study explores some decision structures, including the use of a Boolean variable. It also introduces some rudimentary error-checking concepts.

Statement of problem. We want a program that inputs two 1- to 4-digit positive integer numbers and an operation code. The operation code is a "+", "−", "*", or "/". The program should print output similar to

```
1103 + 1407 = 2510
 317 -  419 = -102
   3 *   15 = 45
```

Preliminary analysis. As we learned in Section 2-4, there are two possible inter-pretations of division for integers. We will write the program to print both answers when division is the requested operation.

We need to design the exact form of the input. As described earlier, we will separate the numeric and character input to avoid some subtleties of input. The program will first ask for the two numbers (using a line with both numbers zero to terminate the loop). It will then request the operation to be performed. We will use a Boolean variable, as discussed earlier in this section, to control the loop. Its value will be true when the user enters the terminating values, false otherwise.

Algorithm and variable list. Based on the preliminary analysis, we may write this variable list:

Constant:	EndOfData	value 0	Used to terminate loop
Input:	Number1	integer	First number
	Number2	integer	Second number
	Operation	char	Operation code (+, −, *, or /)
Output:	Result	integer	Result of operation
	Result2	real	Second answer needed for division
Other:	UserIsDone	boolean	True when user enters terminating values

Our algorithm follows a structure similar to earlier ones. In particular, we will use a procedure to print instructions. [Steps followed by an (*) are not performed when the terminating values have been entered.]

print instruction (using procedure Instructions)
repeat these steps until user enters both numbers as 0:
    prompt for two numbers
    read Number1 and Number2
    prompt for operation (*)
    read Operation (*)
    depending on Operation value, choose a branch: (*)
        '+': Result is sum, print Result
        '−': Result is difference, print Result
        '*': Result is product, print Result
        '/': Result is integer quotient, Result2
           is real quotient, print both
print a closing message and stop

(Of course, there are other possible approaches we could have taken.)

This algorithm, like previous ones in the text, does not deal with errors. In this case study, we will consider two possible error situations. Others are sug-gested in the exercises.

First, it is possible that the operation code entered might not be valid. We might add a fifth branch based on Operation value,

anything else: print an error message

Second, division by 0 is an error. We might modify the "divide" branch to read:

```
'/':   check Number2
          if it is not 0 do these steps:
              calculate Result as the integer quotient
              calculate Result2 as the real quotient
              print both answers
          otherwise do this:
              print an error message
```

We will code the refined algorithm in Pascal.

Test plan. The test plan is fairly simple. We want to exercise all posible paths for the decision structure, especially including the possibility of a faulty operation code or division by 0. In fact, we might include several different faulty codes.

If we reread the statement of the problem, we see that the input is to consist of one- to four-digit integers. This implies a range of 0 to 9999. We will want to include test data that exercises both boundaries (0 and 9999) for each number. In addition, we should include some numbers in between.

These considerations raise an important question. What happens if the numbers are not in the correct range? Ideally, the program should perform error checking here; this is the subject of one of the exercises. As the program stands, there are several possibilities:

1. The answer could be entirely correct. For example:

$$15101 - 14323 = 678$$

2. We could get strange but correct output such as

$$-5 + -4000 = -4005$$

3. The numbers could be so large that the answer (or even the numbers themselves) is too large for the computer to handle, resulting in a run-time error message.

In our test plan, we might include some input in the first two categories. In any case, the test plan does point out the need for further work on the algorithm, as indicated in the exercises.

One final test might involve entering a zero for exactly one of the two numbers. The looping process should not terminate unless *both* are zero. In fact, we will utilize this test table for our testing.

Number 1 zero	Number 2 zero	Test case	Expected result
true	true	0, 0	terminate loop
true	false	0, 5	continue loop
false	true	7, 0	continue loop
false	false	17, 2	continue loop

Write program. Figure 2-14 contains the program that is based on the algorithm, as modified by our error-handling discussion. Various exercises deal with alternate coding approaches, enhancements, and modifications. In particular, we have chosen to use the if–elseif approach to handle the various operation codes. Exercise 6 asks you to rewrite this using the case statement approach.

Observe the use of the Boolean variable UserIsDone. This avoids the pitfall of improper negation of the condition for terminating the loop. (See the shaded lines.)

```
program OperationCodes(Input, Output);
{
     Written by:  XXXXXXXX  XX/XX/XX
         Purpose:  To perform addition, subtraction, multiplication, or
                   division (both integer and real) for two integers.
                      The program also illustrates some error-handling
                   ideas.
Procedures used:  Instructions, to print instructions for user
}
const
  EndOfData = 0;                    {terminating data indicator}

var
  Number1     : integer;           {first number, input}
  Number2     : integer;           {second number, input}
  Operation   : char;              {operation code, input}
  Result      : integer;           {result of operations, output}
  Result2     : real;              {second answer for division, output}
  UserIsDone  : Boolean;           {true if terminating value entered}

procedure Instructions;
begin    { Left to the reader }  end; {Instructions}

begin {OperationCodes}

{*** Before the loop, print instructions.}

  Instructions;

{*** In loop, obtain two numbers and operation; perform operation; print
     answer (two answers for division). Check for two errors: bad
     operation, and division by zero. Stop when both numbers are
     terminating values.}
```

Figure 2-14   Case Study No. 2 (Continued)

```
  repeat
    Writeln;
    Write('Enter two integer numbers (both 0 to stop): ');
    Readln(Number1, Number2);
    UserIsDone := (Number1 = EndOfData) and (Number2 = EndOfData);
    if not UserIsDone then
      begin
        Write('Now enter the operation: ');
        Readln(Operation);
        if Operation = '+' then
          begin
            Result := Number1 + Number2;
            Writeln(Number1, ' + ', Number2, ' = ', Result)
          end
        else if Operation = '-' then
          begin
            Result := Number1 - Number2;
            Writeln(Number1, ' - ', Number2, ' = ', Result)
          end
        else if Operation = '*' then
          begin
            Result := Number1 * Number2;
            Writeln(Number1, ' * ', Number2, ' = ', Result)
          end
        else if Operation = '/' then
          begin
            if Number2 <> 0 then
              begin
                Result := Number1 div Number2;
                Result2 := Number1 / Number2;
                Writeln(Number1, ' / ', Number2, ' = ', Result, ' (integer)');
                Writeln(Number1, ' / ', Number2, ' = ', Result2:1:2, ' (real)')
              end
            else
              Writeln('*** Division by 0 is not allowed! ***')
          end
        else
          Writeln('*** Error made in operation. You entered:', Operation)
      end
  until UserIsDone;

{*** Print final message and stop.}

  Writeln;
  Writeln('Program terminating. Have a nice day.')
end.
```

SAMPLE INPUT AND OUTPUT

```
Enter two integer numbers (both 0 to stop): 45 67
Now enter the operation: *
45 * 67 = 3015
```

Figure 2-14   Case Study No. 2 (Continued)

```
Enter two integer numbers (both 0 to stop): 2 0
Now enter the operation: +
2 + 0 = 2

Enter two integer numbers (both 0 to stop): 23 4
Now enter the operation: /
23 / 4 = 5 (integer)
23 / 4 = 5.75 (real)

Enter two integer numbers (both 0 to stop): 3 19
Now enter the operation: -
3 - 19 = -16

Enter two integer numbers (both 0 to stop): 0 0

Program terminating. Have a nice day.
```

Figure 2-14   Case Study No. 2

Revise/enhance program. Although we will not do so at this point, this program could benefit from some revisions. The main module (not including the const or var declarations or the Instructions procedure) occupies about a page. More important, it has loop and decision structures nested to four levels:

1. a repeat loop
2. an if to avoid processing the terminating data
3. an if-elseif based on the operation code
4. an if-then-else to handle division by zero

Both the length of the module and the level of nesting are close to the limits of easy comprehension. The program should probably be modularized, even as it now stands. If any more sophisticated error checking were incorporated, it would certainly be desirable to modularize further. However, in order to do a good job with the modularization, we will need to develop more tools, which are presented in the next chapter.

REVIEW

Pascal syntax

Case statement

A branch can have a form as indicated by the example:

                10, 11 .. 14, 16 .. 18, 25 : *statement*

Boolean variables and constants

    1. Constant declaration: const

```
constant-name = true;
constant-name = false;
```

    2. Variable declaration: var

```
variable name : boolean;
```

    3. Assignment:

```
variable := any boolean expression
```

    4. Use in if. Examples:

```
if XGreater then . . .
if Valid and (Sex = 'M') then . . .
if Valid and Male then . . .
```

(XGreater, Valid, and Male are boolean variables that have an assigned value.)
Note:

```
if XGreater then . . .
```

means

```
if XGreater = true then . . .

if not Male then . . .
```

means

```
if Male = false then . . .
```

    5. Output: Use Write or Writeln: prints "true" or "false"

    6. Can use in case statement or in "*variable* in [*list*]" condition

DPT   *1.* Cannot read Boolean variables.

    2. Always use begin . . . end for a "then" branch if the branch consists of another decision structure

EXERCISES

1. For a certain honor fraternity, freshmen and sophomores must have a 3.8 grade point average to be eligible. Others must have a 3.5 grade point average.
   *a. Here is a segment of Pascal code that is supposed to print a message if the person is eligible. Does it correctly accomplish its task? If not, revise it so it does.

```
if (Class = 'FR') or (Class = 'SO') then
   if GPA >= 3.8 then Writeln('eligible')
else
   if GPA >= 3.5 then Writeln('eligible')
```

   b. Modify the segment to print a message 'not eligible' if the person is not eligible.
   c. Modify the segment of part (b) to assign a value (true or false) to a Boolean variable Eligible rather than printing a message.

2. a. Consider this segment of Pascal code, which calculates a letter grade based on a numerical average. Some people are taking the course for a "pass-fail," others for a letter grade.

```
if Code = 'P' then
    if Average >= 70 then
        Letter := 'S'
    else
        Letter := 'U'
else
    if Average >= 90 then
        Letter := 'A'
    else if Average >= 80 then
        Letter := 'B'
    else if Average >= 70 then
        Letter := 'C'
    else if Average >= 60 then
        Letter := 'D'
    else
        Letter := 'F'
```

The shaded part is a decision structure within the "then" branch of the main decision. It violates our defensive programming tip by not being included in a begin . . . end grouping. Does the code segment do what it should?

b. These two segments have the same meaning:

```
if Average >= 70 then        if Average >= 70 then
    Letter := 'S'                Letter := 'S'
else                         else if Average < 70 then
    Letter := 'U'                Letter := 'U'
```

Does substituting the right-hand version for the shaded part of the program segment in part (a) change the meaning of that program segment?

c. Comment on the relationship of this example to our defensive programming tip concerning the "dangling else."

3. For each condition listed, choose the appropriate variable names, including a Boolean variable. Give the variable declarations needed (the *var* section), and give an assignment statement to assign an appropriate value to the Boolean variable.

*a. A given number is even

*b. The data is valid (either an 'M' or 'S' for the code, and the number of dependents between 0 and 12)

c. Eligible for an honor fraternity (freshman with 4.0 QPA, sophomore with 3.8 or better, or junior or senior with 3.5 or better)

d. All three values are odd

e. A given number is a multiple of both M and N

f. A given number is either positive or negative

g. Improving (third test better than first two)

*h. vowel (one of 'A', 'E', 'I', 'O', or 'U')

4. Write these decision structures using case statements:

*a.
```
if Grade >= 59.5 then
    Writeln('Passing')
```

b. if Grade >= 59.5 then
   Writeln('Passing')
  else
   Writeln('Failing')

  c. Print an error message if the data is invalid. See Exercise 3(b) for a definition of valid data.

5. a. Rewrite the solutions to Exercises 4(d) and 5(d) of Section 2-5 using the enhancements to the case statement. Which is better for those problems: your original solution or the new one?

  b. Write a decision structure to assign a value of +1, 0, or −1 to a quiz. The quiz is worth 15 points, and scores from 11 to 15 earn a +1, scores below 7 earn −1, all others earn 0.

6. Write segments of Pascal code to assign a value for a Boolean variable as indicated by the following descriptions or questions:

  a. Is the average of the four test scores at least 70?

 *b. Is the test average "close to" the homework average? They are close if they differ by no more than one letter grade. (Using 90 percent = A, etc.)

  c. Repeat part (b) so that scores below 50 are not considered close to a 'D' score.

  d. Are three given values Value1, Value2, and Value3 in increasing order?

 *e. Is Y within 10 units of X?

 *f. Is a four-digit number a "palindrome," that is, the same from front to back? For example, 5115 is; so is 220 because as a four-digit number it would be 0220.

  g. Are three given points (x,y), (z,w), and (t,u) on the same straight line? Assume all values are integers.

  h. Is a person qualified for a rent rebate program? The answer is yes (true) for income of $10,000 or less. It is also yes for income between $10,000 and $13,000 inclusive, provided the number of dependents is at least two. For all others, the answer is no (false).

Exercises 7 to 10 refer to Case Study No. 2.

7. Write the necessary Instructions procedure.

8. Rewrite the if–elseif structure, which handles the operation code, using the case statement.

9. One possible approach for handling input data error is to check the data, print an error message if it is faulty, then "fix" it. Although there are more sophisticated approaches, this approach is better than simply ignoring errors.

  a. Modify the check for the operation code in Case Study No. 2. As soon as Operation is read, check its validity. If it is not valid, print a message like

      Invalid code 'T', changed to '+'

  Then change it to '+' and continue.

  b. Do a similar check for Number1 and Number2. If they are not in the proper 0 to 9999 range, change them to 1.

10. Revise Case Study No. 2 to handle the operations listed below. Include any necessary changes to the test plan.

  +, −, *
  / = real division
  I = integer division

M = mod
S = split and combine. For example,

$$1234 \text{ S } 5678 = 1278$$

D = isolate digit. (Number2 must be in the range 1 to 4, or an error message should be printed.) For example,

$$6279 \text{ D } 3 = 7$$
$$6279 \text{ D } 1 = 6$$
$$279 \text{ D } 1 = 0$$

The remaining exercises deal with programs you will develop yourself.

11. Write complete Pascal programs for the following, using a planning process similar to that used in the various case studies.

*a. Given a year in the range from 1920 to 1990, the program should print a message telling whether or not the year is a leap year. (A leap year is one divisible by 4.)

b. Revise part (a) to work for any year less than 4000. For years in this range, the rule is more complicated. For example, 1900 was not a leap year but 2000 will be. In general, a year divisible by 100 is not a leap year unless it is also divisible by 400.

c. Revise part (b) to print a message 'I can't handle years 4000 or above' if the input year is not less than 4000.

d. Write a program to read a four-digit number representing "military" time. Assume the input is valid. It should add one minute to the time, and print the original time and the new time. Sample output might be:

```
1912 plus one minute is 1913
 759 plus one minute is  800
```

Hint: Use mod and div to split the given time into hours and minutes.

e. Repeat part (d), but input three values: hours, minutes, and either "a.m." or "p.m." Assume valid input. Sample output:

```
11:59 a.m. plus one minute is 12:00 p.m.
```

Hint: Can you think of a way to have 0 print as "00"?

12. Follow the instructions of Exercise 11.

*a. The input consists of these items: a name, the person's gross income, and a code for the county (P = Pembroke, R = Richland, T = Tioga). The three counties have different tax rates: Pembroke County, 2 percent; Richland County, 1.5 percent; and Tioga County, 3 percent. Write a program to print a listing of name, county code, gross income, tax rate, and tax. Print an error message for any input containing an invalid county code.

b. A salesperson's commission is based on two factors: the sales amount and the number of years with the company. The basic commission rate is found by

Sales amount	Rate (%)
Less than $500.00	5
$500.00–$1000.00	7
$1000.01–$1499.99	8
$1500.00 on up	10

In addition, the commission is doubled if the salesperson has worked over 7 years with the company. If the salesperson has worked over 15 years, it is doubled and $5 is added for each year over 15. Write a program to calculate commission rate and commission for each employee.

c. Calculate a customer's bill for an order of some quantity of a single item. We assume there are only four items available, as shown:

Item Number	Unit Price
100	24.03
247	105.00
16	10.35
240	16.00

A discount is allowed for a large order: If the total bill is $1000.00 or over, a 2 percent discount is given; from $800 to $999.99 earns a 1 percent discount.

d. The first input contains a number indicating a beginning inventory (the number of items presently in stock). Each subsequent input consists of a code (P = purchase or S = sale) and a quantity. For a sale, the quantity should be subtracted from the current inventory; for a purchase, added to the inventory. Write a complete program to maintain the running status of the inventory.

If there is insufficient inventory to cover a sale, print a message and reject the sale. If the resulting inventory is below 750 after a sale, issue a "time-to-reorder" message; if it is below 250, issue an "URGENT—time-to-reorder" message.

13. Indicate some tests that should be in a test plan for each of the following exercises.

   *a. Exercise 11(a)   b. Exercise 11(b)
   c. Exercise 11(d)   *d. Exercise 12(b)
   d. Exercise 12(c)   f. Exercise 12(d)

2-7 □□□□□□ USER-DEFINED FUNCTIONS

For some time we have been routinely utilizing Instruction procedures in our examples and exercise solutions. The use of a separate **module** to perform the instruction printing subtask has a number of benefits. Perhaps the major benefit is that the details of instruction-printing do not interfere with developing or displaying the major logic of the program.

In this section, we develop this theme a little further. We will study **functions**, which we can write to perform a subtask consisting of calculating a single value. As we shall see, using a function we write ourselves is similar to using a standard function such as Sqrt.

□ **AN EXAMPLE**   Suppose we wish to write a program to calculate the area of a triangle given the three sides. Following the general method used in earlier programs, we might devise this plan. (Steps with an asterisk are not executed for the dummy data.)

```
print instructions (using procedure Instructions)
repeat these steps until the user enters 0 for A
    issue prompt
    read values A, B, C (the three sides)
    calculate the area based on A, B, C (*)
    print the area (*)
print the final message
```

We choose to write a function whose name will be AreaFn to perform the details of calculating the area. By drawing on our knowledge of user-written procedures and standard functions, we can complete the Pascal code for the main program. In particular, these statements are true:

1. A user-written function must be defined before it is used. We will place its definition after the variable declarations and before the "begin" of the main program.

This is the same as for a user-written procedure.

2. To invoke a user-written function in an assignment statement, we must place the necessary arguments (**parameters**) in parentheses after the function name. These parameters are the values the answer is based on.

This is the same as for a standard function such as Sqrt.

3. In the module that uses the function, we cannot have another variable with the same name as the function. We might choose another variable (perhaps Area) to store the answer from the function.

This is the same as for a standard function.

Figure 2-15 contains the resulting program, with the parts related to the issues discussed above shaded.

To continue with this example, we must learn how to write a function. The key to the process is that, as for a procedure, we simply write the steps necessary to perform the subtask, along with one statement declaring that these steps form a function. As for the procedure, the function can, if desired, declare local variables for its own use.

There are some major differences, however, between a function and the type of procedure we have studied to this point. Before we discuss these issues in detail, let us examine them as they relate to the AreaFn function. The Pascal function is given in Figure 2-16, with lines numbered for easy reference. It uses a mathematical formula for the area based on the sides.

COMMENT   In order to complete the program in Figure 2-15, we would merely insert this code in place of the comment that shows where it goes.

From this example, we can learn a great deal about writing functions.

1. Line 1 declares that AreaFn is a function. The final "real" following the colon says that the value the function calculates is real.

2. Line 1 also describes the parameters for the function. There are three, and all three represent real values. The function will use the names A, B, and C to represent them.

```
program Triangles(Input, Output);
{
       Written by:   XXXXXXX  XX/XX/XX
          Purpose:   To calculate areas of triangles.
Procedures used:   Instructions, to print instructions.
 Functions used:   AreaFn, to calculate the area.
}
const
  EndOfData = 0;

var
  A, B, C     : real;                {sides of triangle, input}
  Area        : real;                {area of triangle, output}

procedure Instructions; begin {stub} end;


{
    At this point in the program we will place the area function
    when it has been developed. Its name will be AreaFn. (See Figure
    2-16.)


}


begin {Triangles}

{*** Before the loop, print instructions.}

 Instructions;

{*** In the loop, read the three sides of the triangle, use
      the area function to find the area, and print the result.
      Quit on entry of A = 0.}

   repeat
     Writeln;
     Write('Enter three sides of triangle (first 0 to stop): ');
     Readln(A, B, C);
     if A <> EndOfData then
       begin
         Area := AreaFn(A, B, C);
         Writeln('The area is ', Area:1:4)
       end
   until A = EndOfData;

{*** After the loop, print closing message and terminate the program.}

     Writeln;
     Writeln('Triangles program terminating.')
```

Figure 2-15 Use of User-Defined Function

```
 1)     function AreaFn(A, B, C : real) : real;
 2)     {
 3)          Written by:   XXXXXXX  XX/XX/XX
 4)            Purpose:   To calculate the area of a triangle
 5)                        based on its three sides.
 6)          Parameters:   A, B, and C are the three sides. This
 7)                        function assumes they do form the
 8)                        sides of a triangle.
 9)     }
10)     var
11)       S              : real;           {semiperimeter (half the perimeter)}
12)
13)     begin {AreaFn}
14)       S := (A + B + C) / 2;
15)       AreaFn := Sqrt(S * (S-A) * (S-B) * (S-C))
16)     end; {AreaFn}
```

Figure 2-16   Code for AreaFn

In the example, we have chosen names that happen to match those used in the main program. *This was not necessary, but it is allowed.*

3. Lines 2 to 9 represent the type of header comments we will use in this text for functions. We include a brief description of the parameters (lines 6 to 8).

4. A function, like a procedure, can declare local variables. Lines 10 to 11 declare the local variable S, the semiperimeter of the triangle. This variable is used within the function, and not in the main program.

5. A function can in turn use another function or procedure. In line 15, the AreaFn function uses the standard square root function (Sqrt).

6. The function sends its answer to the program using it by placing the answer into the function name. Line 15 performs this step.

7. The body of the function is bracketed by begin (line 13) and end (line 16). The final end is followed by a semicolon. We add a comment on each of these lines identifing that these are the beginning and end of the module AreaFn.

**THE FORM OF
A PASCAL
FUNCTION**

□   This example illustrates the general form of a Pascal function:

> 1. A header line identifying the function and its parameters
> 2. Declaration of local constants and variables, if any
> 3. A list of statements forming the ''body'' of the function (bracketed by ''begin'' and ''end;'' and separated by semicolons)
>
> The body must contain at least one statement that gives a value to the function name. It can contain more than one such statement. The entire function (from header line through the final ''end;'') is placed after the variable declarations and before the ''begin'' of the main program.

The header line has this form:

```
function function-name (list of parameters) : type of answer;
```

The "type of answer" can be real, integer, char, or boolean; it cannot be string.[1] It represents the type of value the function calculates and returns.

The "function-name" follows the usual rules for Pascal identifiers. The "list of parameters" can be simple, as in the example, or it can be quite complex. There are alternative ways to express the same list. For example, these two lists are equivalent:

```
A, B, C : real
A : real; B : real; C : real
```

The first says, "There are three parameters: A, B, and C. All three are real." The second says, "There are three parameters. The first is A, which is real. The second is B, which is real. The third is C, which is real."

In general, we can describe the "list of parameters" as containing one or more repetitions of this basic pattern:

```
variable list : type
```

Within each list the variables are separated by commas. If there are several occurrences of the pattern, they are separated by semicolons.

The following sample header lines should help clarify these points.

```
function Lowest(Score1, Score2, Score3 : integer) : integer;

function Lowest(Score1 : integer; Score2 : integer;
                Score3 : integer) : integer;

function LetterGrade(Average : real) : char;

function Average(A, B, C, D, E : integer) : real;

function Raise(Salary : real; Tenured : boolean) : real;

function F(X, Y : real; T, U, V : integer; A, B : char) : real;
```

COMMENT The "type of the answer" does not have to match the type of the parameters.

CAUTION

Strings can be passed as parameters. However, doing so requires the concept of a "named data type", which we have not covered yet. The following is *illegal*:

```
function Bonus(category : string[10]) : real;
```

For now, parameters must be integer, real, char, or boolean.

PARAMETERS ☐ A complete discussion of parameters will be given in Chapter 4. However, a few comments are in order at this point.

The parameters for a function are called **value parameters**. This means that a value comes into the function through the parameter. When the function is used in the main program, the values are calculated and placed into the parameter variables for the function.

For the AreaFn function we just wrote, any of the following would be legal uses, assuming that all the variables are real and have assigned values.

```
Area := AreaFn(A, B, C)
Area := AreaFn(X, Y, Z)
Area := AreaFn(Side1, Side2, Side3)
Area := AreaFn(3.0, 4.0, 5.0)
Area := AreaFn(X+3.5, Y/17.2, (Z+W)/3.2)
```

In each case, the first parameter is evaluated and the value placed into the variable A within the function. A similar comment applies for the second and third parameters.

We can summarize the use of parameters by a function as follows:

1. The program **invoking** the function must supply the correct number of parameters (three, in our example).

2. The values supplied must be of the proper type (real, in our example).

3. The values must have the proper meaning (the three sides of a triangle, in our example).

4. The parameters correspondence occurs by position not by name. The names used can match those in the function (as in our first use given above), but they don't have to (as in all the other sample uses given).

HOW TO WRITE A FUNCTION ☐ There are five general steps involved in writing a function.

1. Decide That a Function is Appropriate. This step occurs as part of the design of the module that will use the function. A function is appropriate whenever there is a subtask that involves calculating *one* value. If the steps involved in the calculation are complex, then certainly a function is in order. Even if the steps are simple, however, using a function can make the main program easier to follow.

For example, the standard function *Round* is not necessary; rounding can be accomplished in a single step without it. However, an assignment such as

```
NumberPerDay := Round(Total / NumberofDays)
```

is far easier to understand with the function than without it.

2. Determine Function Name and Type. We name our function with an identifier descriptive of what it calculates. The only restriction is that the name must be different from any other variable name, procedure name, or function name declared in the main program.

The type of the function is the type of the value it calculates and returns. It can be real, integer, char, or boolean; it cannot be a string.

3. *Identify the Parameters.* A function calculates a value as an answer. If we ask, "What is the answer based on?" we will be identifying the parameters. We choose a variable name for each of these parameters.

In choosing the variable names, we can use the same names that the main program uses for these quantities. This is allowed, but it is not necessary.

4. *Write an Algorithm and Identify Local Variables.* This will, in a sense, be a segment of an algorithm. It will contain only those steps needed to calculate the answer, based on the parameters.

The algorithm should place the final answer into the identifier that is the function name.

To obtain the answer, additional variables may be required. These should be declared as local variables within the function.

5. *Code the Algorithm.* Steps 2 and 3 have identified all the information required for the header line. We declare any local variables identified during step 4, and write the body of the function implementing the algorithm of step 4.

COMMENT If an exercise reads, "Write a function to . . . ," then you should begin at step 2. The authors will already have accomplished step 1.

As an example of the function design process, we will carry out steps 2 to 5 for the following problem. (This problem is essentially Exercise 12(c) of Section 2-6.)

Write a function to calculate a customer's bill for an order of some quantity of a single item. We assume there are only four items available, as shown:

Item Number	Unit Price
100	24.03
247	105.00
16	10.35
240	16.00

A discount is allowed for large orders: If the total bill is $1000.00 or over, a 2 percent discount is given; from $800 to $999.99, a 1 percent discount.

Step 2. Determine Function Name and Type. Because the bill is in dollars and cents, we will use a real function, named BillFn.

Step 3. Identify the parameters. For a function, the parameters are the variables on which the answer depends. In this case, the bill depends on what the item is and on how many of the items are being purchased. We begin our variable list:

Value parameters:	ItemNumber	integer	Item number purchased
	Quantity	integer	Quantity purchased

Step 4. Write an Algorithm and Identify Local Variables. The algorithm contains three major steps: (1) calculate the price; (2) calculate the

total cost before discount; and (3) deduct the discount, if applicable. A more refined algorithm is given below, along with local variables to be added to the variable list. (We are assuming that ItemNumber and Quantity are valid. Perhaps they have been checked in the main program.)

Local variables:	Price	real	Unit price of item
	TotalCost	real	Total cost before discount

Algorithm:
1. calculate Price, based on ItemNumber, as indicated in this table (use a case structure)

ItemNumber −	100	Price −	24.03
	247		105.00
	16		10.35
	240		16.00

2. calculate TotalCost as Price times Quantity
3. calculate BillFn by subtracting a discount based on TotalCost, as indicated in this table (use an if/elseif structure)

TotalCost −	1000.00 or more	Subtract −	2% of TotalCost
	800–999.99		1% of TotalCost
	below 800		nothing

Step 5. Code the Algorithm. We must write the header line, declare the local variables, and write the necessary steps for the body of the function. We have used blank lines to highlight the three major steps of the function. The solution appears as Figure 2-17.

□ **DPT** In writing or using functions, be aware of a few common misconceptions and language subtleties.

1. Functions are written to perform calculations. As a general rule, they will contain no I/O statements. They obtain the values they use from the parameters not from reading. They do not print the answer, but rather send it back to the calling module.

2. Any variables used in the function should be one of these: a parameter, the function name, or a local variable.
Local variables are declared and used strictly within the function. They have no effect outside the function.

3. Each module, on the other hand, should declare only the variables it uses. For example, the main module should *not* declare the local variables used by the function.

4. For the answer to reach the **calling program**, it must be placed into the function name variable.

5. The parameters as supplied by the calling program must match those in the function by type, number, and purpose. The names may or may not match. In fact, the supplied values can be constants or even complicated expressions.

```
function BillFn(ItemNumber, Quantity : integer) : real;
{
       Written by:   XXXXXXX  XX/XX/XX
        Purpose:   To calculate the total bill based on the item
                   ordered and the quantity.
      Parameters:  The first is the item number purchased, the second
                   the quantity of that item which was purchased. Both

                   are assumed to be correct.

}
var
   Price      : real;              {price of item, from the table}
   TotalCost  : real;              {total cost, before discount}

begin {BillFn}

   case ItemNumber of
      100 : Price := 24.03;
      247 : Price := 105.00;
       16 : Price := 10.35;
      240 : Price := 16.00
   end;

   TotalCost := Price * Quantity;

   if TotalCost >= 1000 then
      BillFn := TotalCost - 0.02 * TotalCost
   else if TotalCost >= 800 then
      BillFn := TotalCost - 0.01 * TotalCost
   else
      BillFn := TotalCost

   end; {BillFn}
```

Figure 2-17 Another Function

6. The function type is the type of the answer calculated. It does not have to match the types of the parameters. (In fact, the parameters can be of several different types.)

7. Within the function, we should not use the function name in a condition or on the right side of an assignment statement. For example, consider the BillFn function written in this section. We wrote these lines:

```
TotalCost := Price * Quantity;
if TotalCost >= 1000 then
   BillFn := TotalCost - 0.02 * TotalCost
```

These similar lines are INCORRECT:

```
BillFn := Price * Quantity;
if BillFn >= 1000 then
   BillFn := BillFn - 0.02 * BillFn
```

The use of BillFn in the if statement, and both uses on the right side of the assignment statement, are treated as *invocations of the BillFn function*. This is not what we intended at all. Although the function name looks like any other variable name, it cannot be truly used as a variable. For now, the only proper use of the function name inside a function is on the left side of the assignment statement. (In Chapter 4, we will learn some other uses.)

If we make the error described above, the compiler will detect it. A call to BillFn is supposed to supply two parameters, and these did not. Turbo Pascal gives an error message: '(' expected. This is not very illuminating. What it really expected was a left parentheses followed by the parameter list.

REVIEW

Terms and concepts

module	value parameter
function	invoke
parameter	calling program

Parameters

Parameters (arguments) in the calling program must match those in the function as to number, type, and purpose. They may or may not match in name. Any expression of the proper type can be supplied as a parameter by the calling module.

Pascal syntax

1. Function is declared after variable declarations and before "begin" for the main program.

2. Header statement:

```
function function-name ( parameter list ) : function type;
```

3. Parameter list: one or more occurrences of the following separated by semicolons:

```
list of variables separated by commas : type
```

Considerations for using functions

Writing a function

1. Decide if a function is appropriate (for a subtask to calculate a value).

2. Determine the function type and choose a function name.

3. Identify and name the parameters.

4. Write an algorithm. (Might introduce local variables.)

5. Code as a Pascal function. Write the header line using the function name, parameter information, and function type. Declare local variables. Code the algorithm.

Invoking a function

1. Include a function call, along with required parameters, in an expression. (This is usually in an assignment statement, but it can be in a condition or a call to Writeln.)

2. Supply expressions representing the supplied values for the parameters, using variables or constants of the calling module.

1. Find the errors, if any, in the following function header lines.
   *a. `function Max(A);`
   *b. `function Cube(A; B; C : integer) : integer;`
   c. `function Cube(A : integer) : real;`
   d. `function Maxtwo(A, B: real) : integer;`
   e. `function 2Times(A; integer, B : real) : char`
   f. `function XTimesY(X real, Y real);`
   g. `function Salary(Years : integer;`
                        `Department : string[8]) : real;`

2. Write function header lines for the following:
   *a. A real function XDivY with two real parameters X and Y.
   b. An integer function Largest with three integer parameters A, B, and C.
   *c. A char function LetterGrade with an integer parameter Grade.
   d. A real function Salary with parameters: Department(integer), Years(integer), Bonus(real), Rank(char), and NumberSupervised(integer).

3. Write a function to find the smaller of two real numbers.

*4. Write a function to find the largest of three integer numbers.

5. Write a function to find the smallest of three integer numbers.

6. Write a function to calculate the total surface area of a cone. The formula is
$$V = \pi r \sqrt{(r^2 + h^2)} + \pi r^2$$

7. Write a function to determine the letter grade for a given numerical average. Use the usual 90–80–70–60 scale.

8. Write a function to calculate the final average based on the homework average, test average, and final exam percentage. If the homework average is 0.70 or higher, the final average is the higher of the test average and the final exam percentage. Otherwise, the final average is the sum of 0.3 times the homework average, 0.4 times the test average, and 0.3 times the final exam percentage.

9. a. The vacation days per year are based on the employee type and years experience as defined by the following rules: All type 'A' employees get 7 days and all type 'E' employees get 21 days. Type 'S' employees earn 10 days if they have 6 or fewer years of experience, otherwise 15 days. All other types get 0 days.
      Design a function to calculate the vacation days up to the point of Pascal coding.
   *b. Code the function.

10. a. Write a function to find the larger of two integer numbers.
    *b. Use the function you wrote in part (a) in an assignment statement to accomplish this task: The variable Try should be given an initial value that is the larger of M and N.
    c. Use the function you wrote in part (a) in an assignment statement to accomplish this task: The final grade for the course is to be the exam grade or the average of the two test grades, whichever is larger.

11. a. Write a function Round2 with two parameters: a real number to be rounded and an integer telling the number of places. For example:

> Round2(3.1416, 3) *is* 3.142
> Round2(17.1498, 1) *is* 17.1
> Round2(16.5, 0) *is* 17.0

*b. Use the function you wrote in part (a) to calculate BasketsPerDay as Baskets divided by Days rounded to the nearest hundredth.

c. Repeat part (b), but round to the nearest whole number. What is the difference between this answer and the one supplied by the standard Round function?

d. Use the function of part (a) to find the average on three tests rounded to the nearest tenth.

12. Write functions for the situations described by each of the following exercises from Section 2-5. Note: If the situation calls for printing the answer, instead calculate that answer as the function value. Also, for Exercise 5(a) change the city codes 'MVR', 'MORR', 'JCY', and 'BSTA' to integer codes 395, 217, 152, and 911, respectively.

  a. Exercise 4(c)   b. Exercise 4(e)
*c. Exercise 5(a)   d. Exercise 5(c) (tax only)
*e. Exercise 5(d)

13. In Section 2-6, you wrote some assignment statements and segments of code to assign values to Boolean variables. By choosing appropriate parameters, rewrite the following exercises from Section 2-6 as Boolean functions:

  a. Exercise 3(a)   b. Exercise 3(b)
  c. Exercise 3(c)   d. Exercise 3(h)
  e. Exercise 6(c)   f. Exercise 6(d)
  g. Exercise 6(f)   h. Exercise 6(g)
  i. Exercise 6(h)

14. For each of these exercises from Section 2-6, determine a portion of the program that might reasonably constitute a function. Then write a function to perform the identified calculation subtask.

  a. Exercise 10(b)   b. Exercise 10(d)
  c. Exercise 11(a)   d. Exercise 11(b)
  e. Exercise 11(c)

*15. The library functions Sin and Cos require the parameter values to be supplied in radians. Write functions called DegreeSin and DegreeCos that calculate their values for an angle given in degrees. (Degrees can be converted to radians by multiplying by $\pi/180$.)

16. Write a function Tan that calculates the tangent of an angle supplied in radians. (Watch for an error condition.)

17. See Note 7 at the end of Section 2-4. Use the suggestions given there to write your own Int and Frac functions.

NOTES FOR SECTION 2-7

□ 1. Turbo Pascal does allow functions whose values are strings. This is not standard. At this point in the text, we will not deal with string functions. See Chapter 4 for a discussion including string functions.

2-8
□□□□□□
MODULAR DESIGN AND TESTING

A program that contains subprograms raises some issues on the way in which we test the program. For example, with a main program and one procedure, there are four possibilities:

□
TESTING

1. We could write the entire program, then start testing the whole program as a single unit.

2. We could make sure that the main program works, separately make sure that the procedure works, then put them together and see if they work together.

3. We could make sure that the main program works, then add the untested procedure and make sure that the package works.

4. We could make sure that the procedure works, then add it to the untested main program and make sure that the package works.

Of course, with two subprograms the possibilities increase.

The third and fourth alternatives are examples of **incremental testing**. For programs containing large numbers of subprograms, incremental testing has been found to work better than the other two methods. The first method has the disadvantage that, when an error occurs, it can be difficult to determine which subprogram caused the error. The second method is an improvement, but it has been found that pieces that work perfectly well separately sometimes do not work well when combined. If we combine them all at once, it can be difficult to see which particular combinations are causing the problems.

Method 3 from the above list is an example of **top-down testing**. The top level (main) module is tested first, then the lower level modules are added, one at a time, and the program is tested again. In this form of testing, so-called **stubs** are needed for the subprograms that have not yet been written and tested. We would test the main program with the stub versions of the subprograms. When we get this running properly, we would replace one of the stubs by the actual subprogram and perform more testing of the resulting program. This would be followed by replacing another stub by the actual subprogram and the program as a whole is tested again. This continues until the entire program has been tested.

Method 4 is an example of **bottom-up testing**. The lowest level modules are tested; when they are running correctly, the module that calls them is added and the combination is tested. This form of testing requires a **driver** main program, a substitute for the actual main program that is used to ''drive'' the subprograms that are being tested.

We will have more to say about incremental testing in general, and about top-down and bottom-up testing, in other testing sections later in the text. In the case study that follows, we illustrate simple instances of both top-down testing with stubs and bottom-up testing with drivers.

CASE STUDY NO. 3

This case study develops a complete program that uses a number of subprograms. It is a simplified payroll program. Part of the case study describes some strategies for testing a program that includes subprograms.

Statement of problem. Write a program that calculates weekly pay and the amount of state tax to be withheld from the paycheck. The pay is the hourly rate times the number of hours, except that hours over 40 earn "time and a half." The state tax is based on the following rules:

First, $12 is deducted from the income for each dependent. Then the tax is determined by the following table:

Resulting income	Tax
Less than 0	0
$0–$300	2% of resulting income
Over $300	$15.00 plus 2.5% of the amount over $300

Preliminary analysis. The problem is not well described because it does not specify the necessary input. We will have to discover what input will be required by analyzing the problem. It is clear that we need at least the hourly rate and the number of hours in order to calculate the weekly pay. The tax is based on the pay, which we calculate, and the number of dependents, another part of the input. Finally, we assume that the input will contain an integer clock number.

For output, we will print the clock number, weekly pay, and state tax withholding.

We will not do complete error checking on the input; that will be left to the exercises. However, we do check one possible error: hours less than 0.

One final note: "Time and a half" means that if a person works over 40 hours, then the first 40 are paid at the normal rate and all other hours are paid at 1.5 times the normal rate.

Algorithm and variable list.

1. Main Program. For the main program, we have the following input and output variables, based on our analysis:

Constant:	EndOfData	value 0	Used to terminate loop
Input:	ClockNumber	integer	Employee clock number (also printed)
	HoursWorked	real	Hours worked by employee
	HourlyRate	real	Rate of pay per hour
	Dependents	integer	Number of dependents
Output:	Pay	real	Pay for week
	StateTax	real	State tax withheld for week

The algorithm is quite similar to ones we have written before. [As we have been doing, we mark steps with an (*) to indicate that they are not done for the terminating data.]

print instructions (use procedure Instructions)
repeat these steps until a clock number ≤ 0 is entered:
    issue prompt for clock number
    read ClockNumber
    issue prompt for hours, rate, # dependents (*)
    read HoursWorked, HourlyRate, Dependents (*)
    if HoursWorked < 0 do these two steps: (*)
        print an error message (including HoursWorked)
        set HoursWorked to 0
    calculate Pay (*)
    calculate StateTax (*)
    print ClockNumber, Pay, and StateTax (*)
print a closing message

We have chosen to use a procedure named Instructions for the subtask "print instructions." In addition, we will write functions called PayFn and TaxFn for the "calculate Pay" and "calculate StateTax" subtasks. We refine those two steps as follows:

calculate Pay: `Pay := PayFn(HoursWorked, HourlyRate)`

calculate StateTax: `StateTax := TaxFn(Pay, Dependents)`

In doing so we have supplied as parameters the values on which the calculations are based.

COMMENT   Given in Figure 2-18 is a **hierarchy chart** for the program. This is a visual description of the fact that it contains four modules and that the main module calls the

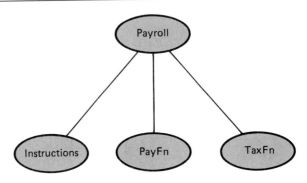

Main program (Payroll):	reads data (some minor checking), calls functions, and prints answers in a loop
Instructions:	procedure that prints instructions
PayFn:	function that calculates weekly pay
TaxFn:	function that calculates state tax withholding

Figure 2-18 Hierarchy Chart

other three. Along with the diagram, we give a short description of what task each module performs.

2. PayFn Function. This completes the design for the main program. Next we design the PayFn function. We have already decided that it should be a real function with two parameters (hours and rate).

The basic algorithm was developed as a part of an earlier example, in Section 2-3 (page 67). That algorithm used the variables Hours and HourlyRate for the hours and rate, respectively. We will make use of the earlier work, so we choose to use these variable names for our parameters.

NOTE One of these variable names happens to match the name used in the main program and the other does not. This is perfectly acceptable. One of the reasons for this flexibility in naming parameters is to make it easy to use previous work on the same or similar problems.

That algorithm also contained two other variables, which will become local variables for the function. We obtain this variable list and algorithm:

Value parameters:	Hours	real	Hours worked
	HourlyRate	real	Hourly pay rate
Local variables:	RegularPay	real	Pay for first 40 hours
	OvertimePay	real	Pay for overtime hours

Algorithm:

```
if Hours > 40 then do these steps:
    calculate RegularPay  (formula 40 * HourlyRate)
    calculate OvertimePay (formula (Hours—40) * HourlyRate * 1.5)
    calculate PayFn as RegularPay + OvertimePay
otherwise do this step:
    calculate PayFn as Hours * HourlyRate
```

3. TaxFn Function. We now design the TaxFn function. It is a real function with parameters representing the pay (a real quantity) and the number of dependents (an integer quantity). We choose names that match those in the main program. In addition to the parameters, we need a local variable for the taxable income.

Value parameters:	Pay	real	Week's pay
	Dependents	integer	Number of dependents
Local variables:	TaxableIncome	real	Taxable income

The algorithm, based on the verbal description, is

```
calculate TaxableIncome
calculate TaxFn based on TaxableIncome, using this table (use an if-elseif
        structure)
```

TaxableIncome:	TaxFn:
<0	0
0–300	0.02 * TaxableIncome
any other	15.00 + 0.025 * (TaxableIncome − 300)

NOTE You might wonder about the use of the local variable TaxableIncome. Could we not just modify the parameter Pay, then use that in our TaxFn calculation? The answer is yes. However, this relies on the fact that *for value parameters*, Pascal is designed so that the Pay variable in the main program is not modified. Value parameters behave much like local variables. There are languages that do not provide this protection. In such languages, the use of the local variable would be mandatory. It is good defensive programming never to change a value parameter.

However, in this example we should use the local variable in any case. In general, it is a good design practice to use different variables where different quantities are being handled. "Pay" is the weekly pay, and "TaxableIncome" is the portion that is taxable. These are not the same concepts, so we should use two different variables.

4. Instructions procedure. We leave the plan for the Instructions procedure to the reader.

COMMENT In working with subprograms, what we did above was typical. We developed and presented each module's plan as a separate piece, starting with the main program and working our way to the subprograms. This is part of what is meant by **top down design**.

Test plan. We now develop the test plan. This consists of two parts: a planned order to write and test the modules and a set of test data for each module. We choose this order: PayFn, TaxFn, main program, and Instructions. Notice that this is "bottom up" in the sense that PayFn and TaxFn are developed before the main program that uses them. On the other hand, it is "top down" in the sense that the main program is developed before its procedure Instructions. Quite frequently in large projects, a mixture of the two methods is used.

When we write a test plan for each separate module, this is sometimes referred to as **unit testing**. We will outline a plan for each module.

NOTE (ON TESTING PHILOSOPHY) In this case study, we present an "idealized" approach to the joint process of testing and program development. This means that, under ideal circumstances, we should follow guidelines similar to those presented here.

But what if circumstances are not ideal? If we do not "have time" to do the thorough testing required, shall we just forget about testing altogether? The answer is no. In testing programs (as in most human endeavors), the choice is not really all or nothing. Even if our test plan is not perfect, any test plan is better than none at all.

There are, of course, risks in taking shortcuts. If at all possible, we should do a thorough testing. If we must skimp, we should try to do the most critical tests in any case. (In general, Boundary tests are probably the most critical.)

With the preceding discussion in mind, we now develop our unit test plans.

Main: Branches and borderlines on bad vs. good hours:

hours = −0.1   hours = −5
hours = 0   hours = 30
hours = 0.1

Note: There are other possible "bad data" situations, which will be explored in the exercises. (In testing the main program, we will repeat some of the branch tests that we have done for the pay and tax functions.)

PayFn: Branches and borderlines on hours:

hours = 39.9   hours = 25
hours = 40.0   hours = 50
hours = 40.1

TaxFn: Branches and borderlines on number of dependents:

dependents = 0   # dependents = 5
dependents = 1

Branches and borderlines on taxable income: For each test, we show the desired taxable income. Because the taxable income depends on the pay and the number of dependents, we also indicate how we plan to achieve the desired taxable income. Notice that we use a variety of values for the number of dependents.

tax. inc. = −1   (pay 23 #dep 2)
tax. inc. =   0   (pay 12 #dep 1)
tax. inc. =   1   (pay 1 #dep 0)

tax. inc. = 299   (pay 299 #dep 0)
tax. inc. = 300   (pay 360 #dep 5)
tax. inc. = 301   (pay 337 #dep 3)

tax. inc. = −50   (pay 10 #dep 5)
tax. inc. = 100   (pay 148 #dep 4)
tax. inc. = 400   (pay 400 #dep 0)

COMMENT We have chosen to test our borderlines 1 dollar below and above rather than 1 cent below and above. At a 2 percent tax rate, a 1 cent difference in income would lead to only a very small change in the tax.

In doing the actual testing, we found that a taxable income of 301 yielded an answer of 15.02 when printed with two decimal places. It wasn't clear that the 2.5 percent rate was being used correctly, so we immediately tried a taxable income of 302, which yielded the correct answer of 15.05.

Instructions: Since the design of the Instructions procedure has been left to the exercises, we also leave the details of the test plan to the exercise. It should include tests of branches based on whether or not instructions are wanted.

Write program. We write the program in the order indicated in our test plan. We begin with the PayFn function. In order to test the function, we need a driver main program. This is a temporary main program written for the sole purpose of testing the function. Because it is temporary, we do not include comments or complicated instructions, and we can use shorter than usual variable names. The function, along with a possible driver is given in Figure 2-19.

```pascal
program Driver(Input, Output);
const
  EndOfData = -1;

var
  Hours  : real;
  Rate   : real;
  Pay    : real;

function PayFn(Hours, HourlyRate : real) : real;
{
    Written by: XXXXXXXX, XX/XX/XX
       Purpose: To calculate the pay for one person.
    Parameters: The first is the number of hours the person worked.
                The second is the hourly rate of pay. Both are assumed
                to be valid.
}
var
  RegularPay  : real;               {pay for first 40 hours}
  OvertimePay : real;               {pay for hours over 40}

begin {PayFn}
  if Hours > 40 then
    begin
      RegularPay := 40 * HourlyRate;
      OvertimePay := (Hours - 40) * HourlyRate * 1.5;
      PayFn := RegularPay + OvertimePay
    end
  else
    PayFn := Hours * HourlyRate

end; {PayFn}

begin {Driver}

  repeat
    Writeln;
    Write('Enter hours and rate (-1 to quit) : ');
    Readln(Hours, Rate);
    if Hours <> EndOfData then
      begin
        Pay := PayFn(Hours, Rate);
        Writeln('Hours = ', Hours:2:2, ' Rate = ', Rate:2:2,
                ' Pay = ', Pay:2:2);
      end
  until Hours = EndOfData;
```

Figure 2-19 Driver Program for a Function (Continued)

```
    Writeln('Driver terminating')
end.
```

SAMPLE INPUT AND OUTPUT

```
Enter hours and rate (-1 to quit) : 34 5.67
Hours = 34.00 Rate = 5.67 Pay = 192.78

Enter hours and rate (-1 to quit) : 45 6.04
Hours = 45.00 Rate = 6.04 Pay = 286.90

Enter hours and rate (-1 to quit) : -1 -1
Driver terminating
```

Figure 2-19   Driver Program for a Function

We test the PayFn function by running the Driver program. If there are any errors in the function, we correct them. When it seems correct, we proceed to the next step.

In the next step, we do exactly the same thing for the TaxFn function. The details are left as an exercise.

We are now ready to write the main program. We do so, inserting the already tested functions in the proper spot. (We should not retype the functions; rather, we should use our system's editor to load them into the proper place in the program.)

We will test the main program together with the two functions that we have already written and tested. However, notice that it also calls for a procedure that has not been written. In order to test the main program, we write a stub for the Instructions procedure. This stub can be very simple; for example,

```
procedure Instructions;
begin
  Writeln('Instructions procedure successfully called')
end;
```

When we run the main program, this message will be printed prior to entering the loop. The actual procedure will be added later. Figure 2-20 contains the program we tested at this point with the actual functions and the stub procedure.

The final step is to replace the stub by the actual Instructions procedure, and run our tests for this procedure. At this point, we have a complete program. We would probably do some more testing, similar to some that we did for the individual pieces, to try to make sure that the program as a whole is working as it should.

Modifications.   One of the advantages of modularity is that it makes modifications easier. For example, we will develop some additions to the program in the next chapter that will not affect any of the subprograms, so they will not have to be retested. As another example, if we modified the pay function, only this function and the program as a whole would have to be retested.

The exercises suggest some modifications to the case study.

```
program Payroll(Input, Output);
{
      Written by:  XXXXXXX  XX/XX/XX
         Purpose:  To calculate pay and state tax for a number of employees.
                   The input consists of a clock number, the number of hours
                   worked, the hourly rate, and the number of dependents.
  Procedures used: Instructions, to print instructions for user.
   Functions used: PayFn, to calculate the pay based on hours and rate.
                   TaxFn, to calculate the tax based on the pay and the
                         number of dependents.
}
const
   EndOfData = 0;                          {terminating data indicator}

var
   ClockNumber : integer;                  {employee clock number, input}
   HoursWorked : real;                     {hours worked, input}
   HourlyRate  : real;                     {rate of pay, input}
   Dependents  : integer;                  {number of dependents, input}
   Pay         : real;                     {pay for week, output}
   StateTax    : real;                     {state tax, output}

procedure Instructions;
begin {Instructions (stub version)}
   Writeln('Instructions procedure successfully called')
end; {Instructions}
```

{*Function PayFn as shown in Figure 2-19 is inserted here.*}

```
function TaxFn(Pay : real; Dependents : integer) : real;
{
     Written by: XXXXXXX, XX/XX/XX
        Purpose: To calculate the tax for one person.
     Parameters: The first is the person's pay for the week. The second
                 is the number of dependents. Both are assumed to be
                 valid.
}
var
   TaxablePay  : real;           {portion of pay used for taxing}

begin {TaxFn}
   TaxablePay := Pay - 12 * Dependents;
   if TaxablePay < 0 then
     TaxFn := 0
   else if TaxablePay < 300 then
     TaxFn := 0.02 * TaxablePay
   else
     TaxFn := 15 + 0.025 * (TaxablePay - 300)

end; {TaxFn}
```

Figure 2-20   Payroll Program (Continued)

```
begin {Payroll}

{*** Before the loop, print instructions.}

  Instructions;

{*** In loop, obtain clock number, hours, rate, and number of dependents.
     Check for dummy value. Check for invalid hours. Calculate and print
     pay and tax.}

  repeat
    Writeln;
    Write('Enter clock number for next employee: ');
    Readln(ClockNumber);
    if ClockNumber > EndOfData then
      begin
        Write('Now enter the hours, rate, and number of dependents: ');
        Readln(HoursWorked, HourlyRate, Dependents);
        if HoursWorked < 0 then
          begin
            Writeln(HoursWorked, ' is invalid; changed to 0.');
            HoursWorked := 0
          end;
        Pay := PayFn(HoursWorked, HourlyRate);
        StateTax := TaxFn(Pay, Dependents);
        Writeln(ClockNumber, ' earned ', Pay:2:2, ' and was taxed ',
                StateTax:2:2)
      end
  until ClockNumber <= EndOfData;

{*** Print final message and stop.}

  Writeln;
  Writeln('Payroll program terminating.')
end.
```

SAMPLE INPUT AND OUTPUT

```
Instructions procedure successfully called

Enter clock number for next employee: 345
Now enter the hours, rate, and number of dependents: 34 5.67 8
345 earned 192.78 and was taxed 1.94

Enter clock number for next employee: 101
Now enter the hours, rate, and number of dependents: 44 6.78 3
101 earned 311.88 and was taxed 5.52

Enter clock number for next employee: 0
Payroll program terminating.
```

Figure 2-20 Payroll Program

REVIEW

Terms and concepts

incremental testing   bottom-up testing
top-down testing   hierarchy chart
stubs   top-down design
driver   unit test

Testing

1. Use an incremental approach (top down, bottom up, or a mixture).

2. Develop a unit test plan for each module.

3. Use drivers and stubs where needed.

■■■■■■ EXERCISES

1. Rewrite the following programs from Section 2-6, using a function for an appropriate calculation subtask. (You will have to identify an appropriate subtask to be placed into a function.)

   a. Exercise 10(d)   b. Exercise 11(a)
   c. Exercise 11(b)   d. Exercise 11(c)

2. Write unit test plans for the functions you identified in Exercise 1.

3. Describe a unit test plan for these exercises in Section 2-7.

   a. Exercise 3   *b. Exercise 4
   c. Exercise 5   d. Exercise 7
   *e. Exercise 9   f. Exercise 11

4. Write a driver program, and test each function referred to in Exercise 3 using your test plan devised in that exercise.

5. Modify Case Study No. 1 (Section 1-4) to calculate and print the letter grade for each student. Use a function that you write and unit test prior to inserting into the case study program. Test the revised program.

*6. Write a complete program, modeled after Case Study No. 2, to accomplish the following. It should read a real number, a one-digit integer number, and a code for the operation to be performed. (The real number is of the form xxx.yyy.) It should use functions where appropriate. The valid operations are

P (part):	123.456	P	1	is	123
	123.456	P	2	is	456
D (digit):	617.354	D	2	is	1
	617.354	D	6	is	4
R (rotate):	123.456	R	1	is	612.345
	123.456	R	-1	is	234.561
	123.456	R	0	is	123.456
S (split & add):	123.456	S	1	is	$1 + 2 + 3 + 4 + 5 + 6 = 21$
	123.456	S	2	is	$12 + 34 + 56$
	123.456	S	3	is	$123 + 456$

The integer number is in these ranges: 1 to 2 for 'P', and 1 to 6 for 'D', -1 to 1 for 'R', and 1 to 3 for 'S'. In each case, the answer is 0 if the integer number is not in the proper range.

7. Write a complete program to calculate wages and state taxes for a number of employees. Input consists of name, clock number, marital status, number of dependents, and job code. Wages are based on department and job code. If we let Department be the first digit of the four-digit clock number, the wages are as indicated in the table (any entry not appearing indicates an error):

Department= 1		Department= 2		Department= 3		Department= 4	
Job	Wages	Job	Wages	Job	Wages	Job	Wages
A	157.00	A	345.00	A	264.00	A	130.00
B	171.00	B	415.00	B	289.00	B	175.00
C	306.00	Any	653.00	C	315.00	C	210.00
D	339.00	Other		D	347.00	Any	239.00
				E	389.00	Other	

State taxes are based on the description given in Exercise 5(c) of Section 2-5.

Exercises 8 to 14 refer to Case Study No. 3.

8. Write an algorithm and a test plan for the Instructions procedure. The person should be able to get instructions by either entering a lowercase or a capital Y.

9. Write a driver program for the TaxFn function. Run the driver program with the function to test the function.

*10. Modify the PayFn function to allow "double time" for all hours in excess of 50. Write a revised test plan.

11. Modify the TaxFn function to deduct 10 percent of the original income from the taxable income prior to calculating the tax. Write a revised test plan.

12. Think of some other possible input error, and modify the main program to check for them. Note: Some errors violate "reasonableness" standards. For example, an hourly wage of $1000 would be unreasonable.

13. Modify both functions to use named constants ("const" declarations). What are the advantages of this? Are there any disadvantages?

14. Add code to create a printed report. Before the loop, print some column headings. Then, for each employee, print (in columns) the clock number, hours worked, hourly rate, dependents, pay, and state tax.

3 USING LOOPS

3-1
□□□□□□
**COMMON
APPLICATIONS
OF LOOPS**

The primary topic of this chapter is loops. In the first section, we will examine some frequently used applications of looping. We will then study loop control in some detail. We begin with a general discussion.

□
**LOOP
PLANNING**

We will discuss loop planning in detail throughout this chapter. However, before we begin the major topic of this section (some common loop applications), let us give a brief overview of the loop planning process.

We may view a loop as consisting of two components. First, we have the actual steps that we wish to have performed repeatedly. This is frequently referred to as the **body** of the loop. For example, the bodies of the loops we have written up to this point have generally contained three major steps: (1) read data values, (2) calculate an answer, and (3) write a line of output.

The second component of a loop is the **loop control**. Whenever we write a loop in a program, we must incorporate some way to **terminate** (or **exit from**) the loop. The loop control consists of the portion that causes the steps of the loop to be performed the proper number of times. In our sample programs so far, the loop control has been of a type we might call "direct user control." The steps in the loop were repeated until the user indicated, by entering a terminal data value, that there was no more data to be read. There are many other possible types of loop control, which we will study in later sections of this chapter. For now, we will continue to use the "terminal data value" loop control used in earlier examples.

In addition to the body and the loop control, there can be other steps closely related to the loop. These steps occur either before or after the loop. For example, many applications of loops require steps, called **initialization** steps, to be performed before the loop. For example, programs that accumulate totals generally must initialize the variable containing the total to zero before the loop. Many other problems require variables to be initialized. Similarly, after the loop, we may need steps that use the information gathered or calculated in the loop. For example, many times we will print totals after a loop.

In this section, we present three common applications of program loops. These are counting how many times some condition occurs as the loop executes; accumulating the total of some set of values; and finding either the largest or smallest of some set of values. In each case, we will concentrate on three major issues:

1. The initialization steps required

2. The steps that should be part of the loop body

3. The steps to be performed following the loop body

COMMENT   These three applications (counting, accumulating, finding largest or smallest) can be used in a variety of programs with complexities that have nothing to do with the specific applications. In order to concentrate our attention on these three applications, we will present them in a context where the program consists of reading some values and calculating and printing some answers. We will examine the steps that must be added to these examples in order to count, to accumulate, or to find the largest or smallest.

□

COUNTING   Consider the following problem. A program is to read a series of nonzero integers. The end of the input will be indicated by a terminal value of 0. For each number, except the 0, the program is to print a message telling whether the number is even or odd. Pascal provides a Boolean function "Odd(n)" which is true if n is odd and false if n is even. The following fragment shows the main loop of the program (EndOfData is the constant 0):

```
repeat
  Write('Enter number (0 to quit): ');
  Readln(Number);
  if Number <> EndOfData then
    if Odd(Number) then
      Writeln(Number:1, ' is odd.')
    else
      Writeln(Number:1, ' is even.')
until Number = EndOfData
```

We would like to modify this example so that our program will print the number of even values at the end. Generally, we need to keep four points in mind when writing a program involving counting:

1. A **counter**, a variable to contain the count value, will be needed. It should normally be an integer variable.

2. This variable must be initialized to 0 before starting the count.

3. Whenever the condition to be counted is reached, one must be added to counter variable.

4. After leaving the loop or the part where the counting occurs, use the counter in some way, perhaps by printing it.

```
EvenCounter := 0;

repeat
  Write('Enter number (0 to quit): ');
  Readln(Number);
  if Number <> EndOfData then
    if Odd(Number) then
      Writeln(Number:1, ' is odd.')
    else
      begin
        Writeln(Number:1, ' is even.');
        EvenCounter := EvenCounter + 1
      end
until Number = EndOfData;

Writeln('There were ', EvenCounter, ' even numbers.')
```

Figure 3-1 Counting

For our specific example, we will use an integer variable, EvenCounter, as our counter variable. The modified program fragment is shown in Figure 3-1. The changes are shaded. Notice that the changes correspond to the considerations listed above. (Notice, also, that the "even" branch of the if–then now contains two steps. We therefore use a begin and end to group these into one compound statement.)

NOTE   In the following example, we will use the terminology **record**, which, as used here, is related to file terminology. In an employee file, for example, the information about one employee is called a record. It would contain the name, social security number, and other information for that employee.

We use record here to signify the collection of data about one entity, usually one person. This data can be supplied by the user through a single Readln or through several Readln's.

This use of the word "record" will occur throughout this section and later in the text.

It is possible, of course, to have a program that does no processing other than the counting, as illustrated in the next example.

Each record contains an identification number and an age. Write a program to determine what percentage of the people represented are age 30 or older.

Here we need two counters because to calculate the percentage we must determine how many are 30 or older and also how many there are all together. Here is the resulting variable list.

Input:	IDNumber	integer	Identification number
	Age	integer	Age
Other:	OldCounter	integer	Number age 30 or older (a counter)
	TotalCounter	integer	Number all together (a counter)
	Percent	real	Percent 30 or older

```
OldCounter := 0;
TotalCounter := 0;

repeat
  Write('Enter I.D. and age (age 0 to quit): ');
  Readln(IDNumber, Age);
  if Age <> EndOfData then
    begin
      TotalCounter := TotalCounter + 1;
      if Age >= 30 then
        OldCounter := OldCounter + 1
    end
until Age = EndOfData;

Percent := (OldCounter / TotalCounter) * 100;
Writeln;
Writeln(Percent:1:2, '% age 30 or over.')
```

Figure 3-2 Two Counters

Once again, we must initialize both counters at 0 before entering the loop that reads data and does the counting. Each time through the loop, add 1 to the OldCounter variable if the Age is 30 or above. This is similar to the previous example. Also add 1 to TotalCounter whether or not Age is 30 or above. After the loop, use the counters to calculate Percent, then print the answer. The program segment appears in Figure 3-2 with the counting steps shaded.

Perhaps the only step of the program that needs to be emphasized is the step that calculates the percentage:

```
Percent := (OldCounter / TotalCounter) * 100
```

First of all, notice that real division (/) is used. Integer division (div) would not work. Second, the program assumes that TotalCounter is not 0. Probably for this problem that is a reasonable assumption; however, there are instances where a count of 0 is very possible, and in those instances, we would want to guard against the possibility of dividing by 0.

ACCUMULATION

Now consider the accumulation process, which finds the total of all the values in a list. For example, we may have a file with employee number and net pay and want to write a program to determine the total payroll for a pay period. Or we may have a list of names and test scores and wish to determine the average score on a test. (To find the average, we would add all the scores and divide by the number of students.) The procedures used in accumulation are similar to those used in counting. First, we need a variable, called an **accumulator**, to keep track of the running total. The required steps before, during, and after the loop are as indicated:

1. Before the loop, initialize the accumulator to 0.

2. In the loop, add the appropriate value to the accumulator. (As in the case of counting, this step can be conditional.)

3. After the loop, use the total. Either print the total obtained or use it in further calculations (such as in obtaining an average).

These steps are analogous to what happens in a cash register at a grocery store checkout. In the cash register, the accumulator can be a piece of hardware within the machine. With each new grocery item, its price is added to the total. In this way, the accumulator maintains a running total. At any point in the process, it will contain the total up to that point (the subtotal). When all the items have been processed, it will contain the final total.

Now let us write a program to print a list of salespeople and to determine the total sales during the week. Assume that each set of input contains a salesperson number, a department number, a basic commission rate, and a sales amount for the week.

This is a typical accumulation problem. We wish to accumulate, or add, the week's sales amount for all employees. To do this, we will use an accumulator. Because real quantities are accumulated, the variable is real. The program will initialize the accumulator to 0 prior to entering the loop, add each sales amount to it in the body of the loop, and print the answer after the loop. In addition to the accumulator, we need variables for the quantities represented in the input.

Input:	IDNumber	integer	Salesperson number
	Department	integer	Department number
	Rate	real	Commission rate
	Sales	real	Sales for week
Other:	TotalSales	real	Total sales for week (printed at end)

The program segment merely incorporates what we have already decided should be done before, in, and after the loop. The loop is controlled by the user entering a terminal data value. See Figure 3-3, where the accumulation steps are shaded.

```
Header;
TotalSales := 0;

repeat
  Write('Enter salesperson number (0 to quit): ');
  Readln(IDNumber);
  if IDNumber <> EndOfData then
    begin
      Write('Now enter department, rate, sales: ');
      Readln(Department, Rate, Sales);
      Writeln(Lst, IDNumber:10, ' ':7, Department:5, ' ':7,
              Rate:5:3, ' ':7, Sales:9:2);
      TotalSales := TotalSales + Sales
    end
until IDNumber = EndOfData;

Writeln; Writeln('Total Sales is ', TotalSales:3:2);
Writeln(Lst); Writeln(Lst, 'Total sales is ', TotalSales:3:2)
```

Figure 3-3 Accumulation

1. This program fragment uses the Turbo feature Writeln(Lst, . . .), introduced in Chapter 2, to print on the printer.

2. The Header procedure invoked at the beginning contains a series of Writeln(Lst, . . .) statements to print column headings at the top of the page.

Suppose that we now consider a slightly more complicated problem. In addition to the accumulation, we will perform other processing in the loop, and not every record will be included in the total. For the same set of input used in the previous example, this time we want to write a program to print a report of commissions earned and to find the average commission earned by department 100.

In this problem, we will again need an accumulator, this time used to calculate the total commission earned by department 100. We will also need a counter to count the people in department 100. As before, we will initialize both the counter and the accumulator to 0 before the loop. After the loop, we will use these values to calculate the average. In doing the counting and accumulating, we include only those in department 100. However, we do calculate the commission for each person, regardless of department number.

Let us use a function CommFn to calculate the commission, and assume that the commission is based on the commission rate and the sales amount. Then the step to calculate the commission can be refined as

$$\text{Commission} := \text{CommFn(Rate, Sales)}$$

Figure 3-4 shows a main program that contains stubs for its three subprograms (two procedures and a function). This version can be used to perform preliminary testing of the main program. The submodules can be added one at a time.

```
program Commissions(Input, Output);
{
          Written by:   XXXXXXXX XX/XX/XX
             Purpose:   To calculate and print a commission report. Included
                        is a summary for department 100 personnel.
    Procedures used:    Header, to print headings
                        PrintLine, to print a detail line
     Functions used:    CommFn, to calculate commission
}
const
  EndOfData    = 0;                           { used to terminate loop }

var
  IDNumber      : integer;                    { salesperson number, input }
  Department    : integer;                    { department number, input }
  Rate          : real;                       { commission rate, input }
  Sales         : real;                       { sales for week, input }

  Commission    : real;                       { commission for week }
  TotalComm     : real;                       { total for dept 100 }
  CountDept100  : integer;                    { count of dept 100 }
  Average       : real;                       { average for dept 100 }
```

Figure 3-4   Accumulation with a Function (Continued)

```
procedure Header;
begin   {Header, stub version }
  Writeln(Lst, 'Header routine output')
end;   {Header}

procedure PrintLine(ID, Dept : integer; Rate, Sales, Comm : real);
begin   {PrintLine, stub version}
  Writeln(Lst, ID:5, Dept:5, Rate:10:2, Sales:10:2, Comm:10:2)
end;   {PrintLine}


function CommFn(Rate, Sales : real) : real;
begin {CommFn, stub version}
  Writeln('CommFn entered with rate = ', Rate:1:2, ' sales = ', Sales:1:2);
  CommFn := 150
end;   {CommFn}


begin   {Commissions}

{*** Print headings, and initialize count and total.}

  Header;
  TotalComm := 0;
  CountDept100 := 0;

{*** Read data, calculate commission, and adjust count and total.}

  repeat
    Write('Enter salesperson number (0 to quit): ');
    Readln(IDNumber);
    if IDNumber <> EndOfData then
      begin
        Write('Now enter department, rate, sales: ');
        Readln(Department, Rate, Sales);
        Commission := CommFn(Rate, Sales);
        PrintLine(IDNumber, Department, Rate, Sales, Commission);
        if Department = 100 then
          begin
            TotalComm := TotalComm + Commission;
            CountDept100 := CountDept100 + 1
          end
      end
  until IDNumber = EndOfData;

{*** Calculate and print average commission.}

  if CountDept100 = 0 then
    Writeln(Lst, 'No one in department 100')
  else
    begin
      Average := TotalComm / CountDept100;
      Writeln;
      Writeln(Lst, 'Average commission for department 100 is ',
              Average:1:2)
    end;
```

Figure 3-4   Accumulation with a Function (Continued)

```
   Writeln;
   Writeln('Commissions program is terminating')
end.
```

SAMPLE INPUT AND OUTPUT

On the terminal:

```
Enter salesperson number (0 to quit): 56
Now enter department, rate, sales: 100 .05 250
CommFn entered with rate = 0.05 sales = 250.00
Enter salesperson number (0 to quit): 34
Now enter department, rate, sales: 99 0.125 1000.10
CommFn entered with rate = 0.13 sales = 1000.10
Enter salesperson number (0 to quit): 0

Commissions program is terminating
```

On the printer:

```
Header routine output
   56  100       0.05     250.00     150.00
   34   99       0.13    1000.10     150.00
Average commission for department 100 is 150.00
```

Figure 3-4   Accumulation with a Function

Now let us plan the function CommFn. We have already named it and established that its parameters are the commission rate and the sales amount. We have this variable list:

Value parameters: Rate   real   Commission rate
                     Sales   real   Sales amount

Suppose the commission is simply rate times sales if sales is less than $250, otherwise it is 1.2 times rate times sales. Then the function is easy to write:

```
function CommFn(Rate, Sales : real) : real;
{
        Written by:   XXXXXXXXXXX, XX/XX/XX
           Purpose:   To calculate one person's commission
        Parameters:   Rate - the commission rate, real
                      Sales - the amount of the sale, real
}
begin {CommFn}
   if Sales < 250 then
     CommFn := Rate * Sales
   else
     CommFn := 1.2 * Rate * Sales
end; {CommFn}
```

This would go in place of the stub version. The other modules are left to the reader.

To summarize, with a problem involving accumulation, a special accumulator variable is needed. Before the loop, initialize the accumulator to 0; in the loop, add to the accumulator, if appropriate; after the loop, either print the total or use the total in further calculations.

□
LARGEST AND SMALLEST

We now discuss using a loop to determine the largest of a set of values. As a simple example, not directly related to the computer, consider the following problem. You (as a person) are given a large stack of cards, each containing a number. You are asked to determine the largest number on any of the cards. You are told that the numbers could be positive, negative, or zero. How would you solve this problem?

Before reading on, stop a moment and consider exactly how you would find the largest number if someone handed you such a deck of cards and you had to sequence through the deck one card at a time. Try to be as detailed as you can in describing your solution.

There are a number of possible solutions to this problem. Perhaps your solution was similar to the following: "Pick up the first card in my left hand. Then repeatedly pick up one card in my right hand until I run out of cards; anytime that the card in my right hand is larger than the one in my left hand, I will replace the card in my left hand. At the end, the card in my left hand will be the one with the largest number on it."

If your algorithm was similar to this one, you have described a method for using a loop to determine the largest item in a list. We know a loop is involved because you will repeat the steps of picking up a card and perhaps replacing the card in your left hand. You are using your left hand as a storage location for the largest value encountered so far and your right hand as a storage location for each of the other cards in succession. Before the loop, when you pick up the first card in your left hand, you are giving an initial (default) value to the largest value; if no other cards have a larger value, then at the end, this one will be the largest.

It might be helpful to write this algorithm in the slightly more formal style we have been using for our other algorithms.

```
Large is assigned the first value
repeat the following until there are no more values
    Next is assigned the next value
    if Next > Large then change Large to the value of Next
print Large
```

This is a form of algorithm that we can use whenever we wish to find the largest using a loop. The following example will illustrate this.

Each set of input contains a name and a yearly salary. The program in Figure 3-5 determines the largest yearly salary. It is based on a specific instance of the general algorithm used above to describe how to find the largest number by hand. Observe how similar the process of finding the largest is to that of counting or accumulating. All three processes involve these properties:

```
program FindLargest(Input, Output);
{
     Written by:  XXXXXXXX  XX/XX/XX
        Purpose:  To demonstrate the process of finding the largest.
                  The program reads a series of names and salaries, and
                  finds the largest salary.
Procedures used:  Instructions, to print instructions for user.
}
const
  EndOfData = ' ';                        {dummy data indicator}

var
  Name         : string[20];             {employee name, input}
  Salary       : real;                   {salary, input}
  LargeSalary : real;                    {largest salary, calculated}

procedure Instructions; begin {stub} end;

begin {FindLargest}

{*** Print instructions and initialize using first data.}

  Instructions;
  Writeln;
  Write('Enter first person''s name: ');
  Readln(Name);
  Write('Enter first salary: ');
  Readln(Salary);
  LargeSalary := Salary;

{*** Repeatedly obtain name and salary. Check each salary against the
     largest so far, changing LargeSalary when appropriate.}

  repeat
    Writeln;
    Write('Enter next name (tap RETURN to quit): ');
    Readln(Name);
    if Name <> EndOfData then
      begin
        Write('Enter next salary: ');
        Readln(Salary);
        if Salary > LargeSalary then
           LargeSalary := Salary
      end
  until Name = EndOfData;

{*** Print largest salary.}

  Writeln;
  Writeln('The largest salary found was ', LargeSalary:1:2)
end.
```

Figure 3-5 Finding Largest Value (Continued)

SAMPLE INPUT AND OUTPUT

```
Enter first person's name: Joe Robertson
Enter first salary: 13000

Enter next name (tap RETURN to quit): Sue Johnson
Enter next salary: 12903

Enter next name (tap RETURN to quit): Sara Michaels
Enter next salary: 17045

Enter next name (tap RETURN to quit):

The largest salary found was 17045.00
```

Figure 3-5 Finding Largest Value

1. A special variable is used to obtain the summary type information (count, or total, or largest value).

2. This variable is initialized prior to the loop.

3. In the loop, this variable is modified based on the values read. This can involve comparisons of various types.

4. After the loop, the summary value is either printed or used to determine other values of interest (for example, an average).

In finding the largest of a set of values, there are two distinct approaches to initializing the variable that will store the largest value. The first is illustrated by the example in Figure 3-5. LargeSalary's initial value is the first person's salary.

Another possible approach is to give this variable a small initial value. Consider this simplified fragment.

```
Large := 0;

repeat
   Readln(Number);
   if Number > 0 then
      begin
         if Number > Large then
            Large := Number
      end
until Number <= 0;

Writeln(Large)
```

We are reading a collection of positive values. Hence, in finding the largest, an initial value of 0 is appropriate. The first number will be larger and will replace Large.

In the preceding examples, the quantity whose largest value we wished to find happened to be one of the fields in our input. Of course, this need not be the case. For example, our input might contain the hourly rate and number of hours and we might wish to find the largest gross pay. To do so, we would have to calculate the pay for each person and compare this pay with the largest we had found so far.

Another point that may very well have struck you as you read through the example of Figure 3-5 is that you might want to know, in addition to the value of the largest salary, the name of that employee who has the largest salary. To do so, we simply need another variable to keep track of the desired information. Add the declaration

```
LargeName : string[20];   name of person with largest salary
```

Because this variable is associated with LargeSalary, it is given a value whenever LargeSalary is given a value. Before the loop, LargeSalary is assigned the value of the first person's salary, and we should follow this by

```
                LargeName := Name;
```

If it turns out that this first salary is the largest, then LargeName will have the first person's name stored.

Within the loop, we replace the step

```
          if Salary > LargeSalary then
             LargeSalary := Salary
```

by the step

```
          if Salary > LargeSalary then
            begin
              LargeSalary := Salary;
              LargeName := Name
            end
```

Because we have found a new largest salary, we need to record both that salary and the associated name. (Notice that we need a begin and end to form a compound statement within the if.)

Finally, after the loop, we can print both the largest salary and the associated name:

```
        Writeln('The largest salary, ', LargeSalary:1:2,
           ' was earned by ', LargeName)
```

There are two further topics to be discussed concerning the preceding example. The first is the matter of ties. Suppose there are two people in the company with the same largest salary. Our program will identify only the first person. (Why?) Although this can be fixed, it is relatively difficult to do, especially prior to studying arrays in depth (Chapter 6). We will, therefore, ignore the possibility of ties.

The second topic relates to the alternate method for initializing LargeSalary. Because the salaries are nonnegative, we could use a value of -1 as the initial value. If we did so, then only these two steps would be required before the loop:

```
Instructions;
LargeSalary := -1;
```

When the first data value is read, the Salary will be compared to LargeSalary. It will be bigger, so LargeSalary and LargeName will be given the values from this first employee.

COMMENT When the possible range of values is known, using a default value is easier. On the other hand, initializing with the first data value is more general, since it does not depend on knowing the range of values.

Consider, however, the problem of finding the largest salary earned by a female. In this instance, we could not initialize using the first data value. We would have to use the *first data value for a female*. This would complicate our program substantially, so we would be inclined instead to use a default of −1, as in the previous example.

In short, it is important for you to know both methods of initialization.

Until now, all the examples have had to do with finding the largest value in a list. Finding the smallest is similar, with only two differences:

1. When initializing the variable (perhaps called Small), start either with the first value or with a number larger than the possible range of values.

2. In the loop, change Small when a smaller value than the current smallest is found.

For example, the program given in Figure 3-6 reads name, age, and sex code and finds the name, age, and sex of the youngest person. Key portions are shaded.

Keep in mind that for a problem in which we are to find the largest of some value, and perhaps other information concerning the record possessing that largest value, special variables are needed for the largest (say Large) and for all the other information concerning the record with the largest value. Before the loop, either initialize Large to a suitable small value or initialize Large and all the other variables based on the first data. In the loop, change Large and all the associated special variables whenever a record is found with a larger value than that currently stored in Large. After the loop, either print the answers or use them in further calculations.

Finding the smallest value is similar.

CASE STUDY NO. 3 *(Continued)*

As a comprehensive illustration of the topics discussed in this section, we will modify the program written in Section 2-8 as Case Study No. 3. The main program for that case study appears in Figure 2-20, on page 152.

```
program FindSmallest(Input, Output);
{
     Written by:   XXXXXXXX  XX/XX/XX
        Purpose:   To demonstrate finding the smallest and associated
                   information. The program finds the name, age, and
                   sex of the youngest person.
Procedures used:   Instructions, to print instructions for user.
}
const
  EndOfData = ' ';                      {dummy data indicator}

var
  Name         : string[20];           {employee name, input}
  Age          : integer;              {age, input}
  Sex          : char;                 {sex code, input}
  SmallAge     : integer;              {smallest age}
  SmName       : string[20];           {name of youngest}
  SmSex        : char;                 {sex of youngest}

procedure Instructions; begin {stub} end;

begin {FindSmallest}

{*** Print instructions and initialize.}

  Instructions;
  SmallAge := 200;             {high default value}

{*** Repeatedly obtain input data. Check each age against youngest so
     far, changing SmallAge and all associated variables when a younger
     person is found.}

  repeat
    Writeln;
    Write('Enter name (hit return to quit): ');
    Readln(Name);
    if Name <> EndOfData then
      begin
        Write('Age: ');
        Readln(Age);
        Write('Sex code: ');
        Readln(Sex);
        if Age < SmallAge then
          begin
            SmallAge := Age;
            SmName := Name;
            SmSex := Sex
          end
      end
  until Name = EndOfData;

{*** Print answers.}
```

Figure 3-6   Finding Smallest Value (Continued)

```
      Writeln;
      Writeln('The youngest person was ', SmName);
      if SmSex in ['M', 'm'] then
         Write('He ')
      else
         Write('She ');
      Writeln('is ', SmallAge:1, ' years old.')
end.
```

SAMPLE INPUT AND OUTPUT

First run:

```
Enter name (hit return to quit): Sally Frisling
Age: 9
Sex code: F

Enter name (hit return to quit): Joe Salzburg
Age: 21
Sex code: M

Enter name (hit return to quit): Mike Sawyer
Age: 15
Sex code: m

Enter name (hit return to quit):

The youngest person was Sally Frisling
She is 9 years old.
```

Second run:

```
Enter name (hit return to quit): Barry Purnell
Age: 45
Sex code: m

Enter name (hit return to quit):

The youngest person was Barry Purnell
He is 45 years old.
```

Figure 3-6   Finding Smallest Value

Statement of problem. Case Study No. 3 calculated wages and state tax withholding for a number of employees. We wish to modify that program to report how many employees had tax withholding of $10 or less, who had the largest amount of tax and what that amount was, and what the average pay was.

Preliminary analysis. One of the advantages of modularity is that modifications can be restricted to specific portions of the program. For example, the modifications do not change the methods for calculating the wages or the tax withholding, so those two functions will remain entirely unchanged. The only changes will involve the main program. (You might want to consider minor changes to the Instructions procedure, but those will not be presented here.)

Algorithm and variable list. In a problem of this type, we need to plan for the additional variables needed. All the variables originally used in the main program will still be used. Here is a list of the additional variables:

Others:			
	LowCount	integer	Number with tax < 10 (Counter)
	Large	real	Largest tax
	LClock	integer	Clock number for person with largest tax
	TotalPay	real	Total pay (Accumulator)
	EmpCount	integer	Number of employees (Counter)
	Average	real	Average pay

The rest of the planning involves inserting the proper steps before the loop, in the loop, and after the loop, using standard methods for these types of problems.

Test Plan. When a program is modified, it should be run again using the original test plan that was used when it was developed. This ensures that those things that used to work still do work. (This is sometimes called **regression testing**.) In addition, devise additional tests relating to the steps added. Details of the types of tests needed will be covered in the next subsection.

Write program. The complete modified main program is shown in Figure 3-7. Changes are shaded, and we have run the program for the same input as in the original case study. Again, note that the functions would not be modified.

```
program Payroll(Input, Output);
{
    Written by:   XXXXXXXX  XX/XX/XX
        Purpose:  To calculate pay and state tax for a number of employees.
                  The input consists of a clock number, the number of hours
                  worked, the hourly rate, and the number of dependents.
        Modified: XXXXXXXX  XX/XX/XX - to report how many employees had
        tax withholding of $10 or less, who had the largest
        amount of tax and what that amount was, and what the
        average pay was.
            These changes affect only the main program.
    Procedures used:  Instructions, to print instructions for user.
      Functions used: PayFn, to calculate the pay based on hours and rate.
                      TaxFn, to calculate the tax based on the pay and the
                             number of dependents.
}
const
    EndOfData = 0;                          {terminating data indicator}

var
    ClockNumber : integer;                  {employee clock number, input}
    HoursWorked : real;                     {hours worked, input}
```

Figure 3-7 Case Study No. 3 (Payroll) (Continued)

```
  HourlyRate   : real;            {rate of pay, input}
  Dependents   : integer;         {number of dependents, input}
  Pay          : real;            {pay for week, output}
  StateTax     : real;            {state tax, output}

  LowCount     : integer;         {# with tax < $10}
  LargeTax     : real;            {largest state tax}
  LClock       : integer;         {clock number of person with most tax}
  TotalPay     : real;            {total pay for week}
  EmpCount     : integer;         {counter of employees}
  Average      : real;            {average pay for week}

  procedure Instructions; begin {stub} end;

  {function PayFn, as shown in Figure 2-19 is inserted here}

  {function TaxFn, as shown in Figure 2-20 is inserted here}

begin {Payroll}

{*** Before the loop, print instructions and initialize.}

  Instructions;
  LowCount := 0;
  LargeTax := 0;
  TotalPay := 0;
  EmpCount := 0;

{*** In loop, obtain clock number, hours, rate, and number of dependents.
     Check for dummy value. Check for invalid hours. Calculate and print
     pay and tax. Also modify summary information (counters, etc.)}

  repeat
    Writeln;
    Write('Enter clock number for next employee: ');
    Readln(ClockNumber);
    if ClockNumber > EndOfData then
      begin
        Write('Now enter the hours, rate, and number of dependents: ');
        Readln(HoursWorked, HourlyRate, Dependents);
        EmpCount := EmpCount + 1;
        if HoursWorked < 0 then
          begin
            Writeln(HoursWorked, ' is invalid; changed to 0.');
            HoursWorked := 0
          end;
        Pay := PayFn(HoursWorked, HourlyRate);
        TotalPay := TotalPay + Pay;
        StateTax := TaxFn(Pay, Dependents);
        Writeln(ClockNumber, ' earned ', Pay:2:2, ' and was taxed ',
                StateTax:2:2);
        if StateTax < 10 then
          LowCount := LowCount + 1;
        if StateTax > LargeTax then
```

Figure 3-7   Case Study No. 3 (Payroll) (Continued)

```
        begin
          LargeTax := StateTax;
          LClock := ClockNumber
        end
      end
   until ClockNumber <= EndOfData;

{*** Print summary information and stop.}

   Writeln;
   if EmpCount = 0 then
     Writeln('No employees entered')
   else
     begin
       Average := TotalPay / EmpCount;
       Writeln(LowCount:1, ' employees had less than $10 withheld');
       Writeln('Clock #', LClock:1, ' paid the most tax -- $', LargeTax:1:2);
       Writeln('The average pay was $', Average:1:2)
     end;
   Writeln;
   Writeln('Payroll program terminating.')
end.
```

SAMPLE INPUT AND OUTPUT

```
Enter clock number for next employee: 345
Now enter the hours, rate, and number of dependents: 34 5.67 8
345 earned 192.78 and was taxed 1.94

Enter clock number for next employee: 101
Now enter the hours, rate, and number of dependents: 44 6.78 3
101 earned 311.88 and was taxed 5.52

Enter clock number for next employee: 0

2 employees had less than $10 withheld
Clock #101 paid the most tax -- $5.52
The average pay was $252.33

Payroll program terminating.
```

Figure 3-7   Case Study No. 3 (Payroll)

TESTING   □   It may require several runs of the program to adequately test a program involving counting, accumulation, or finding the largest/smallest. Among the most important types of tests are these:

Finding the largest:
1. Largest first (no ties)
2. Largest last (no ties)
3. Largest in middle (no ties)
4. All the same value

Counting:
1. No data input at all
2. Data input, but count is still 0 for what is being counted
3. Everything in the input list is in the category being counted

Accumulation: *1*. This is similar to counting.

It may help to understand these tests if they are viewed as the boundary values for the answers to questions such as:

1. Where in the list is the largest found?
2. How many ties are there?
3. How many items in the list of data?
4. How many items in the category being counted or accumulated?

As we mentioned earlier, boundary situations are those that are most likely to yield errors in our programs. Hence, these types of tests are the most fruitful because they are the most likely to uncover the errors that can be in the program.

☐
DPT The most frequently encountered pitfalls in writing programs using the methods of this section may be briefly described as follows:

1. Forgetting to initialize counters and accumulators.

2. Improper initialization of "Large" or "Small" variables. There are two choices. We can give the variable a value based on the first input data. In this case, also initialize any associated variables (for example, LargeName) being used to maintain additional information concerning the record with the highest value.

On the other hand, we can initialize based on the known range of values. If we do so, initialize Large (or Small) in such a way that the first record is certain to contain a larger (or smaller) value. If we choose this approach, the associated variables such as LargeName need not be initialized.

Notice that both approaches require that there be at least one set of valid data. If it is conceivable that there will be no input, we should handle this possibility, perhaps by displaying a message "no valid data."

3. Improper assignment statements. A typical error of this type is

```
if Salary > LargeSalary then
   begin
      Salary := LargeSalary;
      Name := LargeName
   end
```

The two assignment statements are both reversed. Remember that the variable to be changed should be on the left-hand side. LargeSalary and LargeName are to be changed, write

```
if Salary > LargeSalary then
   begin
      LargeSalary := Salary;
      LargeName := Name
   end
```

Terms and concepts

body	counter
loop control	record
terminate	accumulator
exit from	regression testing
initialization	

Algorithm techniques

Counting

Before loop: initialize to 0
    In loop: add 1 to counter, if appropriate
After loop: print or use answer

Accumulation

Before loop: initialize to 0
    In loop: add to accumulator, if appropriate
After loop: print or use answer

Finding the largest

Before loop: initialize to a "small" value, or value from first record
    In loop: change Large and associated variables when new value is larger
After loop: print or use answer

Finding the smallest

Before loop: initialize to a "large" value or a value from the first record
    In loop: change Small and associated variables when new value is smaller
After loop: print or use answer

■■■■■
EXERCISES

1. For each of the following, determine appropriate initial values for Large for an algorithm to find the largest of the quantity indicated. Then determine appropriate initial values for Small for an algorithm to find the smallest.
   *a. age
   b. age of elementary school children
   c. IQ
   d. salary of managers in a small company
   e. number of children in a family
   *f. numbers ranging from −23000 to +1700
   g. balances in checking accounts that just had an overdraft
   h. balances in checking accounts

*2. Each record (that is, set of input data) has a name and a letter grade (A, B, C, D, or F). Write a program to count the number who passed and the number who failed.

3. Each record has a name and a numerical average. Write a program that, for each record, will calculate the variable Result as follows: If the numerical average is 60.0 or higher, the variable should be given the value 'pass', otherwise the value 'fail'. The program should print the name, numerical average, and Result for each person, and tell how many passed.

4. a. In a certain company, a bonus is based on the number of years worked and a skill code (a one-character code). For skill level 'E', the bonus is $15 for each year worked. Write a program to read a set of records, each with name, years worked, and skill code, and print a list of the bonuses for persons with skill level 'E'.
   *b. Modify your program to print the following summary information: percentage of employees with skill level 'E'; total bonus for skill level 'E' employees.
   c. Modify your program to show which skill level 'E' employee had the largest bonus.

5. Each record has an ID number, sex code, age, and number of children.

   a. Write a program to count the number of females under age 21.
   b. Write a program to find the average number of children for persons under age 25.
   c. Write a program to find the age and ID number of the oldest person with no children. (Assume that there is such a person.)
   d. Revise part (c) to find the age and ID number of the youngest person who has children.

6. Each record contains, for a single course, the number of credits and a letter grade (A, B, C, D, or F). There is one record for each course taken by John Smith during his college career. Write a program to calculate his grade point average. The quality point average is the total of the quality points divided by the total number of credits. (A--4 quality points per credit; B--3 per credit; C--2 per credit; and D--1 per credit.)

*7. Modify the latest version of Case Study No.1 (Figure 2-9, Section 2-3) to count how many passed, how many failed, and the percentage of those who were exempted from the final.

8. Modify Case Study No. 2 (Section 2-7) to count how many of each possible operation were performed.

9. Devise test plans for the following:
   *a. Exercise 2
   *b. Exercise 4(b)
   c. Exercise 4(c)
   d. Exercise 5(b)
   e. Exercise 5(c)

10. Write a program to handle all the transactions on a single checking account during a month. Input will start with a record indicating an account number, account type, and a beginning balance. This will be followed by a number of transaction records, each containing a code (C--check; D--deposit) and an amount.

Output should be a table with each transaction and the resulting balance, as illustrated below:

```
ACCOUNT # 12345      BEGINNING BALANCE = 123.14    TYPE = R
--------------------------------------------------------------
     CODE                    AMOUNT                 BALANCE
     ----                    ------                 -------
     C                       150.00                 -26.86
     ***OVERDRAFT - - $5.00 CHARGE ***              -31.86
     D                        30.00                  -1.86
     C                         1.00                  -2.86
     ***OVERDRAFT - - $5.00 CHARGE ***               -7.86
     D                       100.00                  92.14
     C                        10.05                  82.09

                                 CLOSING BALANCE = 82.09
```

The following summary information should be given: minimum balance, number of bad checks, and total of the checks not including the bad checks.

3-2
□□□□□□
PASCAL LOOPING STRUCTURES

Pascal has three looping structures. We have seen the repeat–until loop, which we have used in all our programs to this point. In those programs, the condition that terminated the loop was that the user entered a terminal data value. In this section, we will study the repeat–until looping structure in more detail. In addition, we will learn about the other two looping statements available in Pascal. These are the while–do loop and the for–do loop.

In writing programs, there are two related tasks. We must design the algorithm, that is, determine what the program should do and how it should do it. And we must write the program in some suitable programming language. In connection with loops, this implies that there are two topics to study: how to design loops and how to write loops in Pascal. In this section, the basic form of the three Pascal loops will be studied and a few examples will be presented. The next section begins a thorough study of the techniques of loop design that will enable us to make good use of these three looping structures.

This section also introduces two concepts not directly related to loops. They are random numbers and arrays. We will use these concepts in some of our examples in this and later sections. With random numbers, we can develop some interesting examples of loops that involve simulation of random events such as coin tossing. Arrays will be the subject of a complete chapter (Chapter 6). However, we can begin to gain familiarity with the concept now. Subsequent sections will utilize, from time to time, this important concept first introduced here.

□
REPEAT–UNTIL LOOPS

We begin with **repeat–until** loops, which we have been using previously in the book. Recall that the general form of the loop is

```
repeat
  statement(s)
until  condition
```

It is not necessary to use a begin and end to delimit the body of the loop because the two key words "repeat" and "until" already delimit the loop. Recall also that the meaning of the loop is to execute the statements forming the body of the loop repeatedly until the condition is true. The body of the loop executes one or more times. The precise semantics (meaning) of the repeat–until are:

1. Perform the loop body.
2. If the condition is true, terminate the loop, otherwise go back to step 1.

We can summarize this by saying that

---

the test for terminating a repeat–until loop occurs at the bottom of the loop.

The condition used after the keyword "until" can be a Boolean constant, a Boolean variable, or a more complex Boolean expression. Any condition that could be used in an if statement can also be used in a repeat–until loop.

As an extreme example of a repeat-until loop to keep the computer busy for a long time, we could (but, of course, we wouldn't) use the construct:

```
repeat until false;
```

This example is extreme for two reasons. First of all, it uses the Boolean constant "false" for its condition. Second, the body of the loop is empty. This is an infinite loop; it will run forever. Another extreme example that we are not likely to use in a program is:

```
repeat until true;
```

which will act as though no statement is there at all.

To gain further understanding of the repeat–until loop, consider this program segment:

```
I := 5;
repeat
   Writeln(I);
   I := I + 5
until I > N
```

The table gives a list of the numbers printed for various values of the variable N. It also indicates what value the variable I has following termination of the loop.

N	Numbers Printed	Value of I After Loop
17	5, 10, 15	20
20	5, 10, 15, 20	25
5	5	10
4	5	10

Because the loop termination condition is not checked until the bottom of the loop, the loop always executes at least once. Note especially the last line of the table (N = 4). Even though I is already greater than 4 when the loop begins, the body will execute once, printing 5 and changing I to 10.

□
**WHILE–DO
LOOPS**
The **while–do** loop (which we will call the "while" loop), like the repeat–until loop, is a "condition-based loop." That is, there is a condition whose truth or falsity determines how long the repetition continues. The general form of this looping construct is:

```
while  condition  do
     statement that forms body of loop
```

In most circumstances, the statement that forms the body of the loop is a compound one, so that our general form will usually have the appearance:

```
while  condition  do
   begin
       body of loop
   end
```

The condition, like that in the repeat–until loop, can be any Boolean constant, Boolean variable, or more complex Boolean expression.

The meaning of the while loop is to continue to execute and reexecute the body of the loop as long as the condition remains true. Two extreme examples, analogous to those for the repeat–until loop, are

```
while  true  do;
```

which executes an empty loop body forever; and

```
while  false  do;
```

which is an empty loop that executes 0 times. Although a silly example, the second loop does illustrate the important point that a *while loop executes 0 or more times*.

To contrast the repeat–until loop with the while loop, consider these two program segments:

```
I := 5;                    I := 5;
repeat                     while I <= N do
  Writeln(I);                begin
  I := I + 5                   Writeln(I);
until I > N                    I := I + 5
                             end
```

First, note that the loop bodies are identical (a Writeln and an assignment). However, the while loop requires a begin and an end to group the two statements of the loop body into one compound statement.

An important point to observe relates to the conditions controlling the two loops. In the repeat–until, we have "I > N", and in the while, we have "I <= N". These are negations of each other. In the while loop, the condition expresses "how long the program stays in the loop" (as long as I<=N). In the repeat–until loop, on the other hand, the condition expresses "when the program terminates the loop'' (when I>N). In general, the conditions for similar repeat–until and while loops will be negations of each other.

On the surface, then, these two loops are similar in meaning. However, the table illustrates a fundamental difference between the two looping structures.

Value of N	Printed by repeat–until	Printed by while–do
5	5	5
4	5	none

The semantics of the while loop are:

1. If the condition is true, go to step 2, otherwise the loop terminates.

2. Perform the loop body, then go back to step 1 to check the condition again.

Thus, if N is 5, the loop body is executed, printing I (5) and changing I to 10. Because the condition is now false, the loop terminates. On the other hand, if N is 4, the loop terminates immediately without ever performing the loop body.

We can summarize these semantics of the while loop by saying that:

> The test for terminating a while loop occurs at the top of the loop.

□ **REPEAT VERSUS WHILE**

It may be helpful to summarize the key differences between these two condition-based looping structures:

> 1(a) Repeat–until tests after each execution of the body
> 1(b) While tests before each execution of the body
> 2(a) Repeat–until condition is true to exit the loop
> 2(b) While condition is false to exit the loop
> 3(a) Repeat–until body is always performed at least once
> 3(b) While body might not be performed.

□ **FOR-DO LOOPS**

In this subsection, we consider the **for–do** (or just ''for'') loop. This loop counts the number of times the computer executes the body of a loop and terminates the loop after a certain number of executions. The general form is

```
for control variable := start to end do
    statement that forms body of loop
```

As with the while loop, the statement that forms the body of the loop is most frequently a compound one, so that our general form will usually have the appearance:

```
for control variable := start to end do
   begin
      body of loop
   end
```

The control variable successively takes on the values from the indicated starting value to the indicated ending value. An alternative form, discussed below, uses the key word **downto** in place of the key word **"to"** in the **"for"** statement.

Perhaps the easiest way to understand the meaning of the for loop is to examine the output of the following program fragment for various values of the variables Start and End.

```
for I := Start to End do
   Writeln(I)
```

Start	End	Numbers Printed
1	4	1, 2, 3, 4
13	19	13, 14, 15, 16, 17, 18, 19
2	2	2
3	2	None

The for loop can also count "down" from the starting value to the ending value as in:

```
for I := Start downto End do
   Writeln(I)
```

Again, we can summarize the semantics of this loop:

Start	End	Numbers Printed
4	1	4, 3, 2, 1
17	12	17, 16, 15, 14, 13, 12
5	5	5
5	6	None

We can summarize the for loop as follows:

1. The control variable successively takes on the values from the indicated starting value to the indicated ending value. For each value assumed by the control variable, the loop body is executed once.

2. The starting and ending values can be given by constants, variables, or more complex expressions. For now, the control variable and these expressions should all be integers.

3. If the for statement uses "to" and the final value is less than the initial value, then the body will not be executed. Likewise, if the for statement uses "downto" and the final value is greater than the initial value, the body will not be executed.

4. After the loop terminates, the control variable is "undefined." This means that the program cannot depend upon it having some specific value.

5. The control variable can be used within the loop body, but it may not be modified.

6. If any variables are involved in the starting and ending values, they should not be modified within the loop. Doing so will not modify the behavior of the loop, but it will be confusing to the reader of the program.

7. A for loop, in contrast to a while or repeat loop, cannot be infinite. It will terminate after a predetermined number of passes.

NOTES
1. This loop is sometimes referred to as a count-controlled loop, which means that it is possible to know exactly how many times the loop body will be executed. The control variable can be thought of as "counting" the passes through the loop.

2. The logic of the loop "for I := 1 to N" is essentially equivalent to the following while loop form:

```
I := 1;
while I <= N do
   begin
      { loop body }
      I := I + 1
   end
```

□ RANDOM NUMBERS

We pause momentarily in our study of Pascal loops to introduce the notion of **random numbers**. These give us many interesting applications where loops are appropriate.

Many computer languages include functions that generate "random" numbers. What this means is that every time the function is used, a value results in what looks like a random pattern. Turbo Pascal provides the function Random(N), where N represents any positive integer expression. This function returns a random number greater than or equal to zero and less than N. For example, the following fragment might print the sequence of values 3, 2, 7, 0, 3, 1, 9, and 8:

```
for I := 1 to 8 do
   begin
      Value := Random(10);
      WriteLn(Value)
   end
```

The numbers printed are all in the range from 0 to 9, and they might well be the result of spinning a spinner with 10 possible, equally likely values (0, 1, . . . , 9) on it.[1]

COMMENTS
1. These functions are sometimes called "pseudorandom number generators." This refers to the fact that the output looks random, but it actually follows a set (but complicated) rule.

2. Turbo Pascal also has a "Randomize" procedure. It "seeds" the random number generator. This causes the sequence of random numbers to be different each time the program is run.

This procedure should be invoked once by your program, prior to the first use of the Random function.

Summarizing, then, Turbo Pascal has a Random number generator named Random, it is of type integer, and it has a single integer parameter N. The value it returns is an (apparently) random integer in the range from 0 to N − 1. Each of the possible values is equally likely to occur. Thus, the assignment statement

```
Value := Random(10) + 1
```

assigns Value a randomly chosen integer from 1 to 10 inclusive and each value is equally likely to occur. Note that Random(10) produces values from 0 to 9, and adding one then makes the values range from 1 to 10.

To obtain a different sequence of random numbers each time the program is run, use a call to the Randomize procedure.

Random functions such as this can be used to perform a variety of **simulations** of events in the real world that occur with randomness. For example, the function given in Figure 3-8 simulates rolling a pair of dice. Each "Random(6) + 1" gives a value from 1 to 6 and represents one of the dice. The total on the two dice is placed into the function name RollOfDice. Notice that this function is unusual: it has no parameters. The answer is obtained using Random, not based on parameters.

CAUTION

For the simulation to be valid, each outcome must be equally likely. This is the reason for simulating each die by a separate call to the Random function.

```
function RollOfDice: integer;
{
     Written by:  XXXXXXXXX, XX/XX/XX
          Purpose:  To simulate the roll of a pair of dice
}
var
   Roll1 : integer;        {first die}
   Roll2 : integer;        {second die}

begin  {RollOfDice}
   Roll1 := Random(6) + 1;
   Roll2 := Random(6) + 1;
   RollOfDice := Roll1 + Roll2
end;   {RollOfDice}
```

Figure 3-8 Simulating Rolling Dice

In this subsection, we present a number of examples of the use of count-controlled and condition-based loops. In each case, we will show only a program segment so that we can concentrate our attention on the looping process itself. In Section 3-3, we will develop some complete programs from scratch.

Suppose we wish to estimate the number of rabbits that would be present in an area after 10 years if the number of rabbits doubles each year and there are two rabbits to start. We could count the rabbits using a variable Rabbits and the years using a variable Years. Both Years and Rabbits would be integers. At the start, Rabbits would be 2. After the first year, Rabbits would be 4 and Years would be 1. After the second year Rabbits would be 8 and Years 2. Figure 3-9 contains two solutions.

Notice how much simpler the second code fragment is than the earlier one. We do not have to write the initialization statement, the modification statement, nor the test for leaving the loop. They are all included in the "for" statement. Once you are familiar with the for statement, it is much clearer to read a fragment like the second one. It takes a few seconds of study to determine from the while loop just what the initial and final values are and, in fact, that the while was being used for a count-controlled loop.

You should also notice that in this case there is only one statement in the body of the for loop, and thus we could omit the begin and end to get:

```
Rabbits := 2;
for Years := 1 to 10 do
  Rabbits := Rabbits * 2;
Writeln('After 10 years there are ', Rabbits:1, ' rabbits')
```

Solution #1

```
Rabbits := 2;

Years := 1;
While Years <= 10 do
  begin
    Rabbits := Rabbits * 2;
    Years := Years + 1
  end;   {while}

Writeln('After 10 years there are ', Rabbits:1, ' rabbits')
```

Solution #2

```
Rabbits := 2;

for Years := 1 to 10 do
  begin
    Rabbits := Rabbits * 2
  end;   {for}

Writeln('After 10 years there are ', Rabbits:1, ' rabbits')
```

Figure 3-9   While and For Loops

```
Count7 := 0;

for I := 1 to 1200 do
  begin
    Dice := RollOfDice;
    if Dice = 7 then
      Count7 := Count7 + 1
  end;  {for}

Writeln(Count7:1, ' 7''s occurred in 1200 rolls')
```

Figure 3-10 Counting Sevens

NOTE The comments "{for}" and "{while}" are included following the "end;" of the loops at the programmer's option. As in other such situations, we will make a judgment on whether the readability of the program is enhanced or not by the use of a comment. As programmers, we should keep in mind that comments can be illuminating, neutral, or annoying; we should strive for the first kind, ignore the second, and avoid the third.

On the other hand, it is true that programmers tend to underestimate the illuminating value of comments within their own work.

For another example, the fragment in Figure 3-10 simulates an experiment in which we roll a pair of dice 1200 times, counting the number of 7's that occur.

Our next example (shown in Figure 3-11) is a procedure that prints a row of asterisks. In addition to the looping structure, it illustrates an important aspect of procedures:

> Procedures can have value parameters, just like those for functions.

This procedure has one parameter, called Number, which tells how many asterisks to print. We assume that Number lies between 0 and 70, so that the asterisks will easily fit on a single line.

We use a count-controlled (for) loop. We could use either a repeat–until or a while loop, but a for loop is easiest to write and understand for this example.

Two points should be observed, in addition to the looping structure and the parameter. First, we use Write rather than Writeln in the loop, so that all the asterisks stay on one line. The Writeln after the loop terminates the line. Second, we declare I, the loop's control variable, as a local variable within the procedure.

So far our examples have been count-controlled (for) loops. We now consider some condition-based loops (while and repeat–until loops).

Figure 3-12 contains a program segment that accepts an unknown number of exam scores as input, terminated by the value −1. It calculates the average of the scores and prints the number of scores read and the resulting average to one decimal place. Along with the program segment, we show some sample runs.

```
procedure Asterisks(Number : integer);
{
     Written by:   XXXXXXXXX, XX/XX/XX
        Purpose:   To print a line containing 0 to 70
                   asterisks.
     Parameters:   Number - how many asterisks to print
                   (assumed to be in the range 0 to 70)
}

var
  I : integer;                  {for loop control variable}

begin   {Asterisks}

  for I := 1 to Number do
    begin
      Write('*')
    end;  {for}

  Writeln
end;  {Asterisks}
```

Figure 3-11   Printing N Asterisks

(Note: For the sample runs, the program segment was expanded into a complete program.)

In this example, the program reads the first test score prior to the loop, then the remaining test scores in a loop. As long as the score entered is not −1, the looping continues. The loop body counts and accumulates the scores using the techniques covered in Section 3-1. After the loop, the average score is printed.

Figure 3-13 contains our first example of the repeat–until loop. In the example, we make use of random numbers and the dice rolling function (RollOfDice), which was introduced previously. The purpose of the program is to roll the pair of dice the first time to obtain a value, called the "point," which we will subsequently attempt to match. Then we roll the dice over and over until we match the point with a roll. We count the number of rolls that it takes to match the point and when we finally do match it, we print the number of rolls that it took.

For our second repeat–until example, we return to Case Study No. 1, developed in Chapter 1. That case study calculated the total on three exam scores for a number of students, terminated by a null student name. For this example, we change the specification of the problem to state that there is no terminating value for the student name, but after the processing of the test scores total for a student, the user will be asked if the processing is to continue or not. See Figure 3-14.

The type of loop presented in this example can be used for many interactive programs that are to repeatedly perform an activity until the user decides to terminate the progression by stating that the activity is not to continue. Many educational programs of the "drill-and-practice" variety have this basic structure.

Notice the use of the condition "Answer in ['N', 'n']" to terminate the loop. This causes the loop to terminate if the user tries to say no with a lowercase "n." Even though the program asked for uppercase input, it seems reasonable to interpret a lowercase "n" as desiring termination of the input process.

Program Segment

```
{*** Read and total scores.}

  Total := 0;
  Number := 0;
  Write('Enter score (-1 to quit): ');
  Readln(Score);

  while  Score <> -1  do
    begin
      Total := Total + Score;
      Number := Number + 1;
      Write('Enter score (-1 to quit): ');
      Readln(Score)
    end;  {while}

{*** Calculate and print average.}

  Writeln;
  if  Number > 0  then
    begin
      Average := Total / Number;
      Writeln(Number:1, ' exam scores were processed.');
      Writeln('The average is: ', Average:1:1)
    end
  else
    Writeln('*** No scores were input ***')
```

SAMPLE INPUT AND OUTPUT

Run 1:

```
Enter score (-1 to quit): 89
Enter score (-1 to quit): 56
Enter score (-1 to quit): 77
Enter score (-1 to quit): 83
Enter score (-1 to quit): 92
Enter score (-1 to quit): -1

5 exam scores were processed.
The average is: 79.4
```

Run 2:

```
Enter score (-1 to quit): -1

*** No scores were input ***
```

Figure 3-12 Average Value

Program Segment

```
{*** Roll the point.}

  Randomize;
  Point := RollOfDice;
  Writeln('The point is: ', Point:1);
  Writeln;

{*** Roll until a match occurs; count the tries.}

  Count := 0;

  repeat
    Roll := RollOfDice;
    Writeln('This try: ', Roll:1);
    Count := Count + 1
  until  Roll = Point;

  Writeln;
  Writeln('It took ', Count:1, ' tries to match the point: ', Point:1);
```

SAMPLE INPUT AND OUTPUT

Run 1:

```
The point is: 4

This try: 9
This try: 9
This try: 7
This try: 5
This try: 10
This try: 10
This try: 8
This try: 11
This try: 7
This try: 4

It took 10 tries to match the point: 4
```

Run 3 (Note: run 2 took 49 tries to match the point 10)

```
The point is: 7

This try: 7

It took 1 tries to match the point: 7
```

Figure 3-13 Repeat–Until Loop

Program Segment

```
{*** Process name and scores until the user decides to quit.}

   repeat
     Writeln;
     Write('Enter the name: ');
     Readln(Name);
     Write('Now enter the three scores: ');
     Readln(Score1, Score2, Score3);
     Total := Score1 + Score2 + Score3;
     Writeln('The total is ', Total:1, ' for ', Name);
     Writeln;
     Write('Do you wish to continue (Y,N)? ');
     Readln(Answer);
   until Answer in ['N', 'n']
```

SAMPLE INPUT AND OUTPUT

```
Enter the name: John Smith
Now enter the three scores: 75 88 92
The total is 255 for John Smith

Do you wish to continue (Y,N)? Y

Enter the name: Joe Jones
Now enter the three scores: 83 65 78
The total is 226 for Joe Jones

Do you wish to continue (Y,N)? n
```

Figure 3-14 Case Study No. 1 Revisited (Grades)

□

DPT—LOOPS

1. The repeat–until loop body is always executed at least once. The while loop body can be executed 0 times. In either case, the condition is *not* continuously monitored by the computer. It is checked only at the bottom of the loop (for a repeat–until) or at the top (for a while loop). Notice that this is the reason we have consistently had checks such as "if Name <> EndOfData then" in our loops.

2. Two particularly insidious pitfalls exist when using for loops. These relate to semicolons and to using begin and end. We begin with the for loop.

To illustrate the problem, consider the program fragment of Figure 3-10, which is reproduced here but with two commonly made errors.

```
Count7 := 0;                          Count7 := 0;
for I := 1 to 1200 do;                for I := 1 to 1200 do
  begin                                 Dice := RollOfDice;
    Dice := RollOfDice;                 if Dice = 7 then
    if Dice = 7 then                      Count7 := Count7 + 1;
      Count7 := Count7 + 1            Writeln(Count7:1, ' 7''s out of 1200')
  end;  {for}
Writeln(Count7:1, ' 7''s out of 1200')
```

In the left-hand example, a semicolon is placed after the key word "do." This causes the loop to have a single null statement as its body. The computer will execute this null statement 1200 times, then execute the compound statement once. The answer printed will be either 0 or 1.

The result of the second error, in which the begin and end is missing, is similar. This time the loop body consists of the single statement "Dice := RollOfDice." After this is executed 1200 times, the if and Writeln are executed, with an answer of 0 or 1.

Because the compiler does not detect these errors, we must take extra care to avoid them. Defensive programming suggests that we double check each for loop for the presence of an unwanted semicolon after the "do." The second pitfall can be avoided by consistently using a begin and end even for single-statement loops.

3. The same possibilities for errors exist with the while loop. The consequences are, if anything, more disastrous than with the for loop. Consider, for example, these two modifications of the example of Figure 3-12.

```
while  Score <> -1  do;
   begin
      Total := Total + Score;
      Number := Number + 1;
      Write('Enter the score (-1 to quit): ');
      Readln(Score)
   end; {while}

while  Score <> -1  do
      Total := Total + Score;
      Number := Number + 1;
      Write('Enter next score (-1 to terminate): ');
      Readln(Score);
```

The compiler will accept each of these as legal and meaningful Pascal. However, the meaning is not what we intended. In the first segment, we have an empty loop

```
while Score <> -1 do;
```

followed by a compound statement. In the second, we have the loop

```
while Score <> -1 do
      Total := Total + Score;
```

followed by three statements not in the loop body.

What happens when we execute the program? If the score entered is not −1, the program will loop forever. This is the most likely occurrence. If the user enters a −1 to abort the program, it will instead ask for one more score and print a meaningless answer.

4. Another potential problem exists with the while loop or the repeat–until loop. This problem could be caused by the omission of or erroneous coding of the line that has the potential of changing the value of the condition. In the example considered above, if the line

```
Readln(Score)
```

is either missing or in error, the loop can continue forever or terminate at the wrong time. The most common mistake in this example might be the omission of the statement, but another possibility would be reading another variable (perhaps Number) rather than Score. This kind of error can be avoided by the consistent use of meaningful variable names. It would be far more likely that a mistake could occur if the variables "A" and "B" were used rather than Number and Score. We should make it a regular practice to ensure that the condition used for loop control can change its value to terminate the loop, and that the change will occur in exactly the correct manner.

A FIRST LOOK AT ARRAYS

In this subsection, we will see a brief, simple introduction to **arrays** in Pascal. As we will see, an array is a type of variable that allows us to work with lists of related values. Although simplified, this first look will be sufficient for us to understand some meaningful examples in the sections to come. Later, we will study arrays in more detail (Chapter 6).

We all know about the value of being able to have lists of things. As an example in a program context, recall Case Study No. 1, developed in Chapter 1. In that case study, we made use of three variables for test scores: Score1, Score2, and Score3. Suppose that we had 10 scores. Would we want to use 10 variable names? What about 100 scores? Let us use the concept of a list to help out. We could think of the 3 (10, or 100) scores as a list with a *single* name Scores. To illustrate, in our previous way of thinking about this problem, we might write

Score1: 89

Score2: 78

Score3: 91

for a particular set of scores. Thinking of the scores as a list, we might write:

Scores: 89, 78, 91

for the same set of scores. We can now locate the first score by its position on the list, rather than by a separate variable name. So it is with Pascal arrays. If we declared Scores as an array (we will see how below), then we can refer to the first score as Scores[1], the second as Scores[2], and so on.

You are probably thinking that we haven't really gained anything. In fact, what we have said so far can be summarized as:

Old Way of Thinking	New Way of Thinking
Score1: 89	Scores[1]: 89
Score2: 78	Scores[2]: 78
Score3: 91	Scores[3]: 91

But, here is a *big* advantage: Suppose that I is a variable that contains one of the numbers 1, 2, or 3. How can we refer to the Ith score? Compare:

Old Way of Thinking	New Way of Thinking
??????????	Scores[I]

COMMENT   A frequent error made by beginning programmers is assuming that Score1 would work for the "old way of thinking." *It would not.* However, it is the right idea. What we need is an array, so that we can use the similar form Scores[I].

Suppose that we wanted to calculate the total of the three scores. Compare:

Old Way of Thinking

```
Total := Score1 + Score2 + Score3
```

New Way of Thinking

```
Total := 0;
for I := 1 to 3 do
   begin
      Total := Total + Scores[I]
   end   {for}
```

COMMENT   Study the "new way of thinking" carefully. Here's how it works:

1. Total starts at 0.

2. The first pass through the for loop, I has the value 1. The reference to Scores[I] therefore refers to Scores[1]. This is added to Total, so Total is now equal to the first score.

3. The second pass through the loop, I is 2, so Scores[I] refers to Scores[2]. After this is added to Total, Total is equal to the sum of the first two scores.

4. On the third (and final) pass, I is 3, so Scores[I] refers to Scores[3]. Total becomes equal to the sum of the three scores.

This use of a for loop to gain access to each array value is typical of a large number of algorithms using arrays.

Another big advantage of this new list (array) way of thinking comes when the lists are longer. For example, suppose that we wanted to calculate the total of 20 scores. Compare:

Old Way of Thinking

```
Total := Score1 + Score2 + Score3 + Score4 + Score5
         + Score6 + Score7 + Score8 + Score9 + Score10
         + Score11 + Score12 + Score13 + Score14 + Score15
         + Score16 + Score17 + Score18 + Score19 + Score20
```

```
Total := 0;
for I := 1 to 20 do
  begin
    Total := Total + Scores[I]
  end    {for}
```

Suppose that we wanted to calculate the total of 100 scores. Compare:

```
Exercise for the unconvinced reader
```

```
Total := 0;
for I := 1 to 100 do
  begin
    Total := Total + Scores[I]
  end    {for}
```

For the discussion that follows, assume that we have an array called Scores that contains five scores:

```
Scores: 76, 87, 80, 85, 88
```

In the array notation, this means that

Scores[1]	*is*	76
Scores[2]	*is*	87
Scores[3]	*is*	80
Scores[4]	*is*	85
Scores[5]	*is*	88

If we wish to refer to the third score, then we will say that its **value** is 80. With this terminology in mind, consider the following table, for which we suppose that the variable I has the value 3, the variable J has the value 5, and the variable K has the value 7:

Reference	Value	Comment
Scores[1]	76	
Scores[3]	80	
Scores[I]	80	Scores [3] since I is 3
Scores[I+1]	85	Scores [4] since I + 1 is 4
Scores[I] + 1	81	One more than Scores [3]
Scores[J]	88	Scores [5]
Scores[K]	Illegal	Scores [7] does not exist
Scores[K−3]	85	Scores [4] since K − 3 is 4

There are three points to note well:

1. It is okay to use I+1 as an indicator of which score we want, but be sure to do the arithmetic in the proper place. That is, the two legal expressions:

```
Scores[I]+1
Scores[I + 1]
```

almost always have different values. The first means "one more than the Ith score." The second means "the (I+1)st score."

2. Reference to a score (for example, Scores[7]) that is not on the list is illegal.

3. We will refer to the expression that appears inside of the square brackets ([]) as an **index** (sometimes called a **subscript**) of the array. We can extend the previous table to include this concept as:

Index	Reference	Value
1	Scores[1]	76
3	Scores[3]	80
I	Scores[I]	80
I+1	Scores[I+1]	85
I	Scores[I] + 1	81
J	Scores[J]	88
K	Scores[K]	Illegal
K − 3	Scores[K−3]	85

Now suppose that we are going to have 20 scores for each student of a course, but that it is midterm and we only have values for 10 of each student's scores. We have here two variations of the concept of **size** of the array Scores. Because there will be 20 scores, we have the **potential size** or **maximum allowable size** of 20 for the array. Because there are now 10 scores, we have the **actual size** of 10 for the items in the array that are in use.

The price that we have to pay for this more powerful way of referring to data is that we must declare each array within the Pascal module that uses it. In the declaration of an array, include both type and size information. The size information will be for the potential size of the array. For now, we will suggest a simplified scheme for declaring our arrays. First of all, assume that the arrays will be lists of integer numbers. The second assumption has to do with the size of an array.

Assume that if a program has to use two or more arrays, then they can have the same size. Remember that size refers to the potential (maximum allowable) number of items in the array and not the actual number of items in the array that are in use. Further assume that the potential size of 1000 will suffice for all of our early work with arrays. The way that we will declare our arrays will be to include the following among our declarations in the main module:

```
const
    MaxIndex = 1000;                    {size of arrays}

type
    IntegerArray = array[1 .. MaxIndex] of integer;
```

For each particular array (Scores, for example), we will include among our declarations:

```
var
    Scores      : IntegerArray;       { Test scores }
```

To illustrate, consider the example program in Figure 3-15, which is Case Study No. 1 rewritten using an array. In this case, the actual number of elements of the array that are being used is 3. Note that we have changed the way that the data is input from all on one line to the use of a separate line for each data item. Also, the example has been simplified so that it deals with only one student. The array usage is shaded.

NOTE This program can be and was written earlier without arrays. However, the use of arrays gives some additional flexibility. If the values of the individual scores were needed after computing the total, then it would be difficult to write the program without arrays if the number of scores were increased. For example, suppose we needed to compute the number of grades that were within 10 percent of the average grade, and furthermore the number of grades was to be a variable N. We can compute the average using code like this:

```
Total := 0;

for I := 1 to N do
    begin
        Readln(Scores[I]);
        Total := Total + Scores[I]
    end;   {for}

Average := Total / N;
```

Once we have the average, we can count the number of scores within 10 percent of the average by

```
Count := 0;

for I := 1 to N do
    begin
        if (Scores[I] <= 1.1 * Average)
                and (Scores[I] >= 0.9 * Average) then
            Count := Count + 1
    end;   {for}
```

```
program TestScores(Input, Output);
{
  Written by:  XXXXXXXX  XX/XX/XX
     Purpose:  To calculate the total on three tests, and
               print that total for one student.
}
const
  MaxIndex = 1000;                   {size of arrays}

type
  IntegerArray = array[1 ..  MaxIndex] of integer;

var
  Name    : string[20];              {student name, input}
  Scores  : IntegerArray;            {test scores, input}
  Total   : integer;                 {total of test scores, calculated}
  I       : integer;                 {loop index}

begin {TestScores}

{*** Read name and scores; calculate and print total.}

  Writeln;
  Write('Enter the name: ');
  Readln(Name);
  Writeln('Now enter the scores');
  Total := 0;

  for I := 1 to 3 do
    begin
      Write('Enter score ', I:1, ' : ');
      Readln(Scores[I]);
      Total := Total + Scores[I]
    end;

  Writeln('The total is ', Total:1, ' for ', Name);

{*** Print message and stop the program.}

  Writeln;
  Writeln('TestScores program is terminating.')
end.
```

SAMPLE INPUT AND OUTPUT

```
Enter the name: John Smith
Now enter the scores
Enter score 1 : 78
Enter score 2 : 85
Enter score 3 : 91
The total is 254 for John Smith

TestScores program is terminating.
```

Figure 3-15   Using an Array

DPT—ARRAYS ☐ *1.* Remember that arrays must be declared. The actual size of an array can never exceed the potential size of an array. To avoid problems, use our suggested declaration scheme for your early work with arrays.

2. Don't write the expression Scores[I] + 1 when you mean the expression Scores[I+1]. Think about what the two expressions mean.

3. Be careful not to refer to an array item that is past the potential size of the array. This is illegal and should produce a run-time error from Pascal.[2]

4. Be careful not to refer to an array item that is past the actual size of the array. This error will not be picked up by Pascal, but the value that you get will likely be meaningless.

5. Use square brackets "[]" for your array references and don't use parentheses "()". If you use parentheses instead of square brackets in the example of Figure 3-15, in Turbo Pascal you will get the error message

```
I/O are not allowed.
```

This message is not particularly illuminating as a solution for fixing the problem, so be careful to avoid the problem.

■■■■■■ REVIEW

Terms and Concepts

repeat–until   value
while–do   index
down to   subscript
for–do   size
random number   potential size
simulations   actual size
array

Pascal syntax

Loops

1. Procedure can have value parameters.

2. General form of repeat–until loop:

```
repeat
    statement(s)
until  condition
```

3. General form of while–do loop:

```
while  condition  do
    statement that forms body of loop
```

4. Usual form of while–do loop:

```
while  condition  do
  begin
    body of loop
  end
```

5. General form of for–do loop (can use "downto" for "to")

```
for control variable := start to end  do
    statement that forms body of loop
```

6. Usual form of for–do loop (can use "downto" for "to")

```
for control variable := start to end  do
  begin
    body of loop
  end
```

Arrays

1. For now, declare an array called Scores using the following among the declarations:

```
const
  MaxIndex = 1000;                    {size of arrays}

type
  IntegerArray = array[1 .. MaxIndex] of integer;

var
  Scores   : IntegerArray;        {test scores}
```

2. Refer to the Ith element of the array Scores by the expression:

```
Scores[I]
```

DPT

Loops

1. A while loop executes 0 or more times.

2. A repeat–until loop executes 1 or more times.

3. You usually need a begin and end to enclose the body of a for loop or a while loop.

4. Be careful that you *do not* place a semicolon directly after the "do" of the for loop or the while loop.

5. Make sure that the condition part of a while loop can become false sometime during the execution of the loop.

6. Make sure that the condition part of a repeat–until loop can become true sometime during the execution of the loop.

Arrays

1. Declare arrays.

2. Scores[I+1] and Scores[I] + 1 are different.

3. Do not violate array bounds.

4. Use "[]" and not "()" for arrays.

Exercises 1 to 14 can be solved without arrays.

*1. Trace the following segments by determining what values are printed and the value of I following loop termination.

a.
```
I := 6;                          (Trace for N = 6, 7, 15)
while I < N do
  begin
    Writeln(I);
    if Odd(I) then
      I := I + 3
    else
      I := I + 5
  end
```

b.
```
I := 6;                          (Trace for N = 6, 7, 15)
repeat
  Writeln(I);
  if Odd(I) then
    I := I + 3
  else
    I := I + 5
until I >= N
```

c.
```
I := 1                           (Trace for N = 10, 1, 0)
while I <= N do
  I := I + 1;
  Writeln(I)
```

d.
```
I := 1;                          (Trace for N = 10, 1, 0)
repeat
  I := I + 1;
  Writeln(I)
until I > N
```

*2. Show the output from the program fragment:

```
N := 4;
while  N < 100  do
  begin
    N := Sqr(N);
    Writeln(N)
  end
```

*3. Show the output from the program fragment:

```
S := 0;
for I := 1 to 10 do
  begin
    Writeln(I);
    S := S + I
  end;
Writeln(S)
```

4. Hand-trace this program segment for the indicated input values of the variables I and J. What values are printed by the Writeln?

```
                    Readln (I,J);
                    repeat
                      I := 2 * I;
                      if I <= J then
                          I := I + 1
                    until I > J;
                    Writeln(I)
```

a. 2, 4   c. 0, 12
b. 3, 14   d. −1, 0

*5. Each segment is supposed to print a table of the powers of 2 that are less than or equal to N, where N is known to be at least 2. By hand-tracing with different values of N, determine whether or not they are correct.

```
a. Readln(N);
   I := 0;
   P := 1;
   repeat
     Writeln(I,P);
     if P <= N then
        begin
          I := I + 1;
          P := P * 2
        end
   until P > N
b. Readln(N);
   I := 0;
   P := 1;
   while P <= N do
      begin
        Writeln(I,P);
        I := I + 1;
        P := P * 2
      end
c. Readln(N);
   I := 0;
   P := 1;
   Writeln(I,P);
   while P <= N do
      begin
        I := I + 1;
        P := P * 2;
        Writeln (I,P)
      end
d. Readln(N);
   I := 0;
   P := 1;
   S := 0;
   while P <= N do
      begin
        Writeln(I,P);
        I := I + 1;
        S := S + P;
        P := S + 1
      end
```

6. Write program segments to print tables of feet and inches for:

*a. feet from 1 to 30
b. feet from 30 back to 1
c. feet from 1 to N
d. feet from N back to 1

*7. a. Write a program segment to compute the sum

$$1 + 2 + \ldots + 75$$

Hint: See exercise 3.

b. Write a function to find the sum of the integers between (and including) two given integers. Assume that the first is less than or equal to the second.

c. Using the function written in part (b), write an assignment statement to find the sum of the N integers beginning at First. For example, if First is 7 and N is 3, the answer is 24 (7 + 8 + 9).

8. *a. How could Random be used to simulate a situation with equally likely outcomes ranging from 5 to 15?

*b. How could Random be used to simulate a roulette wheel with numbers from 1 to 30, plus 0 and 00?

c. How could Random be used to simulate a situation with equally likely outcomes 3, 6, 9, 12, 15, and 18?

9. Write a program fragment to throw a pair of dice and print the value thrown until it is 7 (print the value 7).

10. Write a program fragment to throw a pair of dice and print the value thrown as long as it is not a 7 (do not print the value 7).

11. a. Write a program to simulate generating 1000 random numbers in the range 1 to 10,000, and print the largest number generated.

b. Write a program to simulate generating 1000 random numbers in the range 1 to 1000, and count how many times the number generated matches the control variable.

12. *a. Write a program fragment to print all multiples of 19 that are less than 642 (19, 38, 57, and so on).

b. Extend part (a) to write a procedure that prints all multiples of M that are less than N.

13. a. Modify the rabbits example so that, instead of doubling each year, it either stays the same, doubles, or triples, with each equally likely. Hint: Use Random.

b. Modify part (a) to print the population at the end of each year for 10 years rather than after the entire 10 years.

c. Modify part (b) to print the population at the end of each year up to and including the year the population exceeds 10,000.

14. A sum of $200 is deposited and compounded at 5 percent annually. Write program fragments to do the following. Note: This is similar to the rabbits example, but instead of doubling each year, the amount is multiplied by 1.05.

a. Print the amount in the account at the end of each year for nine years.

*b. Print the amount in the account at the end of each year until the amount exceeds $475.

Exercises 15 to 20 refer to arrays.

*15. Suppose the array Ages contains the values:

Ages: 12, 23, 45, 2

Suppose that the variable Oldest has the value 3 and the variable Terrible has the value 4.

a. What is the value of the expression Ages[2]?
b. What is the value of Ages[Oldest]?
c. What is the value of Ages[Terrible]?
d. Show how to refer to the value 12.
e. Show how to declare the array in a program.

*16. Suppose the array Days contains the values:

Days: 31, 28, 31, 30, 31, 30, 31, 31, 30, 31, 30, 31

a. What is the value of the expression Days[2]?
b. What is the value of the expression Days[2] + 1 (which you might use in a leap year)?
c. Write a fragment of Pascal to print all of the values of the array Days.
d. What Pascal statement could you use to change the value of Days[2] to 29?

*17. Determine the values printed by the following program segments, where A is an integer array as described in this section:

```
a. for I := 1 to 7 do
       begin
          A[I] := I
       end;  {for}
   for I := 7 downto 1 do
       begin
          Writeln(A[I])
       end;  {for}
b. for I := 1 to 5 do
       begin
          A[I] := 2*I - 5
       end;  {for}
   J := 3;
   A[J + 2] := A[J] + 2;
   A[1] := A[J] - J;
   for I := 1 to 5 do
       begin
          Writeln(A[I])
       end;  {for}
c. for I := 1 to 15 do
       begin
          if I mod 3 = 0 then
             A[I] := I + 5
          else
             A[I] := I
       end;  {for}
   I := 1;
   while A[I] <= 12 do
       begin
          if A[I] >= 5 then
             Writeln(I, A[I]);
          I := I + 1
       end;  {while}
```

18. Change the Pascal program of Figure 3-15 so that it uses six scores instead of three.

19. Modify your answer to Exercise 18 to change the declaration of the constant MaxIndex to 4 instead of 1000. That is, use the lines

```
const
    MaxIndex = 4;                    {size of arrays}
```

Compile your program and run it. What happens? (Turbo users: Try this both with and without the {$R+} compiler option.)

20. Modify the answer to Exercise 18 so that after printing the value of Total it prints the value of Scores[10]. Compile the program and run it. What happens? What is the interpretation of the value printed for Scores[10] within the context of the program?

21. In the discussion of the old way of thinking and the new way, we did not have a correct alternative to offer for the "new way" statement

```
Writeln(Scores(I))
```

There is a possible alternative given by the following case statement:

```
case I of
    1 : Writeln(Score1);
    2 : Writeln(Score2);
    3 : Writeln(Score3)
end {case}
```

What do you think of this alternative? Which approach, the new or the old, would you prefer if there were 20 scores? If there were 100?

□
NOTES FOR SECTION 3-2

1. The Random function is not standard. However, many versions of Pascal contain similar functions to generate random numbers. Consult your instructor or a reference manual. See Appendix E.

2. For Turbo Pascal, the compiler directive {$R+} should be placed at the beginning of the program to cause the computer to perform this check.

3-3
□□□□□
PLANNING LOOPS

In the first two sections of the chapter, we have covered several applications of loops. These include counting, accumulating totals, and finding largest or smallest values in a list of input. In addition, we have learned about two new looping constructions: the for loop and the while loop.

By imitating the sample program segments of the last two sections, you have (we hope) written some looping structures similar to the examples. However, you may not yet feel confident to design loops for applications that are not exactly like those examples. It is impossible to make a small set of rules which will cover all possible programs that involve looping. However, some general planning strategies that can be useful in loop design can be described. In this section, a possible approach to loop planning is presented and illustrated in a number of examples.

□
THE LOOP PLANNING PROCESS

The general approach to loop design can be outlined in four steps:

1. Recognize the need for a loop.
2. Plan the loop control.

3. Design the loop body and any necessary initialization and finalization steps.

4. Double check the loop control.

As we will see, in actual practice the steps interact. For example, the loop control can affect the initialization steps.

Let us begin with a brief description of the four steps.

1. Recognize the need for a loop.

The purpose of a loop is to provide repetition. A program that must repeat one or more steps will usually include a loop for this purpose.

Part of recognizing the need for a loop involves identifying, in a general way, what is to be repeated. It may be helpful to think in terms of what one **pass** through the loop (that is, one repetition of the loop body) will accomplish. For example, for a specific program this might be:

Completely process one set of user input, or
Print one element of the array, or
Simulate one roll of a pair of dice, or
Double the number of rabbits

In the third step, where we plan the body of the loop, this general statement of the purpose of the loop is refined.

2. Plan the loop control.

Planning **loop control** involves identifying the conditions under which the loop will terminate. For example, the four loops described above might terminate:

When the user enters a special terminal data value, or
When all the array elements have been printed, or
When the roll is a 7, or
When the number of rabbits exceeds 10,000

NOTE   Identifying a termination condition for a loop is equivalent to identifying under what conditions the loop will continue. For example, we can say that "the loop will terminate when the user enters a length of 0" or that "the loop will continue as long as the user does not enter a length of 0." Similarly, we can say that "the loop will terminate when the number of rabbits exceeds 10,000" or that "the loop will continue as long as the number of rabbits is 10,000 or less."

In general, the conditions for termination and for continuation of the repetition are negations of each other.

The types of loop control can be categorized as follows:

1. Count Control. Most frequently, this involves a specific number of repetitions of the loop body. A for loop is the most appropriate structure.

2. Direct User Control. We have seen two types of direct user control. In the first, the user enters a special terminal value to indicate the end of a set of data. In the second, the program specifically asks the user if the process is to be repeated, and reads a yes or no answer. We can develop "standard" ways to handle these types of loops, consistent with our personal programming style. Up to this point in the text, we have used repeat–until loops for these types of problems.

3. *File Control.* When we learn about files in Chapter 5, we will see that loops are sometimes controlled by terminating upon reaching the end of the file. At that time, we will learn some standard ways to write this type of program.

4. *General Condition.* This is a catchall category for any loop that does not fit one of the previous categories. For this type of loop, we will choose an appropriate repeat–until or while–do looping structure. Sometimes the choice of which to use is obvious and sometimes it is not. There can be tradeoffs to consider. This subject is discussed in more detail in the next subsection on choosing between the repeat and the while loops.

3. Design the loop body, initialization, and finalization.

The loop body consists of the steps to be repeated. As we learned in Section 3-1, certain types of looping tasks include specific types of **initialization** and **finalization** steps. For example, in a program to find the average age of a group of individuals, we would initialize a counter and accumulator to 0 prior to the loop. After the loop, we would calculate the average by dividing the accumulator by the counter and print the result.

The exact nature of the initialization steps may relate to our choice of looping structure. For example, for a while loop, we may have to include some preliminary steps to make sure that the condition for the loop "makes sense" the first time we execute the loop body. Thus, designing the initialization portion and the choice of loop control in step 2 may interact with each other.

By the end of this step, our algorithm should be ready (or almost ready) to write in Pascal.

4. Double check the loop control.

Some of the reasons for this double check can be summarized by these three phrases:

Don't be "off by 1."
Don't be "off by ½."
Don't write infinite loops.

These relate to three common errors involving loop control. The first phrase warns against writing loops that execute one too many times or one too few times. For example, consider this fragment:

```
Write('Enter a number: ');
Readln(Limit);
Writeln('The multiples of 17 that are less than ', Limit:1);
Multiple := 17;
```

```
repeat
  Writeln(Multiple);
  Multiple := Multiple + 17
until Multiple >= Limit;
```

For any Limit that is less than 17, the fragment is incorrect; we should have used a while loop.

The second phrase (*Don't be "off by ½."*) warns that frequently there are some steps in the loop body that should not be executed during the last pass through the loop. For example, we have written many repeat–until loops that skip the calculations and printing for the terminal data value entered by the user.

The third phrase (*Don't write infinite loops.*) indicates that we should always make sure that the termination condition can eventually become true. As we discussed in the DPT portions of the previous section, this can be caused by Pascal errors such as erroneous semicolons or forgetting begin–end pairs. It can also be caused by errors in reasoning. For example, the following loop, although it is "correct" Pascal, is faulty.

```
I := 1;
Sum := 0;
Readln(N);

repeat
  Sum := Sum + I;
  I := I + 2
until I = N;
```

For example, if N is even, the loop will not terminate. To remedy this, we would change the termination condition to "until I >= N;".

One way to double check the loop control is to **hand-trace** the loop with specific values. If the loop control involves a value that would cause many passes through the loop, we may mentally replace this value with a smaller one. For example, if the loop is to terminate when an account balance exceeds $5000.00, we might trace an equivalent loop that terminates when the balance exceeds $500.00. This process does not "prove" that the program is correct, but it can help us locate faulty reasoning. For example, consider this fragment to find the sum of the numbers from 1 to 100:

```
Sum := 0;
I := 1;

repeat
  Sum := Sum + I;
  I := I + 1
until I >= 100;
```

If we hand-trace this using 3 instead of 100, we will observe the following:

First pass through the loop: Sum is set to 0 + 1 = 1
                                I is set to 2
Second pass through the loop: Sum is set to 1 + 2 = 3
                                I is set to 3

Since the condition "I >= 3" is now true, the loop terminates. But it didn't find the sum of the numbers from 1 to 3, only from 1 to 2. Our loop control is off by 1. (Notice that we should really have used a count-controlled for loop, which would avoid this problem for this example.)

To illustrate the loop planning process we have outlined, let us design a program to find the squares of numbers input by the user. The numbers are to be in the range from 1 to 100, terminated by a value of 0. The program also will indicate what percentage of the input was greater than 50.

1. Recognize the need for a loop. A loop is needed because several numbers supplied by the user are to be handled. Each pass through the loop will process one set of input.

2. Plan the loop control. This loop is under direct user control: an entry of 0 terminates the process. We can, therefore, use our standard techniques for this type of problem. The loop will be a repeat–until, terminating when the number entered is 0.

3. Design the loop body and any necessary "initialization" and "finalization" steps. The body of the loop consists of these steps to be repeated:

issue a prompt
read a number
calculate and print the square
increment the count of numbers entered
see if the number was over 50; if so, increment the count of numbers over 50

Before the loop, we initialize both counts to 0; after the loop, we calculate and print the percentage.

4. Double check the loop control. If we code the algorithm as it stands, we will be "off by ½." That is, we will execute some steps for the terminal 0 value entered by the user. All the steps beginning with the calculation should be omitted for this last pass. (We have frequently placed an asterisk in our algorithms beside these types of steps.)

<table>
<tr><td>

□
**LOOP
CONTROL—
WHILE–DO
VERSUS
REPEAT–UNTIL**

</td><td>

Figure 3-16 shows one possible fragment of Pascal code for the loop designed in this example.

It uses our usual techniques for writing this type of loop. However, consider the program fragment in Figure 3-17, which accomplishes the same thing in a different way. This fragment **primes the loop** by reading the first value. (This terminology is intended to suggest the act of "priming" a pump by adding water.) As long as the Number obtained is not 0 (EndOfData), the program calculates and prints the square and does the counting. When the Number is 0, it terminates.

</td></tr>
</table>

If you examine the two segments, you will see that there are tradeoffs:

1. The repeat–until form includes an extra level of nesting. This can make the program harder to understand. In addition, there is the danger that we will forget to skip the processing for the terminal data value.

```
Entered := 0;
Over50 := 0;

repeat
  Write('Enter number (0 to quit): ');
  Readln(Number);
  if Number <> EndOfData then
    begin
      Square := Sqr(Number);
      Writeln(Number:1, ' squared is ', Square:1);
      Entered := Entered + 1;
      if Number > 50 then
        Over50 := Over50 + 1
    end
until Number = EndOfData;

Percent := Over50 / Entered * 100;
Writeln(Percent:1:2, '% were over 50');
```

Figure 3-16 Percentage Calculation-Repeat Loop

2. The repeat–until loop body contains its steps in the "natural" order: read, calculate, print. The while loop body has steps in this order: calculate for the value already read, print, read another value to get ready for the next pass. This can be troublesome for beginners, although we can get used to it. In addition, there is the danger that we will forget the priming read.

3. The while loop duplicates the read step: it appears before the loop and at the bottom of the loop. This can lead to problems if this step is modified. (Placing the step in a procedure would help avoid this problem.)

In short, the decision of which approach to use for this type of problem is not obvious. Your authors, after extensive discussion, chose the first approach as a

```
Entered := 0;
Over50 := 0;
Write('Enter number (0 to quit): ');
Readln(Number);

while Number <> EndOfData do
  begin
    Square := Sqr(Number);
    Writeln(Number:1, ' squared is ', Square:1);
    Entered := Entered + 1;
    if Number > 50 then
      Over50 := Over50 + 1;
    Write('Enter number (0 to quit): ');
    Readln(Number)
  end;

Percent := Over50 / Entered * 100;
Writeln(Percent:1:2, '% were over 50');
```

Figure 3-17 Percentage Calculation-While Loop

starting point for the textbook examples. Many Pascal programmers (including authors of other texts) choose the second approach.

Sometimes, as in this example, there are tradeoffs, and the choice is at least partially a matter of personal style. However, there are times when one or the other loop structure seems more appropriate. We offer a few general guidelines. They are not meant to cover all possible situations, but they do indicate some of the possibilities.

1. A while loop executes its body 0 or more times. If it is possible that the loop should terminate immediately without executing the loop body at all, a while loop should be used. For example, a loop to print all the multiples of 17 that are less than some user supplied number should be a while loop.

2. A while loop is ideal for activities that involve performing a first action, then repeating a similar action if necessary. For example, in checking the validity of input data, we can write code such as:

```
Write('Enter a number in the range 0 to 100');
Readln(Number);

while (Number < 0) or (Number > 100) do
  begin
    Writeln('Invalid entry of ', Number:1);
    Write('Please reenter (in the range 0 to 100)');
    Readln(Number)
  end;
```

The first read and the one in the loop are similar but not quite the same. In particular, the prompt is different.

3. A repeat–until loop may be better for some types of problems where the loop body must be executed in order for the termination condition to make sense. For example, in a loop to count the number of dice rolls until a 7 is reached, we might write:

```
RollCount := 0;

repeat
  Roll := RollOfDice;
  RollCount := RollCount + 1
until Roll = 7;
```

An equivalent while loop would have to perform the roll (and count it) prior to the loop. Loop priming, which duplicates the entire loop body, is generally not an ideal structure.

This last statement can supply some further insight into which loop type to use. First, identify the condition that is to control the loop and also the steps that form the initialization for the loop and the body of the loop. If the condition "makes sense" before the loop executes for the first time, then a while loop is indicated. If the entire body of the loop must be executed once before the condition should be tested, then a repeat–until loop is the best choice. If, as frequently happens, the condition first makes sense after part but not all of the loop is executed, we must make an intelligent choice. If we use a repeat–until loop, part of the loop body may have to be skipped on the last pass through the loop. If we use a while–do loop, we may have to move the first part of the loop body before the loop to prime the loop and duplicate those steps at the bottom of the loop to prepare for the next pass through the loop.

For our first example, let us write a function called SmallDivisor, which finds the smallest divisor (other than 1) of a given number. (A divisor of an integer I is an integer which yields no remainder when it is divided into I.)

SmallDivisor(15)	should be 3
SmallDivisor(14)	should be 2
SmallDivisor(29)	should be 29
SmallDivisor(175)	should be 5

The function will have one parameter, Number, an integer assumed to be greater than 1. Since this is our first example, we will discuss it explicitly in terms of the planning steps described earlier. In our later examples, the use of those steps will be implicit, even if we do not make an issue of it.

1. *Recognize the Need for a Loop.* How would you go about finding the smallest divisor of some large number such as 19,327? You would perhaps start trying numbers in a definite pattern: first try 2, then 3, then 4, then 5, and so on. If we imitate this manual solution, we will be repeating a process: try a potential divisor to see if it works. Thus a loop is appropriate.

   At this point, we can see the need for these two variables:

Input parameter:	Number	integer	Number to find divisor of; the number is assumed to be greater than 1
Local variable:	Potential	integer	A potential divisor; takes on the values 2, 3, etc.

2. *Plan the Loop Control.* The appropriate loop control is the "general condition" type. We cannot use count control because we do *not* want to try all the potential divisors from 2 to the given number. We want to stop when we find a divisor, that is, when Number mod Potential is 0.

   In the verbal description of how we would solve the problem, we indicated that our first attempt would be with Potential equal to 2. Because the given number could be even, this initial value could already be the desired answer. This implies that we should use a while loop rather than a repeat loop.

3. *Design the Loop Body, Initialization, and Finalization.* As part of planning the loop control, we have already identified an initialization:

   ```
   Potential := 2
   ```

   (This is typical—the planning steps tend to interact.)

   In the loop body, we must add 1 to Potential; after the loop we assign the answer to the function name.

4. Double Check the Loop Control. In rough form, our algorithm is

> set Potential to 2
> see if it is a divisor; as long as it isn't do this:
>   add 1 to Potential

We might hand-trace this for several possible inputs: perhaps 14, 5, and 45.

For 14:	Potential : 2
	loop terminates, answer is 2
For 5:	Potential : 2
	not a divisor, so Potential := 3
	not a divisor, so Potential := 4
	not a divisor, so Potential := 5
	loop terminates, answer is 5
For 45:	Potential : 2
	not a divisor, so Potential := 3
	loop terminates, answer is 3

COMMENT   These inputs were chosen by observing that a number's smallest divisor lies between 2 and the number itself. The first two inputs exercise the boundaries of this possible range. In hand-tracing, as in testing, boundaries are extremely important considerations.

Based on this tracing, we appear to have avoided the three common pitfalls (off by 1, off by ½, infinite loop).

See Figure 3-18 for the function. There are several things to observe about that function. First, Potential is declared as a local variable for the function. Second, the mod operator checks for divisibility. Third, the while loop is written using a begin and end even though there is only one step in the loop; this is a matter of personal style (and defensive programming).

There is one other, fairly subtle, point. You might wonder, since in the last step of the program, we simply assign Potential to SmallDivisor, why we couldn't just use SmallDivisor itself in the loop. To be precise, would this work?

```
SmallDivisor := 2;
while Number mod SmallDivisor <> 0 do
  begin
    SmallDivisor := SmallDivisor + 1
  end;  {while}
```

The answer is no. Recall our previous defensive programming tip that in writing a function, we should not use the function name anywhere except on the left side of an assignment statement. If we use it in a condition or on the right side of the assignment statement, the compiler will treat it as an invocation of the function and will expect parameters. Although we will learn (in Chapter 4) how to make good use of this ability of a function to invoke itself, for now we should follow the rule described above.

```
function SmallDivisor(Number : integer) : integer;
{
    Written by :   XXXXXXXXX   XX/XX/XX
       Purpose:    To find the smallest divisor of a given number.
    Parameters:    Number - the number whose divisor is to be found
                   (assumed to be bigger than 1)
}
var
  Potential : integer;                    {a potential divisor of Number}

begin    {SmallDivisor}
  Potential := 2;

  while Number mod Potential <> 0 do
    begin
      Potential := Potential + 1
    end;   {while}

  SmallDivisor := Potential
end;   {SmallDivisor}
```

Figure 3-18   Smallest Divisor of a Number

As a second example, let us write a function to find the number of different divisors of a given number. We are not counting 1 nor the number itself as divisors.

NumDivisors(15)	should be 2 because 3 and 5 are divisors
NumDivisors(7)	should be 0 because there are no divisors other than 1 and 7
NumDivisors(36)	should be 7 because 2, 3, 4, 6, 9, 12, and 18 are divisors

This problem is so similar to the previous one that we might be tempted to just use the same loop control. However, there is an important difference that changes the loop control. The previous example found a *particular divisor,* and the loop could terminate when that divisor was found. This example determines a *count*; we must examine *every* integer between 1 and the number (excluding 1 and the number). We do *not* want to terminate the loop when we find a divisor. A count-control loop can be used.

We will need an input parameter Number, a local variable Potential as a trial divisor, and a local variable Counter to count the number of divisors found. The Pascal code for NumDivisors is shown in Figure 3-19.

As another example, let us use the RollOfDice function (written in Section 3-2) to write a procedure that simulates a game of chance. In this game, a pair of dice is rolled once to establish a "goal." The dice are then rolled repeatedly until the goal is matched on a future roll. The player pays $10 to play the game and wins $1 for each successful roll that does not match the goal. We wish to simulate one play of the game and print an appropriate message showing the results.

We will use these variables: Goal, to record the first roll; Roll, for the subsequent rolls; and Money, to keep track of the player's money.

Each pass through the loop will simulate one attempt to match the goal. The

```
function NumDivisors(Number : integer) : integer; .
{
   Written by:   XXXXXXX   XX/XX/XX
      Purpose:   To find the number of divisors of a given number.
   Parameters:   Number - the number whose divisors are to be
                 counted (assumed to be bigger than 1)
}
var
  Potential  :  integer;              { a potential divisor }
  Counter    :  integer;              { number of divisors found }
begin  {NumDivisors}
  Counter := 0;

  for Potential := 2 to Number - 1 do
    begin
      if Number mod Potential = 0 then
        Counter := Counter + 1
    end;  {for}

  NumDivisors := Counter
end;  {NumDivisors}
```

Figure 3-19   Count of Divisors of a Number

loop will terminate when there is a match, that is, when Roll = Goal. We have the
following initialization, loop body, and finalization steps:

Initialization:	obtain the Goal value
	set the Money to −10 (you pay $10 to play)
Loop body:	obtain the Roll value
	print the Roll value
	add 1 to the Money
Finalization:	print a message (depending on whether Money is positive,
	negative, or zero)

We now consider whether to use a while loop or a repeat loop. The termination
condition (Roll = Goal) does not make sense until we have rolled the dice. We
therefore choose a repeat loop. We must be cautious, however, not to be "off by
½." The final step of the loop body should *not* be executed if the roll matched the
goal. For example, if the Goal is matched on the 13th roll, as illustrated in the
second sample run of the program, the player would win only $2 ($12 minus the
$10 to play).

The planning described above leads us to the procedure presented in
Figure 3-20.

Sometimes a problem is "almost" a count-control problem. For example, to
find the sum $1 + 2 + \ldots + 400$, we could use

```
Sum := 0;
for I := 1 to 400 do
  begin
    Sum := Sum + I
  end;   {for}
```

What might we do to find the sum $2 + 4 + \ldots + 266$?

```
procedure MatchRoll;
{
         Written by:     XXXXXXXXXX, XX/XX/XX
            Purpose:     To simulate one play of a game of chance.
         Parameters:    None
   Functions used:      RollOfDice, to simulate rolling a pair of dice.
}
var
   Goal    : integer;         {result of first roll, the "goal"}
   Roll    : integer;         {subsequent rolls of the dice}
   Money   : integer;         {player's money}

begin     {MatchRoll}

{*** Obtain goal and initialize player's money}

   Goal := RollOfDice;
   Writeln('The goal is ', Goal:1);
   Money := -10;

{*** Roll until goal is matched, winning $1 for each successful roll.}

   repeat
     Roll := RollOfDice;
     Writeln('This roll: ', Roll:1);
     if Roll <> Goal then
        Money := Money + 1
   until Roll = Goal;

{*** Print the results.}

   if Money > 0 then
     Writeln('You won $', Money:1)
   else if Money = 0 then
     Writeln('You broke even')
   else
     Writeln('You lost $', Abs(Money):1)

end;     {MatchRoll}
```

SAMPLE INPUT AND OUTPUT

First run:

```
The goal is 8
This roll: 8
You lost $10
```

Second run:

```
The goal is 7
This roll: 11
This roll: 4
```

Figure 3-20   Game of Chance (Continued)

```
This roll: 4
This roll: 11
This roll: 4
This roll: 5
This roll: 9
This roll: 8
This roll: 6
This roll: 8
This roll: 8
This roll: 12
This roll: 7
You won $2
```

Figure 3-20 Game of Chance

One approach is to imitate the logic of the for loop with a while loop, as described in the previous section. We would like to go from 2 to 266, but by 2's. We can write

```
Sum := 0;
I := 2;
while I <= 266 do
  begin
    Sum := Sum + I;
    I := I + 2
  end;    {while}
```

COMMENT Some programming languages, such as FORTRAN, COBOL, and BASIC, expand the notion of the count-control loop to include a "step size." Unfortunately, Pascal does not; we must simulate the idea, perhaps as indicated in this example.

For the final example, we will consider a problem involving an integer array. For this problem, we recall the definitions of *potential size* and *actual size* for an array. The potential size is the declared size (MaxIndex in the declaration scheme we suggested). The actual size is the number of meaningful values presently stored in the array.

NOTE We are suggesting using a large potential size (MaxIndex = 1000). This means that the actual size will usually be considerably smaller. This avoids some subtle pitfalls that we will discuss in detail in Chapter 6.

There are two frequently used ways to indicate the actual size of an array. The first uses a separate variable to keep track of this value. The second places a **delimiter** in the array following the last meaningful value. The delimiter plays the same role that a terminating input value does. It can be any chosen value that could not possibly be mistaken for a meaningful value.

Assuming that this second method is used with a delimiter of −MaxInt, let us write code to find the sum of an array called A. We need a loop because there are several values to be summed. In our preliminary planning, we observe that each pass through the loop will add one of the array values to the sum. We will accomplish this by causing a variable I to take on the values 1, 2, ... Then we can use A[I] to refer successively to A[1], A[2], ...

Because we do not know how many values there are, we will use the "general condition" form of loop control, terminating the loop when we reach the delimiter. To deal with the question of whether to use a while loop or a repeat–

until loop, we ask: Could it be possible that the loop body might be executed 0 times? The answer is yes if A[1] contains the delimiter.

Further planning leads to the following:

Initialization: set the sum to 0
start the subscript at 1

Loop Body: add the array element to the sum
add 1 to the subscript

Finalization: ??

The finalization step might be to print the sum. However, we choose to write a function for this task, so the finalization step assigns the answer to the function name.

The function, based on this planning process, appears as Figure 3-21. Several points are worth noting:

1. An array can be passed as a parameter to a function. We declare the parameter using the identifier IntegerArray defined in the main program. (More details on arrays as parameters are given in Chapter 4.)

2. The termination condition is "A[I] contains the delimiter." As usual in a while loop, the controlling condition tells how long the loop should continue and is the negation of the condition for terminating.

3. If we forget the loop's begin and end or the step "I := I + 1", the program may execute forever.

```
function  ArraySum(A : IntegerArray) : integer;
{
           Written by:  XXXXXXXXX, XX/XX/XX
              Purpose:  To find the sum of an array which uses
                        a delimiter of -MaxInt.
            Parameter:  A, the array to be summed
}
var
  Sum  : integer;                    {array sum}
  I    : integer;                    {subscript}

begin    {ArraySum}
  Sum := 0;
  I := 1;

  while A[I] <> -MaxInt do
    begin
      Sum := Sum + A[I];
      I := I + 1
    end;  {while}

  ArraySum := Sum
end;    {ArraySum}
```

Figure 3-21 Summing an Array with a Delimiter

4. Sum and I are local variables for the function. (Recall that this means that they are declared and used within the function, not in the math program.)

□
DPT A number of points have been raised in this section. We review them briefly.

1. In writing a while loop, the condition for the loop must make sense when the loop is first executed. This may require some "priming" steps prior to the loop. Some or all of these steps may have to be duplicated at the bottom of the body of the loop.

2. We should double check our loops to make sure that we are not "off by 1." One way to accomplish this is by hand-tracing the execution of the loop. If the loop will execute a large number of times, we can make an appropriate modification of the loop for the purpose of this tracing.

3. We should also avoid being "off by ½." We should check to see if there are any of the steps in the loop that should not be executed on the final pass through the loop.

4. Check for initialization steps. Many times the correct initial value for some variable is a value other than zero.

■■■■■■
REVIEW

Terms and concepts

pass (through a loop)   hand-tracing
loop control   priming a loop
initialization   delimiter
finalization

Loop planning

Steps in loop design

1. Recognize the need for a loop.
2. Plan the loop control.
3. Design the loop body and any necessary "initialization" and "finalization" steps.
4. Double check the loop control.

Types of loop control

1. Count control
2. Direct user control
3. File control
4. General condition

Choosing while or repeat

1. Sometimes there is no obvious choice; there are tradeoffs.
2. Use a while loop if the body can be executed 0 times.
3. Use a while loop to execute an action, and then perform a similar action 0 or more times.
4. Use a repeat–until if the body must be executed once before the termination condition "makes sense."

DPT

1. May need priming steps for while loop to cause a condition to "make sense" on first pass.
2. Don't be "off by 1."
3. Don't be "off by ½."
4. Double check the initialization steps.

■■■■■■ EXERCISES

1. By modifying the initialization of Potential, rewrite the SmallDivisor function (Figure 3-18) to use a repeat loop instead of a while loop. Which design seems better?

2. Modify the MatchRoll procedure (Figure 3-20) to use a while loop. Is the revised approach better?

3. Each record has an ID number, yearly income, number of years worked for the company, and a four-letter department code.
   *a. Write a program to find the ID number and yearly income of the person who earned the most during the year.
   b. Modify this program to print how many years this person has worked for the company and his department code (this will require two more special variables).
   c. Write a program to find the average number of years worked by persons in department 'TRNG'.
   d. Write a program to find the ID number and income of the person who earned the least during the year.

4. Each record contains a name, four test scores, the final exam score, and a quiz grade. Give a program to print the final average and resulting letter grade for each student. Also, find who had the highest and lowest scores on the final exam, which of the four tests had the highest class average, and how many received an A for the course. (Grades are based on 90 percent for an A, 80 percent for a B, and so on.)

*5. The loop given below repeatedly divides a positive integer number by 10 until the result is 0. For example, for the number 1372, the results would be 137, then 13, then 1, then 0.

```
Readln(Number);
repeat
   Number := Number div 10
until Number = 0
```

Modify the segment to obtain a count of the digits in the Number that was read.
Would the program work for Number = 0? For Number < 0?

*6. Write a function to find the sum of the digits of a given positive integer. Hint: Use Exercise 5 and the fact that for a positive number N, the expression N mod 10 "picks off" its rightmost digit.

7. Write a function to find the largest digit of a given positive integer. For 1632, the answer would be 6. For 989, the answer would be 9. Hint: See Exercise 6.

8. Write a function HighPower(Number) that for a given positive number finds the highest power of 2 that divides into the number. For example, HighPower(6) is 1 (2^1 is the highest power that divides into 6). Likewise, HighPower(24) is 3 (2^3 is the highest), and HighPower(175) is 0 (2^0 is the highest). Hint: Repeatedly divide the number by 2 until an odd number is obtained.

9. In this section, we wrote a function that found the smallest divisor (other than 1) of a number. Using a similar idea, write a function that finds the largest divisor (other than N itself) of a number N. Hint: Start high and work your way down; then the first divisor found will be the largest.

*10. Using an idea similar to that in the SmallDivisor function of this section (Figure 3-18), write a function GCD(M,N). The input parameters are positive integers. The answer is the "greatest common divisor" of M and N, that is, it is the largest number that divides evenly into both M and N. Hint: Start at the smaller of M and N and work your way down.

11. See Exercise 10. Write a function LCM(M,N) that finds the "least common multiple" of M and N. This is the smallest number into which both M and N divide evenly.

12. The algorithms suggested in Exercises 10 and 11, respectively, for the greatest common divisor and least common multiple of M and N run very slowly for large values of M and N. There are a number of better algorithms.

Probably the most popular and fastest algorithm for calculating the GCD of two positive integers is an algorithm credited to Euclid. One form of Euclid's algorithm is

set Big, Small to the larger and smaller of M, N
repeat these steps in a loop
    set R to Big mod Small (if R is 0, you are done, so terminate the loop)
    Big := Small
    Small := R
set GCD to Small

a. Hand-trace this algorithm for the following pairs of numbers:
  (i) 45, 10   (ii) 10, 45   (iii) 100, 48
  (iv) 105, 32   (v) 10000, 4994   (vi) 500, 735
b. Code the algorithm as a function.
c. Temporarily modify each of the functions in Exercises 10 and 12(b) to count and print the number of assignment statements executed. Write a main program that inputs a series of pairs of numbers and calls each function. Compare the speed of the two functions in terms of the number of assignment statements.
d. Modify the LCM function to take advantage of this relationship:

```
GCD(M,N) * LCM(M,N) = M * N
```

13. a. In this section, we wrote a function that calculated the number of divi-

sors of a given integer. In this exercise, write a procedure that for a given N prints a table listing its divisors.

*b. Write a main program that reads a series of records, each containing an integer. For each such integer, it should use the procedure from part (a) to print a table of divisors of the integer.

14. Write a segment of Pascal code for the following:
   a. Print a table of feet and inches for feet = 1, 2, . . . , 20.
   *b. Repeat part (a) for feet = 5, 10, . . . , 150.
   c. Repeat part (a) for feet = 0.00, 0.25, 0.50, . . . , 4.75, 5.00.

15. a. How could Random be used to simulate the toss of a coin?
   *b. Simulate tossing a coin 1000 times, counting the number of heads.
   c. Simulate tossing a coin 1000 times, counting the number of times the toss does not match the previous toss.
   *d. Simulate tossing a coin 1000 times, determining the longest streak of consecutive heads.

16. Write a program fragment that generates a series of random numbers in the range 1 to 10, counting how many numbers must be generated until two consecutive numbers are the same.

17. We can estimate the probability of a particular outcome occurring in a random experiment by performing the experiment a large number of times and finding for what percentage the outcome occurs. For example, if we roll a pair of dice 12,000 times and there are Count7 7's, then the probability of getting a 7 is approximated by Count7/12000. Using this idea, write program segments for the following. (Note: These can also be solved mathematically.)
   *a. What is the probability that the roll on a pair of dice is between 4 and 8?
   b. If two people each roll a pair of dice, what is the probability that their rolls will be identical?
   c. If you toss three coins simultaneously, what is the probability that only one is a head?
   d. If you draw a card at random from a set of 10 cards numbered 1 to 10, what is the probability that it has an even number?
   *e. If you draw two cards from the set of 10 cards in part (d), replacing the first before drawing the second, what is the probability that both have even numbers?
   f. For the situation in part (e), what is the probability that the sum of the numbers on the cards is at least 15?

18. Write a program to simulate 200 rolls of a single die, counting how many 1's, 2's, 3's, 4's, 5's, and 6's occur. In addition to printing the counts, use the Asterisks procedure of the previous section (Figure 3-11) to print a graph of the answer. For each outcome, the graph contains a row of asterisks, with one asterisk for each occurrence. Sample output:

```
1 : ******************************
2 : ***********************************
3 : *********************************
4 : *****************************
5 : ***********************************
6 : *********************************
```

19. *a. Write a function with two parameters N and Total. The function should

count how many random numbers in the range 1 to N must be generated to obtain a sum of the numbers generated that is greater than Total.

b. By placing the call to the function in part (a) in a loop that is executed 15,000 times, calculate the average number of random numbers that must be generated in the range 1 to 100 to obtain a sum greater than 500.

20. In this exercise, we describe a technique sometimes known as the "Monte Carlo" method.

a. Consider the following diagram containing a quarter of a circle with a radius 1 and a square with a side 1.

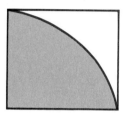

If we randomly dropped a large number of darts onto the figure, we would expect that the following ratio would be approximately true:

$$\frac{\text{Number in quarter circle}}{\text{Total number dropped}} = \frac{\text{Area of quarter circle}}{\text{Area of square}}$$

Since the area of the quarter circle is $\pi/4$ and the area of the square is 1, we get an estimate for π given by

$$\pi = 4\left(\frac{\text{Number in quarter circle}}{\text{Total number dropped}}\right)$$

We can simulate this situation by generating a large number of pairs of number (x,y) in the range from 0 to 1. If $x^2 + y^2 \le 1$, then the point is inside the quarter circle. Write a program to estimate π using this technique. Hint: The Random function used without a parameter will generate a real number between 0 and 1.

b. The idea in part (a) can be extended to other functions. Consider the following diagram.

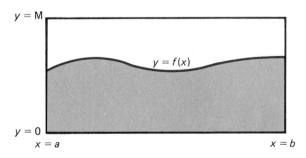

If we generate a large number of random points (x,y) with $a \le x \le b$ and $0 \le y \le M$, we would expect that the ratio below would be true:

$$\frac{\text{number of points with } y \le f(x)}{\text{total number of points}} = \frac{\text{area of shaded portion}}{\text{area of rectangle}}$$

Use this method to approximate the area under the curve $y = x^2$ between 0 and 1. (The exact answer is $\frac{1}{3}$.)

c. Repeat part (b), using $y = 3x^3 - x$ between 1 and 2. (The exact answer is 9.75.)

*21. Write a function to calculate $n!$ for given n. ($n!$ is $n*(n-1)*(n-2)*\cdots*2*1$.) Hint. Finding the product of the first n integers is similar to finding their sum.

22. Write a function that, given an integer N and a real number X, computes X raised to the Nth power by multiplying X by itself the proper number of times. (It should handle the case that N is 0 or a positive number.)

*23. The expression e^X for a given real number X is given by the infinite series

$$1 + X + \frac{X^2}{2} + \frac{X^3}{2 \cdot 3} + \frac{X^4}{2 \cdot 3 \cdot 4} + \cdots +$$

Write a function Exp(X,N) that calculates the sum of the first N terms of this series. Hint: In a "for I := 1 to N do" loop, each term can be calculated from the previous term by multiplying the previous term by X/I.

24. Write a function Exp(X) that calculates the sum of the terms of the series in Exercise 23 up to and including the first term whose value is less than the current value of the sum times 0.00001.

25. The derivative of a function $y = f(x)$ at a point a is given by

$$\lim_{h \to 0} \frac{f(a + h) - f(a)}{h}$$

To demonstrate the limit process, some calculus textbooks print tables showing the value of the expression

$$\frac{f(a + h) - f(a)}{h}$$

for values of h getting closer and closer to 0. Write a program to generate such a table for $h = \frac{1}{2^n}$, $n = 1, \ldots, 14$ and for $h = -\frac{1}{2^n}$, $n = 1, \ldots, 14$. Use these functions and points.

a. $y = x^2$, $a = 2$ (the limit is 4)
b. $y = \sqrt{x}$, $a = 16$ (the limit is $\frac{1}{8}$)
c. $y = \frac{1}{x}$, $a = 3$ (the limit is $-\frac{1}{9}$)

26. The area under a positive curve can be approximated by finding the areas of a collection of rectangles. Refer to the diagram below.

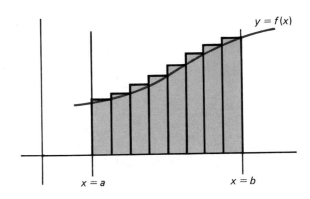

If we divide the region from a to b into n subintervals, then the area of the first rectangle is $hf(a + h)$, where $h = \frac{b-a}{n}$. The area of the second rectangle is $hf(a + 2h)$, the area of the third is $hf(a + 3h)$, and so on.

Use this idea to write a program which approximates the area under the curve $y = x^2 - 5$ between $x = 3$ and $x = 10$. Divide the interval into $n = 28$ regions. Repeat the process with $n = 56$, and with $n = 224$. (The actual area is $289\frac{1}{3}$.)

27. Give test plans for the following exercises:
  *a. Exercise 3(a)   *b. Exercise 3(c)
   c. Exercise 5   d. Exercise 7
   e. Exercise 8   f. Exercise 9
  *g. Exercise 10   *h. Exercise 21
   i. Exercise 22   j. Exercise 23

Exercises 28 to 32 deal with integer arrays as described in the previous section.

*28. Modify the function ArraySum (Figure 3-21) to use a separate variable to keep track of the actual size. That is, there are two parameters: the array and the actual size, N. Use a count-control loop.

*29. For an array that uses a −Maxint delimiter to indicate the actual size, write a segment of code to calculate the actual size as the variable N. For the array

$$12, \quad 4, \quad -6, \quad -\text{Maxint}, \quad . \quad . \quad .$$

the answer is 3.

*30. For an array without a delimiter and the size as a variable N, write code to place a −Maxint delimiter in the array.

31. For each of the following, solve the problem twice by using the delimiter approach and the approach with a separate "size" variable.
  *a. Find the largest value in an array.
  *b. Count the even numbers in an array.
   c. Read an array, with input terminated by a dummy entry of −Maxint.
   d. Print an array, printing one number per line.

32. Give test plans for the following:
  *a. Exercise 29   *b. Exercise 30
   c. Exercise 31(a) *d. Exercise 31(b)
   e. Exercise 31(c)   f. Exercise 31(d)

3.4
NESTED LOOPS AND COMPLEX LOOP TERMINATION

Many problems require combinations of the techniques discussed in Sections 3-1 to 3-3. Frequently, loops must be contained within other loops, leading to **nested loops**. In addition, the terminating conditions for loops frequently involve more than one condition. This is especially true for loops that perform **searches**. These topics will be discussed in this section, along with the important topic of validating user input.

NESTED LOOPS

Just as decisions can be nested, so also loops can be nested. As an example, consider the following program segment:

```
for Row := 1 to 5 do
   begin
```

```
        for Seat := 1 to 8 do
          begin
            Writeln('Row #', Row:1, '  Seat #', Seat:1)
          end   {for Seat loop}
      end   {for Row loop}
```

The variable Row successively takes on the values 1, 2, 3, 4, and 5. For each value of Row, the inner for loop is executed, causing Seat to take on the values 1, 2, 3, 4, 5, 6, 7, and 8. Thus, the output for this segment begins with these lines:

```
              Row #1   Seat #1
              Row #1   Seat #2
              Row #1   Seat #3
              Row #1   Seat #4
              Row #1   Seat #5
              Row #1   Seat #6
              Row #1   Seat #7
              Row #1   Seat #8
              Row #2   Seat #1
              . . . . . .
```

As a second example, consider this segment that, 5 times in a row, counts the number of rolls of the dice it takes to obtain a 7.

```
      for I := 1 to 5 do
        begin
          Count := 0;

          repeat
            Roll := RollOfDice;
            Count := Count + 1
          until Roll = 7;

          Writeln('A 7 was rolled on roll #', Count:1)
        end;   {for}
```

This illustrates that a repeat–until loop can be one of the steps within a for loop. Conversely, consider this example:

```
      repeat
        Count := 0;

        for I := 1 to 100 do
          begin
            Roll := RollOfDice;
            if Roll = 2 then Count := Count + 1
          end;   {for}

        Writeln('There were ', Count:1, ' two''s rolled')
      until Count >= 3
```

This segment, which contains a for loop nested in a repeat loop, counts how many of 100 rolls of the dice are 2's. It continues to do so until a count of at least 3 occurs.

COMMENTS   *1.* We follow our usual indentation pattern for loops by indenting the body of each loop.

2. The terms **inner loop** and **outer loop** are frequently used in describing nested loops. In the previous example, the for loop is the inner loop and the repeat loop is the outer loop.

3. Loops can be nested to any depth. However, we should limit the levels of nesting (of both loops and decisions) to a reasonable number. Subprograms can be useful in this regard.

4. Loops can be nested; they may not overlap. The inner loop must be completely contained within the outer loop.

Nested loops occur quite naturally during the program design process. It is not necessary when beginning the design of a program to know at the outset that nested loops will be involved. For example, suppose we wish to print all the divisors of a series of input numbers. We might begin with an algorithm something like this:

```
print instructions
repeat these steps until the user enters a terminal value (≤0)
      issue a prompt
      read N
      print the divisors of N (not done if N is the terminal value)
print a closing message
```

Now, to print all the divisors of N will involve a count-controlled loop that, for each number I ranging from 1 to N, checks to see if I is a divisor of N. We will therefore have a for loop nested within a repeat loop.

COMMENT Alternatively, we could use a procedure to print the divisors. The loop for printing would be in the procedure rather than nested within the main program's loop.

There is one situation, however, where we can immediately realize that nested loops can be appropriate. This situation is illustrated by the following example. Suppose that the user wishes to obtain a listing of the total sales for a number of employees. To do so, the user inputs the employee name, followed by a list of sales amounts terminated by a 0. Thus, the input will follow this pattern:

```
employee name
sales amount
......
terminal amount of 0
next employee name
sales amount
......
terminal amount of 0
......
```

The data itself consists of repetitions of repetitions. The set of data for an employee is repeated, and the sales figures are repeated within each set of employee data. As a general rule, we can state:

> Nested repetitions of data imply nested loops in the program.

The program in Figure 3-22 reads the data and prints a report on the printer as well as at the terminal. It includes a count of the employees processed. Notice the placement of initialization and print steps for the employee counter and for the sales amount accumulator. The counter is initialized once, before the outermost loop (the repeat loop), and is printed after this same loop. The accumulator, on the other hand, is initialized within the repeat loop, but prior to the while loop, and is printed following the while loop. This is appropriate because this total should be reinitialized to 0 for each new employee, and it should be printed for each employee.

```
program ReadSales(Input, Output);
{
      Written by:  XXXXXXXX  XX/XX/XX
          Purpose:  To read and total a number of sales for a number of
                    employees. The program illustrates the maxim:
                    nested repetitions of data imply nested loops.
   Procedures used:  Instructions, to print instructions.
                    Header, to print headings.
}
const
   EndOfData = 0;                  { loop control }

var
   Name   : string[20];          { employee name, input }
   Sales  : real;                { sales amount, input }
   Total  : real;                { total sales, calculated }
   Answer : char;                { continue? }
   Count  : integer;             { number of employees }

procedure Instructions; begin {stub} end;

procedure Header;
begin  {Header - stub version}
   Writeln(Lst, ' ':10, 'Name', ' ':12, 'Total sales');
   Writeln(Lst, ' ':10, '----', ' ':12, '----- -----')
end;  {Header}

begin {ReadSales}

{*** Initialize and print instructions and headings. }

   Count := 0;
   Instructions;
   Header;

{*** Read name. }
```

Figure 3-22   Counting and Accumulation with Nested Loops (Continued)

```
      repeat
        Write('Enter name: ');
        Readln(Name);
        Count := Count + 1;

  {*** Read and total sales figures. }

        Total := 0;
        Write('Sales: ');
        Readln(Sales);

        while Sales <> 0 do
          begin
            Total := Total + Sales;
            Write('Sales: ');
            Readln(Sales)
          end;   {while}

  {*** Print total, ask user if done. }

        Writeln('The total is ', Total:1:2);
        Writeln(Lst, Name:20, Total:10:2);
        Writeln;
        Write('Any more? ');
        Readln(Answer)
      until not (Answer in ['Y', 'y']);

  {*** Print summary for entire set of data and quit.}

      Writeln;
      Writeln('There were ', Count:1, ' employees.');
      Writeln(Lst);
      Writeln(Lst, 'There were ', Count:1, ' employees.');
      Writeln;
      Writeln('ReadSales program terminating.')
    end.
```

SAMPLE INPUT AND OUTPUT

Terminal

```
Enter name: Bob Ransome
Sales: 100
Sales: 53.40
Sales: 125.07
Sales: 0
The total is 278.47

Any more? y
Enter name: Joe Hocking
Sales: 0
The total is 0.00

Any more? Y
Enter name: Mary Wilkinson
```

Figure 3-22   Counting and Accumulation with Nested Loops (Continued)

```
Sales: 450
Sales: 0
The total is 450.00

Any more? n

There were 3 employees.

ReadSales program terminating.
```

Printer

```
        Name              Total sales
        ----              ----- -----
     Bob Ransome          278.47
     Joe Hocking            0.00
   Mary Wilkinson         450.00
```

Figure 3-22 Counting and Accumulation with Nested Loops

COMMENT As you can see from the printer output, some adjustment in the spacing is needed to achieve better alignment. After this adjustment, the Header procedure would no longer be a stub.

The design process for a program involving nested loops is similar to that described in the previous section for single loops. As we have indicated, we may or may not immediately realize that nested loops are needed. However, once we do realize this, we should plan each loop using our usual loop design methods.

In considering the placement of initialization and finalization steps, it may be helpful to do two things: (1) identify the primary "purpose" of each loop and (2) visualize the loops as dividing the program into segments. For example, for the program of Figure 3-22, we would have

outer loop beginning (one pass = 1 employee)

inner loop beginning (one pass = 1 sale)

inner loop end

outer loop end

We can then summarize as shown:

Region Number	Summary
1	Steps done once prior to handling all the employees
2	Steps done once for each employee, prior to handling the employee's sales
3	Steps done once for each sale
4	Steps done once for each employee after the employee's sales
5	Steps done once after all employees are processed

□
MORE THAN ONE TERMINATION CONDITION

For some loops, there is more than one possible condition for terminating the repetition. These loops are designed in much the same way as the simpler loops with a single termination condition. We simply use the Boolean operators "and" and "or" to write a compound condition for loop continuation (for a while loop) or termination (for a repeat loop). For example, the segment of code given below simulates a game of chance with these rules: Generate a random integer from 1 to 25. If the number is 1, 2, 3, or 4, you win $5, otherwise you lose $1. Starting with $20, we play the game until we either go broke or double our money.

```
Money := 20;

repeat
  Number := Random(25) + 1;   {random number between 1 and 25}
  if Number < 5 then
    Money := Money + 5
  else
    Money := Money - 1
until (Money = 0) or (Money >= 40);

if Money = 0 then
  Writeln('You went broke')
else
  Writeln('You doubled your money to ', Money:1)
```

COMMENT
It may be useful in working with loops using multiple-termination conditions to use an **assertion** (a Boolean expression known to be true) to verbalize the situation on leaving the loop. In our example, we might insert the comment:

```
{Either Money is $0 or it is at least $40}
```

right after the loop.

This assertion can help us decide what should be done next (frequently a decision structure).

To illustrate this comment, consider the following slightly modified segment, which limits play to 30 rolls:

```
NRolls := 0;
Money := 20;
```

```
repeat
  Number := Random(25) + 1;
  NRolls := NRolls + 1;
  if Number < 5 then
    Money := Money + 5
  else
    Money := Money - 1
until (Money = 0) or (Money >= 40) or (NRolls = 30);

{Either Money = $0, or Money >= $40, or NRolls = 30}

if Money = 0 then
  Writeln('You went broke')
else if Money >= 40 then
  Writeln('You doubled your money to ', Money:1)
else
  Writeln('You neither went broke nor doubled your money. ',
          'You have ', Money:1)
```

In an "or" condition, it is possible that more than one of the individual conditions is true. This leads to a defensive programming tip:

Be careful in writing decision structures after loops with compound termination conditions. More than one part of the condition can be true.

In our example, if we wrote

```
if NRolls = 30 then
  Writeln('You neither went broke nor doubled your money. ',
          'You have ', Money:1)
else if Money = 0 then
  Writeln('You went broke')
else
  Writeln('You doubled your money to ', Money:1)
```

we would be incorrect. (Why?)

In addition, we must take special care to avoid some pitfalls described earlier. We must make sure, in particular, that:

1. The condition used for loop control makes sense on the first pass through the loop

2. The condition makes sense on the last pass (that is, when the loop terminates)

3. We are not "off by ½."

We illustrate these ideas with two examples.

For the first, let us simulate a game of chance in which we roll a pair of dice. The object of this game is to roll 10 consecutive numbers greater than 3. If we succeed we win, and if we fail we lose.

At first glance this looks like it might be a count-controlled loop, however, the game should terminate immediately if a 2 or a 3 is rolled. Since the Pascal for loop is designed to execute precisely the number of times indicated, it will not be appropriate. We will, therefore, write code to explicitly count the rolls using a variable RollCount. We will initialize this to 1, which is consistent with the semantics of the for loop "for RollCount := 1 to 10 do . . . ." The loop should terminate when RollCount indicates that we have rolled 10 rolls or when a 2 or 3 is rolled, whichever occurs first.

Because we must roll the dice to check for a 2 or 3, we use a repeat–until loop. A Pascal segment is given in the first half of Figure 3-23. However, it has some problems. Before you read on, and without looking at the second half of the figure, try to locate the bugs.

As the first half of the figure stands, the loop is off by 1 and also off by ½. If we never roll a 2 or 3, the loop executes only nine times. If we do roll a 2 or a 3, the RollCount reported will be one greater than the roll on which it actually occurred. With the loop the way we have written it, RollCount keeps track of which pass of the loop is occurring, and the step which adds 1 is getting ready for the next pass. This step should be omitted if a roll of 2 or 3 has occurred. The second half of the figure illustrates one correct solution. Other possible approaches, and other issues related to this example, are explored in the exercises.

FAULTY PASCAL CODE

```
RollCount := 1;

repeat
   Roll := RollOfDice;
   RollCount := RollCount + 1
until (Roll <= 3) or (RollCount = 10);

if Roll <= 3 then
   Writeln('You lost with a ', Roll:1, ' on try #', RollCount:1)
else
   Writeln('Congratulations, you win.')
```

CORRECTED CODE

```
RollCount := 1;

repeat
   Roll := RollOfDice;
   if Roll > 3 then
     RollCount := RollCount + 1
until (Roll <= 3) or (RollCount > 10);

if Roll <= 3 then
   Writeln('You lost with a ', Roll:1, ' on try #', RollCount:1)
else
   Writeln('Congratulations, you win.')
```

Figure 3-23 Wrong and Right Way to Exit a Loop

For the second example, we will write Pascal code that works with an array of integers named Nums. As in our previous array example, we will assume that values have been read into the array. Moreover, we will assume that the actual size is indicated by a variable rather than by using the delimiter method. Thus, we assume that a variable Count contains the number of values read in. For example, Nums might contain the integers

$$3, 15, -101, 214, -66, 14$$

with Count having the value 6.

We can use the following program segment to print the values in the array:

```
for I := 1 to Count do
   begin
      Writeln(Nums[I])
   end    {for}
```

This works even if Count has the value 0 due to the semantics of the Pascal for loop. In our example, we will *not* assume that Count is positive.

What we wish to do in this example is to modify the program segment to print only up to the first negative value in the array. For the array values given above, only the 3 and the 15 would be printed. Because the loop should terminate (possibly) prior to printing all the values, the for loop is no longer appropriate. However, perhaps we can modify the following equivalent representation of the for loop logic:

```
I := 1;

while I <= Count do
   begin
      Writeln(Nums[I]);
      I := I + 1
   end    {while}
```

Our planning might go something like this: The loop should continue as long as I is less than or equal to Count and Nums[I] is positive . We are tempted to make a simple modification to the while loop, writing

```
while (I <= Count) and (Nums[I] > 0)do . . .
```

To consider whether this is correct, we must look in particular at whether the condition makes sense on the last pass when the loop terminates. For the condition to make sense, both halves must make sense:

```
I <= Count
Nums[I] > 0
```

Now if the loop terminates because it has found a negative value in the array, both parts are fine. However, suppose the loop terminates because it has printed all the array values. In this case, the variable I will have a value one greater than Count, and the reference to Nums[I] will make no sense. For example, if Count is 3, the array contains values Nums[1], Nums[2], and Nums[3]. The reference to Nums[4] in this condition refers to something that does not exist. (This is especially bad if Count is equal to the declared size of the array. Then Nums[I] would refer to a location beyond the end of the array. This error might or might not be detected by the compiler; see Chapter 6 for details.)

```
I := 1;
MoreToPrint := true;

while (I <= Count) and MoreToPrint do
  begin
    if Nums[I] < 0 then
      MoreToPrint := false
    else
      begin
        Writeln(Nums[I]);
        I := I + 1
      end {if}
  end  {while}
```

Figure 3-24   Avoiding a Pitfall with Arrays

One way to resolve this problem is illustrated in Figure 3-24. This is a well-known pitfall in dealing with arrays; you should study carefully the solution given in the figure. (In the chapter on arrays we will have more to say about this pitfall.)

The examples just given are typical of many problems in which loops have more than one termination condition. In each example, we could view the loop as performing a process that would either succeed or fail. For example:

Success	Failure
Doubling money	Going broke
Rolling 10 times	Getting a 2 or 3 before 10 rolls
Printing the entire array	Reaching a negative value

The broad class of **searching algorithms** has this same "succeed or fail" characteristic. We will be studying this class in some detail in Chapter 5 (in connection with files) and in Chapter 6 (in connection with arrays). In a searching algorithm, we have this general form:

repeat the steps of a loop:
    (if we find what we are searching for, terminate the loop)
    (if we reach the end of the data without finding it,
        terminate the loop)

Observe that we may not examine all the data. As soon as we find the desired item, we want to terminate. One common approach is to use a flag (a Boolean variable) to cause this termination to occur, as we did in the array printing example of Figure 3-24.

Another "typical" feature of this type of program is that the loop is followed by a decision structure. This decision structure is used to choose an action based on which individual condition caused the loop to terminate.

□ Perhaps you have heard the phrase "garbage in, garbage out." This is a rather cynical reaction to shortcomings that are sometimes found in programs. The phrase indicates that if you supply the program with invalid data, you may very well get answers that are not to be trusted.

Unfortunately, that is an accurate observation for some programs in current use. There are some programs in which no effort is made to see if the data being supplied makes sense. Certainly there is some excuse for this with beginning programmers, and it is not always possible to anticipate every possible error in input. However, we can make an effort to avoid this type of lazy programming.

Already in this text, we have indicated some techniques involved in "**editing**" (or **validating**) the input, that is, making sure that it has an appropriate value. For example, recall Case Study No. 2, which read two numbers and an operation symbol, and applied that operation to the two numbers. In that case study, the program checked user input for two errors: attempting to divide by 0 and entering an invalid operation symbol. In this subsection, we examine some commonly used methods for examining the input as soon as it is read and not proceeding any further unless it is valid. This is not always possible to do: the validity of the data may depend on some calculation not yet performed. However, it is frequently possible.

Consider, for example, the program segment of Figure 3-25, which obtains user input for the variable Score.

```
{*** Read and total scores.}

  Total := 0;
  Number := 0;
  Write('Enter the score (-1 to quit): ');
  Readln(Score);

  while  Score <> -1  do
    begin
      Total := Total + Score;
      Number := Number + 1;
      Write('Enter the score (-1 to quit): ');
      Readln(Score)
    end;   {while}

{*** Calculate and print average.}

  Writeln;
  if  Number > 0   then
    begin
      Average := Total / Number;
      Writeln(Number:1, ' exam scores were processed.');
      Writeln('The average is: ', Average:1:1)
    end
  else
    Writeln('*** No scores were input ***')
```

Figure 3-25 Reading without Data Validation

An algorithm for this program segment might contain a step:

read value for Score

Suppose we replace this algorithm step by

read a valid value for Score

We can view the task of obtaining Score and making sure that it is valid as a subtask. We might choose to write a Pascal procedure to perform the task.

A procedure to read a value for Score might begin by issuing a prompt and reading Score. Then the procedure would check the value read to make sure it was valid. If it was not valid, the procedure should print an error message and read a new value for Score. Notice, moreover, that this new value might also be invalid. Thus, the procedure should continue printing an error message and reading a new value "as long as" the Score is not valid. We have described this rough algorithm:

issue a prompt
read Score
as long as the Score is not valid, do these steps:
    print an error message
    read a new value for Score

A Pascal procedure to accomplish this task is contained in Figure 3-26. It accepts any score greater than or equal to −1 as valid. (A score of −1 is valid because that is the dummy value for the loop.)

```
procedure GetScore(var Score : integer);
{
   Written by:   XXXXXXXX   XX/XX/XX
      Purpose:   To accept a valid score (-1 or higher).
    Parameter:   Score, the score read (passed back to the calling
                 program)
}
begin {GetScore}
  Write('Enter the score (-1 to quit): ');
  Readln(Score);

  while  Score < -1  do
    begin
      Writeln('You entered an invalid score: ', Score:1);
      Writeln('The score must be positive (or -1 to quit)');
      Write('Re-enter the score: ');
      Readln(Score)
    end   {while}

end; {GetScore}
```

Figure 3-26 Data Validation Procedure

This procedure, like some of the procedures developed earlier in this chapter, has a parameter. However, the way it uses its parameter is new. This is our first example of a **var parameter**.

All our previous parameters have been **value parameters**, which means that the calling program passes a value into the submodule (function or procedure). A var (short for "variable") parameter, on the other hand, is used when the submodule is passing information back to the calling program using the parameter. The parameter is "vary-able"; the submodule can modify the value of the parameter. As a result, the calling program must supply a matching variable for the parameter. This matching variable in the calling program will be modified whenever the parameter is modified within the submodule.

If the data is invalid, the GetScore procedure prints the value that the user entered prior to printing an error message. Although this was not required by the problem description (or even the algorithm), it is a good idea.

CAUTION

If a procedure has a *var* parameter, then the statement that invokes that procedure must supply a *variable* to match that parameter. *Constants and expressions cannot match var parameters*. This is one of the important distinctions between value and var parameters.

We now consider what changes would be made to the original program segment as a result of writing this procedure to edit (validate) the input. Figure 3-27 is the revised program segment that now uses the GetScore procedure. The changes are shaded. As far as the calling program segment is concerned, the process of prompting the user, accepting input, checking the input, and persisting until the input is valid is all contained in the one statement

```
GetScore(Score)
```

NOTE   As is frequently the case, the calling module and the submodule use the same name (Score) for the parameter. We remind you, however, that this is not a requirement of the Pascal language. If the person writing the submodule had chosen a different variable name, the program segment would still have worked the same. The parameter correspondence is by position in the list of parameters, not by name.

Note that the keyword "var" in the parameter list is that which determines that the value of the parameter can be changed and passed back to the caller. If the keyword "var" were omitted from the header line of procedure GetScore, then the program would still compile correctly. However, the value of Score in the main program could not be changed by the procedure GetScore, so that Score would have some accidental "random" value that would depend on factors outside of the user's control. A way to avoid this problem is to *test each module*

```
{*** Read and total scores.}

  Total := 0;
  Number := 0;
  GetScore(Score);

  while  Score <> -1  do
    begin
      Total := Total + Score;
      Number := Number + 1;
      GetScore(Score)
    end;   {while}

{*** Calculate and print average.}

  Writeln;
  if  Number > 0  then
    begin
      Average := Total / Number;
      Writeln(Number:1, ' exam scores were processed.');
      Writeln('The average is: ', Average:1:1)
    end
  else
    Writeln('*** No scores were input ***')
```

Figure 3-27   Reading Using the Data Validation Procedure

separately. An independent test of the GetScore procedure would quickly show the effects of the absence of the keyword "var".

We show a sample driver program for the procedure GetScore as Figure 3-28. In this case, we wish to test the procedure to be sure that it handles negative, zero, and positive integers correctly.

```
program Driver(Input, Output);
{
        Written by:  XXXXXXXXX  XX/XX/XX
           Purpose:  To test the GetScore procedure.
   Procedures used:  GetScore, to get a score of -1 or higher.
}
var
  Score      : integer;                    { Valid score from GetScore }
  I          : integer;                    { Loop index }

{procedure GetScore as shown in Figure 3-26 is inserted here}

begin {Driver}

{*** Call GetScore 3 times}
```

Figure 3-28   A Driver for Testing (Continued)

```
      for I := 1 to 3 do
        begin
          Writeln;
          Writeln('GetScore called.');
          GetScore(Score);
          Writeln('Value returned from GetScore: ', Score:1)
        end;

  {*** Print terminating message and stop program.}

      Writeln;
      Writeln('Driver program is terminating.')
    end.
```

SAMPLE INPUT AND OUTPUT

```
GetScore called.
Enter the score (-1 to quit): -5
You entered an invalid score: -5
The score must be positive (or -1 to quit)
Re-enter the score: -2
You entered an invalid score: -2
The score must be positive (or -1 to quit)
Re-enter the score: -1
Value returned from GetScore: -1


GetScore called.
Enter the score (-1 to quit): -2
You entered an invalid score: -2
The score must be positive (or -1 to quit)
Re-enter the score: -2
You entered an invalid score: -2
The score must be positive (or -1 to quit)
Re-enter the score: 23
Value returned from GetScore: 23


GetScore called.
Enter the score (-1 to quit): 15
Value returned from GetScore: 15


Driver program is terminating.
```

Figure 3-28   A Driver for Testing

When we use the driver program to test the GetScore procedure, we precede each call of GetScore with the message "GetScore called." If the program should hang up or abort, we can tell that it happened in that procedure. We also print a message when GetScore returns, and we include the value returned to produce a record of the testing. (The outputs are shaded in the figure.) In the driver, we have called GetScore three times in order to try three different test cases:

> Case 1: −5 (bad input)
> −2 (bad input)
> −1 (good input)

Case 2: −2 (bad input)
         −2 (bad input)
         23 (good input)

Case 3: 15 (good input)

Although this is not an exhaustive test plan, it does have sufficient cases (including the boundary between good and bad input) for us to have a large degree of confidence that the procedure works correctly.

□ **DPT** The DPT subsections of Sections 3-1 to 3-3 should be reviewed. In addition, there are some specific tips relating to the material of this section.

1. Check for initialization and finalization steps. For nested loops, make sure the steps are associated with the correct loop. It can be helpful to verbalize what each pass through the loop accomplishes. For example, in the program of Figure 3-22, each pass through the outer loop processes one employee, and each pass through the inner loop processes one sales amount for the employee. The step to initialize the counter of employees should occur prior to the loop that processes the employees. The step to initialize the sales accumulator should occur for each employee, so it is placed within the outer loop, but before the inner loop.

2. Examine loops with compound ("multiple") conditions for continuation or termination especially carefully. The entire condition should make sense on the first pass and on the last pass. The possibility of being "off by ½" is greater for this type of loop than for those where the condition is a simple condition.

3. Take care in writing decision structures after loops with multiple-termination conditions. Sometimes more than one of the individual conditions can occur during the same pass through the loop. In this case, the order in which the individual conditions are examined can be important.

4. Use a var parameter only if a value is to be passed from the procedure to the calling program using that parameter. Using a var parameter when one is not required can lead to inadvertently modifying a value in the calling program that should not have been modified.

5. Use a var parameter, on the other hand, if appropriate. Failure to do so will prevent the value that is obtained in the subprogram from being passed to the calling program.

6. When a procedure does use a var parameter, the statement that invokes the procedure must use a *variable* to match that parameter.

■■■■■■
REVIEW

Terms and Concepts

nested loop	searching algorithm
searches	editing input
inner loop	validating input
outer loop	var parameter
assertion	value parameter

Pascal syntax

Var parameter form:

```
var list of parameters
```

Var parameter use:
To allow a subprogram to send a value back to the calling program

Program design

1. Nested loops: Each loop is designed in the usual way; each loop is coded in the usual way.

2. Nested data repetitions can imply nested loops are needed.

3. More than one termination condition: Use a compound condition in the while or repeat loop control.

4. Loops with compound termination conditions are frequently followed by a decision structure.

5. General form of algorithm to edit input:

prompt
read data
as long as the data is not valid do the following:
    error message
    prompt for reentering data
    read data

6. General form of search loop:

set flag to indicate not yet found
initialize so first pass examines first item
as long as not yet found and more to examine do:
    examine an item; if it is the one sought, set flag
    to indicate found; if not, move on to the next item

DPT

1. Check the initialization and finalization steps. For nested loops, associate them with the correct loop.

2. For loops with compound termination conditions:
    a. Condition must make sense on the first and last passes.
    b. Do not be off by ½.
    c. Take care in writing a following decision structure.

3. Use a var parameter when, and only when, that parameter is being used to pass back a value to the calling program.

4. Only variables can match var parameters.

5. Test each module separately.

■■■■■■
EXERCISES

*1. For each program segment below, find the output that would be produced.

```
a. for I := 1 to 3 do
     begin
       Sum := 0;
       for J := 1 to 4 do
         Sum := Sum + J;
       Writeln(Sum)
     end
```

```
b. Sum := 0
   for I := 1 to 3 do
      begin
         for J := 1 to 4 do
            Sum := Sum + J;
         Writeln(Sum)
      end
c. J := 1;
   repeat
      I := 1;
      while I <= J - 2 do
         begin
            Writeln(I);
            I := I + 3
         end;
      J := J + I
   until J >= 15
```

2. Using the program of Figure 3-22, what changes would you make for each of the following?

   a. As it stands, the program's printer output is not done well. Change the output to align the columns better and to right-justify the name within its allotted 20 columns.

   *b. How many individual sales did each person have?

   *c. What was the total sales amount for the entire company?

   d. Who had the highest total sales?

   *e. What was the largest individual sales amount for the entire company? Who had it?

   f. How many individuals had no sales?

   g. Among those employees who had at least five individual sales, who had the lowest total?

3. a. For the program segment of Figure 3-23, write a correct segment that uses a while loop with RollCount initialized to 1.

   b. Following the lead of a typical for loop, we initialized RollCount to 1 in Figure 3-23. Another possibility is to initialize to 0. Write a correct segment that does so by using either a while or a repeat loop.

   c. What other corrections can fix the problems of the faulty code?

*4. Write a complete Pascal program to produce the output:

```
Row 1   Seat 1  _____
        Seat 2  _____
                        . . . .
        Seat 7  _____
Row 2   Seat 1  _____
        Seat 2  _____
                        . . . .
        Seat 7  _____
                        . . . .
Row 5   Seat 1  _____
        Seat 2  _____
                        . . . .
        Seat 7  _____
```

*5. Simulate an election in which candidate A is expected to receive 60 percent of the vote and candidate B 40 percent. There are 30,000 votes, and your loop should simulate each vote. Hint: Generate a random number from 1 to 10, with 1 to 6 indicating a vote for A and 7 to 10 a vote for B.

Your program should answer three questions: How many times in the counting was the vote tied? What was the last time the vote was tied? What was the largest lead candidate A ever had? Output might be similar to this:

```
The vote was tied 100 times.
The last tie occurred when counting the 917th ballot.
At ballot 23417 A was ahead by 7913 votes, his largest
lead.
```

6. *a. Write a program that reads a beginning balance, an interest rate, and an ending balance. It should print the amount in a savings account at the end of each year until the current balance exceeds the ending balance which was read. Interest for each year is calculated by multiplying the interest rate by the current balance.
   b. Modify part (a) to allow a deposit to be made at the end of each year.
   c. Modify part (a) to place an asterisk in the left margin for the first year (if any) in which the current balance exceeds twice the original balance.
   d. Modify part (a) to print, for each year, the beginning balance and the ending balance for that year on a single line.

7. a. Write a program segment that simulates rolling a pair of dice until a 5, 6, or 7 is rolled. If it took an even number of rolls and a 5 or 7 occurred, it should print the message "you win," otherwise it should print the message "you lose."
   *b. Write a program segment that repeats the action for part (a) a total of 100 times. Instead of printing "you win" and "you lose", it should count and print the number of wins and losses.

8. A deposit of $10,000 is compounded annually at 8 percent. At the end of each year, after the interest has been added, $1000 is to be withdrawn from the account.

   a. Write a program that prints the balance in the account every year up to, but not including, the year in which $1000 cannot be withdrawn.
   b. Modify the program to show how many $1000 withdrawals were made and the amount that remains the final year.

9. Write procedures to input each of the following lists of variables with the indicated restrictions. For this exercise, the error message handling can simply print a single error message "invalid data."

   a. Name and sex code, where the sex code must be either "M" or "F".
   *b. Four test scores, each of which must be in the range 0 to 100, inclusive.
   c. A single integer that must be larger than 2 and no more than 10,000.
   d. Two integers that must both be positive and even.
   e. A color code (three characters) that must be either "RED", "GRE", "BLU", "BLA", "WHI", or "ORA".

*10. Modify the procedures in Exercises 9(b) and 9(d) to have the error message tell exactly what is wrong with the input data.

11. a. Write a program that generates a random number in the range 1 to 1000 and then asks the user to guess the number. The program should terminate with a message telling how many tries it took the user to guess the number. For incorrect guesses, it should print the messages "too high" or "too low."

b. Modify the program to allow no more than seven guesses.

*12. By thinking about your guessing strategy for Exercise 11, write a program in which the computer tries to guess the number the user is thinking of. Hint: The program might want to keep track of a range in which it knows the answer lies.

13. For each number from 1 to 200, print a list of its divisors in a form similar to this:

```
Divisors of 1:    1

Divisors of 2:    1
                  2

Divisors of 3:    1
                  3

Divisors of 4:    1
                  2
                  4

           . . . .
```

14. Suppose we generate random numbers in the range from 1 to 10. On the average, how many numbers would have to be generated until two consecutive numbers are the same? To answer the question, write a program to perform the experiment 1000 times.

*15. A person offers you a game of chance that involves rolling a pair of dice until either 2, 7, or 11 comes up. If 2 or 11 comes up, you win $5, otherwise you lose $2. Should you play the game (assuming you are a betting person in the first place)? To answer the question, write a program to play the game 1000 times.

16. Some state lotteries operate on the following principle: You bet $1, choose a number in the range 0 to 999, and win $500 if your number is drawn in the lottery. A person described a sure-fire system to win: Bet on the same number every day, eventually it's bound to turn up. This exercise explores the wisdom of that system.

a. Assume that the person has $1500 with which to play the lottery 300 times a year for 5 years (50 weeks a year, 6 days a week). Write a program to allow the user to choose his number, then simulate 5 years of play. At the end of the simulated 5 years, tell the person how much of the original $1500 is left.

b. Suppose 1000 people all tried this system. What would be the average amount left after the 5 years? To answer the question, write a program to simulate the 5 years of play 1000 times using a single chosen number.

c. Modify part (b) to simulate each of the 1000 people choosing a different number to play for the 5 years.

17. Suppose that 5000 people all decide to play the daily number lottery game until they either go broke or win once. Each person starts with $1000. Based on a simulation of the situation, answer these questions: What percentage will go broke? What percentage will quit with more than $1000? What percentage will quit with between 0 and $1000? (See Exercise 16 for a description of the lottery game.)

*18. Modify the procedure MatchRoll of Figure 3-20 so that if a roll of the dice (after the first roll) comes up with either a match of the goal or the value of 7, then the loop will terminate. The program should print the message "you win" if the goal was matched or "you lose" if a 7 was rolled. (If the first roll of the dice comes up with a 7, then roll for another point.) (Hint: Use another repeat–until loop for the rolling of the point and change the condition of the original repeat–until loop.)

19. Write a program to simulate a simplified Game of Craps. The simplified rules of the game are as follows:

   a. Roll the dice for a first time. If the roll is a 7 or 11, then you win; if the roll is a 2 or 12, then you lose; otherwise, the point is equal to the roll.
   b. If you have a point, then roll the dice repeatedly until you match the point (which makes you a winner) or you roll a 7 (which makes you a loser).

20. Use the program from Exercise 19 to write another program that simulates the running of 100 games of craps. Instead of printing whether you are a winner or loser, use variables Wins and Losses to count the number of times that you win and lose. Ask someone who knows some probability theory (or a gambler) what the odds of winning at Craps are. Compare the results from the program with the theoretical odds.

21. A given real function Approx(X) computes an approximation to the answer to some problem, starting with an initial approximation X. For example, if we write

   XNew := Approx(XOld)

   then XNew is a new approximation that is hopefully better than the previous approximation XOld.

   Write a loop to compute a series of approximations starting with an initial value XOld equal to 1.0. The loop should compute XNew := Approx(XOld) and then replace XOld by XNew before redoing the calculation. The loop should terminate when either

   $$\left| \frac{XNew - XOld}{XNew} \right| < 1.0 \times 10^{-4}$$

   or when 50 iterations of the loop have been completed. Print a message showing which occurred and the latest value of XNew.

22. Write a program for each of the following situations:
   *a. Each record has a beginning balance and an interest rate. The interest is compounded annually: the balance after one year is the original balance plus the interest for that year, the interest for the second year is based on this new balance, and so on. Write a program that, for each record, will show how many years it takes for the balance in the account to be more than twice the starting balance.
   b. The setup is the same as for part (a). However, for each record, the algorithm should print out a table showing the year number, the beginning balance for that year, the interest for the year, and the ending balance for the year up through and including the year in which the balance exceeds twice the starting balance. Print one new page per record.
   c. Modify part (b) so that it does not print a line of information for the final year, when the balance goes over twice the starting balance.

d. Repeat part (a), but with no data records. Instead, use a beginning balance of $1000.00 and interest rates of 4 to 20 percent in steps of 0.25 percent, that is, 4 percent, 4.25 percent, 4.5 percent, etc.)

23. Find and print the smallest divisor of each odd number from 3 to 201.

24. The input data consist of repetitions of this pattern:

> account record for a checking account
> 0 or more transaction records for this account
> terminal transaction record (code "L")

For each account, generate output similar to that illustrated in Exercise 10 of Section 3.1.

Then modify the program to do the following for each account:
a. Count the checks and deposits.
b. Determine the lowest and highest balance.
c. Calculate the average check amount.
d. Calculate the service charge for the month. The first record of each group will contain an account type (R, S, or V). For regular (R) accounts, the service charge is $3.00 unless the minimum balance is at or above $750, in which case it is 0. For special (S) accounts, the charge is $0.20 per check. For VIP (V) accounts, the charge is based on the average of the minimum and maximum balances. If this is less than $500, there is a $7.00 charge; $500 to $1,000, a $5.00 charge; over $1,000, free.

25. Using the Random function to simulate the throw of a pair of dice, write programs for the following:
*a. Simulate an experiment in which we roll the dice once, then attempt to match that number on future rolls. If we succeed in five or fewer rolls, print how many rolls it took, otherwise print a message reporting failure.
b. Write a program to repeat the experiment of part (a) 10,000 times, reporting the percentage of successes and the average number of rolls for the successes. For example, the output might be:

```
Succeeded 75% of the time, with 3.72 average rolls
for each successful experiment.
```

c. Simulate a game in which two players will roll dice. Player A starts with $15 and player B with $23. When they roll, the player with the higher number wins $1. They agree to go until one or the other is broke or 100 rolls, whichever occurs first. Print an appropriate message at the end.
d. Place the game in part (c) in a loop to simulate it a number of times in order to answer the question: Is the game fair?

26. To see if a number $N (\geq 2)$ is prime, it suffices to check for divisors in the range from 2 to $\sqrt{N}$. If no divisors are found, then N is prime. Using this fact, write a Boolean function which tells if a number is prime or not.

27. For a function $y = f(x)$, finding a root for the function means finding a value x that yields $y = 0$. For many functions (the continuous functions), the following is true: if $f(a)$ and $f(b)$ have different signs, then there must be at least one root between a and b.

One way to approximate that root is by the *bisection method*, described as follows: Let m be the midpoint of the interval from a to b. If $f(m) = 0$, then you have found a root, so quit. If $f(a)$ and $f(m)$ have opposite signs, there must be a root between a and m; if not, there must be a root between m and b. In either case, you can repeat this process with one or the other subinterval. Since the subintervals will get smaller as you proceed, you will be getting closer and closer to the root. Quit after some predetermined number of passes.

Write a program which uses this method to approximate the root of $y = x^3 + 4.5x^2 - 0.19x - 0.14$ that lies between 0 and 1. Stop after 30 iterations and use m as the approximation, unless a root is found before 30 iterations have occurred.

28. a. Write a program to simulate a drunk attempting to cross a footbridge with no railing. See the figure. Label the squares on the bridge as illustrated by the examples.

Assume that the drunk is equally likely to stagger left, right, forward, or backward. Print an indication of the location after each stagger, and a message at the end: "backed off the bridge," "fell in the water," or "made it across."

b. Put part (a) in a loop which executes 1000 times. Replace the prints by counting steps. Tell how many times each of the three possible outcomes occurred.

c. Repeat part (a) and (b) with the probability of staggering forward 0.4, staggering left or right 0.25, and staggering backward 0.1, Hint: Generate a random number from 1 to 20, with 1 to 8 representing forward, 9 to 13 left, 14 to 18 right, and 19 to 20 back.

29. Give test plans for the following:

a. Exercise 2(c)
c. Exercise 6(c)
e. Exercise 9(c)
*g. Exercise 24, without modifications

*b. Exercise 6(a)
*d. Exercise 9(b)
f. Exercise 12
h. Exercise 24, with parts (a) to (d)

Exercises 30 to 34 refer to integer arrays as discussed in Section 3-2.

*30. Write a program to read an array of 10 integers and to print the first integer that is greater than or equal to the average of the 10 numbers. Hint: After you calculate the average of the numbers, use a repeat–until loop to search the array.

31. Repeat Exercise 30 using a while loop.

32. Should you repeat Exercise 30 using a count-control (for) loop?

33. Write a program to read an array of an unknown number of positive integers (terminated by a 0) and to print the *position* and the value of the first integer that is greater than or equal to the average of the numbers that are input.

34. Put the steps of Exercise 30 in a loop, and terminate by asking the user if the steps are to be run through again.

3-5 ANTIBUGGING, DEBUGGING, AND TESTING

Many sections of a textbook represent material to be mastered, perhaps through memorization, preferably through concentrated practice and understanding. Many sections of this book fall in that category. For example, you should come to thoroughly understand counting applications; if you are asked to do any problem that involves counting, the techniques involved should be fairly automatic.

This section has a somewhat different flavor. In it we attempt to gather together some ideas that will aid you in writing correct programs and in feeling confident that they are correct. The section does not cover any new algorithmic techniques as such. We will not be learning how to search through a file or how to find the largest of a set of numbers. It does contain some techniques and ideas that can form a part of your program development style no matter what the specific program is designed to accomplish.

In some of your early programs, the program logic was relatively simple. On the other hand, all the rules about how to write the Pascal statements were new and perhaps confusing. As a result, your programs may have generated many "compiler" error messages. (This type of error includes, for example, such things as forgetting the final parenthesis in a Writeln statement, leaving out a semicolon, or misspelling the word "integer" in a declaration.) It is possible that once you got past the list of errors generated by the compiler and your misunderstandings about the Pascal language, your programs ran correctly.

By this time, on the other hand, your programs are becoming more complex, but you are getting used to the Pascal language. It is possible that you are able to resolve compiler-generated errors with little difficulty. However, you may be discovering that even with "no errors" (that is, no compiler-detected errors), the program just is not doing what it should. In the first subsection, we discuss antibugging and debugging, two related techniques that seek to avoid this situation or to allow you to correct this situation as easily as possible.

The second subsection is on program testing. We have included sections on this topic from time to time in the text, and we will continue to do so. Here we attempt to pull together some of the ideas into a single summary discussion of program testing.

We begin with two related concepts: antibugging and debugging. Both terms come from the common use of the word **bug** to describe an error in a computer program. They tend to relate to the types of errors that occur after you have obtained a "clean compile." Errors that the compiler detects are not the primary subject of this section. Those errors can generally be fixed by careful examination of the subject line of code, comparing it to the required syntax (form) for that type of statement. The errors we are discussing are the more subtle errors, which frequently require more work to uncover.

The purpose of **antibugging** is to avoid bugs, and the purpose of **debugging** is to help you uncover and remove those bugs that do occur. The two concepts are closely related. Of course, if the antibugging is done sufficiently well, then no debugging is necessary. In a way, debugging can be thought of as adding more antibugging to the system to flush out those bugs that the original antibugging was not sufficient to prevent.

We will cover these concepts by presenting a list of ideas that can be useful either in antibugging or in debugging. Where it is appropriate, we will indicate differences between using the ideas for antibugging and using them for debugging. Following the list, we discuss a few issues that arise when using these ideas.

1. Awareness of pitfalls. This is emphasized throughout the text, especially in the DPT subsections. By being aware of what some common errors are, we can avoid making those errors. This is a form of antibugging. On the other hand, if errors do occur, we can review the known pitfalls to see if we have made any of the common errors and to see if the particular pitfall accounts for the observed behavior of the program. This is a form of debugging.

2. Hand-tracing. This refers to "playing computer" and executing the algorithm or program by hand.

Deciding on the data to hand-trace is in some ways similar to deciding on test data. We want to use that data which is most likely to uncover any errors, just as we do in testing.

It is sometimes useful to hand-trace a slightly modified form of an algorithm. For example, if an output table is to contain 40 lines per page, it could take a long time to hand-trace sufficiently to make sure that exactly 40 lines are printed prior to moving to a new page. We might want to write and hand-trace the same program modified to print three lines per page. If the modified program works correctly, we can have some assurance that the original program will also work.

3. Echo printing of input. Sometimes a program appears to be performing calculations incorrectly when actually it is the input of the data that is at fault. As a simple example, we might have this:

```
Write('Enter pay rate and hours worked: ');
Readln(Hours, Rate)
```

The user who, in response to the prompt, types a line containing 5.50 and 40 will not realize that the program interprets this as 5.5 hours at $40 an hour.

To avoid this type of problem, we could always echo print all input to the program. This would be antibugging. Alternatively, we could insert the echo prints when errors do occur. This would be debugging.

4. Edit (validate) input. This topic was discussed in Section 3-4. If we check all input for correctness and reasonableness, we can avoid many problems. For example, the error described in the previous paragraph would be uncovered by an input procedure that made sure that the pay rate was in the expected range.

5. Diagnostic prints (trace prints). This idea expands upon the idea of echo printing the input. **Trace prints** are print statements that trace the execution of the program. A few examples are as follows:

(a) If the program does many complex calculations, it might be desirable to print the partial answers as they are calculated. For example, in a function that calculates the total taxes for an individual, each specific tax could be printed as soon as it is calculated. The print statement could use a variable name, as in

```
Writeln('SocSec = ', SocSec:1:2)
```

or a more meaningful message as in

```
Writeln('Social security withheld = ', SocSec:1:2)
```

Which you use is up to you; the output from these print statements will not be seen by the final user of the program.

(b) Trace prints can be useful in examining the progress of a loop. For example, in Figure 3-19, we wrote a function to calculate the number of divisors of a given integer. At the bottom of the loop in that function, we might print Number, Potential, Number mod Potential, and Counter to verify that the count is occurring properly. Similarly, a program to locate a particular name in a file might print each name that it reads within the search loop.

(c) Trace prints are frequently used in programs that involve a number of subprograms. They might consist of a print statement at the beginning of each subprogram and one at the end of each. The one at the beginning might print the message "Entering subprogram xxxxx," where xxxxx is the subprogram name. This print might also print the value of the parameters. (This is similar to echo printing all user input.) The print statement at the end could print the message "Leaving subprogram xxxxx" and again print the parameters.

For the trace prints to aid our error detection, we would compare the output to that we expect to see. This implies that we are hand-tracing the program or algorithm to determine what to expect. By seeing exactly where the output begins to differ from what we expect, we can focus our efforts on the portion of the program that is causing the error.

The term **diagnostic prints**, which is frequently used to describe trace prints, conveys the idea of using these prints as a debugging tool to "diagnose" errors. Many programmers, however, do not wait until errors occur; they routinely include trace prints in all their programs.

NOTE   Programs that involve random numbers may need trace prints even to know if the answer is correct. For example, if the program is supposed to count the number of 7's rolled in a dice simulation, we should print each dice roll to check the answer.

(Of course, we might temporarily modify the program to perform the simulation only 10 to 20 times rather than 12,000 times.)

The various prints (echo prints of input and trace prints) raise an important issue. There can very well be differences between the program during development and the program as delivered. The extra prints are useful in uncovering and fixing bugs, but the person who is running the finished program certainly does not want to see them. This person is interested only in the final answer, not in all the details of how the program reached that answer. Thus, the final version must not print the trace messages.

There are several ways to remove the extra print statements. The simplest is to delete them. However, this has the disadvantage that if they are needed later (for example, when modifications are made to the program), they must be done over. Another alternative frequently used is to "comment them out." This means to place them in brackets, as illustrated here:

```
{  Writeln('Length = ', Length:1:2);  }
```

If the prints are needed again, the comment brackets can be removed. A variation of this might involve something like this:

```
{Debug :  Writeln('Length = ', Length:1:2); }
```

This makes them stand out more, and thus they are easier to locate when they need to be reactivated. In addition, they look different from ordinary comments.

Other possibilities exist for handling this problem; some will be discussed in later sections.

□
TESTING   In this subsection, we summarize a number of **testing** concepts, most of which have been presented in more detail earlier in the text. Because whole textbooks have been written on the subject, our treatment here will obviously be on an elementary level. By the time you finish the course that uses this text, you will not be an expert tester. (Of course, neither will you be an expert programmer. Each skill will require further development in later courses and experience.) However, you can be aware of the need for testing and have some ability to come up with a reasonable test plan for the types of programs you are writing.

We should emphasize that the purpose of testing is to find bugs. For some (perhaps most) people, testing is psychologically difficult: They do not really want to find bugs in the program they have just developed so carefully. For that reason, many companies that develop computer software have groups whose primary job is to test the programs written by other people. In the context of a programming course, however, you will generally be doing your own testing. It may help to adopt the attitude, when a test case indicates a problem, that the bug was there and would probably have been noticed by the person grading the program. The fact that your test uncovered the bug is therefore a benefit, not something to get upset about.

We begin with some general testing concepts. This is followed by a few specific pointers for testing programs that use some of the "standard" algorithm concepts we study, such as counting and searching. Finally, top-down and bottom-up testing are discussed. Further explanations of all these topics can be found in the various testing subsections throughout the text.

1. Check your answers. Some of the test cases should contain data for which the correct answer is easily determined, preferably without using a calculator. This will allow you to see at a glance whether there are obvious bugs in the program. However, this does not imply that you should ignore the other test cases. After you have verified that the program is working correctly for those that are easy to check, check all the answers. *Never stop work on a program for which there are known errors.* Some of the techniques described in the previous subsection can be helpful in tracking down and removing the bugs.

2. Class testing. This is sometimes referred to as branch testing because it frequently relates to branching in the program. For example, when a program contains a decision structure

```
if Value < 1000 then
  Rate := 0.04
else if Value < 5000 then
  Rate := 0.07
else
  Rate := 0.10
```

we can identify three branches or classes for the variable Value: under 1000, 1000 or greater but less than 5000, 5000 or greater.

However, we generally should base our analysis of what classes there are on the problem description in addition to, or instead of, the actual algorithm or program. Even if the programmer found some way to calculate the Rate without using a decision structure, the testing should treat the calculation of Rate as one involving three classes for Value. As a simple example, in rounding a real number to the nearest integer, we can identify two classes of input: input with fractions less than 0.5 and input with fractions 0.5 or greater. The rounding process treats these two classes of input differently, so we want to test both classes. The fact that the built-in Round function is used rather than a decision structure does not change the need for that testing.

Class testing frequently involves ranges of values, as in the previous example. It sometimes involves specific values rather than ranges. For example, if the price of a window depends upon its color, we might identify these classes for the color: white, brown, cream, etc.

In class testing, we want to include test cases that exercise each identifiable class. In fact, if the class consists of a range of values, we should generally include a number of realistic, randomly chosen values within that class.

3. Bad data. In the previous example, which calculated the variable Rate, we actually missed at least one important class: Value less than 0. This represents an error class for which the program should ideally generate some sort of error message. In addition, the problem statement or analysis can indicate that values larger than 100,000 are considered unreasonable and probably indicate a data entry error. If so, then another class of bad data (larger than 100,000) exists and should be tested.

Just as we generate test cases for each class of good data, we generate test cases for each error class. It is important to note here that each error should be tested separately. For example, if the sex code must be "M" or "F", and the grade must lie between 0 and 100, we identify three classes of bad data:

Sex code incorrect
Grade less than 0
Grade greater than 100

Each should be tested by itself. A single record with an incorrect sex code and a grade less than 0 is not adequate.

4. Boundary values. Experience has shown that errors are more likely to occur for boundary values than for any other values. Thus, test cases that exercise the boundaries are likely to be more valuable in uncovering bugs.

Boundary values are frequently related to class testing. If a class consists of a range of values, then there are boundaries at each end of the range. For example, in the calculation of Rate based on Value (described above), we can identify these boundaries:

0	(between good data and bad data)
1,000	
5,000	
100,000	(between good data and bad data)

Since 1000 is the lowest number in the class for which the Rate is to be 0.07, we include a test case with Value equal to 1000. We also want to test the upper boundary of the class where the Rate is 0.04, so we include a value just below 1000, perhaps 999, or 999.99, or even both. A similar discussion holds for the other boundaries.

A couple of comments may help here. First, we might wish to test both just below and just above the boundary. In the previous example, we would add test cases 1000.01, or 1001, or both. Second, the actions for the two classes are sometimes not distinguishable for numbers very close to the boundary. For example, consider this decision structure:

```
If Amount <= 500 then
   Tax := 50
else
   Tax := 50 + 0.10 * (Amount - 500)
```

If Amount is 500.01, then Tax would be 50.001, which would appear as 50.00 if printed as a dollars and cents figure (using Amount:1:2, perhaps). Because this cannot be distinguished from the answer for 500.00, we might include a test case a little further from the boundary (for example, 500.10).

Finally, we should note that some boundaries are related to output rather than input. For example, if we are supposed to print exactly 45 lines per page, we should include a test where the output ends on the 45th line of a page and a test where it ends on the first line of the following page.

5. Special cases. This is closely related to boundary testing, and in fact, you may wish to view them as the same thing. An example of a special case test might involve a program finding the average check amount for a month in a checking account. We would want to include a test where there were no checks at all.

For many, if not all, "special case" tests, we can view the test as a boundary test in connection with a "how many?" or a "where?" question. For example, if we ask, "How many of the transactions for the month were checks?" the answer would be, "Anywhere from no checks to all checks." Our special case where there were no checks is one of the two boundaries for the possible range of answers to the question. Similarly, in looking for the largest of a set of numbers, we could ask, "Where in the list could the answer occur?" The answer is, "Anywhere from first to last," and we have two boundaries (first and last) for that range.

6. Compound conditions. Consider the following description of who gets a bonus: Any employee with an attendance record of 95 percent, or who sold more than 500 units, or who recruited at least one new customer receives a bonus. This can be coded as a simple if–then construction. However, in testing the program, it is not really sufficient to just test both branches. We should test various combinations of the three conditions involved. As you can see in the following table, there are eight possible combinations.

Attendance > 95%	Sold > 500	Recruited
No	No	No
No	No	Yes
No	Yes	No
No	Yes	Yes
Yes	No	No
Yes	No	Yes
Yes	Yes	No
Yes	Yes	Yes

We should check all combinations in a situation such as this. As usual, the "boundaries" (all no, all yes, exactly one no, exactly one yes) are the most critical tests.

A particularly important example of compound conditions occurs in validating input data. To be valid, the data typically must meet a number of criteria. This implies a number of combinations, similar to those for the example above. Experience has shown that for each way in which the data could fail to be acceptable, there should be a test case that is correct except for that one particular item.

7. Path testing. In a program with several different decision structures, it is desirable to test all possible paths through the program. For example, consider the segment:

```
if Category = 3 then
   Bonus := 100
else
   Bonus := 250;
if Total > 1000 then
   Bonus := Bonus * 2;
```

There are four possible paths: (1) category 3, total > 1000; (2) category 3, total ≤ 1000; (3) category not 3, total > 1000; and (4) category not 3, total ≤ 1000. We should test all possibilities.

As you can imagine, for a large program, the number of paths can grow quite rapidly. This is one strong argument for modularity. We write small modules and test them independently using drivers. Some of the tests for each module might involve thorough path testing of that module.

8. Loop termination. In Section 3-4 we studied loops with more than one termination condition. For this type of loop, we should include at least one test case for each possible termination condition. As a simple example, consider a search loop that is looking for the name "John Jones" in a data file. Since he might not be in the file, we would use a loop with two conditions for termination; either we find "John Jones" or we reach the end of the file and therefore know he is not in the file. Both possibilities should be tested for in our test plan. (Notice that the idea this is based on is similar to that for path testing.)

9. Include random tests. Sometimes when we carefully plan our tests, we can fall into the trap that our tests are too orderly. For a grading program, for example, our test sequence might go: 100, 90, 89, 80, 79, etc. These are all important boundary tests for a 90–80–70–60 grading scale. However, it would be good to mix up the tests. In addition, we would want to include some random testing.

This point was driven home to one of the authors in a recent program. The user was allowed to perform a sequence of activities. It turned out that a certain activity we called X worked fine unless it came right after activity Y. In testing, he never had that particular combination. However, during the demonstration of the product, the combination arose. How much better it would have been to uncover the bug during testing rather than during demonstration!

We now consider how some of the general concepts listed above apply in specific types of algorithms. We are especially interested here in "special case" tests. For example, for a counting problem, we might identify the following tests:

No data input
Data input, but count is 0
Everything input is in the class being counted

A similar list would apply for accumulation. For finding the largest (or smallest) value, we could list tests such as:

No data input
Exactly one data item (would be both largest and smallest)
First is largest (no ties)
Largest in middle (no ties)
Last is largest (no ties)
All values the same

In a program that searches for a particular value in a file (or a set of user input, or an array), we can list tests such as:

Not found
Found, only one in file
Found, first one in file (file containing > 1 record)
Found, last one in file (file containing > 1 record)
Found, somewhere in middle of file

Generalizing this last situation slightly, we can come up with the following types of tests for algorithms that use either count control or general condition loops:

Loop terminates on first pass through loop
Loop terminates on last possible pass through loop

We now turn to a brief review of **top-down** and **bottom-up testing**. To illustrate the difference, consider the following hierarchy chart of modules. The main module A uses modules B and C to accomplish subtasks. B in turn uses subprograms D and E, whereas C uses a subprogram F.

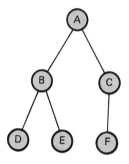

In both types of testing, we test one module at a time in the context of modules that are already tested. For example, one possible order for top-down testing is

A   (stubs for B and C)
B   (using the tested A, and stubs for D, E, and C)
D   (using the existing A and B, and stubs for E and C)
E   (using the existing A, B, and D, and a stub for C)
C   (using the existing A, B, D, and E, and a stub for F)
F   (using the existing A, B, D, E, and C)

Other orders are also possible, such as A, B, C, D, E, and F.
In bottom-up testing, on the other hand, we would start with the lowest level modules, perhaps in this order:

D   (using a driver)
E   (using a driver)
B   (using a driver to call it, and the existing D and E)
F   (using a driver)

C   (using a driver, and the existing F)
A   (using the existing B, C, D, E, and F)

Again, other orders are possible, such as F, C, D, E, B, and A.

Sometimes it is helpful to combine the two techniques. For example, suppose that the logic of main program A depends heavily on parameters it obtains from B and that those parameter values cannot be easily imitated by a stub. We might first develop the subsystem consisting of B, D, and E. The resulting order might be B, D, E, A, C, and F.

SUMMARY □ This concludes our discussion of antibugging, debugging, and testing. We remind you that this section, in contrast with many others in the text, can be most useful as a reference to be applied to your programming projects. It, together with DPT and testing subsections throughout the text, can be useful in writing programs that avoid bugs and in discovering, uncovering, and removing those that do occur.

REVIEW

Terms and concepts

bug   diagnostic print
antibugging   testing
debugging   top-down testing
trace print   bottom-up testing

Antibugging and debugging tips

1. Be aware of pitfalls.
2. Hand-trace algorithms and programs.
3. Echo print input.
4. Edit (validate) input.
5. Use trace prints.

Testing

Tips

1. Check answers.
2. Test all classes.
3. Test with bad data.
4. Use boundary values.
5. Use special cases (boundary values for ''how many'' or ''where'').
6. Test combinations for compound conditions.
7. Test all paths (use small modules to make this easier).
8. Test all possible loop termination conditions.
9. Include random tests.

Specific tests for counting problems, etc.

1. Counting (accumulation is similar)
   No data input
   Data input, but count is 0
   Everything input is in the class being counted

2. Finding the largest (or smallest)
   No data input
   Exactly one data item (would be both largest and smallest)
   First is largest (no ties)
   Largest in middle (no ties)
   Last is largest (no ties)
   All values the same

3. Searching in file (array search similar)
   Not found
   Found, only one in file
   Found, first one in file (file containing > 1 record)
   Found, last one in file (file containing > 1 record)
   Found, somewhere in middle of file

4. Any loop with count or general condition control
   Loop terminates on first pass through loop
   Loop terminates on last possible pass through loop

4
MORE ON SUBPROGRAMS

4-1
▫▫▫▫▫
PARAMETERS AND GLOBAL VARIABLES

Pascal subprograms (procedures and functions) have been introduced earlier. In this chapter, we examine these concepts in more depth. In the first two sections, we discuss a number of important issues, including

Value parameters versus var parameters
Global versus local variables
Use of arrays and strings as parameters
Subprograms that invoke other subprograms
Recursion

The third section presents some case studies that use procedures and functions as tools in the top-down design of complete programs.

By the end of this chapter, you will have an almost complete picture of the technical aspects of Pascal subprograms. Chapter 10 explores recursion in more depth, and a few miscellaneous topics are left until Appendix A.

More importantly, by the end of this chapter, you should be able to use subprograms as a tool in your program design.

▫
REVIEW AND TERMINOLOGY

A Pascal program consists of a number of **modules**. The **main module** (or **main program**) is always present; there may or may not be **submodules** (**subprograms**).

In Pascal, there are two types of subprograms: **procedures** and **functions**. We generally use a function for a subtask whose purpose is to calculate one value. A procedure is used for any other subtask. The main program can **invoke** (or **call**) any subprogram. A procedure is invoked by using its name as a statement; a function is invoked by including it as part of an expression, frequently in an assignment statement.

It is possible for one subprogram to invoke a second subprogram. In this case, we can use the terms **calling program** (or **calling module**) and **called program** (or **called module**) in describing the situation. If module A invokes module B, for example, then module A is the calling module and module B the called module.

The terms **parameter** and **argument** are frequently used interchangeably. For example, in a function declared with the header

```
function AreaFn(A, B, C : real) : real;
```

the variables A, B, and C are the parameters. These are sometimes called the **formal parameters**. When we use the function in an assignment statement such as

```
Area := AreaFn(Side1, Side2, Side3)
```

the variables Side1, Side2, and Side3 are supplied as parameters to match the formal parameters A, B, and C. To distinguish between these two uses of the word, we sometimes refer to Side1, Side2, and Side3 as the **actual parameters**. Some reserve the word "argument" to mean "actual parameter."

Formal parameters and actual parameters correspond by position within the list of parameters. The names may or may not be the same. However, the types must match. If a function expects to receive a real value as its second parameter, then the second parameter must be real. Moreover, the purpose of the parameters must match. For the function with header

```
function Volume(Radius, Height : real) : real;
```

the actual parameters supplied when the function is invoked should represent the radius and height in that order. Reversing the order would almost certainly cause erroneous answers.

□
REASONS FOR SUBPROGRAMS

There are at least four reasons for using subprograms. We mention them briefly here. These themes, especially the fourth, are expanded upon throughout the text.

1. Repetition. Sometimes a task must be executed several times within a program. If so, writing the task as a procedure or function precludes having to place the detailed steps for the task in several places in the program. In fact, by using parameters judiciously, it may be possible to unify several almost identical tasks as a single submodule.

2. Universal use. Some procedures might be needed in more than one program. Perhaps a large group of programmers all need the same procedure. By writing a subprogram and making it available to the entire group, we can avoid duplication of effort. (This saves not only the effort of copying the code, but also that of creating the code in the first place.)

3. Teamwork. A large portion of programming in the "real world" is done by programming teams. Rather than having the whole team work on the whole program, the program is generally divided into subprograms. Each subprogram will be written by one or two members of the team.

4. Modularity. Using subprograms enables us to break a large project up into more manageable pieces. This is important not only during the initial development of a project, but also during subsequent modification. Modularization allows us to focus our attention on the specific task at hand during development. For the person who must later modify the program, it makes the program easier to understand. In addition, it allows that person to concentrate on the piece that needs to be changed.

Of these four reasons, the most important is the last. As we have seen in some of our examples involving subprograms, it is extremely useful to be able to allocate subtasks to either functions or procedures. This aids in the **top-down design** of our program. As we design the main program, we identify various tasks or calculations that we allocate to procedures or functions. This allows us to complete the design of the overall solution to our problem without getting bogged down in the details of the subtasks. We then come back and design the subprogram for each identified subtask. Of course, if the subtask is complex, we may in turn identify further subtasks. This would lead to one subprogram in turn invoking another subprogram. We continue in this fashion until we have designed the entire program to solve our particular problem. Because we start with the main program and work our way down to successively more and more detailed pieces, we refer to this as "top-down" design and refinement.

NOTE Top-down design is similar to but different from top-down testing. In coding and testing a program that has already been designed, it can make sense to use top-down testing, or bottom-up testing, or some suitable combination. However, the design process should always be top-down.

□

VALUE AND VAR PARAMETERS

Parameters are the primary means of communication between a calling program and a called program. Values used by the submodule are passed into the submodule, and answers can be passed back. As a simple example, consider this procedure that calculates the quotient and remainder of two integers.

```
procedure QuotRem(I, J : integer; var Quotient, Remainder : integer);
begin
   Quotient := I div J;
   Remainder := I mod J
end;
```

The parameters I and J are used to pass values to the procedure; the parameters Quotient and Remainder pass back the answers.

In this example, I and J are **value parameters** and Quotient and Remainder are **var parameters**. The way these parameters work is totally different. To discuss the difference, consider the following simple main program.

```
program Sample(Input, Output);
var
   A, B, Q, R : integer;

{procedure QuotRem goes here}

begin
   A := 34;
   B := 6;
   QuotRem(A, B, Q, R);
   Writeln(Q, R)
end.
```

When QuotRem is invoked, the actual parameters A, B, Q, and R "correspond to" the formal parameters I, J, Quotient, and Remainder, respectively. For the two value parameters A and B, the present value is calculated and sent to the procedure's variables I and J, respectively. Thus, I and J are 34 and 6, respectively.

For the var parameters, however, no values are calculated. Rather, the procedure is informed of where in the computer memory the variables Q and R are stored. It then uses those locations for any reference to its formal parameters Quotient and Remainder. Thus, the assignment

`Quotient := I div J`

divides I (34) by J (6) *and places the result directly into the variable Q in the calling program.* At this instant, Q already contains the answer 5. The next step, likewise, places its answer (4) directly into the variable R in the main module. When the procedure terminates, the answers are there, ready to be printed by the Writeln statement. Figure 4-1 summarizes this discussion.

Notes:
1. When the procedure is invoked, the expression "A" is evaluated and the value (34) is placed in the QuotRem variable I.

2. Likewise, the value of the second argument ("B") is placed into J.

3. The variable Quotient in the QuotRem procedure has no storage space of its own. The procedure call establishes the correspondence between it and the main program's variable Q.

4. Likewise, the procedure call establishes that Remainder in QuotRem refers to R in the main program.

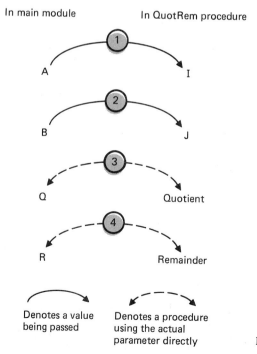

In main module   In QuotRem procedure

A   ①   I

B   ②   J

Q   ③   Quotient

R   ④   Remainder

Denotes a value being passed   Denotes a procedure using the actual parameter directly

Figure 4-1 Parameter Passing

This fundamental difference in how the parameters are handled helps explain various "rules" and "notes" concerning value and var parameters. Among these are:

---

1. The actual parameter for a value parameter can be any expression of the proper type. It need not be a variable. For example,

    QuotRem(A+B, 17, Q, R)

    would be legal.
    Reason: The value of the actual parameter is calculated and passed into the formal parameter variable in the submodule. Therefore, the actual parameter can be an expression.

2. The actual parameter for a var parameter must be a variable (of the proper type). It cannot be a constant or other expression.
    Reason: The formal parameter variable in the submodule does not occupy its own memory space. Instead, it works directly with the corresponding actual parameter in the computer memory.

3. Changing a value parameter in a submodule has no effect in the calling module.
    Reason: The communication using a value parameter consists *solely* of sending a value to the submodule when the submodule is invoked.

4. Changing a var parameter in a submodule immediately changes the corresponding actual parameter.
    Reason: The communication using a var parameter consists of the submodule *working directly with* the corresponding actual parameter.

☐ **PARAMETERS—TYPE MATCHING**

The communication that occurs through parameters is based on the *position* in the parameter list. It is not based on the name. Thus, in our previous example, we had these correspondences:

Main Module	QuotRem
A	I
B	J
Q	Quotient
R	Remainder

The names used in the calling program may or may not match.

However, the number, use, and type must match. In the example, the main module must supply four actual parameters, each of type integer. These parameters must represent the two numbers to be divided and the resulting quotient and remainder, in that order. In this subsection, we examine type matching for parameters in some detail.

For example, suppose we have an integer function whose header is given as

```
function Double(Number : integer) : integer;
```

It should not be surprising that assignments such as

```
Twice := Double(Number)
```

and

```
Again := Double(Twice)
```

are legal (Provided Twice, Number, and Again are integer). Also, because the parameter is a value parameter, we can write

```
Four := Double(2)
```

or

```
Final := Double((2 * I - 5) mod 3)
```

In addition, because a single element of an integer array is an integer variable, we can declare an integer array as

```
type
   IntegerArray = array[1 .. 1000] of integer;

var
   Grades : IntegerArray;
```

and then use an assignment such as

```
Grades[I + 1] := Double(Grades[I])
```

We can summarize this by saying that

> For a formal parameter of type integer, the actual parameter can be an integer variable or a single member of an integer array. If the parameter is a value parameter, it can be any integer expression whatsoever.

NOTE Similar comments apply for real, char, or Boolean parameters. That is, when we learn about arrays of reals, for example, we will see that a real array element can match a real parameter.

Parameters can also be arrays. For example, consider the function in Figure 4-2. The two parameters are List, an "IntegerArray," and N, the number of integers in the list. The type IntegerArray has been declared in the main module, as we have been doing for several sections now.

```
function ArraySum(List : IntegerArray; N : integer) : integer;
{
  Written by:   XXXXXXXXXXX, XX/XX/XX
      Purpose:  To add the numbers in an array
   Parameters:  The array to be summed, and an indication of how
                many numbers are stored in the array.
}
var
  I : integer;          {for loop control}
  Sum : integer;        {used to accumulate the sum}

begin
  Sum := 0;

  for I := 1 to N do
    begin
      Sum := Sum + List[I]
    end; {for}

  ArraySum := Sum
end;
```

Figure 4-2   Array Parameter

To use an array as a parameter, it must be given a named type. The following is *illegal* as a header:

```
function ArraySum(List : array[1 .. 1000] of integer; N : integer)
    : integer;
```

We must use the type name "IntegerArray" and *not* the definition of what that type means. A similar comment applies to the use of strings as parameters. For example, the following procedure header might seem reasonable to the reader; however, it is *illegal*.

```
procedure PrintLine(Name : string[20]; Age : integer;

    Department : string[6]);
```

The shaded parts are illegal. Rather, we must, in the main module, include type declarations such as

```
type
   String20 = string[20];
   String6  = string[6];
```

Then the procedure header would be

```
procedure PrintLine(Name : String20; Age : integer;
    Department : String6);
```

In the calling program, the actual parameters corresponding to Name would be declared as String20 rather than as string[20].[1]

We can summarize this discussion as follows:

When using arrays or strings as parameters, the formal and actual parameters must be of the same type. That type must be a named type defined in the "type" declarations of the main module.[2]

□

CHOOSING PARAMETERS

Understanding the preceding discussion is valuable, but the real test comes in applying it to programs. In this section, we describe some general advice on choosing parameters.

1. The parameters for a function represent values on which the function answer is based. They are called **input parameters** to emphasize the fact that the information flows into the subprogram from the calling program. They should be value parameters because the function should not modify its input.

2. For a procedure, we can have a mixture of input parameters and **output parameters**. Output parameters represent "answers" determined by the procedure. Put another way, they represent the *information passed back to the calling module*. Output parameters *must* be var parameters. Values passed into the procedure (input parameters), on the other hand, should be value parameters.

CAUTION

A potential for confusion exists in this terminology. Notice that the terms *input* and *output,* when used to describe parameters, have nothing to do with reading from the keyboard or printing to the screen. An output parameter, for example, is one calculated by the procedure and returned to the calling module. *That does not mean that the procedure should print its value.*

Since we cannot invent our own terminology, we must learn to recognize the distinction between, for example, an input parameter and input from the user.

3. Sometimes a procedure has a parameter representing a value that is passed in, modified, then passed back. For example, a procedure can modify a bank balance by adding a deposit or subtracting a withdrawal. Such a parameter, called an **update parameter**, must be a var parameter.

4. There can be efficiency considerations that override this advice for array parameters. For example, consider the ArraySum function of Figure 4-2. Because the parameter List is a value parameter, it will occupy storage space in the function. When the function is invoked, the actual parameter will automatically be copied (all 1000 integers) to the formal parameter. If the array were a var parameter, it would not occupy space and no copying would be needed. Instead, the function would work directly with the calling module's array, which is the actual parameter.

For this reason, many programmers habitually use var parameters for all arrays. However, see the caution that follows.

Defensive programming argues against the practice of making all arrays var parameters. Value parameters protect the programmer from inadvertently modifying a parameter in the calling program. If we use a var parameter, we must take extra care that any modification of the parameter is *intended to modify* the corresponding actual parameter.

Thus, there is a design tradeoff between defensive programming and efficiency. Unless the program contains an exceptional number of subprogram calls, we suggest that value parameters be used as a general rule. For most interactive applications, the extra time for copying the array to the value parameter will not be noticeable.[3]

COMMENT ON TERMINOLOGY

The terms input parameter, output parameter, and update parameter are "generic" terms. That is, they apply to writing subprograms in a number of languages that support parameters for subprograms. They describe the desired use of the parameter: as information flowing into the subprogram (input), as information flowing out of the subprogram (output), or as a combination (update).

The notion of value parameters and var parameters, on the other hand, is strictly Pascal. It represents Pascal's way of implementing the general concepts of input, output, and update parameters.

□

GLOBAL AND LOCAL VARIABLES; SCOPE

At this point in the text, a program is of this form

> Program header line
> Constant definitions ("const")
> Type definitions ("type")
> Variable declarations for the main module
> Zero or more procedures and functions
> Main module action steps (begin . . . end.)

Our discussion here is limited to this context. See Appendix A for a more complete discussion.

Each of the procedures and functions in the scenario described above can, in turn, declare its own constants, types, and variables. For example, the first procedures we learned about were Instructions procedures that declared a variable "Answer." These variables are called **local variables**; they are usable "locally" within the particular procedure or function. They are not accessible in the main program or in any of the other procedures or functions.

Consider the following meaningless program:

```
program Demo(Input, Output);
var
    I, J : integer;
```

```
procedure Manipulate;
var
  I, N : integer;
begin {Manipulate}
  I := 1;
  N := 2;
  J := I + N
end;  {Manipulate}

begin {Demo}
  I := 10;
  J := 11;
  Manipulate;
  Writeln(I, J)
end.
```

The main module (Demo) has two variables I and J. The procedure has two variables I and N. The I variable in the Manipulate procedure is not the same as that in Demo. Examine the following diagram:

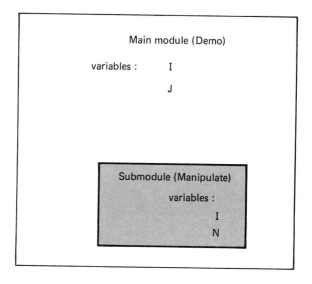

To understand how Pascal interprets these variables, imagine that the box enclosing the submodule Manipulate is a one-way mirror, with the outside surface silvered. From within Manipulate, we can see out, but it is impossible to see in.

Thus, within Manipulate, three variables are "visible": the local variables I and N and the **global variable** J. The variable I in the main module is not visible because the compiler will assume that any reference to I means the locally defined I.

Within Manipulate, therefore, any references to I and N refer to the local variables I and N. However, Manipulate also references (and changes) J. Because J is not declared locally, it is assumed to be global. The reference to J will refer to the globally defined J in the main module.

> Any variable used in a submodule, which is not declared either as a local variable or a parameter for that submodule, is assumed to be global. If the main module has a variable by that name, that main module variable will be used. (If not, a syntax error—undefined variable—exists.)

In our example, the assignments I := 1 and N := 2 do not affect the main module. The assignment J := I + N changes J in the main module to 3. The Writeln prints the unchanged I (10) and the modified J (3).

COMMENTS

1. The "visibility" of a variable is called its **scope**. Scope is discussed in more depth in Appendix A. For the programs that we will write:

(a) The scope of anything defined in the main program includes the entire program. However, local declarations of the same name will "hide" the global version. (The variable I in our example illustrates this "hiding" process.)

(b) The scope of anything defined within a subprogram is that subprogram only.

2. The term "global" refers to the fact that the main program's declarations are visible throughout the entire program.

It is possible to contrive perfectly horrendous examples illustrating the results of this global default. For our purposes, however, we need to concentrate on three issues:

1. Accidental globals can be a disaster. Defensive programming requires that we take extra care that all variables used in a module are declared in the module (either as parameters or as local variables). This prevents the submodule from having unwanted "side effects." The only exception is when we specifically design the module to use global variables.

2. Global type declarations are useful, indeed necessary. To pass arrays and strings as parameters, for example, the type (IntegerArray, String6, etc.) should be declared in the main module.

3. Intentional global variables should be used sparingly, if at all. The primary means of communication among modules should be parameters. Some languages, such as BASIC and COBOL, force modules to communicate via global variables. Sometimes this seems easier than parameters for introductory level programs. However, experience has shown that using globals leads to increased program complexity. Excessive use of globals makes it harder to get large programs working and harder to modify them.

A little reflection on some of the reasons for using subprograms helps clarify this. For example, one important reason is modularity. This term implies units that perform predictable tasks with specified input. By using parameters, we have a complete list of the input and output for the subprogram, right in the subprogram header. If globals are used, we must study the code itself to see which variables are used and which are modified. Moreover, if a variable does not have the desired value, it can be quite a task to track down which module changed it.

Two other considerations relate to the concepts of "universal use" and "teamwork." First, to be truly universally useful, a module must not require certain declarations in the calling program. For example, the standard subprograms (Writeln, Sqrt, etc.) do not require us to declare certain variables in order to use them. All their communication occurs through the parameters. Second, part of the advantages of allocating pieces of a project to different team members is lost if they must collaborate on all the variable names. Using local variables and parameters, it is possible to concentrate one's attention on the key issues: What data does each module need, what data does it generate, and what procedures are needed to transform the input data to the output data?

In the next section, we do present an example where global variables are useful. However, our general rule is to use parameters rather than globals for communication.

□
DPT
 1. The most insidious difficulties with Pascal subprograms involve inadvertent side effects. If a subprogram fails to declare a variable it uses, the compiler will look in the main program for a variable of that name. If it fails to find one, that is good—it will print an error message for the undefined variable.

On the other hand, if it does find a variable by that name, it will assume that the reference in the submodule meant to refer to this variable as a global variable.

Special care must be taken with for loop control variables. The use of variables I, J, and K for these variables is very common. Hence, the likelihood of the main module containing a variable of the same name increases.

One possible way to detect this involves unit testing each module. When we test a module, we can use a driver with "unusual" variable names. Perhaps each variable name in the driver could begin with a sequence such as "XXXX." Any variable not declared in the submodule would almost certainly fail to have the same name as a variable in the driver routine. This would allow the compiler to detect undeclared local variables for the module.

2. Attention must also be paid to the choice of value and var parameters. If a parameter is used to pass a value into the module, it should be a value parameter. Var parameters should be reserved for parameters that communicate answers to the calling module.

Two things can go wrong here. If a parameter should be declared as var, failing to do so will prevent the calling module from getting its answer. On the other hand, suppose we use var for what should have been a value parameter. Then, if the submodule modifies the parameter, the corresponding variable in the calling program will be modified.

Another point must be remembered for value and var parameters. If the parameter is a var parameter, we cannot supply an expression as the actual parameter. If we do, the compiler will detect the error and try to tell us what is wrong. The actual compiler message can vary. For example, if we use an expression such as I+J, it will stop at the plus sign and tell us that it expected either a comma (if there is another parameter following) or a right parenthesis (if this is the last parameter). If we use a number, it will tell us that the number is an illegal identifier.

3. Remember that variables defined within a subprogram are local. They cannot be used outside that subprogram.

4. When a subprogram has several parameters, we must pay close attention to the order of the parameters. When we invoke the submodule, we must supply the actual parameters in the proper order.

5. Parameters must match by type. This can be a little confusing with arrays. For example, suppose List has been declared as an integer array; consider this program segment.

```
for I := 1 to 50 do
   begin
      Root := Sqrt(List[I]);
      Writeln(List[I]:10, Root:10)
   end; {for}
```

The first 50 elements of the array "List" are passed, one at a time, to the standard Sqrt function. This function's parameter is a single number. Since each List[I] is one number, the invocation is correct.

On the other hand, the function ArraySum of Figure 4-2 has an integer array (type IntegerArray) as its first parameter. The step

```
Sum := ArraySum(List,50)
```

will calculate the sum of the first 50 elements of the array List. Notice that in this case we pass the entire array. There is no subscript.

■■■■■■
REVIEW

Terms and concepts

module	parameter
main module	argument
main program	formal parameter
submodule	actual parameter
subprogram	top-down design
procedure	value parameter
function	var parameter
invoke	input parameter
call	output parameter
calling program	update parameter
calling module	local variable
called program	global variable
called module	scope

Reasons for subprograms

1. Repetition

2. Universal use

3. Teamwork

4. Modularity

Value versus var parameters

1. Value

(a) Actual parameter can be any expression (of proper type).

(b) Value of expression is passed to the formal parameter when the subprogram is invoked.

(c) Nothing is passed back to the calling program.

(d) Usually supplies input values to the subprogram.

2. Var

(a) The actual parameter must be a variable.

(b) No value is passed to the subprogram; instead, the subprogram works directly with the calling program's actual parameter.

(c) Changes (within the subprogram) to the formal parameter immediately modify the calling program's actual parameter.

(d) Usually supplies "answers" to the calling program or updates a variable of the calling program.

Type matching for parameters

1. Any expression of the proper type matches a value parameter.

2. An integer variable or one element of an integer array matches an integer var parameter. (Similarly for real, Boolean, char).

3. Arrays can be passed to match arrays of the same type. The type *must be a named type* declared in the "type" section of the main program.

4. Strings can be passed to match strings *of the same named type.*

Global vs. local variables

1. Local: declared within the subprogram where it is used.

2. Global: not declared within the subprogram where it is used, but declared in the main program.

3. When interpreting the use of a variable, the compiler:

(a) Checks for a local declaration first

(b) Checks for a global declaration if there is no local one

(c) Generates an error message if there is neither a global nor a local declaration

DPT   *1.* Declare all local variables. Be especially careful to declare control variables of for loops (I, J, etc.)

2. Unit test modules.

3. Avoid the use of global variables.

4. Use value parameters to supply input to a subprogram. Use var parameters to supply answers to the calling program or to update a variable.

5. Do not attempt to use a subprogram's local variables (or its formal parameters) outside that subprogram.

6. Do not supply an expression for a var parameter.

7. Watch the order of the parameters.

8. Remember that parameters must be named types. (Use IntegerArray, not array[1..1000] of integer; use String20, not string[20]).

9. Only arrays can match array parameters.

10. Either simple variables or single array elements can match nonarray var parameters.

EXERCISES

*1. Suppose that the main program contains these declarations:

```
const
  MaxIndex = 1000;
type
  IntegerArray = array[1..MaxIndex] of integer;
var
  L : IntegerArray;
  I, J, K, T, U, V : integer;
  B, C, X : real;
  S : string[20];
```

For each of the following, you are given a procedure or function header and an invocation of that procedure or function. Decide whether each is legal; if not, explain why not.

a. `procedure P1(A, B : integer);`

   . . . .

  `P1(I, J, K);`

b. `function F1(A, B : real) : integer;`

   . . . .

  `T := F1(B, C);`

c. `function F2(X : array[1..1000] of integer) : integer;`

   . . . .

  `U := F2(L);`

d. `procedure P2(A : integer; B : real) : real;`

   . . . .

  `X := P2(T, U);`

e. `function F3(I : integer) : integer;`

   . . . .

  `F3(I);`

f. `procedure P3(L : integer);`

   . . . .

  `P3(L);`

g. `procedure P4(var R : integer);`

   . . . .

  `P4(L[5])`

h. `procedure P5(A : integer; var B : integer);`

   . . . .

  `P5(7, V + 12);`

i. `Function F4(Q : string[20]) : integer;`

   . . . .

  `I := F4(S);`

*2. The following is a procedure to swap two integer numbers.

```
procedure Swap(var N1, N2 : integer);
var
  T : integer;                    {temporary variable}
```

```
begin  {Swap}
   T  := N1;                          {save a copy of N1}
   N1 := N2;
   N2 := T
end;   {Swap}
```

a. What would be printed if we use this procedure in a program containing these steps?

```
I := 5;
J := 16;
Swap(I, J);
Writeln(I, J)
```

b. Repeat part (a) assuming that the Swap procedure failed to declare its parameters as var parameters.

c. What would happen if the Swap procedure failed to declare its local variable T?

3. Suppose that an integer array named A has been declared using our usual method and contains these as its first 10 values:

$$5 \quad 2 \quad 6 \quad 17 \quad -3 \quad 4 \quad 9 \quad -2 \quad 15 \quad -53$$

*a. Is this use of the procedure Swap from Exercise 2 legal?

```
Swap(A[1], A[5])
```

If so, what would the array look like after the procedure invocation?

b. Repeat part (a) for this invocation:

```
Swap(A, A[10])
```

*c. What would be printed by this program segment?

```
for I := 1 to 5 do
   begin
      Swap(A[I], A[11-I])
   end;  {for}
for I := 1 to 10 do
   Write(A[I] : 6);
Writeln
```

What is the purpose of the final Writeln?

d. What would be the effect of this program segment?

```
for I := 1 to 9 do
   begin
      Swap(A[I], A[I+1])
   end;  {for}
```

e. What would be the effect of this program segment?

```
for I := 1 to 9 do
   begin
      if A[I] > A[I+1] then
         Swap(A[I], A[I+1])
   end;  {for}
```

4. The following is a procedure that prints the digits of a positive integer in order from right to left.

```
    procedure RightToLeft(N : integer);
    var
      Number : integer;        {holds "working copy" of N}
    begin  {RightToLeft}
      Number := N;

      repeat
        Writeln(Number mod 10);     {print right digit}
        Number := Number div 10     {then strip it off}
      until Number = 0

    end;  {RightToLeft}
```

    a. Hand-trace the procedure with various values of the parameter N to see how it works.

*b. Is the variable Number really needed? That is, could we just write the loop as follows?

```
            repeat
              Writeln(N mod 10);
              N := N div 10
            until N = 0
```

*c. What would happen in part (b) if N were inadvertently listed as a var parameter?

5. Each of the following procedure and function headers is illegal. For each, indicate the type declarations that the main program needs and modify the header line to be legal.

*a. procedure Shift(var Scores : array [1..1000] of integer);

*b. procedure Print(Name : string[20]; Initials : string[2];
                     Score : integer);

c. function Inorder(String1, String2 : string[15]) : boolean;

d. function Largest(A : array[1..75] of integer; N : integer);

6. Type and run the following program. What happens? Why?

```
            program Exercise6(Input, Output);
            var
              I : integer;
            procedure PrintRow(RowNumber : integer);
            begin  {PrintRow}
              Write('Row # ', RowNumber:1, ':');
              for I := 1 to 10 do
                Write(RowNumber*I:5);
              Writeln;
            end;  {PrintRow}
            begin  {Exercise6}
              for I := 1 to 10 do
                PrintRow(I)
            end.
```

7. For each of the following, write a header line for a function or procedure to do the indicated task. *Do not write the entire submodule.*

    You will need to identify parameters and decide whether they should be value or var parameters. If you make any assumptions about type declarations, identify those assumptions.

*a. Calculate a person's commission based on a sales amount and commission rate.

*b. Convert a date from Julian form to the usual form. For example, day 1 is January 1, day 33 is February 2, etc. The answer consists of a month and a day within that month. Assume that this is not a leap year.

c. Modify part (b) to include a parameter telling the subprogram whether or not this is a leap year.

d. Reverse a number viewed as a four-digit number. For example, 4172 would become 2714 and 319 would become 9130.

e. Sort an array containing 1000 integers.

f. Repeat part (e) assuming that a variable N indicates how many of the possible 1000 places in the array actually contain numbers.

g. Split a name into first and last names. For example, for "John Smith" the answers would be "John" and "Smith".

h. Add a bonus to the salary. The amount of the bonus depends on three things: the person's rank, department, and number of years in the company.

4-2 PROCEDURES AND FUNCTIONS

□□□□□□

In this section, we study the syntax (form) and semantics (meaning) of Pascal subprograms. To a great extent, the section merely brings together material you have studied previously. However, there are at least two major additions to your knowledge:

1. In previous sections, we have not used subprograms that invoked other subprograms (except for the built-in subprograms such as Readln or Sqrt). As we will see, you can write subprograms that invoke other subprograms you have written.

This capability is extremely important in top-down design. When we break a program into subtasks, some of those subtasks can still be complicated. We will want to subdivide them further, and this will involve subprograms invoking other subprograms.

2. We introduce the important notion of **recursion**. This involves a subprogram invoking itself to solve a simpler version of the same problem. There are certain types of problems for which a **recursive** solution (one using recursion) is the easiest to create and to understand.

Subprograms can in turn invoke other subprograms. For example, we can have the pattern of calls suggested by this hierarchy chart:

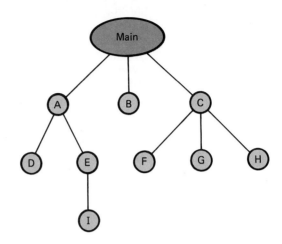

This suggests that the main module uses modules A, B, and C to perform needed subtasks. In turn, module A invokes both modules D and E, and module E invokes I. We refer to this situation as **nested invocations** (invocations within invocations). When module I completes its task, control returns to module E; when E completes, control returns to module A; and when A completes, control returns to the main module.

To write a program with the indicated hierarchy, it is only necessary to remember this rule:

In Pascal, everything must be declared before it is used.

Thus, for instance, because module A uses module E, the declaration for module E must precede that for module A. One possible program layout is this:

Program header
Constants, types, and variables for main module (globals)
Module D
Module I
Module E
Module A
Module B
Module F
Module G
Module H
Module C
Main module

Each module declares any necessary parameters and local variables. As another example, consider the following:

```
program Nested(Input, Output);
var
  Number : integer;
{
  This program illustrates nested invocation.
}

function Double(I : integer) : integer;
begin  {Double}
  Double := 2 * I
end;   {Double}
procedure Triple (var X : integer);
begin  {Triple}
  X := Double(X) + X
end;   {Triple}

begin  {Nested}
  Number := 10;
  Writeln('Before call : ', Number:1);
  Triple(Number);
  Writeln('After call : ', Number:1)
end.
```

The main program uses the Triple procedure to triple the value of the variable Number. The procedure accomplishes this by invoking the function Double (which calculates twice the number), then adding the number to that. Double must be declared before Triple.

COMMENT In addition to nesting invocations, it is possible to nest declarations. That is, we can declare one procedure within another. In the previous example, Double is used only by the Triple procedure, not by the main program. It could therefore be declared within Triple.

For an advanced programmer, there are some advantages to nested definition. For very large programs with a chance of inadvertent duplicate module names, defining a module where it is used is sometimes useful.

On the other hand, nested definition increases the likelihood of accidental use of globals. Since this is a common pitfall encountered by beginners, we have chosen to defer our detailed discussion of this concept to Appendix A. (Any program we will write in this text can be written quite effectively without using nested declarations.)

□
PROCEDURES VERSUS FUNCTIONS In both form and use, there are many similarities between procedures and functions. The major difference between the two can be summarized as follows: a function returns exactly one value, and that value is returned to the calling program by the function name. This fact has implications for both form and use.

Both types of subprograms have this general form:

> **Header line**
> declarations of local constants, types, and variables
> Body (a compound statement)

There are three differences between the two:

1. In the header line, one uses the word *function*, the other the word *procedure*.

2. The header line for a function includes an indication of the type of the answer.

3. The body of a function must include at least one assignment statement giving a value to the function name. A procedure *cannot* give a value to the procedure name.

The header lines have this form:

```
function function-name parameter-list : function-type;
```

```
procedure procedure-name parameter-list;
```

The *parameter-list* is optional. If it is present, it consists of one or more repetitions of the following pattern, enclosed in parentheses, separated by semicolons.

```
var list of variables separated by commas : type
```

The keyword "var" is optional. If it is included, the parameters *in that list* are **var parameters**, otherwise they are **value parameters**. The type of the parameters can be any named type (Boolean, char, String20, IntegerArray, etc.).

For a function, the header line contains a *function-type*. This can be any of the following:

integer
real
Boolean
char
a named string type[1]

It cannot be an array type. If we wish to return an array answer to the calling program, it must be a var parameter of a procedure. (A function returns exactly one value, and Pascal does not view an array as being a single value.)

The methods used to invoke a procedure differs from that used to invoke a function. A procedure is invoked by using its name, with necessary parameters, as a single statement. For example,

```
Triple(Number)
```

invokes the Triple procedure, passing the parameter Number. A function is invoked by using it in an expression, as in these three examples.

```
I := 1;
repeat
  I := I + 1
until  Double(I) > 17

Y := Double(X) - 35 div Double(Z)

Writeln(T:1, ' times 2 = ', Double(T):1)
```

In addition to the differences in form, there are differences in use. These differences arise from the view that *the job of a function is to calculate its answer.* It should have no other effects (known as side effects). This view is not enforced by the compiler, but it is a commonly accepted programming practice. In accordance with this view, we have the following "rules."

---

1. All parameters for a function are value parameters. Procedures can use value or var parameters or a mix of the two.

2. Functions should not do any input or output (exception: temporary diagnostic prints, as described in Section 3-5). A procedure may or may not include I/O, depending on whether or not that is part of its identified subtask.

3. Functions should *never* use global variables. (Procedures should "almost never" use global variables.)

The following table summarizes some of the important differences between a function and a procedure.

Item	Function	Procedure
Name	Has a type (integer, etc.)	Does not have a type
	Function name is assigned a value within the function	Procedure name is never assigned a value
Use	Used to calculate a single real, boolean, char, integer, or string value	Used to perform a task other than calculating a single value
	Invoked by using in an expression	Invoked by using its name as a statement
Parameters	Uses value parameters	Can use value or var parameters

□ **WRITING A SUBPROGRAM**

In writing any type of subprogram, it is important to identify precisely the task to be performed. For example, many of our algorithms have been of this form:

print instructions
repeat these steps until user enters terminal value

```
obtain input
if not terminal input then do these steps:
    calculate answers
    print answers
```

We can use subprograms to refine the step "calculate answers." If so, these subprograms would probably not involve any I/O operations. They would receive input from the main program through value parameters and send back answers using var parameters (or through function names).

On the other hand, we can have subprograms whose task specifically involves input or output. For example, a procedure to obtain valid input would issue prompts, read values, and check for validity. Thus, some procedures do include I/O.

The key to proper design is defining precisely what task the subprogram is to accomplish.

We can summarize the steps for writing a subprogram as follows:

1. Identify the task to be performed. Determine whether to use a function or a procedure. Choose a name for the subprogram, and determine the type (real, etc.) if it is to be a function.

2. Decide on parameters. "Answers" passed to the calling program are var parameters. Values needed to perform the task are value parameters. Any parameter that is updated (used as input and then modified) must be a var parameter.

(All parameters for a function should be value parameters.)

3. Devise a plan for the submodule. This can involve identifying further subtasks. Both an algorithm for the required actions and a list of local variables should be generated.

Remember that the algorithm for a function must include assigning a value to the function name.

4. Write the subprogram in Pascal. The first and second steps listed above supply information for the header line. The third step supplies the local variable declarations and the body of the subprogram.

These four steps are always necessary. The degree to which they must be written will depend on two things: the complexity of the task and your skill as a program designer and programmer. For most programmers, jotting down some notes and thoughts will enhance the process.

□

EXAMPLES Let us write a number of example functions and procedures. These examples are mostly relatively simple. Their purpose is to illustrate some of the variety possible in working with Pascal subprograms. The examples here are not recursive. In the next subsection, we present some recursive examples. In addition, Section 4-3 contains some complete program case studies.

For the first example, we will find the largest and smallest of three given integers. Since there are two answers, we will write a procedure rather than a function. We will name the procedure MaxMin.

The parameters include the three given integers, which we will name Num1, Num2, and Num3. These are value parameters. The answers, which will be var parameters, are Maximum and Minimum, also integer.

We are now ready to devise an algorithm. Several different ones are possible. However, the one given below has certain advantages.

Give Maximum and Minimum default values of Num1
compare them to Num2 and adjust if necessary
compare them to Num3 and adjust if necessary

One major advantage is that this algorithm can easily be adapted to more than three numbers. In fact, it is based on our standard method of finding the largest or smallest of a long list of input.

We can now write this in Pascal. There are no local variables. The step "compare them to Num2 and adjust if necessary" becomes

```
if Num2 > Maximum then
   Maximum := Num2;
if Num2 < Minimum then
   Minimum := Num2;
```

See Figure 4-3 for the complete subprogram and a sample call.

For our next example, let us do some string processing. Suppose we are given three variables containing the city, state, and zip code of an individual. We would like to build a line suitable for an address on an envelope, similar to the following:

```
Jefferson City, TN 37760
```

Since there is one answer, a function seems more appropriate than a procedure. In Turbo Pascal, this will be possible. Turbo Pascal allows functions of a predefined string type. Therefore, we choose to write a function of type String30 (= string[30]). This will have as parameters the City, State, and ZipCode and will simply use concatenation to obtain the address line. See Figure 4-4. Notice that the types String30, String20, String2, and String5 must be globally defined.[2]

For our next example, let us write a subprogram to check three integers to see if they are in increasing order. Because the answer is either yes or no, a Boolean function is appropriate. For parameters, we need the three numbers to be checked, which we will call First, Second, and Third.

No local variables are involved. The algorithm is quite simple, but we do need to resolve one issue. Does "increasing order" allow duplicates? Are 6, 6, and 8 in increasing order? This could be answered either way, but for this example, we choose to assume the answer is no. The function appears as Figure 4-5. Study both the function and the alternate approach given for the function body.

To illustrate subprograms that deal with arrays, let us calculate the elementwise sum of two arrays. Here is what we mean. A and B are two variables of

SUBPROGRAM

```
procedure MaxMin(Num1, Num2, Num3 : integer;
                 var Maximum, Minimum : integer);
{
    Written by:  XXXXXXXX, XX/XX/XX
       Purpose:  To calculate the largest and smallest of three numbers.
    Parameters:  Num1, Num2, Num3 - input, the three numbers
                 Maximum - output, the largest
                 Minimum - output, the smallest
}
begin   {MaxMin}

{*** Give Maximum and Minimum default values.}

  Maximum := Num1;
  Minimum := Num1;

{*** Compare to second number.}

  if Num2 > Maximum then
    Maximum := Num2;
  if Num2 < Minimum then
    Minimum := Num2;

{*** Compare to third number.}

  if Num3 > Maximum then
    Maximum := Num3;
  if Num3 < Minimum then
    Minimum := Num3
end;   {MaxMin}
```

SAMPLE CALL (I, J, K, Large, and Small are integer variables)

```
Readln(I, J, K);
MaxMin(I, J, K, Large, Small);
Writeln(' The largest is ', Large:1,
        ' and the smallest is ', Small:1)
```

Figure 4-3 Procedure with Two Tasks

type IntegerArray, each containing N values. For example, if N is 5, then A and B might be

```
A : 6, 1, 3, -5, 2
B : 2, 5, -3, 1, 7
```

We wish to calculate Sum, found by adding corresponding elements of A and B. For the example, Sum would be

```
Sum : 8, 6, 0, -4, 9
```

TYPES DECLARED GLOBALLY

```
type
  String30 = string[30];
  String20 = string[20];
  String2  = string[2];
  String5  = string[5];
```

SUBPROGRAM

```
function AddressLine(City : String20; State : String2;
                                      Zip : String5) : String30;
{
    Written by:  XXXXXXX, XX/XX/XX
       Purpose:  To concatenate a city, state, and zip code into an
                 address.
    Parameters:  City - input, the city part of the address
                 State - input, the state part of the address
                 Zip - input, the zip code part of the address
}
begin  {AddressLine}
  AddressLine := City + ', ' + State + ' ' + Zip
end;  {AddressLine}
```

SAMPLE CALL

```
Writeln(Name);
Writeln(StreetAddress);
CityState := AddressLine(City, State, ZipCode);
Writeln(CityState)
```

Figure 4-4   String-Valued Function

To do so, we need a procedure. Conceptually there is a single answer (Sum), but that answer is an array. Pascal does not allow a function to have an array type as its type. Hence, we will write a procedure.

There are four parameters we need: the two arrays A and B; the answer array Sum; and the variable N, which shows how many values the arrays contain. Of these, only the answer (Sum) will be a var parameter.

The algorithm needs to accomplish the following steps:

$$Sum[1] := A[1] + B[1];$$
$$Sum[2] := A[2] + B[2];$$
$$\cdots$$
$$Sum[N] := A[N] + B[N];$$

If we use a for loop to cause the variable I to take on the values 1 through N, then the body of that for loop would be

$$Sum[I] := A[I] + B[I]$$

SUBPROGRAM

```
function InOrder(First, Second, Third : integer) : Boolean;
{
    Written by:   XXXXXXXX, XX/XX/XX
       Purpose:   To see if three given numbers are in strictly
                  increasing order.
    Parameters:   First, Second, Third - input, the numbers to be tested.
}
begin   {InOrder}
  if (First < Second) and (Second < Third) then
    InOrder := true
  else
    InOrder := false
end;   {InOrder}
```

ALTERNATE BODY

```
begin
  InOrder := (First < Second) and (Second < Third)
end;
```

SAMPLE CALL

```
Readln(Score1, Score2, Score3);
if InOrder(Score1, Score2, Score3) then
  Writeln('Improving')
else if InOrder(Score3, Score2, Score1) then
  Writeln('Going steadily downhill')
else
  Writeln ('Neither steadily increasing nor steadily decreasing')
```

Figure 4-5   Boolean Function

The first time through the loop, I will be 1, and Sum[1] will be calculated as A[1] + B[1]. The second time through, Sum[2] will be calculated as A[2] + B[2], and so on. Observe that I is a local variable for the procedure. See Figure 4-6 for the subprogram and a driver main program used to test the procedure. The procedure and the statement invoking it are shaded. Study the matchup of the formal parameter (A, B, Sum, N) to the actual parameters (Arr1, Arr2, Answer, N).

You may wish to adapt the driver to write drivers to test your own subprograms which have array parameters.

One approach to printing tables of output involves using procedures to print detail lines and headers. As a simple example of one possible approach, consider the program of Figure 4-7, which has lines numbered for reference purposes. That program is similar to one we wrote in Chapter 2 (Figure 2-10). It prints a table of square roots for numbers input by the user. In Chapter 2, we simply assumed that the list would occupy no more than one page. If it did go beyond one page, headers appeared only on the first page.

```
program Driver(Input, Output);
{
      Written by:  XXXXXXXX  XX/XX/XX
         Purpose:  To test the AddArrays procedure.
  Procedures used:  AddArrays, to add two arrays.
}
const
  MaxIndex  = 1000;                   {array size}
  EndOfData = 0;                      {terminal value}

type
  IntegerArray = array[1..MaxIndex] of integer;

var
  Arr1, Arr2 : IntegerArray;          {the two arrays to add, input}
  N          : integer;               {the size of the arrays, input}
  Answer     : IntegerArray;          {the sum array, output}
  I          : integer;               {loop control variable}

  procedure AddArrays(A, B : IntegerArray;
                      var Sum : IntegerArray; N : integer);
  {
        Written by:  XXXXXXXX, XX/XX/XX
           Purpose:  To add two arrays elementwise.
        Parameters:  A, B - input, the arrays to be added
                     Sum - output, the sum array
                     N - input, the present size of the arrays (that is,
                         the number of actual values in the arrays)
  }
  var
    I : integer;                        {control variable - for loop}

  begin  {AddArrays}

    for I := 1 to N do
      begin
        Sum[I] := A[I] + B[I]
      end  {for loop}

  end;  {AddArrays}

begin {Driver}
  Write('Enter array size (0 to stop): ');
  Readln(N);

  while N <> EndOfData do
    begin

{*** Get first array.}

      Writeln('Enter first array, one number per line');

      for I := 1 to N do
        begin
          Readln(Arr1[I])
        end;  {for loop}
```

Figure 4-6 Procedure to Calculate an Array (Continued)

```
{*** Get second array.}

        Writeln('Enter second array, one number per line');

        for I := 1 to N do
          begin
            Readln(Arr2[I])
          end;  {for loop}

{*** Use procedure to calculate sum.}

        AddArrays(Arr1,Arr2,Answer,N);

{*** Print answer.}

        Writeln('The sum array is: ');

        for I := 1 to N do
          begin
            Writeln(Answer[I])
          end;  {for loop}

{*** Prepare for next pass.}

        Writeln;
        Write('Enter array size (0 to stop): ');
        Readln(N)
      end;  {while}

{*** Print termination message and stop.}

     Writeln;
     Writeln('Driver program terminating.')
   end.
```

SAMPLE INPUT AND OUTPUT

```
Enter array size (0 to stop): 3
Enter first array, one number per line
4
-6
7
Enter second array, one number per line
-6
6
203
The sum array is:
-2
0
210

Enter array size (0 to stop): 0

Driver program terminating.
```

Figure 4-6 Procedure to Calculate an Array

The hierarchy chart illustrates the overall structure of the program:

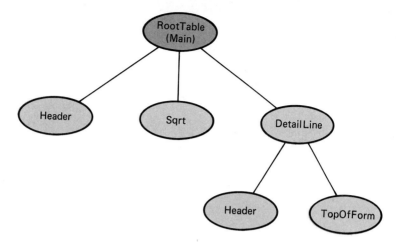

RootTable:	Reads values in a loop and calculates square roots using Sqrt
Header:	Procedure to print column headings on printer (it is used both by DetailLine and the main module)
Sqrt:	Built-in square root function
DetailLine:	Procedure to print one line of output on printer, advancing to a new page with new headings when the previous page is full
TopOfForm:	Procedure to send a "form feed" to the printer, to advance to a new page

```
 1)    program RootTable(Input, Output);
 2)    {
 3)          Written by:    XXXXXXXXX  XX/XX/XX
 4)             Purpose:    To create a table of square roots on the printer,
 5)                         with new headings on each new page.
 6)      Functions used:    Sqrt, the built in square root function
 7)     Procedures used:    TopOfForm (called by DetailLine), to advance to
 8)                            a new page.
 9)                         Header (called by DetailLine as well as main
10)                            module), to print headings.
11)                         DetailLine, to print one line of the table.
12)    }
13)
14)    const
15)       EndOfData  = -1;                  { terminating value }
16)       MaxLines   = 45;                  { maximum lines per page }
17)
18)    var
19)       Number    : integer;             { user input }
20)       LineCount : integer;             { global variable for line count }
21)       PageNumber: integer;             { global variable for page number}
22)
```

Figure 4-7   Header and DetailLine Procedures (Continued)

```
23)    procedure TopOfForm;
24)    {
25)            Written by:  XXXXXXXXXX   XX/XX/XX
26)               Purpose:  To advance to a new page on the printer. This
27)                         procedure assumes the printer recognizes the
28)                         standard top-of-form control character.
29)            Parameters:  None
30)    }
31)    begin  {TopOfForm}
32)      Writeln(Lst, Chr(12))
33)    end;  {TopOfForm}
34)
35)    procedure Header;
36)    {
37)            Written by:  XXXXXXXXXX   XX/XX/XX
38)               Purpose:  To print headings at the top of a page.
39)            Parameters:  None
40)          Globals used:  Page Number, printed and incremented by 1.
41)    }
42)    begin  {Header}
43)      Writeln(Lst, ' ':29, 'TABLE OF SQUARE ROOTS', ' ':10, 'page ',
44)              PageNumber: 1);
45)      Writeln(Lst);
46)      Writeln(Lst, ' ':28,  'Number        Square Root');
47)      Writeln(Lst, ' ':27, '--------        -------------');
48)      Writeln(Lst);
49)      PageNumber := PageNumber + 1
50)    end;  {Header}
51)
52)    procedure DetailLine(Number : integer; Root : real);
53)    {
54)            Written by:  XXXXXXXXXX   XX/XX/XX
55)               Purpose:  To print a detail line (one line of a table).
56)                         If the page is full, it first advances to a
57)                         new page and prints headings.
58)            Parameters:  Number - input, the integer number to be printed
59)                         Root - input, the square root, also to be printed.
60)          Globals used:  LineCount, used to see if it is time to start a
61)                         new page; set back to 0 for each new page.
62)        Procedures used:  TopOfForm, to advance to a new page.
63)                          Header, to print headings.
64)    }
65)    begin  {DetailLine}
66)
67)    {*** Check for full page.}
68)
69)      if LineCount = MaxLines then
70)         begin
71)           TopOfForm;
72)           Header;
73)           LineCount := 0
74)         end:  {if}
75)
```

Figure 4-7   Header and DetailLine Procedures (Continued)

```
76)        {*** Print the line and increment the count of lines on this page.}
77)
78)          Writeln(Lst, ' ':29, Number:4, ' ':7, Root:10:4);
79)          LineCount := LineCount + 1
80)       end;  {DetailLine}
81)
82)
83)       begin {RootTable}
84)
85)       {*** Initialize line counter and page number, and print headings.}
86)
87)          LineCount   := 0;
88)          PageNumber  := 1;
89)          Header;
90)
91)       {*** Read numbers in a loop, calculate square roots and print.}
92)
93)          repeat
94)            Writeln;
95)            Write('Enter a number (-1 to terminate): ');
96)            Readln(Number);
97)            if  Number <> EndOfData then
98)              begin
99)                Writeln('The square root is ', Sqrt(Number):10:4);
100)               DetailLine(Number, Sqrt(Number))
101)             end;  {if}
102)          until  Number = EndOfData;
103)
104)       {*** Print terminating message and stop program.}
105)
106)          Writeln;
107)          Writeln('RootTable program is terminating.')
108)       end.
```

SAMPLE INPUT AND OUTPUT
Terminal:

```
Enter a number (-1 to terminate): 6
The square root is    2.4495

Enter a number (-1 to terminate): 4
The square root is    2.0000

Enter a number (-1 to terminate): 10
The square root is    3.1623

Enter a number (-1 to terminate): 0
The square root is    0.0000

Enter a number (-1 to terminate): 1231
The square root is   35.0856

Enter a number (-1 to terminate): 97
The square root is    9.8489
```

Figure 4-7   Header and DetailLine Procedures (Continued)

```
Enter a number (-1 to terminate): 50
The square root is      7.0711

Enter a number (-1 to terminate): -1

RootTable program is terminating.
```

Printer (with MaxLines temporarily changed to 3 rather than 45):
  First page:

```
              TABLE OF SQUARE ROOTS          page 1

          Number          Square Root
          -------         -------------

             6               2.4495
             4               2.0000
            10               3.1623
```

Second page:

```
              TABLE OF SQUARE ROOTS          page 2

          Number          Square Root
          -------         -------------

             0               0.0000
           1231              35.0856
             97               9.8489
```

Third page:

```
              TABLE OF SQUARE ROOTS          page 3

          Number          Square Root
          -------         -------------

             50               7.0711
```

Figure 4-7 Header and DetailLine Procedures

The program in Figure 4-7 contains some interesting features. First, notice that the header printing routine prints and then increments a PageNumber variable (lines 43 and 49). That variable is not included as a parameter or a local variable; hence it is global. The main program initializes its value at 1 (line 88), and the Header procedure updates it.

COMMENT PageNumber could not be local. If it were, it would never change its value.

The TopOfForm routine (lines 23 to 33) indicates a method of going to the top of a new page. The character represented by Chr(12) is (for most printers) a "form feed." This causes the printer to advance the paper to what it thinks is the top of a new page. Provided the paper was at the top of a page when the printer was turned on, this will generally work out correctly. We choose to use a procedure to perform this activity because the technique, although short, is "messy"; it is better to hide the details.

The DetailLine procedure not only prints the output line, but also counts how many have been printed. If 45 lines have been printed, it calls Header (line 72) to advance to a new page prior to printing the line. The global variable LineCount, which is initialized to 0 by the main program (line 87), is incremented by DetailLine (line 79). Whenever a new page is begun, it is reset to 0 (line 73).

The global constant MaxLines (declared in line 15) indicates how many lines we want on each page. This is used by DetailLine to see if the page is "full" (line 69). This proved useful in preliminary testing of the program. We changed its value (temporarily) to 3, which allowed us to test multiple pages of output more quickly.

Finally, observe that the main program passes the value "Sqrt(Number)" for the DetailLine procedure's second parameter (line 100). Because that parameter is a value parameter, this is legal.

This example can appear complicated at first. However, you should study it carefully. It contains some ideas you may wish to use (or improve upon) in programs that create tables of printed output.

□
RECURSION   Pascal subprograms are allowed to call themselves. A subprogram that calls itself is a **recursive** subprogram, and the process of calling oneself is called **recursion.**

Recursion is an extremely useful tool in certain areas of computer science. For some applications, it represents the easiest approach to understanding and solving a problem. In addition, it is frequently easier to *prove* a subprogram's correctness when the subprogram is written recursively.

In this subsection, we will examine a few recursive subprograms. Our purpose is twofold. First, we wish to develop a mode of thinking that lends itself to finding recursive solutions to problems. Second, we want to understand how recursion actually works. We begin this study here; Chapter 10 provides a more in-depth examination of the topic.

For our first example, consider the problem of raising an integer number to an integer power. We wish to calculate

$$a^n$$

where both a and n are integers and n is not negative. Suppose we decide to write a function with header

```
function Power(A, N : integer) : integer;
```

How do we go about it?

One possibility is to observe that the following property holds:

$$a^n = a \cdot a^{n-1}$$

A naive approach might be this:

```
function Power(A, N : integer) : integer;
begin  {Power}
  Power := A * Power(A, N-1)
end;  {Power}
```

Although naive, this is almost correct, and it captures the spirit of recursion very nicely:

Restate the problem in terms of a "simpler" form of the same problem.

In this case, a^{n-1} is "simpler" than a^n because the exponent is one less.

To see what is wrong with this function, let us trace its execution for A = 4 and N = 3. When the function is invoked, space is set aside in the computer memory for the two value parameters. We can visualize the situation as shown:

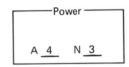

The first step that Power takes is to invoke itself with actual parameters A and N − 1 (4 and 2, respectively). This causes additional space to be set aside for a second "instance" of the two value parameters:

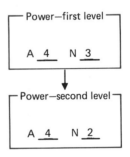

The arrow signifies that the first-level Power has invoked the second-level Power.

The second-level Power in turn invokes a third level, which invokes a fourth level, which invokes a fifth level. At this point, we have

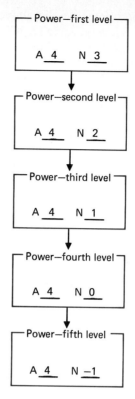

As you can see, the fifth level will in turn call a sixth level, and so on forever. What we need is a way to terminate this process.

The figure above can suggest a possibility. The fourth-level version of Power has to calculate 4 to the 0 power, which is simply 1. Suppose we rewrite the Power function as shown in Figure 4-8.

```
function Power(A, N : integer) : integer;
{
       Written by:  XXXXXXXX, XX/XX/XX
          Purpose:  To raise an integer to an integer power. If the
                    numbers are too large, overflow may yield an
                    incorrect result.
       Parameters:  A - input, the number to raise to the power
                    N - input, the power (must be 0 or higher)
   Functions used:  Power is called recursively.
}
begin  {Power}
  if N = 0 then
    Power := 1
  else
    Power := A * Power(A, N-1)
end;  {Power}
```

Figure 4-8 Recursive Function for a^n

In the tracing we did above, the fourth-level Power now will not invoke a fifth level. Since its value for N is 0, it will instead return the answer 1 to the third level. The third level will multiply this answer times A (which is 4), returning the answer 4 to the second level. The second level will multiply this by A, sending 16 to the first level. Finally, the first level will multiply this by 4, returning the answer 64 to the original caller.

There are two important principles of recursion illustrated by this example. (We have stated one previously.) They are

---

1. For the general case, phrase the answer in terms of a simpler version of the same problem.
2. Identify one or more simple base cases for which the answer is easy to calculate *without a recursive call*.

We can now identify what "simpler" means: closer to the base cases. This ensures that the process will not keep on invoking new levels infinitely.

In the example, N = 0 was identified as a base case where the answer is easy. For larger values of N, the relationship

$$a^n = a \cdot a^{n-1}$$

gave the answer in terms of a simpler version of the same problem.

COMMENT This function works only for positive values of N. In the exercises, you will be asked to consider negative values. The function would have to be real to handle this. For example, 4 to the −1 power means 1 divided by 4 to the 1 power, which is 0.25.

Now let us consider a nonnumerical application of recursion. Given a string, we wish to "double" it.[3] For example, the following values of the string yield the indicated answers:

String	Answer
'A'	'AA'
'Sam'	'SSaamm'
'DoubleIt'	'DDoouubblleeIItt'
''	'' (the null string doubled is still null)

To solve this problem, we use the two principles of recursion listed above.

1. Phrase an answer in terms of a simpler version of the same problem. For strings, one way to get a simpler string is to remove the first character. The resulting string is shorter and therefore simpler. (It is closer to the base case.) We call ourselves with this shorter string, using the answer obtained to build our answer.

2. Identify a simple base case: if the string is null, the answer is simply the null string.

In writing recursive subprograms, it is not necessary to trace the subprogram as we did for Power. (Once we have written it, however, tracing can help us understand how it really works.) When writing the subprogram, we think as follows:

Assuming the recursive call does calculate the correct answer for the simpler problem, how can I use that to calculate the answer for the original problem?

In our example, suppose our string is 'fine'. We will call ourselves with the simpler string 'ine' and trust that the answer will be correct ('iinnee'). To finish the problem, we concatenate 'f' on the front of this twice. Figure 4-9 contains the solution which is based on this observation.

NOTES   *1.* We have used a procedure Split to split a string into two pieces: the first character and the rest of the string. In writing recursive subprograms using strings, you can utilize this procedure as illustrated here. One of the exercises indicates one way this procedure could be written.

```
procedure DoubleString(AString : String255; var Doubled : String255);
{
      Written by:   XXXXXXX, XX/XX/XX
         Purpose:   To 'double' a string by duplicating each character.
      Parameters:   AString - input, the string to be doubled, assumed no
                              longer than 127 characters
                    Doubled - output, the doubled string
  Procedures used:  Split, to split off the first character of the string.
                    DoubleString is called recursively.
}
var
   First        : String255;                {the first character}
   Rest         : String255;                {the rest of the string}
   RestDoubled  : String255;                {the rest, doubled recursively}

begin   {DoubleString}
   if AString = '' then
     Doubled := ''
   else
     begin
       Split(AString, First, Rest);
       DoubleString(Rest, RestDoubled);
       Doubled := First + First + RestDoubled
     end   {if}
end;   {DoubleString}
```

Figure 4-9   Doubling a String Recursively

2. The named type String255 has been defined globally as string[255], Turbo's maximum size. Our procedure "works" for any input string whose length is 127 or less. (However, on testing the program, we find that for long strings we run out of memory space because each level of the recursive DoubleString procedure contains its own copies of the value parameter AString and the local variables First, Rest, and RestDoubled. See the exercises for some possible enhancements.)

□
DPT

1. Subprograms must be declared before they are used. This implies that the lower level subprograms in the hierarchy chart will come first in the program.

2. Each module declares its own local variables. These cannot be accessed outside the module.

3. Make sure you understand precisely what task each module is to perform, and write the module to perform that task. For example, many procedures are designed to calculate answers for the calling program, which will use them and perhaps later print them. If the procedure's subtask does not include printing the answers, then it should not print them. (A function should never include any I/O.)

4. Use parameters as the primary means of communication. Do not use globals without giving the use careful thought.

5. Be careful in your choice of value and var parameters. Value parameters should be used to supply values to the subprogram. Var parameters are used to pass answers back to the calling program or to modify a variable in the calling program.

6. A function cannot be used to calculate an array answer. Instead, the array should be a var parameter for a procedure.

7. Always include an assignment to the function name in a function. Never assign a value to a procedure name.

8. Remember that any reference to the function name, other than on the left side of an assignment statement, represents a recursive call. If this is what was intended, great. If not, use a local variable to obtain the answer, then assign the answer to the function name.

9. When writing a recursive function or procedure, make sure you identify the base case or cases that do not involve a recursive call. Without this, the recursive process will have no way to stop.

Exactly what will happen depends on the problem. One possibility is a "stack overflow" (Turbo runtime error FF). This simply means that the program has run out of memory. (Each new level of the subprogram contains space for its value parameters and also any local variables.) Another possibility is that the program attempts to do some illegal activity and terminates.

■■■■■■
REVIEW

Terms and concepts

recursion
recursive
nested invocation
header line

parameter list
var parameter
value parameter
function type

Pascal syntax

Program layout:

Program header line
Global constants, types, and variables
Procedures and functions
Main module body (compound statement)

Form of subprogram:

Header line
Local constants, types, and variables
Body of subprogram (compound statement)

Header line form:

```
procedure procedure-name parameter-list;
function function-name parameter-list : function-type
```

Parameter list (optional):

One or more repetitions, in parentheses, separated by semicolons, of:

```
var variables separated by commas : type
```

"Var" is optional; default is value parameter

Function-types allowed:

Integer   Boolean   Named string type (Turbo extension)
Real   Char

Function versus procedure   See table on page 279.

Writing a subprogram
1. (a) Identify the subtask.
   (b) Choose a function or procedure.
   (c) Choose a name (and a type if a function is chosen).
2. Decide on parameters (value and var).
3. Write an algorithm, identifying local variables.
4. Code in Pascal.

Recursion   Two principles:

1. Write the general case using a recursive call to solve a simpler version of the same problem.
2. Identify base case(s) not involving a recursive call.

DPT

1. Declare before use.
2. Local variables are usable only in the module.
3. Identify subtasks precisely.
4. Avoid global variables.
5. Be careful in choosing between value and var parameters.
6. Remember a function answer cannot be an array.
7. Always assign an answer to the function name (in the function). Never assign a value to a procedure name.
8. Avoid unintentional recursion.
9. When using recursion, don't forget the base case(s).

■■■■■■
EXERCISES

*1. Write a subprogram to calculate the volume and surface area of a sphere of radius R.
$$V = \frac{1}{3}\pi r^3$$
$$S = 4\pi r^2$$

2. If P dollars are deposited in a savings account earning interest I compounded annually, then after N years the amount present is given by
$$A = P(1 + i)^n$$
Write a subprogram to calculate A and also the total interest earned, given P, I, and N.

*3. Write a subprogram to determine the state tax based on the following rules. First, $500 is deducted from the income for each dependent. Then a standard deduction of 10 percent of the original income is subtracted. Finally, the tax is determined by the following table.

Resulting Income	Tax
Less than 0	0
0–10,000	2% of resulting income
Over 10,000	$200.00 plus 2.5% of amount over $10,000

4. *a. Write a subprogram to find the largest and smallest of two integers I and J.
   b. Write a subprogram to find the largest and smallest of five integers.

5. Write a subprogram to calculate the letter grade, given the number grade, based on the following table. (What type of variable is the answer?)

Number	Letter
90 up	H
75–89.999	C
Under 75	F

*6. Write a subprogram with three integer parameters. This subprogram will find the range of the numbers, that is, the difference between the largest of the three and the smallest of the three. Use the MaxMin procedure, developed in this section, to calculate the largest and the smallest.

*7. Write a Boolean function that determines whether or not two given real numbers are within 0.00001 of each other.

8. One way to approximate the square root of a real number X is by the method of iteration, as given by Newton. This consists of choosing a first approximation (perhaps X itself), then repeatedly getting a new (and better) approximation by using the formula:

$$a_{new} = \frac{1}{2}\left(a_{old} + \frac{X}{a_{old}}\right)$$

Thus, we have a loop involved. We will continue until

$$|a_{new} - a_{old}| < 0.00001$$

(Use the function from Exercise 7.)

Write a subprogram to approximate the square root of X in this manner. Then write a main program that invokes your program and also the built-in Sqrt function. Print both answers and compare them. How good is your subprogram? How fast?

9. a. Write a subprogram that, given an integer and a position, finds the digit in that position of the integer. For example, for the number 29867, we would have the following answers for various positions.

Position	Answer
1	7
2	6
3	8
4	9
5	2
Any other	0

b. Using this subprogram, print the digits of a number in reverse order, one per line.

10. Write Boolean functions for the following:

a. Given four integer test scores, see whether or not the average is at least 60.

*b. Repeat part (a), but the parameter is an integer array containing 14 weekly quiz scores; see if the average is at least 12.0.

c. Given a character, determine whether it is a vowel.

d. Given three integers Value, Low, and High, see whether Value lies between Low and High, inclusive.

*e. Given a four-digit integer, determine whether or not it is a "palindrome" (reads the same front to back as back to front). Examples: 1001 and 3443 are; 6117 is not. Also, 110 is because 110 is 0110 as a four-digit number.

f. See whether a given point (x,y) lies within the "unit square" from (0,0) to (1,1).

g. See whether a given point (x,y) lies within a circle with center $(0,0)$ and a given radius.

11. Use the function written in Exercise 10(d) as a tool for the following:

    *a. Write a GetScores procedure that reads three test scores and makes sure each lies between 0 and 100 inclusive.

    b. Write a segment of code to see if at least one of the integers I and J lies between 500 and 553, inclusive.

    c. Write a segment of code to see if an integer A is at least ½ of B and no more than twice B.

12. a. Write a function to simulate the following game. It should generate random numbers in the range 1 to 100, continuing until a generated number is divisible by 10. If the sum of the numbers generated (including the last one) is 1000 or more, the result is 'W' (win); for 500 to 999, it is 'T' (tie); and for less than 500, it is 'L' (lose).

    b. In a large number of plays, what percentage of wins, losses, and ties might you expect? Write a program to find out.

13. Turbo Pascal supplies some facilities for working with strings that we have not discussed yet. For example, a string is treated as very similar to an array of characters. For the following descriptions, StrngVar represents any string variable. We can write

    ```
    StrngVar[I]
    ```

    to obtain the Ith character of the string. If Name has the value 'John Smith', for example, then Name[1] is 'J' and Name[7] is 'm'.

    In addition, there are some useful functions. One is

    ```
    Length(StrngVar)
    ```

    which calculates the present length of the string. Another is

    ```
    Copy(StrngVar, Position, Number)
    ```

    The answer is a substring of StrngVar, beginning at position Position and having Number characters. These examples illustrate the functions:

    ```
    Length('Tom Jones') is 9
    Length('')          is 0

    Copy('ABCDEFG', 3, 4)   is 'CDEF'
    Copy('Alphabet', 1, 1)  is 'A'
    Copy('Tom', 4, 2,)      is ''    (null, 4 is beyond end)
    Copy('Tom', 2, 5)       is 'om'  (only copies what is there)
    ```

    Using these functions, do the following:

    *a. Write a procedure to print a string, one letter per line. For the string 'find', the output would be

    ```
    f
    i
    n
    d
    ```

    *b. Write a function to count the blanks in a string.

    *c. Write the Split procedure that was used in this section.

d. Find the middle character (or characters) in a string. For 'hop', the answer would be 'o', for 'Mary' it would be 'ar'.

*e. Write a SplitLast procedure that takes off the last rather than the first character.

f. Write a procedure that removes both the first and the last characters.

14. a. Write a subprogram to find the sum of an array. The parameters are A, an IntegerArray, and N, which indicates how many values are in the array.

b. Modify part (a) to "drop the lowest value." For the list

$$3, 7, 2, 5$$

the sum would be 15. Hint: As you are calculating the sum, find the lowest value. Then subtract that from the sum.

c. Modify part (a) to drop the two lowest values.

*15. Write a subprogram to find the smallest and largest values in an integer array. The parameters include a variable telling how many values are in the array.

*16. As part of a check printing program, it is desired to print a line such as

EXACTLY 55 DOLLARS AND 04 CENTS

Write a procedure to accomplish this, given a real number containing the amount to be printed.

17. Repeat Exercise 16, but print words instead of numbers:

EXACTLY FIFTY FIVE DOLLARS AND FOUR CENTS

Assume the dollars are in the range 0 to 99.

18. a. As it stands, the Power function is not very good on a microcomputer with MaxInt of 32767. For example, it says that 11 to the power 4 is 14641 (which is correct) and that 11 to the power 5 is 29979 (which is not even close). Modify the function so that it will return a value of 0 when its answer is going to be wrong. Hint: Consider how you can tell that A * Power(A, N−1) is going to be larger than MaxInt.

b. Another approach to the problem mentioned in part (a) would be to make the function a real function rather than an integer function. This will expand its range of usefulness. Although the resulting answers may not be completely accurate for large values, they will at least be reasonably close. Make the suggested change.

c. Modify the Power function to handle negative integer powers. Use the fact that

$$a^{-n} = 1/a^n$$

*19. Write a recursive function to calculate n! (n factorial). This is defined as $n! = n \cdot (n - 1) \cdot \ldots \cdot 3 \cdot 2 \cdot 1$. Hint: $n! = n * (n - 1)!$

*20. Write a recursive GCD function to find the greatest common divisor of two positive integers m and n. An algorithm due to Euclid states that if m divides evenly into n, then the answer is m. Otherwise, it is the same as the greatest common divisor of (n mod m) and m.

21. Write an LCM function to find the least common multiple of two positive integers m and n. Hint: For any two positive integers m and n, it is true that

LCM(m,n) * GCD(m,n) = m * n

22. A famous sequence of numbers is the collection of Fibonacci numbers, defined as

$$F_0 = 0$$
$$F_1 = 1$$
$$F_n = F_{n-1} + F_{n-2} \qquad \text{for } n \geq 2$$

Using these rules, we can list the first few Fibonacci numbers:

$$0, 1, 1, 2, 3, 5, 8, 13, 21, 34, 55, \ldots$$

Observe that each one is the sum of the previous 2.

    Write a recursive function Fibonacci(N) that calculates F_N for a given N.

23. The usual definition for the binomial coefficients is expressed in terms of factorials:

$$\binom{n}{k} = \frac{n!}{k!(n-k)!} \qquad (0 \leq k \leq n)$$

However, it is also possible to give a recursive definition. There are two base cases: if $k = 0$, then the answer is 1; if $n = k$, then the answer is 1. The general case is given by

$$\binom{n}{k} = \binom{n-1}{k-1} + \binom{n-1}{k}$$

Use this definition to write a recursive function Binomial (N,K).

24. By imitating the example in this section, write a recursive subprogram to do the following string manipulations. You can utilize the Split procedure.

    a. Reverse a string. For 'ABCD', the answer is 'DCBA'.
  *b. See if the string contains a given character. Hint: There are two base cases: (1) the null string and (2) a string whose first character matches the given character.
    c. Count the blanks in a string
    d. Create a string with all blanks removed. Hint: For the complex case, you either will or will not concatenate the first character with the result from the recursive call.

25. a. If you test the DoubleIt procedure in the text, you will find that "stack overflow" occurs for long strings. This simply means that the program has run out of memory due to having several versions of DoubleIt, each with a value parameter and three local variables. Experiment to discover the longest string that does not cause stack overflow. You will need to write the Split procedure [Exercise 13(c)] to run this experiment.
    b. Modify the Split procedure and the DoubleIt procedure to make the first parameter type char rather than String 255. Does this increase the size string that can be handled? If so, suggest other similar modifications.

26. Describe a unit test plan for these exercises in this section.

a. Exercise 3	*b. Exercise 4
*c. Exercise 5	d. Exercise 6
e. Exercise 7	f. Exercise 9
g. Exercise 13(a)	h. Exercise 13(b)
i. Exercise 13(c)	j. Exercise 13(d)

k. Exercise 14(a)　　l. Exercise 14(b)
m. Exercise 15　　*n. Exercise 16
o. Exercise 19　　*p. Exercise 20
q. Exercise 24(a)　　*r. Exercise 24(b)
s. Exercise 24(c)　　t. Exercise 24(d)

NOTES FOR SECTION 4-2

1. Standard Pascal allows us to define the notion of a string as an array of characters. It does not allow us to declare a function of type string. If we wish to return a string answer to the calling program, it must be a var parameter of a procedure. Turbo Pascal has relaxed this restriction.

2. Some versions of Pascal which do support string types and concatenation may not allow functions to return a string answer. In this case we would simply use a procedure, with AddressLine as an output parameter.

3. This example uses Turbo Pascal's string declarations and concatenation. For other versions of Pascal which support string types, minor modifications will be needed. You should read through the example even if your Pascal does not have a string type built in.

4-3 CASE STUDIES

In this section, we present three case studies that use a number of the ideas developed to this point in the text.

CASE STUDY NO. 4

Statement of problem. Write a program to print all the prime numbers between 1 and N, where N is a value supplied by the user.

Preliminary analysis. A prime number is a positive integer larger than 1 that has no divisor other than itself and 1. The first few primes are

$$2, 3, 5, 7, 11, 13, 17, \ldots$$

The number 4 is not prime (it is divisible by 2) nor is 15 (it is divisible by both 3 and 5). Notice that the number 1 is *not* a prime as mathematicians define the concept.

We will want to put limits on the values of N that are allowed. Suppose we specify that N must lie between 2 and 1000, inclusive.

Algorithms and variable list.

1. Main Module. We begin with a general description of what we must do to solve the problem:

```
print instructions
read a valid value for N
for each integer I in the range from 2 to N, do the following:
    check I to see if it is prime
    if it is, then print I
```

There are four "obvious" candidates for submodules:

- A procedure to print instructions
- A procedure to read a valid value for N
- A Boolean function to see if a number is prime
- A procedure to print a number.

We will use a procedure for printing in order to print 20 numbers on the terminal, then pause until the user is ready to continue. (If we did not do this, the numbers would be displayed too rapidly to read.)

For our variable list, we have the following:

Constant:	MaxLines	value 20	Maximum number of lines to be printed per screen
Input:	N	integer	Indicates the desired range
Output:	I	integer	Printed if prime
Other:	LineCount	integer	Used to print MaxLines lines per screen

LineCount will be a global variable, initialized to 0 in the main module and updated in the printing module. We will compare it to MaxLines to see if the screen is full.

The hierarchy chart at this point is

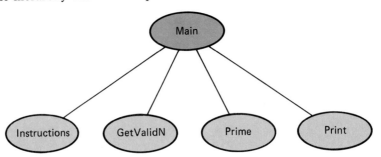

2. GetValidN Procedure. This is very similar to the validation procedures we have written before. The logic is

```
issue prompt
read N
while N is not valid do the following:
    error message
    read N again
```

The variable N must be a var parameter.

3. Print Procedure. In some ways, this is similar to the procedure we used in the previous section. However, we will pause just after printing the twentieth value rather than just before printing the twenty-first. Using the global variable LineCount, we write:

print Number
add 1 to LineCount
if LineCount = MaxLines then do the following:
    issue a message
    wait for user to hit return
    reset LineCount to 0

The accompanying variable list is:

Input parameter:	Number	integer	The number to be printed
Global variable:	LineCount	integer	Keeps track of lines printed
Global constant:	MaxLines	value = 20	Maximum number of lines to be printed per screen

4. Prime Function. A number is prime if its smallest divisor (other than 1) is the number itself. Hence, we can do the following

use a function Divisor to get SmallDivisor
if SmallDivisor = Number, our answer is True,
            otherwise it is False

The variables are

Input parameter:	Number	integer	The number to check
Other:	SmallDivisor	integer	The smallest divisor (other than 1)

At this point, our hierarchy chart is

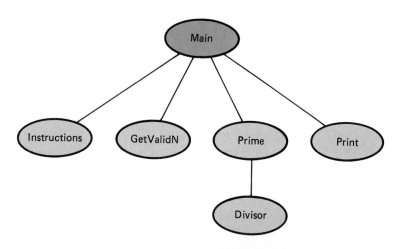

5. Divisor Function. This function can be written by using a search loop, starting at 2 and continuing until we find a divisor for the number.

We use these variables:

Input parameter: Number integer The number for which to find a divisor (assumed to be ≥2)

Other: PotentialDivisor integer Takes on values 2, 3, . . . until a divisor is found

Since 2 can itself be a divisor, we need a while loop rather than a repeat–until loop.

```
set PotentialDivisor to 2
while we still do not have a divisor do this:
        add 1 to PotentialDivisor
assign the final value of PotentialDivisor as the function answer
```

Test plan. We will use a top-down testing strategy augmented by a unit test for the critical module (the Divisor function). The planned tests include the following:

GetValidN: borderlines on valid : 1, 2, 1000, 1001
others in between

Print: borderlines on total number printed:
1, 20, 21, 40, 41
others in between

Prime: branches: is prime, is not
number of factors : 1 (example, $9 = 3 \cdot 3$)
>1 (example, $105 = 3 \cdot 5 \cdot 7$)

Divisor: branches: smallest divisor = Num
smallest divisor not = Num
smallest divisor = 2

Except for GetValidN, all of these tests will occur naturally as a part of the process of running the program.

Write in Pascal. We begin at the top level with stubs for GetValidN, Prime, and Print (Figure 4-10). Observe that we document as we go along. When we run this with a valid value of N, all the numbers from 2 to N are printed without pause.

Next we refine the procedure GetValidN and run its unit tests. This is followed by the procedure Print. Observe that because the stub version of Prime still reports that all numbers are prime, it is easy to verify that exactly twenty numbers per screen are being printed. It is also easy to force the boundary tests on the total number printed.

We now write the Prime function with a stub for Divisor. Because we want to check both branches of the Prime function, we have the stub sometimes reporting that the smallest divisor is equal to the number and sometimes not. See Figure 4-11 for the current version of the program. (Changes from Figure 4-10 are shaded.)

```
program FindPrimes(Input, Output);
{
      Written by:   XXXXXXXX  XX/XX/XX
         Purpose:   To find and print the primes between 2 and a
                    user supplied limit value. They are printed
                    20 per screen, pausing after each screenful.
   Procedures used: Instructions, to print instructions
                    GetValidN, to edit the limit value.
                    Print, to print each prime and pause after
                       each screen.
   Functions used:  Prime, to check to see if prime.
                    Divisor, to find the smallest divisor of a number
                       (called by the Prime function).

}
const
  Maximum = 1000;                     {maximum limit allowed}
  MaxLines= 20;                       {maximum number of lines per
                                        screen}

var
  N           : integer;              {indicates the desired range, input}
  I           : integer;              {loop control, printed if prime}
  LineCount   : integer;              {used to see when screen is full}

procedure Instructions; begin {stub} end;

procedure GetValidN(var N : integer);
{
    Written by:   XXXXXXXX, XX/XX/XX
       Purpose:   To obtain a valid limit from the user.
   Globals used:  Constant Maximum, the largest value allowed for N.
     Parameters:  N - output, the valid limit (will lie between 2 and
                     Maximum, inclusive)
}
begin  {GetValidN}  {stub version}
  Writeln;
  Write('Enter a number in the range 2 to ', Maximum:1, ': ');
  Readln(N)
end;  {GetValidN}

function Prime(Number : integer) : boolean;
{
     Written by:   XXXXXXXX, XX/XX/XX
        Purpose:   To see if a given number is prime.
     Parameters:   Number - input, the number to be checked
   Functions used: Divisor is used to find the smallest divisor of
                   the number.
}
begin  {Prime}  {stub version}
  Prime := true
end;  {Prime}
```

Figure 4-10 Case Study No. 4 (Find Primes) (Continued)

```
procedure Print(Number : integer);
{
        Written by:   XXXXXXXX, XX/XX/XX
           Purpose:   To print a number on the screen, pausing at
                      the bottom of each screen.
     Globals used:    Variable LineCount, which has been initialized to 0
                        prior to the first call of Print.
                      Constant MaxLines indicating the maximum lines per
                        screen.
      Parameters:     Number - input, the number to be printed
}
begin  {Print}    {stub version}
  Writeln(Number:6)
end;  {Print}


begin {FindPrimes}

{*** Print instructions, and initialize global line counter.}

  Instructions;
  LineCount := 0;

{*** Ask the user for the desired range.}

  GetValidN(N);

{*** Loop to check each number in the range.}

  for I := 2 to N do
    begin
      if Prime(I) then
        Print(I)
    end;  {for loop}

{*** Terminate.}

  Writeln('FindPrimes program terminating')
end.
```

Figure 4-10   Case Study No. 4 (Find Primes)

COMMENTS   *1.* In the Prime function, we do not really need the local variable SmallDivisor. We could write the body as

```
if Divisor(Number) = Number then
    Prime := true
else
    Prime := false
```

2. In fact, we could write

```
Prime := (Divisor(Number) = Number)
```

The condition "Divisor(Number) = Number" is either true or false, and the answer for Prime is the same true or false value.

```
program FindPrimes(Input, Output);
{
      Written by:   XXXXXXXX  XX/XX/XX
         Purpose:   To find and print the primes between 2 and a
                    user supplied limit value. They are printed
                    20 per screen, pausing after each screenful.
   Procedures used: Instructions, to print instructions.
                    GetValidN, to edit the limit value.
                    Print, to print each prime and pause after
                       each screen.
    Functions used: Prime, to check to see if prime.
                    Divisor, to find the smallest divisor of a number
                       (called by the Prime function).
}
const
   Maximum = 1000;                            {maximum limit allowed}

var
   N            : integer;       {indicates the desired range, input}
   I            : integer;       {loop control, printed if prime}
   LineCount    : integer;       {global variable used to see when
                                      screen is full}

procedure Instructions; begin {stub} end;

procedure GetValidN(var N : integer);
{
      Written by:   XXXXXXXX, XX/XX/XX
         Purpose:   To obtain a valid limit from the user.
      Globals used: Constant Maximum, the largest value allowed for N.
        Parameters: N - output, the valid limit (will lie between 2 and
                       Maximum, inclusive)
}
begin  {GetValidN}
   Writeln;
   Write('Enter a number in the range 2 to ', Maximum:1, ': ');
   Readln(N);
   while (N < 2) or (N > Maximum) do
      begin
         Write('Illegal number entered. Try again: ');
         Readln(N)
      end  {while}

end;  {GetValidN}


function Divisor(Num : integer) : integer;
{
      Written by:   XXXXXXXX, XX/XX/XX
         Purpose:   To find the smallest divisor of a number.
        Parameters: Num - input, the number to be checked (assumed to
                       be at least 2)
}
```

Figure 4-11   Case Study No. 4 (Find Primes) (Continued)

```
begin  {Divisor}  {stub version}
  if Odd(Num) then
    Divisor := Num
  else
    Divisor := Num - 1
end;  {Divisor}


function Prime(Number : integer) : boolean;
{
     Written by:  XXXXXXXX, XX/XX/XX
        Purpose:  To see if a given number is prime.
     Parameters:  Number - input, the number to be checked
  Functions used:  Divisor is used to find the smallest divisor of
                   the number.
}
var
  SmallDivisor : integer;              {smallest divisor of Number}

begin  {Prime}
  SmallDivisor := Divisor(Number);
  if SmallDivisor = Number then
    Prime := true
  else
    Prime := false
end;  {Prime}


procedure Print(Number : integer);
{
     Written by:  XXXXXXXX, XX/XX/XX
        Purpose:  To print a number on the screen, pausing at
                  the bottom of each screen.
    Globals used:  Variable LineCount, which has been initialized to 0
                   prior to the first call of Print.
                   Constant MaxLines indicating the maximum lines per
                   screen.
     Parameters:  Number - input, the number to be printed
}
begin  {Print}
  Writeln(Number:6);
  LineCount := LineCount + 1;
  if LineCount = 20 then
    begin
      Writeln;
      Write('Tap RETURN to continue:');
      Readln;
      LineCount := 0
    end  {if}
end;  {Print}


begin {FindPrimes}

{*** Print instructions, and initialize global line counter.}
```

Figure 4-11   Case Study No. 4 (Find Primes) (Continued)

```
   Instructions;
   LineCount := 0;

{*** Ask the user for the desired range.}

   GetValidN(N);

{*** Loop to check each number in the range.}

   for I := 2 to N do
     begin
       if Prime(I) then
         Print(I)
     end;  {for loop}

{*** Terminate.}

   Writeln('FindPrimes program terminating')
end.
```

Figure 4-11   Case Study No. 4 (Find Primes)

Finally, we refine the Divisor function. Because this is a critical module, we give it a special unit test with a driver. (Notice that in the context of our current program, we could not tell if this function is correct. For example, if it reported that the smallest divisor of 36 is 18 and the smallest divisor of 49 is 3, our program would appear to be correct.) Figure 4-12 contains the driver with the function and a sample run. In Figure 4-13, we present a sample run of the entire program with the stub Divisor function replaced by that in Figure 4-12.

```
program DivisorDriver(Input, Output);
{
     Written by:   XXXXXXXX  XX/XX/XX
        Purpose:   To test the Divisor function.
 Functions used:   Divisor, to find the smallest divisor of a number
}
const
  EndOfData = 0;                        {terminating value for loop}

var
  N             : integer;             {number to find smallest divisor of}

function Divisor(Num : integer) : integer;
{
     Written by:   XXXXXXXX, XX/XX/XX
        Purpose:   To find the smallest divisor of a number.
     Parameters:   Num - input, the number to be checked (assumed
                         to be at least 2)
}
var
  PotentialDivisor : integer;          {takes on values 2, 3, . . .}

begin  {Divisor}
  PotentialDivisor := 2;
```

Figure 4-12   Driver for Smallest Divisor Function (Continued)

```
    while Num mod PotentialDivisor <> 0 do
      begin
        PotentialDivisor := PotentialDivisor + 1
      end;  {while}

    Divisor := PotentialDivisor
  end;  {Divisor}
```

```
  begin  {DivisorDriver}

    repeat
      Writeln;
      Write('Enter an integer (2 or higher, 0 to quit): ');
      Readln(N);
      if N <> EndOfData then
        Writeln('The smallest divisor is ', Divisor(N):1)
    until N = EndOfData;

    Writeln;
    Writeln('Driver program terminating')
  end.
```

SAMPLE INPUT AND OUTPUT

```
    Enter an integer (2 or higher, 0 to quit): 2
    The smallest divisor is 2

    Enter an integer (2 or higher, 0 to quit): 47
    The smallest divisor is 47

    Enter an integer (2 or higher, 0 to quit): 77
    The smallest divisor is 7

    Enter an integer (2 or higher, 0 to quit): 100
    The smallest divisor is 2

    Enter an integer (2 or higher, 0 to quit): 0

    Driver program terminating.
```

Figure 4-12   Driver for Smallest Divisor Function

SAMPLE INPUT AND OUTPUT FOR FINAL PROGRAM

```
Enter a number in the range 2 to 1000: 100
    2
    3
    5
    7
   11
   13
   17
```

Figure 4-13   Sample Run for Case Study No. 4 (Continued)

```
      19
      23
      29
      31
      37
      41
      43
      47
      53
      59
      61
      67
      71

Tap RETURN to continue:
      73
      79
      83
      89
      97
FindPrimes program terminating
```

Figure 4-13   Sample Run for Case Study No. 4

Enhancements. This case study has adopted a "brute force" approach to finding primes: check each candidate by locating its smallest divisor. Moreover, the process of finding the smallest divisor has been carried out in the most straightforward manner. As a reader, you should be aware that many improvements are possible. The exercises suggest several of these improvements.

CASE STUDY NO. 5

Statement of problem. Write a program that reads a series of integers from the terminal. For each number input, the program should factor the number. For example, for the series of inputs 35, 100, and 17, the output would be similar to this:

```
        5   7
        2   2   5   5
       17
```

Preliminary analysis. Let us restrict the input to positive numbers greater than or equal to 2. We can use a slightly modified revision of the procedure GetValidN from the previous case study. Also, we observe that the first number to be printed is the smallest divisor of the number. In the previous case study, we wrote a function Divisor that we can use to find that smallest divisor. A tentative hierarchy chart is

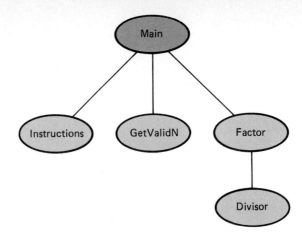

"Factor" is the procedure that will do the factoring.

It is always a good idea to consider whether previously written modules are either exactly or almost what we need for the current program.

Algorithms and variable lists

1. Main Module. We need only one variable and one constant.

Constant:	EndOfData	value 1	Terminating entry
Input:	N	integer	Number to be factored

The algorithm is

repeat these steps until the user enters the terminating value
    read a valid N (use GetValidN)
   if N is not the terminal value,
      factor the number N (use Factor)

2. GetValidN Procedure. This is almost identical to the procedure in Case Study No. 4. For this case study, a valid number is 1 (the terminating value) or higher.

3. Divisor Function. This function was written and unit tested as part of Case Study No. 4. We will use editor commands to obtain an exact copy of the function to use in the present program. No further planning, writing, or unit testing is required.

4. Factor Procedure. This procedure is the heart of the case study. To aid in writing it, let us suppose the number to be factored is 63. If we did this by hand, we might use two steps:

$$63 = 3 \cdot 21 = 3 \cdot 3 \cdot 7$$

First we find one factor (the smallest one), obtaining $3 \cdot 21$; then we factor 21. Similarly, for 245 and 100, we might write

$$245 = 5 \cdot 49 = 5 \cdot 7 \cdot 7$$

$$100 = 2 \cdot 50 = 2 \cdot 2 \cdot 25 = 2 \cdot 2 \cdot 5 \cdot 5$$

For a prime such as 17, we simply write

$$17 = 17$$

This discussion suggests a possible solution to our problem. We can state it in three steps:

   (1) Find the smallest divisor and write it
   (2) Calculate the "rest of the number": divide by the smallest divisor
   (3) Factor the rest of the number if any.

For the first two steps, we will need these variables:

Input parameter:	N	integer	The number to factor
Local variables:	FirstFactor	integer	The smallest divisor
	Quotient	integer	N div FirstFactor

In Pascal, we will write

```
FirstFactor := Divisor(N);
Writeln(FirstFactor);
Quotient := N div FirstFactor;
```

How do we factor the rest of the number (the variable Quotient)? There are several approaches; one is to simply call the Factor procedure recursively:

```
Factor(Quotient)
```

Will this work? The answer is, "Yes, almost." Remember the two important concepts of recursion:

   a. Call yourself with a simpler version of the same problem.
   b. Write a nonrecursive solution for the "simplest" (base) inputs.

Since Quotient is smaller than N, the first is satisfied. However, the second is not; we would have infinite recursion. To fix this, we note that when the number N is prime, we do not have anything left to factor. In this case, Quotient will have the value 1. We want to call Factor recursively only if Quotient is greater than 1:

```
if Quotient > 1 then
   Factor(Quotient)
```

Test plan. What tests are needed for the Factor procedure? To answer this, we consider the question, "How many factors could N have?" The answer is, "One or more." This leads to two types of test input: primes and nonprimes.

   A few other considerations can be included in the test plan. We should have numbers where the same factor is repeated several times, and some numbers where there is no such repetition. Some of our answers should be easy to check. We should test some large numbers whose answers we know. (We can do this by starting with the desired answer and multiplying it on a calculator.)

   Based on these considerations, we devise the following list of tests with the expected answers. (Note: The program as designed will print one factor per line.)

17	17					
15	3	5				
64	2	2	2	2	2	2
119	7	17				
700	2	2	5	5	7	
31407	3	19	19	29		
4171	43	97				
9409	97	97				

Write program. The program with a sample run containing some of the tests from the test plan appears in Figure 4-14.

Enhancements. One possibility, developed in the exercises, is to print the factorization on a single line rather than one number per line. We could also insert a multiplication symbol (*) between successive factors.

```
program PrintFactors(Input, Output);
{
      Written by:   XXXXXXX  XX/XX/XX
         Purpose:   To read a series of numbers and print a complete
                    factorization of each.
Procedures used:    Instructions, to print instructions.
                    GetValidN, to obtain a valid input number.
                    Factor, a recursive procedure to perform the
                       factorization.
 Functions used:    Divisor, to find the smallest divisor of a number
                       (called by the Factor procedure).
}
const
  EndOfData = 1;                     {terminating input value}

var
  N            : integer;            {number to be factored, input}

procedure Instructions; begin {stub} end;
```

{*procedure GetValidN as shown in Figure 4-11 is inserted here with minor modifications (valid range is 1 or higher)*}

{*function Divisor as shown in Figure 4-12 is inserted here*}

```
procedure Factor(N : integer);
{
      Written by:   XXXXXXX, XX/XX/XX
         Purpose:   To print the factors of a given number.
      Parameters:   N - input, the number to be factored
Procedures used:    Factor is called recursively.
 Functions used:    Divisor is used to find the smallest divisor of
                    the number.
}
var
  FirstFactor : integer;            {smallest divisor of N}
  Quotient    : integer;            {the part left after FirstFactor is
                                     factored out}

begin   {Factor}

{*** Find and print the first factor.}

  FirstFactor := Divisor(N);
  Writeln(FirstFactor:5);
```

Figure 4-14   Case Study No. 5 (Recursive Factoring) (Continued)

```
{*** If the number was not prime, factor the rest of the number}

    Quotient := N div FirstFactor;
    if Quotient > 1 then
      Factor(Quotient)
end;  {Factor}


begin {PrintFactors}
  Instructions;

  repeat
    GetValidN(N);
    if N <> EndOfData then
      Factor(N)
  until N = EndOfData;

  Writeln;
  Writeln('PrintFactors program terminating')
end.
```

SAMPLE INPUT AND OUTPUT

```
Enter a number in the range 1 or higher (1 to quit): 17
   17

Enter a number in the range 1 or higher (1 to quit): 15
    3
    5

Enter a number in the range 1 or higher (1 to quit): 64
    2
    2
    2
    2
    2
    2

Enter a number in the range 1 or higher (1 to quit): 9409
   97
   97

Enter a number in the range 1 or higher (1 to quit): 1

PrintFactors program terminating
```

Figure 4-14 Case Study No. 5 (Recursive Factoring)

CASE STUDY NO. 6

In Section 4-2, we wrote a program (Figure 4-7) that created a printed list of numbers with their square roots. In this case study, we will use some of the ideas from that program. In addition, we will include some array processing ideas.

Statement of problem. For each salesperson in a company, records are kept on the amount of sales in each month of the year. A printed report is desired that, for each person, indicates three items:

Name
12 monthly sales figures
Total sales for the year

In addition, the final page of the report should indicate the totals for the company for each month.

Preliminary analysis. Input will consist of a name and 12 sales figures. Although we could use 12 distinct variables for the sales figures, a better design would use a "real array" declared as follows:

```
const
   MaxIndex = 12;

type
   RealArray = array[1 .. MaxIndex] of real;

var
   SalesArr = RealArray;
```

Observe how similar this is to declaring integer arrays of size 1000, which we have done several times previously.

When we plan the output for this program, ideally we would like:

```
name     Jan. sales     Feb. sales . . . Dec. sales     Total sales
```

However, a "typical" microcomputer printer will print 80 columns and all this information will not fit in one line. We therefore decide on a layout like this for each person:

```
name           Jan sales      Feb sales      March sales
               Apr sales      May sales      June sales
               July sales     Aug sales      Sept sales
               Oct sales      Nov sales      Dec sales      Total sales
```

Program design. In this case study, we will not present the detailed design for each module. Rather, we will discuss the design of the program from a broader perspective.

One can view this program as containing two relatively independent components: I/O and calculations. One approach to solving the problem would be to work on one component first and then add the other. For example, we might postpone concerns about getting a "nice" output report (with headers, new pages when appropriate, etc.). Alternatively, we could tackle this aspect first. Using the program of Figure 4-7 as a starting point, we chose the latter approach. We wrote TopOfForm, Header, and DetailLine procedures, and a driver to test them. The final version of this driver program appears in Figure 4-15, along with sample input and output. (Portions to be discussed in the notes below are shaded.)

We ran this program several times, testing:

(a) Exactly one salesperson.

(b) First page exactly full, no second page.

(c) First page full, one entry on second page.

(d) Two pages full, several entries on third pages.

NOTES

1. Observe the treatment of LineCount in the DetailLine procedure (shaded). Each person's print adds five lines of output. When we do not increment LineCount by 1, it is safer to use ">=" in the comparison with MaxLines.

2. The Header procedure prints the global PageNumber, then increments it.

3. When we ran the test originally, the names were right-justified. Usually, lists of names will be left-justified, as in

Bill Johnson
Timothy Axenhall
Jo Coy

To achieve left justification, we used a local variable PrintName in the DetailLine procedure. (This method is applicable in Turbo Pascal with its string type.)

4. The DetailLine procedure uses

```
for I := 1 to 80 do Write(Lst, '-');
Writeln
```

to print a row of dashes.

5. The Name parameter for DetailLine must be a named type (String20, not string[20]).

6. The driver routine initializes global variables, assigns values to the items to be printed, and calls DetailLine the number of times indicated by the user.

```
program Driver(Input, Output);
{
      Written by:  XXXXXXXXXX  XX/XX/XX
         Purpose:  To test the header printing, page, and detail
                   line routines for compatibility.
  Procedures used: Instructions to print instructions.
                   Header to print headings.
                   TopOfForm (called by DetailLine) to advance to a new
                      page.
                   DetailLine to print a set of detail lines for one
                      individual.
}
const
  MaxIndex = 12;              { size of arrays }
  MaxLines = 45;              { maximum lines per page }
```

Figure 4-15 Driver for Printing Format (Continued)

```
type
  String20  = string[20];
  RealArray = array[1 .. MaxIndex] of real;

var
  PageNumber : integer;          { page number }
  LineCount  : integer;          { line count  }
  Name       : String20;         { name to be printed }
  SalesArr   : RealArray;        { sales array to be printed }
  YearTotal  : real;             { total sales to be printed }
  I          : integer;          { loop control }
  NPeople    : integer;          { number of salespeople to print, input }

procedure Instructions; begin {stub} end;
```

{*procedure TopOfForm, as shown in Figure 4-7, is inserted here*}

```
procedure Header;
{
        Written by:    XXXXXXXXX  XX/XX/XX
           Purpose:    To print headings at the top of a page.
        Parameters:    None
 Globals modified:     PageNumber is incremented after printing.
}
var
  I        : integer;                   { loop control to print dashed line }

begin  {Header}
  Write(Lst, ' ':27, 'LIST OF EMPLOYEE SALES');
  Writeln(Lst, ' ':21, 'page ', PageNumber:1);
  Writeln(Lst);
  Writeln(Lst, ' ':8,  'NAME', ' ':27, 'MONTHLY SALES',
               ' ':16, 'TOTAL SALES');
  Writeln(Lst);
  Writeln(Lst, ' ':30, 'January     February         March');
  Writeln(Lst, ' ':30, ' April          May           June');
  Writeln(Lst, ' ':30, '   July        August     September');
  Writeln(Lst, ' ':30, 'October     November      December');
  for I := 1 to 80 do Write(Lst,'-');
  Writeln(Lst);
  Writeln(Lst);
  PageNumber := PageNumber + 1
end;   {Header}


procedure DetailLine(Name : String20; Sales : RealArray; Total : real);
{
        Written by:    XXXXXXXXX  XX/XX/XX
           Purpose:    To print a detail line (one line of a table).
                       If the page is full, it first advances to a
                       new page and prints headings.
        Parameters:    Name - input, the salesman name
                       Sales - input, the array of 12 sales figures
                       Total - input, the total sales for the salesman
```

Figure 4-15   Driver for Printing Format (Continued)

```
   Procedures used:   TopOfForm, to advance to a new page.
                      Header, to print headings.
   Globals modified:  LineCount is used to control the call to Page and
                      Header; following those calls it is reset to 0, and
                      it is incremented for each person printed.
   }
   var
   I           : integer;              { loop control to print sales }
   PrintName : String20;               { name right padded with blanks }

begin  {DetailLine}  {stub version - adapted from Figure 4-7}

{*** Check for full page.}

   if LineCount >= MaxLines then
      begin
        TopOfForm;
        Header;
        LineCount := 0
      end;   {if}

{*** Print the lines and increment the count of lines on this page.}

   PrintName := Name + '                         ';
   Write(Lst, PrintName:20,' ':4);                    {name}
   for I := 1 to 3 do Write(Lst, Sales[I]:13:2);      {Jan - Feb - Mar}
   Writeln(Lst);

   Write(Lst, ' ':24);
   for I := 4 to 6 do Write(Lst, Sales[I]:13:2);      {Apr - May - Jun}
   Writeln(Lst);

   Write(Lst, ' ':24);
   for I := 7 to 9 do Write(Lst, Sales[I}:13:2);      {Jul - Aug - Sep}
   Writeln(Lst);

   Write(Lst, ' ':24);
   for I := 10 to 12 do Write(Lst, Sales[I]:13:2);    {Oct - Nov - Dec}
   Write(Lst, ' ':3, Total:13:2);                     {total sales}
   Writeln(Lst);
   Writeln(Lst);
   LineCount := LineCount + 5

end;   {DetailLine}

begin {Driver}

{*** Initialize the global variables.}

   PageNumber := 1;
   LineCount := 0;

{*** Set up variables to be printed.}
```

Figure 4-15 Driver for Printing Format (Continued)

```
  for I := 1 to 12 do SalesArr[I] := 100 * I;
  Name := 'name';
  YearTotal := 7800;

{*** Perform the trial run.}

  Instructions;
  Write('How many people do you want to print? ');
  Readln(NPeople);
  Header;

  for I := 1 to NPeople do
    begin
      DetailLine(Name, SalesArr, YearTotal)
    end   {for}

end.
```

SAMPLE INPUT AND OUTPUT

At terminal:

```
How many people do you want to print? 2
```

On printer:

	LIST OF EMPLOYEE SALES		page 1
NAME	MONTHLY SALES		TOTAL SALES
	January	February	March
	April	May	June
	July	August	September
	October	November	December
name	100.00	200.00	300.00
	400.00	500.00	600.00
	700.00	800.00	900.00
	1000.00	1100.00	1200.00	7800.00
name	100.00	200.00	300.00
	400.00	500.00	600.00
	700.00	800.00	900.00
	1000.00	1100.00	1200.00	7800.00

Figure 4-15 Driver for Printing Format

With the "easy but messy" details of printing the report out of the way, we can concentrate our attention on the rest of the program.

As far as variables are concerned, we need these:

Input:	Name	String20	Salesperson name
	SalesArr	RealArray	12 sales figures

Output:	YearTotal	real	Individual's total for year
	TotalSales	RealArray	Company totals (12 totals, one per month)
Other:	I	integer	For loop
	PageNumber	integer	Global for page number
	LineCount	integer	Global count of detail lines printed

In a loop, we want to

read employee name
read 12 sales figures
calculate the total for the year
add to the company totals
print the data (DetailLine)

Before the loop, we must

initialize global variables for output control
   (PageNumber, LineCount)
print headings on the first page
set the company totals to 0

After the loop, we print the company totals on a new page.

In studying the steps listed here, we chose to modularize as indicated in this hierarchy chart, which emphasizes the portion of the program we are working on now:

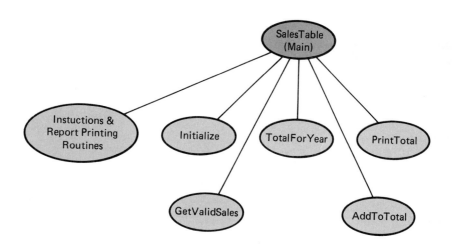

Initialize:	Procedure to set company totals to 0.
GetValidSales:	Procedure to obtain sales amount for one month.
TotalForYear:	Function to calculate total sales for one employee.

AddToTotal: Procedure to add one employee's sales amounts to the company totals.

PrintTotal: Procedure to print the company summary.

The complete program appears as Figure 4-16; a small sample run appears as Figure 4-17. The program is long, but it has been modularized so that no one piece is very complicated. You should examine the main module and each procedure, using the hierarchy chart as a guide to the overall structure of the program.

```
program SalesTable(Input, Output);
{
        Written by:  XXXXXXXXXX  XX/XX/XX
           Purpose:  To create a table listing the names and monthly sales
                     figures for a number of sales employees. In addition,
                     the total sales for each month are calculated and
                     printed on a separate page.
   Procedures used:  Instructions to print instructions.
                     TopOfForm (called by DetailLine and PrintTotal), to
                        advance to a new page.
                     Header (called by DetailLine as well as main module),
                        to print headings.
                     DetailLine, to print one line of the table.
                     GetValidSales to obtain a valid sales figure for one
                        month.
                     Initialize to initialize the array of sales totals.
                     AddToTotal to add each salesperson's sales figures to
                        the running total.
                     PrintTotal to print the total sales.
    Functions used:  CommisFn to calculate a monthly commission.
}
const
  EndOfData    = '';           { terminating value for name }
  MaxIndex     = 12;           { size of arrays }
  MaxLines     = 45;           { maximum lines per page }
  MaximumAmount = 5000.0;      { maximum sales amount }

type
  String20  = string[20];
  RealArray = array[1 .. MaxIndex] of real;

var
  I           : integer;       { loop control }
  PageNumber  : integer;       { global variable for page number }
  LineCount   : integer;       { global variable for line count  }
  Name        : String20;      { salesperson name, input }
  SalesArr    : RealArray;     { 12 sales figures for salesperson, input }
  TotalSales  : RealArray;     { 12 total sales figures for company }
  YearTotal   : real;          { total sales to be printed }

procedure Instructions; begin {stub} end;
```

Figure 4-16 Case Study No. 6 (Sales Report) (Continued)

```
{procedure TopOfForm, as shown in Figure 4-7, is inserted here}

{procedures Header and DetailLine, as shown in Figure 4-15, are inserted here}

procedure GetValidSales(Month : integer; var Amount : real);
{
        Written by:  XXXXXXXXX  XX/XX/XX
           Purpose:  To obtain a valid sales figure (in the range from
                     0 to MaximumAmount, a global constant.
        Parameters:  Month - input, the month number to be read
                     Amount - output, the value of the amount read
}
begin  {GetValidSales}
  Writeln;
  Writeln('Month # ', Month:1);
  Write('Enter sales amount (0 - ', MaximumAmount:1:2, '): ');
  Readln(Amount);

  while (Amount < 0.0) or (Amount > MaximumAmount) do
    begin
      Write('Illegal amount entered, try again: ');
      Readln(Amount)
    end;  {while}

end;  {GetValidSales}


procedure Initialize(var Total : RealArray);
{
        Written by:  XXXXXXXXX  XX/XX/XX
           Purpose:  To set the total array to all zeros.
        Parameters:  Total - output, the array to be initialized
}
var
  I    : integer;                          { loop control }

begin  {Initialize}

  for I := 1 to 12 do
    begin
      Total[I] := 0.0
    end  {for loop}

end;  {Initialize}


procedure AddToTotal(OnePerson : RealArray; var CompanyTotal : RealArray);
{
        Written by:  XXXXXXXXX  XX/XX/XX
           Purpose:  To add one person's sales to the company total.
        Parameters:  OnePerson - input, the array of sales for one person
                     CompanyTotal - update, the company total array
}
var
  I    : integer;                          { loop control }
```

Figure 4-16 Case Study No. 6 (Sales Report) (Continued)

```
begin  {AddToTotal}

  for I := 1 to 12 do
    begin
      CompanyTotal[I] := CompanyTotal[I] + OnePerson[I]
    end  {for loop}

end;  {AddToTotal}

procedure PrintTotal(CompanyTotal : RealArray);
{
        Written by:  XXXXXXXXX  XX/XX/XX
           Purpose:  To print the company totals on a new page.
        Parameters:  CompanyTotal - input, the company total array
   Procedures used:  TopOfForm, to advance to a new page for the totals.
}
var
   I     : integer;                        { loop control }

begin  {PrintTotal}

  TopOfForm;
  Writeln(Lst,' ':12, 'TOTALS FOR COMPANY');
  Writeln(Lst);
  Writeln(Lst, '        Month                Total');
  Writeln(Lst, '   ----------------------------------');
  Writeln(Lst);

  for I := 1 to 12 do
    begin
      Writeln(Lst, I:12,' ':10, CompanyTotal[I]:12:2)
    end  {for loop}

end;  {PrintTotal}


function TotalForYear(Sales : RealArray) : real;
{
        Written by:  XXXXXXXXX  XX/XX/XX
           Purpose:  To calculate the total sales for one person for the
                     year, based on the array of 12 sales figures.
        Parameters:  Sales - input, the salesperson's set of figures
}
var
   I     : integer;                        { loop control }
   Sum   : real;                           { accumulates the total }

begin  {TotalForYear}
   Sum := 0.0;

   for I := 1 to 12 do
     begin
       Sum := Sum + Sales[I]
     end;  {for loop}
```

Figure 4-16   Case Study No. 6 (Sales Report) (Continued)

```
      TotalForYear := Sum
   end;  {TotalForYear}


begin {SalesTable}

{*** Print instructions, initialize the global variables, and print the
     first set of headings.}

   Instructions;
   PageNumber := 1;
   LineCount := 0;
   Header;

{*** Initialize total sales array to all zeros.}

   Initialize(TotalSales);

{*** Read names and sales in a loop, calculate individual yearly total,
     add to company totals, and print lines containing the information
     for one employee.}

   repeat
     Writeln;
     Write('Enter name (tap RETURN to quit):  ');
     Readln(Name);
     if  Name <> EndOfData then
       begin
         for I := 1 to 12 do                    { get sales figures }
           begin
             GetValidSales(I, SalesArr[I])
           end;  {for}

         YearTotal := TotalForYear(SalesArr);  { calculate yearly total }
         AddToTotal(SalesArr, TotalSales);     { add this person to total }
         DetailLine(Name, SalesArr, YearTotal) { print data }
       end  {if}
   until Name = EndOfData;

{*** When no more input, print the total array and stop the program.}

   PrintTotal(TotalSales);
   Writeln('SalesTable program terminating.')
end.
```

Figure 4-16   Case Study No. 6 (Sales Report)

SAMPLE INPUT AND OUTPUT (PARTIAL)

At terminal:

```
Enter name (tap RETURN to quit):  Bill Frederickson
```

Figure 4-17   Sample Run for Case Study No. 6 (Continued)

```
Month # 1
Enter sales amount (0 - 5000.00): 100


Month # 2
Enter sales amount (0 - 5000.00): 200
                . . . .
Month # 12
Enter sales amount (0 - 5000.00): 100



Enter name (tap RETURN to quit):  Sally Fielding


Month # 1
Enter sales amount (0 - 5000.00): 5001
Illegal amount entered, try again: 5000


Month # 2
Enter sales amount (0 - 5000.00): 5000.01
Illegal amount entered, try again: 5000


Month # 3
Enter sales amount (0 - 5000.00): -1
Illegal amount entered, try again: -.01
Illegal amount entered, try again: 0
                . . . .

Month # 12
Enter sales amount (0 - 5000.00): 432

Enter name (tap RETURN to quit):
SalesTable program terminating.
```

On printer (first page):

	LIST OF EMPLOYEE SALES			page 1
NAME		**MONTHLY SALES**		**TOTAL SALES**
	January	February	March	
	April	May	June	
	July	August	September	
	October	November	December	
Bill Frederickson	100.00	200.00	300.00	
	400.00	500.00	600.00	
	600.00	500.00	400.00	
	300.00	200.00	100.00	4200.00
Sally Fielding	5000.00	5000.00	0.00	
	100.00	500.00	356.45	
	308.78	3800.00	405.50	
	100.00	150.00	432.00	16152.73

Figure 4-17 Sample Run for Case Study No. 6 (Continued)

On printer (second page):

```
              TOTALS FOR COMPANY

        Month                 Total
    ----------------------------------------

            1                5100.00
            2                5200.00
            3                 300.00
            4                 500.00
            5                1000.00
            6                 956.45
            7                 908.78
            8                4300.00
            9                 805.50
           10                 400.00
           11                 350.00
           12                 532.00
```

Figure 4-17 Sample Run for Case Study No. 6

EXERCISES   Exercises 1 to 4 refer to Case Study No. 4.

*1. Write a program to read an integer N, then print the first N primes. (If N is 7, the answers are 2, 3, 5, 7, 11, 13, and 17.) Write a test plan.

2. Write a program that reads a series of input integers. For each, print a message telling whether or not the number is prime.

3. a. It is a waste of time in Case Study No. 4 to check the even numbers: The only even number that is prime is 2. Revise the case study to print 2 before the loop, then check the numbers 3, 5, 7, 9, . . . in the loop.
   b. If we revise the main program as in part (a), then we are only checking odd numbers. We can revise the Divisor function to take advantage of this fact. (It can look for divisors among 3, 5, 7, . . . instead of 2, 3, 4, ...) Make this revision.
   c. Can the revised Divisor function be used in Case Study No. 5? Explain your answer.

*4. If a number N is going to have a divisor other than N, then the smallest divisor will be $\leq$ Sqrt(N).
   a. Explain why.
   b. Revise the Divisor function to take advantage of this fact.

Exercises 5 to 7 refer to Case Study No. 5.

5. Modify Case Study No. 5 to print the factors on a single line. Hint: Use Write rather than Writeln. When is it appropriate to send a carriage return using Writeln?

6. Modify Exercise 5 to obtain output similar to

                 2 * 2 * 5 * 5

7. Modify Exercise 6 to obtain output similar to

             100 = 2 * 2 * 5 * 5

Exercises 8 to 9 refer to Case Study No. 6

8. Modify Case Study No. 6 to precede the name with an asterisk (*) if the total sales are under $10,000. If any names are marked, place a footnote on the final page explaining the asterisk.

9. Add other summary statistics to the final page for Case Study No. 6:
   a. Which months had the lowest and highest company totals?
   b. What was the company grand total?
   c. How many employees had at least one month with no sales?
   d. Who had the highest total sales? What was his or her total?

In the remaining exercises, you will develop subprograms or complete programs. For some, ideas developed in the case studies can be useful.

10. Write the main program for the following situation. (You will want to decide which steps might be done as subprograms and what parameters would be required.)

   Each set of input data contains employee ID number, rank, number of units manufactured, basic bonus rate, and number of years experience. Your program should calculate and print basic pay and bonus pay for each employee. It should also print the ID of the person of rank 'A' with the most units produced and the average years of experience of the employees.

   The basic pay consists of $200 for code 'A', $300 for code 'B', and $355 for code 'C', plus $5 for each year of experience.

   The bonus pay is based on the number of units manufactured: 0 if under 100; basic bonus rate times basic pay if 100 to 150; 1.5 times as much if over 150.

11. *a. Write a Boolean function RelativelyPrime(A, B) that returns true if A and B are relatively prime, false otherwise. Use the GCD function developed earlier: GCD(A, B) is the greatest common divisor of A and B.
   b. Write a driver to test the function.

12. a. Write a Boolean function Near(Test, Homework) to do the following. Input will consist of two real numbers between 0.0 and 1.00, representing a test percentage and a homework percentage. The function will return true if the homework percentage is no more than one letter grade below the test percentage (using 90 percent = A, 80 percent = B, etc.); otherwise it will return false.

   For example, for a test percentage of 0.958 and a homework percentage of 0.8012, the answer is true. For 0.901 and 0.795, the answer is false.

   b. Write a main program that reads a series of data containing name, test percentage, and homework percentage. For each person, it should calculate and print the final average and the corresponding letter grade. Use subprograms where appropriate. For any subprogram you use, describe its parameters and logic.

   Note: The final average is

   $$0.7 \times \text{test percentage} + 0.3 \times \text{homework percentage}$$

   However, for a person for whom the homework percentage is lower than the test percentage but "near" as defined in part (a), the final average is just the test percentage.

   c. Give a test plan for the Near function.

13. A "prime pair" is a pair of primes exactly two apart. For example, 11 and 13 form a prime pair, as do 29 and 31. Write a program to print all the prime pairs between 2 and N, where N is supplied by the user.

14. Write a program to find the roots of a quadratic equation, using the following general design.

Recall that, for a quadratic equation $ax^2 + bx + c = 0$, the roots are given by

$$\frac{-b + \sqrt{b^2 - 4ac}}{2a} \quad \text{and} \quad \frac{-b - \sqrt{b^2 - 4ac}}{2a}$$

There are three distinct possibilities:

(1) $b^2 - 4ac$ is positive. Then there are two distinct real roots. For example, if $b^2 - 4ac = 4$, we might have

$$\frac{-1 + \sqrt{4}}{2} = \frac{-1 + 2}{2} = 0.5$$

$$\frac{-1 - \sqrt{4}}{2} = \frac{-1 - 2}{2} = -1.5$$

(2) $b^2 - 4ac$ is zero. Then there is a single real root. For example,

$$\frac{-2 + \sqrt{0}}{2} = -1.0$$

(the other root is the same).

(3) $b^2 - 4ac$ is negative. Then there are two complex number solutions, $m + ni$ and $m - ni$, where

$$m = -b/2a$$

and

$$n = \frac{\sqrt{-(b^2 - 4ac)}}{2a}$$

For example, with $b^2 - 4ac = -4$, we might have

$$\frac{-1 + \sqrt{-4}}{2} = \frac{-1}{2} + \frac{2i}{2} = -0.5 + 1.0i$$

$$\frac{-1 - \sqrt{-4}}{2} = \frac{-1}{2} - \frac{2i}{2} = -0.5 - 1.0i$$

(Note: The quantity $b^2 - 4ac$ is referred to as the **discriminant**, and the letter D is used to indicate it.)

Your output should appear in a form similar to the following, with new headings on each page.

A	B	C	Type	First Root	Second Root
1.00	-2.00	-3.00	2 real	3.00	-2.00
1.00	-2.00	10.00	2 complex	1.00 + 3.00 I	1.00 - 3.00 I
1.00	-2.00	1.00	1 real	1.00	

a. Write a DetailLine procedure to print the output line in the proper form. It should have six parameters: A, B, C, Number1, Number2, and Type.

A, B, and C are the coefficients of the original equation. Type is an integer that is either 1, 0, or −1, the "sign" of the discriminant (1 for positive, 0 for zero, −1 for negative). Number1 and Number2 are real; what they represent depends on the value of Type:

(1) If Type is 1 (D is positive), then Number1 and Number2 are the two distinct real roots.

(2) If Type is 0 (D is 0), then Number1 is the single real root and Number2 is meaningless.

(3) If Type is −1 (D is negative), then Number1 and Number2 are the real and imaginary parts of the complex solutions (m and n above). You can assume that Number2 is positive. The answers are

```
Number1 + Number2 i
Number1 - Number2 i
```

b. Write a GetData procedure that reads data records containing A, B, and C, the coefficients of a quadratic equation. We will insist that A must be a positive number; print an error message for faulty input.

c. Write a procedure that calculates three values. The first is the sign of the discriminant $D = b^2 - 4ac$. The second and third are

$$-b/2a \quad \text{and} \quad (|D|)^{1/2}/2a$$

d. Using the routines developed in parts (a) to (c), write a program that reads a series of inputs, each containing A, B, and C, and prints a table of solutions to the corresponding equations.

15. Modify the program of Exercise 14 to remove the restriction that A must be positive. (Notice that if A is 0, the equation is $bx + c = 0$, which has 1 real solution $x = -c/b$. However, if both A and B are 0, print an error message.)

16. Print a table of square roots for all the integers from 1 to 500, 50 per page.

17. Repeat Exercise 16, but for the real numbers 0.1, 0.2, . . . , 49.9, and 50.0.

18. An instructor gives five tests but allows each student to take either three, four, or five. (A student who takes fewer than three is treated as having taken three.) Write a program to create a printed grade report in a form similar to this:

Name	Grades				#	Total	Average	Letter Grade
John Jones	100	−	− 95	90	3	285	95	A
Sue Smith	− 100	60	90	90	4	340	85	A
Bill Jacobs	50	40	−	− −	3	90	30	F

Round the average to the nearest integer. Include various statistics, such as:

a. How many took test 5?

b. What was the average on test 5?

c. What percentage received each letter grade?

d. Were there any F's other than by people who apparently "gave up."

19. Write an elementary school arithmetic tutorial package. The basic idea is to pose questions to a student and check the answers. In its simplest form, for example, the program might do the following 10 times:

pose an addition problem

read the student's answer

if the answer is right, add 1 to a count; if not, print the correct answer

At the end, it could print a count of how many were right. However, you should go beyond this simplest form. Here are some suggestions.

a. Include several operations: add, multiply, find least common denominator, etc. Allow the user to choose which he wants.

b. Allow up to three attempts to get the correct answer.

c. Calculate a score where getting the answer on the first try is worth more than getting it on the second try, and so on.

d. Allow the user to set a difficulty level, with a higher level getting harder problems (bigger numbers).

20. In this exercise, we explore some ideas related to the game of blackjack. In a simplified version of the game, an ace is worth 11 points; cards 2 to 10 are worth the face value; and jack, queen, and king are worth 10. The object is to get as high a score as possible without going over 21 by drawing cards from a deck.

*a. We can simulate the cards with integers 0 through 51, as shown here:

0 - ace of clubs

1 - 2 of clubs

. . . .

9 - 10 of clubs

10 - jack of clubs

11 - queen of clubs

12 - king of clubs

13 - ace of diamonds

. . . .

25 - king of diamonds

. . . .

Write a procedure that, given an integer in the range 0 to 51, prints the card description. Hint: A case structure with 52 branches will work, but is not very pleasant. Can you think of a way to use mod and div to solve this?

b. Write a function that, given a number between 0 and 51, calculates its value. See the hint for part (a).

*c. Simulating the draw of a card is a little tricky. If we assume that the card supply consists of an infinite number of decks, then

```
Card := Random(52)
```

will work.

If we have only one deck, on the other hand, we must avoid repeating a card. One possibility is a global Boolean array Dealt with index values 0 through 51, where Dealt[I] is true if and only if card I has already been dealt.

Write a function Card that simulates drawing a card. It should utilize the global Dealt array to avoid redealing a card that was previously dealt. Note: Declaring Boolean arrays is similar to declaring integer or real arrays.

d. Combine the ideas presented here to simulate one play of a game of blackjack. It should deal two cards, then repeatedly ask the user if it is to continue. Print a message such as "You quit with 17 points" or "You went over 21".

  e. Modify part (d) to allow several games. Shuffle the deck after each game.
  f. Modify part (d) to have the user play against the computer. Deal two cards to the user; deal two to the computer but only print the second. Deal cards to the user until told to quit or the cards go over 21. If the cards go over 21, the computer wins. If not, print the first computer card, then deal cards to the computer with the strategy: "stay" (stop) on a total 16 or higher. If the computer goes over 21, the user wins; otherwise the user wins if her total is *greater than* the computer's. Shuffle the deck after each game.

21. Many enhancements to the previous exercise are possible. We suggest a few for your consideration.
  a. Aces are worth either 1 or 11, whichever yields the higher score not over 21. (The choice can change after subsequent draws.)
  b. Drawing five cards whose total is not over 21 is an automatic win for the user.
  c. Betting could be allowed with a house limit and with the player staked to an initial amount.
  d. The deck could be shuffled less frequently. (With our somewhat primitive way of telling which cards have been dealt, this could slow down the drawing of a card.)

22. It is possible to run simulations to determine probabilities for the blackjack game. These can be done with any version of the game you have written. Notice that the printing of the cards should be removed for these simulations.
  a. How many times out of 1000 would you expect the dealer to exceed 21 using the strategy of stopping at 16 or higher?
  b. Would a user strategy of stopping at 17 or higher likely win or lose more often? Run the game 1000 times to find out.
  c. The user can see one but not both of the dealer's cards. Suppose the user chooses to stop at 17 if the dealer shows a 10 or higher (including an ace) and at 14 otherwise. How many out of 1000 might the user expect to win?

23. Write a program that, given a series of integers, calculates the score for a game of bowling. Each integer in the series represents the number of pins knocked down by one ball. A sample game is shown here.

Frame	Balls	Score for Frame	Total	Comment
1	3,6	9	9	Open frame
2	4,6	17	26	Spare—10 plus next ball
3	7,3	20	46	
4	10	30	76	Strike—10 plus next 2 balls
5	10	23	99	
6	10	15	114	
7	3,2	5	119	
8	5,1	6	125	
9	8,2	20	145	
10	10	19	164	Strike in last frame gets 2 extra balls (spare would get one)

The following are some tips that may help you in your design.

a. To record the score from strikes and spares, you must "look ahead" at future balls. This is a lot easier to do if you store the series of integers in an integer array.

b. For starters, you might write a program to:

(1) Read a game into an array (terminate by an entry of −1)

(2) Print output similar to that above, but with only three columns filled in (frame, balls, and comment—either "strike," "spare," or "open"). Ignore the "extra" balls for now.

Assume the data is valid.

c. Once you get part (b), finishing the problem may not be too difficult. You should, if possible, include detection of illegal situations such as this:

Frame 1 : 3,6

Frame 2 : 4,7—impossible

ELEMENTARY DATA STRUCTURING

5-1
TEXT FILES

A **text file** is organized as a number of lines, each consisting of a varying number of characters. The concept is similar to a (perhaps long) page of typewritten words. The file can be read from or written to either line by line or character by character. We can think of reading from a text file as similar to input via a keyboard and writing to a text file as similar to output to a display screen or printer. Thus, we are already familiar with most of the details of reading and writing lines of text files. In fact, most of the programs that we have discussed thus far can be modified to obtain input from a text file instead of a keyboard and to produce output to a text file instead of a screen or printer. We can either read from a text file or write to it, but not both simultaneously. In order to use a text file, we must first activate it (**open the file**); then we can read from or write to (not both) the file; finally, when we are finished, we must deactivate it (**close the file**).

COMMENT

Versions of Pascal tend to differ in their handling of files. We present the Turbo Pascal methods in detail here. For text files, the changes you would have to make for other versions of Pascal are minor and easy to adapt to. For details consult your instructor or reference manual.

□
BASIC TEXT FILE OPERATIONS

Suppose we wish to work with a file that has the name "FRIENDS.ME." We must tell the Pascal compiler how to refer to the file by declaring a **file designator** variable as follows:

```
var
    MyFile  : text;
```

Notice that variable is of a new type, the **text** type. We are free to choose the name of the file designator variable in the same way as with variables of the other types that we have discussed. Next, in the executable code (after the "begin") of the program, we specify the file name with the **Assign** command as follows:

```
Assign(MyFile, 'FRIENDS.ME');
```

This notifies the compiler that when we refer to a file by means of the file designator MyFile, we mean the file that is called FRIENDS.ME on the disk.[1]

If we wish to create a new file of friends' names, we can open the file with the **Rewrite** command:

```
Rewrite(MyFile);
```

If a file with the assigned name (FRIENDS.ME, for our example) already exists, it will be erased and replaced by the new file. After the file has been opened, we can write to the file by using the procedures Write and Writeln in conjunction with the file designator. For example, if we wish to write "Sally Jones" to the file, we could use the statement:

```
Writeln(MyFile, 'Sally Jones');
```

When we are finished with the file activities, we must close the file with the **Close** command:

```
Close(MyFile);
```

The program in Figure 5-1 illustrates these ideas. This program creates a file called FRIENDS.ME and writes two friends' names into it. After you have run the program, check the contents of the file FRIENDS.ME by using your text editor. You should see that the contents of the file are

```
My Friends

Sally Jones
John Smith
```

□
**FILE
PROCESSING
ACTIVITIES**

A text file can be created by using a program similar to the one in Figure 5-1 or by using a text editor such as the Turbo editor. In any case, once a file has been created, there are various activities that we can perform on the file. Among these are

Display the file
Print the file
Add lines to the file
Find a particular line in the file
Change a particular line in the file

We will now discuss each of these activities.

□
**DISPLAYING
AND PRINTING
TEXT FILES**

Suppose that we wish to display the file FRIENDS.ME on the screen. We must first declare our file designator as follows:

```
FriendsList   : text;
```

We have used a different name for the file designator variable to emphasize that you have the choice of naming the variable as you wish. We assign the file name to

```
program Friends(Input, Output);
{
        Written by:  XXXXXXXX  XX/XX/XX
          Purpose:  To write the names of some friends on a file.
  Procedures Used:  Instructions - to print instructions.
}
var
  MyFile  : text;                          { File designator }

procedure Instructions; begin {stub} end;

begin {Friends}

{*** Print instructions and designate the file.}

  Instructions;
  Assign(MyFile, 'FRIENDS.ME');

{*** Open the file.}

  Rewrite(MyFile);

{*** Write to the file.}

  Writeln(MyFile, '    My Friends');
  Writeln(MyFile);
  Writeln(MyFile, 'Sally Jones');
  Writeln(MyFile, 'John Smith');

{*** Close the file.}

  Close(MyFile);

{*** Print terminating message and stop program.}

  Writeln;
  Writeln('Friends program is terminating.')
end.
```

Figure 5-1 Writing to a Text File

the file designator with the statement:

```
            Assign(FriendsList, 'FRIENDS.ME');
```

We use a different statement for opening the file for reading than we did for opening the file for writing. For reading the file, we open the file by using the **Reset** statement:

```
            Reset(FriendsList);
```

We read lines from the file by using the Readln procedure along with a string variable. Suppose that we have declared the string variable Line in the var section of the program. Then, we can read one line of the file with the statement:

```
            Readln(FriendsList, Line);
```

The first time that we use the Readln statement, we will read the first line of the file; the second time, we will read the second line; and so on.

Pascal provides a Boolean function **Eof** to help us in reading exactly the correct number of lines of a text file. We can test to see if we have read the entire file by the test:

```
if  Eof(FriendsList)  then . . .
```

If we are reading lines of the file in a loop, then we can use one of the looping constructs:

```
while  not Eof(FriendsList) do . . .
```

or

```
repeat . . .

until  Eof(FriendsList)
```

Eof(*file designator*) is true exactly when there are no more data left in the file that can be read. In a program that reads using Readln, it becomes true immediately after the last line is read. We should use the construct

```
while  not Eof(file designator) do . . .
```

for a loop where we are not sure if there are *any* data left to be read. If we are certain that there are data that can be read, then we can use the construct

```
repeat . . .

until  Eof(file designator)
```

We can display each line that is read from the file by the statement:

```
Writeln(Line);
```

Finally, when we are through, we close the file with the statement:

```
Close(FriendsList);
```

In Figure 5-2, we illustrate the above discussion by means of a program that will read and display the file FRIENDS.ME. Note that we have chosen a string variable of size 20 for reading lines of the file. In our experience, we have found that 20 characters is a reasonable maximum when dealing with people's names (at least in America).

COMMENT We chose to use a while loop in this program. This allows the program to function correctly even if the file is empty.

After you study the program of Figure 5-2, you may note that the dependence on the particular file FRIENDS.ME is slight. In Figure 5-3, we give a general-purpose program to read and display any text file whose lines are at most 80 characters in length. We allow the user to specify file names with lengths of up to 14 characters. This allows a filename such as

```
B:THISFILE.TXT
```

to be used. The major differences between this program and the one in Figure 5-2 are shaded.

```
program Display(Input, Output);
{
        Written by:  XXXXXXXX  XX/XX/XX
           Purpose:  To read and display the file  FRIENDS.ME.
    Procedures Used:  Instructions - to print instructions.
}
var
  FriendsList  : text;                    { File designator }
  Line         : string[20];              { For lines of the file }

procedure Instructions; begin {stub} end;

begin {Display}

{*** Print instructions and designate the file.}

  Instructions;
  Assign(FriendsList, 'FRIENDS.ME');

{*** Open the file.}

  Reset(FriendsList);

{*** Put heading on the screen.}

  Writeln;
  Writeln('  Lines of the file: FRIENDS.ME');
  Writeln;

{*** Read and display lines of the file.}

  while  not Eof(FriendsList)  do
    begin
      Readln(FriendsList, Line);
      Writeln(Line)
    end; {while}

{*** Close the file.}

  Close(FriendsList);

{*** Print terminating message and stop program.}

  Writeln;
  Writeln('Display program is terminating.')
end.
```

Figure 5-2   Reading from a Text File

You can use the program of Figure 5-3 to display the Pascal programs that you have written so far. You may find other text files that you can also display using the program.

We can print the contents of a text file on the printer by using the built-in file designator Lst in the Writeln statements of the program of Figure 5-3.

```
program FileDisplay(Input, Output);
{
        Written by:   XXXXXXXX  XX/XX/XX
           Purpose:   To read and display the contents of a text file.
   Procedures Used:   Instructions - to print instructions.
}
var
   AnyFile       : text;                    { File designator }
   FileName      : string[14];              { Name of the file }
   Line          : string[80];              { For lines of the file }

procedure Instructions; begin {stub} end;

begin {FileDisplay}

{*** Print instructions and ask the user for the filename.}

   Instructions;
   Write('Enter the filename: ');
   Readln(FileName);

{*** Designate the file.}

   Assign(AnyFile, FileName);

{*** Open the file.}

   Reset(AnyFile);

{*** Put heading on the screen.}

   Writeln;
   Writeln('  Lines of the file: ', FileName);
   Writeln;

{*** Read and display lines of the file.}

   while  not Eof(AnyFile)  do
     begin
       Readln(AnyFile, Line);
       Writeln(Line)
     end; {while}

{*** Close the file.}

   Close(AnyFile);

{*** Print terminating message and stop program.}

   Writeln;
   Writeln('FileDisplay program is terminating.')
end.
```

Figure 5-3 User-Specified File Name

For example, to put the heading on the printer, we could use the lines:

```
Writeln(Lst);
Writeln(Lst, '  Lines of the file: ', FileName);
Writeln(Lst);
```

(Recall that the use of Lst to denote the printer is specific to Turbo Pascal on a PC. Other versions will use other methods.)

SUMMARY OF FILE-HANDLING SYNTAX

□ In the examples so far, we have been introduced to the various text file handling procedures available in Turbo Pascal. Before presenting further examples of their use, let us give a brief summary. The Pascal elements are as follows:

```
var
   file designator : text;

Assign(file designator, file name);

Reset(file designator);

Rewrite(file designator);

Readln(file designator, . . .);

Writeln(file designator, . . .);

Eof(file designator);

Close(file designator);
```

In a typical program that uses a text file, we choose a variable name to represent the file (the *file designator*). We use Assign to indicate the *file name* (a character string) to which the file designator refers. We use either Reset or Rewrite to open the file (for input or output). We use Readln or Writeln to read or write lines, respectively, of the file. If we are reading, we can use the Boolean function Eof to see if there are more data to be read. Finally, after processing is complete, we close the file using Close.

(Notice that the form and meaning of Readln and Writeln are the same as for the standard files Input and Output. That is, they behave as they would for terminal I/O.)

ADDING LINES TO A TEXT FILE

□ Suppose that we have just made a new friend, Nancy Doe, and wish to add her name to the FRIENDS.ME file. We can accomplish this by use of the following steps:

copy the file FRIENDS.ME to the file TEMP.FIL
read the lines of the file TEMP.FIL and write them
    to the file FRIENDS.ME.
write the new line to the file FRIENDS.ME

Copying one file to another requires that we have two files open at the same time, one for reading (Reset) and one for writing (Rewrite). We need two file designators and we must be sure to close both files when the copying is complete. After the files are open, the copying could be accomplished with the loop below:

```
while  not Eof(Infile)  do
   begin
      Readln(InFile, Line);
      Writeln(OutFile, Line)
   end {while}
```

The copy operation is a good candidate for use of a procedure. We use the procedure Copy, which has the header line:

```
procedure Copy(var SourceFile, TargetFile : text);
```

Note that we are using descriptive names for the source file (copied from) and the target file (copied to).

NOTE File parameters are required to be var parameters.

In the main program, let us assume that the file designator InFile is used for the source file and that the file designator OutFile is used for the target file. When we wish to perform the copy operation, we invoke the procedure with the statement:

```
Copy(Infile, Outfile);
```

In Figure 5-4, we show the complete program for adding a friend to our list.

```
program AddFriend(Input, Output);
{
        Written by:   XXXXXXXX  XX/XX/XX
           Purpose:   To add a friend's name to the file.
  Procedures Used:    Instructions - to print instructions;
                      Copy - to copy one text file to another.
}
var
   InFile  : text;                    { File designator for source file }
   Outfile : text;                    { File designator for target file }
   Line    : string[80];              { One line of file }

procedure Instructions; begin {stub} end;

procedure Copy(var SourceFile, TargetFile : text);
{
        Written by:   XXXXXXXX  XX/XX/XX
           Purpose:   To copy one text file to another. The files must be
                      open.
        Parameters:   SourceFile - file to copy from (var);
                      TargetFile - file to copy to (var).
}
begin {Copy}
   while  not Eof(SourceFile)  do
      begin
```

Figure 5-4 Updating a Text File (Continued)

```
        Readln(Sourcefile, Line);
        Writeln(Targetfile, Line)
      end {while}
end; {Copy}
```

```
begin {AddFriend}

{*** Print instructions and designate the files.}

   Instructions;
   Assign(InFile, 'FRIENDS.ME');
   Assign(OutFile, 'TEMP.FIL');

{*** Open the files.}

   Reset(InFile);
   Rewrite(OutFile);

{*** Copy the source file to the target file.}

   Copy(Infile, Outfile);

{*** Close the files.}

   Close(InFile);
   Close(OutFile);

{*** Reassign the files.}

   Assign(InFile, 'TEMP.FIL');
   Assign(OutFile, 'FRIENDS.ME');

{*** Open the files.}

   Reset(InFile);
   ReWrite(OutFile);

{*** Copy the source file to the target file.}

   Copy(Infile, Outfile);

{*** Write the new name to the target file.}

   Writeln(OutFile, 'Nancy Doe');

{*** Close the files.}

   Close(InFile);
   Close(OutFile);

{*** Print terminating message and stop program.}

   Writeln;
   Writeln('AddFriend program is terminating.')
end.
```

Figure 5-4 Updating a Text File

□ The method of file creation that we used in Figure 5-1 is crude and inflexible. A better manner of building files is for the user to respond to prompts with the information for the file in an **interactive** way. For example, if we wish to build a file of friends that includes both the names of the friends and their phone numbers, we could prompt the user for the information:

> file name
>
> list of friends and phone numbers

In Figure 5-5, we show a program that creates a file as described above.

```
program Build(Input, Output);
{
      Written by:  XXXXXXXX  XX/XX/XX
         Purpose:  To build a file of friends.
  Procedures Used:  Instructions - to print instructions.
}
const
  EndOfData  =  '$END';

var
  FriendsFile  : text;                    { File designator }
  FileName     : string[14];              { Name of the file }
  Name         : string[20];              { Name of friend }
  Phone        : string[8];               { Phone number of friend }

procedure Instructions; begin {stub} end;

begin {Build}

{*** Print instructions and ask the user for the filename.}

  Instructions;
  Write('Enter the filename: ');
  Readln(FileName);

{*** Designate the file.}

  Assign(FriendsFile, FileName);

{*** Open the file.}

  Rewrite(FriendsFile);

{*** Put heading on the file.}

  Writeln(FriendsFile, '     Friends Names and Phone Numbers');
  Writeln(FriendsFile);

{*** Get names and phone numbers for file.}
```

Figure 5-5 Interactive Text File Building (Continued)

```
   repeat
     Writeln;
     Write('Enter name ($END to quit): ');
     Readln(Name);
     if  Name <> EndOfData then
       begin
         Write('Enter phone number: ');
         Readln(Phone);
         Writeln(FriendsFile, Name);
         Writeln(FriendsFile, Phone)
       end {if}
   until  Name = EndOfData;

 {*** Close the file.}

   Close(FriendsFile);

 {*** Print terminating message and stop program.}

   Writeln;
   Writeln('Build program is terminating.')
 end.
```

Figure 5-5 Interactive Text File Building

Note that the form of the file is

```
Friends Names and Phone Numbers

Joan Smith
111-2222
Bill Jones
222-1111
```

The reason why we put the names and phone numbers on separate lines of the file is a bit complicated. Suppose that we used the same line for name and phone number. A sample line of the file might be

```
Joan Smith   111-2222
```

Now suppose that we wish to read lines of the file and recover the name and phone number. How can we tell our program that the name should be "Joan Smith" rather than "Joan" and the phone number should be "111-2222" rather than "Smith 111-2222"? It would require some tricky use of formatting when building the file and subsequent care when reading the file to achieve the desired results. We will discuss some further formatting issues in Chapter 8. We will find a simple and satisfactory solution for dealing with this file in the next section of the text; but for now, we will use separate lines for separate data items to avoid difficulty.

□ **SEARCHING AND MODIFYING TEXT FILES** For our next example, we will present a program that will ask the user for the name of a friend and will display the friend's phone number. This program will provide an example of a **search** of a file. The basic idea is to ask the user for the name of the friend, to skip over the heading lines of the file, to read names and phone numbers from the file until the friend is found, and to display the phone number for the friend. Can we trust the user to ask for the name of a friend that is in the file? To answer this question, we quote from an axiom of interactive programming:

Never trust the user!

Our searching strategy must take into account that we may not find the friend's name in the file. We can use the Eof function to signal that we have searched the entire file in vain.

Note that there are two ways for the search to terminate: successfully finding a friend or unsuccessfully reaching the end-of-file. We choose to design the search in the following way:

while friend has not been found and end-of-file has not occurred:
    read name and phone number
if friend was found, print phone number; otherwise print not found

Note that in the program we use a compound condition in searching for the friend's name:

```
while  (Friend <> Name) and (Not Eof(FriendsFile))  do . . .
```

The loop can terminate in one of two ways:

1. Friend = Name (the friend has been found).
2. Eof(FriendsFile) is true (end of file has occurred).

After the loop, we wish to check to see which condition caused the search to end. The condition that will always work correctly is

$$Friend = Name$$

If we substituted the condition

$$Eof(FriendsFile)$$

in order to check how the loop has terminated, we would get the wrong result if the desired name were the *last name in the file*. This is a subtle point worthy of some reflection. (What is the value of Eof(FriendsFile) before the last name is read? Before the last phone number is read? After the last phone number is read?)

NOTE The answers are false, false, true. Thus, if the last name is the one we seek, Eof(FriendsFile) will be true after the loop.

One other step of the program is worthy of special note. When we write a while loop, we must always be sure that the condition for the loop is defined when the loop begins. In our case, the condition is

$$(\text{Friend} <> \text{Name}) \text{ and } (\text{Not Eof(FriendsFile)})$$

Before we read the first name, the variable Name is undefined. We therefore must assign some value to it, so that "Friend <> Name" will make sense. We choose a null value because this could not inadvertently be equal to the name we are searching for.

Figure 5-6 shows a program that creates a file as described above.

```
program Search(Input, Output);
{
      Written by:  XXXXXXXX  XX/XX/XX
         Purpose:  To search for a friend and display her phone number.
  Procedures Used:  Instructions - to print instructions.
}
var
  FriendsFile  : text;                  { File designator }
  FileName     : string[14];            { Name of the file }
  Friend       : string[20];            { Name of friend to find }
  Name         : string[20];            { Name from file }
  Phone        : string[8];             { Phone number of friend }

procedure Instructions; begin {stub} end;

begin {Search}

{*** Print instructions and ask the user for the filename.}

  Instructions;
  Write('Enter the filename: ');
  Readln(FileName);

{*** Designate the file.}

  Assign(FriendsFile, FileName);

{*** Open the file.}

  Reset(FriendsFile);

{*** Skip heading lines of the file.}

  Readln(FriendsFile);     {Reads the line "Friends Names and Phone Numbers"}
  Readln(FriendsFile);     {Reads the blank line}

{*** Get name from the user.}

  Writeln;
  Write('Enter the friend''s name: ');
  Readln(Friend);

{*** Search the file for the name.}
```

Figure 5-6 Searching a Text File (Continued)

```
Name := '';                    { Required so while condition is defined}

while  (Friend <> Name) and (Not Eof(FriendsFile))  do
   begin
      Readln(FriendsFile, Name);
      Readln(FriendsFile, Phone);
   end; {while}

{*** Display the results of the search.}

if  Friend = Name  then
   Writeln('The phone number is: ', Phone)
else
   Writeln('*** Friend not found.');

{*** Close the file.}

Close(FriendsFile);

{*** Print terminating message and stop program.}

Writeln;
Writeln('Search program is terminating.')
end.
```

Figure 5-6   Searching a Text File

As our final example of text file processing, we will present a program that will allow us to change the phone number of one of our friends. This program is a combination of the concepts of adding lines to a file, as illustrated in Figure 5-4, and searching a file, as illustrated in Figure 5-6. We will allow the user to specify the friend's name and, if we find the friend in the file, we will ask the user for the new phone number. The steps for the program are:

ask the user for the filename
open the file
copy the file to TEMP.FIL
ask the user for the friend's name
search TEMP.FIL for the friend while copying back to the file
if found, ask the user for the new phone number and write to
   the file; otherwise, tell the user that the friend was not
   found
copy the remainder of TEMP.FIL back to the file

We will use the Copy procedure once again in order to perform the copying activities in the program, as shown in Figure 5-7. Two items in the figure are especially noteworthy. First, after files have been closed, they can be reassigned. Second, the Copy procedure is invoked a second time to finish the copying operation. It will copy starting at the current record of Infile until end of file is reached.

```
program Change(Input, Output);
{
        Written by:   XXXXXXXX   XX/XX/XX
           Purpose:   To change a friend's phone number.
  Procedures Used:    Instructions - to print instructions;
                      Copy - to copy one file to another.
}
var
  InFile      : text;              { File designator for source file }
  Outfile     : text;              { File designator for target file }
  FileName    : string[14];        { Name of the file }
  Friend      : string[20];        { Name of friend to find }
  Name        : string[20];        { Name from file }
  Phone       : string[8];         { Phone number of friend }
  Line        : string[80];        { Line of file }

procedure Instructions; begin {stub} end;

{procedure Copy, as shown in Figure 5-4, is inserted here}

begin {Change}

{*** Print instructions and ask the user for the filename.}

  Instructions;
  Write('Enter the filename: ');
  Readln(FileName);

{*** Designate the files.}

  Assign(InFile, FileName);
  Assign(OutFile, 'TEMP.FIL');

{*** Open the files.}

  Reset(InFile);
  Rewrite(OutFile);

{*** Copy the source file to the target file.}

  Copy(Infile, Outfile);

{*** Close the files.}

  Close(InFile);
  Close(OutFile);

{*** Reassign the files.}

  Assign(InFile, 'TEMP.FIL');
  Assign(OutFile, FileName);

{*** Open the files.}
```

Figure 5-7   Interactive Text File Update (Continued)

```
      Reset(InFile);
      ReWrite(OutFile);

   {*** Skip heading lines of the file.}

      Readln(InFile, Line);
      Writeln(OutFile, Line);
      Readln(InFile, Line);
      Writeln(OutFile, Line);

   {*** Get name from the user.}

      Writeln;
      Write('Enter the friend''s name: ');
      Readln(Friend);

   {*** Search for the name while copying the file.}

      Name := '';

      while  (Friend <> Name) and (Not Eof(Infile))  do
        begin
          Readln(Infile, Name);
          Writeln(OutFile, Name);
          Readln(InFile, Phone);
          if  Friend = Name then
            begin
              Writeln('The old phone number is: ', Phone);
              Write('Enter the new phone number: ');
              Readln(Phone)
            end; {if}
          Writeln(OutFile, Phone)
        end; {while}

   {*** Act on the results of an unsuccessful search.}

      if  Friend <> Name  then
        Writeln('*** Friend not found.');

   {*** Finish the copying operation.}

      Copy(Infile, Outfile);

   {*** Close the files.}

      Close(InFile);
      Close(OutFile);

   {*** Print terminating message and stop program.}

      Writeln;
      Writeln('Change program is terminating.')
   end.
```

Figure 5-7   Interactive Text File Update

The program of Figure 5-7 assumes that the filename of the file of friends is not called TEMP.FIL because that is the file that is used for copying. Another assumption is that the user will enter the correct name for the file. The program will fail to work correctly if either of the above assumptions are incorrect. You should experiment with this program by making one or both of the assumptions incorrect. A program that is intended for serious use should not make any assumptions; the program should be designed to handle all contingencies. We will discuss the handling of input/output errors (such as trying to read from a nonexistent file) in Section 5-3.

□
TEXT FILES AS STANDARD I/O

The examples in this section have dealt with a file as the primary focus of the program. For example, we have had programs to create a file, to print its contents, to search for a value in a file, and to modify a value in a file.

As we indicated in the first paragraph of the section, text file processing has much in common with processing input from a terminal or output to either a terminal or a printer. We describe briefly several types of programs in which text files can be used as substitutes for the standard input and output devices.

When the amount of input to be supplied to a program is large, it may be more convenient for the user to build a text file using an editor, then run the program with that data. Suppose it turns out, upon examining the result of running the program, that some of the input is faulty. Then that input can be corrected (using an editor) and the program run again. This may be much simpler than rerunning an interactive program and having to redo all the input, including the correct input.

Two specific examples of this come to mind. The first is the Turbo Pascal compiler. It accepts your program as a text file rather than interactively one line at a time. When there is a problem, you do not have to retype the entire program.

Second, even for a program that will be interactive, this idea can be useful during debugging and testing. Suppose your test plan includes 34 individual test cases and that the 26th uncovers a bug. After you fix the bug, you should start over with the testing. This is easy if your test cases are in a text file. When the entire run is bug free, you can then change the input to the terminal and run through the tests one final time. (The input text file can be saved for future testing in case modifications are made to the program.)

In a similar way, we can use a file for output rather than the terminal, especially if the amount of output is extensive.

As an example, suppose we are debugging and testing as described in the previous paragraph. The output from the 34 test cases might flash by so quickly on the screen that we are unable to see it. We can send the output to a file instead and examine it using a text editor after the program runs.

A similar example occurs in many production programs. Along with the interactive input and output, the program can be building a text file (called a **trace file**). The trace file contains a complete record of all output from the program and all user input. If a problem develops while the program is running, the file can be examined to isolate the difficulty. It can, if it is built carefully, even be used to rerun the program up to the point of the difficulty.

Finally, text files can be used in place of printer output. Consider this situation: You are to write a program that creates a printed report, but you do not personally own a printer (or the printer is in the shop). By redirecting all the output that would have gone to the printer to a text file, you can build a file version of the report. Later, when you have access to a printer, you can print the file (using the operating system's print command) to obtain a printed report.

By using this idea, it is even possible to write programs that generate two or more printed reports simultaneously.

An additional advantage can be achieved using this technique. It is possible to obtain multiple copies of the report without having to run the program again, simply by printing multiple copies of the text file containing the report.

□
DPT

1. Before we can make use of a file designator, we must associate it with the name of some file by use of the built-in Assign procedure. If we forget to use the Assign procedure, the compiler will not detect the omission, but we will encounter a run-time I/O error when we attempt any input or output operation using the file designator.

2. We must open a file before we can perform input or output operations on it. Also, we must use Reset if we wish to read from the file and Rewrite if we wish to write to the file. If we fail to open the file before attempting to use it, the compiler will not detect the omission, but we will encounter a run-time I/O error when we attempt to read from or write to the file. If we attempt to read from a file that has been opened with Rewrite or to write to a file that has been opened with Reset, a run-time I/O error will occur.

3. There is a danger in using Rewrite to open a file. If the file already exists, then it is deleted as soon as the Rewrite is executed. Be careful not to carelessly lose valuable files through this side effect of Rewrite.

4. If we attempt to open a file using Reset and the file does not exist, then a run-time I/O error will occur. We will explain a mechanism for controlling this situation in Section 5-3.

5. After using a file, we should close it. If we forget to close a file that has been opened with Reset and attempt to reopen the file with either Reset or Rewrite, no error will result and nothing is wrong except our programming style. If we forget to close a file that has been opened with Rewrite, we are very likely to lose some of the data that we have written to the file. If we get in the habit of always closing files, we will not encounter any difficulty.

6. Always use the file designator when performing input and output activities with a file. If we forget to include the file designator in our input and output statements, then we will find ourselves using the keyboard and printer instead of the file.

7. After searching a file in a loop with a compound exit condition, do not use the function Eof after the loop has terminated as a check on how termination occurred. Remember that as soon as the last line in a file has been read, Eof(*file designator*) becomes true.

8. Do not assume that the user of your program will always do the correct thing, spell words correctly, or even type what he or she is intending to type. You already have had enough experience at using your own programs to realize that even a knowledgeable user makes mistakes (often!). Attempt to write programs that protect the user from mistakes instead of punishing the user for making mistakes. We will provide some special techniques for making programs "bullet-proof" (immune from user errors) later in the book.

□
TESTING   We have given several example programs that illustrate file searching. There are certain test cases that should always be tested when searching a file for a particular instance of a data item.

Empty file. Your program should not falter when it encounters a file that contains no data. You can produce an empty file to use in testing with the following Pascal program:

```
program EmptyFile(Input, Output);
var
  AnyFile : text;
begin {EmptyFile}
  Assign(AnyFile, 'EMPTY.FIL');
  Rewrite(AnyFile);
  Close(Anyfile)
end.
```

Target item is first. Your program should be tested with a file in which the first data item is the only one that should be successfully found.

Target item is last. Your program should be tested with a file in which the last data item is the only one that should be successfully found.

Target item is between first and last. Your program should be tested with a file in which some middle data item is the only one that should be successfully found.

Multiple target items. Your program should be tested with a file in which there are at least two data items that should be successfully found. Even more thorough testing would have several files in which the data items are in the first and last positions, two middle positions, etc.

No target item. Your program should be tested with a file in which there are no data items that should be successfully found, although some of the data items should be close (for example: Smith, Simth).

If we wished to test the program of Figure 5-6, searching for Joan Smith, we might use the following set of test files:

Empty File:

Target Item First:

```
Friends Names and Phone Numbers
```

```
                        Joan Smith
                        111-2222
                        Bill Jones
                        222-1111
```

Target Item Last:

```
                Friends Names and Phone Numbers

                Bill Jones
                222-1111
                Joan Smith
                111-4444
```

Target Item in Middle:

```
                Friends Names and Phone Numbers

                Bill Jones
                222-1111
                Joan Smith
                111-2222
                Carol Doe
                333-4444
```

Multiple Target Items (first phone number should be reported):

```
                Friends Names and Phone Numbers

                Carol Doe
                333-4444
                Joan Smith
                111-2222
                Bill Jones
                222-1111
                Joan Smith
                999-9999
```

No Target Item:

```
                Friends Names and Phone Numbers

                Bill Jones
                222-1111
                Joan Simth
                111-2222
                Carol Doe
                333-4444
```

■■■■■■
REVIEW

Terms and concepts	text file	text (variable type)
	open a file	Reset

close a file   Eof
file designator   interactive
Assign   search
Rewrite   trace file
Close

Pascal syntax   Text file manipulation: All examples use "MyFile" as the file designator.

1. To declare the file designator:

```
var
    MyFile   : text;
```

2. To associate the file name with the file designator:

```
Assign(MyFile, 'FRIENDS.TXT');
```

3. To open the file for output:

```
Rewrite(MyFile);
```

4. To open the file for input:

```
Reset(MyFile);
```

5. To write to the file:

```
Writeln(MyFile, 'John Smith');
```

6. To read from the file:

```
Readln(MyFile, Name);
```

7. To test for the end of the file:

```
if Eof(MyFile) then . . .
```

or

```
while not Eof(MyFile) do . . .
```

or

```
repeat . . .
until  Eof(MyFile)
```

8. To close the file:

```
Close(MyFile);
```

DPT   *1.* Assign a file name to the file designator before using it.

2. Open a file with Reset before reading or Rewrite before writing.

3. Rewrite deletes an existing file.

4. Opening a nonexistent file with Reset causes a run-time error.

5. Close files after using them.

6. Always use the file designator when reading or writing a file.

7. Don't test Eof outside of a loop that has used Eof as part of a compound exit condition.

8. Never trust the user.

TESTING   To test a program that is searching a file for a particular object, use at least the following test cases:

1. Empty file
2. Target item first
3. Target item last
4. Target item in the middle
5. Multiple target items
6. No target item, some close

EXERCISES

*1. Write a program to build a text file called SHOPPING.LST with the following contents:

```
              A Shopping List
              ----------------
              2 Frozen Pizzas
             10 Bags of chips
              4 Cans of soup (assorted)
              1 Case of cola
```

2. Write a program to add the two lines

```
              3 Boxes of cough drops
              1 Bottle of aspirin
```

to the file SHOPPING.LST:

a. To the beginning of the file.
b. To the end of the file.
c. Between lines 5 and 6 of the file (after the chips).

3. Modify the programs of Exercises 1 and 2 as follows:

*a. Obtain input from the user to be placed into the file you are creating.
b. Allow the user to insert new data after any line of the file. For each line of the original file, do these steps:

   Read the line
   Write the line to the output file
   Ask the user if he wishes to add lines
       if so, read 0 or more lines and add them to the output file

4. Modify the program of Figure 5-3 so that after each segment of 23 lines are displayed, the user is prompted to tap a key to continue.

5. Modify the program of Figure 5-3 to output to the printer instead of displaying on the screen. Also, print a heading and page number at the top of each page except the first. Finally, print at most 58 lines of text on each page.

6. Modify the program of Figure 5-1 by omitting the Close statement. Run the modified program. Look at the file FRIENDS.ME by using your text editor. What effect does omitting the Close statement have?

7. Write a program to produce a text file with the following contents:

```
program SelfMade(Input, Output);
var
  N : integer;
begin {SelfMade}
  N := 6;
  Writeln(N)
end.
```

After you have successfully created the file with your program, see if the text file can be compiled and run as a program in its own right. In a trivial way, you just wrote a program that wrote a program.

*8. Write a program that will read a text file and print each line, allowing the user to choose one of three options. The user can choose to delete the line, retype it, or leave it unchanged. For convenience, this last option should be chosen just by hitting return.

9. Write a program combining the ideas of Exercises 3 and 8.

10. Write a program that allows the user to interactively build a file of student names, student numbers, and scores on an examination. A sample set of lines of the file should appear as:

```
John Smith
111-33-5555
85
```

*11. Use the program from Exercise 10 (or a text editor) to build a file that has several students with the same score on the examination. Write a program that asks the user for a score and then lists all students who have earned that score on the display. Example input and output are as follows:

```
Enter a score: 85

Students with a Score of 85:
    John Smith    111-33-5555
    Nancy Doe     222-11-4444
    *** list complete


Enter a score: 66

Students with a Score of 66
    *** list complete


Enter a score: -1

    *** Scores program terminating.
```

12. Write a program that processes the file created in Exercise 11 by asking the user for a student number and displaying the name and score for the student. Example input and output are as follows:

```
Enter a student number: 111-33-5555

The student is:
    John Smith    85


Enter a student number: 333-33-3333
```

```
*** Student not found.

Enter a student number: $END

*** Search program terminating.
```

13. Write a program that processes the file created in Exercise 11 by adding 5 points to Nancy Doe's score.

14. Revise Exercise 10 to allow multiple tests by making the first data item in the file N, the number of tests.

15. Write a program that uses the file created in Exercise 14 to add another test score for each student.

16. This exercise deals with a textfile that, for each person, contains the following data:

> Name
> Age
> Sex
> Marital status
> Earned income for previous year
> Number of children

You can build the file using the ideas of Exercise 10 or using a text editor.

a. Write a procedure to read the data for one person. This procedure will be used in part (b).

b. Write programs (or program segments) to answer these questions concerning the data file.
   (1) How many people are in the file?
   (2) What percentage are single (code 'S')? Female (code'F')? Either single or female?
   (3) Who has the largest earned income? How old is that person?
   (4) What is the marital status of Mary Wikinson?
   (5) What is the average number of children for married males between the ages of 40 and 60?
   (6) Who is the *first* person in the file who is either Widowed (code 'W') or divorced (code 'D'), has no children, and has an income over $50,000?

17. a. Tell what changes you would make to Case Study No. 6 (Figure 4-16) if the data were on a text file rather than obtained from the user as the program runs.
    b. Which approach do you think would be preferable to the user of the program: the original approach or the one suggested in part (a)?
    c. Tell how you could modify Case Study No. 6 to create an output file containing name and total sales for each employee.

18. a. Choose any program that you have written and revise it to read its input from a text file.
    b. Choose any program that you have written and revise it to create a trace file (see page 352) containing a complete record of the program run.
    c. Choose any program that you have written that creates a printed report

and revise it to send the report to a file instead. Print the file using the operating system's print command.

19. A text file consists of repetitions of the following data:

> Student information
>
> One or more groups of course information for the student
>
> A line containing the string XXX

The student information consists of name, total semester hours taken prior to this semester, and total quality points earned prior to this semester. Each group of course information consists of course department (e.g., CPS), course number (e.g., 121), semester hours credit for the course, and letter grade for the course. The course information groups represent courses taken during this semester.

*a. Design the exact file structure and give a small sample file for two students.

*b. Write a program to read the file. For each student, it should display the information on the screen, then use Readln to wait for the user to tap return.

c. Modify part (b) to create a printed grade report for each student, indicating name, list of courses (department, number, grade, and quality points for course), total semester hours for the semester, total quality points for the semester, and quality point average for the semester. (Quality points for each course are found by multiplying the semester hours for the course by 4 for an A, 3 for a B, 2 for a C, 1 for a D, or 0 for an F. Quality-point average is quality points divided by semester hours.)

d. Write a program to create an output text file containing this information for each student: name, semester hours taken including this semester, and total quality points earned including this semester.

> The output file should follow the same general form as the input file. It can then be used as a starting point for building next semester's input file.

e. Add a printed report to the program in part (d). Send the printed output to a file for future printing. The columns of the report are name, total semester hours, total quality points, and quality-point average. See part (c) for information on quality-point calculations.

*21. A text file contains the following information:

> A record Counting the number of departments
>
> Department information (code, number of professors) for the first department
>
> Name and salary information for each professor in the first department
>
> Department information (code, number cf professors) for the second department
>
> Name and salary information for each professor in the second department
>
> And so on

Write a program to read the text file and generate a report in this form:

```
Department              Professor          Salary
----------              ---------          ------
    XXX          XXXXXXXXXXXXXXXXX          XXXXX
                 XXXXXXXXXXXXXXXXX          XXXXX
                 XXXXXXXXXXXXXXXXX          XXXXX
    XXX          XXXXXXXXXXXXXXXXX          XXXXX
                 XXXXXXXXXXXXXXXXX          XXXXX
                     .   .   .
```

Then show what changes to make to accomplish the following:

a. Find and print the average salary in each department.
b. Find and print the average salary in the entire school.
c. Count the number earning over $28,000 in the entire school.
d. Find and print the person with the highest salary in each department.
e. Find the number of departments that have an average salary in excess of $20,000.
f. Find the largest average salary for a department. For example, the answer might be:

```
BIO department has highest average salary: 25533.00
```

22. Give test plans for the following.

a. Exercise 3(b)
c. Exercise 8
e. Exercise 12
g. Exercise 16(b)(2)
i. Exercise 16(b)(4)

b. Exercise 4
d. Exercise 11
f. Exercise 13
h. Exercise 16(b)(3)
j. Exercise 16(b)(5)

□

NOTES FOR SECTION 5-1

1. With other implementations of Pascal, some other method may have to be used to associate an external file with an internal file designator. This may require that the file designators for each file used by the program be listed in the program heading. The association of the actual file name to this file designator may have to be accomplished by the user prior to running the program. Turbo Pascal makes no use of the list of files in the heading line, instead using the Assign statement to associate file designators to files.

In addition, a few versions of Pascal force the programmer to deal with concepts of buffers and pointers in order to deal with files. Turbo Pascal's approach is easier, using the familiar procedures Read, Readln, Write, and Writeln.

The specific Pascal Reference Manual will have further information on this matter.

5-2
□□□□□□
RECORDS AND SETS

In this section, we will introduce a powerful data structuring technique by means of the Pascal **record** construct. We will continue our discussion of files that was begun in the last section. Finally, we will learn some more about the Pascal **set** data structure.

RECORDS   □

Especially when dealing with files, it is frequently the case that certain data items are associated with one another. For example, in the last section, we discussed a text file that consisted of friends' names and phone numbers. The two data items Name and Phone are associated because of their relationship with one particular individual. Recall that we stored the name and phone number in a rather awkward manner: on two separate lines of the file. Pascal provides a better way of dealing with this information via the record structure.

COMMENT   Historically, the term "record" originally referred to files. However, the concept of grouping related data is an important one, whether files are involved or not. In our discussion of records, some examples will involve files and others will not.

We begin by adapting the programs of the previous section, which dealt with text files to files of records.

A record consists of data entities called **fields** that have values. The general form of the definition of a record occurs in the "type" section of a Pascal module and has the following form:

```
type
   identifier = record
                   list of field declarations
                end;
```

In our example, we want to have a record called PersonalData, which has two fields: Name and Phone. We declare this data structure in the "type" area of our declarations as follows:

```
type
   PersonalData = record
                     Name    : string[20];
                     Phone   : string[ 8]
                  end;
```

We also must declare a variable of type PersonalData, which can hold the values for one particular instance of a friend. We make this declaration in the "var" area of our program as follows:

```
var
   Friend   : PersonalData;
```

We can refer to the individual fields of a record variable by means of the construction:

record variable name.field name

Therefore, for our example, we can refer to the fields of the variable Friend by means of the designations:

```
Friend.Name
Friend.Phone
```

If we want to use our records for a file (and we do), then we declare a file type as follows:

```
type
   PersonalData = record
```

```
                                        Name    : string[20];
                                        Phone   : string[ 8];
                                      end;
                 PersonalFile = file of PersonalData;
```

We also declare a file designator variable in the "var" section:

```
                 var
                     Friend      : PersonalData;
                     FriendsFile : PersonalFile;
```

We open a file of type PersonalFile with Reset or Rewrite, as shown in the previous section. A major difference is that we use Read and Write rather than Readln and Writeln with this new file type. We must take care not to use Readln and Writeln except for text files; otherwise, we will encounter run-time input/output errors when we execute our program. We also read and write entire records in this new setting. Another difference is that we can no longer view our file's contents with a text editor. We rewrite the programs of Figures 5-5 and 5-6 using the record concept, as shown in Figures 5-8 and 5-9. Major differences are shaded.

COMMENT   As for text files, there are differences in how versions of Pascal deal with files of records. The differences are similar to those for text files. Consult your instructor or reference manual.

```
program Build(Input, Output);
{
        Written by:   XXXXXXXX  XX/XX/XX
           Purpose:   To build a file of friends.
   Procedures used:   Instructions - to print instructions.
}
const
  EndOfData  =  '$END';

type
  PersonalData = record
                   Name    : string[20];
                   Phone   : string[8];
                 end;
  PersonalFile = file of PersonalData;

var
  Friend             : PersonalData;      { Instance of record }
  FriendsFile        : PersonalFile;      { File designator }
  FileName           : string[14];        { Name of the file }

procedure Instructions; begin {stub} end;

begin {Build}

{*** Print instructions and ask the user for the filename.}
```

Figure 5-8 Writing to a File of Records (Continued)

```
          Instructions;
          Write('Enter the filename: ');
          Readln(FileName);

      {*** Designate the file.}

          Assign(FriendsFile, FileName);

      {*** Open the file.}

          Rewrite(FriendsFile);

      {*** Get names and phone numbers for file.}

          repeat
            Writeln;
            Write('Enter name ($END to quit): ');
            Readln(Friend.Name);
            if  Friend.Name <> EndOfData then
              begin
                Write('Enter phone number: ');
                Readln(Friend.Phone);
                Write(FriendsFile, Friend)
              end {if}
          until  Friend.Name = EndOfData;

      {*** Close the file.}

          Close(FriendsFile);

      {*** Print terminating message and stop program.}

          Writeln;
          Writeln('Build program is terminating.')
        end.
```

Figure 5-8   Writing to a File of Records

```
    program Search(Input, Output);
    {
          Written by:   XXXXXXXX   XX/XX/XX
             Purpose:   To search for a friend and display her phone number.
      Procedures used:  Instructions - to print instructions.
    }
    type
      PersonalData = record
                       Name    : string[20];
                       Phone   : string[8];
                     end;
      PersonalFile = file of PersonalData;
    var
      FriendsFile  : PersonalFile;                    { File designator }
```

Figure 5-9   Searching a File of Records (Continued)

```
    FileName      : string[14];          { Name of the file }
    ToFind        : string[20];          { Name to find }
    Friend        : PersonalData;        { Instance of record }

  procedure Instructions; begin {stub} end;

  begin {Search}

  {*** Print instructions and ask the user for the filename.}

    Instructions;
    Write('Enter the filename: ');
    Readln(FileName);

  {*** Designate the file.}

    Assign(FriendsFile, FileName);

  {*** Open the file.}

    Reset(FriendsFile);

  {*** Get name from the user.}

    Writeln;
    Write('Enter the friend''s name: ');
    Readln(ToFind);

  {*** Search the file for the name.}

    Friend.Name := '';           {Required so while condition is defined}

    while   (Friend.Name <> ToFind) and (not Eof(FriendsFile))   do
      begin
        Read(FriendsFile, Friend)
      end; {while}

  {*** Display the results of the search.}

    if  Friend.Name = ToFind   then
      Writeln('The phone number is: ', Friend.Phone)
    else
      Writeln('*** Friend not found.');

  {*** Close the file.}

    Close(FriendsFile);

  {*** Print terminating message and stop program.}

    Writeln;
    Writeln('Search program is terminating.')
  end.
```

Figure 5-9   Searching a File of Records

Because the file to contain the friends' names and phone numbers is no longer available for use with a text editor, we no longer use the concept of heading lines in the file. In the following subsection, we discuss some additional aspects of the record structure.

UTILITIES

There is one disadvantage of using files of records instead of text files. Text files can be created using an editor, and they can also be examined using an editor. This is not true for files of records.

It would therefore be very useful, when writing a program which works with non-text files, to first write simple programs for file creation and file display.

Appendix E (UTILITIES) contains a framework for writing file creation and display utilities. To use these frameworks, you will only need to write a procedure to read one record and a procedure to display one record.

□
**OPERATIONS
WITH
RECORDS**

Assignment. We can assign the entire contents from one record to another record of the same type. For example, if Friend and NewFriend are both declared to be of type PersonalData, then the statement:

```
Friend := NewFriend;
```

is equivalent to the two statements:

```
Friend.Name := NewFriend.Name;
Friend.Phone := NewFriend.Phone;
```

This is a convenience when a record contains many fields.

Processing a single record. Pascal allows a shorter way to refer to fields than the examples we have seen: NewFriend.Phone, for example. The shorter route involves the Pascal keyword **with**. The general form of the with–do construction is

```
with  record variable name  do
   begin
      list of statements
   end
```

In between the "begin" and "end" of the with–do construct, we can use the names of the fields of the record without using the record variable and a dot (.) as a prefix.

As an example, suppose that we wish to read the name and phone number of NewFriend from the keyboard. Our first style for doing this would be as follows:

```
Write('Enter the name: ');
Readln(NewFriend.Name);
Write('Enter the phone number: ');
Readln(NewFriend.Phone);
```

The shorter method uses the form:

```
with NewFriend do
  begin
    Write('Enter the name: ');
    Readln(Name);
    Write('Enter the phone number: ');
    Readln(Phone)
  end;
```

Note that because we have told Pascal that we are dealing with NewFriend, we do not have to use the record identifier as a prefix for the field names.

Records as parameters. We can pass records as parameters to procedures or functions. For example, if we wanted to use a detail line print procedure Detail to print the name and phone number of a friend, then we could declare the procedure with the heading:

```
procedure Detail(Friend : PersonalData);
```

We could then invoke the procedure from our program with the statement:

```
Detail(Friend);
```

As another example, consider the following segment of code. It works with records whose fields are Name and Age. The variables Person and Large are records of this type.

```
Large.Name := '';
Large.Age := 0;

repeat
  GetRecord(Person, Quit);
  if  not Quit then
    begin
      if  Person.Age > Large.Age  then
          Large := Person
    end {if}
until Quit;

PrintRecord(Large)
```

This segment reads a series of input consisting of Name and Age. After the loop, it prints the name and age of the oldest person (assuming no ties). We have, of course, written a number of programs similar to this. This one is notable in several ways:

1. The data that "belongs together" (name and age) is associated by putting it in a record.

2. We use variables which are records as parameters to two procedures: GetRecord, PrintRecord.

3. If a larger age is found, we assign

```
Large := Person
```

This makes a record of both the name and age of the person whose age is larger. If the record contained ten fields, all ten fields would be copied by the one assignment statement.

Arrays of records. We can use the array concept with records as well as with other types of variables. For example, if we wanted to be able to deal with a list of 10 friends, we could use the declarations:

```
type
  PersonalData = record
                     Name    : string[20];
                     Phone   : string[8]
                 end;
  PersonArray = array[1 .. 10] of PersonalData;

var
  Friends    : PersonArray;
```

NOTE   We could accomplish the declaration by

```
var
    Friends : array[1 .. 10] of PersonalData;
```

However, the former method of declaring the array is more general and is recommended over the first. One advantage is that it allows the passing of the array Friends to a subprogram.

To illustrate a few possible ways we could work with arrays of records, suppose that the PersonArray type is declared globally (that is, in the main program's declarations). Then we can declare a procedure ReadPeople as follows:

```
procedure ReadPeople(List : PersonArray);
```

We can invoke the subprogram ReadPeople this way:

```
ReadPeople(Friends);
```

If we wish to refer to the name field of the fifth record in the array, we can use the form:

```
Friends[5].Name
```

We can do extensive processing with the sixth record in the array by using the construct:

```
with  Friends[6]  do
  begin
       . . . .
  end
```

Finally, we can print the names in the Friends array by:

```
for I := 1 to 10 do
  begin
     Writeln(Friends[I].Name)
  end
```

Arrays of records will be dealt with in greater detail in Chapter 6.

We have used the concept of a Pascal set in some of our examples in previous sections of the book. In particular, when a user is asked a yes or no question, we have checked for a valid response by means of the Boolean expression:

```
Ans in ['Y','y','N','n']
```

In this subsection, we will discuss some additional details on Pascal sets.

A set in Pascal is similar to the mathematical notion: a collection of objects. Each object that is in the set is called a **member** or **element** of the set. Two sets are equal if they have exactly the same elements, regardless of order. All of the elements of a set must be of the same Pascal type. The legal types for elements in sets are

> Integer
> Boolean
> Char
> User-defined scalar types (see Section 5-3)

Constant sets are specified by listing the elements of the set between a pair of square brackets (for example, ['Y','y','N','n']). Some examples of set constants are

```
[1,3,5]
['a','b','c']
[ ]
```

The third example above is the **empty set**, the set with no elements. We can also specify a constant set by means of ellipsis (..). Thus, we can specify the set of all uppercase letters between A and F by:

```
['A' .. 'F']
```

We declare a set type by specifying the type of the elements that may belong to sets of that type. The type of the elements of the set is called the **base type**. For example, if we wanted to work with sets of integers less than 100, we could declare the set type as

```
type
   SmallNumbersSet  = set of 1 .. 99;
```

NOTE   We have seen the notation value .. value (as in 1 .. 99) before: in defining array types and in listing the branches of a case statement. This notation indicates a subrange of the integers. Subranges will be examined in more detail in Section 5-3.

If we wish to work with sets of characters, then we could declare the set type as

```
type
   CharacterSet  = set of char;
```

We declare variables to have a set type in the var section of the program. For example, if we want the variables A and B to be sets of numbers less than 100, we can use the declarations:

```
type
   SmallNumbersSet   = set of 1 ..99;
var
   A, B  : SmallNumbersSet;
```

Assignment. We can assign a set value to a set variable of the same type. Thus, if A is declared of type SmallNumbersSet as above, we can use the statement

$$A := [17,23,41];$$

to give A a value. If B is also of type SmallNumbersSet, then we can also assign a value to A with the statement

$$A := B;$$

Union. If A and B are variables of the same set type, then we can form the **union** of A and B by the expression A + B. This new set A + B is comprised of all of the elements that are in either A or B. For example, if

$$A \quad is \quad [1,3,5] \quad and \quad B \quad is \quad [4,6]$$

then

$$A + B \quad is \quad [1,3,5,4,6]$$

Remember that order does not matter with sets, so that we can also say that

$$A + B \quad is \quad [6,3,4,1,5]$$

We do not allow repetition in sets. For example, if

$$C \quad is \quad [1,3,5] \quad and \quad D \quad is \quad [5,6]$$

then

$$C + D \quad is \quad [1,3,5,6]$$

Intersection. If A and B are variables of the same set type, then we can form the **intersection** of A and B by the expression A * B. This new set A * B is comprised of all of the elements of A that are also members of B. For example, if

$$A \quad is \quad [1,3,5] \quad and \quad B \quad is \quad [4,6]$$

then

$$A * B \quad is \quad [\ ]$$

As another example, if

$$C \quad is \quad [1,3,5] \quad and \quad D \quad is \quad [5,6]$$

then

$$C * D \quad is \quad [5]$$

Difference. If A and B are variables of the same set type, then we can form the **difference** of A and B by the expression A − B. This new set A − B is comprised of all of the elements of A that are not members of B. For example, if

```
     A  is  [1,3,5]   and  B  is  [4,6]
```
then

```
            A - B  is  [1,3,5]
```

As another example, if

```
     C  is  [1,3,5]  and  D  is  [5,6]
```
then

```
            C - D  is  [1,3]
```

Note that in general A − (A − B) is equal to A * B. Note also that D − C is [6], which is totally different from C − D. In general, A − B and B − A are not equal.

Membership test. We have already encountered the Pascal keyword **in**. In general, if A is a variable of set type and if X is a variable of the base type of A, then we can construct the Boolean expression "X in A", which is true if X is an element of A. We must be careful not to attempt to test mismatched types with the membership test.

Set equality. We can compare two variables of the same set type for equality by use of the "=" operator. Thus, if A and B are variables of the same set type, we can construct the Boolean expression:

```
                A = B
```

which is true if A has exactly the same elements as does B. Remember that order does not count, so that

```
        [1,3,5] = [3,5,1]
```

is true. We can use the operator "<>" to test for inequality.

Set inclusion. We can compare two variables of the same type to see if one is a **subset** of the other by means of the operators "<," "<=," ">," and ">=." If A and B are two variables of the same set type, then we can construct the following Boolean expressions:

A < B	true if every element of A is also an element of B and A is not equal to B
A <= B	true if every element of A is also an element of B
A > B	true if every element of B is also an element of A and B is not equal to A
A >= B	true if every element of B is also an element of A

For example, these are true conditions:

```
        [1,5] < [3,1,5,6]
        [6,3,2] >= [3,2]
        [1,2,3] >= [1,2,3]
```

but these are not:

$$[1,5] < [2,6]$$
$$[1,2,3] > [1,2,3]$$

Input and output. No automatic input and output of sets is allowed with keyboard, display, printer, or text files. We can read and write sets with files declared to be of set type in a fashion similar to that of records.

However, we can write our own code to print sets one element at a time. For example, these steps can be used to print a set A of the type SmallNumberSet defined above. (The numbers in the set will be printed one per line.)

```
for I := 1 to 99 do
   begin
      if I in A then
         Writeln(I)
   end   {for}
```

Similarly, we can read a set of this type by reading the numbers one at a time and using a step such as

```
A := A + [I]
```

where I is the number read. (A would be initialized to [ ].)

Set construction. Sets can be constructed using constants or variables of the base type. For example, if A is a set with base type char and if X and Y are variables of type char, then we can construct a set as follows:

```
A := ['a', X, 'b', Y];
```

If X has the value 'c' and Y has the value 'd' in the above expression, then the resulting value of A is ['a', 'c', 'b', 'd']. Below is a Pascal fragment to test the validity of the example just cited:

```
var
   A    : set of char;
   X, Y : char;

X := 'c';
Y := 'd';
A := ['a', X, 'b', Y];
if  A = ['a', 'c', 'b', 'd']  then
   Writeln('The example is valid.')
else
   Writeln('The example is invalid.');
```

Parameters. Sets can be passed as parameters with some care. A valid scenario for passing a set as a parameter is shown in the fragment:

```
type
   Kind = set of char;      { This is a named type }
               . . . .
var
   A    : Kind;
```

```
      procedure BeCareful(S : Kind);

   BeCareful(A);
```

The main point is that for passing set parameters, *named types* must be used. The scenario below is invalid and will be rejected by the compiler:

```
   var
      A     : set of char;

   procedure BeCareful(S : set of char);

   BeCareful(A);
```

The situation with set parameters is similar to that we have already seen with arrays, strings, and records.

□
AN EXAMPLE

We will develop an example use of sets for obtaining valid input from a user. Quite often, a program has to ask the user for a response that consists of a single character. For example, in answering a yes-or-no question, we often consider any of Y, y, N, or n to be valid responses. If a menu has the options

S(top the process)
R(estart the process)
C(ontinue the process)

then we would consider any of S, s, R, r, C, or c to be valid responses. We will write a subprogram called AskUser, which will accept a prompting message for the user and a set of valid responses as its two parameters and which will return a valid response from the user. The steps in the subprogram are

print the prompting message
read response from user
while the response is invalid do the following:
    ask user to try again
    read response from user
return the valid response

It is convenient for the user to be able to type a response by just hitting the appropriate key and not having to hit the return key afterwards. Turbo Pascal provides the capability through the use of built-in file designator Kbd.[1] If X is a char variable, then the statement

```
            Read(Kbd, X);
```

will read a single character into the variable X without the need for the return key. (It will not display the character typed on the screen.)

In the example program shown in Figure 5-10 we exercise the AskUser function in two of the most common contexts in which it would be used. Note that in the first, we use variables in the invocation of the function; whereas in the second, we use constants. Either method is valid.

```
program Ask(Input, Output);
{
        Written by:  XXXXXXXXX  XX/XX/XX
           Purpose:  To ask the user to respond.
  Procedures used:  Instructions - to print instructions.
   Functions used:  AskUser - to obtain valid input.
}
type
  Letters  = set of char;
  Sentence = string[40];

var
  Responses    : Letters;          { Valid responses }
  Prompt       : Sentence;         { Message to user }
  Answer       : char;             { Answer from user }

procedure Instructions; begin {stub} end;

function AskUser(Message : Sentence; Valids : Letters) : char;
{
        Written by:  XXXXXXXXX  XX/XX/XX
           Purpose:  To ask the user to respond.
        Parameters:  Message - a string to be displayed, input;
                     Valids -  a set of valid responses, input.
}
var
  Keystroke    : char;                  { User input }

begin {AskUser}
  Write(Message);
  Read(Kbd, Keystroke);
  Writeln(Keystroke);

  while  not (Keystroke in Valids)  do
    begin
      Write('*** Invalid response, please reenter: ');
      Read(Kbd, Keystroke);
      Writeln(Keystroke)
    end; {while}

  AskUser := Keystroke
end; {AskUser}


begin {Ask}

{*** Print instructions.}

  Instructions;

{*** Show typical "yes/no" setup.}

  Responses := ['Y','y','N','n'];
  Prompt := 'Do you wish to continue (Y,N)?';
```

Figure 5-10 Using a Set to Validate Input (Continued)

```
      Answer := AskUser(Prompt, Responses);
      Writeln('Your answer was: ', Answer);

   {*** Show sample menu setup.}

      Writeln('S(top the process)');
      Writeln('R(estart the process)');
      Writeln('C(ontinue the process)');
      Answer := AskUser('Selection: ',['S', 's', 'R', 'r', 'C', 'c']);
      Writeln('Your answer was: ', Answer);

   {*** Print terminating message and stop program.}

      Writeln;
      Writeln('Ask program is terminating.')
   end.
```

SAMPLE INPUT AND OUTPUT

```
Do you wish to continue (Y,N)?q
*** Invalid response, please reenter: w
*** Invalid response, please reenter: y
Your answer was: y
S(top the process)
R(estart the process)
C(ontinue the process)
Selection: y
*** Invalid response, please reenter: n
*** Invalid response, please reenter: s
Your answer was: s

Ask program is terminating.
```

Figure 5-10   Using a Set to Validate Input

□
DPT   *1.* When we are dealing with nontext files, we use Read and Write and *do not use* Readln and Writeln. If we use Readln or Writeln in a program, then the compiler will detect and report the error.

2. We must be sure to use the "." when dealing with a field of a record when not within a "with–do" construct. For example, suppose that we have a record declared as

```
type
   PersonalData = record of
                        Name    : string[20];
                        Phone   : string[8]
                  end;

var
   Friend   : PersonalData;
```

Suppose that in our program (and not in a "with Friend do" construct) we unintentionally omit the prefix and write

```
              Name := 'Joan Smith';
```

One of two things will happen:

(a) If there is no string variable Name in the program, then the compiler will report an "undeclared variable" error.

(b) If there is a string variable Name in the program, then the compiler will not report any problem. This could cause the program to act erroneously without causing a compiler or run-time error. This problem could be very hard to correct.

3. The preceding tip raises a very subtle point. It is legal to have a program containing these declarations:

```
type
   String20    = string[20];
   InputRecord = record
                    Name : String20;
                    Age  : integer
                 end;
var
   Person : InputRecord;
   Name   : String20;
   Age    : integer;
```

The identifiers Name and Age are not considered to be duplicates because the actual names of the fields within the record are

```
              Person.Name
              Person.Age
```

Inside a with statement, as indicated by tip number 1, the field name would take precedence over the variable name. Thus, the output of the fragment

```
Person.Name := 'Sam';
Name := 'Sue';
with Person do
   Name := 'Mary';
Writeln(Name, ' ', Person.Name)
```

would consist of "Sue" and "Mary".

Our defensive programming tip is to try to avoid this situation because it has the potential for confusion. Do not include a field name and a variable name that are the same.

COMMENT   On the other hand, using identical field names within two different record structures can be appropriate. For example, this might be useful:

```
type
   String20 = string[20];
   InputRecord =  record
                     Name                 : String20;
                     Score1, Score2, Score3 : integer
                  end;
   OutputRecord = record
                     Name  : String20;
                     Total : integer
                  end;
```

4. We must take care to use the file designator in all of our Read and Write statements that are intended to work with a file. If we omit the file designator, then we will read from the keyboard and we will write to the display screen.

5. We must be sure to use a subscript when dealing with a field of one element of an array of records. Suppose that we have declared the array of records:

```
Friends   : array[1 .. 10] of PersonalData;
```

It would be an error to attempt to refer to one of the elements as in the following example:

```
Friends.Name := 'Joan Smith';
```

The compiler will detect and report this error.

6. We must use a named type when passing a record as a parameter to a subprogram. The compiler will detect an attempt to declare a parameter as a record in the heading of a procedure or function.

7. When we specify a range of values, we must use two dots as in:

```
5 .. 99
```

A common mistake is to use three dots instead of two, as we do when using an elipsis in our writing. Also, some electronic spreadsheets allow the use of three dots to specify ranges of rows or columns. An example of the misuse of range specification is the following:

```
if  'C' in ['A' ... 'F']  then
    Writeln('You won''t see this message!');
```

The compiler will detect this error.

8. When we wish to specify a range of characters, we must use quotes around the characters at the beginning and end of range as in the example:

```
'A' .. 'F'
```

Suppose that we omit the quotes, as in the example:

```
if  C in [A .. F]  then
    Writeln('Will you see this message?');
```

One of two things will happen:
   (a) If any one of C, A, or F have not been declared as variables, then the compiler will report an undeclared variable error.
   (b) If C, A, and F have been declared as variables, then the statement can be legal. For example, if all three have been declared as integer variables and if A has the value 4, C has the value 2, and F has the value 6, then the condition

```
C in [A .. F]
```

is legitimate and has the value of false. The main principle that will help us to avoid this kind of situation is the use of meaningful variable names in our programs. It is unlikely that the variables C, A, and F would be the best choices in a program.

9. Two sets must have the same base type in order for them to be involved in set operations. For example, we cannot construct the set union:

```
[1, 2, 3] + ['A', 'B', 'C']
```

The compiler will detect this kind of type mismatch error.

10. Input and output of sets as text is not allowed. If we attempt to print a set as in the example:

```
Writeln([1, 2, 3]);
```

the compiler will detect the error.

11. Use of the set membership condition "in" requires that the element being tested be of the base type of the set. Thus, the condition:

```
1 in ['A' .. 'F']
```

is not false, it is illegal. The compiler will detect this error.

12. We must remember the significance of using single quotes. We have already discussed this point in DPT item number 7 above. But for reemphasis, remember:

```
[X, Y, Z]  is different from  ['X', 'Y', 'Z'].
```

13. We must be aware of the restrictions that apply to the use of sets.[2] First, the base type of the set must be integer, Boolean, char, or any other of the types that will be discussed in Section 5-3. When using integers in sets, we must use values between 1 and 256, inclusive. Because of this restriction, the following declaration is illegal:

```
A = set of integer;
```

To help you to remember that you should only use integer values between 1 and 256 when dealing with sets of integers, run the following program:

```
program WatchOut(Input, Output);
begin {WatchOut}
  if 257 in [257]  then
    Writeln('You won''t see this message!')
  else
    Writeln('So, watch out!')
end.
```

■■■■■■
REVIEW

Terms and *concepts*	record	base type
	set	union (+)
	field	intersection (*)
	with	difference (−)
	member	in
	element	subset (<, <=, >, >=)
	empty set	named type

Records

1. Define a record structure in the type section:

```
type
  identifier = record
                 list of field declarations
               end;
```

2. Declare a variable to have a record type in the var section:

```
var
  variable name    : record type name;
```

3. Refer to a single field of a single record:

```
record variable name.field name
```

4. Process a single record using the with–do construct:

```
with record variable name  do
  begin
    list of statements
  end;
```

5. Declare an array of records in the var section; for example:

```
Friends    : array[1 .. 10] of PersonalData;
```

6. Refer to a field of an element of an array of records, as shown in the example:

```
Friends[5].Name
```

7. Pass a record as a parameter using named type, as shown in the example:

```
procedure Print(List : PersonalData);
```

Files of records

1. Define a type for a file of records:

```
file type name = file of record type name;
```

2. Define a file designator for a file of records:

```
file designator  : file type name;
```

3. Use Read and Write for input and output activities with a file of records:

```
Read(file designator, record variable name);
```

or

```
Write(file designator, record variable name);
```

Sets

1. Define a constant set using square brackets, as shown in the example:

```
[1, 3, 5]
```

2. Declare a set type in the type section, as shown in the example:

```
SmallNumbersSet = set of 1 .. 99;
```

3. Refer to the empty set by:

```
[ ]
```

4. If A and B are of the same set type, then the set operations are

Assignment	A := B
Union	A + B
Intersection	A * B
Difference	A − B
Equality tests	A = B
	A <> B
Subset tests	A < B
	A <= B
	A > B
	A >= B

5. If A is of set type and X has the base type of A, then we can test to see if X is a member of A with the Boolean expression:

```
X in A
```

6. If X, Y, and Z are elements of the same base type, then we can construct the set containing the values of the variables:

```
[X,Y,Z]
```

DPT

1. Do not use Readln and Writeln with nontext files.

2. Be sure to use the "." when dealing with a field of a record when not within a "with–do" construct.

3. Do not use duplicate names for variables and field names.

4. Make sure that you use the file designator in your Read and Write statements that are intended to work with a file.

5. Be sure to use a subscript when dealing with a field of one element of an array of records.

6. Use a named type when passing a record as a parameter to a subprogram.

7. When specifying a range of values, use two dots as in:

```
5 .. 99
```

Do not use three dots.

8. When specifying a range of characters, use quotes around the characters at the beginning and end of range:

```
'A' .. 'F'
```

9. Two sets must be of the same base type in order for them to be involved in set operations.

10. Input and output of sets as text is not allowed.

11. Use of the set membership condition "in" requires that the element being tested be of the base type of the set.

12. Note that [X, Y, Z] is different from ['X', 'Y', 'Z'].

13. There can be no more than 256 elements in a set.

EXERCISES

*1. Write declarations or expressions to represent each of the following:

a. The field Phone of the record variable Friend is assigned the value '555-1212'.

b. The record type Complex is to consist of the two real number fields: RealPart and ImaginaryPart.

c. The variable Number is of type Complex.

d. If the field Name of the record variable Friend is equal to 'Joan Smith', then print "Found".

e. The set consisting of the numbers 1, 2, and 3.

f. The set consisting of the characters '1', '2', and '3'.

g. If the value of the variable N is a member of the set consisting of the numbers between 3 and 9, inclusive, then print "Yes".

h. The variable A is to have sets of characters as its values.

2. Write a procedure or function for each of the following:

*a. Given a record variable of type PersonalData, print a detail line consisting of the phone number, a colon, and the name.

b. Given a record variable of type PersonalData, get input from the user for the name and phone number.

*c. Given a record variable of type Complex [see Exercise 1(b)], calculate the sum of the squares of the real and imaginary parts.

d. Given a character set variable, ask the user for characters to be members of the set.

e. Given a set of characters and one character that is a member of the set, ask the user to enter a character that is a member of the set. Check for valid input and return a value of true if the user enters the given character and return a value of false otherwise. (This might be part of a program for administering a multiple-choice examination.)

*3. Extend the record structure of Figure 5-9 by adding the fields:

Address   (string of size 80)
Month of birth   (integer)

4. Write a Pascal program to interactively build a file of records of the form:

Company	
Name	(string)
Address	(string)
City	(string)
State	(string)
Zip code	(string)
Number of employees	(integer)

5. Write a Pascal program to deal with the file created by use of the program from Exercise 4. The program should accept the company name as input and should print the number of employees of the company.

*6. a. Write a Pascal program to list the contents of the file from Exercise 4 on the printer. You should use appropriate headings.

   b. Modify the program of part (a) to also print the following summary information:
      (1) The number of companies
      (2) The percentage of "large companies (more than 700 employees)
      (3) The company with the most employees and the number of employees
      (4) The number of the companies that are New York (state = NY) companies
      (5) The California company (state = CA) with the most employees (assume there is at least one California company)
      (6) Repeat (5) without the assumption. If there is no California company, the program should say so

7. Using the file from Exercise 4 as input, write a program to create an output file containing only the name and number of employees for those companies from North Carolina (state = NC) employing 50 or fewer employees.

*8. Write a program to consist of two loops:

   First loop:
   Read integers between 50 and 100 and store them in a set A. The loop should terminate when the user enters a 0. Use set union to add to the set.

   Second loop:
   Read integers and tell the user whether or not each integer is in the set.

9. Write a program to check that your compiler will not allow you to pass set parameters in a manner similar to the statement:

```
procedure Check(A : set of char);
```

10. Write a calculator program that provides the following menu:

```
                    OPTIONS
                    ───────

          A(dd two numbers)
          S(ubtract two numbers)
          Q(uit)
```

Use the AskUser function to get the user request for a menu option. Use a Case statement for the different menu options.

11. Write a program to allow the user to complete (in any order) a list of five unrepeatable tasks:

```
              F(ill in a blank)
              S(olve an addition problem)
              G(uess a number)
              N(ame a famous person)
              R(ead a joke)
```

Use the set difference operator to reduce the set of options, and when there are no more options left, quit. Hint: There are no options left when the set of options is equal to [ ].

12. Write a program to build a set of all prime numbers between the numbers N and M that are input by the user. The numbers N and M must be in the range from 1 to 256, inclusive. Then, in a loop, let the user enter a number and have the program say whether or not the number is a prime. Hint: Use set union to incrementally build the set.

13. Write a test plan for the following exercises:

*a. Exercise 2(c)   b. Exercise 2(d)
*c. Exercise 5   d. Exercise 6(a)
e. Exercise 6(b)(3)   f. Exercise 6(b)(4)
g. Exercise 6(b)(6)   *h. Exercise 8
i. Exercise 12

□
NOTES FOR SECTION 5-2

1. The built-in file designator Kbd is not available in most other versions of Pascal. We consider the capability provided with this feature to outweigh the nonportability issue, and we therefore will use the Kbd designator. To modify our programs for versions of Pascal which do not have this feature, we would simply change Read(Kbd, X) to ReadLn(X). The user would have to hit RETURN following the choice.

2. The maximum number of elements that can be in a set varies among different Pascal implementations.

5-3
□□□□□□
USER-DEFINED DATA TYPES

Pascal provides a powerful and flexible means of dealing with data in the form of user-defined data types. We have seen some examples of this facility when we dealt with arrays, records, files, and sets. In this section, we will discuss some additional possibilities for structuring data through data typing. Defining the structure of data is a significant part of the total program design effort. Choosing an appropriate structure for the data can make writing the program more straightforward than choosing an unnatural, awkward structure for the data. For example, we could deal with time in minutes and seconds by using two integer variables Minutes and Seconds; or we could use a single real variable Minutes. If we have to perform time arithmetic, we will appreciate having chosen the latter data structure. (However, due to the limitation of real accuracy, we might have to use the former structure in a program where total accuracy is critical.)

In this section, we will deal with scalar types, enumerated types, ordinal types, subrange types, type checking, and more information on records. We will also illustrate input/output error trapping for two common situations.

□
SCALAR TYPES

Pascal provides the standard **scalar types**: integer, real, Boolean, and char. All of these except real are also referred to as **ordinal types** because it makes sense to think of them as being in order, one after another. Ordinal types are sometimes referred to as **enumerated types**. When we are looking at an element of an ordinal type, it usually is meaningful to talk about the previous and the next element. The first and last elements of an ordinal type are exceptions. For example:

Type	Element	Previous	Next
integer	4	3	5
Boolean	false	—	true
char	'd'	'c'	'e'[1]

Pascal provides three built-in functions to help in dealing with ordinal types. The function **Ord** tells us the serial order of an element within its ordinal type. If X is an element of an ordinal type, then Ord(X) is an integer value expressing its position within the type. In general, Ord begins its count at 0 rather than 1. For integers, Ord(X) is X itself. The following table gives some example values of Ord:

Type	Element	Ord(element)
integer	0	0
integer	1	1
integer	−4	−4
Boolean	false	0
Boolean	true	1
char	'a'	97
char	'A'	65
char	'3'	51[2]

Note that for an integer, Ord acts as an identity. Also note that the values of Ord for false and true are reasonably chosen (you wouldn't want true to be associated with zero would you?). The values of Ord for char variables cannot appear to be either reasonable or obvious. These values depend on the particular character code set that is used for the implementation of Pascal that you are using. The values in the table above for the char variables assume that we are using an IBM PC that uses a popular character code set called ASCII. (See Appendix F.) Other implementations of Pascal can use other character code sets, but ASCII is used on most microcomputers at present. Figure 5-11 shows a program that will allow you to print your character code set for reference.[3]

For elements of char type, the **Chr** function is the inverse of the Ord function. That is, for any char variable X:

$$Chr(Ord(X)) = X$$

Also, for any integer variable I that has a value from 0 to 255:

$$Ord(Chr(I)) = I$$

Because of the order that is associated with ordinal types, we can use the relational operators:

$$= \quad <> \quad < \quad > \quad >= \quad <=$$

These operators behave in the manner that the Ord function dictates. For example, if X and Y are elements of the same ordinal type, then X < Y is true if and only if Ord(X) < Ord(Y) is true. One concrete example is the ethical inequality:

```
program CodeSet(Input, Output);
{
        Written by:  XXXXXXXX  XX/XX/XX
           Purpose:  To print the code set from 27 onward.
}
var
  I    : integer;                              { Loop index }


begin {CodeSet}

{*** Print headings on the printer.}

  Writeln(Lst, ' ':34, 'My Code Set');
  Writeln(Lst, ' ':34, '-----------');
  Writeln(Lst);
  Writeln(Lst);
  Writeln(Lst, ' ':28, 'Ord Value', ' ':6, 'Character');
  Writeln(Lst);

{*** Generate the code set.}

  for I := 27 to 255 do
    Writeln(Lst, ' ':32, I:3, ' ':13, Chr(I));

{*** Print terminating message and stop program.}

  Writeln;
  Writeln('CodeSet program is terminating.')
end.
```

Figure 5-11 Printing the ASCII Code

false < true. You can test this inequality with the small program shown as Figure 5-12.

Pascal provides two additional functions that can be used with ordinal types: **Pred** and **Succ**. For any element X of an ordinal type that is not the first element of

```
program Ethics(Input, Output);
{
        Written by:  XXXXXXXX  XX/XX/XX
           Purpose:  To illustrate the ethical inequality.
}


begin {Ethics}
  if  (false < true)  then
    Writeln('All is well.')
  else
    Writeln('Something is wrong.');
  Writeln;
  Writeln('Ethics program is terminating.')
end.
```

Figure 5-12 An Ethics Lesson

the type, Pred(X) is the element of the ordinal type that precedes X. The relationship between Pred and Ord is

$$Ord(Pred(X)) = Ord(X) - 1$$

Pred(X) is not meaningful when X is the first element of the ordinal type. Note that if X is an element of any ordinal type except integer, then X is the first element of the type if and only if Ord(X) = 0. Thus, when moving "backwards" through an ordinal type using the Pred function, we should stop when Ord returns the value 0. For any element X of an ordinal type that is not the last element of the type, Succ(X) is the element of the ordinal type that follows X. The relationship between Succ and Ord is

$$Ord(Succ(X)) = Ord(X) + 1$$

Succ(X) is not meaningful when X is the last element of the ordinal type. Note that we cannot detect the last element of an ordinal type in as easy a manner as for the first element of the type. However, we can define an integer constant to check the Ord function for the detection of the last element of the type.

□
**USER-DEFINED
ORDINAL
TYPES**

Pascal allows for **user-defined ordinal types**, declared by naming the elements of the type in the order of the type, from first element to last. For example, one can specify a type consisting of adventure game character classes as follows:

```
type
   Classes = (Dwarf, Elf, Halfling, Human, Cleric, MagicUser);
```

Note that the identifier Dwarf, for example, represents a **constant** of the type Classes. The Pascal compiler will not allow any duplication of identifiers within a program unit. So we could not use the type Classes as specified above along with a real (or any other type) variable Dwarf within the same program unit. We can declare variables to have a user-defined ordinal type, as shown in the example:

```
var
   Class   : Classes;
```

The variables and constants of a user-defined ordinal type can be used in a similar manner to other ordinal types with some restrictions.

As another example, we could define

```
type
   Days = (Sun, Mon, Tue, Wed, Thur, Fri, Sat);
var
   Today : Days;
```

Assignment. If Class is a variable of the type Classes, then we can use the assignment statement

```
Class := Cleric;
```

If PrimaryClass and SecondaryClass are two variables of the type Classes, then we can use the assignment statement

```
SecondaryClass := PrimaryClass;
```

Comparison. If Class is a variable of the type Classes, then we can use any of the comparisons

```
Class = Human;
Class <> Human;
Class < Human;
Class <= Human;
Class > Human;
Class >= Human;
```

If Today and PayDay are two variables of the type Days, then we can use any of the comparisons

```
Today = PayDay;
Today <> PayDay;
Today < PayDay;
Today <= PayDay;
Today > PayDay;
Today >= PayDay;
```

Use of the functions Ord, Pred, and Succ. If Today is a variable of type Days, then we can use any of the expressions

```
Ord(Today)
Pred(Today)    if the value of Today is not Sun
Succ(Today)    if the value of Today is not Sat
```

For example,

```
Ord(Sun)     is   0
Ord(Wed)     is   4
Pred(Sat)    is   Fri
Succ(Wed)    is   Thur
```

Input and output. We *cannot* use any of the functions Read, Write, Readln, or Writeln with variables or constants of a user-defined ordinal type to the display screen, to the printer, or to any text file. However, we can perform input and output activities with files of a user-defined ordinal type and we can use files of records that include user-defined ordinal types as fields. We also can simulate text input and output activities by use of arrays, as shown below.

Indexes of arrays. We can employ the constants of a user-defined ordinal type as the indexes of an array. For example, for use in output activities, we can declare and initialize an array as follows:

```
type
   Classes = (Dwarf, Elf, Halfling, Human, Cleric, MagicUser);
   ClassesStrings = array[Classes] of string[9];

var
   PrintName  : ClassesStrings;

begin
   PrintName[Dwarf] := 'Dwarf';
   PrintName[Elf] := 'Elf';
   PrintName[Halfling] := 'Halfling';
```

```
PrintName[Human] := 'Human';
PrintName[Cleric] := 'Cleric';
PrintName[MagicUser] := 'MagicUser';
```

COMMENT The array indexes (Dwarf, Elf, etc.) are of type Classes. The values stored in the array ('Dwarf', 'Elf', etc.) are strings. In Pascal we cannot use strings as array indexes, and we cannot print user-defined ordinal variables. Thus, we need solutions like that given by the PrintName array.

The initialization activities should be done in a procedure subprogram in order to "hide" all of the assignment statements from the major logic of the main program. We can now simulate output of a value of the variable Class of the type Classes by the statement

```
                Writeln(PrintName[Class]);
```

If the variable Class currently has the value Cleric, for example, this will print the string 'Cleric' because the value of PrintName [Cleric] is 'Cleric'. We shall provide you with more details on arrays in Chapter 6.

For loop index. We can employ the constants of a user-defined ordinal type to control a for loop. For example, suppose that we have defined the ordinal type DaysOfWeek as follows:

```
type
   DaysOfWeek = (Sun, Mon, Tue, Wed, Thr, Fri, Sat);
```

We also do the initialization activity described above in an initialization procedure:

```
procedure Initialize;
{
    Written by:   XXXXXXXX   XX/XX/XX
        Purpose:  To initialize PrintName array.
  Globals used:   PrintName array - changed.
}
begin {Initialize}
  PrintName[Sun] := 'Sunday';
  PrintName[Mon] := 'Monday';
  PrintName[Tue] := 'Tuesday';
  PrintName[Wed] := 'Wednesday';
  PrintName[Thr] := 'Thursday';
  PrintName[Fri] := 'Friday';
  PrintName[Sat] := 'Saturday'
end; {Initialize}
```

If we wish the user to input the amount of sales for each day of a week in order to compute a total, we could use the following code fragment (assuming that the variables DaysSales and WeekTotal have both been declared as real and that the variable Day has been declared to have type DaysOfWeek):

. . . . .

```
WeekTotal := 0.0;
for Day := Sun to Sat do
```

```
begin
  Write('Enter the sales for ', PrintName[Day], ': $');
  Readln(DaysSales);
  WeekTotal := WeekTotal + DaysSales
end; {for}
```

. . . . .

If we used "for Day := Mon to Fri do", then this fragment would ask for sales only for the days Monday through Friday.

In summary, we have seen that user-defined ordinal types allow the programmer to make clear his or her intentions within the code of the program. This clarity can make the jobs of program design, coding, debugging, and program maintenance easier and less time-consuming.

□
SUBRANGE TYPES

Pascal allows us to define ordinal types that contain part of the values of a given ordinal type lying between two values. This construction of a **subrange type** can be accomplished using built-in ordinal types or user-defined ordinal types. We specify the subrange values by means of the construction:

first value in the subrange .. last value in the subrange

Some examples follow:

2 .. 5 represents the subrange of integers 2, 3, 4, and 5

'd' .. 'g' represents the subrange of chars 'd', 'e', 'f', and 'g'[4]

Halfling .. Cleric represents the subrange of the type Classes defined above consisting of Halfling, Human, and Cleric.

We have seen subranges used in our preliminary discussions of arrays wherein we defined the type:

```
type
  IntegerArray = array[1 .. 100] of integer;
```

In this case, the subrange 1 .. 100 is used to limit the legal indexes for the arrays of the type. This use of the concept of subrange is typical: to limit the values that can be used for a given situation. For example, in adventure games, characters have certain assigned qualities, such as dexterity, wisdom, and intelligence. In some such games, the values of these qualities are obtained from a roll of an 18-sided die. In addition, values under 6 are considered to be too low to be useful. So, we have a working rule that the values of these character qualities are to lie between the values 6 and 18, inclusive. This concept can be embodied in a Pascal program via a type declared as follows:

```
type
  RolledValue = 6 .. 18;
```

We can then declare character qualities as variables of type RolledValue as follows:

```
var
    Dexterity    : RolledValue;
    Wisdom       : RolledValue;
    Intelligence : RolledValue;
```

We could accomplish the same result without an explicit type name by means of the lines of code:

```
var
    Dexterity    : 6 .. 18;
    Wisdom       : 6 .. 18;
    Intelligence : 6 .. 18;
```

We consider the use of a named type to be better programming style because it allows the use of the variables Dexterity, Wisdom, and Intelligence to be passed as parameters. Use of a named type also makes it relatively easy to change the subrange to 7 .. 18, if desired.

□ **TYPE AND RANGE CHECKING**

Pascal provides for two levels of checking for the legality of certain activities such as value assignment, input/output, array referencing, and parameter passing. At *compile time*, Pascal performs **type checking** in which each instance of the above listed activities is checked to see if the types involved are legal for the context. Earlier in this book, we discovered that the compiler will not allow an assignment statement that has an integer variable on the left side and a real variable on the right side. This was our first example of type checking. As programmers, we should be grateful that the compiler attempts to stop us from doing things that are likely to cause erroneous results from our program. As we have introduced different data types in this book, we have attempted to indicate what activities can legitimately be performed with each type. For example, we cannot write the values of a user-defined ordinal type on the display screen; an attempt to do so will be detected as the compiler does its type checking.

In general, activities performed with objects of subrange types of the same base type will pass through type checking. For example, if X is a variable of type RolledValue as defined above and if Y is a variable of type integer or any subrange of the integer type, then the assignment statement:

$$X := Y;$$

is deemed legal by the compiler.

In other type checking activities, the compiler will only allow variables of a *named* type to be passed as parameters. Also, indexes of arrays must be of the same base type as that used in the declaration of the array.

The other kind of checking occurs at both compile time and *run time* and is called **range checking**. The main purpose of having subrange types in Pascal is to allow for the detection of invalid values for variables that can occur as the program runs. The invalid values can result from bugs in the program or they can result from invalid user input.

TURBO NOTE

In Turbo Pascal, the default compiler option is for run-time range checking not to be performed. (The program will run faster if range checking is disabled.) However, we can activate range checking by including the compiler option {$R+} at the top of our programs. We suggest that you activate range checking for all programs as they are under development. Once the program has been completely debugged, range checking can be deactivated by deleting the {$R+} compiler option.

The following are some of the common violations of range restrictions:

1. Array index out of range. If we have declared that the array X has indexes that are integers in the range from 3 to 6, inclusive, then the array reference X[7] is invalid. Also, the array reference X[2] is invalid. The above two errors are detected by the compiler whether run-time range checking is active or inactive. A slightly different set of circumstances is found in the following lines:

```
Y := 7;
Z := X[Y];
```

This range violation will not be detected at compile time, but will be detected at run time if range checking has been activated.

2. Assignment outside of subrange. Suppose that the type Classes and a subrange type Elite have been declared as follows:

```
type
    Classes = (Dwarf, Elf, Halfling, Human, Cleric, MagicUser);
    Elite = Halfling .. Cleric;
```

Also, suppose that the variable HiClass has been declared to be of type Elite. Then the assignment statement

```
HiClass := Dwarf;
```

is a range violation that will be detected at run time if run-time error checking is activated.

3. Numeric value out of range. If real number values exceed the maximum possible value, then a run-time error will occur whether or not range checking is activated. For example, the following statement will result in a run-time error for some implementations of Pascal:

```
X := Exp(1000);
```

In the above statement, we are attempting to produce a value of order of magnitude 1 followed by 435 zeros.

4. Illegal value for function. Recall that the Chr function is defined for the ordinal values of the character set used in the implementation of Pascal. Under most circumstances, the expression Chr(300) is illegal and will result in a run-time error if range checking is activated. Examples of the same kind are the attempt to refer to the predecessor of the first element or the successor of the last element of an ordinal type. The expressions Pred(false) and Succ(true) are illegal and will result in run-time errors if range checking is activated.

5. Input of an integer of overlarge magnitude. If the user responds to a Read or Readln of an integer with a value that is above Maxint or below -Maxint, then an input/output error will occur. This error can be trapped in a manner similar to that described below in the subsection on error trapping.

□
ERROR TRAPPING

There are two circumstances that are annoyances when dealing with files. If you have been running the example programs of this chapter, you have probably experienced both of the situations. The first situation occurs when you are asked for the name of an existing file in order that the information be displayed or changed. If you make a spelling mistake in entering the name of the file, the program **aborts** in a run-time input/output error. The second situation can cause you to lose valuable files in addition to being an annoyance. It arises when you are asked for the name of a file that is to be created. If a file by the same name already exists, then it is deleted and any information that was in the file is lost. If you accidently enter the name of one of your highly prized programs, then your hard work can be lost.

Turbo Pascal provides a solution to both of the above problems by means of **error trapping**.[5] By default, Turbo Pascal will abort the program when an input/output error is detected. There are a pair of compiler directives that control the handling of input/output errors:

> {$I−}   *no program abort when input/output errors are detected*
> {$I+}   *resumes abort when input/output errors are detected*

In addition, Turbo Pascal provides a built-in function IOResult that indicates the presence of an input/output error when the compiler directive {$I−} is in effect. The values of IOResult are interpreted as follows:

> IOResult = 0   *means that no input/output error has occurred*
> IOResult <> 0   *means that some input/output error has occurred*

By using the compiler directives and the built-in function Ioresult, we can cause our programs to behave properly. For example, Figure 5-13 contains a function Exists that will tell if a file with a given name exists on the disk. Also shown in the figure is a procedure OpenRead which invokes the Exists function. If the file specified by the user does not exist, another chance is given to correctly specify the file name.

Any program which reads from a file will need to contain code similar to that in Figure 5-13. The easiest way to accomplish this is to put the code in subprograms, as illustrated in the figure. These subprograms can then be inserted in any program which needs them.

NOTE OpenRead as shown in Figure 5-13 opens a text file. For any other file type, you would simply change the parameter type (shaded in the figure) to match the file to be opened.

This type of module is sometimes referred to as a "utility" module. It can be utilized in a large variety of programs. Another useful utility would be OpenWrite, to open a file for output Appendix E (Utilities) contains such a module, along with the OpenRead and Exists presented here.

```
function Exists(FileName : String14) : boolean;
{
      Written by:  XXXXXXXX  XX/XX/XX
         Purpose:  To check a given file name for existence, using
                   the Turbo Pascal special features IOResult and the
                   $I compiler directive.
      Parameters:  FileName - input, the name of the file to be
                   checked
}
var
  DummyFile   : test;                    { Used to check file name }

begin    {Exists}
  Assign(DummyFile, FileName);
  {$I-}                                  { Turn off error messages }
  Reset(DummyFile);                      { Try to open for input }
  {$I+}                                  { Turn on error messages }
  Exists := IOResult = 0;         { Call IOResult function to see if o.k. }
  Close(DummyFile)                { Don't leave files lying around open }
end;   {Exists}


procedure OpenRead(var InputFile : text);
{
      Written by:  XXXXXXXX  XX/XX/XX
         Purpose:  To obtain the name of an existing file from the
                   user, and open it for reading.
      Parameters:  InputFile - the file to be opened
   Functions used: Exists, to see if the file exists.
}
var
  FileName  : String14;                  { Name of file on disk }
  ValidName : boolean:                   { Name entered exists }

begin    {OpenRead}

  repeat
    Write('Enter the filename: ');
    Readln(FileName);
    ValidName := Exists(FileName);
    if not ValidName then
      Writeln('*** File does not exist.')
  until ValidName;

  Assign(InputFile, FileName);    { Open the file for output }
  Reset(InputFile)
end;   {OpenRead}
```

Figure 5-13   Trapping I–O Errors

□
MORE ON RECORDS

In this subsection, we will look at a slightly richer record structure that combines some of the ideas that we have been developing in this section. The record structure that we will discuss represents some of the attributes of an adventure game character. Our record structure is defined as follows:

```
Character = record
            Name            : String20;
            Class           : Classes;
            Dexterity       : RolledValue;
            Constitution    : RolledValue;
            Wisdom          : RolledValue;
            Strength        : RolledValue;
            Intelligence    : RolledValue;
            Charisma        : RolledValue
          end;
```

The type String20, Classes, and RolledValue must have been defined prior to defining the type character.

The name of the character is a string of up to 20 characters and would include the examples: Gandalf the Grey, Garvin, and Mirro the Ugly. The type Classes is the same as discussed above:

```
Classes = (Dwarf, Elf, Halfling, Human, Cleric, MagicUser);
```

The type RolledValue is a subrange type that was also discussed above:

```
RolledValue = 6 .. 18;
```

The other fields of the record represent qualities of the character that determine the limits of the character's activities during a game. In the two programs that are shown as Figures 5-14 and 5-15, we provide the means to build a file of characters and to search that file, respectively. Portions of those programs, which are shaded, will be discussed briefly.

Note the use of the array PrintName to provide for the display of the identification of the character class. The array is assigned its values by the procedure Initialize.

The Build program of Figure 5-14 makes considerable use of the random generator function Random to produce the simulated dice rolls and also to choose the character class for each character. The simulated dice rolls are supposed to be random numbers in the range from 6 to 18, inclusive. The random generator Random can be invoked with an integer variable or constant N, so that Random(N) will be returned as an integer value between 0 and N − 1, inclusive. To get the random numbers in the range that we want (6 to 18), we use the expression

```
Random(HighRollLess5) + 6;
```

where HighRollLess5 has the value 13.

In order to choose a random member of the enumerated type Classes, we begin at the first element (Dwarf) and, at random, execute 0 or more instances of the Succ function to arrive at a random element in the enumerated type. Note that because the number of elements in the type is 6, we want to execute between 0 and 5 instances of Succ. This is accomplished via the lines

```
Class := Dwarf;
for I := 1 to Random(ClassesSize) do
    Class := Succ(Class);
```

where ClassesSize has the value 6.

Input/output error trapping is utilized via the Exists function and OpenWrite procedure to prevent the user from inadvertently deleting a file.

```
program Build(Input, Output);
{
        Written by:   XXXXXXXX   XX/XX/XX
           Purpose:   To build a file of characters.
   Procedures used:   Instructions - to print instructions;
                      Initialize - to initialize PrintName array.
    Functions used:   Exists - to check for existence of a file.
}
const
   EndOfData = '$END';                { Terminating value }
   ClassesSize = 6;                   { Number of classes }
   HighRollLess5 = 13;                { Highest possible roll minus 5}

type
   String20 = string[20];
   Classes = (Dwarf, Elf, Halfling, Human, Cleric, MagicUser);
   ClassesStrings = array[Classes] of string[9];
   RolledValue = 6 .. 18;
   Character = record
                    Name          : String20;
                    Class         : Classes;
                    Dexterity     : RolledValue;
                    Constitution  : RolledValue;
                    Wisdom        : RolledValue;
                    Strength      : RolledValue;
                    Intelligence  : RolledValue;
                    Charisma      : RolledValue
                end;
   FileType = file of Character;
   String14 = string[14];             { For filename }
var
   MyChar     : Character;                   { Instance of record }
   AnyFile    : FileType;                    { File designator }
```

Figure 5-14   A Comprehensive Example—Build a File (Continued)

```
   PrintName     : ClassesStrings;          { For printing classes }
   I             : integer;                 { Loop index }

procedure Instructions; begin {stub} end;

procedure Initialize;
{
        Written by:  XXXXXXXXX  XX/XX/XX
           Purpose:  To initialize array PrintName.
      Globals used:  PrintName array - changed.
}
begin {Initialize}
  PrintName[Dwarf] := 'Dwarf';
  PrintName[Elf] := 'Elf';
  PrintName[Halfling] := 'Halfling';
  PrintName[Human] := 'Human';
  PrintName[Cleric] := 'Cleric';
  PrintName[MagicUser] := 'MagicUser'
end; {Initialize}
```

{function Exists, as shown in Figure 5-13, is inserted here}

{procedure OpenWrite, as shown in Appendix E, is inserted here; with type
    text changed to type FileType.}

```
begin {Build}

{*** Print instructions and initialize.}

  Instructions;
  Initialize;
  Randomize;

{*** Ask the user for the filename and open the file.}

  OpenWrite(AnyFile);

{*** Get names for file.}

  with MyChar do
    begin

      repeat
        Writeln;
        Write('Enter name ($END to quit): ');
        Readln(Name);
        if Name <> EndOfData then
          begin
            Class := Dwarf;
            for I := 1 to Random(ClassesSize) do
              Class := Succ(Class);
            Writeln('The class is: ', PrintName[Class]);
            Dexterity := Random(HighRollLess5) + 6;
```

Figure 5-14 A Comprehensive Example—Build a File (Continued)

```
                    Writeln('The dexterity is: ', Dexterity);
                    Constitution := Random(HighRollLess5) + 6;
                    Writeln('The constitution is: ', Constitution);
                    Wisdom := Random(HighRollLess5) + 6;
                    Writeln('The wisdom is: ', Wisdom);
                    Strength := Random(HighRollLess5) + 6;
                    Writeln('The strength is: ', Strength);
                    Intelligence := Random(HighRollLess5) + 6;
                    Writeln('The intelligence is: ', Intelligence);
                    Charisma := Random(HighRollLess5) + 6;
                    Writeln('The charisma is: ', Charisma);
                    Write(AnyFile, MyChar)
                end {if}
            until Name = EndOfData

        end; {with}


    {*** Close the file.}

        Close(AnyFile);

    {*** Print terminating message and stop program.}

        Writeln;
        Writeln('Build program is terminating.')
    end.
```

SAMPLE INPUT AND OUTPUT

```
Enter the filename: chars.fil
File already exists. Delete(Y,N)?y

Enter name ($END to quit): Gandalf the Grey
The class is: Dwarf
The dexterity is: 6
The constitution is: 7
The wisdom is: 12
The strength is: 15
The intelligence is: 10
The charisma is: 11

Enter name ($END to quit): Dalvin
The class is: MagicUser
The dexterity is: 16
The constitution is: 18
The wisdom is: 7
The strength is: 14
The intelligence is: 6
The charisma is: 15

Enter name ($END to quit): $END

Build program is terminating.
```

Figure 5-14 A Comprehensive Example—Build a File

The program Search of Figure 5-15 allows the user to specify the name of a character and receive the other information associated with the character. The procedure Initialize is once again used to establish the array of print names for the character classes. Input/output error trapping is utilized to detect the situation where the user specifies a file that does not exist. The file searching technique is similar to that used earlier in this chapter.

```
program Search(Input, Output);
{
        Written by:    XXXXXXXX  XX/XX/XX
          Purpose:    To search for a character and display its
                      information.
   Procedures used:   Instructions - to print instructions;
                      Initialize - to initialize PrintName array.
    Functions used:   Exists - to check for existence of a file.
}
type
  String20 = string[20];
  Classes = (Dwarf, Elf, Halfling, Human, Cleric, MagicUser);
  ClassesStrings = array[Classes] of string[9];
  RolledValue = 1 .. 18;
  Character = record
                   Name          : String20;
                   Class         : Classes;
                   Dexterity     : RolledValue;
                   Constitution  : RolledValue;
                   Wisdom        : RolledValue;
                   Strength      : RolledValue;
                   Intelligence  : RolledValue;
                   Charisma      : RolledValue;
                 end;
  FileType = file of Character;
  String14 = string[14];

  var
    MyChar     : Character;          { Instance of record }
    AnyFile    : FileType;           { File designator }
    PrintName  : ClassesStrings;     { Array of print names }
    ToFind     : string[20];         { Name to find }


{procedure Initialize, as shown in Figure 5-14, is inserted here}

{function Exists, as shown in Figure 5-13, is inserted here}

{procedure OpenRead, as shown in Figure 5-13, is inserted here
      with type text changed to type FileType}

begin {Search}

{*** Print instructions and initialize.}
```

Figure 5-15 A Comprehensive Example—Search a File (Continued)

```
  Instructions;
  Initialize;

{*** Ask the user for the filename and open the file.}

  OpenRead(AnyFile);




{*** Get name from the user.}

  Writeln;
  Write('Enter the character''s name: ');
  Readln(ToFind);

{*** Search the file for the name.}

  with MyChar do
    begin
      Name := '';              { Null value in case no characters in file}

      while (Name <> ToFind) and (not Eof(AnyFile)) do
        begin
          Read(AnyFile, MyChar);
        end; {while}

{*** Display the results of the search.}

      if Name = ToFind then
        begin
          Writeln('The class is: ', PrintName[Class]);
          Writeln('The dexterity is: ', Dexterity);
          Writeln('The constitution is: ', Constitution);
          Writeln('The wisdom is: ', Wisdom);
          Writeln('The strength is: ', Strength);
          Writeln('The intelligence is: ', Intelligence);
          Writeln('The charisma is: ', Charisma)
        end
      else
        Writeln('*** Character not found.')
    end; {with}

{*** Close the file.}

  Close(AnyFile);

{*** Print terminating message and stop program.}

  Writeln;
  Writeln('Search program is terminating.')
end.
```

Figure 5-15   A Comprehensive Example—Search a File (Continued)

SAMPLE INPUT AND OUTPUT

```
Enter the filename: chars.fle
*** File does not exist.
Enter the filename: chars.fil

Enter the character's name: Gandalf the Grey
The class is: Dwarf
The dexterity is: 6
The constitution is: 7
The wisdom is: 12
The strength is: 15
The intelligence is: 10
The charisma is: 11

Search program is terminating.
```

Figure 5-15   A Comprehensive Example—Search a File

□
DPT

1. Perhaps the most important defensive programming tip is to make sure that range checking is in effect. With Turbo Pascal this means to use the compiler option {$R+} during development, which allows the compiler to detect illegal references outside the proper range.

Without this, almost anything can happen when we make an illegal reference. For example, if we write

$$Y := A[I]$$

and I is out of range, Y's value will be totally meaningless. Even worse,

$$A[I] := Y$$

will "clobber" some memory location by placing the value of Y in it. This could, for example, give some other variable the value of Y, give some other variable a meaningless value, or even modify part of the program.

2. We must not use the functions Ord, Pred, or Succ on variables of type real. These errors will be detected by the compiler.

3. Do not use Pred on the first element of an ordinal type or Succ on the last element. These may not produce an error message, but they have no reasonable meaning.

4. Do not use duplicate identifiers within a program unit. They will produce a compiler error.

One possibility for violating this rule occurs when we create user-defined ordinal types. For example, suppose we have a type declaration

$$Days = (Sun, Mon, Tue, Wed, Thr, Fri, Sat)$$

Then we cannot use Days or any of Sun, Mon, and so on as variable names. More subtly, we cannot define another type as

$$Weekdays = (Mon, Tue, Wed, Thr, Fri)$$

The duplicate use of Mon, for example, is illegal. (However, we can define Weekday using the subrange type Mon .. Fri.)

5. Do not try to input or output variables or constants of a user-defined ordinal type to the display, printer, or any text file. These activities will result in a compiler error.

We have demonstrated techniques that use arrays to simulate output of variables of a user-defined data type by using a PrintName array. You can use similar notions to read in such a value. (See the exercises.)

6. Use input/output error trapping techniques for friendlier programs. Remember that the programmer is responsible for the behavior of a program, even when it is being used by an ignorant or hostile user.

REVIEW

Terms and concepts

scalar type	user-defined ordinal types
ordinal type	constant
enumerated type	subrange
Ord	type checking
Chr	range checking
Pred	abort
Succ	error trapping

Pascal syntax

1. Functions for ordinal types:
(a) Ord(X) shows the position of X within the type.
(b) Succ(X) gives the successor of X.
(c) Pred(X) gives the predecessor of X.

2. Declare user-defined ordinal type by listing the constants of the type, as in this example:

```
type
    Classes = (Dwarf, Elf, Halfling, Human, Cleric, MagicUser);
```

3. Specify the limits of a subrange by separating the first and last elements with two dots:

first value .. last value

4. Turbo: IOResult = 0 indicates no error occurred ({$I−} directive must be in use).

DPT

1. Use range checking (in Turbo, the {$R+} compiler option) during development.

2. Do not use the functions Ord, Pred, or Succ on variables of type real.

3. Do not use Pred on the first element of an ordinal type. Do not use Succ on the last element of an ordinal type.

4. Do not use duplicate identifiers within a program unit.

5. Do not try to input or output variables or constants of a user-defined ordinal type as text.

6. Use input/output error-trapping techniques.

1. Evaluate the following as would your implementation of Pascal:

   a. `Ord('b')`
   b. `Succ('I')`
   c. `Pred(true)`
   d. `Ord(-5)`
   e. `Succ(Pred('t'))`
   f. `Ord(Chr(75))`
   g. `Chr(Ord('d'))`
   h. `Succ(Chr(68))`
   i. `Pred(4)`
   j. `Pred('4')`
   k. `Succ(9)`
   l. `Succ('9')`

*2. Suppose that we have defined a type as follows:

   ```
   type
        Outcomes = (Lose, Draw, Win);
   ```

   Evaluate the following:

   a. `Ord(Lose)`
   b. `Pred(Win)`
   c. `Succ(Draw)`
   d. `Lose < Draw`
   e. `Win = Lose`

*3. Write an integer function Roll that returns a random integer between 6 and 18, inclusive.

4. Write an integer function Roll(Low, High : integer) that returns a random integer between Low and High, inclusive.

5. Either of the functions of Exercises 3 and 4 would prove useful for the program of Figure 5-13. Discuss pros and cons of each of the functions and choose one of them to use. Rewrite the program of Figure 5-13 using the function that you have chosen.

*6. Write a function ClassFun(Name : String09) of type Classes that uses PrintName as a global variable and String09 as a global named type. Class-Fun should return one of the values Dwarf, Elf, etc., depending on a match between the appropriate element of PrintName and the input parameter Name.

7. Use the function ClassFun from Exercise 6 above to modify the program of Figure 5-13 so that the class of the character is input by the user along with the name of the character.

*8. a. Write a function of type Outcomes (see Exercise 2) as follows: Two pairs of dice are rolled. If the first pair's result is greater than the second, you win; if less, you lose; if equal, you draw.
   b. Using the function of part (a), write a program that plays the following game. Two players start with $20 and $14, respectively. They will roll the dice 100 times or until one goes broke, whichever occurs first. The winner on each roll wins $1 from the other player. The program should tell what happened.
   c. Is the game described in part (b) fair? To answer the question, simulate the game 1000 times, calculating the average amount of money each player has left at the end of the game.

9. For type char, the Ord function has an inverse function (the Chr function). For other types, no such function exists. However, it is possible to write such functions ourselves.[6]

   *a. For the type Day = (Sun, Mon, Tue, Wed, Thr, Fri, Sat), write a function:

```
function DayValue(N : integer) : Day;
```
Assume that N is an integer between 0 and 6, and use a case statement to assign the answer.
   b. Rewrite the function to use a for loop to obtain the answer. Start a variable at the value Sun and apply the Succ function N times.
   c. Which approach do you prefer? (See also Exercise 10.)

10. Using the ideas of Exercise 9, write a function:

```
function UppercaseValue(N : integer) : Uppercase;
```
The type Uppercase is defined as 'A' .. 'Z', and we assume the ASCII code, so that this consists of precisely the uppercase letters.
   Which of the approaches of Exercise 9 is better here?

*11. (Inspired by Steve's of Somerville, MA.) Define the following types:

Fruits:	Includes strawberries, raspberries, plums, and bananas
Flavors:	Includes vanilla, chocolate, tinroof, and tuttifruiti
Toppings:	Includes chocolatechips, nuts, candybars, and hardcandy
Sundaes:	A record which includes a name, 3 flavors, 1 fruit, and 3 toppings

12. Write Pascal programs to build and search for sundaes as defined in Exercise 11.

*13. a. Define a procedure TimeAdd(Time1, Time2 : Times; var Sum : Times). Times is a record type that includes the two integer fields Minutes and Seconds.
   b. Define a procedure TimeSub similar to TimeAdd.

14. Define the record types:

Point:	Includes two real fields: X and Y
Line:	Includes 3 real fields: Ycoeff, Xcoeff, and Constant

We want to interpret the record type Point to represent points in a coordinate plane. We want to interpret Line to represent a line in a coordinate plane via its equation:

```
(Ycoeff)*Y + (Xcoeff)*X + (Constant) = 0
```

Write the following functions:

   a. IsLine—Boolean; input parameter of type Line; returns true if the equation represents a line. (Hint: At least one of Ycoeff or Xcoeff must be nonzero.)
   b. OnLine—Boolean; determines if the input parameter of type Point lies on the input parameter of type Line.

15. Give test plans for the following:

   a. Exercise 4   *b. Exercise 6
   *c. Exercise 9   d. Exercise 10
   *e. Exercise 13(a)   f. Exercise 13(b)
   g. Exercise 14(a)   h. Exercise 14(b)

1. This example assumes the ASCII character code set.

2. These examples assume the ASCII character code set.

3. We begin with 27 because the first 26 elements of the ASCII code set are used for "control codes," which can cause your printer to perform some unwanted actions.

The upper limit might be different for some versions of Pascal on some computers, but 255 is reasonably standard.

4. This example assumes the ASCII character code set.

5. Some versions of Pascal provide for no input/output error trapping.

6. Turbo Pascal does supply what it calls a "retyping" facility, which makes this unnecessary. For example,

```
Day(0) would be Sun
Day(4) would be Wed
```

We simply put the name of the type as if it were a function name.

This is definitely not standard. As the exercise indicates, it is quite easy to achieve the same results with a function of type Day.

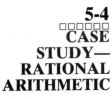

5-4 CASE STUDY— RATIONAL ARITHMETIC

In this section, we will present two case studies. In the first, we will develop portions of a package to deal with rational numbers (fractions). In order to represent the data, we will use the record data structure. (As we indicated when we first discussed records, the record concept is frequently used when files are not involved. This case study illustrates this type of use.) As the program design proceeds, we will present the venerable **Euclidean Algorithm** for determining the greatest common divisor of two integers as a function that is needed for several of the activities involved with rational numbers.

The second case study illustrates the use of the modules in the package by developing a working program that acts as a "calculator" for rational numbers, but which contains only two functions. In order to present the user interface, we will use sets to specify valid menu options. We will suggest several other functions in the exercises at the end of the section.

CASE STUDY No. 7 (A RATIONAL NUMBER PACKAGE)

Statement of problem. The real variables in Pascal are usually only approximately accurate representations. For example, the constant ⅓ as used in the statement

```
X := 1/3
```

will not provide the exactness that it appears to have. We might expect that following the assignment above we could use X as an accurate representation of the rational number ⅓. However, if we execute the lines of code below (with X declared as a real variable)

```
X := 1/3;
if  3*X = 1  then
  Writeln('I''m surprised!')
else
  Writeln('I knew it was an approximation!');
```

we will see that real variables do not provide a faithful representation for rational numbers. In this case study, we will develop a set of modules to provide a more faithful representation.

Preliminary analysis. There are an infinite number of mathematical representations for a given rational number. For example, 1/2, 5/10, 25/50, −7/−14, and so on are all representations for the same number. However, there is a unique preferred representation, namely the one in which the numerator and denominator have no common factors and the denominator is positive.

Since the mathematical representation of a rational number contains two integer numbers, it is natural to choose a computer representation that uses two Pascal integer variables. In our case, we will use a record with two integer fields to represent a single rational number:

```
RationalNumber = record
                     Numerator   : integer;
                     Denominator : integer
                 end;
```

The use of this data structure allows us to deal with a rational number as a single entity when we are communicating with subprograms, and it allows us to deal with the numerator and denominator individually when necessary.

We must next decide on the operations to perform. We obviously will need to provide addition, subtraction, multiplication, and division. In addition to these, it would be desirable to have operations for reading and writing rational numbers, converting a rational number to an integer or a real number, and converting an integer to a rational number. We might also provide comparison of rationals and possibly other operations. Refer to Table 5-1 for a summary of the operations mentioned above.

Table 5-1 Operations to be provided by rational arithmetic package

Addition
Subtraction
Multiplication
Division
Input
Output
Convert rational to real
Convert rational to integer
Convert integer to rational
Compare for equality
Compare for less than
Compare for less than or equal

Note that some of the operations can be expressed in terms of others. For example, subtraction involves a change of sign followed by addition. Division

Table 5-2 Operations separated into primitive and composite operations

---

Primitive
  Addition
  Multiplication
  Input
  Output
  Convert rational to integer
  Convert rational to real
  Convert integer to rational
  Compare for equality
  Compare for less than
Composite
  Subtraction
  Division
  Compare for less than or equal

---

involves inverting one rational and multiplying. This suggests a separation of the operations into primitive and composite operations, as shown in Table 5-2.

We must next decide on the form of the operations. Most operations will take several steps to perform, so it seems reasonable to use subprograms. Many operations in Table 5-1 produce a rational result. Because we cannot have Pascal functions of a record type, we will use procedures for these operations. Input and output activities are normally not appropriate for functions, so we will use procedures for these activities also. It is natural to expect comparison operations to produce conditions to be used in if–then, while–do, and repeat–until constructs, so we will use Boolean functions for these operations. Finally, we will use an integer function and a real function for the conversion of a rational number to integer and real, respectively.

The arithmetic operations require two operands and one result. We could use another argument to indicate success or failure of the operation. However, in order to simplify the argument lists of the subprograms, we will adopt the following convention: any error will cause an error message and the program will terminate.

Some of the operations are commutative and others are not. For example, $\frac{1}{2} + \frac{1}{3}$ is the same as $\frac{1}{3} + \frac{1}{2}$, but $\frac{1}{2} - \frac{1}{3}$ is not the same as $\frac{1}{3} - \frac{1}{2}$. When we add two rational numbers to produce the sum, there are six different ways to arrange the parameters for the addition procedure. We will choose our arrangement based on the principles:

1. Input parameters will come before output parameters.

2. The two operands for the operation will be arranged in the natural order for the operation that we use in arithmetic.

Summarizing our discussion so far, we have decided to use the following procedures:

```
procedure Add(FirstNumber , SecondNumber : RationalNumber;
              var Sum : RationalNumber);
procedure Subtract(FirstNumber , SecondNumber : RationalNumber;
              var Difference : RationalNumber);
procedure Multiply(FirstNumber , SecondNumber : RationalNumber;
              var Product : RationalNumber);
procedure Divide(FirstNumber , SecondNumber : RationalNumber;
              var Quotient : RationalNumber);
```

We will adopt the convention that all rational numbers that appear as parameters of the operations of Table 5-1 will have the following reduced form:

1. The numerator and denominator have no common factor bigger than 1.
2. The denominator is positive.

In order to produce this internal consistency of representation in the package, we will use the procedure:

```
procedure Reduce(Number : RationalNumber;
              var ReducedNumber : RationalNumber);
```

Algorithms and Programs. We will select a few of the operations for detailed discussion and leave the others for the exercises.

A simple method of adding the two rational numbers A/B and C/D is shown in the equation:

$$\frac{A}{B} + \frac{C}{D} = \frac{AD + BC}{BD}$$

The equation shows us that the algorithm for addition is essentially two steps:

set the numerator to $AD + BC$
set the denominator to BD

Because of our desire to maintain the reduced form for all of our results, we will add a third step:

reduce the answer

This algorithm becomes the Pascal procedure of Figure 5-16. Note the use of the with–do construct to simplify the calculation of the numerator and denominator. Also, notice that Sum is used as the input and the output in the call to the Reduce procedure. This is very similar to the dual use of a variable in an assignment statement such as:

```
I := I + 1
```

However, it can be dangerous if both parameters are var parameters. Because that is not the case here, we are safe. An alternate approach would be to use a local variable ReducedSum, and replace the line

```
Reduce(Sum, Sum)
```

by the steps

```
Reduce(Sum, ReducedSum);
Sum := ReducedSum
```

The next procedure is intended to accept the input of a rational number from the user. We will call this procedure ReadOne because it will read one rational number. This procedure must not allow the user to input a denominator of 0, which would produce an invalid rational number. The steps in the algorithm for ReadOne are

prompt the user for the numerator
read the numerator
prompt the user for the denominator
read the denominator
as long as the denominator is zero do these steps:
    print a message
    read a new value for the denominator
reduce the rational number

The Pascal code for ReadOne is shown in Figure 5-17.

```
procedure Add(FirstNumber , SecondNumber : RationalNumber;
              var Sum : RationalNumber);
{
        Written by:  XXXXXXXX  XX/XX/XX
           Purpose:  To add two fractions.
        Parameters:  FirstNumber - input, first fraction to add
                     SecondNumber - input, second fraction to add
                     Sum - output, sum of the two fractions
   Procedures used:  Reduce - to reduce a fraction to lowest terms.
}
begin {Add}
  with  Sum  do
    begin
      Numerator :=
        FirstNumber.Numerator*SecondNumber.Denominator +
        SecondNumber.Numerator*FirstNumber.Denominator;
      Denominator :=
        FirstNumber.Denominator * SecondNumber.Denominator
    end; {with}
  Reduce(Sum, Sum)
end; {Add}
```

Figure 5-16 Adding Rational Numbers

```
procedure ReadOne(var Number : RationalNumber);
{
        Written by:   XXXXXXXX  XX/XX/XX
           Purpose:   To read a fraction.
        Parameters:   Number - output, fraction to be entered by user
   Procedures used:   Reduce - to reduce a fraction to lowest terms.
}
begin {ReadOne}
  with  Number  do
    begin
      Write('     Enter numerator: ');
      Readln(Numerator);
      Write('     Enter denominator: ');
      Readln(Denominator);

      while Denominator = 0 do
        begin
          Writeln;
          Write(' Denominator of 0 not allowed. Please reenter: ');
          Readln(Denominator)
        end;  {while}

    end; {with}
  Reduce(Number, Number)
end; {ReadOne}
```

Figure 5-17 Reading Rational Numbers

The next procedure, which we will call WriteOne, will be for output of a rational number on the terminal. We will not attempt to produce any fancy output for this discussion, but will simply perform the following steps:

print a blank line
print the numerator preceded by "Numerator:"
print the denominator preceded by "Denominator:"
print a blank line

The code for the procedure WriteOne appears as Figure 5-18.

```
procedure WriteOne(var Number : RationalNumber);
{
        Written by:   XXXXXXXX  XX/XX/XX
           Purpose:   To print a fraction.
        Parameters:   Number - input, fraction to be printed
}
begin {WriteOne}
  Writeln;
  with  Number  do
    begin
      Writeln('     Numerator: ', Numerator);
      Writeln('     Denominator: ', Denominator)
    end; {with}
  Writeln
end; {WriteOne}
```

Figure 5-18 Writing Rational Numbers

The Reduce procedure has two major jobs: to eliminate any common factor bigger than 1 from the numerator and denominator and to provide for a positive denominator. The steps in the algorithm for Reduce are

determine the greatest common divisor (gcd) of the numerator and denominator
divide the numerator by the gcd
divide the denominator by the gcd
if the denominator is negative, then negate both numerator and denominator

The process of determining the greatest common divisor of two integers is a natural candidate for a subprogram. The best method for producing the gcd is an algorithm attributed to the Greek mathematician Euclid (ca. 300 B.C.). The algorithm is based on the idea that for any two positive integers N and M (not 0), we can find integers Q (quotient) and R (remainder) so that

$$N = Q*M + R$$

and such that R is less than M. Some examples:

N	M	Equation
12	10	12 = 1*10 + 2
34	7	34 = 4*7 + 6
20	3	20 = 6*3 + 2
43	8	43 = 5*8 + 3

The simplest way to find the numbers Q and R is to let Q be the integer part of N/M and let R be N − Q*M. The basis of the Euclidean Algorithm is that the gcd of N and M is the same as the gcd of M and R. Thus, the basic idea is a recursive one:

To find the gcd of N and M:

if M is zero, N is the gcd
otherwise:
    determine Q and R
    find the gcd of M and R

The following is an example that traces the recursion for the two numbers 1101 and 24:

N	M	Q	R
1101	24	45	21
24	21	1	3
21	3	7	0
3	0		

The above example calculates the gcd of 1101 and 24 as 3. Note that there is no requirement that N be larger than M because the two numbers switch places in the first step if N is smaller.

Usually, the gcd of two integers is expected to be positive even if one or both of the integers is negative. We will accomplish this requirement by calculating the gcd of the *absolute values* of the numerator and denominator in Reduce. The code for Reduce and the recursive Gcd function appear in Figure 5-19.

```
function Gcd(N, M : integer) : integer;
{
        Written by:  XXXXXXXX  XX/XX/XX
          Purpose:   To calculate the greatest common divisor
                     of two positive integers by means of
                     the Euclidean Algorithm.
        Parameters:  N - input, first number for gcd
                     M - input, second number for gcd
   Functions used:  calls itself recursively
}
begin {Gcd}
  if  M = 0  then
    Gcd := N
  else
    Gcd := Gcd(M, N mod M)
end; {Gcd}

procedure Reduce(Number : RationalNumber;
              var ReducedNumber : RationalNumber);
{
        Written by:  XXXXXXXX  XX/XX/XX
          Purpose:   To reduce a fraction to lowest terms:
                     1.   Numerator and denominator have no common
                          factor bigger than 1.
                     2.   The denominator is positive.
        Parameters:  Number - input, fraction to be reduced
                     ReducedNumber - output, reduced fraction
   Functions used:  Gcd - to compute the greatest common divisor;
                     Abs - to calculate the absolute value.
}
var
  CommonFactor : integer;                    { Greatest common factor }

begin {Reduce}
  with  Number  do
    CommonFactor := Gcd(Abs(Numerator), Abs(Denominator));
  ReducedNumber.Numerator := Number.Numerator div CommonFactor;
  ReducedNumber.Denominator := Number.Denominator div CommonFactor;
  with  ReducedNumber  do
    if  Denominator < 0  then
      begin
        Denominator := -Denominator;
        Numerator := -Numerator
      end {if}
end;  {Reduce}
```

Figure 5-19 Greatest Common Divisor (Reducing Rational Numbers)

The final operation that we will discuss is the compare for less than. In designing the algorithm for this operation, we must consider how it is that we know that

$$\text{5/8 is less than }^{11}/_{16}$$
$$\text{3/5 is less than }^{61}/_{99}$$

We can tell very simply which of two fractions is smaller by using a calculator to divide the denominators into the numerators and comparing the resulting decimals. This is the strategy that we will adopt for our algorithm for our operation, which we will call Less:

divide the numerator of the first number by its denominator
divide the numerator of the second number by its denominator
if the first quotient is less than the second, then return true;
    otherwise, return false

The code for the operation is given in Figure 5-20. Note that the value of the function Less is produced by the assignment statement:

```
Less := (FirstQuotient < SecondQuotient)
```

Because the right side of the assignment statement provides a value of type Boolean, the statement is valid. It is also meaningful because it clearly states that the value of the function Less is directly dependent on the sizes of the quotients for the two fractions.

CASE STUDY NO. 8 (AN APPLICATION OF THE RATIONAL NUMBER PACKAGE)

The purposes of this case study are twofold:
    1. To demonstrate how the rational number package (or, more generally, any package) might be used
    2. To illustrate a program that provides the user with a menu of choices

Statement of problem. Hand-held calculators typically work with decimal numbers. Write a program that acts as a calculator but works with fractions instead.

Preliminary analysis. We will approach this problem using "menu-driven" logic. That is, we will display the possible options and let the user decide which one to choose. This will simulate the existence of the function keys on a typical calculator. Contrary to what most calculators do, we will input first the operation and then the fraction(s) the operation should use. (Thus, we are using *prefix* input, whereas most calculators would use *infix* input with the operation in the middle or *postfix* input with the operation entered last.)

Algorithms, data, and program. The logic of the main program is as follows:

print instructions
repeat the following until the user wants to quit:

```
function Less(FirstNumber, SecondNumber : RationalNumber) : Boolean;
{
        Written by:  XXXXXXXX  XX/XX/XX
           Purpose:  To compare two fractions to determine if the first
                     is less than the second.
        Parameters:  FirstNumber - input, first fraction to compare
                     SecondNumber - input, second fraction to compare
}
var
  FirstQuotient  : real;        { The first number "divided out" }
  SecondQuotient : real;        { The second number "divided out" }

begin {Less}
  with  FirstNumber  do
    FirstQuotient := Numerator / Denominator;
  with  SecondNumber  do
    SecondQuotient := Numerator / Denominator;
  Less := (FirstQuotient < SecondQuotient)
end; {Less}
```

Figure 5-20   Comparing Rational Numbers

present the user a menu and get user choice
depending on the choice, perform appropriate activity
print message and terminate program

The main program declares our record type for rational numbers, three variables for use as rational numbers, a variable for the user choice from the menu, and a set to be used for valid menu options. The declarations of the main program are

```
type
  Letters = set of char;
  RationalNumber = record
                     Numerator   : integer;
                     Denominator : integer
                   end;

var
  FirstNumber, SecondNumber, ThirdNumber
             : RationalNumber;        { Rational numbers for working }
  Option       : char;                { User choice of menu option }
  ValidOptions : Letters;             { Valid menu options }
```

In the spirit of top-down design, the main program delegates most of its activities via calls to subprograms. To print the instructions, the procedure Instructions is used, as was shown earlier in this book. To display the menu and obtain a valid user option, the procedure Menu is used. To perform the appropriate activity, the procedure Handle is called. The only details that the main program is involved in are the establishment of the valid menu options and the printing of the terminating message. The code for the main program is as shown:

```
begin {Calculator}
  ValidOptions := ['R', 'r', 'A', 'a', 'Q', 'q'];
```

```
{*** Print instructions.}

  Instructions;

{*** Main loop.}

  repeat

{*** Display Menu and get user option.}

    Menu(ValidOptions, Option);
    Page(Con);                              { Clear screen }

{*** Handle user choice.}

    Handle(Option)
  until  Option in ['Q', 'q'];

{*** Print terminating message and stop program.}

  Writeln;
  Writeln('Calculator program is terminating.')
end.
```

The decision to have the main program establish the valid menu options was made because two subordinate program units depend on the valid options. The communication of the valid options to the Menu procedure is done via a parameter, but the procedure Handle has the valid options as elements of a case statement, as we shall see. If an option is to be added to the list of valid options, then the following must be changed:

the set in the main program must be enlarged
another menu line must be added in Menu
another case must be added in Handle

The procedure Page is used to clear the screen. We use the procedure Pause in several places throughout the program. Its purpose is to cause the user to tap a key on the keyboard before activity can continue. The code for the procedure is as follows:

```
procedure Pause;
{
      Written by:  XXXXXXXX  XX/XX/XX
         Purpose:  To wait for user keystroke.
}
var
  Answer  : char;                           { User keystroke }

begin {Pause}
  Writeln;
  Writeln(' ':27, '<Tap any key to continue.>');
  Read(Kbd, Answer)
end; {Pause}
```

As we have seen earlier in the chapter, we use the Turbo Pascal built-in file designator Kbd in order to accept any key without the requirement of the user tapping the return key. Many users find the space bar a more convenient target than the return key when tapping a key to continue. Small details such as this can make the difference between a **user-friendly** and a **user-hostile** program. (However, for versions of Pascal without the Kbd feature, a ReadLn could replace the Read of Kbd. The user would have to tap RETURN to continue.)

The Menu procedure displays the options to the user and obtains a valid choice. The procedure is as follows:

```
procedure Menu(ValidOptions : Letters; var Option : char);
{
         Written by:   XXXXXXXX   XX/XX/XX
            Purpose:   To display the menu and obtain the user choice.
         Parameters:   ValidOptions - input, the set of legal options
                       Option - output, the option selected by the user
   Procedures used:    Page - to clear the screen.
}
const
  Margin = 23;                           { Left margin for menu }
  Bel = 7;                               { ASCII Bel character }

var
  Answer   : char;                       { User response }

begin {Menu}
  Page(Con);                             { Clear the screen }
  Writeln(' ':34, 'MENU OPTIONS');
  Writeln(' ':34, '------------');
  Writeln;
  Writeln(' ':Margin, 'R(educe fraction to lowest terms)');
  Writeln(' ':Margin, 'A(dd two fractions)');
  Writeln(' ':Margin, 'Q(uit)');
  Writeln;
  Write(' ':Margin+5, 'Tap option: ');

  repeat
    Read(Kbd, Answer);
    if  not (Answer in ValidOptions)  then
      Write(Chr(Bel))
  until  Answer in ValidOptions;

  Writeln(Answer);
  Option := Answer
end; {Menu}
```

We use the local constant Margin to determine the left "edge" of the menu display. As we add options to the calculator, the number of spaces that we want to indent each option will very likely change. Once again, we use the built-in file designator Kbd so that we can accept the user choice as a single keystroke. Note that we do not print the invalid keystrokes on the screen, but we do cause the computer to "beep" by use of the Bel character.[1] Once a valid keystroke has been tapped, we print the valid choice on the screen.

The procedure Handle actually performs the useful work of the program. The module is organized as a case structure according to the option that the user has selected. Note that both the uppercase and lowercase alternatives for each choice are listed together, separated by a comma, to lead in to the case. We use the "else" for the case structure to detect an invalid option. This error message is useful only during debugging of the program because once the program begins to work as designed, invalid options cannot be selected by the user. Note that in order to reduce a fraction to lowest terms, the program need only read and write the fraction because the procedure ReadOne calls Reduce before returning the user input. The code for the module is as follows:

```
procedure Handle(Option : char);
  {
        Written by:   XXXXXXXX   XX/XX/XX
          Purpose:   To perform the appropriate activities depending
                     on the user choice.
        Parameters:  Option - input, user choice
   Procedures used:  ReadOne - to get a fraction from the user;
                     WriteOne - to print a fraction;
                     Pause - to wait for a user keystroke;
                     Add - to add two fractions.
  }
begin {Handle}
    case  Option  of
      'R', 'r':
        begin
          Writeln(' ':25, 'REDUCE FRACTION TO LOWEST TERMS');
          Writeln(' ':25, '-------------------------------');
          Writeln;
          ReadOne(FirstNumber);
          Writeln;
          Writeln('The reduced number is:');
          WriteOne(FirstNumber);
          Pause
        end;
      'A', 'a' :
        begin
          Writeln(' ':32, 'ADD TWO FRACTIONS');
          Writeln(' ':32, '-----------------');
          Writeln;
          Writeln('Enter the first fraction: ');
          Writeln;
          Readone(FirstNumber);
          Writeln;
          Writeln('Enter the second fraction: ');
          Writeln;
          Readone(SecondNumber);
          Add(FirstNumber, SecondNumber, ThirdNumber);
          Writeln('The sum of the fractions is:');
          WriteOne(ThirdNumber);
          Pause
        end;
      'Q', 'q' :
        Writeln;
```

```
      else
        Writeln('*** illegal option: ', Option,
                ' detected in procedure Handle')

      end {case}
  end; {Handle}
```

Now that we have discussed all of the modules of the program, it is time to put things together. To comply with the idea of defining elements before using them, it will be helpful to view the hierarchy of the program. We show the program hierarchy in an alternative "paragraph" form in which indentation indicates subordination of modules:

```
main program
        Instructions
                Page
                Pause
        Menu
                Page
        Page
        Handle
                ReadOne
                Reduce
                        Gcd
                                Gcd
                Pause
                Add
                        Reduce
                        Gcd
                                Gcd
        WriteOne
```

We can see from the hierarchy that the following order of defining modules will ensure that each module is defined before it is used:

```
            Page
            Pause
            Instructions
            Menu
            Gcd
            Reduce
            Add
            ReadOne
            WriteOne
            Handle
```

This order is by no means unique, but it does have the virtue of keeping subordinate modules close to calling modules to some extent. The assembled program appears as Figure 5-21, with a sample run given in Figure 5-22.

Documentation. As becomes apparent when one uses a package of modules to develop a program, the documentation for such a package is different from that for a program. The fundamental reason is that the class of user is different.

If we think about the user of a program, we might picture a person sitting at a terminal running the program. Such a person needs to know enough about computers to get the computer going and initiate the program. He or she needs to know about the use of the return key, the back space key, and other similar features of the computer. However, the user need not know how to program in Pascal. (Most users are not programmers in any language.) Accordingly, the user documentation should avoid technical jargon. It should explain how to start the program, what type of input will be expected, what type of output will be generated, how to handle any error situations, and similar topics.

On the other hand, the user of a package of modules is definitely a programmer. She or he may not be proficient in the language in which the package was written. For example, many packages are written in assembly language for a specific machine, for efficiency reasons. However, the user will understand terms such as subprogram, input parameter, and other technical terms. Moreover, these technical terms will be very important. She or he will want to know what parameters must be supplied to the modules of the package in order for them to work properly. The user will want to know what declarations must be included in the main program for use by the modules in the package. She or he will want to know precisely what output values will result from given input values to modules. (The user will not, however, care about the details of how the magic happens: the algorithm and the code will not be important.) The user's guide for a package of modules is therefore much more technical than a typical user's guide.

Appendix B has more to say on this matter and suggests a simplified outline for documentation for programs and for packages.

```
program Calculator(Input, Output);
{
         Written by:  XXXXXXXX  XX/XX/XX
            Purpose:  To provide a calculator for fractions.
    Procedures used:  Instructions - to print instructions;
                      Page - to clear the screen;
                      Menu - to display the menu and get the
                             user option;
                      Handle - to perform the user option.

}
```

{The declarations on page 413 are inserted here.}

```
procedure Instructions; begin {stub} end;
```

{The following modules are inserted here:
Page from Appendix E;
Pause from page 414;
Menu from page 415;
Gcd from Figure 5-19;
Reduce from Figure 5-19;
Add from Figure 5-16;
ReadOne from Figure 5-17;

Figure 5-21 Menu-Driven Calculator (Continued)

WriteOne from Figure 5-18;
Handle from page 416}

```
begin {Calculator}
  ValidOptions := ['R', 'r', 'A', 'a', 'Q', 'q'];

{*** Print instructions.}

  Instructions;

{*** Main loop.}

  repeat

{*** Display Menu and get user option.}

    Menu(ValidOptions, Option);
    Page(Con);

{*** Handle user choice.}

    Handle(Option)
  until  Option in ['Q', 'q'];

{*** Print terminating message and stop program.}

  Writeln;
  Writeln('Calculator program is terminating.')
end.
```

Figure 5-21   Menu-Driven Calculator

SAMPLE INPUT AND OUTPUT

```
                       MENU OPTIONS
                       -----------

                       R(educe fraction to lowest terms)
                       A(dd two fractions)
                       Q(uit)


                          Tap option: r

                       REDUCE FRACTION TO LOWEST TERMS
                       -------------------------------

        Enter numerator: 11
        Enter denominator: 33

The reduced number is:

        Numerator: 1
        Denominator: 3
```

Figure 5-22   Sample Input and Output for Case Study No. 8 (Continued)

```
                              <Tap any key to continue.>
                                   MENU OPTIONS
                                   -----------

                            R(educe fraction to lowest terms)
                            A(dd two fractions)
                            Q(uit)

                                Tap option: A

                                ADD TWO FRACTIONS
                                -----------------

           Enter the first fraction:

                  Enter numerator: 2
                  Enter denominator: 0

              Denominator of 0 not allowed. Please re-enter: 3

           Enter the second fraction:

                  Enter numerator: 6
                  Enter denominator: -4
           The sum of the fractions is:

                  Numerator: -5
                  Denominator: 6


                              <Tap any key to continue.>
                                   MENU OPTIONS
                                   -----------

                            R(educe fraction to lowest terms)
                            A(dd two fractions)
                            Q(uit)

                                Tap option: q


           Calculator program is terminating.
```

Figure 5-22   Sample Input and Output for Case Study No. 8

■■■■■■
EXERCISES

Exercises 1 to 7 relate to the case studies of this section.

1. Write modules for one or more of the modules that were mentioned in this section but not fully discussed:

    a. Subtract
          Make use of the procedure Add to write this one.
    b. Multiply

c. Divide

　　Make use of the procedure Multiply to write this one.

d. Convert rational to real

e. Convert rational to integer

f. Compare for equality

　　Do not do this the same way as for Less. Take advantage of the fact that all fractions are in a standard form in order to just compare numerators and denominators.

2. In the code for Add, the product of the denominators is used as the denominator of the unreduced sum. This is not how schoolchildren do this problem; instead, the concept of least common denominator is used. This concept makes use of the mathematical idea of the least common multiple (LCM) of two integers: the smallest integer that is a multiple of each of the two integers. Because we already have a function to compute the gcd of two numbers, we can take advantage of the relationship:

　　LCM of N and M = (product of N and M)/(gcd of N and M)

a. Write a LCM function to compute the least common multiple of two integers. In order to keep the numbers generated by the calculation as small as possible, calculate the LCM of N and M as:

```
LCM := N * (M/GCD(N,M))
```

b. Use the LCM function to change the method used in Add to arrive at the denominator of the unreduced sum.

3. Add some more user options to the fraction calculator of Figure 5-21. Some possible options to add:

```
S(ubtract two fractions)
M(ultiply two fractions)
D(ivide two fractions)
I(nvert a fraction)
```

4. Add an option to the fraction calculator of Figure 5-21:

```
C(onvert a fraction)
```

Make this new option lead to a submenu:

```
CONVERSION MENU OPTIONS
----------------------
   R(eal conversion)
   I(nteger conversion)
   Q(uit this menu)
```

5. Use the ideas of this section to write a Pascal program for fraction drill and practice. Your program should pose random problems in the categories:

```
R(educe fraction to lowest terms)
A(dd two fractions)
M(ultiply two fractions)
D(ecimal equivalent of a fraction)
```

The program should tell the user if the answer to a problem is correct or not and a running score should be kept. The user should get a "report card" when the session ends.

6. a. Write a program using the rational arithmetic package to read three rational numbers A, B, C and compute and print D1 = (A + B)/C and D2 = (A − B)/C.

b. Write a program using the rational arithmetic package to read rational numbers A, B, and C and an integer number X. Calculate and print P = A * X + B * X + C. The answer should be printed as an integer if possible.

c. Repeat part (b), but print the answer as a real number.

d. Repeat part (c), but first convert A, B, C, and X to real numbers. Compare the answer to that of part (c).

7. For a quadratic equation $ax^2 + bx + c = 0$, where a, b, and c are integers, the solutions may or may not be rational numbers. If the quantity $b^2 - 4ac$ (the so-called *discriminant* of the equation) is a positive perfect square (1, 4, 9, 16, 25, and so on), then the solutions are rational. Write a program to read values for a, b, and c, and either print a message "no rational solutions" or else print the rational solutions. You may wish to refer to Exercise 14 of Section 4-3 for more information on quadratic equations.

Exercises 8 to 15 involve writing packages of subprograms which use Pascal's record types to represent various data.

8. In Exercise 14 of Section 5-3, we defined two record types:

Point: includes two real fields: X and Y
Line: includes three real fields: Ycoeff, Xcoeff, and Constant

This choice of record for a line is based on the standard form of the equation of a straight line:

(Ycoeff) * Y + (Xcoeff) * X + (Constant) = 0

Using these record definitions, write subprograms for the following:

a. Determine whether or not two lines are parallel.
b. Determine whether or not two lines are perpendicular.
c. Determine whether or not two lines are the same.
d. Given a line and an X value, find the corresponding Y value.
e. Given a line and a Y value, find the corresponding X value.
f. Given a line and a point, determine whether or not the point is on the line.
g. Given a line and two points, determine whether or not the points are on the same side of the line.

9. Another possible representation for a line is based on the fact that two distinct points determine a line. Thus, we define a line as a record consisting of two points. Repeat Exercise 8 for this representation.

10. A third possible representation for a line is based on the slope-intercept equation for a line:

$$y = mx + b$$

Provided the line is not vertical, we can represent the line as a record containing slope m and intercept b. To handle vertical lines, we might choose a record with three components:

vertical: A boolean field indicating if the line is vertical
slope: A real field
intercept: The x intercept for a vertical line $x = c$; otherwise the y intercept (b in the equation)

Repeat Exercise 8 for this representation.

11. Write routines to convert from any of the three representations in Exercises 8 to 10 to any other representation.

12. Revise Exercise 10 to use rational numbers (as developed in this section) rather than real numbers for the slope and intercept portions of the record.

13. Using real numbers for dollars and cents operations can lead to accuracy problems. An alternate approach might be to keep each money value as a record containing two integer fields representing the dollars and the cents, respectively. For this situation:

   a. Write a subprogram to add two such figures. Notice that there are two parts to the answer. Given 101, 50 representing $101.50, and 45, 63 representing $45.63, the answer should be 147, 13 representing $147.13. You can assume that the numbers are positive.

   b. Write a subprogram to subtract two such figures. Assume that the first amount is larger than the second.

   c. Write a subprogram similar to part (b) except that it does not assume that the first amount is larger than the second. Instead, it has another parameter that is used to report to the main program whether or not it was able to do the subtraction. If it is able, it sets this parameter to true and does the subtraction; if not, it sets this parameter to false.

   d. Write a subprogram to multiply two such figures. Assume that both are positive, and round the answer to the nearest cent. For example, 145.01 times 1.10 should be 159.51.

   e. Modify part (d) to make the second figure represent a real number with three decimal places. For example, 1, 85 to represent 1.085.

   f. Write subprograms to compare two such dollar and cents figures. One, called Equal, should tell whether or not they are equal. The second, called Larger, should tell whether or not the first is larger than the second.

   g. Extend your representation scheme to include a Boolean field that indicates if the number is positive or negative, and rewrite the various subprograms.

   h. Write a program for Exercise 14 of Section 3-2 that uses this representation for money rather than using real numbers.

   i. Write a program for Exercise 24 of Section 3-4 that uses this representation for money rather than using real numbers.

14. On many microcomputers, the value for MaxInt is 32767. This imposes a stringent limit on the size of integers than can be used. There are various ways to extend the range of values; one is suggested by analogy with what we did in Exercise 13 to represent money.

   For example, to represent positive numbers with up to nine digits, we could think of the number as we typically write it by hand, as in these examples:

$$213,567,198$$
$$3,175,000$$

We might choose to use a record with three integers to represent the number of millions, thousands, and units. Using this representation, write subprograms for the following:

   a. Add two integers.
   b. Subtract two integers, assuming the first is larger.
   c. Compare two integers to see if they are equal.

d. Compare two integers to see if the first is larger.

e. Multiply two integers. Caution: If you multiply two 3-digit numbers, the result may be larger than MaxInt. Can you suggest some solutions to this problem?

15. Refer to Exercise 14. Add a field to the record indicating whether or not the number is positive. Write routines to find the absolute value, to compare, to add, and to subtract two integers using this representation scheme.

□

NOTES FOR SECTION 5-4

1. This is a standard ASCII character for ringing the bell on a teletype. For most microcomputers, this should produce a "beep." In the early years of computer usage, Teletype terminals had bells inside that rang when the Chr(13) code was encountered. Some modern terminals produce a whistle and some produce a chime when this code is input or output. See Appendix F for a discussion of the ASCII code set.

ONE-DIMENSIONAL ARRAYS

6-1
DEFINING AND USING ARRAYS

In this chapter, we study arrays in some detail. The concept of an array was first introduced in Chapter 3, and we have used them in Chapters 4 and 5. Our purpose in this chapter is therefore twofold:

1. To review and consolidate what you already know about arrays
2. To examine some more sophisticated applications of arrays

The first section of this chapter is mostly review. In the second section, we examine some uses of arrays to structure the data used by our program. The third section discusses two important concepts related to arrays: sorting and searching. Finally, we present some case studies in the fourth section.

□ THE NEED FOR ARRAYS

An **array** can be thought of as a list of values. The values must be of the same type, and they are generally related in some way. For example, we might declare an array as

```
AverageTemp : array[1 .. 31] of real;
```

Our program can then use AverageTemp to store a list of 31 real values. For example, those values might represent the average temperature in Tempe, Arizona, for the 31 days of March, 1988. We would refer to the first value as AverageTemp[1], the tenth as AverageTemp[10], and so on. (Notice that we would know that AverageTemp[23] refers to the average temperature on March 23; the computer would know only that it refers to the 23rd value in the array named AverageTemp.)

As a general rule, we can state that:

> An array is probably the proper choice of data type when the program needs to store a list of related values of the same type.

To illustrate this, we briefly describe some situations in which we might consider using an array and some in which an array is probably inappropriate. (Some of these examples are developed more fully later in the section.)

1. *Given a list of 40 test grades for a class, find how many are greater than the average.* To solve this problem, we would read the grades, add them, and divide by 40 to calculate the average. We would then have to compare each grade to the calculated average. Rather than ask the user to reenter the grades, we would want to store the grades in an array as we read them. We then could compare the values in the array to the average, in order to find the desired count.

2. *Given a list of 40 test grades for a class, find the average.* This is similar to the previous problem, but we do not need an array. We can read the grades one at a time, as shown in this segment:

```
Sum := 0;
for I := 1 to 40 do
   begin
      Readln(Grade);
      Sum := Sum + Grade
   end;
Average := Sum / 40
```

As we read each grade, we do everything that is required for that grade prior to reading the next. We do not need to store all 40 grades, so we do not need an array.

3. *Data for each employee consists of name and 12 monthly pay figures. Print the name, the 12 pay figures, and the total pay for each person.* To solve this problem, it is convenient to store the 12 pay figures in an array as we read them, then print the array along with the name and total. By making clever use of Write rather than Writeln, we could avoid using an array. However, the program design will be ''cleaner'' if we use an array.

4. *Simulate rolling a pair of dice 12,000 times, and tell how many 2's, 3's, etc., are rolled.* For this, we will need 11 counter variables. We could use Count2, Count3, . . . , Count12 as variables. However, it is useful to think of the counters as a list of values and use a declaration such as

```
Count : array[2 .. 12] of integer;
```

Count[7] would be the number of 7's rolled, and so on. This allows us, for example, to print the results using

```
for I := 2 to 12 do
   begin
      Writeln(I:2, ' occurred ', Count[I]:4, ' times. ')
   end
```

(You might consider how you would print the results using variables Count2, Count3, etc.)

Notice that we would *not* need an array of size 12,000 to store the 12,000 simulated rolls. We would generate one at a time, adding to the appropriate counter.

5. *Given I, a number between 1 and 12 representing a month, print the month name.* This can be solved without an array, of course. For example, we could use the structure suggested here:

```
case I of
  1  :  Writeln('January');
           . . . .
end {case}
```

However, if an array Month were set up by the program to contain the 12 month names, then we could simply use

```
Writeln(Month[I])
```

to accomplish the task. (We used a similar idea in Section 5-3 to print the adventure game classes.)

□

ARRAY DECLARATION

Arrays can be declared in Pascal using a declaration of the form

```
array[index type] of component type
```

For example, in the declaration

```
array[1 .. 100] of integer
```

the index type is "1 .. 100" and the component type is "integer." This says that:

1. The **subscript** (**index**) must be an integer in the range 1 to 100.
2. Each value (component) in the array is an integer.

The example given above illustrates the most common form for the index type: a subrange of the integers from 1 to some number greater than 1. However, declarations such as

```
array[2 .. 12] of integer
```

or

```
array[-500 .. 500] of real
```

are also allowed when they are appropriate for the problem to be solved.[1]

COMMENT   If a subscript range has a negative lower bound and a positive upper bound, then 0 is one of the valid subscripts.

The "component type" can be any of the following: integer, real, Boolean, char, a string type, or a programmer-defined scalar or subrange type.

COMMENT In Section 6-2, we will see that the index type and component type can be defined in a more general fashion than that considered in this section.

There are several ways to declare a specific variable to be an array. For example, to declare an array of 50 names, we could write

```
var
   Names : array[1 .. 50] of string[20];
```

or we could write

```
const
   MaxIndex = 50;

type
   String20  = string[20];
   NameArray = array[1 .. MaxIndex] of String20;

var
   Names : NameArray;
```

The second approach has several advantages. First, by using the constant MaxIndex, it is easier to adjust the array size in the future. Second, the array Names can be passed as a parameter to a procedure or function because it is of a named type. (Likewise, Name[3] could be passed as a parameter because it is of the named type String20.) As we shall see, there are other advantages to be gained by using named types. Therefore, we will almost always use named types when declaring arrays.

□
ARRAY REFERENCE Suppose that we have these declarations:

```
type
   CountArray = array[2 .. 12] of integer;
   RealArray  = array[-5 .. 25] of real;

var
   Count : CountArray;
   X     : RealArray;
   I, J  : integer;
```

More often than not, a program step that refers to one of these arrays would be referencing a specific value of the array. To do so, it would use

```
array-name [ subscript ]
```

The subscript (index) can be any integer expression in the proper **subscript range**. For example, if I and J currently have the values 5 and 3, respectively, then each of these is a valid reference:

```
Count[7]
Count[I]         refers  to  Count[5]
Count[2 * I]     refers  to  Count[10]
X[-I + J]        refers  to  X[-2]
```

COMMENT: If we use the Turbo compiler directive {$R+}, discussed in Section 5.3, the computer will detect subscripts that are **outside the range** of valid subscripts.

A reference to an element of the Count array can be used anywhere an integer variable could be used. For example, we could write steps such as these:

```
Count[3] := 0
if Count[I] > Count[I+1] then . . .
Readln(Count[J])
X[I] := Sqrt( X[I+1] )
```

In particular, an array element can be used as an argument passed to a function or procedure to match a corresponding parameter of the same type. Since $X[I+1]$ is a numeric value, it can be passed to the Sqrt function. For any function with an integer parameter, we could pass Count[12] to match that parameter.

Less frequently, a program step will refer to the array name without using a subscript. Such a reference refers to the *entire array*. The most frequent example involves passing an entire array as a parameter to a subprogram. In such a case, the parameter in the subprogram *must be of the same named type*.

Another instance in which we would use the array name without a subscript involves array assignments. For example, the assignment

```
A := B
```

could be used to cause the entire array B to be copied to array A. This is possible only if the arrays are of *precisely* the same type. For example, it is legal with the declarations:

```
type
   IntegerArray = array[1 .. 50] of integer;

var
   A : IntegerArray;
   B : IntegerArray;
```

It is illegal with the similar declarations:

```
var
   A : array[1 .. 50] of integer;
   B : array[1 .. 50] of integer;
```

□ **ARRAY ALGORITHMS—COUNT-CONTROLLED**

The easiest program segments to write dealing with arrays are those that use a "count-controlled" logic. We can describe segments of this type generically as follows:

```
for I := start to end do
   begin
      steps which process array element A[I]
   end;  {for}
```

For example, the program in Figure 6-1 carries out the task referred to earlier in this section: read exactly 40 grades and count how many are larger than the average. Some portions are shaded for emphasis. First, we have used a named constant for the number of grades. In our preliminary testing, we changed this to a smaller value. Second, the variable I is used both to control the "for" loop and as a subscript for the array. The for loop causes I to take on the values 1 through 40, and therefore the reference "Grades[I]" refers to Grades[1] the first time through the loop, Grades[2] the second time, and so on.

```
program CountGrades(Input, Output);
{
    Written by:  XXXXXXXXX  XX/XX/XX
        Purpose:  To read a list of grades (of a fixed length), and
                  count how many are greater than the average.
}
const
  MaxIndex = 40;                          { size of grade array }

type
  GradeArray  = array[1 .. MaxIndex] of integer;

var
  Grades   : GradeArray;         { list of grades }
  I        : integer;            { loop control, and subscript }
  Sum      : integer;            { sum of grades }
  Average  : real;               { average of grades }
  Count    : integer;            { how many are > average }

begin

{***  Read the grades and find the sum.}

  Sum := 0;

  for I := 1 to MaxIndex do
    begin
      Write('Enter grade #', I:1, ': ');
      Readln(Grades[I]);
      Sum := Sum + Grades[I]
    end;  {for}

{***  Find and print the average.}

  Average := Sum / MaxIndex;
  Writeln;
  Writeln('The average is ', Average:1:2);

{***  Count how many are larger than the average, and print answer.}

  Count := 0;

  for I := 1 to MaxIndex do
    begin
      if Grades[I] > Average then
        Count := Count + 1
    end;

  Writeln(Count:1, ' grades are larger than the average.')
end.
```

Figure 6-1   Number of Above Average Grades

COMMENT It happens that this example uses an array of integers. We can write similar examples using arrays of other "component types." For example, we can declare an array as indicated here:

```
type
  VoicePart = (bass, tenor, alto, soprano);
  VoiceArray = array[1 . . 50] of VoicePart;

var
  Voice : VoiceArray;
```

Assuming that some earlier steps in the program have supplied values to this array, code such as the following could be used to count the tenors in the array:

```
TenorCount := 0;
for I := 1 to 50 do
  begin
    if Voice[I] = tenor then
      TenorCount := TenorCount + 1
  end;  {for}
```

As another example, let us write a function that finds the largest grade in an array GradeList. To do so, we maintain a variable Large that at all times contains the largest value encountered so far. We compare each value in the array with this largest value. Our "step which processes array element A[I]" is in this case:

```
if GradeList[I] > Large then
  Large := GradeList[I]
```

Before the loop, we must give Large an initial value; otherwise, the comparison "GradeList[I] > Large" would be meaningless the first time through the loop. We have two choices: start at a low value (0 is low enough for this example) or start with the first value. In working with an array, it is easy to start with the first value, so we do:

```
Large := GradeList[1]
```

Figure 6-2 contains the function. Observe that:

1. We have included a parameter that indicates the number of students. This allows the function to be used more generally than if it used the array size for its loop control.

2. The for loop index I goes from 2 to NumberOfStudents. There is no need to compare the first grade with itself.

3. We need a local variable Large to obtain the answer. As our last step, we copy the answer to the function name. (Without this, a step "if GradeList[I] > Largest" would be considered a recursive call to the function.)

In Figure 6-3, we present a slight modification. In addition to the largest value, we wish to know the **position** (that is, the subscript) for which the value occurred. To do so, we add an additional variable LargePosition. Because there are now two answers, we use a procedure rather than a function. Whenever we assign a value to Large, we also assign a value to LargePosition to keep track of

```
function Largest(GradeList : GradeArray; NumberOfGrades : integer) : integer;
{
     Written by:   XXXXXXXXX  XX/XX/XX
        Purpose:   To find the largest value in an array of grades.
     Parameters:   GradeList - input, the array of grades to examine
                   NumberOfGrades - input, a count of how many students
                                    there are
}
var
   Large     : integer;                   { used to get the largest }
   I         : integer;                   { loop control and subscript }

begin  {Largest}
   Large := GradeList[1];

   for I := 2 to NumberOfGrades do
      begin
        if GradeList[I] > Large then
          Large := GradeList[I]
      end;   {for}

   Largest := Large
end;   {Largest}
```

Figure 6-2   Largest Value in an Array

CAUTION

We can pass the current length of an array as a parameter to a procedure or function. The subprogram can use that parameter to make sure it works only with the portion of the array which contains meaningful data.

However, the declared size of the array is fixed. It cannot be defined or redefined by the subprogram. It is set by the type declaration in the main program.

---

where Large obtained its value. For example, if at the end, LargePosition has the value 3, this means that the third grade was the largest. (It is useful to notice that GradeList[LargePosition] is the largest, and hence we do not really need to pass back Large to the calling program.)

CAUTION

One of the most frequent errors made in working with arrays is confusing a subscript with the array element to which it refers. In working with arrays, we must always ask, "Do I want to refer to the subscript or to the array element indicated by the subscript?"

```
procedure Largest(GradeList : GradeArray; NumberOfGrades : integer;
                  var Large, LargePosition : integer);
{
     Written by:  XXXXXXXXX  XX/XX/XX
        Purpose:  To find the largest value, and its subscript, in an
                  array of grades.
     Parameters:  GradeList - input, the array of grades to examine
                  NumberOfGrades - input, a count of how many students
                                   there are

                  Large - output, the largest number found
                  LargePosition - output, the position where the largest
                                  was found (in case of a tie, it is the
                                  first position where a largest was
                                  found)
}
begin  {Largest}
  Large := GradeList[1];
  LargePosition := 1;

  for I := 2 to NumberOfGrades do
    begin
      if GradeList[I] > Large then
        begin
          Large := GradeList[I];
          LargePosition := I
        end  {if}
    end;  {for}

end;  {Largest}
```

Figure 6-3 Position of Largest Value in an Array

As another example, let us write a procedure to print an integer array. For this, we will use two parameters: the array and an indication of how many values are in the array. We assume, as we have in the previous examples, that the lowest subscript is 1. We would like our procedure to print eight values per line.

We begin with steps that print one value per line, then modify the procedure to print eight per line. We might write:

```
for I := 1 to NumberOfGrades do
  begin
    Writeln(Grades[I]:7)
  end;  {for}
```

Each Writeln invocation prints the grade followed by a carriage return to move to the next line. What we must do to get eight grades per line is to only send a carriage return after every eight grades, so we might write:

```
for I := 1 to NumberOfGrades do
  begin
    Write(Grades[I]:7);
    if I mod 8 = 0 then
      Writeln
  end;  {for}
```

Each individual grade is written (using Write not Writeln) without a carriage return. When I is 8, 16, 24, and so on, I mod 8 will be 0 and the Writeln will send a carriage return.

This version almost works; however, if NumberOfGrades is not evenly divisible by 8, the last line of grades will not get a carriage return. Thus, we add

```
if NumberOfGrades mod 8 <> 0 then
     Writeln
```

after the loop. The details of writing this as a procedure are left to the reader.

□
ARRAY ALGORITHMS— CONDITION-CONTROLLED
In the preceding subsection, we examined several types of problems where a count-controlled loop ("for" loop) is an appropriate structure. Some looping processes involving arrays, however, cannot use such a structure. An important class of problems where this is true is that involving an **array search**.

In Chapter 5, we wrote several programs that involved searching in a file. As we discovered, the loops involved in those searches used a compound condition for termination. We wanted to terminate the loop "successfully" as soon as the desired item was found or "unsuccessfully" if the entire file was traversed without finding the desired item.

A similar approach can be used in searching an array. If for an array A, the subscripts range from 1 to N, we can cause an index variable I to assume the values 1, 2, and so on using this basic logic:

initialize I to 1
as long as the search is not complete,
    add 1 to I to move to the next array element.

When is the search complete? If A[I] is the item sought, it is complete (we have found it). If I goes beyond N (the number of items in the array), it is also complete (the item is not there). We may be tempted to write the condition "the search is complete" as

```
(I > N) or (A[I] = ValueSought)
```

However, this contains a subtle flaw. If I is greater than N, the reference to A[I] is illegal (at best, meaningless). One common solution to this problem is to use a Boolean variable Found to indicate success in the search. Our basic logic becomes

initialize Found to false, I to 1
as long as the search is not complete:
    if A[I] is the sought value, set Found true;
    otherwise add 1 to I.

This general approach is illustrated by the function of Figure 6-4, which searches for a given integer in an array of integers. This technique (using a Boolean variable to indicate success) can be useful in solving any problem that involves searching for the occurrence of some condition in an array.

```
function Search(A : IntegerArray; Key, N : integer) : integer;
{
    Written by:   XXXXXXXXX  XX/XX/XX
        Purpose:  To locate a given value in an array. The answer is
                  the subscript where found (0 if not found).
     Parameters:  A - input, the array to search in
                  Key - input, the value to search for
                  N - input, the portion of the array in use
}
var
  Found     : boolean;                  { used to indicate success }
  I         : integer;                  { loop control and subscript }

begin  {Search}
  Found := false;                       { assume not there as default }
  I := 1;

  while (I <= N) and (not Found) do
    begin
      if A[I] = Key then
        Found := true
      else
        I := I + 1
    end;  {while}

  if Found then
    Search := I
  else
    Search := 0
end;  {Search}
```

Figure 6-4   Searching an Array

As another example of a condition-based loop using an array, we will write code that reads up to ten nonzero integers into an integer array of size 10. We would like the procedure to stop after 10 numbers have been read or when the user enters a terminating (0) value. Moreover, the 0 should not be placed into the array, and a parameter N should indicate how many numbers were actually input.

One approach to this problem involves "simulating" the for loop. To read exactly 10 numbers, we could use the for loop on the left or the equivalent while loop on the right:

```
                                      I := 1;
    for I := 1 to 10 do               while I < = 10 do
      begin                             begin
        Readln(Number);                   Readln(Number);
        A[I] := Number                    A[I] := Number;
      end    {for}                        I := I + 1
                                        end   {while}
```

If we use a for loop, we must read exactly 10 values. With the while loop, we can quit when the input number is 0. One idea is to use the Boolean variable UserIs-Done initialized to false. In the loop, because we do not want to put the 0 in the array, we write

```
          if Number = 0 then
             UserIsDone := true
          else
             A[I] := Number
```

The while loop condition is modified to

```
          while (I < = 10) and (not UserIsDone) do
```

After the loop, we can calculate the size of the array as

```
                    N := I - 1
```

With these changes, the while loop solution becomes

```
          I := 1;
          UserIsDone := false;
          while (I <= 10) and (not UserIsDone) do
             begin
                Readln(Number);
                if Number = 0 then
                   UserIsDone := true
                else
                   A[I] := Number;
                I := I + 1
             end;   {while}
          N := I - 1
```

(You should convince yourself that this is correct for the boundary values N = 0, 1, 9, and 10.)

□

INITIALIZATION, COPYING, AND SHIFTING

We have considered a few examples of processing an entire array. These examples have included important algorithm classes, such as finding the largest and searching, which were considered at length in earlier chapters. We now consider some array processing methods that have no analogues in earlier chapters.

It is frequently necessary to initialize arrays to some known value. To initialize all elements of an array X with 100 elements to some value, for example Z, we could write

```
          for I := 1 to 100 do
             begin
                X[I] := Z
             end   {for}
```

Of course, Z could be replaced by a constant such as 0, ' ', or other value, as might be needed.

Another common initialization is to place values equal to the index of the element into each element; for example, X[1] = 1, X[2] = 2, . . . , X[100] = 100. This can be accomplished by

```
          for I := 1 to 100 do
             begin
                X[I] := I
             end   {for}
```

In addition to initializing arrays, we frequently wish to copy one array, or part of one array, into another. As we have seen, if A and B are the same named type, the assignment

```
A := B
```

can be used to copy all of B to A. Suppose now that we want to copy only the first ten elements of B to the first ten elements of A. A simple loop such as

```
for I := 1 to 10 do
   begin
     A[I] := B[I]
   end  {for}
```

will suffice.

On the other hand, suppose we want to copy elements 1 to 5 and 10 to 15 of B into the first 11 positions of A. One approach is to copy B[1] to B[5] to A[1] to A[5], as in the first example, then copy B[10] to B[15] to A[6] to A[11].

There are several approaches to writing a loop to move B[10] to B[15] to A[6] to A[11]. We might make a table of subscripts, as follows:

A *Subscript* Comes from B *Subscript*	
6	10
7	11
8	12
9	13
10	14
11	15

After studying this table, we might write

```
for I := 1 to 5 do
   begin
     A[I] := B[I]
   end;  {for}
for I := 1 to 6 do
   begin
     A[I+5] := B[I+9]
   end  {for}
```

The second loop was written by first noting that we wished to move six elements. This led to the loop for I = 1 to 6. Now we know we want our loop body to be of the form

```
A[??] := B[??]
```

We must come up with the proper formulas for the A subscript and the B subscript. To determine the formula for the A subscript, we note that

when I is 1, the subscript is 6
when I is 2, the subscript is 7
and so on

The subscript is always 5 more than I, and hence the proper formula is I+5. Similar reasoning leads to the formula I+9 for the B subscript.

1. The second loop could be replaced by

```
for I := 6 to 11 do
   begin
      A[I] := B[I+4]
   end  {for}
```

In this case, we have chosen the index range to match the destination subscripts. By having I take on the values 6 to 11, we avoid the need to determine a formula for the A subscript. The formula for the B subscript is found by observing that it is always 4 more than the A subscript.

2. If we do not wish to devise a formula for B's subscript, we might use this alternate approach:

```
J := 10;
for I := 6 to 11 do
   begin
      A[I] := B[J];
      J := J + 1
   end  {for}
```

By initializing J to 10 prior to the loop and incrementing it each time through the loop, we have J take on the values 10 to 15.

An array operation that is frequently used is shifting. Shifting is similar to copying, but involves only one array. As an example, let us write code to shift the array A to the left by one position. This means to copy A[2] to A[1], A[3] to A[2], and so on. If A contains 50 values, our last copy would copy A[50] to A[49]. We might then set A[50] to 0, or decrease a variable representing the actual length by 1. The code would be

```
for I := 1 to 49 do
   begin
      A[I] := A[I+1]
   end; {for}
A[50] := 0
```

Next consider a shift to the right. We might be inclined to write code which copies A[1] to A[2], then A[2] to A[3], and so on. However, this will not work, since A[2] will be changed before we copy it to A[3]. The solution is to work from right to left: first copy A[49] to A[50], then A[48] to A[49], and so on. The code to do so is left as an exercise.

□
PROCESSING SINGLE ELEMENTS

In the examples we have considered in this section, the subscripts of the array elements have been set by the index of a loop or have been obtained using a formula in terms of that index.

The loops are of the general form

```
for I := 1 to N do
   begin
      process A[I]           [ or A[formula involving I] ]
   end  {for}
```

Frequently, however, we need to work with a single element of an array. We will need a subscript, but because we are not in a loop, the subscript will not be a loop index.

It sometimes happens that, in reading values for an array, we do not read the entire array at once. Instead, each input record can contain a subscript along with the value to be placed in the array at that position. For example, the input

```
7 150.25
```

would indicate that the value 150.25 is to be placed into A[7].

It is possible to read such an input record using

```
Readln(I, A[I])
```

This practice is dangerous because it makes the program vulnerable to data entry errors. For example, we might have an array with 10 elements in it and the data value read for I might be 25. A reference to A[25] will either be recognized as an error (if we remembered to include the Turbo {$R+} compiler directive) or be treated as a reference to some part of the computer memory outside of the array A. A much better approach is to read the array value into a temporary variable. We then check that the subscript is in the valid range before placing the value in the array. Thus, the Readln statement above would be better written as

```
Readln(I, Temp);
if (I >= 1) and (I <= 10) then
  A[I] := Temp
else
  Writeln('Subscript value ', I:1, ' is illegal ')
```

A second situation involving subscripts that are not loop indexes can be illustrated by the following problem. We are to simulate rolling a pair of dice 12,000 times and to count the number of times each possible number (2 through 12) occurs.

As we discussed in the subsection "The Need for ARRAYS," it is convenient to use an array (with possible subscripts from 2 to 12) for the counters. The array can be declared as

```
type
  CountArray = array[2 .. 12] of integer;
var
  Counter : CountArray;
```

The first step in the program would involve initializing the entire array to 0:

```
for I := 2 to 12 do
  begin
    Counter[I] := 0
  end;  {for}
```

The steps to do the counting can be written as

```
for I := 1 to 12000 do
  begin
    Roll := RollOfDice;  {use the function we wrote earlier}
    Counter[???] := Counter [???] + 1
  end;  {for}
```

Our only problem is determining the proper subscript. However, that is easily solved. If the roll is 2, we want to increment Counter[2]; if it is 3, we want to increment Counter[3]; and so on. The variable Roll gives the desired subscript. Thus, the counting step should be

```
Counter[Roll] := Counter[Roll] + 1
```

As a final indication of the use of subscripts other than the loop index itself, consider the following situation. Each child in a nursery school has been assigned to one of six different groups, numbered 1 to 6. An array Group contains the group assignments for the children. There are N children. Count how many are in each group.

We have a program segment similar to the one involving dice rolls:

```
for I := 1 to N do
  begin
    calculate subscript CountSub for Counter array;
    Counter[CountSub] := Counter[CountSub] + 1
  end   {for}
```

What is the proper value for CountSub? It is the person's group number, namely Group[I]:

```
CountSub := Group[I];
Counter[CountSub] := Counter[CountSub] + 1
```

NOTE We may combine the steps as

```
Counter[Group[I]] := Counter[Group[I]] + 1
```

□
TESTING
In working with arrays, there are two natural boundaries: the first element in the array and the last element in the array. Moreover, in speaking of the last element in the array, we can mean one of two things: the last element the array is capable of holding or the last element it actually holds. For example, consider an array Names of size 50, capable of holding names for a class of 50. For a given class, it might actually contain only 33 students. The "last" element of the array could be thought of as Names[33] or as Names[50].

Likewise, in an array such as the Names array, we have boundaries on how "full" the array is. Put another way, if NStudent indicates the number of students in the class, then there are boundaries at NStudent=0, NStudent=1, and NStudent=50.

Most testing involving arrays uses these considerations together with those for the specific problem. For example, in finding the largest grade in an array Grade of size 50 that currently contains NStudent grades, we can identify tests such as these:

Value of NStudent: 0, 1, 50, in between, 51 (an error)

Location of largest (assuming no ties):
  position 1, with NStudent > 1
  position NStudent, with NStudent = 1

position NStudent, with NStudent > 1
position NStudent, with NStudent = 50
in between 1 and NStudent

Number of ties for largest:

none
all scores the same
in between none and all

As another example, similar tests would apply for an array search. Among the most important tests would be these:

value not found

value found:
in first position
in last position in use (N), with N < declared array size
in last position in use (N), with N = declared array size

□
DPT   *1.* Do not use subscripts in place of array elements and vice versa. In any reference to an array, we must ask, "Do we want to refer to the location (the subscript) or the value in that location of the array?"

2. Think carefully about the formula for subscripts. Because so many standard processes involve a reference A[I], we may have a tendency to assume that all subscripts will always be a loop-control variable I. In this section, we have seen several examples where the proper subscript is not the loop-control variable.

3. Avoid subscripts out of range. An out-of-range subscript can be caused by the errors indicated in items 1 and 2. In addition, some common causes are
a. Failing to check the input that indicates a subscript
b. Adding values to an array without checking if the array is full
If we include the Turbo compiler directive {$R+}, the computer will detect this error. If we forget this directive, the out-of-range array reference will be allowed. This reference will refer to (and perhaps modify) some part of the computer memory outside the array—perhaps another variable, a constant, or even the program itself. This can cause almost any type of error to occur.

4. Think carefully when using arrays as arguments for subprograms. If the subprogram expects an array as a parameter, then pass the whole array [for example, Print(Scores)]. If the subprogram expects a single value, pass an array element [for example, Y := Sqrt(Total[I])].

5. Parameters must be of a named type. For example,

```
function Sum(A : IntegerArray) : integer;
```

is legal, but

```
function Sum(A : array[1 .. 100] of integer) : integer;
```

is *illegal*.

6. Be especially wary of compound conditions involving subscripts. Any condition such as the ones below are suspect:

```
a. (I > N) or (A[I] = Value)
b. (I <= N) and (A[I] <> Value)
c. (I > 0) and (A[I] > Temp)
```

The problem is that Pascal can evaluate both halves of the condition even if only the first half is needed to determine whether the condition is true or false. If the valid subscripts for the array A are 1 to N, then these three conditions are faulty because

a. If I > N is true, then A[I] = Value is illegal (an out-of-range subscript).
b. If I <= N is false, then A[I] <> Value is illegal.
c. If I > 0 is false, then A[I] > Temp is illegal.

COMMENTS   *1.* As we discussed in our array search example, a common solution to this last problem is to introduce a Boolean variable such as Found, which represents the second half of the compound condition. This variable is initialized prior to the loop and changed within the loop body.

2. Versions of this bug can be found in the sample programs of many computer science textbooks. What this should say to you as a student is that it is an exceptionally dangerous bug: even experienced programmers can easily make this mistake. You must be especially alert to avoid the problem.

■■■■■■
REVIEW

Terms and concepts

array	out of range
subscript	position
index	array search
subscript range	

Pascal syntax

Array declaration:

```
array[index type] of component type
```

where the index type can be of the form low .. high, and the component type can be integer, real, string type, etc.

Array reference:

```
array-name[subscript]
```

where the subscript can be any integer expression in the proper range, as is given in the declaration of the array

The compiler directive {$R+} causes the computer to check for a subscript out of range.

Array algorithms

Frequently used form (count-controlled):

```
initialization, if needed;
for I := 1 to N do
```

```
              begin
                process involving A[I]
              end  {for}
```

Searching:

```
          Found := false;
          I := 1;
          while (I <= N) and (not Found) do
            begin
              if A[I] = Value then
                Found := true
              else
                I := I + 1
            end;  {while}
          {at this point, take action based on whether or not
           found}
```

Working with a single element:

Subscript based on some action, such as searching, formula calculation, and reading data.

Testing 1. Natural boundaries for arrays:

> First element
> Last possible element
> Last element actually present

2. Portion of array in use:

> None
> Completely in use
> In between

DPT 1. Do not confuse a subscript and the corresponding array element.

2. Do not use a wrong subscript.

3. Avoid a subscript out of range.

4. Pass arrays to match array parameters, array elements to match real, integer, etc., parameters.

5. Parameters must be of a named type.

6. Be wary of compound conditions such as

$$(I > N) \text{ or } (A[I] = \text{Value})$$

EXERCISES

Many of these exercises ask you to write subprograms involving arrays. To do so, you must make intelligent assumptions about the context.

For example, in Exercise 3, you must assume that the type for the array has been declared in the main program, and you must make an assumption about what that type is called. Also, you should assume that N represents the portion in use, and that the lowest subscript is 1.

(If a specific array size such as 50 or 100 is mentioned, you can use a global constant such as MaxIndex in place of the specific constant.)

1. Give the appropriate constant, type, and variable declarations to declare the following arrays:

   *a. An integer array with subscripts ranging from 0 to 100.
   *b. A real array with subscripts ranging from −50 to 75.
   *c. A Boolean array with subscripts ranging from 22 to 53.
   d. An array of days of size 100. The array values are Monday, Thursday, etc. Use an appropriate user-defined scalar type.
   e. An array representing the positions played by a 28-member baseball team. Possible positions are P, C, 1B, 2B, SS, 3B, and OF.
   f. An array to contain the names of up to 250 students in an introductory calculus section.
   g. An array to contain the classes (FR, SO, JR, SR, CONTED, or GRAD) of approximately 1750 students at a small liberal arts college.

2. a. Give appropriate declarations and Pascal code to create an array containing the names of the months.
   *b. Repeat part (a) for an array containing the 16 single characters "0" through "9" and "A" through "F". (The subscript for "0" should be 0, for "1" should be 1, and so on.)

3. Assume that we have an array A containing N elements. Write subprograms to:

   *a. Find the value of the smallest element in A.
   *b. Find the location of the first element equal to the smallest.
   c. Find the location of the last element equal to the smallest.
   d. Count the number of elements equal to the smallest.
   e. Print the subscripts of all array elements equal to the smallest. Hint: This will require two loops.

4. a. By making minor modifications to the procedure in Figure 6-3, write a function that finds the position of the largest value in an array.
   b. Can you accomplish this task without using a variable such as Large to contain the largest value? Hint: In Figure 6-3, GradeList[LargePosition] is the same as Large.

5. a. Given is code to read an array, terminating when the user enters a 0; N is the array size.

```
I := 0;
Readln(Number);
while Number <> 0 do
  begin
    I := I + 1;
    A[I] := Number;
    Readln(Number)
  end;    {while}
N := I
```

   Modify this segment to limit the array to 10 numbers. Compare this to the segment on page 439 that accomplishes the same task.
   b. Trace your solution, and that on page 439, for situations where the resulting value of N should be 0, 1, 9, and 10.

*6. On page 440, we gave the following solution to a problem of counting how many children in a kindergarten are assigned to each of six groups. (We assume the Counter array has been initialized to 0.)

```
for I := 1 to N do
   begin
      CountSub := Group[I];
      Counter[CountSub] := Counter[CountSub] + 1
   end   {for}
```

A student has proposed the following alternative solution:

```
for I := 1 to 6 do
   begin
      for J := 1 to N do
         begin
            if Group[J] = I then
               Counter[I] := Counter[I] + 1
         end   {for J}
   end   {for I}
```

Compare the two solutions as to efficiency. If N is 150, how many steps are involved for each?

7. Write subprograms for the following for an integer array A. Assume the array is of size 50, but that it presently contains only N values.

  a. Find the average of the values.
  *b. Find what percentage of the values are positive.
  *c. Set a variable Location to contain the subscript of the first negative value in the array (Location is to be 0 if there are no negative values).
  d. Set a Boolean variable to true if none of the array values are 0, otherwise to false.
  e. Add a new value to the end of the array. The variable NewValue contains the value to be added. Assume that N < 50.
  f. Repeat part (e), but remove the assumption that N < 50. Set a Boolean variable to indicate if the array was full.
  g. Repeat part (f), but assume that if that value is already present in the array, it should not be added.
  h. Repeat part (g), but assume that the numbers in the array are in increasing order and that they should still be in increasing order after the new value is inserted.

8. The standard deviation of a group of N values of A can be defined as

$$\sqrt{\frac{1}{(N-1)} \sum_{i=1}^{N} (A_i - \overline{A})^2}$$

(The Σ (summation) notation indicates the sum of the indicated values for i from 1 to N.) Write a subprogram that will compute $\overline{A}$ (the average of the A values), then compute the sum of the values $(A_i - \overline{A})^2$, and finally compute the standard deviation.

9. We are given two arrays A and B of N elements each. Write a subprogram to compute

$$P = A_1 * B_1 + A_2 * B_2 + \ldots + A_N * B_N$$

*10. Suppose an array of N integers is known to contain only 0's and 1's. Write code to get all the 0's at the beginning of the array and all the 1's at the end of the array.

11. Given an array representing the positions played by a 28-member baseball team, count the pitchers. [See Exercise 1(e)].

12. Given an array representing the voice parts of a 75-member choir, what is the ratio of tenors to sopranos?

13. Using the array defined in Exercise 2(a), write a subprogram to convert a date to printable form. The input is a record containing three fields (month, day, and year); the output is a string. For example, for input 11 7 89, the output would be 'November 7, 1989'.

14. Using the array defined in Exercise 2(b), write subprograms for the following:

   *a. Given an integer in the range 0 to 15, the output is the corresponding character from "0" to "9", "A" to "F".
   b. Given a character in the range "0" to "9" or "A" to "F", the output is the corresponding integer in the range 0 to 15.

15. Write a subprogram to calculate a student's score on a 100-point true-false test. The input consists of two Boolean arrays of size 100: the answer key and the student's answers.

16. Assume that we have real arrays A and B, each containing 100 elements. Write subprograms for the following:

   *a. Copy B to A.
   *b. Copy the first 50 locations of B to the last 50 locations of A, that is, copy B[1–50] to A[51–100].
   *c. Copy B[17–23] to A[1–7].
   d. Copy B[First] through B[Last] to the first locations of A. Assume that First and Last are variables containing numbers in the range 1 to 100, with First ≤ Last.
   e. Copy the next six numbers, starting at the first nonzero number in B, into A[1–6]. You can assume that there is a nonzero number in B, located prior to or at location 95.
   f. Repeat (e), but copy six numbers or fewer. For example, if B[98] is the first nonzero number, you should copy only three numbers: B[98], B[99], and B[100]. If there are no nonzero numbers, don't copy any. Set a parameter to indicate how many were copied.
   g. Shift A one place to the right, setting A[1] to 0.
   h. Shift A two places to the left.
   i. Shift A two places to the right.
   j. Shift A in a given direction by a given amount. The parameters are A (the array), a char variable telling which direction to shift (value 'L' or 'R'), and an integer N telling how far to shift (assume N > 0).

17. A large data file contains the SAT scores for all the students in an incoming freshman class. The scores can range from 200 to 800.

   a. Write a program segment that counts how many students had each of the possible scores. What is a suitable type definition for the array of counters?
   b. Modify the code to also find which score occurred most frequently.

c. Give two ways to find the average score.

d. Modify part (a) to count scores in ranges of 10 points each: 200 to 209, 210 to 219, etc. Hint: Use integer division by 10.

e. Modify part (a) to count scores in the ranges 200 to 300, 301 to 400, . . . , 701 to 800.

18. a. Write a subprogram to interchange two integers A and B. Use this subprogram to interchange the elements in positions I and J of an integer array A.

b. Using the subprogram of part (a), write code to reverse the elements of an array A of five elements. For example, if A = (2, 4, 6, 8, 10), then the code should change A to (10, 8, 6, 4, 2). (Set this up so that elements 1 and 5 are interchanged followed by elements 2 and 4.)

c. Repeat part (b), but allow the number of elements to be N. Does N have to be odd? Hint: First do the specific cases where N = 51 and where N = 50.

19. a. Write code for scanning an array A and whenever A(I) > A(I+1) interchanging A(I) and A(I+1). If the array has N elements, how many comparisons should be made? What is the value of the last element of A after the algorithm has been performed?

b. Enclose your solution to part (a) in a loop that causes J to take on the values 1 through N − 1. Trace this algorithm using N = 5 and A = (1, 4, 5, 3, 2).

*20. Write a subprogram to compare two arrays A and B of N elements each to see if the arrays are identical. In other words, the subprogram should see if the Ith element of A is the same as the Ith element of B for all I from 1 to N. If the arrays are identical, the answer is true; otherwise, false. Hint: This can be viewed as a search problem.

21. Write a subprogram to check if each element of A occurs only once in A. The answer is true if each does and false if some element occurs more than once. Hint: This can be viewed as a search problem.

22. Write a subprogram to check if each element of A occurs at least once in an array B. Hint: This can be viewed as a search problem.

23. a. A is an array of N elements, where N is larger than 7. Write code to locate the largest element in positions 7, 8, up to N, and interchange it with the element in position 7.

b. Redo part (a), but instead of using element 7, make that position variable, perhaps J.

c. Enclose your solution to part (b) in a loop that causes J to take on the values 1 through N − 1. Trace this subprogram using N = 5 and A = (1, 4, 5, 3, 2).

24. Each record in a file contains a name and 12 monthly take-home pay figures. We can use this segment of code to read and print the file:

```
while not Eof(InputFile) do
  begin
    GetInput(InputFile, Name, Pay);
    DetailLine(Name, Pay)
  end   {while}
```

GetInput is a procedure that reads a name and 12 pay figures from the file.

DetailLine is a procedure that prints the data, with headings when appropriate. We assume that these procedures have already been written. (Note: For a complete program, we would have to add steps to open and close the file, initialize line and page counts, and so on. In this exercise we do not deal with these issues. See Exercise 25.)

Show how to modify this segment of code to do the following:

*a. Also print the total yearly take-home pay for each person.
  b. Find and print the name of the person who had the highest total take-home pay.
  c. Find the highest take-home pay for each of the twelve months. Hint: Use an array LargePay of size 12.
  d. Find who had the highest take-home pay in each month:

```
In month 1 xxxxxxxxxxxx had the largest pay - xxxxx.xx
                           etc.
```

  e. Modify part (d) to print messages like

```
In January xxxxxxxxxxxx had the largest pay - xxxxx.xx
                           etc.
```

Hint: Use a string array of size 12 containing the names of the months.

25. a. Write the GetInput procedure for Exercise 24 under the assumption that the file is a text file consisting of 13 lines for each person: name, January pay, and so on.
  b. Redo part (a) assuming that the file is of Pascal records each consisting of a name and 12 pay figures.
  c. Using either file description from part (a) or (b), write a complete program accomplishing everything outlined in Exercise 23.

26. Give test plans for the following exercises in this section.
  a. Exercise 3   b. Exercise 7(a)
  c. Exercise 7(b)   d. Exercise 7(c)
  e. Exercise 7(f)   f. Exercise 7(g)
  g. Exercise 7(h)   h. Exercise 16(d)
  i. Exercise 18(c)   j. Exercise 20
  k. Exercise 22

□
NOTES FOR SECTION 6-1

1. Turbo Pascal has a limited amount of memory space available, which places limits on the total size of all the arrays declared. What the exact limits are depends on the specific program. However, a few arrays each of size 1000, for example, will generally not exceed this limit.

6-2
□□□□□□
ARRAYS AND DATA STRUCTURES

In the previous section, we examined arrays in some detail, expanding the knowledge we had been gradually building over the previous three chapters. In that section, we placed a number of restrictions on the arrays under consideration: (1) the subscripts were integers; (2) the component type was integer, real, char, string, or a user-defined scalar type; and (3) we dealt (mostly) with one array at a time. In this section, we remove these restrictions and consider the important topic of **data structures**.

ARRAYS IN PASCAL

□ We begin with a more complete description of Pascal arrays. We can declare an array type using a declaration of the form

array[index-type] of <code>component-type</code>

As we have seen, a common form for "index-type" is a range of integers from 1 to some number greater than 1. However, there are other possibilities including these:[1]

    1. A subrange of the integers, such as

```
    2  .. 12
 -500  .. 500
```

    2. Either "boolean" or "char".

    3. A subrange of char, such as

```
'a' .. 'z'
'0' .. '9'
'A' .. 'J'
```

    4. A user-defined enumerated or subrange type, as illustrated by these examples:

```
type
   Suits = (Clubs, Diamonds, Hearts, Spades);
   ValidGrade = 0 .. 100;
   Days = (Sun, Mon, Tue, Wed, Thr, Fri, Sat);

   Distribution = array[Suits] of 0 .. 13;
   Summary = array[ValidGrade] of integer;
   HourArray = array[Mon .. Fri] of real;
```

We access an element of an array by giving the array name and the **subscript**, or **index**, in an expression of the form

array name[index]

The "index" can be any expression of the proper type. For example, suppose we declare these arrays, using the type definitions given above:

```
var
   GradeCount  : Summary;
   HandCount   : Distribution;
   Hours       : HourArray;
   LetterCount : array[char] of integer;
```

Then these are valid array references:

```
Hours[Mon]
GradeCount[73]
HandCount[Hearts]
LetterCount['w']
```

Moreover, if Score is an integer variable in the range 0 to 100, Today is a "Days" variable in the range Mon to Fri, and ThisCharacter is a char variable, then these are legal:

```
Hours[Today]
GradeCount[Score]
LetterCount[ThisCharacter]
```

In fact, we can use any legal expression of the proper type as a subscript.

The "**component type**" in the array declaration can be any legal type. This specifically includes arrays and records. We defer the consideration of "arrays of arrays" to the next chapter. However, we will consider arrays of records extensively in the remainder of this section.

□

DATA STRUCTURES

The term **data structure** refers to "structuring data." Thus, a data structure is a way of organizing data in a meaningful way. In this text, we have already seen numerous examples of data structures, including the following:

Strings. Turbo Pascal uses the string data type to organize a series of individual characters into a meaningful entity.

Records. Records are one of the most useful tools for structuring data. For example, we can organize information about a person (name, age, and so on) as a record with a field for each piece of information. A slightly different example occurred in the case study of Section 5-4, where we used a record to structure the two parts of a fraction: numerator and denominator.

Arrays. Arrays allow us to organize a large number of related items of the same type.

Files. Files provide two important services. Most people probably think first of the "long-term storage" aspect of files. However, they also provide a structuring of the data they store.

Most computer science curricula include at least one course whose primary topic is data structures. Thus, it is obvious that we cannot cover the entire topic in this section. However, we will indicate, primarily by examples, how arrays and records can be used in various combinations to organize data in meaningful ways.

□

PARALLEL ARRAYS AND ARRAYS OF RECORDS

Consider the following simple example. We wish to read the names and grades for 40 individuals and print the name of each person whose grade is larger than the average grade.

This is a slight extension of the program of Figure 6-1. We can solve the problem by modifying that program, as shown in Figure 6-5. The changes are shaded.

Notice especially the step that prints the name:

```
if Grades[I] > Average then
    Writeln(' ':3, Names[I])
```

If, for example, the third grade in the Grades array exceeds the average, then this will print the third name in the Names array. Because of the manner in which the

```
program PrintNames(Input, Output);
{
    Written by:  XXXXXXXXX  XX/XX/XX
       Purpose:  To read a list of names and grades (of a fixed length),
                 and print the names whose grades are greater than the
                 average.
}
const
  MaxIndex = 40;                      { size of grade array }
type
  String20    = string[20];
  NameArray   = array[1 .. MaxIndex] of String20;
  GradeArray  = array[1 .. MaxIndex] of integer;

var
  Names     : NameArray;              { list of names }
  Grades    : GradeArray;             { list of grades }
  I         : integer;                { loop control, and subscript }
  Sum       : integer;                { sum of grades }
  Average   : real;                   { average of grades }

begin

{***  Read the names and grades and find the sum.}

  Sum := 0;

  for I := 1 to MaxIndex do
    begin
      Write('Enter name  #', I:1, ': ');
      Readln(Names[I]);
      Write('Enter grade #', I:1, ': ');
      Readln(Grades[I]);
      Sum := Sum + Grades[I]
    end;  {for}

[***  Find and print the average.]

  Average := Sum / MaxIndex;
  Writeln;
  Writeln('The average is ', Average:1:2);

{***  Print names whose grades are larger than the average. }

  Writeln;
  Writeln('Names whose grades are larger than average:');

  for I := 1 to MaxIndex do
    begin
      if Grades[I] > Average then
        Writeln(' ':3, Names[I])
    end  {for}

end.
```

Figure 6-5 Parallel Arrays

names and grades were stored in the array, the third name corresponds to the third grade, and thus the program prints the correct name.

We say that the name and grade arrays are **parallel arrays**. As another example, we might have parallel arrays ClockNumber, Age, Sex, and Salary, each of size 50. We can think of these arrays as the columns of a table, as illustrated.

ClockNumber	Age	Sex	Salary
1149	25	M	12,500
1614	20	F	14,000
2319	35	F	17,250
1003	50	M	16,750
3914	39	M	22,000
⋮	⋮	⋮	⋮

Notice that, in the table, the arrays are parallel to each other (vertically).

Pascal, with its record structure, provides an alternative way to organize the data in our example program. Rather than using two parallel arrays Name and Grade, we might use a single array of 40 records, where each record has a name component and a grade component. Figure 6-6 illustrates the differences involved with this approach.

```
program PrintNames(Input, Output);
{
    Written by:  XXXXXXXXXX  XX/XX/XX
       Purpose:  To read a list of names and grades (of a fixed length),
                 and print the names whose grades are greater than the
                 average.
}
const
  MaxIndex = 40;                      { size of grade array }

type
  String20    = string[20];
  StudentRecord = record
              Name  : String20;
              Grade : integer
            end;
  StudentArray = array[1 .. MaxIndex] of StudentRecord;

var
  Student : StudentArray;             { list of names and grades }
  I       : integer;                  { loop control, and subscript }
  Sum     : integer;                  { sum of grades }
  Average : real;                     { average of grades }
```

Figure 6-6 Array of Records (Continued)

```
begin

{***  Read the names and grades and find the sum. }

  Sum := 0;

  for I := 1 to MaxIndex do
    begin
      Write('Enter name  #', I:1, ': ');
      Readln(Student[I].Name);
      Write('Enter grade #', I:1, ': ');
      Readln(Student[I].Grade);
      Sum := Sum + Student[I].Grade
    end;  {for}

{***  Find and print the average. }

  Average := Sum / MaxIndex;
  Writeln;
  Writeln('The average is ', Average:1:2);

{***  Print names whose grades are larger than the average. }
{***  For illustrative purposes, use 'with' statement for this loop. }

  Writeln;
  Writeln('Names whose grades are larger than average:');

  for I := 1 to MaxIndex do
    begin
      with Student[I] do
        if Grade > Average then        { that is, Student[I].Grade }
          Writeln(' ':3, Name)         { that is, Student[I].Name  }
    end   {for}

end.
```

Figure 6-6 Array of Records

Conceptually, parallel arrays and arrays of records are the same. We can visualize each in terms of a table, as illustrated earlier. For languages that do not provide a record structure, we are forced to use the parallel array idea. However, in Pascal we have a choice.

Many of the array-processing techniques we have learned can fruitfully be used in the context of tables (either as parallel arrays or as arrays of records). For example, Figures 6-7a and 6-7b each give code to locate a student in the data structure and tell his grade. The first assumes parallel arrays, and the second assumes an array of records. They both assume that the data has been read earlier in the program. The significant differences are shaded.

NOTE   As usual when there are two ways to accomplish a task, there are tradeoffs to be considered when choosing between parallel arrays and arrays of records. Fortunately, the thought processes involved in the two methods are similar. This is

```
{***  Read a name to search for. }

  Writeln;
  Write('Enter a name to search for: ');
  Readln(NameToFind);

{***  Locate name and print grade, or error message. }

  Found := false;
  I := 1;

  while (I <= MaxIndex) and (not Found) do
    begin
      if Names[I] = NameToFind then
        Found := true
      else
        I := I + 1
    end;   {while}

  if Found then
    Writeln('The grade is ', Grades[I]:1)
  else
    Writeln('Name not found.')
```

Figure 6-7a   Searching Parallel Arrays

```
{***  Read a name to search for. }

  Writeln;
  Write('Enter a name to search for: ');
  Readln(NameToFind);

{***  Locate name and print grade, or error message. }

  Found := false;
  I := 1;

  while (I <= MaxIndex) and (not Found) do
    begin
      if Student[I].Name = NameToFind then
        Found := true
      else
        I := I + 1
    end;   {while}

  if Found then
    Writeln('The grade is ', Student[I].Grade:1)
  else
    Writeln('Name not found.')
```

Figure 6-7b   Searching an Array of Records

illustrated by the small number of differences between Figure 6-7a and Figure 6-7b.

Generally, the array of records more closely matches our usual notion of a table as a set of rows, each row describing one entity. This is a plus for the array of records method. Using parallel arrays, it is up to the programmer to tie together the related data.

On the other hand, suppose we modified the code in Figures 6-7a and 6-7b as follows: Write a procedure which finds the subscript of a given name. Using parallel arrays, we would pass the name array to the procedure. The same procedure could be used in other programs with arrays of names. Using the array of records representation, we would have to pass in the entire data structure (the array of records called student). The procedure would not be usable (without some changes) in another program needing a procedure to locate a name in an array. (In addition, the procedure could inadvertently modify a part of the data structure totally unrelated to its purpose of looking for a name.)

□ **RECORDS CONTAINING ARRAYS**

In defining a record data type, we are allowed to use an array as one of the fields of the record. To illustrate this, we will design a program that reads payroll data from a file and prints a report. For each person, the data consists of these components:

Name

Pay rate

Hours worked each of 7 days (Sunday through Saturday)

The basic logic of the program will involve repeating these steps for each employee:

read the data
calculate the total hours
calculate the pay
print the name and pay

An appropriate data structure involves several of the ideas developed in this section:

```
type
  String20      = string[20];
  DaysOfWeek    = (Sun, Mon, Tue, Wed, Thr, Fri, Sat);
  HourArray     = array[DaysOfWeek] of real;
  WorkerRecord  =
    record
      Name      : String20;
      PayRate   : real;
      Hours     : HourArray
    end;
  WorkerFile    = file of WorkerRecord;

var
  Worker        : WorkerRecord;          { individual's data }
  MasterFile    : WorkerFile;            { master worker file }
```

Leaving for later the details of opening and closing files, we can write the body of the main program as

```
while not Eof(MasterFile) do
  begin
    Read(MasterFile, Worker);
    TotalHours := TotalFn(Worker.Hours);
    Pay := Worker.PayRate * TotalHours;
    DetailLine(Worker.Name, Pay)
  end;   {while}
```

We have chosen to use a function to calculate the total hours, passing it the Hours array portion of the Worker record as its parameter. (Its parameter is of type HourArray.) We have also chosen to use a procedure to print the output. We can begin with a stub version, later adding refinements such as printing headers, etc.

The entire program is presented in Figure 6-8. Of special interest is the TotalFn function. It adds the weekday hours; any in excess of 40 are scaled by a factor of 1.5 ("time and a half"). Weekend hours are "double time," reflected in the scaling factor of 2.0. Notice the use of

```
for Day := Mon to Fri
```

to loop through the five weekdays (Monday through Friday), and of

```
HourList[Day]
```

to refer to the array elements.

NOTE   An array such as HourList, which uses an enumerated type for its subscripts, raises an interesting issue. With integer subscripts, we are used to expressions such as

```
A[I+1]
A[I-1]
```

To do a similar thing with enumerated types, we would have to use the functions Succ and Pred. For example, if Day has the value Wed, then

```
HourList[Succ(Day)]
```

would refer to the hour for Thursday, and

```
HourList[Pred(Day)]
```

to the hours for Tuesday.

We use the OpenRead procedure discussed in Chapter 5 to handle the details of opening the file.

We now consider an important data structure with an entirely different flavor. In dealing with arrays in the preceding section, we frequently maintained a count of how many values were in the array. We used a separate variable for that purpose.

```
program PayReport(Input, Output);
{
     Written by:     XXXXXXXXX  XX/XX/XX
        Purpose:     To read data from a payroll file, and print a pay
                     report.
  Functions used:    TotalFn to find the total hours, adjusted for overtime
                     rules.
 Procedures used:    OpenRead to open the master file.
                     DetailLine to print a line of the report.
}
type
   String20      = string[20];
   DaysOfWeek    = (Sun, Mon, Tue, Wed, Thr, Fri, Sat);
   HourArray     = array[DaysOfWeek] of real;
   WorkerRecord =
     record
       Name      : String20;
       PayRate   : real;
       Hours     : HourArray
     end;
   WorkerFile    = file of WorkerRecord;

var
   Worker        : WorkerRecord;          { individual's data }
   MasterFile    : WorkerFile;            { master worker file }
   TotalHours    : real;                  { total hours for week }
   Pay           : real;                  { pay for week }


function TotalFn(HourList : HourArray) : real;
{
     Written by:     XXXXXXXXX  XX/XX/XX
        Purpose:     To add up all the hours, adjusting for double time
                     (for weekends), and time and a half (for over 40 hours
                     during regular week).
     Parameters:     HourList - input, array of hours for week
}
var
   Day           : DaysOfWeek;            { loop control and subscript }
   Total         : real;                  { local variable for total }

begin  {TotalFn}

{*** Total weekday hours. }

   Total := 0;

   for Day := Mon to Fri do
```

Figure 6-8 Record Containing an Array (Continued)

```
        begin
          Total := Total + HourList[Day]
        end;   {for}

{*** Adjust for time and a half (over 40 hours). }

     if Total > 40 then
        Total := 40 + (Total - 40) * 1.5;

{*** Add in weekend at double time. }

     Total := Total + 2 * (HourList[Sun] + HourList[Sat]);

{*** Send answer back. }

     TotalFn := Total
   end;    {TotalFn}
```

{*function Exists, as shown in Appendix E, is inserted here*}

{*procedure OpenRead, as shown in Appendix E, is inserted here, with text type changed to WorkerFile*}

```
procedure DetailLine(Name : String20; Pay : real);
begin  {DetailLine - stub version; full version left as exercise}
   Writeln(Name, ' ', Pay:1:2)
end;   {DetailLine}

begin   {PayReport}

{*** Open file. }

   OpenRead (MasterFile);

{*** Read records and process pay report. }

   while not Eof(MasterFile) do
     begin
       Read(MasterFile, Worker);
       TotalHours := TotalFn(Worker.Hours);
       Pay := Worker.PayRate * TotalHours;
       DetailLine(Worker.Name, Pay)
     end;   {while}

{*** Close file and terminate. }

   Close(MasterFile);
   Writeln;
   Writeln('PayReport program is terminating.')
 end.
```

Figure 6-8   Record Containing an Array

Another approach that is sometimes used associates the array size more closely with the array, as indicated by these data declarations:

```
const
  EndOfData   = -1;                    { terminates input }
  MaxSize     = 50;                    { maximum size of array }

type
  IntegerList =
    record
      Len     : integer;                         { length of list }
      Values  : array[1 .. MaxSize] of integer   { values in list }
    end;
```

When we pass a parameter of type IntegerList to a subprogram, its current length (Len) automatically goes along. We do not have to remember to pass it as a separate parameter.

NOTE   In a subprogram that has this type of variable as a parameter, we might wish to use the Pascal "with" statement. See Figure 6-9.

☐
OTHER COMBINATIONS

As we indicated earlier, our intention here is simply to suggest some data structuring ideas. For our final example, we consider a combination of ideas from the previous two subsections. We will have an array of records, where each record contains an array. Specifically, we will deal with an array of student records, where each student record has these components:

Name
4 test grades
Final exam grade
10 program grades
Final average
Letter grade

We define our data structure as follows:

```
const
  MaxStudents = 50;

type
  String20 = string[20];
  TestArray = array[1 .. 4] of integer;
  ProgramArray = array[1 .. 10] of integer;
  StudentRecord =
    record
      Name     : String20;
      TestList : TestArray;
      Exam     : integer;
      ProgList : ProgramArray;
      Average  : real;
      Letter   : char
    end;
  StudentList = array[1 .. MaxStudents] of StudentRecord;

var
  Student      : StudentList;     { array of student records }
```

```
procedure AddToEnd(var List : IntegerList; Number : integer;
                   var OK : boolean);
{
       Written by:  XXXXXXXXX  XX/XX/XX
          Purpose:  To add a number to the end of a list, if possible.
       Parameters:  List - update, the list to add to
                    Number - input, the number to add
                    OK - output, whether or not the list was full
      Globals used:  MaxSize - global constant telling maximum size of list
}
begin  {AddToEnd}
  with List do
    begin
      if Len = MaxSize then
        OK := false
      else
        begin
          OK := true;
          Len := Len + 1;
          Values[Len] := Number
        end  {if}
    end  {with}
end;  {AddToEnd}
```

Figure 6-9   Keeping the Actual Size with an Array

The program in Figure 6-10 has three major steps:

   1. Read the data for the class: How many students? How many tests so far? How many programs so far? And what is the student list?

   2. Add the scores for a test to each student's record.

   3. Rewrite the data to the same files.

Besides illustrating data structures, the program illustrates one approach to maintaining data on files over a period of time. We can read the entire set of data from the file into memory, allow the user to perform a number of steps that modify the data in various ways, then write the data back to the file. (This is the approach used by the Turbo Pascal editor in working with the files containing your programs.) One difficulty arises in this example because we have two different types of data. First, we have the list of student records, which can be stored using a file declared as "file of StudentRecord." Second, we have the "control" information: how many students, how many tests, how many programs? There are a number of ways to approach this problem. The program illustrates one possibility, using a **control file** to store control information about the **data file**. The data file has the data for the students in the class, and the control file has the information about the number of students, tests, and programs. (Chapter 11, on files, will indicate other file-related ideas.)

```
program EnterTest(Input, Output);
{
        Written by:  XXXXXXXXX  XX/XX/XX
           Purpose:  To allow the user to enter test scores for the class.
   Procedures used:  OpenFiles to open the files.
                     ReadFiles to read the files into the program data
                        structure.
                     WriteFiles to write the program data structures
                        back to the files.
                     GetValidScore to obtain a score in the range 0 to 100.
}
const
   MaxStudents  = 50;                              { limit on array size }

type
   String20     = string[20];
   TestArray    = array[1 .. 4] of integer;
   ProgramArray = array[1 .. 10] of integer;
   StudentRecord =
     record
       Name     : String20;
       TestList : TestArray;
       Exam     : integer;
       ProgList : ProgramArray;
       Average  : real;
       Letter   : char
     end;
   ControlRecord =
     record
       NStudents : integer;
       NTests    : integer;
       NPrograms : integer
     end;
   StudentList  = array[1 .. MaxStudents] of StudentRecord;
   StudentFileType = file of StudentRecord;
   ControlFileType = file of ControlRecord;

var
   Student     : StudentList;           { array of students }
   Control     : ControlRecord;         { control information }
   StudentFile : StudentFileType;       { master student file }
   ControlFile : ControlFileType;       { control file }
   I           : integer;               { loop control }


procedure OpenFiles(var Master : StudentFileType;
                    var ControlFile : ControlFileType);
begin   {OpenFiles - stub version; full version left as exercise}
   Assign(Master, 'STUDENT.DAT');
   ReSet(Master);
   Assign(ControlFile, 'STUDENT.CTR');
   ReSet(ControlFile)
end;   {OpenFiles}
```

Figure 6-10   Array of Records Containing Arrays (Continued)

```
procedure GetValidScore(var Score : integer);
begin  {GetValidScore - stub version; full version left as exercise}
  Readln(Score)
end;  {GetValidScore}


procedure ReadFiles(var StudentFile : StudentFileType;
                    var ControlFile : ControlFileType;
                    var Student: StudentList;
                    var Control : ControlRecord);

{
     Written by:  XXXXXXXXX  XX/XX/XX
        Purpose:  To read the data from the control and student files
                  into the internal data structure.
     Parameters:  StudentFile - the file designator for the student file
                  ControlFile - the file designator for the control file
                  Student - output, the array of student records
                  Control - output, the control record
}
var
  I        : integer;                          { loop control }

begin  {ReadFiles}
  Read(ControlFile, Control);

  for I := 1 to Control.NStudents do
    begin
      Read(StudentFile, Student[I])
    end; {for}

end;  {ReadFiles}

procedure WriteFiles(var StudentFile : StudentFileType;
                     var ControlFile : ControlFileType;
                     Student : StudentList;
                     Control : ControlRecord);
{
     Written by:  XXXXXXXXX  XX/XX/XX
        Purpose:  To write the data from the internal data structures
                  back to the original files.
     Parameters:  StudentFile - the file designator for the student file
                  ControlFile - the file designator for the control file
                  Student - input, the array of student records
                  Control - input, the control record
}
var
  I        : integer;                          { loop control }

begin  {WriteFiles}
  Rewrite(ControlFile);
  Rewrite(StudentFile);
  Write(ControlFile, Control);

  for I := 1 to Control.NStudents do
```

Figure 6-10 Array of Records Containing Arrays (Continued)

```
      begin
        Write(StudentFile, Student[I])
      end; {for}

  end;  {WriteFiles}


begin  {EnterTest}

{*** Open files and read the data. }

  OpenFiles(StudentFile, ControlFile);
  ReadFiles(StudentFile, ControlFile, Student, Control);

{*** See if another test can be entered. If so, print each student
     name and read the test score. }

  if Control.NTests >= 4 then
    Writeln('There have already been 4 tests.')
  else
    begin
      Control.NTests := Control.Ntests + 1;

      for I := 1 to Control.NStudents do
        begin
          with Student[I] do
            begin
              Write('Score for ', Name, ': ');
              GetValidScore(TestList[Control.Ntests])
            end   {with}
        end   {for}

    end;   {if}

{*** Write the resulting data structure back to the files. }

  WriteFiles(StudentFile, ControlFile, Student, Control);

{*** Close files and terminate. }

  Close(StudentFile);
  Close(ControlFile);

  Writeln;
  Writeln('EnterTest program is terminating.')
end.
```

Figure 6-10   Array of Records Containing Arrays

TESTING   □   The comments presented in Section 6.1 on testing involving arrays should be reviewed. In addition, some of the topics covered in this section raise some new testing issues.

For example, consider a program that reads an array of student records from a file, allows the user to make a series of changes, then writes the records back to the file. Suppose that among the possible changes to the data are these:

Delete a student
Add a student
Change a grade

In this type of program, we might want to test the relationship of various steps performed in sequence. This is sometimes called **sequence testing** or **combination testing**. For example, these are some important tests:

- delete a name, then try to delete the same name again
- delete a name, do some other steps, then add the same name
- try to add the same name twice in a row
- change a test, then later change it again for the same person
- add a name, change a test, and delete the name
- add enough names to "overflow" the array
- with the array full, try to add a name that is already there
- delete all names, then add a name

In this type of problem, the results of a specific step depend on what has come before. The rules for determining the important test sequences, in a context such as this, are not as precise as those for boundary or class testing considered earlier. Writing a good test plan is always a creative process, although we can give some general guidelines. Testing for this type of problem involves even more creativity than those we have been dealing with earlier.

□
DPT
   1. The most important defensive programming tip, perhaps, is an offensive programming tip: Choose your data structures wisely. Data structures that adequately reflect the "real world situation" will be much easier to understand as you develop your program. Hastily chosen data structures can lead to a great amount of frustration later. Carefully chosen data structures can make the program easier to write and easier to understand.

   2. Remember that subscripts are necessary to access an element of an array. For example, in the data structures used in Figure 6-10, the reference

```
Student[5]
```

would refer to the fifth student record. Within that record,

```
Student[5].TestList[3]
```

would refer to that student's third test. To access the fifth student's third test, we need both subscripts in the form indicated by the example.

   3. The subscript must be an expression of the proper type. For example, if we declare:

```
type
   Days = (Sun, Mon, Tue, Wed, Thr, Fri, Sat);

var
   Hours = array[Days] of real;
```

then Hours[1] makes no sense, but Hours[Sun] does.

4. Don't forget to use range checking (in Turbo, the {$R+} compiler directive) during development.

5. When we define complex data structures involving records, it is a good idea to use named data types for each component of the record. For example, use

```
type
   String20 = string[20];
   TestArray = array[1 .. 5] of integer;
   StudentRecord =
      record
         Name : String20;
         Test : TestArray
      end;
```

This allows us to pass individual components, if necessary or convenient, as parameters to subprograms.

6. All other tips relating to arrays (especially in Sections 3-2 and 6-1) and to records (Sections 5-2 to 5-4) must be kept in mind when dealing with combinations of these structures.

■■■■■■
REVIEW

Terms and concepts	data structures	control file
	subscript	data file
	index type	sequence testing
	component type	combination testing
	parallel array	

Pascal syntax

1. Index type for an array declaration can be:
a. Subrange of integers, e.g., 1 .. 50 or −3 .. 5
b. Boolean
c. Char
d. Subrange of char, e.g., 'a' .. 'z'
e. User-defined enumerated type or subrange type, e.g. Days or Mon .. Fri

2. Array reference : *array-name*[*index*]

Data structure examples

1. Strings

2. Records

3. Arrays

4. Files

5. Parallel arrays

6. Arrays of records

7. Records containing arrays

8. Other combinations, e.g., arrays of records, where each record contains an array

Sequence (combination testing); for example:

> add same name twice
> delete name, then add back
> change same value twice
>   etc.

DPT

1. Choose data structures carefully.

2. Use subscripts to access array elements, e.g., Student[5].Test[3].

3. Subscript must be of the proper type.

4. Use the {$R+} directive.

5. Use named data types for record components.

EXERCISES

1. Define data structures for each of the following. Give the type and var declarations and show how to access each part of the data structure. (For example, Student.Grade[I], etc.)

   a. One entry for a mailing list: name, address, expiration date, and a special eight-character code.
   b. Data for a family consisting of a husband, wife, and up to five children. Include name and age for each person.
   *c. A list of rainfall figures for one year for one state. The data consists of the state name and 12 monthly rainfall figures.
   *d. Repeat part (c), but store the data for all 50 states at once.
   e. Repeat part (d), but simultaneously store the data for seven years. For each year, the data consists of the year (e.g., 1992) and the data for the 50 states.
   f. A table containing data for up to 100 employees: name, social security number, and last year's salary.
   *g. A polynomial having up to 20 terms, each consisting of a real coefficient and an integer exponent.
   *h. An answer key for a multiple-choice test containing up to 100 questions. Each question has possible answers a, b, c, d, or e, and has a point value assigned to it.
   i. A student's answer sheet for the test described in part (h).
   *j. An array to contain the characters '0', '1', . . . , '9'. The array should be set up in such a way that the element with subscript 5 contains '5', and so on. Also give the assignments to initialize the array.
   *k. An array called Vowel, indexed by capital letters 'A' through 'Z', to make it easy to answer the question, "Is this capital letter a vowel?" For example, Vowel['T'] would be false. Also give the assignments to initialize the array.

2. The person designing the data structure for a class list has chosen to use a group of parallel arrays: Name, Test1, Test2, Test3, Test4, Test5, Test6, Exam, Average, and Letter. Name[I] contains the name of the Ith student, Test1[I] her score on the first test, and so on.

   Suppose that the names, test grades, and exam grades have already been read and that there are N students. Write segments of Pascal code to do the following:

*a. Compute the values for the Average array.

*b. Print the names of all students who received the highest average. Notice that there may be several tied for highest.

c. Print the highest and lowest score for each test.

d. Compute the average score for each test.

e. Assuming that the function LetterGrade calculates a letter grade, given a numeric average, write code to calculate the values for the Letter array.

3. Repeat Exercise 2, but assume that students can withdraw. When they do, the information remains in the arrays; however, their letter grade is given the value 'W'.

    a–d. Repeat parts (a) to (d) of Exercise 2, but ignore all students who have withdrawn.

    *e. Write code to count the number of students who have withdrawn and print the percentage of withdrawals.

    f. Write code that, given a student name, will locate that student and mark him as withdrawn. If the student has already withdrawn or if the name is not present, print error messages.

*4. Repeat Exercise 2 with a different choice for the data structure. Use an array of records, each record having these fields: name, an array of six test scores, exam score, final average, and letter grade.

5. Was there any significant advantage to either of the data structures in Exercises 2 and 4? Which strategy would be more appropriate if there were three tests and 14 weekly quizzes? Which would be better if there were variables indicating how many scores have been entered so far?

6. In this exercise, we explore three possible data structures to represent a list of campers and the cabins to which they are assigned. There are 20 cabins, with names such as "BlackHawk," "Wigwam," and so on. For each data structure, we will use an array of records, one record per camper. The record will have the camper's name and a representation of the cabin. The differences will be in how we represent the cabin.

    Data structure No. 1: the cabin is given by a string variable containing the name of the cabin.

    Data structure No. 2: the cabin is an integer code representing the cabin number.

    Data structure No. 3: the cabin is a user-defined scalar type defined in the form CabinType = (BlackHawk, Wigwam, . . .).

    For each part of the exercise, give code to solve the problem for each data structure. (You may need to define additional data, such as printname arrays; if so, describe them in words.)

a. Print a list of campers: name and cabin name.

b. Read a camper's name and print his or her cabin name (or an error message).

c. For each cabin, print the cabin name and a count of the campers in the cabin.

d. Read a name and cabin name for a camper to be added to the list. Make sure the cabin name is one of those allowed and that the camper's name is not a duplicate.

7. a. Write a program that declares an array CountLetter indexed by the range type 'A' .. 'Z'. It should initialize the array to contain all zeros, then read

a series of single-character inputs from the user. The array should be used to count how many of each letter ('A' to 'Z') are input. Output consists of a series of lines such as

```
B was entered 3 times
```

Skip any for which the count was 0.

b. Extend part (a) to include all characters. Hint: The index type is "char" and a loop

```
for I := Chr(0) to Chr(255)
```

can be used to move through the array.

c. Extend part (a) to read strings rather than single characters. Hint: For a string InputString, InputString[I] is the Ith character, and Length(Input-String) uses the built-in Length function to determine how many characters are in InputString.

8. Suppose that an array of 100 records contains data for NEmpl employees. Each record contains the employee number, name, sales, age, sex, department, and group. Give segments of code for the following. Assume that the data has been read earlier in the program.

*a. Give the appropriate declarations to declare the array.

*b. There are 10 groups. Find the total sales for each of the 10 groups, putting the answers in an array of size 10. Then read an employee number and new sales amount; add this amount to that employee's sales figure and to the total for each group.

c. Suppose that an array ValidDepartment of size 17 contains a list of all the valid department codes. Print the employee number of all employees whose department entry is presently invalid.

d. Add a new employee to the end of the list. Check for these errors: invalid department code, employee number already in use, and list full.

e. Count how many are in the following age groups: under 20, 20 to 29, 30 to 39, 40 to 49, 50 to 59, 60 or over. Use an array of counters.

f. Count how many are in each department. Hint: The ValidDepartment array of part (c) can be used to convert a valid department name to a number from 1 to 17.

9. a. Write a program to interactively build an array of records of the form: father's name, mother's name, number of children, and children's names (array of up to 8). At the end, print the array and write it to a file.

b. Write a program to read the file created in part (a) into an array, and print the array on the terminal.

10. Do the following for the example of Figure 6-8:

a. Write the DetailLine procedure.

b. Write a program to create the file used by the program. It should read data from an appropriate text file, check for errors in the data, and write it to the file of records.

11. Do the following for the example of Figure 6-10:

a. Write a program to create the files used by the program. At the beginning of the semester, the number of tests and programs is 0. Thus, the program should simply read a series of names and write the appropriate values to the data and control files.

b. Write the open-files procedure. It should ask the user for a "base name" and use that to build the file names. For example, if the user enters HIST305, the file names would be HIST305.DAT and HIST305.CTR. The procedure should print a message if the files do not exist. Hint: Use an Exists function as shown in Appendix E. You may also wish to imitate the logic of the OpenRead procedure of Appendix E.

c. Write the GetValidScores procedure.

d. Write a program to dump the data in the files. It should print the control record, then each student record. For each student, print all four test scores and all 10 program scores, even if not all have been entered yet.

Note: Unless the create program put meaningful data (such as 0) in the fields of the record, the dump program may show until later programs fill in the data.

e. Describe what additional programs would be needed to make the system useful to an instructor. Do you think it would be better to have a separate program for each task or to use a single menu-driven program with each task an option on the menu?

*12. One very useful data structure in various applications is called a *stack*. A stack is a list where items are inserted and removed from one end of the list only. The term is suggestive of a stack of cafeteria trays or a stack of papers in an "in" box. A stack has the *last in first out* property. The item removed from a stack is always the last one that was placed on the stack.

One way to implement a stack of integers is as a record defined by

```
type
  Stack =
    record
      Top : integer;
      Values : array[1 .. MaxIndex] of integer
    end;
```

"Top" contains the subscript of the top element in the stack. It is 0 for an empty stack, increases by 1 each time an item is added to the stack, and decreases by 1 each time an item is removed. Observe that this data structure is similar to the one discussed on page 459.

Write the following subprograms:

a. Procedure CreateEmpty(var S : Stack). It causes S to be an empty stack by setting S.Top to 0.

b. Function IsEmpty(S : Stack): Boolean. It sees if S is empty.

c. Procedure Push(var S : Stack; Item : integer; var Overflow : boolean). It "pushes" an item on the stack. "Overflow" indicates whether the push succeeded. If there was no more room on the stack, it is set to true, otherwise to false.

d. Procedure Pop(var S : Stack; var Item : integer; var Underflow : Boolean). It "pops" an item from the stack, placing its value into the variable Item. Underflow is set true if there was no item on the stack, otherwise false.

*13. Using the stack operations defined in Exercise 12, write a program to reverse a series of integer inputs. Push each input on the stack, then pop each item from the stack.

14. Define subprograms to perform various operations on lists of integers. Use the data structure:

```
type
  Integerlist =
    record
      Length : integer;
      Values : array[1 .. MaxIndex] of integer
    end;
```

For example,

$$\text{Length} = 3$$
$$\text{Values} = 6, 7, 9$$

would represent a list of three integers.

  a. Read a list of integers.

*b. Print a list, eight numbers per line.

  c. Given a list and a value, place the value on the end of the list if it is positive, otherwise on the front of the list. Assume there is room for it.

*d. Concatenate two lists. For example, consider

A.Length = 3	B.Length = 2
A.Values = 6, 7, 9	B.Values = 1, 8

If C is the answer, it would be

$$\text{C.Length} = 5$$
$$\text{C.Values} = 6, 7, 9, 1, 8$$

Assume that A.Len + B.Len ≤ MaxIndex.

  e. Repeat part (d) without the assumption. The result should be truncated to the first MaxIndex values.

  f. Extract a sublist. The parameters are:

    List : a list

    Posn : starting position for the sublist

    Len : the length of sublist desired

    Sublist : the resulting sublist.

Assume that Posn and Len are such that the desired sublist is entirely contained within the list and that Len ≥ 0.
The original list is unchanged.

  g. Repeat part (f), but without the assumptions on Posn and Len. If Posn < 1, Posn > List.Length, or if Len < 0, the resulting list should be empty. If Posn lies within the list and Len would go beyond the end, stop at the end. (For a list of length 5 with Posn = 4 and Length = 15, the resulting list would have only the fourth and fifth values of the original list.)

  h. Repeat part (f), but modify the original list by removing the extracted sublist.

  i. Insert a list into a given position "Posn" in another list. Assume that the position is between 1 and the length of the list into which it is being inserted.

  j. Repeat part (i), but without the assumption. If Posn < 1, place the new list at the front of the other; if Posn > the length of the list, place the new list at the end.

15. Suppose we have an array of up to 75 records for choir members. Among the fields are name, voice part, and range (e.g., 'John Smith', bass, high) would denote a "first bass," that is a bass with a higher range than a "second bass." The voice parts are soprano, alto, tenor, and bass; the ranges are high and low. There are Number members in the choir at present. Give code for each of the following; use subprograms if appropriate. Except for part (c), assume that the data has already been read.

   *a. Give the necessary declarations for the array.
   *b. Declare and initialize "printname" arrays for the voice part and range. Using these, print a list of the choir.
   c. Read values for the array from the terminal.
   d. What percentage of the choir is soprano?
   e. What percentage of the tenors are "first tenors" (high range)?
   f. Given a name, tell his or her voice part and range.
   g. Declare an array of four counters indexed by the voice part data type. Use this array to count the number of each voice part.

16. A file contains 50 records, each consisting of the name of a state and 12 monthly rainfall figures. Give code for the following:

   a. Give appropriate declarations [see Exercises 1(c) and 1(d)].
   b. Read the file into an array of size 50.
   c. Rewrite the array to the file.
   d. Given the name of a month, find the average rainfall for that month.
   e. Given the name of a state, find which month had the largest rainfall.
   f. Find the total rainfall for each state.
   g. Find which state had the highest total rainfall. If there were ties, print all the states with the highest total.

*17. a. Using the random-number generator, write a function with two parameters: Range and Previous. The function should generate an integer in the range 1 .. Range, with the generated number not equal to Previous.
   b. Repeat part (a), but with Range, Previous1, and Previous2. The number generated should not equal either Previous1 or Previous2.
   c. Expand on this idea by having an array Previous containing N different values. The number generated should not equal any of the values in the array. Note: In order to be assured of eventual success, assume that N < Range.

18. One of the authors was given a chance to win a prize at a movie rental store. The game slip had nine hidden numbers. The goal was to uncover any three of the nine numbers; if the total was 15 or more, the author would win the prize.

   After failing to win, your author proceeded to uncover all nine numbers. They were 2, 9, 2, 5, 8, 9, 8, 6, and 5. What was the probability that the author would lose? To answer this, write a function of type win or lose that simulates one play of the game. Invoke the function 5000 times, counting how many are losses.

   Hint: For the function, use an array of size 9 containing the nine values. Generate three different numbers in the range 1 .. 9, and add those three array elements. The functions written in Exercises 17(a) and 17(b) can prove helpful. You may wish to allow the user to enter the values for the array to make the game more general.

19. a. One way to simulate shuffling a deck of 52 cards is to generate random numbers in the range 1 .. 52, making sure that each number is different from all those that came before. Using the function of Exercise 17(c), write a procedure to generate an array of size 52, containing the numbers 1 to 52 shuffled.

   b. The problem with the approach in part (a) is that toward the end it may take quite some time to find a number that does not duplicate some earlier number. A better approach is this. Put the numbers 1 to 52 in the array. Then generate 52 random numbers in the range 1 .. 52. If Num is the Ith number generated, swap A[I] with A[Num]. Write a procedure to do this.

   c. Write a program to compare the times for the two methods. See Appendix E for a Turbo Pascal procedure to print the current time. To obtain a meaningful test, you may want to invoke each procedure a number of times in a loop.

20. We can use the shuffling procedure of Exercise 19, suitably modified, to simulate the following experiment: Shuffle five cards, numbered from 1 to 5, into random order, then count how many cards are in their ''correct'' position. For example, if the cards are in the order 5, 2, 4, 1, and 3, then the 2 is in the correct position. For the order 1, 5, 3, 2, and 4, both the 1 and the 3 are in the correct position.

   a. On the average, how many would we expect to be in the correct position? To answer this, write a program to simulate the experiment a large number of times.

   b. Suppose there were 10 cards, numbered 1 to 10. On the average, how many would we expect to be in the correct position?

   c. Suppose there were 52 cards, numbered 1 to 52. On the average, how many would we expect to be in the correct position?

□
NOTES FOR SECTION 6-2

1. Strictly speaking, a declaration such as

```
array[integer] of . . .
```

is also allowed. However, this array is too large to fit in the Turbo Pascal memory allocation. In fact, some subranges of the integers are also too large.

How large is "too large" depends on how many other variables are declared in the program.

A similar comment would apply for other versions of Pascal.

6-3
□□□□□□
SORTING AND SEARCHING

Two important applications involving arrays are **searching** and **sorting**. The first involves looking for a specific value in an array and reporting its location (subscript). If it is not found, that fact should also be reported. The second application involves arranging the elements of an array in increasing or decreasing order. For simplicity, we will imagine that the arrays are integer arrays. However, the techniques developed will apply to any data type for which order comparisons make sense. This specifically includes integers, real, strings, and user-defined scalar types.

For each application, we present two solutions. The first will be easier to understand, and the second will be faster. For very small arrays, speed may not be important. However, for large arrays, it becomes important, so it is valuable to examine solutions that are faster than the first "naive" solution we may devise.

For this and the other applications, let us assume we are dealing with an integer array A with subscripts ranging from 1 to a constant MaxIndex. We also assume that the array actually contains N values, with $0 \leq N \leq$ MaxIndex.

In searching problems, we are also given a value to look for in the array. The **linear search** is the one we have already seen. We simply start at the first element A[1] and proceed through the array until one of two conditions occurs:

1. We reach the end of the portion of the array containing values.

2. We find the value we are looking for.

As we learned in Section 6-1, we have to take some care in writing the condition for the loop. See Figure 6-11 for a subprogram that accomplishes the search.

There are actually two "answers" from this subprogram. They answer the questions: (1) Is the value present? (2) If so, in what location? However, by setting

```
function Search(A : IntegerArray; Key, N :  integer) : integer;
{
    Written by:   XXXXXXXXX  XX/XX/XX
        Purpose:  To locate a given value in an array. The answer is
                  the subscript where found (0 if not found).
     Parameters:  A - input, the array to search in
                  Key - input, the value to search for
                  N - input, the portion of the array in use
}
var
  Found     : boolean;                   { used to indicate success }
  I         : integer;                   { loop control and subscript }

begin  {Search}
  Found := false;                        { assume not there as default }
  I := 1;

  while (I <= N) and (not Found) do
    begin
      if A[I] = Key then
        Found := true
      else
        I := I + 1
    end;  {while}

  if Found then
    Search := I
  else
    Search := 0
end;  {Search}
```

Figure 6-11 Linear Search of an Array

the location to 0 if the value is not found, we can convey the answer to both questions in a single variable.

COMMENT As a general rule of program design, using "trickery" to convey two answers as if there were only one is not good programming style.

However, using a 0 to indicate "not found" is widely used and thoroughly understood within the computer science community. Thus, this use is generally accepted.

By making a slight modification to the linear search, we can simplify it a good deal. Its major complexity arises from not knowing whether we will find the value in the array. Suppose, before we enter the loop, we do an assignment

```
A[N + 1] := Value;
```

Now, we can write our loop as

```
I := 1;
while A[I] <> Value do
  begin
    I := I + 1
  end;  {while}
```

Because we have placed the value into the array, we know it is there, so we don't need the test I <= N in the "while" condition. After the loop, we can write

```
if I = N + 1 then
   Location := 0
else
   Location := I
```

If I is N + 1, then the only occurrence of the value was the one we put in, so we set Location to 0 to show that the value was not in the original array.

CAUTION

If N = MaxIndex, the size of the array, this will not work. The rest of our program must treat the array such that N always stays less than MaxIndex.

Some people always declare arrays to be one larger than they really need, so that techniques such as this will always work. For example, the declaration

```
array[1 .. 51] of integer
```

might be used for an array to store up to 50 (*not* 51) student grades.

Efficiency. To discuss the **efficiency** (speed) of the linear search algorithm of Figure 6-11, we ask this question:

On the average, how many passes through the loop will be required?

474 □ *ONE-DIMENSIONAL ARRAYS*

Intuitively, we can reason as follows. We might get lucky and find the value at A[1], requiring one pass. Or it might require two, three, or four passes. At worst, it will require N passes. On average, we would expect about N/2 (higher if many are not found).

Computer scientists describe this by saying that the linear search has average time **O**(N) (read as "**order** N" or "**big oh** of N"). Roughly speaking, this means that the time will be "approximately proportional to N." If the array size doubles, so will the average time for the search.

□

BINARY SEARCH

If the array is in order, we can use a more efficient search known as the **binary search**. The easiest way to understand this method is by looking at an example. Suppose we have the array pictured below.

$$15 \quad 23 \quad 36 \quad 42 \quad 79 \quad 101 \quad 125 \quad 140 \quad 142$$

The numbers are in increasing order. Because N is 9, we know that whatever value we are looking for is between position 1 and position 9, inclusive, if it is there. For our example, assume we are looking for the value 101.

Suppose we initialize a variable Low to 0 and a variable High to 10 (= N + 1). Then *the value, if it is there, must be strictly between position Low and position High.* ("Strictly between" means "between but not including.")

Rather than check the positions in order, let's check the middle item of the array. We calculate

```
Middle := (Low + High) div 2
```

and examine A[Middle]. In this case, Middle is 5, so we examine A[5], which is 79. If we were looking for the value 79, we would be done—the location would be 5.

Because the number we are looking for (101) is larger than the one at position Middle (79) and *because the array is in increasing order*, we know it must be above the Middle position. If we do

```
Low := Middle
```

then this is our situation:

1. Low is 5.

2. High is 10.

3. If the value is there, it must be strictly between position Low and position High.

We again go to the middle of the possible positions, setting Middle to (5 + 10) div 2 = 15 div 2 = 7, and examine A[7]. This time the number we look for is less than A[Middle], so we know it must be to the left of the Middle position. We set

```
High := Middle
```

and have

1. Low is 5.

2. High is 7.

3. If the value is there, it must be strictly between position Low and position High.

This time, we set Middle to $(5 + 7)$ div $2 = 6$, and A[6] is our desired value, so we quit with the answer 6.

Suppose, now, that we had been searching for 40. The following table summarizes what would happen:

	Low	High	Middle	New Low	New High
First pass	0	10	5	0	5
Second pass	0	5	2	2	5
Third pass	2	5	3	3	5
Fourth pass	3	5	4	3	4

At the start of the fifth pass, we have

1. Low is 3.

2. High is 4.

3. If the value is there, it must be strictly between position Low and position High.

But this cannot be: nothing can be *strictly* between positions 3 and 4. This is how we detect that an element is not present in the array: when High − Low = 1.

The function in Figure 6-12 reflects this discussion. It uses a Boolean variable Found to indicate success, with High − Low ≤ 1 indicating failure.

COMMENTS   *1.* The condition "if the value is there, it must be strictly between position Low and position High" is an example of a **loop invariant**. It is true when we start the loop, and we make sure that it remains true for each successive pass.

The concept of a loop invariant can be made very formal and used in proving that programs are correct (**program verification**). For our purposes in this introductory text, we use loop invariants primarily in an informal way. We might not even use the term invariant, but rather think in terms of what is true on each successive pass. Such reasoning can help us understand how the loop accomplishes its task and thus can help us write correct loops.

2. Another key aspect of the correctness of the program of Figure 6-12 is that the distance between Low and High is becoming smaller on each successive pass. Thus, if the value is not in the array, the loop will eventually terminate when High − Low is 1.

3. Notice that if the array is empty (N = 0), then Low starts at 0, High at 1, and we leave the loop immediately with Found still false.

Efficiency. To examine the efficiency of the binary search, imagine an array of size 31. Each pass through the loop eliminates the middle number from consideration and also half of the remaining numbers. For example, after the first pass, we

```
function BinarySearch(A : IntegerArray; Key, N :  integer) : integer;
{
      Written by:   XXXXXXXXX   XX/XX/XX
         Purpose:   To locate a given value in an array. The answer is
                    the subscript where found (0 if not found).
                        Because a binary search is used, the array must be in
                    increasing order.
      Parameters:   A - input, the array to search in
                    Key - input, the value to search for
                    N - input, the portion of the array in use
}
var
   Found     : boolean;                    { used to indicate success }
   Low       : integer;                    { lower end of subarray }
   High      : integer;                    { higher end of subarray}
   Middle    : integer;                    { middle of subarray }

begin   {BinarySearch}
   Found := false;                         { assume not there as default }
   Low := 0;
   High := N + 1;

   while (High - Low > 1) and (not Found) do
     begin
       Middle := (Low + High) div 2;
       if A[Middle] = Key then
         Found := true
       else if A[Middle] > Key then
         High := Middle
       else
         Low := Middle
     end;   {while}

   if Found then
     BinarySearch := Middle
   else
     BinarySearch := 0
 end;   {BinarySearch}
```

Figure 6-12   Binary Search of an Array

have found the number, or know that it is between positions 0 and 14, or know that it is between positions 16 and 32.

In the worst possible case, this will happen:

At start	31 numbers left to examine
After one pass	15 numbers left to examine
After two passes	7 numbers left to examine
After three passes	3 numbers left to examine
After four passes	1 number left to examine
After five passes	Have found the number or know that it is not there

Thus, five passes is the most it could take.

Now, because $2^5 = 32$, we have $\log_2 32 = 5$. Thus, the number of passes is approximately the **log base 2** of the array size. We say that the binary search has a worst-case behavior O(logN), where the base 2 is understood. For an O(logN) algorithm, doubling the array size adds a constant amount of time to the running time.

Although the average number of passes is more difficult to calculate, it is also O(logN).

Notice that for an array of size 1024, logN is 10, whereas N/2 is 512. Thus, the binary search would be expected to be significantly faster than the linear search. However, it does require that the array be sorted.

SELECTION
SORT

We now turn to sorting algorithms. Given an array A containing N values, we wish to rearrange the array so that the values are in increasing order. Our first method is sometimes called the **selection sort**.

The underlying idea is to select the number that should be in the first position in the array and to put it there. We then select the number that should be in the second position in the array and put it there. We continue in this fashion until the proper numbers have been selected for and placed into each position in the array.

In order to understand the selection sort algorithm, we begin with some preliminary examples.

First, let us write a segment of Pascal to determine the subscript SmLoc of the smallest element in A. We have written algorithms of this type before. We use a for loop indexed by the variable J. (The reason for the use of J rather than I will become apparent later.)

```
SmLoc := 1;

for J := 2 to N do
   begin
     if A[J] < A[SmLoc] then
        SmLoc := J
   end;  {for}
```

Next we write code to exchange A[1] and A[SmLoc]. For example, if SmLoc is 7, this will exchange A[1] and A[7]. To accomplish this, we will write a procedure capable of swapping any two integers. We can then invoke the procedure to swap A[1] and A[SmLoc] by a step such as

```
Swap(A[1], A[SmLoc])
```

To write the procedure, we will need two var parameters, which we will call X and Y. We will use a temporary location to keep the value of X, moving data as indicated by the diagram, in the order indicated.

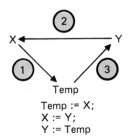

```
Temp := X;
X := Y;
Y := Temp;
```

To make use of the ideas just developed, we must generalize them slightly. Rather than starting at position 1, let us start at position I. We will, therefore, write code to determine the subscript SmLoc of the smallest element in A[I] through A[N] and then exchange A[I] with A[SmLoc]. For example, if A is the array shown below and I is 4, then SmLoc will be 7.

$$6 \quad 9 \quad 10 \quad 25 \quad 15 \quad 27 \quad 13 \quad 14 \quad 20 \quad 31$$

After swapping A[4] and A[7], we will have A as follows:

$$6 \quad 9 \quad 10 \quad 13 \quad 15 \quad 27 \quad 25 \quad 14 \quad 20 \quad 31$$

The code to accomplish this follows, with the generalizations shaded.

```
SmLoc := I;

for J := I + 1 to N do
   begin
     if A[J] < A[SmLoc] then
        SmLoc := J
   end;  {for}

Swap(A[I], A[SmLoc])
```

The selection sort method consists of applying this algorithm segment repeatedly. Starting with an array A that is not sorted, we determine the subscript SmLoc of the smallest number in A[1] through A[N], then exchange A[1] with A[SmLoc]. For example, if A is

$$21 \quad 17 \quad 3 \quad 16 \quad 12 \quad 10 \quad 19 \quad 9$$

then after this first swap we have

$$3 \quad 17 \quad 21 \quad 16 \quad 12 \quad 10 \quad 19 \quad 9$$

We now determine the subscript SmLoc of the smallest number in A[2] through A[N], and exchange A[2] with A[SmLoc], with the results shown:

$$3 \quad 9 \quad 21 \quad 16 \quad 12 \quad 10 \quad 19 \quad 17$$

As you can see, the first exchange located and placed into A[1] the smallest number in A. The second placed the proper number (the smallest of the remaining numbers) into A[2]. A third exchange will determine the subscript SmLoc (it turns out to be subscript 8) of the smallest number in A[3] through A[N], exchanging A[3] with A[SmLoc]:

$$3 \quad 9 \quad 10 \quad 16 \quad 12 \quad 21 \quad 19 \quad 17$$

After each such exchange, one more number is in its correct location. After N − 1 exchanges, N − 1 numbers will be correct and the Nth will therefore also be correct. Our algorithm is

```
for I := 1 to N-1 do
   begin
     determine the subscript SmLoc of the smallest
        element in A[I] through A[N], then exchange A[I]
        with A[SmLoc]
   end  {for}
```

To obtain the final procedure, we replace the body of the loop with the code written earlier that accomplishes the required task. See Figure 6-13.

Efficiency. The selection sort is easy to analyze. In determining the efficiency of sorting algorithms, the most frequent technique is to count array comparisons. Because each pass through the inner loop does one comparison, this is equivalent

```
procedure Swap(var X, Y : integer);
{
    Written by:   XXXXXXXXX  XX/XX/XX
       Purpose:   To swap two integers.
    Parameters:   X, Y - update, the integers to be swapped
}
var
  Temp      : integer;                   { temporary variable for swapping }

begin  {Swap}
  Temp := X;
  X := Y;
  Y := Temp
end;  {Swap}


procedure SelectionSort(var A : IntegerArray; N :  integer);
{
       Written by:   XXXXXXXXX  XX/XX/XX
          Purpose:   To sort an array, using the selection sort technique.
       Parameters:   A - update, the array to sort
                     N - input, the portion of the array in use
  Procedures used:   Swap, to swap two array elements
}
var
  I,J        : integer;                 { loop control}
  SmLoc      : integer;                 { location of smallest }
  Temp       : integer;                 { used for swapping }

begin  {SelectionSort}

  for I := 1 to N - 1 do
    begin

      SmLoc := I;

      for J := I + 1 to N do
        begin
          if A[J] < A[SmLoc] then
            SmLoc := J
        end;  {for J}

      Swap(A[I], A[SmLoc])
    end;  {for I}

end;  {SelectionSort}
```

Figure 6-13 Selection Sort

to counting the total passes through the inner loop. The following table should help.

When I is	J starts at	and ends at	No. of passes
1	2	N	N − 1
2	3	N	N − 2
3	4	N	N − 3
⋮	⋮	⋮	⋮
N − 3	N − 2	N	3
N − 2	N − 1	N	2
N − 1	N	N	1

The total is $1 + 2 \ldots + (N - 1)$, which can be shown to be equal to[1]

$$\frac{N(N - 1)}{2} = \frac{1}{2} N^2 - \frac{1}{2} N$$

This is roughly proportional to N^2 (for large N, the $\frac{1}{2}N$ is insignificant). We therefore have an $O(N^2)$ algorithm. For such an algorithm, doubling the array size quadruples the time.

The selection sort is satisfactory for small arrays, but not for larger ones.

□ **QUICK SORT**   One of the fastest known sorting algorithms is the **quick sort**. Many variations of the underlying idea have been developed. We present one of the simpler forms.

The quick sort is easiest to understand as a recursive procedure, although it can be written nonrecursively. The basic idea is this:

1. Rearrange the given array so that:
a. Its first element has been moved to its proper spot. Let us call this the "pivot location" and use the variable name PivotSub for this subscript.
b. Everything to the left of position PivotSub is less than or equal to A[PivotSub].
c. Everything to the right of position PivotSub is greater than or equal to A[PivotSub].
This is called the **partition** step.
2. Do a recursive call to sort the subarray to the left of position PivotSub.
3. Do a recursive call to sort the subarray to the right of position PivotSub.

Because when we call ourselves recursively, we will be sorting subarrays of the original array, we have three parameters:

A: The array to be sorted. This is modified, so it is a var parameter.
Low: The lowest subscript of the part to be sorted.
High: The highest subscript of the part to be sorted.

If Low < High, there are at least two elements in the subarray. If not, then there is nothing to do to accomplish the sort of the subarray. This is our base case, which we must have in any recursive algorithm.

NOTE The program that originally calls the QuickSort procedure will do so as shown here:

```
QuickSort(A, 1, N)
```

This says the subarray to be sorted is the entire array.

As an example, suppose the array is

$$23 \quad 6 \quad 24 \quad 17 \quad 29 \quad 12 \quad 19 \quad 28 \quad 8$$

After the partition, if it is done correctly, we will have PivotSub = 6, with this situation

A[1] to A[5] contains 6, 17, 12, 8, 19 in some order	A[6] is 23	A[7] − A[9] contains 24, 29, 28 in some order

If the recursive calls work, they will sort A[1] to A[5] into the order 6, 8, 12, 17, and 19 and A[7] to A[9] into the order 24, 28, and 29. The entire array will then be sorted.

Let us use a Partition procedure for the partition step. It will require the parameters A, Low, and High and returns the value for PivotSub. The quick sort itself is fairly easy; it simply reflects everything we have just said, using the procedures Partition and QuickSort:

```
if Low < High then
   begin
      Partition(A, Low, High, PivotSub);
      QuickSort(A, Low, PivotSub - 1);
      QuickSort(A, PivotSub + 1, High)
   end  {if}
```

To complete the quick sort, we must now write the Partition procedure. We present a version of the general method that seems to be most frequently described in discussing the quick sort. There are a number of other possible ways to do this; some are explored in the exercises.

The method is easy to describe intuitively, although it is probably more subtle than most algorithms we have seen in this text. For illustration, consider this small array:

$$23 \quad 6 \quad 24 \quad 17 \quad 29 \quad 12 \quad 19 \quad 28 \quad 8$$

For simplicity, we will assume that this is the entire array, so that Low is 1 and High is 9. The ideas will work equally well for a piece of an array.

The idea is this. We use two pointers (variables containing subscripts) that we will call I and J. We will start I at the left end of the array and J at the right end. We will then move them together until they meet or cross, constantly maintaining this conditon (the loop invariant):

Everything to the left of position I is less than or equal to the pivot, and everything to the right of J is greater than or equal to the pivot.

When I and J meet or cross (that is, I ≥ J), we can swap the pivot with the Jth element; then everything to the right of position J will still be greater than or equal to the pivot, and everything to the left of J will also be to the left of I and be less than or equal to the pivot. This is the desired result.

To see how this works, we will step through the algorithm for the array given above.

First, starting at the left (not including the pivot number 23), locate a number that is bigger than or equal to the pivot number. Then, starting at the right, locate a number less than or equal to the pivot number. The numbers we locate are colored, with the variables I and J containing their subscripts:

In order to maintain the loop invariant as I and J continue moving, we must swap the Ith and Jth elements:

Continuing, we move I to the right again, then J to the left again, obtaining

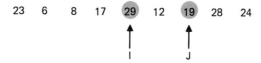

After the swap, we have

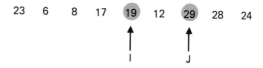

Once more we move I, then J, obtaining

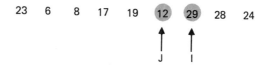

Because I and J have crossed, we do not swap. To finish the partition, we need only place the pivot in its proper position, by swapping it with A[J], and observe that J is the PivotLocation.

You may wonder why J, and not I, is the PivotLocation. To answer this, recall our invariant:

Everything to the left of position I is less than or equal to the pivot, and everything to the right of J is greater than or equal to the pivot.

If I and J are equal, then either one would do. However, if they have crossed, then I is to the right of J. The invariant would say that A[I] is greater than or equal to the pivot. If we swap the pivot with A[I], we will be moving a large value into the left subarray. *We do not want that.*

The final result of the partition process is

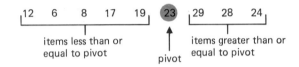

The complete Partition and QuickSort procedures are given in Figure 6-14. The Swap procedure referred to is that of Figure 6-13.

COMMENT Because the recursive calls to QuickSort sort a piece of the array, there are three parameters: the array and the lower and upper bounds of the piece to be sorted. To sort the entire array, the main program would include a call such as

```
QuickSort(GradeArray, 1, NumberOfStudents)
```

The argument "1" must be supplied as the lower bound of the array.

```
procedure Partition(var A : IntegerArray; Low, High :  integer;
                    var PivotLocation : integer);
{

        Written by:   XXXXXXXXX  XX/XX/XX
           Purpose:   To partition an array into three parts:
                      1. values less or equal to the pivotal element
                      2. the pivotal element
                      3. values greater than or equal to the pivotal
                         element
        Parameters:   A - update, the array to partition
                      Low, High - input, the portion of the array to partition
                      PivotLocation - output, the location for the pivotal
                                      element
  Procedures used:   Swap, to swap two array elements

}
var
  I       : integer;              { used to locate large values }
  J       : integer;              { used to locate small values }
  Pivot   : integer;              { the pivotal element }
```

Figure 6-14 Quick Sort (Continued)

```
begin  {Partition}
  I := Low;
  J := High + 1;
  Pivot := A[Low];

  repeat

{***  Move I to right looking for a value greater than or equal to
      the pivot.}

    repeat
      I := I + 1
    until (I = High) or (A[I] >= Pivot);

{***  Move J to left looking for a value less than or equal to
      the pivot.}

    repeat
      J := J - 1
    until A[J] <= Pivot;

{***  Swap if the values are out of order.}

    if I < J then
      Swap(A[I], A[J])

  until I >= J;

{*** Put the pivotal element in the proper place, and return the
     value of its subscript to the calling module.}

  Swap(A[Low], A[J]);
  PivotLocation := J
end;  {Partition}

procedure QuickSort(var A : IntegerArray; Low, High :  integer);
{
      Written by:  XXXXXXXXX  XX/XX/XX
         Purpose:  To sort an array, using the quick sort technique.
      Parameters:  A - update, the array to sort
                   Low, High - input, the portion of the array to sort
Procedures used:  Partition, to partition the array into two pieces
                     (the smaller numbers and the larger numbers)
                   QuickSort (recursively), to sort the two pieces
}
var
  PivotSub : integer;                      { location of pivotal element }

begin  {QuickSort}
  if Low < High then
    begin
      Partition(A, Low, High, PivotSub);
      QuickSort(A, Low, PivotSub - 1);
      QuickSort(A, PivotSub + 1, High)
    end  {if}
end;  {QuickSort}
```

Figure 6-14   Quick Sort

Efficiency. In the best case, each Partition splits the array exactly in half and that this algorithm is $O(N\log N)$. In the worst case, the algorithm is $O(N^2)$. The worst case occurs when the array is already in order. In the average case, the algorithm is also $O(N\log N)$. For an algorithm that is $O(N\log N)$, doubling the array size multiplies the time by a factor just barely more than 2. This factor gets smaller as N gets larger.

This is much better than an $O(N^2)$ algorithm. Thus, for large arrays, we would definitely choose the quick sort rather than the selection sort.

It is important to note that the efficiency of the quick sort depends partially on the efficiency of the partition process. It is possible to replace the Partition procedure with another that accomplishes the same goal but is either faster or slower than that we described. This will effect the speed of the quick sort. However, as long as the partition is $O(N)$, the quick sort will be $O(N\log N)$.

Some of the work that has been done in speeding up the quick sort has concentrated on making the partition faster. Other work has concentrated on

---

To help you get a better feel for the different efficiency ratings discussed in the section, we present below a table showing the values of logN, N logN, and N^2 for various values of N. The column labelled "ratio" will be discussed below.

N	logN	NlogN	N^2	Ratio
16	4	64	256	4.00
32	5	160	1024	6.40
64	6	384	4096	10.67
128	7	896	16,384	18.29
1024	10	10,240	1,048,576	102.40
2048	11	22,528	4,194,304	186.18
4096	12	49,152	16,777,216	341.33
8192	13	106,496	67,108,864	630.15

Of course, when we say an algorithm is O(expression), that means that it is approximately proportional to the expression. For example, quick sort might take approximately .01 NlogN and selection sort approximately .001 N^2. If so, then the ratio of selection sort time to quick sort time would be

$$\frac{.001\ N^2}{.01\ NlogN} = 0.1\ \frac{N^2}{NlogN}$$

The column "Ratio" is the ratio N^2/NlogN (which is also N/logN). As you can see, with these hypothetical times, the two would be approximately equal for N = 64 ($0.1 \times 10.67 \times 1$). For N = 2048, quick sort would be almost 20 times as fast.

Some of the exercises are designed to give you further insight into the significance of the efficiency discussions.

---

trying to make sure that the partition splits the array as nearly in half as possible. Thus, if you examine a half dozen quick sort programs in papers or texts, you will find that the major differences occur in how the partitioning works.

DPT AND
TESTING

□ We already know about some of the pitfalls to watch for from our previous study of arrays and of the linear search. Specifically, we must take care that our array references do not include subscripts beyond the legal array limits. If they do, we will know if we have used the {$R+} compiler option. If not, our program may run very strangely. It may actually appear to work for several runs, then begin to not work. Remember that searching programs are especially prone to this type of error. Avoid compound conditions that could possibly lead to errors, such as:

```
while (I > 0) and (A[I] > Key) do
```

Remember the fairly widely used solution to this problem: a Boolean variable such as Found to indicate success.

   The sorting and searching algorithms presented in this section have their own pitfalls, which seem to occur with regularity. For example, in the binary search as we have written it, our loop invariant states that the item to be found is *strictly* between positions Low and High. To make this true at the start, we must set Low to 0 (not 1) and High to N + 1 (not N).

COMMENT   See the exercises for a version of the binary search with a slightly different loop invariant.

   Another pitfall involves the partition algorithm. Notice that in the loop involving I, we must include the test for I = High. If we do not, the condition A[I] >= Pivot might never become true if the first element is the largest in the array. The variable I would go beyond the end of the array, leading to thoroughly unpredictable results (unless we have set the {$R+} option). As a matter of fact, the partition algorithm as described here is extremely subtle. It is probably safe to say that bugs appear in many presentations of the quick sort.

   Searching and sorting, then, seem to be relatively dangerous activities, prone to error. What can be done about this? One possibility is to make more careful use of assertions about the loops (loop invariants). A second is to make extensive use of hand-tracing with small sample arrays. Yet another is to do very careful testing. We will list a number of tests we feel are important for any searching or sorting algorithm. First, for searching:

   1. An important boundary test relates to the actual size (N) of the array. Try arrays of size 0, 1, and MaxIndex, where MaxIndex is the declared (potential) size of the array.

   2. Two other important boundaries are closely related. We would want to try searching for the first and last items in the array. However, this has two possible interpretations: by the "first," we could be referring to A[1] or we could be referring to the smallest value. Both interpretations should be tested.

   In addition to the boundaries, we should search for other items in the array that are present.

3. We should exercise the possibility that the item sought is not present. Of special interest are values less than the smallest or greater than the largest.

4. Finally, we would suggest a totally exhaustive test for a relatively small array. For example, we might set up an array such as this:

10 20 30 40 50

and search for 5, 10, 15, 20, 25, 30, 35, 40, 45, 50, and 55 (in some random order). Notice that we have searched for each item that is there and between each pair of items, as well as below the first and above the last.

If the search does not require the array to be ordered, we might try the same test with a rearranged array, perhaps 30, 40, 10, 50, and 20.

The tests we suggest for sorting are similar:

1. Test arrays of size 0, 1, and MaxIndex.

2. Test an array that is already in order and one that is in exactly reversed order. (Also, naturally, test some in random order.)

3. Test arrays with and without duplicates; perhaps include an array for which the entire array consists of the same value.

4. For some small arrays, try every possible ordering. In a graduate class, a student was assigned to present a variation on the quick sort that had been published in a leading computer science journal. She was to explain the method to the class and give some analysis of the efficiency. Within a few days, she reported that the algorithm did not work. What she had tried (and the author of the article apparently had not) was testing the method on some small arrays. In particular, she tried all possible orders of the three numbers 1, 2, and 3. For more than one of these, the algorithm failed.

REVIEW

Terms of concepts	searching	binary search
	sorting	loop invariant
	linear search	program verification
	efficiency	log base 2
	O notation	selection sort
	order	quick sort
	big oh	

Searching and sorting algorithms	Linear search:	Start at the beginning, keep going until found or reach the end
		Order is O(N)
	Binary search:	Look in the middle, keep cutting the part of the array to search in half, until found or there is no part left to search
		Array must be in order
		Order is O(logN)

<table>
<tr><td>Selection sort:</td><td>Repeatedly find the smallest of those left, and swap it with the first of those left
Order is $O(N^2)$</td></tr>
<tr><td>Quick sort:</td><td>Partition the array based on a pivot element, then sort the subarrays to the left and right of the pivot element recursively
Order is $O(N\log N)$</td></tr>
</table>

Efficiency **The approximate results on time from doubling the size of the array:**

$O(\log N)$:	adds a constant amount of time
$O(N)$:	doubles the time
$O(N\log N)$:	multiplies the time by a factor slightly above 2; the larger the array, the smaller the factor
$O(N^2)$:	quadruples the time

DPT
1. Hand-trace the algorithms for some small arrays.
2. Avoid the known bugs.
3. Avoid conditions such as

```
(I > 0) or (A[I] . . .)
```

Testing

Searching

1. Test arrays of size 0, 1, and MaxIndex.
2. Search for the first and the last items, and items in between.
3. Search for the smallest and the largest items, and items in between.
4. For some small arrays, try searching for each item.
5. Search for numbers less than the lowest in the array, greater than the highest, and in between but not there.

Sorting

1. Test arrays of size 0, 1, and MaxIndex.
2. Test arrays already in order and in reverse order.
3. For some small arrays, try every possible ordering.

■■■■■■
EXERCISES

1. Under the assumption that the array is in increasing order, the linear search algorithm could be modified to give up as soon as it encounters a value larger than the one sought. Comment on this as compared to the binary search.

*2. If a searching method is of order $O(N)$ and it takes an average of 10 ms to locate a value in an array of a given size, how long would you expect it to take if the array size is doubled. Note: ms stands for milliseconds; 1 ms = $\frac{1}{1000}$ of a second.

*3. Suppose that you are using an order $O(N^2)$ sorting algorithm, and it takes about 2 seconds to sort an array of size 60. About how long would you expect it to take for an array of size 120? 250? 500? 1000? 2000? 4000?

*4. Suppose that you are using an order $O(NlogN)$ sorting algorithm, and it takes about 5 seconds to sort an array of size 60. About how long would you expect it to take for an array of size 120? 250? 500? 1000? 2000? 4000? Note: The time is scaled by a factor of approximately $2 + 2/logN$.

5. Suppose that you are using an order $O(N)$ algorithm, and it takes about 3 ms to sort an array of size 60. About how long would you expect it to take for an array of size 120? 250? 500? 1000? 2000? 4000? See the note in Exercise 2.

6. Suppose that you are using an order $O(logN)$ algorithm, and it takes about 10 ms to sort an array of size 60. Assuming that each doubling adds 25 ms to the time, about how long would you expect it to take for an array of size 120? 250? 500? 1000? 2000? 4000?

7. Hand-trace the partition algorithm given in the section for these arrays:

a. 10, 12, 9, 14, 7, 21
b. 2, 22, 7, 24, 100, 5, 13, 4, 1, 23
c. 1, 2, 3, 4, 5
d. 5, 4, 3, 2, 1
e. 10, 10, 10, 10

8. For the following array, trace the binary search for each element of the array. For each, find the number of passes through the loop it takes to find the value.

101   122   123   203   417   500 623

9. An alternate version of the binary search uses the loop invariant "the value, if it is there, lies at or between the positions Low and High." This method initializes Low to 1 and High to N. Write the algorithm.

Caution: This approach contains a notorious pitfall into which many professional programmers have stumbled. Hand-trace your solution with some small arrays. Make sure you avoid an infinite loop by ensuring that the subarray remaining is smaller for each pass.

*10. Write a recursive form of the binary search. Note: By rights, the array being searched should be a value parameter. However, in a recursive routine, passing an array as a value parameter uses considerable time and space because each level must maintain its own copy of the array. Make the array a var parameter.

*11. What is the maximum number of passes that it could take to locate a value using the binary search of this section in an array of size 63? Of size 127? Of size 80?

12. a. Generate a random array of size 2000, and sort it using the selection sort. How long does it take? Repeat for the quick sort.
b. Modify the two sorts of part (a) to count the number of key comparisons that occur. Run each to compare the two in terms of this count.

13. A colleague once made a bet with an unsuspecting friend. He wagered that he could locate a person in the white pages of the phone book in 20 guesses or less. For each guess, the friend must merely indicate whether the actual name came before or after the guess in the phone book.

The local phone book contains perhaps 20,000 entries. Did the colleague win the bet? If so, can you explain how?

*14. a. An array contains N student records, each with a last name, first name, the final average, and space for a letter grade. To aid in figuring grades, the professor desires a listing of the students in order from highest to lowest average. Write a procedure to sort the array and print the listing.

b. For the final grade list, the names must be in alphabetical order. Write a procedure to print a listing of name and letter grade in alphabetical order by last name.

15. An array contains 50 records, each with a state name and 12 monthly rainfall figures. Write a procedure to print a listing of the states, in order from lowest to highest total yearly rainfall.

16. See Exercise 15. A naive approach might involve calculating the total rainfall for some of the records over and over again. Suggest a data structure that would allow you to calculate the total for each state only once. Note: You cannot, as the person writing the procedure, change the description of the parameters. However, you can define local variables. You may wish to write your procedure to set up the local variables, then call the procedure that actually accomplishes the sorting.

*17. a. Write a procedure that has as parameters an array, its current size (N), and a value to be inserted into the array. The array is in increasing order, and N < MaxIndex is the declared size of the array. Insert the value into the array so that the array is still in order. Hint: If the value is bigger than the last, put it at the end. If not, move the last one over 1 and compare the value to the next to last. Continue until you find the proper spot.

b. Your procedure in part (a) should be O(N). Present a reasonable argument that this is so.

c. A student proposed accomplishing part (a) by just placing the new value at the end, then calling quick sort to reorder the array. Comment on the efficiency of this approach.

18. a. By using the procedure of Exercise 17(a) repeatedly, write a sorting algorithm. Insert A[2] into the (sorted) subarray A[1], then insert A[3] into the (now sorted) subarray consisting of A[1] and A[2], and so on. This is the *insertion sort*.

b. By counting the number of array comparisons for the worst possible case, determine the efficiency of the insertion sort.

19. One version of the *bubble sort* has this form:

```
for I := 1 to N-1 do
   begin
      for J := 1 to N-I do
         begin
            if A[J] > A[J+1] then
               Swap(A[J], A[J+1])
         end  {for J}
   end  {for I}
```

Analyze the efficiency of this algorithm by counting the number of array comparisons.

20. An easy way to accomplish the partition process for an array is to simply copy the array to another array. Then, starting with subscript 2 of the other

array, return the values to the original array. If they are less than the pivot, they go to the front of the array; if not, to the end. Use two pointers, one starting at Low and increasing and the other starting at High and decreasing. Write the code for this approach. Is it easier to understand? Is it better?

21. See exercise 20. Another approach[2] to the partition process can be based on a possible solution to Exercise 10 in Section 6-1. In that exercise, you were asked to arrange an array containing only 0's and 1's in such a way that all the 0's came before all the 1's. A possible solution is the following:

```
LastZero := 0;
for I := 1 to N do
  begin
    if A[I] = 0 then
      begin
        Swap(A[LastZero+1], A[I]);
        LastZero := LastZero + 1
      end {if}
  end; {for}
```

The variable LastZero keeps track of where you have placed a 0; when another 0 is found, it is swapped into the next available spot and LastZero is incremented.

a. Trace this code for some sample arrays to make sure you understand it.

*b. This code can be thought of as partitioning the array into two pieces: the 0's and the 1's. Using the basic idea of the code, write code for the following. You are given an array of size N. Partition the subarray from position 2 to N so that everything that is less than A[1] comes first and then comes everything that is not less than A[1].

c. Generalize the solution to part (b) to obtain a Partition procedure. Note: After you obtain the result of part (b), swap the first element with the last one that is smaller than it.

d. Trace your code from part (c) for the arrays of Exercise 5 as well as for the one traced in this section for the Partition procedure.

e. Explain in your own words how this method works. Is it easier to understand than the one in Figure 6-14?

f. Test your code by writing it as a procedure and including it in the quick sort of Figure 6-14.

22. The quick sort performs best if the pivot element is always in the middle of the subarray being sorted. If an array is already partially sorted, this does not happen. This exercise describes two approaches to solving this problem.

a. Modify the partition procedure to swap A[Low] with A[RandomLoc] prior to beginning, where RandomLoc is a subscript in the range Low .. High generated randomly.

b. Modify the partition procedure to swap A[Low] with the one of A[Low], A[High], or A[(Low + High) div 2] that is the median of those three values prior to beginning. The median of three numbers is the middle one. For example, the median of 5, 16, and 10 is 10; the median of 20, 12, and 20 is 20; and the median of 7, 7, and 7 is 7.

*23. Write a procedure to *merge* two sorted arrays. Input consists of arrays A and B and the size of each. Output consists of array C and its size. Assume that the sum of the sizes of A and B is less than or equal to MaxIndex, the declared size of the three arrays.

The two input arrays are in increasing order, and the output arrays should be also. For example, if we merge the arrays A and B illustrated here, the answer is the array C as shown:

$$A = 5 \quad 6 \quad 8 \quad 12 \quad 13$$
$$B = 4 \quad 6 \quad 7 \quad 9$$
$$C = 4 \quad 5 \quad 6 \quad 6 \quad 7 \quad 8 \quad 9 \quad 12 \quad 13$$

Hint: Maintain pointers for each array. Use a decision structure based on whether the A element or the B element is larger.

24. a. Modify the procedure of Exercise 23 as follows: Input consists of an array A and three subscripts Start1, Start2, and End2. In addition, a "scratch" array is passed for the procedure to use. The arrays to be merged are both subarrays of A, namely A[Start1] through A[Start2 − 1] and A[Start2] through A[End2]. Merge these into the scratch array, then copy the result back to A[Start1] through A[End2].

   b. Using the procedure of part (a), write a procedure to sort an array by this method: Use a recursive call to sort the left half of the array, use a recursive call to sort the right half of the array, then use the merge procedure to merge the two halves into a single sorted array.

   This is called the *recursive merge sort*. Provided the procedure of part (a) is written properly, it is of order O(NlogN).

   c. Repeat Exercise 12 for the recursive merge sort of part (b).

□
NOTES FOR SECTION 6-3

1. The formula we use is

$$\sum_{i=1}^{n} = \frac{n(n + 1)}{2}$$

Substituting N − 1 for *n*, we obtain

$$\frac{(N − 1)(N − 1 + 1)}{2} \quad \text{or} \quad \frac{N(N − 1)}{2}$$

2. This approach appeared in the "Programming Pearls" column of the *Communications of the ACM*, April 1984, Vol. 27, No. 4. The author of the column, Jon L. Bentley, states that he learned the method from Nico Lomuto of Alsys, Inc.

6-4 CASE STUDIES

In this section, we will develop two case studies that indicate the broad range of possible applications of arrays. The first is a business-related application in which we use arrays to store information on prices, customer discounts, and so on. In the second, we write a package of modules that could be used in programs that need to manipulate polynomials.

CASE STUDY No. 9

Statement of problem. A small, locally owned store wants to computerize its point-of-sale operations. It sees a number of benefits to be derived from this automation, including automatic updating of inventory records and granting of discounts to preferred customers.

Preliminary analysis. A system such as this involves quite a few activities. We will implement only a few of them, and even then in only a simplified way. Some enhancements are suggested in the exercises.

To accomplish some of the desired point-of-sale and inventory functions, we will use a file containing information about the items the store stocks. Likewise, a file will contain a list of preferred customers. The following table represents sample information from the two files:

Item number	Inventory	Price	Customer number	Discount
101	249	3.89	4398	2%
247	1300	24.99	3898	½%
93	500	0.78	6756	1%
16	55	100.04	4528	½%
89	453	6.34		

For simplicity, let us assume that the customer file contains no more than 75 records, and the item number file no more than 500. As we did for the program of Figure 6-10, we will use a control file to record the current status of the data. This file will contain one record with two fields: current number of items and current number of preferred customers.

There are techniques, beyond the scope of our knowledge at this point, that would allow us to work directly with the data in the files. Instead, we will read the file data into arrays, work with the arrays, and then rewrite the arrays to the files.

We will use a menu-driven program similar to that in Case Study No. 8 (Section 5-4). In fact, rather than begin from scratch, we will build our menu system by modifying the menu portion of the program of Figure 5-20. We choose to implement these four actions for the case study:

P—purchase: Obtain an item number and quantities, adjust the inventory, and calculate the bill.
C—new customer: Add a new customer to the preferred list.
S—save: Save the data to the files.
Q—quit: Warn the user if there is a change since the data was last saved.

Overall data requirements. This analysis indicates the need for these variables:

1. A control record with two fields: number of items and number of customers

2. An array of item records, each with three fields: item number, current inventory, and price

3. An array of customer records, each with two fields: customer number and base discount

4. A Boolean variable indicating whether the arrays have been changed

5. A set of valid options

6. The user option

7. File designators for the three files

In addition, the various modules will require local variables to be determined as we write the modules. In this case study, we choose to use the data listed in items (1) to (4) above as global data throughout the program. The alternative would involve passing the arrays and control information as parameters to almost every subprogram.

Main program (and menu handling procedures). The main program will initialize the data described above, then process user requests in a loop. As mentioned, it is adapted from Figure 5-20 of Case Study No. 8. By using the code from the previous work as a starting point, we significantly reduced the time required to get started.

Figure 6-15 contains a first attempt at the program. Most of the modules are stubs. We have added an option D, which "dumps" the data. This will be helpful for debugging purposes, but will be removed from the version of the program delivered to the user.

```
program PointOfSale(Input, Output);
{
        Written by:  XXXXXXXXX   XX/XX/XX
           Purpose:  To handle point-of-sale procedures.
    Procedures used:  Instructions - to print instructions;
                      Page - to clear the screen;
                      Menu - to display the menu and get the
                             user option;
                      Handle - to perform the user option.
}
const
  MaxCust = 75;                         { Customer array size }
  MaxItem = 500;                        { Item array size }
  Bel = 7;                              { ASCII Bel character }

type
  Letters = set of char;
  ControlRec = record
                 NItem  : integer;      { # of items presently }
                 NCust  : integer       { # of customers presently }
               end;
  ItemRec = record
              ItemNumber : integer;
              Inventory  : integer;
              Price      : real
            end;
  CustomerRec = record
                  Number   : integer;
                  Discount : real
                end;
```

Figure 6-15 Case Study No. 9—First Cut (Continued)

```
     ItemArray = array [1 .. MaxItem] of ItemRec;
     CustomerArray = array [1 .. MaxCust] of CustomerRec;
     CFile = file of ControlRec;
     CustFile = file of CustomerRec;
     ItFile = file of ItemRec;

   var
     Item          : ItemArray;      { Array of item information }
     Customer      : CustomerArray;  { Array of customer information }
     Modified      : boolean;        { Has data been changed? }
     ControlRecord : ControlRec;     { The control record }
     ControlFile   : CFile;          { The control file }
     CustomerFile  : CustFile;       { The list of customers }
     ItemFile      : ItFile;         { The list of items }
     Option        : char;           { User choice of menu option }
     ValidOptions  : Letters;        { Valid menu options }
     Answer        : char;           { User answer to yes/no}
```

*{procedures Pause, Instructions, and Menu are inserted here. They are
        minor modifications of the procedures of Figure 5-20}*

```
procedure Purchase;
begin   {Purchase - stub version }
  Writeln('Purchase procedure invoked');
  Pause
end;   {Purchase}

procedure NewCustomer;
begin   {NewCustomer - stub version }
  Writeln('NewCustomer procedure invoked');
  Pause
end;   {NewCustomer}

procedure SaveData;
begin   {SaveData - stub version }
  Writeln('SaveData procedure invoked');
  Pause
end;   {SaveData}

procedure DumpData;
{
       Written by:  XXXXXXXX  XX/XX/XX
          Purpose:  To dump the data on the screen to aid in
                    testing and debugging.
    Globals used:  The following are used for the dump:
                    ControlRecord.NItem
                    ControlRecord.NCust
                    Item
                    Customer
                    Modified
```

Figure 6-15   Case Study No. 9—First Cut (Continued)

```
      Procedures used:  Pause - to wait for a user keystroke
   }
   var
      I      : integer;                       { Loop control }

   begin  {DumpData}
      if Modified then
        Writeln('Data has been modified since save')
      else
        Writeln('Data has NOT been modified since save');
      Pause;
      Page(Con);

      Writeln('There are ', ControlRecord.NItem:1, ' items');
      Pause;
      Page(Con);

      for I := 1 to ControlRecord.NItem do
        with Item[I] do
          begin
             Writeln('Item number: ', ItemNumber:1);
             Writeln('Inventory:   ', Inventory:1);
             Writeln('Price:       ', Price:1:2);
             Pause;
             Page(Con)
          end;   {with}

      Writeln('There are ', ControlRecord.NCust:1, ' customers');
      Pause;
      Page(Con);

      for I := 1 to ControlRecord.NCust do
        with Customer[I] do
          begin
             Writeln('Customer number: ', Number:1);
             Writeln('Discount:        ', Discount:1:2);
             Pause;
             Page(Con)
          end;   {with}

      Writeln('End of Dump');
      Pause
   end;   {DumpData}


   procedure Quit;
   begin  {Quit - stub version }
      Writeln('Quit procedure invoked');
      Pause
   end;   {Quit}
```

{procedure Handle is inserted here. It is a minor modification
    of the procedure of Figure 5-20}

Figure 6-15 Case Study No. 9—First Cut (Continued)

```
procedure Initialize;
begin  {Initialize - stub version}
  ControlRecord.NItem := 3;
  ControlRecord.NCust := 2;
  Item[1].ItemNumber := 101;
  Item[1].Inventory := 10;
  Item[1].Price := 1.56;
  Item[2].ItemNumber := 202;
  Item[2].Inventory := 20;
  Item[2].Price := 2.56;
  Item[3].ItemNumber := 303;
  Item[3].Inventory := 30;
  Item[3].Price := 3.56;
  Customer[1].Number := 1;
  Customer[1].Discount := 0.01;
  Customer[2].Number := 2;
  Customer[2].Discount := 0.02;
  Customer[3].Number := 3;
  Customer[3].Discount := 0.03;
  Modified := false;
end;  {Initialize}



begin {PointOfSale}
  ValidOptions := ['P', 'p', 'C', 'c', 'S', 's', 'Q', 'q', 'D', 'd'];

{*** Print instructions.}

  Instructions;

{*** Load data from files.}

  Initialize;

{*** Main loop.}

  repeat

{*** Display Menu and get user option.}

    Menu(ValidOptions, Option);
    Page(Con);

{*** Handle user choice.}

    Handle(Option)
  until  Option in ['Q', 'q'];

{*** Print terminating message and stop program.}

  Writeln;
  Writeln('PointOfSale program is terminating.')
end.
```

Figure 6-15 Case Study No. 9—First Cut

Purchase procedure and its subprograms. This procedure will consist of the following steps:

1. Clear the screen, input an item number, and make sure it is valid.
2. Input the quantity desired, between 0 and the available inventory.
3. Adjust the inventory (and indicate that the arrays have been modified).
4. Calculate the cost before discount.
5. Input the customer number and determine the discount.
6. Determine the net cost.
7. Display lines of information on the purchase.

We will use subprograms for steps (1), (2), and (5).

We can now identify required variables and write the body of the Purchase subprogram.

Global variables:	Item	array of item records	used to access the price for the item
	Modified	Boolean	Has data been modified?
Local variables:	ItemSub	integer	Subscript of item number entered
	Quantity	integer	Number purchased
	Gross	real	Cost before discount
	Discount	real	Discount percentage
	Net	real	Cost after discount

We do not directly deal with the item number or customer number. Rather, the procedures that read them will report the item number subscript and the discount percentage.

In the Pascal code below, we have numbered the lines based on the general description of the steps given above.

```
1.   GetValidItem(ItemSub);
2.   GetAmount(Quantity, ItemSub);
3.   with Item[ItemSub] do

         Inventory := Inventory - Quantity;

3.   Modified := true;
4.   Gross := Quantity * Item[ItemSub].Price;
5.   GetCustomer(Discount);
6.   Net := Gross - Discount * Gross;
7.   Writeln;
7.   Writeln(Gross:10:2, ' <--- Gross');
7.   Writeln(Discount*Gross:10:2, ' <--- Discount');
7.   Writeln(Net:10:2, ' <--- Net');
7.   Pause
```

1. *GetValidItem Procedure.* The general logic of the procedure consists of repeating these steps until a valid number is entered:

   a. Prompt and read the item number.

   b. Use a lookup function to calculate the subscript for the item number.

   c. Handle three possibilities:

   Not found

   Found, but no inventory

   Found, valid

   Based on this statement of the algorithm, we can identify variables and write the required code. Notice the use of the Bel character to "beep" for an error.

Global variables:	Item	Array of item records	Used to check inventory
Parameters:	ItemSubsc	integer	Output parameter (therefore var)
Local variables:	ItemNum	integer	User input
	Valid	Boolean	Is input valid?

```
repeat
  Writeln;
  Write('Enter item #: ');
  Readln(ItemNum);
  ItemSubsc := ItemLookup(ItemNum);
  if ItemSubsc = 0 then
    begin
      Valid := false;
      Writeln(Chr(Bel), 'Item does not exist. Please try again')
    end
  else if Item[ItemSubsc].Inventory <= 0 then
    begin
      Valid := false;
      Writeln(Chr(Bel), 'Out of stock. Please try again')
    end
  else
    Valid := true
until Valid
```

COMMENTS

1. At first, we wrote a while loop for this, but we changed to a repeat loop. Try writing a while loop yourself. Caution: Do not write a condition such as (ItemSubsc <> 0) and (*condition using ItemSubsc*). Why not?

2. We could not exchange the first two branches of the if–then–else–if decision structure. Why not?

3. ItemLookup Function. This is a standard array Lookup function. See Figure 6-16.

4. GetAmount Procedure. See Figure 6-16. Observe that this procedure needs the parameter ItemSub in order to check that the quantity entered does not exceed the inventory for that item.

5. GetCustomer Procedure (and CustomerLookup Function). These are similar to the subprograms for the item number. Notice, however, that if the customer number is not found in the customer array, this is not an error. It simply means that the discount is zero. See Figure 6-16.

NewCustomer procedure. We will perform the following steps:

    a. Obtain a customer number and a discount.

    b. Handle these possibilities:

        The customer number is already in the array.

        There is no more room in the array.

        Everything is OK. Add to the array.

In step (2a), we will use the CustomerLookup function described above. In step (2c), we should signal that the data has changed by setting the global Modified flag to true.

Based on this discussion, we can describe the variables and write the code.

Global variables:	Customer	Array of customer records	Record added to end
	ControlRecord.Ncust	integer	# of customer, modified
	Modified	Boolean	Has data been modified? (Set to true)
Global constants:	MaxCust		Max. # of customers
Local variables:	CustomerNo	integer	New customer #
	Disc	real	New discount

```
Write('Enter customer number, discount: ');
Read(CustomerNo, Disc);
if CustomerLookup(CustomerNo) <> 0 then
  begin
    Writeln(Chr(Bel), 'Customer already in file');
    Pause
  end
else if ControlRecord.NCust = MaxCust then
  begin
    Writeln(Chr(Bel), 'Customer list is full. ',
            'Must modify program.');
    Pause
  end
else
  begin
    with ControlRecord do
      begin
        NCust := NCust + 1;
        Customer[NCust].Number := CustomerNo;
        Customer[NCust].Discount := Disc
      end;  {with}
    Modified := true;
    Writeln('Added to list');
    Pause
  end  {if}
```

```
program PointOfSale(Input, Output);
```

*{The main program declarations and the Pause, Instructions, and Menu procedures are
        unchanged.}*

```
function ItemLookup(ItemNum : integer) : integer;
{
        Written by:  XXXXXXXX  XX/XX/XX
           Purpose:  To look for an item number in the item array
        Parameters:  ItemNum - input, the number to look for
      Globals used:  Item - to check the item number
                     ControlRecord.NItem - to know array size
}
var
  I          : integer;                    { Array subscript }
  Found      : boolean;                    { Loop control }

begin   {ItemLookup}
  I := 1;
  Found := false;

  while (not Found) and (I <= ControlRecord.NItem) do
    begin
      if ItemNum = Item[I].ItemNumber then
        Found := true
      else
        I := I + 1
    end;  {while}

  if Found then
    ItemLookup := I
  else
    ItemLookup := 0
end;  {ItemLookup}

procedure GetValidItem(var ItemSubsc : integer);
{
        Written by:  XXXXXXXX  XX/XX/XX
           Purpose:  To input item number and determine subscript
        Parameters:  ItemSubsc - output, the subscript of the item
                                 entered
      Globals used:  Item - to check for out of stock
    Functions used:  ItemLookup - to look up item number in array
}
    var
      ItemNum      : integer;              { Item number, user input }
      Valid        : boolean;              { Is input valid? }

begin   {GetValidItem}
```

{The body of the procedure is given in the discussion on page 500.}

```
end;   {GetValidItem}
```

Figure 6-16   Case Study No. 9—Refined (Continued)

```pascal
procedure GetAmount(var Quantity : integer; ItemSub : integer);
{
        Written by:  XXXXXXXX  XX/XX/XX
           Purpose:  To obtain a valid quantity for an item
        Parameters:  Quantity - output, the quantity desired
                     ItemSub - input, the item's subscript
      Globals used:  Item - to access the inventory
}
var
  Limit     : integer;                      { Inventory available }

begin  {GetAmount}
  Limit := Item[ItemSub].Inventory;
  Write('Quantity desired (maximum ', Limit:1, '): ');
  Readln(Quantity);

  while (Quantity <= 0) or (Quantity > Limit) do
    begin
      Write(Chr(Bel), 'Quantity desired (maximum ', Limit:1, '): ');
      Readln(Quantity)
    end   {while}

end;   {GetAmount}

function CustomerLookup(CustNum : integer) : integer;
{
        Written by:  XXXXXXXX  XX/XX/XX
           Purpose:  To look for a customer number in the customer array
        Parameters:  CustNum - input, the number to look for
      Globals used:  Customer - to check the number
                     ControlRecord.NCust - to know array size
}
var
  I         : integer;                      { Array subscript }
  Found     : boolean;                      { Loop control }

begin  {CustomerLookup}
  I := 1;
  Found := false;

  while (not Found) and (I <= ControlRecord.NCust) do
    begin
      if CustNum = Customer[I].Number then
        Found := true
      else
        I := I + 1
    end;   {while}

  if Found then
    CustomerLookup := I
  else
    CustomerLookup := 0
end;   {CustomerLookup}
```

Figure 6-16 Case Study No. 9—Refined (Continued)

```
procedure GetCustomer(var Disc : real);
{
        Written by:  XXXXXXXXX  XX/XX/XX
           Purpose:  To input customer number and determine discount
        Parameters:  Disc - output, the discount
      Globals used:  Customer - to get the discount
    Functions used:  CustomerLookup - to look up item number in array
{
var
  CustNum        : integer;              { Customer number, user input }
  CustSub        : integer;              { Customer subscript }

begin   {GetCustomer}
  Writeln;
  Write('Enter customer #: ');
  Readln(CustNum);
  CustSub := CustomerLookup(CustNum);
  if CustSub = 0 then
    Disc := 0.0
  else
    Disc := Customer[CustSub].Discount
end;   {GetCustomer}

procedure Purchase;
{
        Written by:  XXXXXXXXX  XX/XX/XX
           Purpose:  To handle a customer's purchase.
      Globals used:  Item - to access the price
  Globals modified:  Modified - changed to true
   Procedures used:  GetValidItem - to obtain item subscript
                     GetAmount - to obtain quantity desired
                     GetCustomer - to get customer percentage
                     Pause - to wait for a user keystroke
}
var
  ItemSub    : integer;              { Subscript of item }
  Quantity   : integer;              { Number purchased }
  Gross      : real;                 { Cost before discount }
  Discount   : real;                 { Discount percentage }
  Net        : real;                 { Cost after discount }

begin   {Purchase}

    {The body of the procedure is given in the discussion on page 499.}

end;   {Purchase}

procedure NewCustomer;
{
        Written by:  XXXXXXXXX  XX/XX/XX
           Purpose:  To add a new customer
      Globals used:  ControlRecord.NCust - to see if array is full
                     MaxCust - to see if array is full
  Globals modified:  Modified - changed to true
                     Customer - new customer added at end
```

Figure 6-16   Case Study No. 9—Refined (Continued)

```
     Procedures used:  Pause - to wait for a user keystroke
      Functions used:  CustomerLookup - to check for a duplicate
}
var
  CustomerNo  : integer;                    { New customer # }
  Disc        : real;                       { New discount }

begin   {NewCustomer}

  {The body of the procedure is given in the discussion on page 501.}

end;   {NewCustomer}

procedure SaveData;
{
        Written by:   XXXXXXXX   XX/XX/XX
           Purpose:   To save the data to the files
      Globals used:   ControlFile - the control file handle
                      CustomerFile - the customer file handle
                      ItemFile - the item file handle
                      The following are written to the files
                        ControlRecord
                        Item
                        Customer
 Globals modified:   Modified - set to false
}
var
  I       : integer;                       { Loop control }

begin   {SaveData}
  Rewrite(ControlFile);
  Write(ControlFile, ControlRecord);
  Close(ControlFile);

  Rewrite(ItemFile);
  for I := 1 to ControlRecord.NItem do
    begin
      Write(ItemFile, Item[I])
    end;   {for}
  Close(ItemFile);

  Rewrite(CustomerFile);
  for I := 1 to ControlRecord.NCust do
    begin
      Write(CustomerFile, Customer[I])
    end;   {for}
  Close(CustomerFile);

  Modified := false;
  Writeln('Data has been saved to files');
  Pause
end;   {SaveData}
```

{procedure DumpData, as shown in Figure 6-16, is inserted here}

Figure 6-16   Case Study No. 9—Refined (Continued)

```
procedure Quit;
{
        Written by:  XXXXXXXX  XX/XX/XX
           Purpose:  To quit, first allowing a save if anything has
                     changed since the last save.
      Globals used:  Modified - to see if a save should be offered
   Procedures used:  SaveData - to save data to the files;
}
begin  {Quit}
  if Modified then
    begin
       Write(Chr(Bel));
       Writeln('Data modified since last save');
       Write('Do you wish to save (Y, N): ');
       Read(Kbd, Answer);

       while not (Answer in ['Y', 'y', 'N', 'n']) do
         begin
            Write(Chr(Bel));
            Read(Kbd, Answer)
         end;  {while}

       Writeln(Answer);
       Writeln;
       if Answer in ['Y', 'y'] then SaveData
    end  {if}
end;  {Quit}

{procedure Handle is unchanged.}

 procedure Initialize;
 {
        Written by:  XXXXXXXX  XX/XX/XX
           Purpose:  To open files and read data
   Globals modified: ControlFile - the control file handle
                     CustomerFile - the customer file handle
                     ItemFile - the item file handle
                     The following are read from the files
                        ControlRecord
                        Item
                        Customer
                     Modified - set to false
 }
 var
   I      : integer;                          { Loop control }

 begin  {Initialize}
   Assign(ControlFile, 'sales.ctr');
   Assign(ItemFile, 'sales.itm');
   Assign(CustomerFile, 'sales.cst');

   Reset(ControlFile);
   Read(ControlFile, ControlRecord);
   Close(ControlFile);
```

Figure 6-16   Case Study No. 9—Refined (Continued)

```
    Reset(ItemFile);
    for I := 1 to ControlRecord.NItem do
      begin
        Read(ItemFile, Item[I])
      end;  {for}
    Close(ItemFile);
    Reset(CustomerFile);

    for I := 1 to ControlRecord.NCust do
      begin
        Read(CustomerFile, Customer[I])
      end;  {for}

    Close(CustomerFile);

    Modified := false
  end;  {Initialize}


begin {PointOfSale}

  {Main program is unchanged.}

end.
```

Figure 6-16 Case Study No. 9—Refined

SaveData and Quit procedures. These are fairly straightforward. See Figure 6-16. We simply comment on their use of the Modified flag. The SaveData procedure sets it to false because now the data has not been modified since the last save. The Quit procedure allows the user to save the data if the Modified flag is true.

Test plan. We will not write a complete test plan, but rather describe a few tests to remind you of some of the testing strategies:

- Item number not in list
- Item number for item with 0 inventory
- Item number first in list; last in list; in between
- Quantity = entire remaining inventory
- Quantity one more than remaining inventory
- Quantity = 0; = 1
- Password correct, except it has trailing blanks
- New customer already in array − first, last, in between
- Customer array full
- Try to add same new customer twice
- Do several purchases of same item, driving inventory to 0 eventually
- Add several customers in a row to fill the array
- New customer already in array, with array full (should tell us "already in array", *not* "array full")

CASE STUDY No. 10

In this case study we will prepare a package of subprograms rather than a single program. The modules in the package will enable us to write programs that manipulate polynomials in a single variable. While we are writing such programs, we will be able to concentrate on the problem we wish to solve and not on the details of how to work with polynomials because the package of subprograms will handle those details.

Statement of problem. Polynomials of degree n or less in a single unknown, say x, can be written as

$$c_0 + c_1x + c_2x^2 + \ldots + c_nx^n$$

where the c's are the coefficients of the individual powers of x.

Such a polynomial can be specified completely by giving the values for the coefficients and the name of the single unknown. We want to have a collection of subprograms for performing arithmetic and other operations on polynomials of a single unknown that we will call X.

Analysis. There are a number of ways to represent polynomials in the computer. Some use techniques not yet covered. The one we present has a number of drawbacks. For example, there is a limit placed on the degree of the polynomials. However, it has the advantage of being one of the easiest to understand.

In the case study, then, we choose to represent the polynomials by real arrays containing their coefficients. For example, a polynomial P will be represented by an array C declared as

```
type
   Polynomial = array[0 .. MaxDegree] of real;

var
   P : Polynomial;
```

(MaxDegree is a constant defined in the const section.)

Note that we are taking advantage of the fact that we can specify a lower bound other than 1 for the array subscripts. Thus, the coefficient of X^K in the polynomial is the element of the array with subscript K.

We will next decide on the operations to be performed. We normally would like to provide addition, subtraction, multiplication, and division. (Division is fairly difficult and, therefore, we will not do that in this example.) Other operations that we can provide are the evaluation of a polynomial for a given value of X and integration and differentiation by X. More computer related operations would be reading and writing polynomials, finding the degree of a polynomial, comparing two polynomials to see if they are the same polynomial, and copying one polynomial into another. We shall also include some special cases of multiplication, namely by a constant and by X. Refer to Table 6-1 for a summary of these operations.

We must next decide on the form our operations will take. Most of the operations will require a number of steps to complete, and so it seems reasonable to use subprograms for the operations. Most of the operations will have a polyno-

Table 6-1 Operations to be provided by polynomial package

(a) Addition
(b) Subtraction
(c) Multiplication
(d) Multiplication by a constant
(e) Multiplication by X
(f) Evaluate a polynomial
(g) Integrate a polynomial
(h) Differentiate a polynomial
(i) Read a polynomial
(j) Write a polynomial
(k) Find the degree of a polynomial
(l) Compare two polynomials for equality
(m) Copy a polynomial

mial for a result. In Pascal, a function cannot return an array as the function value, and the polynomials are being represented by arrays. It therefore seems reasonable to use procedures for these operations. Operations (f), (k), and (l) do return single values and thus could be implemented using functions.

Let us name the subprograms with names that start with "Poly" for polynomial and end with characters in some sense descriptive of the operation. Thus, we will use names like PolyAdd, PolySub, PolyMult, and PolyEval. By starting with the characters Poly, the routines will usually be listed together in any automatically generated alphabetical lists of subprograms used in any program. Although this is not a consideration in using Turbo Pascal, it is in many production environments.

The arithmetic operations require two operands and one result. Also, we will sometimes use another argument to indicate success or failure of the operation.

The operation

```
R := OP1 - OP2
```

could be represented with six different orderings of R, OP1, and OP2. However, it would be very confusing to the user of the routine to have OP1 follow OP2 or to have OP1 separated from OP2 by the result R. Therefore, the two reasonable choices for the ordering of these three seem to be R, OP1, OP2 and OP1, OP2, R. As we did in Case Study No. 7 (Section 5-4), we will choose the order OP1, OP2, R.

For example, the first routine would have this header line:

```
procedure PolyAdd(P, Q : Polynomial;
                  var Result : Polynomial);
```

Result is the array representing the result polynomial, and P and Q are the arrays representing the operand polynomials.

One remaining question is the size of the arrays to be used. We will pick 50 as the maximum degree of the polynomials, writing

```
const
   MaxDegree = 50;
```

in the main program. This global constant will be referenced by many of the submodules.

Algorithms and programs. Most of the algorithms are very simple and short, so in many cases we will omit the variable lists. Also, because we have many short programs, we will show them right after the discussion of the algorithm.

Addition of two polynomials is performed by adding the coefficients of the same power of X. The sum of

$$5x^5 - 4x^2 + 6$$

and

$$6x^5 + 2x^3 + 3$$

is

$$11x^5 + 2x^3 - 4x^2 + 9$$

The first and second polynomials are represented by arrays containing

$$6 \quad 0 \quad -4 \quad 0 \quad 0 \quad 5$$

and

$$3 \quad 0 \quad 0 \quad 2 \quad 0 \quad 6$$

as their first six elements (in positions 0 through 5). The result is represented by the array

$$9 \quad 0 \quad -4 \quad 2 \quad 0 \quad 11$$

The algorithm uses a count-control loop to add each corresponding array element. This can be easily coded in Pascal, as shown in Figure 6-17.

The subtraction routine is very similar to the addition routine. Multiplication, on the other hand, is much more complex. The product of two polynomials

---

```
procedure PolyAdd(P, Q: Polynomial;
                  var Result: Polynomial);
{
    Written by :   XXXXXXXXX   XX/XX/XX
        Purpose :  To add two polynomials
  Globals used :   MaxDegree, constant for maximum degree
    Parameters :   P, Q - input, the polynomials to add
                   Result - output, the resulting sum
}
var
  I      : integer;                {loop control}

begin  {PolyAdd}

  for I := 0 to MaxDegree do
    begin
      Result[I] := P[I] + Q[I]
    end    {for}

end;   {PolyAdd}
```

Figure 6-17 Adding Two Polynomials

$$p_0 + p_1x + p_2x^2$$

and

$$q_0 + q_1x + q_2x^2 + q_3x^3$$

is

$$p_0q_0 + (p_0q_1 + p_1q_0)x + (p_0q_2 + p_1q_1 + p_2q_0)x^2$$
$$+ (p_0q_3 + p_1q_2 + p_2q_1)x^3 + (p_1q_3 + p_2q_2)x^4 + p_2q_3x^5$$

The first polynomial has three terms and the second four terms. The product has twelve individual terms, each a product of one P term and one Q term. In other words, each P coefficient is multiplied by each Q coefficient. The power of x in the product associated with the term p_iq_j is just $i + j$.

The degree of the product polynomial is the sum of the degrees of the two factors. This is one place where it will be convenient to have a routine to compute the degree of a polynomial. Let us define that routine as an integer function named PolyDegree. It will have a single parameter, which is a polynomial. We will write the function later.

In order to multiply each term of polynomial P by each term of polynomial Q, we will need a nested loop structure. We will use the variables IP and IQ as indices for the loops. For the degrees of P and Q, we will use the variables PDegree and QDegree. Similarly, we will use IR and RDegree for the index and degree, respectively, associated with the result polynomial Result.

The rough algorithm for the multiplication routine would be:

1. Compute the degree of Result and check for a legal value.

2. Initialize the coefficients of Result to zero.

3. Compute all the products of the terms of P and Q, adding them into the appropriate terms of Result.

The first step becomes

```
PDegree := PolyDegree(P);
QDegree := PolyDegree(Q);
RDegree := PDegree + QDegree;
if RDegree > MaxDegree then
  OK := false
else
                 . . . .
```

The output parameter OK will be used to indicate to the calling program whether the multiplication was possible.

Within the "else" branch, we set OK to true and perform the second and third steps of our algorithm.

The second step becomes

```
for IR := 0 to 50 do
  R[IR] := 0.0
```

Notice that we initialize all elements of R to zero and not just the elements from 0 to RDegree. This is done so that later calculations, such as adding or finding the

```
procedure PolyMult(P, Q : Polynomial;
                   var Result : Polynomial; var OK : boolean);
{
    Written by :  XXXXXXXXX  XX/XX/XX
       Purpose :  To multiply two polynomials
  Globals used :  MaxDegree, constant for maximum degree
    Parameters :  P, Q - input, the polynomials to multiply
                  Result - output, the resulting product
}
var
  IR          :  integer;          {index for Result}
  IP          :  integer;          {index for P}
  IQ          :  integer;          {index for Q}
  RDegree     :  integer;          {degree for Result}
  PDegree     :  integer;          {degree for P}
  QDegree     :  integer;          {degree for Q}

begin    {PolyMult}

{*** Calculate Result degree, see if legal.}

  PDegree := PolyDegree(P);
  QDegree := PolyDegree(Q);
  RDegree := PDegree + QDegree;
  if RDegree > MaxDegree then
    OK := false
  else

{*** Set OK, initialize result to 0.}

    begin
      OK := true;

      for IR := 0 to MaxDegree do
        begin
          Result[IR] := 0;
        end;  {for}

{*** Multiply P, Q terms; add to Result terms. }

      for IP := 0 to PDegree do
        begin
          for IQ := 0 to QDegree do
            begin
              IR := IP + IQ;
              R[IR] := R[IR] + P[IP] * Q[IQ]
            end  {for IQ}
        end  {for IP}
    end    {if}
end;    {PolyMult}
```

Figure 6-18 Multiplying Two Polynomials

degree, will work correctly. The main part of the algorithm will be the nested loops multiplying the individual terms and adding to the proper terms in R:

```
for IP := 0 to PDegree do
  begin
    for IQ := 0 to QDegree do
      begin
        IR := IP + IQ;
        R[IR] := R[IR] + P[IP] * Q[IQ]
      end  {for IQ}
  end  {for IP}
```

Combining the pieces, we obtain the procedure shown in Figure 6-18.

Let us now work on the PolyDegree function used in PolyMult. The degree of a polynomial P is the highest power of X that appears in the polynomial. This corresponds to the subscript of the last nonzero coefficient for the polynomial. A simple way to find that element is to search the array from the last term back until we find a nonzero element. Note that if all the elements are zero, then the polynomial represents the constant zero and the degree is zero.

This can be written using our usual searching techniques, as outlined here:

1. Set Found to false and I to MaxDegree.

2. In a loop, examine P[I]. If it is nonzero, set Found to true; otherwise decrement I.

3. The loop terminates when Found is true or I reaches 0.

4. After the loop, I will be the answer. Notice this is true no matter which condition causes the loop termination.

Based on this discussion, we write the function given in Figure 6-19.

Now let us consider the routine for evaluating a polynomial. It will require two arguments: the array of coefficients and the value of X. The routine will return only a single value and therefore can be a function. Let us call the function PolyEval, with arguments P and X.

A first rough algorithm might look like

PDegree := PolyDegree(P);
Value := P[0];
for I := 1 to PDegree do
    add P[I] times Ith power of X to Value

To compute X to the Ith power, we could use

```
XToI := X;
for J := 2 to I do
  XToI := XToI * X
```

This approach would require $I - 1$ multiplications. To compute the value of a polynomial of degree N would require N multiplications of coefficients by powers of X plus

$$(N - 1) + (N - 2) + (N - 3) + \ldots + 2 + 1$$

```
function PolyDegree(P : Polynomial) : integer;
{
    Written by :   XXXXXXXX  XX/XX/XX
        Purpose :  To find the degree of a polynomial
   Globals used :  MaxDegree, constant for maximum degree
     Parameters :  P - input, the polynomial whose degree is sought
}
var
    I          :  integer;          {array index}
    Found      :  boolean;          {used to quit loop}

begin  {PolyDegree}
  Found := False;
  I := MaxDegree;

  while (I > 0) and (not Found) do
    begin
      if P[I] <> 0 then
        Found := true
      else
        I := I - 1
    end;  {while}

  PolyDegree := I
end;  {PolyDegree}
```

Figure 6-19 The Degree of a Polynomial

additional multiplications to compute the various powers of X. The expression $(N - 1) + \ldots + 2 + 1$ above is equal to

$$\frac{N(N - 1)}{2}$$

and so the total number of multiplications needed is

$$\frac{N^2}{2} - \frac{N}{2} + N = \frac{N^2}{2} + \frac{N}{2}$$

If N were 50, this would require 1275 multiplications. This number can be reduced considerably. Notice first that the powers of X are needed in sequence. Rather than compute the Ith power of X starting from scratch, we can compute it from the $(I - 1)$st power. This leads to the following code:

```
            PDegree := PolyDegree(P);
            XToI := 1;
            Value := P[0];

            for I := 1 to PDegree do
              begin
                XToI := XToI * X;
                Value := Value + P[I] * XToI
              end;  {for}

            PolyEval := Value
```

For this algorithm, the number of multiplications for a polynomial of degree N is just 2N. Note that for N = 50, this is a reduction by a factor of almost 13.

There is still a better method, commonly called **Horner's method**. A polynomial such as

$$p_0 + p_1x + p_2x^2 + p_3x^3 + p_4x^4$$

can be rewritten in a nested form as

$$p_0 + x(p_1 + x(p_2 + x(p_3 + x(p_4)))).$$

This can be evaluated in the order

$$\text{val} := p_4$$

$$\text{val} := p_3 + x * \text{val}$$

$$\text{val} := p_2 + x * \text{val}$$

$$\text{val} := p_1 + x * \text{val}$$

$$\text{val} := p_0 + x * \text{val}$$

When we are finished, val will be the value of the polynomial. We will have used, in this case, only four multiplications. In general, the algorithm would be that shown in the function of Figure 6-20.

Of course, here a polynomial of degree N requires N multiplications. Notice that in this situation the fastest of our three algorithms is also the shortest to write. One should not assume that this last procedure will be twice as fast as the second procedure because there are other operations, such as additions, loop control, etc., involved. Still this should be faster than the others on most conventional computer systems.

```
function PolyEval(P : Polynomial; X : real) : real;
{
    Written by :   XXXXXXXX   XX/XX/XX
        Purpose :  To evaluate a polynomial for a given x value
     Parameters :  P - input, the polynomial to evaluate
                   X - input, the given x value
}
var
  PDegree    : integer;                  {degree of P}
  Value      : real;                     {local copy of answer}
  I          : integer;                  {loop control}

begin
  PDegree := PolyDegree(P);
  Value := P[PDegree];

  for I := PolyDegree -1 downto 0 do
    begin
      Value := P[I] + X * Value
    end;  {for}

  PolyEval := Value
end;  {PolyEval}
```

Figure 6-20 Evaluating a Polynomial (Horner's Method)

The routines for integration and differentiation use similar methods. If you haven't studied calculus yet, you can skip this material without affecting your understanding of the other routines in the package.

The integral of a polynomial is the sum of the integrals of each of the terms plus an arbitrary constant. The integral of the term

$$p_i x^i$$

is

$$\frac{p_i x^{i+1}}{i + 1}$$

The result is a new polynomial, say Result, with the $(i + 1)$st coefficient of Result being the ith coefficient of P divided by $i + 1$. For the degree of Result to be less than or equal to MaxDegree, the degree of P must be less than or equal to MaxDegree $- 1$.

```
procedure PolyIntegrate(P : Polynomial; C : real;
                        var Result : Polynomial; var OK : boolean);
{
    Written by:   XXXXXXXX   XX/XX/XX
       Purpose:   To integrate a polynomial
    Parameters:   P - input, the polynomial to integrate
                  C - input, the constant of integration
                  Result - output, the resulting integral
                  OK - output, indicates whether or not o.k.
  Globals used:   MaxDegree - largest possible degree
}
var
   PDegree   : integer;           {degree of P}
   I         : integer;           {loop control}

begin  {PolyIntegrate}
   PDegree := PolyDegree(P);
   if PDegree > MaxDegree - 1 then
     OK := false
   else
     begin
       OK := true;
       Result[0] := C;

       for I := 2 to PDegree + 1 do
         begin
           Result[I] := P[I-1] / I
         end;  {for}

       for I := PDegree + 2 to MaxDegree do
         begin
           Result[I] := 0
         end   {for}

     end   {if}
end;  {PolyIntegrate}
```

Figure 6-21 Integrating a Polynomial

Let us call our routine PolyIntegrate and use arguments P, C, Result, and OK. P is the original polynomial, C is the arbitrary constant, Result is the result polynomial, and OK indicates success. See Figure 6-21.

For our final example we will write the output routine. This should be a procedure because it returns no value. It needs only the one argument, the polynomial to be printed. Let us call the routine PolyOut. Suppose we print all coefficients except the constant term as

$$(dddddd.ddddd) \quad * \quad X \quad ** \quad (dd)$$

where the d's stand for digits, and the constant term as

$$(dddddd.ddddd)$$

(This uses ** to stand for exponentiation, a common notation.)

Also, let us not print any terms with a zero coefficient; however, we should be sure to print at least one term. We will use a Boolean variable AnyPrinted to indicate whether any terms have been printed. The procedure is shown in Figure 6-22.

Testing. Testing a package of subprograms differs from testing a program in several ways. First, the individual subprograms cannot stand alone, and so you must write programs to call the subprograms. These programs are commonly called drivers. Second, the individual routines tend to be fairly simple, and so tests can sometimes be fairly simple also.

```
procedure PolyOut(P : Polynomial);
{
    Written by:   xxxxxxxx, xx/xx/xx
       Purpose:   To print out a polynomial
  Globals used:   MaxDegree, constant for maximum degree
    Parameters:   P - input, the polynomial to print
}
var
  AnyPrinted  : boolean;            {to make sure we print something}
  I           : integer;           {loop control}

begin   {PolyOut}
  AnyPrinted := false;

  for I := MaxDegree downto 1 do
    begin
      if P[I] < > 0 then
        begin
          Writeln('(', P[I]:12:5, ') * X ** (', I:2, ')');
          AnyPrinted := true
        end   {if}
    end;   {for}

  if (P[0] <> 0) or (not AnyPrinted) then
    Writeln('(', P[0]:12:5, ')')
end;   {PolyOut}
```

Figure 6-22   Output of a Polynomial

Probably the input and output subroutines should be tested first. In that way, you can use those routines when you test the others. A simple way to test these routines is to use a driver program that calls PolyIn (the input routine) and PolyOut in a loop. You can then check the output to see if it matches your input. The driver should also print the array corresponding to the polynomial that has been read by PolyIn to guard against errors in PolyOut and PolyIn that might cancel each other. An example of such an error would be if PolyIn placed the coefficients in the wrong elements of the array and PolyOut picked up the elements in the same wrong manner. The test data for the driver should include polynomials of degree 0, 1, MaxDegree − 1, MaxDegree, and some over MaxDegree. (You may wish to reduce the size of MaxDegree for most of the tests.) Some of the polynomials should consist of just a few nonzero terms, whereas others should have all nonzero terms. The constant 0 should be one of the test values because that will cause a special action in the PolyOut routine.

Once PolyIn and PolyOut are tested and appear to be correct, you can begin testing the others. A driver that reads two polynomials and computes their degrees, adds them, subtracts them, differentiates them, compares for equality, and multiplies by X would be a natural next step and would test a large number of the routines. These operations have been grouped because they each require one or two input polynomials but do not require any additional data. In addition, separate drivers should be used to provide each routine that has error checks with invalid data to check the error handling.

The copy routine can be tested after the routine for comparing for equality. Finally, the last group to be tested could be the routines for evaluating a polynomial, multiplication by a constant, and integration. This group requires both a polynomial and a real value as inputs for each routine.

The detailed unit test plans for the various modules are left as an exercise. To get you started, we list a few possible tests for two of the modules.

For PolyDegree: degree MaxDegree
degree 1
degree 0 (not zero polynomial)
degree 0 (zero polynomial)

For PolyAdd: both polynomials zero
first polynomial zero
second polynomial zero
neither polynomial zero, result not zero
neither polynomial zero, result zero

Documentation. The documentation for a package of subprograms would normally include a description of what operations are provided, how the polynomials are represented, how the user has to define the data arrays that hold the polynomials, and, finally, a detailed description of each routine in the package. The detailed description should include precise descriptions of how to call each routine and precise descriptions of each argument. It would be desirable to include examples of the use of each routine. You can use Pascal terminology, if convenient, to describe these routines because anyone using the package has to know Pascal to write a program calling the routines. Notice that the user documentation for a package such as this differs from that for a program. For a program, Pascal terminology would not be appropriate for the user's guide. See Appendix B.

Exercises 1 to 5 refer to Case Study No. 9.

EXERCISES

1. a. Write a program to initially create the data files used by the case study.
   b. Modify the Initialize procedure to obtain the base part of the file name from the user, and check that files <base>.ctr, <base>.itm, and <base>.cst exist prior to opening them. See the hint for Exercise 11b, Section 6-2.

2. The case study uses a linear search for item number and customer number. What changes would be necessary to use a binary search? Caution: The new customer insertion would change.

3. Modify the Purchase activity as follows:
   a. Allow the user to abort the process of obtaining a valid item number. (This avoids the possibility of being stuck forever in the Purchase procedure if the item numbers entered are all invalid.)
   b. Obtain a list of one or more item numbers and quantities rather than just one.
   c. Double the discount for preferred customers if the total bill is at least $500.
   d. Add sales tax to the bill.
   e. Add to part (b) as follows: When the user can enter several item numbers, it is possible that he or she may want to abort the whole activity. Allow this to occur at any point up to indicating that the list of input is through. This must adjust the inventory properly. Hint: One way to solve this involves building up the purchase information in an array. Assume that there will be no more than 30 individual items input.

4. Modify the new customer procedure as follows:
   a. Require the user to enter a password before a new customer can be entered.
   b. Validate the discount entered. It must lie between 0.0 and 10.0 percent. (It can be 10.0, but not 0.0.)

5. Add the following activities. Note: To avoid "clutter" in your menu, you may want to reorganize the menu. For example, you might have a single menu item for the various "Utility" activities, such as adding an item or a customer, changing a price, etc. Choosing this item would cause a submenu to be displayed for the various utility activities.

   a. Add an item to the list.
   b. Remove an item from the list.
   c. Change a price.
   d. Change a discount percentage.
   e. Change the password. You might wish to store the valid password on the control file.
   f. See part (e). If the control file contains the password, it should not be in character form. Modify the program to store the password on the control file as a record containing: (1) length of the password and (2) an array of the Ord values for the characters in the password.
   g. Query: Given an item, what is the current price and inventory?

h. Query: Given a customer number, what is the discount?

i. Generate an order. Add a field to the item file indicating a cutoff point. When the inventory drops below that point, it is time to reorder. This activity should print a list of all items that should be reordered.

Exercises 6 to 12 refer to Case Study No. 10.

6. a. Design and write an interactive version of the module PolyIn(P, EndOf-Data). You will need to devise a way for the user to indicate that she or he does not wish to enter more data. In addition, you will need a way to terminate the polynomial being entered. EndOfData is a Boolean parameter set to true if the user does not wish to enter a polynomial, otherwise false.

b. Design and write a file version of the module. It should read its data from a text file opened by the main program. (Prompts are not appropriate in this version.)

7. a. Design and write the routines for multiplication of a polynomial by a constant or by X.

b. If you have studied calculus, design and write the routine for differentiation.

c. Design and write the routines for comparing for equality and copying polynomials.

8. Think carefully about how you do polynomial division. Write a routine to divide P by Q, giving a quotient polynomial and a remainder polynomial. Hint: If you think about it, you may be able to write this almost entirely in terms of other routines in the package.

9. Test all of the routines written in Exercises 6 to 8.

10. The family of polynomials known as the Chebyshev polynomials is used in several different areas of mathematics. These polynomials are denoted by

$$T_N(x)$$

where N is the degree of the individual polynomial. The first few of these are defined as

$$T_0(x) = 1$$
$$T_1(x) = x$$
$$T_2(x) = 2x^2 - 1$$

and

$$T_{10}(x) = 512x^{10} - 1280x^8 + 1120x^6 - 400x^4 + 50x^2 - 1$$

The polynomial of degree N can be calculated from those of degree N − 1 and degree N − 2 by the equation:

$$T_N(x) = 2xT_{N-1}(x) - T_{N-2}(x)$$

Write a program using the polynomial package to compute and print the Chebyshev polynomials for N = 0 through N = 15. How would you have to modify the package for N greater than 15?

*11. a. Revise each of the routines developed in the case study to use the following representation of a polynomial.

```
type
  Polynomial = record
                 Degree : integer;
                 Coeff  : array[1 .. MaxDegree] of real
               end;
```

The degree is stored as part of the record, and the coefficient array contains meaningful data only for the portion indicated by the degree.

b. Repeat part (a) for the routines developed in Exercises 6 to 8.

c. What differences would the revised representation of a polynomial make for Exercise 10?

*12. Follow the instructions for Exercise 11 for this data structure. A polynomial will be represented as a list of its nonzero terms. For example, $5x^6 - 4x^3 + 7.5$ would have these values stored:

3 (there are 3 terms)

5.0, 6   a record representing $5x^6$

−4.0, 3   a record representing $-4x^3$

7.5, 0   a record representing 7.5 ($=7.5x^0$)

The terms will be stored in order from the highest degree to the lowest. We will use the declarations:

```
const
  MaxTerms = 50;              {maximum number of terms}
type
  Term =
    record
      Coeff : real;
      Power : integer
    end;
  Polynomial =
    record
      NTerms : integer;
      Terms  : array[1 .. MaxTerms] of Term
    end;
```

Hint: The add routine can be done using the "array merge" type logic, as described in Exercise 21 of Section 6-3.

Exercises 13 to 14 suggest packages of subprograms that could be developed to aid in working with certain types of problems.

13. Integers of long length can be stored in the computer as arrays, one digit per array element. For example, a 15-digit number could be represented as an integer array Number of size 15. Number[1] would contain the first digit of the number, Number[15] the last digit.

*a. Write a procedure to add two such numbers. It should give an indication of whether or not the answer will fit in the array that represents the answer.

b. Subtract two such numbers, indicating whether it is possible to do so.

c. Compare two such numbers to see whether the first is greater than the second. (This might be a Boolean function.)

d. Multiply two such numbers.

e. Use this package to find the sum

$$1 + 2 + 4 + 8 \ldots + 2^1 + \ldots + 2^{63}$$

(The answer is fewer than 30 digits long.)

14. Numbers in base 10 can be represented as arrays, each array element having one digit whose value is 0 to 9 (see Exercise 13). If we limit our digits to 0 to 7, we have a "base 8" number instead of a base 10 number.

For example, in base 8, the array

$$0 \quad 0 \quad 0 \quad 0 \quad 1 \quad 5 \quad 3$$

would represent $1 * 8^2 + 5 * 8 + 3 = 107$.

Write procedures or functions for the following:

*a. Given an array and a base, calculate the value of the number represented by the array in that base.
b. Given a value, convert it to an array in a given base.
c. Print the number represented by an array, given the array and the base.

For example,

array	base	result
0,0,8,0,3	10	803
0,1,5,1,0	8	1510
0,15,10,1,9	16	FA19

Hint: Convert the given array to an array of characters, with leading zeros converted to blanks. Notice that for base 16, the digits are 0 to 9 and A to F, with A = 10, etc. An array containing the characters '0', '1', etc. may help.

d–g. Revise parts (a) to (d) of Exercise 13 to work for arrays representing numbers in any given base.

Exercises 15 to 21 suggest other "case study" type applications.

15. a. A simple encryption ("secret code") method is to jumble the alphabet, replacing, for example, A by D, B by X, C by M, and so on. One way to implement this uses two parallel arrays. The first contains the letters in order, and the second contains the letters in the desired jumbled order (for example, D, X, M, . . .). Give the declarations and assignment statements to create these arrays.
b. Another approach would be to use one array indexed by the char values 'A' to 'Z'. Give the necessary declarations and assignment statements to set this up.
c. Write a subprogram segment to encode a single character. Assume that characters that are not letters are replaced by themselves (CAB$ might become MDX$). Use the representation of either part (a) or part (b).
d. Write a main program that codes or decodes lines of text. It will read a series of lines, each 65 columns long. The first character of each line should contain either a C or D to indicate whether the remaining 64 characters should be coded or decoded.
e. Modify your program to handle both uppercase and lowercase letters.

16. a. Modify Exercise 15 to use the following different encryption method: A is

replaced by G, B by H, C by I, and so on. Each letter is replaced by the sixth letter further along in the alphabet. Some care is required to properly handle the letters near the end; for example, Z is replaced by F. Use only a single array containing the letters in order.

   b. Modify Exercise 15 to replace A by Z, B by Y, C by X, D by W, and so on. Use only a single array containing the letters in order.

17. Write subprograms for the following actions that deal with an array of records containing employee ID, sales, and rate. There are presently NEmployees employees represented in these arrays. Hint: Write a search function first.

   *a. Inquire. Given an ID number, print the sales amount and rate for that employee or print an error message if the given ID is faulty.

   b. New sale. Given a sales amount and ID, add the amount to the Sales figure for that ID (or print an error message). Also calculate the commission as sales amount times rate.

   c. Change the rate. Given a new rate and an ID, change the rate for that employee to the given new rate or print an error message.

   d. Find the largest. Print the ID, rate, and sales amount of the salesman with the largest sales amount.

   e. New employee. Given a new employee ID and rate, add that employee to the end of the list. If the ID is already in use, print an error message.

   f. Sort. Sort the data in order by sales (highest to lowest).

18. Repeat Exercise 17 under the assumption that the array is maintained in increasing numerical order by employee number. Notice that for part (e), the new employee goes at the proper place based on his ID, which is not necessarily at the end of the list. For part (f), create a separate sorted array.

   Hint: Rewrite the search function so it returns the subscript of the first table element larger than or equal to the given key. This will simplify part (e), but it will also require some changes in parts (a) to (c).

19. a. Write a general-purpose procedure to copy a portion of the array B to the array A. Assume A and B are integer arrays, each of size 200.

     The routine will be given A, APosn, B, BPosn, and ArrLength. APosn and BPosn represent the starting positions in the A and B arrays, respectively. ArrLength is the number of items to be copied. You can assume that ArrLength is valid, that is, copying that many items will not run past the end of either A or B.

   b. Rewrite part (a) to handle the possibility that ArrLength may be "too long." The routine should copy up to ArrLength items, taking care to stay within the bounds of both arrays. For example, APosn = 199, BPosn = 3, and ArrLength = 14. Only two items are copied to A[199] and A[200].

20. In Case Study No. 4 (Figures 4-11 to 4-13) we presented a program to find all the primes less than or equal to a number N. To do so, we checked each number I from 2 to N to see if I was prime.

   The method used to see if I is prime can be improved significantly using arrays. To see if I is prime, we checked for divisibility by all the numbers from 2 to I-1. It would suffice to check for divisibility by all the *primes* from 2 to $\sqrt{I}$. If, as we located a prime, we put it into an array of primes, then this check would be easy to accomplish.

   Write a program which carries out this procedure.

21. An efficient method for determining all the primes less than some given value N is the so-called *sieve of Eratosthenes*, which consists of two major phases. The first is to write the positive integers from 2 to N. The second phase is a nested search and marking process. Starting with the first un-marked number in the list, say K (at the start, all the numbers are un-marked), go through the list and mark off all multiples of K.

    The result of applying this process three times to the numbers from 2 to 34 is shown in the list below. The marks (X) are shown above the numbers so that we can indicate at which time the markings occurred. Notice that some numbers are marked more than once. The first mark shows all numbers divisible by 2 except for 2. The second mark shows all values divisible by 3 except for 3. The third mark shows all values divisible by 5 (4 was already marked because it is divisible by 2). Upon completion of the entire marking process, all numbers divisible by some smaller number other than 1 have been marked. The unmarked values thus are primes.

	2	3	4	5	6	7	8	9	10	11	12
Third								X			
Second					X			X			X
First			X		X		X		X		X

	13	14	15	16	17	18	19	20	21	22	23
Third			X					X			
Second			X			X			X		
First		X		X		X		X		X	

	24	25	26	27	28	29	30	31	32	33	34
Third		X					X				
Second	X			X			X			X	
First	X		X		X		X		X		X

    The key to the efficiency of this process is that the marking process does not require any checking of divisibility. In general, the multiples of K are in positions 2K, 2K + K, 2K + 2K, and so on. Also, notice that only values up to K = $\sqrt{N}$ need to be processed.

a. Write Pascal code for initializing an integer array Num, with subscripts ranging from 2 to 2000, to the values 2, 3, . . . , 2000.

b. Write Pascal code that, given the array Num initialized as in part (a), carries out the marking process described for the sieve of Eratosthenes. One way of marking the numbers is to set the array element equal to zero.

c. The values of the numbers do not actually have to be used because the positions of the numbers can indicate their values in this algorithm. Re-write parts (a) and (b) using a Boolean array Marked, with subscripts ranging from 2 to 1000. Initialize the elements to false, and indicate mark-ing by setting an element to true. After marking, we can determine if a value J (2 ≤ J ≤ 2000) is prime by checking to see if Marked[J] is true or false.

d. Write a program to produce a printed table of primes up to 2000 with 10 primes printed on each line. Be sure that the last line is printed whether or not it includes 10 numbers.

22. Compare the efficiency of the programs written in Exercises 20 and 21, by timing them for various values of N.

23. Revise the program of Figure 6-10 (Section 6-2) to develop a menu-driven system that allows various activities with the data on the files. You might include, for example, the ability to initialize the files, add students, delete students, change grades, calculate current averages, set values for tests and programs, and so on.

7

MORE ON ARRAYS

7-1
☐☐☐☐☐☐
**MORE ON
ARRAYS**

In Chapter 6, we introduced the fundamental techniques for dealing with arrays. In this chapter, we will deal with some additional array concepts that can prove useful in your programming. In the first section, we discuss arrays of arrays and the particular case of the representation of matrices. We also discuss some input and output considerations for arrays. In the second section, we present a powerful programming technique and explain how to use arrays to use the technique in Pascal programs.

☐
**ARRAYS OF
ARRAYS**

The form for declaring an array is

        array [*index type*] of *component type*;

The index type is frequently of the form 1 .. N for some integer N, but it can also be, for example, a user-defined scalar type. The component type can, among other types, be integer, real, a string type, or a record type. It can also be an array type. Thus, for example, we can declare an array to consist of three arrays, where each of those arrays consists of four real numbers. There are three ways to accomplish this. First, we could translate what we have written into Pascal more or less directly:

```
type
   ArrayofArrays = array [1 .. 3] of array [1 .. 4] of real;
```

Second, we could predefine the notion of an array of four real numbers, then use that in our definition of the array of arrays:

```
type
   RealArray4    = array [1 .. 4] of real;
   ArrayofArrays = array [1 .. 3] of RealArray4;
```

Finally, Pascal provides an abbreviated form of declaration as follows:

```
type
    ArrayofArrays = array[1 .. 3, 1 .. 4] of real;
```

In this example, we can think of the declaration as: (1) showing the number of arrays (three, indexed by 1 .. 3) and (2) describing each as consisting of four real numbers (indexed by 1 .. 4).

It is important to realize that each of these describes precisely the same type. The three methods simply give alternative ways to describe the type.

If we declare a variable X to be of the type ArrayofArrays, then it will consist of three arrays of four real numbers each. It is useful, at times, to be able to visualize such an array of arrays. A common technique is to list the three arrays one below the other, as illustrated here:

3.6	−1.0	4.2	1.0
2.9	7.8	11.5	0.0
0.5	−0.1	−6.5	10.2

Because of this commonly used visualization, arrays of arrays are frequently referred to as **two-dimensional arrays**.

Within an array of arrays, we can refer to the entire array by using its name (X, in our example). We can also refer to X[1], which is the first array, consisting of the four numbers 3.6, −1.0, 4.2, and 1.0. X[2] is the second array, and X[3] is the third.

It is also possible to refer to the individual numbers within the array of arrays. One way to refer to the number 4.2, for example, is to realize that it is the third number in the array X[1]. Thus, we can write

$$X[1][3]$$

Similarly, X[2][4] refers to the fourth number in X[2], whose value is 0.0 in the illustration above.

Pascal provides an alternative way to say the same thing. Rather than writing X[1][3], we can abbreviate this as X[1, 3]. The two notations mean exactly the same thing: the third number in the array X[1]. Notice that, because of this meaning, both X[4, 2] and X[3, 5] would be illegal. The first says to take the second value of X[4], and there is no X[4]. The second says to take the fifth value of X[3], and X[3] contains only four numbers.

An interpretation of X[I][J] or X[I, J], then, is as follows. The first subscript tells which array to choose, and the second which number within that array. If we are picturing the array in the table form described above, the first subscript tells which row to choose, the second which number within that row.

To further illustrate these ideas, in the context of a meaningful application, we will work extensively with the following example. We wish to use an array to represent the monthly rainfall in inches for several cities of the United States. For each city in the list, Philadelphia, New York, Atlanta, Los Angeles, and Chicago, we will have a list of 12 real numbers representing the rainfall for the 12 months. We wish to obtain a data structure with which we can specify one of the cities, one of the months of the year, and obtain the average rainfall. Some alternative ways of defining the data structure are[1]

1. Separate Declaration.

```
type
  Months = (January, February, March, April, May, June, July,
            August, September, October, November, December);
  Amount = array [Months] of real;
  Cities = (Philadelphia, New_York, Washington_DC,
            Los_Angeles, Chicago);

var
  MonthlyRain : array [Cities] of Amount;
```

2. Joint Declaration.

```
type
  Months = (January, February, March, April, May, June, July,
            August, September, October, November, December);
  Cities = (Philadelphia, New_York, Washington_DC,
            Los_Angeles, Chicago);

var
  MonthlyRain : array [Cities] of array [Months] of real;
```

3. Abbreviated Joint Declaration.

```
type
  Months = (January, February, March, April, May, June, July,
            August, September, October, November, December);
  Cities = (Philadelphia, New_York, Washington_DC,
            Los_Angeles, Chicago);

var
  MonthlyRain : array [Cities, Months] of real;
```

In any of the variations for the declaration of the array, we can refer to November's rainfall in Philadelphia by either of the expressions:

```
MonthlyRain[Philadelphia][November]
MonthlyRain[Philadelphia, November]
```

Note that the second expression is an abbreviation of the first. To put the ideas into perspective, let us look at some possible expressions and attempt to decide on the data type represented.

Expression	Data type
MonthlyRain[Philadelphia, November]	Real
MonthlyRain[Philadelphia]	Array of real
MonthlyRain[January]	Illegal construction
MonthlyRain	Array of arrays of real

We can perform activities appropriate to the type on each type of expression. For example, if we wished to make the rainfall figures for Chicago the same as that of

Los_Angeles for the entire year, then we could execute the statement

MonthlyRain[Chicago] := MonthlyRain[Los_Angeles]

If we wished to make the amount of rainfall for the month of June for New York the same as that of the month of May for Philadelphia, then we could execute the statement

MonthlyRain[New_York, June] := MonthlyRain[Philadelphia, May]

If we wish to make the monthly rainfall statistics for February the same as the rainfall statistics for January, then we could use a variable City of type Cities and the loop:

```
for City := Philadelphia to Chicago do
    MonthlyRain[City, February] := MonthlyRain[City, January]
```

□ **INTERACTIVE INPUT AND OUTPUT OF TWO-DIMENSIONAL ARRAYS**

Suppose that we wish to read in the rainfall values by having the user enter them one at a time. As your own experiences have shown, it is important to clearly indicate to the user what input is required by way of meaningful prompts. We can expect most users to know that a prompt such as "Month2" indicates February, but we cannot expect the user to know that "City2" indicates New York. As we know, we cannot print the constants of the user-defined types Cities and Months in order to prompt the user. However, we can use the idea of a print name and an initialization routine, as shown in Figure 7-1.

Now, if we wish to read in the values for the rainfall from the user by city and then by month for each city, we can use the loops:

```
for City := Philadelphia to Chicago do
    begin
        Writeln('Enter rainfall for ', CityName[City], ': ');
        for Month := January to December do
            begin
                Write(' ':5, MonthName[Month], ': ');
                Readln(MonthlyRain[City, Month])
            end {for}
    end; {for}
```

If we wish to read in the values for the rainfall from the user by month and then by city for each month, we can use the loops:

```
for Month := January to December do
    begin
        Writeln('Enter rainfall for ', MonthName[Month], ': ');
        for City := Philadelphia to Chicago do
            begin
                Write(' ':5, CityName[City], ': ');
                Readln(MonthlyRain[City, Month])
            end {for}
    end; {for}
```

Now, suppose that we have obtained the rainfall values in either of the ways shown above and that we wish to print the values in a table, which appears similar to the following:

assume type declared as above

```
CityName     : array [Cities] of string[20];
MonthName    : array [Months] of string[10];

procedure Initialize;
{
 Written by:  XXXXXXXX  XX/XX/XX
    Purpose:  To set up the print names for cities and months.
}
begin {Initialize}
  MonthName[January] := 'January';
  MonthName[February] := 'February';
  MonthName[March] := 'March';
  MonthName[April] := 'April';
  MonthName[May] := 'May';
  MonthName[June] := 'June';
  MonthName[July] := 'July';
  MonthName[August] := 'August';
  MonthName[September] := 'September';
  MonthName[October] := 'October';
  MonthName[November] := 'November';
  MonthName[December] := 'December';
  CityName[Philadelphia] := 'Philadelphia';
  CityName[New_York] := 'New York';
  CityName[Atlanta] := 'Atlanta';
  CityName[Los_Angeles] := 'Los Angeles';
  CityName[Chicago] := 'Chicago'
end; {Initialize}
```

Figure 7-1   Initialize Print Name Arrays

	Philadelphia	New York	Atlanta	Los Angeles	Chicago
January	2.33	1.40	1.58	4.34	1.35
February	1.11	4.05	3.07	2.52	0.71
March	2.81	3.60	0.31	0.41	4.48
April	3.94	3.91	1.05	1.29	2.73
May	3.40	4.07	1.11	4.25	4.42
June	1.56	2.42	3.39	3.30	1.23
July	4.34	0.67	1.94	1.40	1.60
August	2.22	2.91	1.03	4.56	4.83
September	4.37	4.71	4.22	0.88	0.13
October	2.64	2.19	3.40	4.61	0.66
November	0.70	1.02	2.86	0.21	2.61
December	3.02	0.56	3.37	1.42	2.90

We can accomplish this by the code fragment shown below, which makes use of the Turbo Pascal Length function to find the length of a string.

```
{*** Print column headings. }

Writeln;
Write(' ':10);
for City := Philadelphia to Chicago do
```

```
     begin
       Left := (13 - Length(CityName[City])) div 2;
       Right := 13 - (Left + Length(CityName[City]));
       Write(' ':Left, CityName[City], ' ':Right);
     end; {for}
   Writeln;

{*** Print one row of data for each month. }

   for Month := January to December do
     begin
       Write(MonthName[Month], ' ':10-Length(MonthName[Month]));
       for City := Philadelphia to Chicago do
         Write(MonthlyRain[City, Month]:10:2, ' ':3);
       Writeln
     end; {for}
```

Note the use of the integer variables Left and Right in the code fragment. These variables allow us to center the city names in their allotted 13 spaces without accumulating any "off-by-one" errors that might occur if we had used the expression

```
     (13 - Length(CityName[City])) div 2
```

for both sides. This is another example of a small detail that makes the difference between code that accomplishes the desired result and code that surprises us with its behavior.

□
TEXT FILE
INPUT AND
OUTPUT OF
TWO-
DIMENSIONAL
ARRAYS

If you run a program that interactively obtains data for a large array, you may come to the conclusion that there must be a better way. It is possible to obtain data from a text file instead of from a terminal. Perhaps the most common context is that where the data has been placed onto a text file by the same or another program at an earlier time. However, the method will work for text files created using an editor.

The discussion given here applies only to numeric arrays. For arrays that involve strings, it is difficult although not impossible to write programs that deal with text files. Provided we take some care when we write the array, we can later read a numeric array from the text file and expect its values to be the same as they were when we wrote the array to the file.

We illustrate the methods by again referring to our rainfall array. The code given above for printing the array can be used to place the same data on a text file, simply by declaring a file and placing it in each Write and Writeln statement. This is appropriate if the text file is for persons to examine. If we want to use the file as input to a program at a later date, however, we would not want the row or column headings. The code that follows would place one month's rainfall per line of the text file RainFile:

```
for Month := January to December do
  begin
    for City := Philadelphia to Chicago do
      Write(RainFile, MonthlyRain[City, Month]:10:2, ' ':3);
    Writeln(RainFile)
  end; {for}
```

Similar code could be used to read the data from the file:

```
for Month := January to December do
   begin
      for City := Philadelphia to Chicago do
         Read(RainFile, MonthlyRain[City, Month]);
      Readln(RainFile)
   end; {for}
```

1. The spaces between the figures (written using ' ':3) are a good idea for user-read output. They provide white space between the numbers. They are mandatory if the data is to be read by another program.

2. The Readln(RainFile) step in the last code segment is optional. When the Read runs out of data on a line of a text file, it goes on to the next line automatically. The Readln can be useful, however, to cause the rest of the input line to be skipped. And it is useful in this example to illustrate how similar the code for reading data from a text file is to that for writing it.

3. Note that the order of the loops is important. If we write the data by month, then by city, we should read it in the same order.

□
PROCESSING TWO-DIMENSIONAL ARRAYS

We will continue to refer to our rainfall example to consider some typical processing activities that we may wish to perform on two-dimensional arrays. We will consider three problems to illustrate the techniques needed for common processing situations.

Find the average rainfall in Philadelphia. We will use real variables, TotalRain and AverageRain, whose values we can calculate with the following code fragment:

```
TotalRain := 0;
for Month := January to December do
   TotalRain := TotalRain + MonthlyRain[Philadelphia, Month];
AverageRain := TotalRain / 12;
```

Note that in the loop, we use the expression

```
MonthlyRain[Philadelphia, Month]
```

in which the first subscript is a constant and the second subscript is a variable.

Find the average rainfall in January. We will use the same two real variables as in the previous example. The following code segment can be used to calculate the values:

```
TotalRain := 0;
for City := Philadelphia to Chicago do
   TotalRain := TotalRain + MonthlyRain[City, January];
AverageRain := TotalRain / 5;
```

Whereas in the first example, the constant 12 is an obvious choice to use as the number of months, the number 5 is not such an obvious choice. What if we add a city to the list? It would be better to use a constant named NumberCities that would be set to 5 in this case. When we add a city, we would change the named constant. Perhaps even better would be to simply count the cities within the loop, as shown here:

```
TotalRain := 0;
CityCount := 0;
for City := Philadelphia to Chicago do
  begin
    TotalRain := TotalRain + MonthlyRain[City, January];
    CityCount := CityCount + 1
  end;  {for}
AverageRain := TotalRain / CityCount;
```

Find the average rainfall overall. We will use the same two real variables. In this case, we are being asked to average all the rainfall numbers in the array. It doesn't matter what order is used as long as each number is involved once and only once. We choose one of the two natural alternatives in the following code fragment:

```
TotalRain := 0;
for City := Philadelphia to Chicago do
  for Month := January to December do
    TotalRain := TotalRain + MonthlyRain[City, Month];
AverageRain := TotalRain / 60;
```

Once again, it would be better to use the expression 12 * NumberCities, or to count the number of cities, rather than using the constant 60 to calculate the average.

□
MATRICES   A **matrix** is a mathematical structure that consists of a rectangular table in which we refer to the horizontal groupings as rows and the vertical grouping as columns. A matrix can be written as, for example,

$$\begin{bmatrix} 3 & 2 & 1 \\ 2 & 6 & 7 \end{bmatrix}$$

We usually refer to the size of the matrix by specifying the number of rows and columns, in that order. The example above would be called a "2-by-3" matrix, which is frequently written as "2 × 3." A natural way to represent a matrix within a Pascal program is as a two-dimensional array. We could represent 2-by-3 matrices with integer entries by use of a declaration such as

```
var
  A : array [1 .. 2, 1 .. 3] of integer;
```

In a program that will make extensive use of such 2-by-3 matrices, we would want to declare a global type such as

```
type
  MatrixType = array [1 .. 2, 1 .. 3] of integer;
```

By using the global type, we can pass variables as parameters, which would be a common desire in any program dealing with matrices.

One operation that is often performed upon matrices of the same size is that of **matrix addition**. When we add two matrices, we get a third matrix of the same size that is obtained by adding the two elements in each of the positions of the matrices. For example,

$$\begin{bmatrix} 3 & 2 & 1 \\ 2 & 6 & 7 \end{bmatrix} + \begin{bmatrix} -5 & 4 & 0 \\ 1 & -1 & 6 \end{bmatrix} = \begin{bmatrix} -2 & 6 & 1 \\ 3 & 5 & 13 \end{bmatrix}$$

Let us design a procedure MatrixAdd to add two matrices to obtain a third. In order to create a general-purpose matrix adder, we need to have available the number of rows and columns of the matrices. Therefore, we will alter our declarations slightly to the following:

```
const
   NumberRows = 2;
   NumberCols = 3;

type
   ElementType = integer;
   MatrixType = array[1 .. NumberRows, 1 .. NumberCols]
                of ElementType;
```

If A and B are two matrices that we wish to add to obtain the matrix C, then the algorithm is

loop Row going from 1 to NumberRows:
    loop Col going from 1 to NumberCols:
        set C[Row, Col] to A[Row, Col] plus B[Row, Col]

The two variables Row and Col must be declared as integer variables in the program. Translating the algorithm into Pascal code is quite straightforward, as we see by inspection of the code in Figure 7-2.

```
procedure MatrixAdd(A, B : MatrixType; var C : MatrixType);
{
    Written by:    XXXXXXXX   XX/XX/XX
       Purpose:    To add two matrices.
    Parameters:    A, B - input, the matrices to add
                   C - output, the resulting sum
  Globals used:    NumberRows, NumberCols - constants for matrix size
}
var
  Row      : integer;                        { Loop index }
  Col      : integer;                        { Loop index }

begin {MatrixAdd}

  for Row := 1 to NumberRows do
    for Col := 1 to NumberCols do
      C[Row, Col] := A[Row, Col] + B[Row, Col]

end; {MatrixAdd}
```

Figure 7-2 Adding Two Matrices

```
    procedure ScalarMult(M : ElementType; A : MatrixType;
                         var C : MatrixType);
    {
       Written by:   XXXXXXXX   XX/XX/XX
          Purpose:   To scalar multiply M times A.
       Parameters:   M - input, scalar to multiply by
                     A - input, matrix to multiply
                     C - output, resulting matrix
      Globals used:  NumberRows, NumberCols - constants for matrix size
    }
    var
      Row      : integer;                    { Loop index }
      Col      : integer;                    { Loop index }

    begin {ScalarMult}

      for Row := 1 to NumberRows do
        for Col := 1 to NumberCols do
          C[Row, Col] := M * A[Row, Col]

    end; {ScalarMult}
```

Figure 7-3   Scalar Multiplication of a Matrix

Another standard activity for rectangular matrices is the operation of **scalar multiplication**. The operation consists of multiplying a specified number by each of the elements of the matrix to produce another matrix of the same size. For example, if we multiply the scalar 4 by the matrix

$$\begin{bmatrix} 3 & 2 & 1 \\ 2 & 6 & 7 \end{bmatrix}$$

we get the resulting matrix:

$$\begin{bmatrix} 12 & 8 & 4 \\ 8 & 24 & 28 \end{bmatrix}$$

Once again, we can write a procedure, ScalarMult, to accomplish the operation. The code appears in Figure 7-3.

□ **MATRIX MULTIPLICATION**

For **matrix multiplication,** the number of columns of the first matrix must be equal to the number of rows of the second matrix. The most usual circumstance for this operation is for **square matrices**, where the number of rows is equal to the number of columns. For such matrices, we still would like to maintain the operations of addition and scalar multiplication, so we would probably use a set of declarations such as

```
    const
      NumberRows = 3;
      NumberCols = 3;
```

```
type
  ElementType = integer;
  MatrixType = array [1 .. NumberRows, 1 .. NumberCols]
                 of ElementType;
```

The algorithm for multiplying two matrices is a bit complicated. If we are multiplying the two matrices A and B to obtain the matrix C, then we obtain the individual elements of C by the computations:

```
C[Row, Col] := 0;
for Runner := 1 to NumberRows do
  C[Row, Col] := C[Row, Col] + A[Row, Runner]*B[Runner, Col];
```

Because we must calculate C[Row, Col] for each row and column combination, the code fragment for matrix multiplication is

```
for Row := 1 to NumberRows do
  for Col := 1 to NumberCols do
    begin
      C[Row, Col] := 0;
      for Runner := 1 to NumberRows do
        C[Row, Col] := C[Row, Col] + A[Row, Runner]*B[Runner,Col]
    end; {for Col}
```

As always, the variable Runner must be declared as an integer in the program (most likely, within a MatrixMult procedure, which you can write as an exercise).

□ **MATRIX UTILITIES**

When we are dealing with operations on matrices, it is convenient to have a procedure that will "pretty print" a matrix, horizontally centered on the screen if possible. We will illustrate such a routine for matrices with integer entries. We make use of the built-in Turbo Pascal procedure Str, which converts numbers into strings. This procedure is discussed in detail in Chapter 8. We note that our procedure will work for real matrices, but it formats the numbers in the dreaded "E" form because no degree of precision is specified in the Write statement. The procedure, named MatrixPrint, performs many detailed computations to account for various combinations of numeric ranges, number of columns, etc. The code for MatrixPrint appears in Figure 7-4.

Another convenience for testing matrix routines is a means of quickly generating test matrices. The following fragment of code can be used to generate a random matrix, A, with values from −5 to +5, for testing.

```
Randomize;
for Row := 1 to NumberRows do
  for Col := 1 to NumberCols do
    A[Row, Col] := Random(11)-5;
```

□ **USING PART OF AN ARRAY**

As we have seen when working with arrays in Chapter 6, we frequently declare an array with more room than is used. The same is true for two-dimensional arrays. For example, a program that deals with matrices might very well have many different sizes of matrices at any given time. This can be handled by declaring the type MatrixType to be the largest expected size (say 10 by 10), then keeping track

```
      procedure MatrixPrint(InMatrix : MatrixType);
      {
         Written by:   XXXXXXXXX   XX/XX/XX
            Purpose:   To print a matrix.
         Parameters:   InMatrix - input, the matrix to print
       Globals used:   NumberRows, NumberCols - constants for matrix size
      }
      var
        Width            : integer;            { Width of an element}
        MaxWidth         : integer;            { Max width of element }
        TotalWidth       : integer;            { Total width of matrix}
        Row              : integer;            { Index for rows }
        Col              : integer;            { Index for cols }
        TestString       : string[20];         { String for numbers }
        Entry            : integer;            { Loop index }
        PerRow           : integer;            { Number per row }
        ScreenRows       : integer;            { Number of rows on screen }
        LeftMargin       : integer;            { Spaces on left of row }
        ScrRow           : integer;            { Loop index }

      begin {MatrixPrint}

      {*** Establish the maximum width for an element. }

        MaxWidth := 0;

        for Row := 1 to NumberRows do
          for Col := 1 to NumberCols do
            begin
              Str(InMatrix[Row, Col], TestString);
              Width := Length(TestString);
              if  Width > MaxWidth  then
                MaxWidth := Width
            end; {for}

      {*** Decide on the number of elements per screen row.}

        TotalWidth := NumberCols*(MaxWidth+1) - 1;
        if TotalWidth <= 80 then
          begin
            PerRow := NumberCols;
            LeftMargin := (80 - TotalWidth) div 2;
            ScreenRows := 1
          end
        else
          begin
            PerRow := 80 div (MaxWidth+1);
            LeftMargin := 0;
            ScreenRows := NumberCols div PerRow + 1
          end;

      {*** Print the matrix.}
```

Figure 7-4   Output of a Matrix (Continued)

```
        Writeln;
        for Row := 1 to NumberRows do
          begin
            if LeftMargin > 0 then
              Write(' ':LeftMargin);
            Col := 1;
            for ScrRow := 1 to ScreenRows do
              begin
                for Entry := 1 to PerRow do
                  if Col <= NumberCols then
                    begin
                      Write(InMatrix[Row, Col]:MaxWidth);
                      if Entry < PerRow then
                        Write(' ');
                      Col := Col + 1
                    end; {if}
                Writeln
              end; {for}
            if TotalWidth mod 80 <> 0 then
              Writeln
          end; {for}

        Writeln
      end; {MatrixPrint}
```

Figure 7-4 Output of a Matrix

of the size of each individual matrix separately. This can be done using three variables, declared as in this example:

```
var
  A       : MatrixType;
  ARows   : integer;
  ACols   : integer;
```

Alternatively, we could define a record type consisting of three components: the matrix, the number of rows, and the number of columns:

```
type
  MatrixType =
    record
      Data        : array [1 .. 10, 1 .. 10] of ElementType;
      NumberRows  : integer;
      NumberCols  : integer
    end;
```

No longer are NumberRows and NumberCols global constants that apply to all matrices. Each matrix carries its own size. To illustrate, Figure 7-5 repeats the scalar multiplication example using the record data type.

□ **MORE THAN TWO DIMENSIONS**

You should not be surprised that the notion of arrays of arrays can be generalized. For example, we can declare an array of two-dimensional arrays to obtain a three-dimensional array. One way to accomplish this is illustrated by this example:

```
var
  A   : array [1 .. 3, 1 .. 4, 1 .. 5] of integer;
```

```
procedure ScalarMult(M : ElementType; A : MatrixType;
                     var C : MatrixType);
{
    Written by:   XXXXXXXX   XX/XX/XX
        Purpose:  To scalar multiply M times A.
     Parameters:  M – input, scalar to multiply by
                  A – input, matrix to multiply
                  C – output, resulting matrix
}
var
    Row      : integer;                     { Loop index }
    Col      : integer;                     { Loop index }

begin {ScalarMult}
    C := A;
    with C do
      begin
        for Row := 1 to NumberRows do
          for Col := 1 to NumberCols do
            Data[Row, Col] := M * Data[Row, Col]

      end  {with}
end; {ScalarMult}
```

Figure 7-5   Matrix as a Record with Size Information

This might be called a $3 \times 4 \times 5$ array; it can be conceptualized as consisting of three separate 4-by-5 matrices. To access a single value from the array, we would supply three subscripts. The first picks one of the three 4×5 matrices; the second chooses a row; the third a column. Because of this view of what the array is, we might choose to print the data as three 4×5 arrays.

We will not pursue this subject at length. We should, however, point out that it can be useful in the type of problem typified by our rainfall example. For example, we might declare an array indexed on three subscripts, where the first chooses a year in the range 1980 to 1995, the second chooses the city, and the third chooses the month. With such a declaration,

```
MonthlyRain[1990, Philadelphia, March]
```

would signify the rainfall in Philadelphia in March of 1990.

□ All the defensive programming techniques we learned in connection with arrays in
DPT Chapter 6 apply to two-dimensional arrays as well. In addition, there are some tips that apply specifically for two-dimensional arrays.

1. To access a single value from the array, two subscripts must be supplied. In a matrix application, the first tells the row and the second the column. More generally, the first chooses one of the arrays that make up the two-dimensional array and the second chooses one value from that array.

What happens if we use only one subscript varies with the context. For example, consider a matrix defined as

```
var
    X : array[1 .. 2, 1 .. 3] of integer;
```

We can visualize X as having this form:

$$\begin{bmatrix} 2 & -4 & 5 \\ -6 & 1 & 3 \end{bmatrix}$$

If we write X[1], this refers to the *entire* first row, an array of three integers. This may or may not be what we intended. A reference to X[3], on the other hand, is illegal. There is no way to refer to the columns of the matrix as separate entities.

Similarly, for our declaration

```
var
    MonthlyRain : array [Cities, Months] of real;
```

we need to specify both the city and the month to get a single rainfall figure. A reference such as MonthlyRain[Philadelphia] is legal and refers to the entire array of 12 rainfall figures for Philadelphia. A reference such as MonthlyRain[January], on the other hand, is illegal.

2. In addition to supplying two subscripts, we must supply them in the proper order. When the two subscript types are different, as in the rainfall example, the compiler will catch this error. (This is an added advantage to choosing data types to closely match the problem being solved). If the compiler cannot detect the error, as in the case of matrix applications, we will simply access the wrong data item and get erroneous results.

3. Nested loops are frequently used to process the entire array in some fashion. The outer loop control is based on one of the subscripts, and the inner loop control on the other. For example, to process a matrix by rows, then by columns within each row, we would use the row subscript as the outer loop index. To process the rainfall array by months, then by city for each month, we would use the month subscript as the outer loop index. By thinking about the order in which we wish to process the data, we can properly write the loops.

REVIEW

Terms and concepts

two-dimensional arrays

matrix

matrix addition

scalar multiplication

matrix multiplication

square matrix

Two-dimensional arrays

Declaration

Examples:

1. type

```
ArrayofArrays = array [1 .. 3] of array [1 .. 4] of real;
```

2. type

```
RealArray4     = array [1 .. 4] of real;
ArrayofArrays = array [1 .. 3] of RealArray4;
```

3. type

```
ArrayofArrays = array[1 .. 3, 1 .. 4] of real;
```

Processing and I/O

    1. A single "row" can be processed by letting the row subscript remain constant and the column subscript vary.

    2. A single "column" can be processed by letting the column subscript remain constant and the row subscript vary.

    3. An entire array can be processed by using nested loops, one controlled by varying the row subscript and the other by varying the column subscript.

DPT

    1. Generally need two subscripts when working with two-dimensional arrays.

    2. Don't interchange the subscripts.

    3. Pay attention to which subscript is the outer loop control when writing nested loops to process arrays.

EXERCISES

*1. For the two-dimensional array X shown, what is the size of the array? What is X[3][2]? What is X[2, 4]? What is X[4, 2]?

1	4	−3	2
10	−5	5	7
−6	0	1	11

2. Modify the declarations and the code of Figure 7-1 to use six of your favorite cities.

3. a. Write a Pascal program to read rainfall statistics and display a table such as that shown in this section.
   b. Write a Pascal program to read rainfall statistics and print a table such as that shown in this section on your printer.

4. a. Write a segment of Pascal code to print the rainfall statistics on a printer with 132 columns, one city per line.
   b. Modify the segment to handle printers of smaller width by printing two lines for each city. Label the columns appropriately.

5. Write segments of Pascal code to allow a person to query the rainfall statistics:

   *a. Given a city name, print the total rain for that city.
   b. Given a month, show which city had the most rainfall during that month.
   c. Given a city and a month, print the rainfall.

6. Write code for the following, which deal with a 21-by-28 real matrix.

   *a. Find the largest number in the entire matrix.

b. Modify part (a) to also find which row and column contained the largest value. Assume there are no ties.

c. Modify part (b) to handle ties.

*d. Find the largest number in each row, placing the results in an array Large.

e. Print the sum of each row.

f. For row 5, find the column number of the first positive value (0 if none are positive).

*g. Exchange rows 14 and 19.

*h. Exchange columns 14 and 19.

i. Sort the rows of the matrix so that the row with the largest sum is the first, and so on.

j. Repeat part (i), but sort the columns instead.

7. Write the MatrixMult procedure for multiplying two square matrices, assuming global constants for the array size.

8. Generalize the matrix addition procedure to handle matrices that are only partially used. Part of the output should be a Valid variable set to true or false depending on whether or not the operation was legal.

a. Use separate variables for the sizes.

*b. Use records containing the size to represent matrices.

9. Repeat Exercise 8 for the matrix multiplication procedure of Exercise 7. You should try to handle matrices that are not necessarily square.

10. Write a MatrixRead procedure that prompts the user for input as shown:

```
Enter row 1:
    element for column 1:
    element for column 2:
            . . . .
Enter row 2:
    element for column 1:
            . . . .
```

11. Write a procedure similar to MatrixPrint that has another parameter specifying the number of decimal places for real numbers.

12. Write a Pascal program that acts as a matrix calculator for 3-by-3 matrices. The program should be menu-driven with the main menu:

```
           Main Menu
           ---------

    1 -- Matrix Addition
    2 -- Scalar Multiplication
    3 -- Matrix Multiplication

    4 -- Terminate Session

    Selection?
```

When the user selects an operation, the program should ask the user to input the two matrices or the number and matrix in the case of scalar multiplication. The program should print the user input and then print the answer. Ask the user to touch a key to return to the main menu.

*13. A matrix is called *sparse* if most of the entries are 0's. Suppose that we wish to work with 10-by-10 sparse matrices with entries that are either 0's or 1's. One technique for accepting input for such a matrix is to ask the user to specify the row and column pairs for each of the 1's in the matrix. Write a Pascal program to read a sparse matrix and print it using the MatrixPrint procedure.

14. Modify the program of Exercise 13 so that the nonzero entries in the matrix can be any integer values.

15. Write a program to generate two random 10-by-10 matrices, multiply them, and print the answer using the MatrixPrint procedure. How many individual additions are required in the matrix multiplication operation?

16. In a square matrix, the *main diagonal* is the collection of elements that have their row equal to their column. That is, the main diagonal of the matrix A is the collection of elements A[1,1], A[2,2], etc.

   *a. Write a function to calculate the sum of the elements on the main diagonal of a square matrix.
   b. Write a function to find the largest number on the main diagonal.
   c. Write a function to find the average of the numbers that lie on or below the main diagonal:

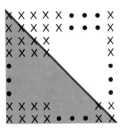

   d. Write a function to find the sum of the numbers on or below the diagonal that runs from the lower left to the upper right.

17. A square matrix A is *symmetric* if A[I, J] is equal to A[J, I] for each I and J from 1 to the number of rows of the matrix.

   a. Write a Boolean function to determine if a given square matrix is symmetric.
   b. Generate 1000 random 2-by-2 matrices with elements ranging from 1 to 6 and calculate the fraction of these that are symmetric. (The probability that such a square matrix is symmetric is the same as the probability of throwing doubles on a pair of dice; can you see why?)

*18. Write a program to declare a 3-by-4-by-5 integer array, fill it with random integers in the range from −5 to 5, and print it as three 4-by-5 matrices.

19. Do the following for the rainfall array indexed by year, city, and month alluded to in the subsection "More Than Two Dimensions":

   *a. Give declarations for the array.
   *b. Write a procedure that, given a year and a city, prints the rainfall figures for that year and city.
   c. Write a procedure that prompts the user for a month *name* and a city *name*, and prints the history of rainfall for that month and city.

d. Write a procedure that answers the question: For a given year, which cities had a total rainfall less than 20 inches?

e. Write a procedure that answers the questions: For a given year, what was the highest rainfall figure? What city had that highest figure? What month?

f. Write a procedure that answers the questions: Within the entire structure, what year, city, month combination had the highest rainfall figure.

20. Write programs for the following.

*a. Read a series of birthdays represented as a month number and a day number. Keep track of how many people were born on each day. When the data has all been read, print a list of all the days on which two or more persons were born. Hint: Use a two-dimensional array of counters to count the birthdays.

b. Repeat part (a), but do not read the data. Instead, generate 30 random birthdays using Random.

c. Place the process of part (b) in a loop to execute 1000 times, and find how many of those 1000 executions resulted in at least one duplicate birthday.

21. a. Write a function to calculate the "number of combinations of n items taken k at a time," whose value is given by

$$\frac{n!}{k!(n - k)!}$$

b. The $k!$ in this formula "cancels with" the last k factors of the $n!$, leaving

$$\frac{n(n - 1)(n - 2) \cdots (k + 1)}{(n - k)!}$$

Revise your function to take advantage of this fact.

(c) If we have many of these to calculate in a program, we might want to set up an array Comb declared as

    array [0..10, 0..10] of integer;

Comb[N, K] will be the number of combinations of N items taken K at a time. It is known that Comb[N, K] can be calculated by

    Comb[N, K] :=   1, if K = 0 or N = K
                    Comb[N-1, K-1] + Comb[N-1, K], otherwise

Use this fact to fill the portion of the array on and below the main diagonal. See Exercise 16.

22. Write a program to play Conway's Game of Life. On an infinite checkerboard, each square has eight neighbors:

This game simulates growth and decay in a collection of interacting organisms, where cells (squares) are born, survive, or die based on how "crowded" are the conditions. The cycle occurs in "generations" by these rules (each square is either *dead* (empty) or *alive*):

> *Birth.* If an empty (dead) square has exactly three live neighboring squares, it will be alive the next generation.

> *Survival.* If a live square has either two or three live neighbors, it will still be alive the next generation.

> *Death.* Any live square that does not survive dies either from overcrowding (more than three neighbors) or isolation (less than two neighbors).

For example,

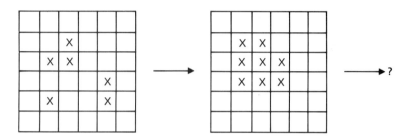

Input to the program will include an initial configuration and an indication of how many generations to print. Output will be one screen (or printed page) per generation (starting with the initial configuration).

Because programming an infinite array is difficult (not to mention printing it), we will restrict ourselves to a 20-by-78 array if using the display or a 50-by-50 array if using the printer. Use the character "*" to denote live and " " (blank space) to denote dead. Treat the squares on the edges as infertile regions where nothing is ever born.

NOTES FOR SECTION 7-1

□ 1. In this example, we are using an underscore character as part of the variable name. This is a Turbo Pascal extension that seems especially appropriate for these identifiers.

7-2
□□□□□□
USING ARRAYS FOR FINITE-STATE PROCESSES

In this section, we will introduce an extremely powerful programming technique known as **data-driven programming**. We will illustrate the technique by solving a problem of providing a flexible means of accepting user input of signed integer numbers. We will design a device, called a **Finite-State Automaton (FSA)**, that represents the solution to the problem. We will then translate the FSA into an **action table** using an array with two subscripts. Finally, we will write a program to simulate the FSA by using the action table.

STATEMENT OF THE PROBLEM

☐ We wish to allow the user to input a signed integer number. Before we give a precise specification of the form of the input, here are some examples of good and bad input:

```
GOOD INPUT:

       2
      +2
       +2
     -  2
     -          34


BAD INPUT:
     +
     -

     23a
     45 6
```

The following description characterizes the form of good input:

Good input consists of a string of:
      0 or more leading blank spaces, followed by
      an optional plus or minus sign, followed by
      0 or more blank spaces, followed by
      1 or more digits, followed by
      0 or more trailing blanks,
that represents an integer value in the range from −Maxint to Maxint, inclusive.

With the above specification, if we are given any string of characters, we can determine if it represents good input or not. What we wish to do for good input is to receive an integer value. For bad input, we wish to know the leftmost position in the string that makes the input invalid.

We are using the simple and familiar example of signed integer input for the purpose of making our presentation easy to follow. We will indicate in the exercises some further applications of the technique.

DESIGNING THE FSA: THE STATE DIAGRAM

☐ A useful way to view a finite-state automaton is as a "board game". We move a token about on the board by starting at some position, moving according to some rules, and ending at a goal position (for a win) or not (for a loss). We will set up to play the board game by reading in the input string, setting a marker on the first character of the string, and placing our token on the start position on the board. We will move the token depending on the character of the input string that is located in the marked position. Our job in designing the FSA is to construct the game board, which is technically called a **state diagram**. The positions on the game board are referred to as **states**.

We begin with a board that consists only of a start state, which we will label "Start".

We will provide paths from the Start state for each character that can validly appear while our token is in the state. In the case of our problem, the valid characters that can appear while we are in the Start state are

Blank space, ' '

Plus sign, '+'

Minus sign, '−'

Digit, '0', '1', . . . '9'

Any other character is invalid. For each valid character, we decide whether the token should remain on the start state or moved toward a goal state. For our list of valid characters, we decide as follows:

Blank space:	stay in the Start state
Plus sign:	move to a new state named Signed
Minus sign:	move to the Signed state
Digit:	move to a new state named Evaluating

For each possibility, we move the marker to the next position in the input string. For invalid characters, we would end the game in an error condition. It is usual practice to draw a path with an arrowhead for each of the valid characters. We label each path with the character (or class of characters, in the case of digits) that causes us to take the path. Before we continue to construct the game board, we have to decide whether or not each of the states that we have so far is a goal state. A goal state has the property that if the input string runs out while we are in the state, then we have successfully accepted the input. The Start and Signed states cannot be goal states because of the input specification. The Evaluating state is a goal state because the string that we have processed in arriving at the state represents a valid signed integer. We will denote goal states by drawing double lines around them. With our two new states and the character paths, we now have the game board:

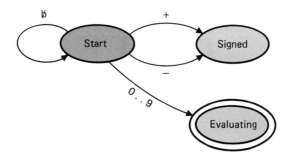

Note that the path for the blank leads back to the Start state. Also, note that the paths for the plus and minus signs both lead to the same state.

We continue to construct the game board by considering the Signed state. If our token is in the Signed state, then the valid characters that could occur in the marked position of the input string are

Blank space: stay in Signed state

Digit: move to Evaluating state

If our token is in the Evaluating state, then the valid characters that could occur in the marked position of the input string are

Blank space: move to a new Waiting state

Digit: stay in Evaluating state

The new Waiting state is a goal state according to our input specification. If our token is in the Waiting state, then the only valid character that can occur in the marked position of the input string is

Blank space: stay in Waiting state

Our game board is now complete. It appears as

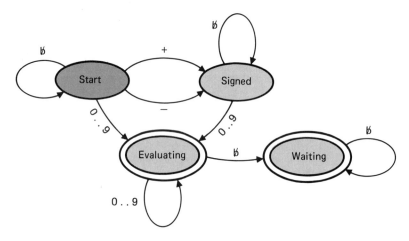

Let us play. Suppose that we have the input string: − 34.

Use a coin as a token and place it on the Start state. We will lead you through the game step by step. We will use a caret (^) as the position marker. At each step of the game, we will show the input string and leave it to you to move your token on the game board.

Step One: current state: Start
input string: − 34
^

marked character: '−'
action: move token to Signed state

Step Two: current state: Signed
              input string: − ꓱ4
                                  ^

              marked character: ' '
              action: move token to Signed state (that is, back to
              Signed state)

Step Three: current state: Signed
              input string: − ꓱ4
                                  ^

              marked character: ' '
              action: move token to Signed state

Step Four: current state: Signed
              input string: − ꓱ4
                                   ^

              marked character: '3'
              action: move token to Evaluating state

Step Five: current state: Evaluating
              input string: − ꓱ4
                                    ^

              marked character: '4'
              action: move token to Evaluating state

Step Six: current state: Evaluating
              input string: − ꓱ4
                                     ^

              marked character: end-of-string
              action: terminate successfully

The above set of steps is a good representation of a successfully played game. For games that do not go so well, we have one more possible action: terminate in error. This action will be taken whenever an invalid character is marked. We can tell that the marked character is invalid by noting that there is no path leading from the current state that is labeled by that character. We will also terminate in error if we reach the end-of-string when we are not in a goal state.

Let us now play two games that do not terminate successfully. For the first game, we will use the input string 3 4. Place your token on the Start state.

Step One: current state: Start
              input string: ꓱ 4
                                 ^

              current character: '3'
              action: move token to Evaluating state

Step Two: current state: Evaluating
              input string: ꓱ 4
                                 ^

              current character: ' '
              action: move token to Waiting state

Step Three: current state: Waiting
input string: ⅎ 4
                    ^

current character: '4'
action: terminate in error

As a final game, we will take as our input string +. Place your token on the Start state.

Step One: current state: Start
input string: +
                    ^

current character: '+'
action: move token to Signed state

Step Two: current state: Signed
input string: +
                    ^

current character: end-of-string
action: terminate in error

□ **DESIGNING THE ACTIONS**

So far, in designing the FSA by means of a state diagram, we have a mechanism for distinguishing between good and bad input. We have not achieved our main purpose, which is to obtain an integer value whenever the input string is valid. We accomplish our main purpose in what appears to be an afterthought: modifying the actions. Our actions have consisted of either moving the token to a state or terminating successfully or in error. We will now concentrate more fully on the actions and attempt to provide all of the capabilities that we need for inputting a signed integer value.

We must add some initializing steps. Because we will be obtaining an integer value, we must have the variable Answer in which to accumulate the value. We will initialize Answer to 0. In order to distinguish between plus and minus signs, we will use the variable Sign, which will have the value of 1 for no sign or for a plus sign and which will have the value of −1 for a minus sign. We will initialize Sign to 1.

For each path in the state diagram, we will have a corresponding named action, but two or more paths can use the same action. In our state diagram, there are three paths that loop back to the current state when the current character is a blank. All three paths can use the same action named Increment. We do not have to perform any additional steps for this action, so its definition is:

Increment: do nothing

When we see a plus sign in the Start state, we will perform an action named SawPlus, which is defined as follows:

SawPlus: set Sign to 1
          move token to Signed state

When we see a minus sign in the Start state, we will perform an action named SawMinus, which is defined as follows:

SawMinus: set Sign to -1
             move token to Signed state

When we see a digit in the Start, Signed, or Evaluating states, we can perform the same action named SawDigit, which is defined as follows:

SawDigit: set Answer to 10*Answer + value of digit
             move token to Evaluating state

When we see a blank space in the Evaluating state, we will perform an action named GoWait, which is defined as:

GoWait: move token to Waiting

Because we are not just playing a board game, but are trying to obtain an integer value, we will place a special end-of-string character at the right end of the string. When we see the end-of-string character while we are in either of the goal states, Evaluating or Waiting, we will perform an action named Done, which is defined as:

Done: set Answer to Sign*Answer
         terminate with success

Finally, whenever we see an invalid character, we will perform an action named Error, which is defined as:

Error: terminate in error

After defining the actions, we can modify the state diagram by adding the name of the appropriate action to each of the paths. The state diagram now appears as

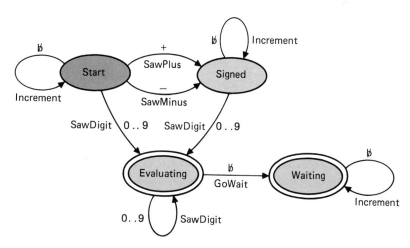

We now modify the rules of the board game slightly. Whenever you move your token, perform the action corresponding to the path. Perform the action

Done if you see the end-of-string while in a goal state. Let us trace the steps of the game with the input string − 34.

Initialization: set token on Start state
set Answer to 0
set Sign to 1

Step One: current state: Start
input string: − 34
      ^

marked character: '−'
action: perform SawMinus
value of Answer: 0

Step Two: current state: Signed
input string: − 34
      ^

marked character: ' '
action: perform Increment
value of Answer: 0

Step Three: current state: Signed
input string: − 34
      ^

marked character: '3'
action: perform SawDigit
value of Answer: 3 (10 * 0 + 3)

Step Four: current state: Evaluating
input string: − 34
      ^

marked character: '4'
action: perform SawDigit
value of Answer: 34 (10 * 3 + 4)

Step Five: current state: Evaluating
input string: − 34
      ^

marked character: end-of-string
action: perform Done
value of Answer: −34 (−1 * 34)

CONSTRUCTING THE ACTION TABLE

We have names for the states and the actions of our finite-state automaton. In addition, we need names for the character classes that determine the paths of the state diagram. In our analysis, we have identified the following classes, which we will give the indicated names:

Blank: consists of the blank space ' '

Plus: consists of the plus sign '+'

Minus: consists of the minus sign '−'

Digit: consists of the decimal digits '0', '1', . . . '9'

EOS: consists of the end-of-string character (to be determined)

Invalid: consists of all other characters

An action table is a tabular representation of a FSA. The table consists of rows labeled by the states and columns labeled by the character classes. Each table entry consists of the name of an action. We fill out the table by inspection of the state diagram. For each path in the state diagram, we fill in the corresponding table position with the appropriate action. Our state diagram translates into the action table:

	Blank	Plus	Minus	Digit	EOS	Invalid
Start	Increment	SawPlus	SawMinus	SawDigit	Error	Error
Signed	Increment	Error	Error	SawDigit	Error	Error
Evaluating	GoWait	Error	Error	SawDigit	Done	Error
Waiting	Increment	Error	Error	Error	Done	Error

We are going to represent this table in a Pascal program as an array with two subscripts. In order to accomplish this data structuring, we will utilize user-defined ordinal types for the states, actions, and character classes. Our type declarations are

```
LegalStates = (Start, Signed, Evaluating, Waiting);
ActionList = (Increment, SawPlus, SawMinus, SawDigit,
              GoWait, Done, Error);
CharClasses = (Blank, Plus, Minus, Digit, EOS, Invalid);
```

The next step is to define an array that will faithfully represent the action table. We declare the array as

```
Action : array [LegalStates, CharClasses] of  ActionList
```

One of the best features of the Pascal language is that it allows us to structure our data so closely to the entities that we are trying to represent.

We have defined the table as the Action array, but we have not placed the table entries within it. Turbo Pascal provides a useful feature for loading the values into an array.[1] To use the feature, we place a const section after the type declarations and we both declare the array and load it with values with the same statement:

```
const
  Action : array [LegalStates, CharClasses] of  ActionList =
    ((Increment, SawPlus , SawMinus,SawDigit,  Error  ,  Error  ) ,
     (Increment,  Error  ,  Error  ,SawDigit,  Error  ,  Error  ) ,
     ( GoWait  ,  Error  ,  Error  ,SawDigit,  Done   ,  Error  ) ,
     (Increment,  Error  ,  Error  ,  Error  ,  Done   ,  Error  ));
```

Some points of the syntax of this loading of values are

1. The entire set of values must be enclosed in parentheses.

2. The values for each row of the array are separated by commas and the whole row is enclosed in parentheses.

3. The rows are separated by commas.

Note that we can arrange the values to appear very similar to the table that is represented by the array.

□
SIMULATING THE FSA IN PASCAL

The Finite State Automaton model has proved to be a powerful problem-solving technique due to several factors: the problems to which it applies are often highly complex; the FSA technique has an orderly structure; the pictorial nature of the state diagrams provides an intuitive, "hands-on" character to the process; and, some important classes of problems are solvable by use of the FSA model. There are several kinds of language analysis problems that fit quite well into the FSA model. Portions of programming language compilers can be systematically constructed using Finite State Automata. If you refer to the syntax diagrams in Appendix D, you can see how a Pascal compiler can use an FSA to detect syntax errors. Decoding of electronic transmissions by hardware devices is also often based on the FSA model. For example, a device monitoring Morse code signals could sound an alert whenever the letter sequence 'SOS' is detected by use of a three state FSA. (Can you see how?)

So far, we have seen a systematic approach to designing the action table for an FSA. To continue the programming effort, we next present a basic algorithm for our simulation of the FSA.

read the input string
append the EOS character onto the input string
set the current state to Start
do the specific initialization for the problem
set the marker to the first character of the input string
repeat the following steps until we terminate:
    get the current character
    get the current character class
    perform the action corresponding to the current state and
        current character class
    set the marker to the next position of the input string

The general algorithm above can be used for a wide variety of situations in which an FSA is an appropriate solution technique. For many circumstances, the value Chr(0) is a good value to use for the EOS character.

We will use a procedure named GetInt to simulate the FSA. GetInt has two output parameters:

    Value   integer
                the integer value that was input; 0, if invalid input

ErrPos: integer
            the position of the first invalid position in the input string; 0, if no
            error

We will use the following variables for the simulation:

InString: string
                input string (with EOS appended)

Marker: integer
                position of the current character in InString

CurrentChar: char
                the current character of InString

CurrentClass: CharClasses
                the character class of the current character

Sign: integer
                multiplier to handle positive and negative values; 1 for
                positive, −1 for negative

Answer: real
                the value being calculated; is compared with Maxint to
                check for value out of range

Finished: Boolean
                an indicator for termination

In order to obtain the character class corresponding to the current character, we will use the function ClassOf(InChar), which will return a value of type Char-Class corresponding to the input parameter InChar and which has the following algorithm:

depending on the value of InChar do the following case:

'0', .. '9':
        set ClassOf to Digit
' ':
        set ClassOf to Blank
'+':
        set ClassOf to Plus
'−':
        set ClassOf to Minus
Chr(0):
        set ClassOf to EOS
otherwise:
        set ClassOf to Invalid

In the actual Pascal code for the ClassOf function, we cannot use Chr(0) as a case constant, so we will handle it as a special condition at the bottom of the case structure. Since ClassOf is to return a value of type CharClass, we will declare that type as a global type. This lack of uniformity of treatment of the CharClass type could be rectified by defining the ClassOf function *within* the GetInt function. If you are interested in this idea of embedded definition, see Appendix A for details.

The code for the FSA simulation, together with a driver program, is shown in Figure 7-6.

```
program Driver(Input, Output);
{
 Written by:   XXXXXXXX  XX/XX/XX
     Purpose:  To test GetInt
}
type
   String255 = string[255];
   CharClasses = (Blank, Plus, Minus, Digit, EOS, Invalid);
                                       { Character classes }

var
   Value    : integer;                 { Value of input integer }
   ErrorPos : integer;                 { Position of error }

function ClassOf(InChar : char) : CharClasses;
{
       Written by:   XXXXXXXX  XX/XX/XX
          Purpose:   To return the character class of an input character.
       Parameters:   InChar - input, character to classify
    Functions used:  Chr - (built-in) to form a character.
}
begin {ClassOf}
   case  InChar  of
     '0' .. '9':
       ClassOf := Digit;
     ' ':
       ClassOf := Blank;
     '+':
       ClassOf := Plus;
     '-':
       ClassOf := Minus;
     else if  InChar = Chr(0)   then
       ClassOf := EOS
     else
       ClassOf := Invalid;
   end {case}
end; {ClassOf}

procedure GetInt(var Value, ErrPos : integer);
{
       Written by:   XXXXXXXX  XX/XX/XX
          Purpose:   To use a state-table to read an integer.
       Parameters:   Value - output, value from input string (0 if invalid)
                     ErrPos - output, position of error (0 if none)
```

Figure 7-6   Finite-State Automaton for Integer Input (Continued)

```
              Globals used:   String255 - global type;
                              CharClasses - global type for character classes.
           Functions used:    ClassOf - to get the class of a character;
                              Chr - (built-in) to form a character.
    }
    type
      LegalStates = (Start, Signed, Evaluating, Waiting);
                                              { States of the FSA }
      ActionList = (Increment, SawPlus, SawMinus, SawDigit,
                   GoWait, Done, Error);
                                              { Actions }

    const
      Action : array [LegalStates, CharClasses] of  ActionList =
            ((Increment, SawPlus , SawMinus,SawDigit,  Error   ,  Error   ) ,
             (Increment,  Error  ,  Error  ,SawDigit,  Error   ,  Error   ) ,
             ( GoWait  ,  Error  ,  Error  ,SawDigit,  Done    ,  Error   ) ,
             (Increment,  Error  ,  Error  ,  Error ,  Done    ,  Error   ));

    var
      InString      : String255;            { Input string }
      Marker        : integer;              { Current position in string }
      Finished      : Boolean;              { Termination indicator }
      State         : LegalStates;          { Current state }
      CurrentChar   : char;                 { Current character }
      CurrentClass  : CharClasses;          { Class of current character }
      Sign          : integer;              { Multiplier for sign }
      Answer        : real;                 { Value under calculation }

    begin {GetInt}
      Readln(InString);
      InString := InString + Chr(0);        { Append end-of-string }
      Marker := 1;
      Finished := false;
      State := Start;
      Answer := 0;
      Sign := 1;

      repeat
        CurrentChar := Instring[Marker];
        CurrentClass := ClassOf(CurrentChar);
        case  Action[State, CurrentClass] of
          Increment :
            begin
            end;
          SawPlus:
            begin
              Sign := 1;
              State := Signed
            end;
          SawMinus:
            begin
              Sign := -1;
              State := Signed
            end;
```

Figure 7-6   Finite-State Automaton for Integer Input (Continued)

```
      SawDigit:
        begin
          Answer := 10*Answer + (Ord(CurrentChar) - Ord('0'));
          if  Answer > Maxint   then
            begin
              Answer := 0;
              Finished := true;
              ErrorPos := Marker
            end
          else
            State := Evaluating
        end;
      GoWait:
        begin
          State := Waiting;
        end;
      Done:
        begin
          Answer := Sign*Answer;
          Finished := true;
          ErrorPos := 0
        end;
      Error:
        begin
          Answer := 0;
          Finished := true;
          ErrorPos := Marker
        end;
      else
        Writeln('System error');
    end; {case}

    Marker := Marker + 1                    { Move to next character }
  until  Finished;

  Value := Round(Answer)
end; {GetInt}


begin {Driver}
  Write('Enter an integer: ');
  GetInt(Value, ErrorPos);
  if  ErrorPos <> 0   then
    Writeln('Error occurred at position ', ErrorPos)
  else
    Writeln('The value is ', Value);

{*** Print message and terminate.}

  Writeln;
  Writeln('Driver program is terminating.')
end.
```

Figure 7-6   Finite-State Automaton for Integer Input

Terms and concepts

data-driven programming

finite-state automaton FSA

action table

state diagram

states

■■■■■■
EXERCISES

1. Play the integer input board game for the following input strings: The character b stands for a blank space.

   a. +b34−
   b. +bbbbb45
   c. bbb2

2. Draw state diagrams for each of the following input situations:

   *a. Dates in the form: xx/xx/xx.
   b. Signed integers with optional trailing exponent part:

   > the letter "E," followed by
   > 0 or more blanks, followed by
   > an optional "+" sign, followed by
   > 1 or more digits, followed by
   > 0 or more trailing blanks.

   c. Signed integers with an optional prefix of "$".
   d. MSDOS filenames.
   e. Arithmetic expressions involving unsigned integers and the operations "+" and "*." Do not allow parentheses, and do not try to evaluate the expression.
   f. Signed real numbers, including signed integers as a special case.
   g. Signed real numbers with optional trailing exponential part:

   > the letter "E," followed by
   > 0 or more blanks, followed by
   > an optional "+" or "−" sign, followed by
   > 1 or more digits, followed by
   > 0 or more trailing blanks.

   h. Dates that are either in the form xx/xx/xx or in the form exemplified by "01Jul86." In either case, print the date in the form month, day, year. For example, either of the input strings 12/25/88 or 25Dec88 will be printed as

   > December 25, 1988.

   i. Phone numbers in the form:

   > (xxx) − xxx − xxxx

   where each of the x's represents a decimal digit.
   j. Unsigned binary numbers using the digits 0 and 1. Evaluate into a decimal integer and print it. Some valid input and corresponding values are

Input string	Value
10	2
111	7
1010	10

k. Unsigned hexadecimal numbers using the digits

$$0, 1, 2, 3, 4, 5, 6, 7, 8, 9, A, B, C, D, E, F$$

Evaluate into a decimal integer and print it. Some examples of valid input and corresponding values are

Input string	Value
10	16
A	10
A1	161
FF	255

3. For each of the situations of exercise 2:

   a. Give examples of good and bad input.
   b. Make a list of the character classes and design the actions.
   c. Write a Pascal program to simulate the corresponding FSA.

4. a. Tell how you would initialize the Action array if you were not able to use Turbo Pascal's "const" technique (page 553).
   *b. Using the special technique, show how to initialize the array PrintName with the subscript type month so that:
        PrintName[January] is 'January'
        PrintName[February] is 'February', etc.
   c. Use the technique to initialize an array indexed by 0 .. 9 containing the characters '0' to '9'.
   d. Use the technique to initialize an array indexed by '0' .. '9' containing the values 0 to 9. Could you use this array to any benefit in the program of Figure 7-6? Hint: Consider the SawDigit action.

5. The techniques of this section are applicable to a class of "string recognition" problems that involve deciding whether a given string belongs to a set of strings composed of the characters "0" and "1" that satisfy some property. For each of the following specifications, design a state diagram and write a Pascal program that either accepts or rejects the string.

   *a. Strings with exactly one occurrence of the pattern "11".
   b. Strings of alternating 0's and 1's. The empty string is acceptable.
   c. Strings with an even number of 0's. The empty string is acceptable.
   d. Strings with no occurrence of the pattern "11". The empty string is acceptable.
   e. Nonempty strings in which each occurrence of 1 is followed by a 0 somewhere to the right.
   f. Strings that begin with 1 and end with 1. The string "1" is acceptable.

g. Any string, including the empty string.

h. Strings that contain no more than two 1's. The empty string is acceptable.

NOTES FOR SECTION 7-2

□   1. This is not a feature of standard Pascal. Other options for loading values into an array are to use an initialization routine that assigns the specific value to each location of the array, or to read the values into the array from a text file.

8

STRING
MANIPULATION

8-1
□□□□□□
**STRING
DATA AND
OPERATIONS**

In this chapter, we will present an in-depth discussion of string handling. Strings are the most common form of nonnumeric data that our programs have to process. Standard Pascal does not provide for a separate string type; hence our discussion in this chapter will be focused on the specific capabilities of Turbo Pascal. Even if you are using an implementation of Pascal that has different string handling facilities, many of the programming techniques presented here will prove useful to you as a programmer.

In this first section, we will discuss string data and the basic operations that apply to string data. In the second section, we will discuss string processing and provide some additional string-processing tools. In the third section, we will take a look at input/output techniques. We will show how the programmer can be completely responsible for the input and output behavior of his or her program.

NOTE   In some versions of Pascal, the only way to handle strings is as arrays of characters. By defining the array to be ''packed,'' a few additional features are obtained, but nothing which comes close to those versions of Pascal which support strings directly.

If you are using a version which does not have strings, you will be especially interested in the second section of this chapter. Beginning on page 594, we show how to implement your own strings as a record consisting of the string length and an array of the characters in the string. The discussion includes implementation of some of the standard string handling subprograms provided by Turbo Pascal.

□
**STRING DATA
TYPES**

We already know much about strings because we have been using them throughout the book. Strings are similar to an array of type char in that they consist of a sequence of characters that can be accessed by use of an index. However, strings form a distinct class of data types with their own special properties. A string can consist of from 0 to 255 characters. Note that during the running of a program, no string can be created that is longer than 255 characters or a run-time error will result. A string variable has a maximum length that is specifed when it is declared. For example, if we wish to work with lines of text that are less than or equal to 80 characters in length, then we might declare a variable Line as follows:

```
var
   Line  : string[80];
```

Remember that the number 80 above specifies the maximum number of characters that Line can contain, not necessarily the actual number of characters that Line does contain. The actual number of characters that Line contains at any time during the running of a program can vary from 0 to 80, inclusive.

When we discussed the string assignment statement, we noted that the attempt to assign more than the maximum number of characters to a string variable results in the truncation of the value. The truncation does not cause a run-time error, but it can produce unwanted results. For example, suppose that we wish to have the user enter his or her name into a variable for later use. A commonly used maximum size for names is 20 characters; but there certainly are names that exceed this length. If the user enters a name longer than 20 characters and the accepting variable has a maximum length of 20, then truncation results.

We can access the individual characters of a string by use of an index. If String1 is a string variable, then String1[1] is the first character of the string, String1[2] is the second character of the string, and so on. If we try to refer to a character position that is beyond the declared length of a string and if range checking is on, then a run-time error results. What happens if we try to refer to a character position that is within the declared length of the string, but that is beyond the actual length of the string? A run-time error does not occur when referring to such a position, *but it is not meaningful.* We must be careful to avoid using character positions that are beyond the actual length of the string because of their meaningless nature. The best way to avoid trouble when dealing with strings is to view them as higher-level data constructs and to use the string operations that Turbo Pascal provides.

□

BASIC STRING OPERATIONS

We can use global string types in our programs so that we can more easily work with procedures and functions that deal with strings. As we shall see later, most programs that deal with strings should contain the type declaration:

```
type
   String255 = string[255];
```

The String255 global type is the most general type of string because it will allow all valid string lengths. It is tempting to simply declare all string variables within a program to be of type String255, but we should resist the temptation because of the possible waste of valuable memory resources. Another common type that will appear in many programs using strings is String80, which can be defined by

```
type
   String80 = string[80];
```

As we have seen already, the string **concatenation** operator in Pascal has the symbol '+'. The result of concatenation can not exceed 255 characters in length or a run-time error will result.

We can compare strings with a similar set of relational operators that are used for other types of objects. **String equality** uses the symbol '=' and has the definition:

$$String1 = String2$$

is true *if:*

the *actual* lengths of String1 and String2 are the same and all of the characters of the two strings from the first up to the actual length are the same.

is false *if:*

the actual lengths of the strings are different or if any character position contains different characters.

If two strings are not equal, then the nonequality relation

$$String1 <> String2$$

is true, otherwise it is false.

The other **string relational operators** depend on the collating sequence of the character set that underlies the implementation of Pascal (which for Turbo Pascal is the ASCII character set). We will discuss the relational operator "<" in detail below; the other relational operators (>, <=, and >=) have analogous definitions. The definition of "<" is as follows:

$$String1 < String2$$

is true if:

in some character position the character for String1 precedes the character in the same position of String2, with all characters prior to this character position matching; or, every character of String1 is equal to the character in the same position of String2 and the actual length of String1 is less than the actual length of String2.

Two important functions that we have used from time to time are **Chr** and **Ord**. Ord(*character*) gives the position of the character in the collating sequence (the ASCII sequence for Turbo Pascal). Chr is the inverse of Ord. That is, given a number *n* in the proper range (0 to 255 for Turbo Pascal), Chr(*n*) is the character in the *n*th position in the collating sequence. Thus, for example, in the ASCII collating sequence, Ord('a') is 97, and Chr(97) is 'a'.

□ **BUILT-IN STRING FUNCTIONS**

Turbo Pascal provides four string functions to aid in our programming with strings. The first of these functions is the *integer*-valued function **Length**. The function is used in the form

$$Length(string\ expression)$$

which returns the actual number of characters in the string expression that is provided as a parameter. Suppose that the string variable X has the value 'abc'. Then the following table of examples shows the nature of the Length function. (We use a dash to signify a blank space to help you see the lengths more clearly.)

StringExpression	Length(StringExpression)
X	3
''	0
X + X	6
X + 'd'	4
'a----'	5
'--a--'	5
X + '-'	4
X + ''	3

Notice that the presence of blank spaces in a string is detected by the Length function and that blanks are counted in the same way as other characters. The Length function permits us to access only the valid character positions in a string. For example, suppose that we wish to print the contents of the string variable X vertically. The following fragment of code will accomplish the task:

```
for I := 1 to Length(X) do
    Writeln(X[I])
```

If we want to print the string "diagonally" down the screen, we could use the fragment

```
for I := 1 to Length(X) do
    Writeln(' ':I, X[I])
```

For compatibility with some other dialects of Pascal, the string-valued function **Concat** is provided. The function is used in the form

```
Concat(list of string expressions)
```

and returns the string that results from concatenation of the parameters from left to right. The value of Concat(X, Y, Z) is the same as X + Y + Z.

The string-valued function **Copy** is provided for extracting substrings of a string. The function is used in the form

```
Copy(string expression, start position, number of characters)
```

and returns the substring that begins in the start position and continues for the number of characters specified. Suppose that the string variable X has the value 'abc'. Then the following table of examples shows the nature of the function Copy:

Stg	Start	Chars	Copy(Stg, Start, Chars)
X	2	2	'bc'
X + X	3	3	'cab'
X	1	3	'abc'
X	2	0	''
X	0	2	Run-time error
X	2	5	'bc'
X	2	−1	''
X	4	1	''
X	−1	3	Run-time error

We note that the starting position cannot be set to 0 or below or a run-time error will result. On the other hand, the starting position can be set to a value beyond the length of the string (actual or declared) with the null string as the resulting value of Copy.

The integer valued function **Pos** is provided to permit searching a string for a specified substring. The function is used in the form

$$\text{Pos}(\textit{search string, object string})$$

and returns the starting position of the *leftmost* occurrence of the search string within the object string. If there is no occurrence of the search string within the object string, then the value of Pos is 0. Suppose that the string variable X has the value 'abc'. Then the following table shows the nature of the function Pos:

Search	Object	Pos(Search, Object)
'b'	X	2
'cb'	X	0
'ca'	X + X	3
'abc'	X	1
'b'	X + X	2
''	X	1
X	''	0
'd'	X	0
''	''	1

The examples that may surprise you are those that involve the null string as the search string. We note that the null string is always found starting in position 1 even when the object string is itself null.

As an example of the use of the string functions, suppose that we are dealing with strings that may contain a substring between pairs of single quotes. Some examples of such strings are:

```
this string contains no substrings of interest
this string also doesn't contain any
this string 'certainly' does contain one
this string also contains 'one'
```

For our example, we will assume that the strings contain at most one substring contained between pairs of single quotes. The goal of the example is to read in a string, extract the substring between the quotes (if any), and print the substring or a message indicating that no substring was found. The substring extraction process will be implemented as a procedure called Extract with three parameters:

InString: (input) string sent in
type = String255

SubString: (output) substring found
type = String255

NotFound: (output) indicates whether substring is found or not
             type = Boolean

The steps of the procedure are as follows:

look for a single quote; if none found, set NotFound to
     true and quit; otherwise:
          set Start to the position of the single quote
          look for a single quote in the substring of the string
               which comes after Start; if none found, set NotFound
               to true and quit; otherwise:
                    set Finish to the position of the second single
                         quote in the string
                    set SubString to the string between Start and
                         Finish
                    set NotFound to false

We present the procedure Extract as part of the program Find in Figure 8-1. Note the correspondence of parameters in the procedure call:

```
Extract(InString, Substring, NotFound)
```

In the case of the first parameter, we have a String80 variable associated with a String255 variable. This is valid for *value* parameters. In the case of the second parameter, which is a *var* parameter, both variables are of type String255 because their types must match exactly.

```
program Find(Input, Output);
{
        Written by:   XXXXXXXX  XX/XX/XX
           Purpose:   To read strings and locate substrings between
                       single quotes.
    Procedures used:   Instructions - to print instructions
                       Extract - to extract substrings
}
const
   EndOfData = '$END';                   { terminates input loop }

type
   String255 = string[255];
   String80 = string[80];

var
   InString    : String80;        { string read in }
   SubString   : String255;       { substring found }
   NotFound    : Boolean;         { indicator for success of search }

procedure Instructions; begin {stub} end;
```

Figure 8-1 Finding Quoted Substrings (Continued)

```
procedure Extract(InString : String255;
                  var SubString : String255; var NotFound : Boolean);
{
        Written by:   XXXXXXXX   XX/XX/XX
           Purpose:   To find a substring between two single quotes.
        Parameters:   Instring - input, the string to look in
                      Substring - output, the substring found (if any)
                      NotFound - output, true means no substring found
    Functions used:   Pos - to locate the single quotes;
                      Copy - to get substrings.
}
const
  Quote = '''';                       { single quote character }

var
  Start    : integer;                 { location of first single quote }
  Finish   : integer;                 { location of second single quote }
  Rest     : String255;               { string after first single quote }

begin {Extract}

{*** Find first single quote, if any.}

  Start := Pos(Quote, InString);
  if  Start = 0  then
    begin
      NotFound := true;
      SubString := ''
    end
  else

{*** Find second single quote, if any.}

    begin
      Rest := Copy(InString, Start+1, Length(InString)-Start);
      Finish := Pos(Quote, Rest);
      if  Finish = 0  then
        begin
          NotFound := true;
          SubString := ''
        end
      else

{*** Establish substring.}
        begin
          SubString := Copy(Rest, 1, Finish-1);
          NotFound := false
        end
    end
end; {Extract}


begin {Find}

{*** Print Instructions }
```

Figure 8-1 Finding Quoted Substrings (Continued)

```
      Instructions;

   {*** Read and process strings.}

      repeat
        Write('Enter the string ($END to quit):');
        Readln(InString);
        if  InString <> EndOfData  then
          begin
            Extract(InString, SubString, NotFound);
            if  Notfound  then
              Writeln('*** No substring found.')
            else
              Writeln('Substring found: ->', SubString, '<-')
          end {if}
      until  InString = EndOfData;

   {*** Print message and terminate.}

      Writeln;
      Writeln('Find program terminating.')
   end.
```

SAMPLE INPUT AND OUTPUT

```
Enter the string ($END to quit):there is none here
*** No substring found.
Enter the string ($END to quit):there is 'one' here
Substring found: ->one<-
Enter the string ($END to quit):there is 'one ' here
Substring found: ->one <-
Enter the string ($END to quit):i don't see one
*** No substring found.
Enter the string ($END to quit):'tis not here
*** No substring found.
Enter the string ($END to quit):not here'
*** No substring found.
Enter the string ($END to quit):'
*** No substring found.
Enter the string ($END to quit):''
Substring found: -><-
Enter the string ($END to quit):
*** No substring found.
Enter the string ($END to quit):'first' thing
Substring found: ->first<-
Enter the string ($END to quit):'only'
Substring found: ->only<-
Enter the string ($END to quit):and 'last'
Substring found: ->last<-
Enter the string ($END to quit):$END

Find program terminating.
```

Figure 8-1 Finding Quoted Substrings

We may note the following tests that are shown in the sample input and output for Figure 8-1. Notice that many of these are boundary tests. For example, we test when the quoted string is at the extreme left and at the extreme right of the input string.

1. A string with no substring to find
2. The null string
3. The null string between quotes
4. A substring at the beginning of the string
5. A substring at the end of the string
6. A substring in the middle of the string
7. A substring that covers the whole string
8. A string with only one quote
9. A string consisting of only one quote
10. A string that has only one quote at the beginning
11. A string that has only one quote at the end
12. A string that has only one quote in the middle

□
BUILT-IN STRING PROCEDURES

Turbo Pascal also provides two procedures that deal with strings. The first of these procedures is **Delete**, which allows for the deletion of a substring of a specified string. The use of the procedure has the form

`Delete(string variable, start position, number of characters)`

This procedure has the side effect of altering the value of the string variable that is supplied as the first parameter. Suppose that the string variable X has the value 'abc'. Then the following table shows the nature of the procedure Delete:

Stg	Start	Chars	Stg after Delete(Stg, Start, Chars)
X	2	1	'ac'
X	2	2	'a'
X	2	3	'a'
X	1	3	''
X	2	0	'abc'
X	2	5	'a'

Note that you can specify more characters than are remaining in the string after the start position, as is shown in the example Delete(X, 2, 5), which causes X to have the value 'a'.

The procedure **Insert** allows a substring to be inserted into a string. The procedure is used in the form

`Insert(substring expression, string variable, start position)`

and has the side effect of changing the value of the string variable by inserting the substring beginning at the start position. Suppose that the string variable X has the value 'abc'. Then the following table shows the nature of the procedure Insert:

SubStr	Stg	Start	Stg after Insert(SubStr, Stg, Start)
'd'	X	2	'adbc'
'd'	X	4	'abcd'
'd'	X	5	'abcd'
'de'	X	1	'deabc'

We note that you can specify a starting position that is beyond the end of the string, but no matter what number you specify, you will get the substring concatenated with the string as the result.

As an example of the string procedures, we will write a program that will read a string and replace any occurrence of the word "thing" with the two words "general object." We will consider a word to have on both sides a nonnumeric, nonalphabetic character. Thus, in the following strings, we find "thing" as a word:

```
The word "thing" is here.
The music is the thing.
We have the thing, and it has us.
The thing's attributes are right.
in the middle of the thing
thing is one of the
```

In the following strings, we will not find "thing" as a word:

```
Something is wrong.
Things go better without bugs.
```

To make our design simpler, we will assume that there is only one occurrence of the substring "thing" within the string. We will use a Boolean function Break to determine if the characters to the left and right of the substring "thing" are nonnumeric and nonalphabetic. We will use the procedure ChangeThing to do the replacement of "thing" by "general object." The procedure has two parameters:

InString: (input) string for replacement

OutString: (output) string with replacements made

The steps for the procedure ChangeThing are as follows:

set OutString to InString
set Start to position of "thing" in OutString
if Start is not zero and if characters to left and right of "thing" are both break characters, then:
    delete "thing"
    insert "general object" into OutString at Start

```
function Break(Character : char) : Boolean;
{
        Written by:   XXXXXXXXX  XX/XX/XX
           Purpose:   To determine if a character is a break
                      character or not. ('0' to '9', 'a' to 'z',
                      and 'A' to 'Z' are not break characters,
                      all others are)
        Parameters:   Character - input, the character to test
}
begin {Break}
  Break := ((Character < '0') or (Character > '9'))  and
           ((Character < 'a') or (Character > 'z'))  and
           ((Character < 'A') or (Character > 'Z'))
end; {Break}

procedure ChangeThing(InString : String255;
                  var OutString : String255);
{
        Written by:   XXXXXXXXX  XX/XX/XX
           Purpose:   To replace the word "thing" with "general object".
        Parameters:   Instring - input, the string to work with
                      Outstring - output, the resulting string with the
                                  replacements made
   Procedures used:   Delete - to delete "thing";
                      Insert - to insert "general object".
    Functions used:   Pos - to locate a substring;
                      Break - to determine break characters.
}
var
  Start   : integer;                     { location of "thing" }

begin {ChangeThing}

{*** Initialize. Put blanks at front and rear to avoid special cases.}

  OutString := ' ' + InString + ' ';

{*** Replace "thing" if there.}

  Start := Pos('thing', OutString);
  if  (Start <> 0) then                        { if 'thing' is there }
    if (Break(OutString[Start-1])) and         { check for breaks }
       (Break(OutString[Start+5]))  then
       begin
         Delete(OutString, Start, 5);
         Insert('general object', OutString, Start)
       end;  {if}

{*** Remove the extra blanks at front and rear.}

  OutString := Copy(OutString, 2, Length(OutString)-2)
end; {ChangeThing}
```

Figure 8-2   Changing Substrings

If you think about the above steps, you can uncover a subtle flaw in the logic. If the word "thing" occurs at the extreme left of Instring, then there is no character to its left to be a break character. A similar problem arises if the word is at the extreme right. Instead of handling these situations as special cases, we choose to demonstrate a technique that is frequently useful. We add an extra blank at the front and rear of our string when we start, then take them off when we are done. Now the word "thing" cannot be at either the extreme left or the extreme right.

We show the code for ChangeThing in the program of Figure 8-2.

COMMENT The algorithm condition

if Start is not zero and if characters to left and right of "thing"

is changed to

if Start is not zero then
    if characters to left and right of "thing"

This avoids examining OutString[Start-1] when Start is 0, which would generate a range check error.

We will make the program of Figure 8-2 more useful in the exercises.

□ **STRING-NUMERIC CONVERSIONS**   Turbo Pascal supplies two procedures that implement numeric to string and string to numeric conversions. The procedure **Str** allows the conversion of a numeric expression into a string in the same form as is produced by Write or Writeln. The procedure is used in the form

```
Str(numeric expression, string variable)
```

and has the effect of assigning the "output representation" of the numeric value to the string variable. The numeric expression can include formatting as in the case with Write and Writeln. The following table shows the nature of the procedure Str:

NumExp and Format	Stg after Str(Numexp and Format, Stg)
1	'1'
1:3	' 1'
−2.5	' −2.5000000000E+00'
−2.5:6:2	' −2.50'
23.46:7:1	' 23.5'
−8	'−8'

The precise form of the use of the procedure Str is shown in the example

```
Str(-2.5:6:2, Stg)
```

COMMENT We will use Stg to denote a string variable in a number of examples throughout the chapter. We do not wish to use Str because of the confusion with the Str function. We cannot use String; that is a reserved word in Turbo Pascal.

The procedure **Val** allows us to convert a string that represents a numeric expression into a number. The use of the procedure has the form

```
Val(string expression, numeric variable, error variable)
```

and has the effect of assigning to the numeric variable the value represented by the string. If the string does not validly represent a numeric expression, then the first invalid position of the string is returned in the error variable. The string can represent either a real or integer variable and the numeric variable should be declared to be of the appropriate type. The following table shows the nature of the procedure Val:

		After Val(Stg, Num, ErrPos)	
Stg	*type of Num*	*Num*	*ErrPos*
'1'	integer	1	0
' 1'	integer	0	1
'1a'	integer	1	2
'−'	integer	0	0
'3+4'	integer	3	2
'−3.4+'	real	−3.4	5
'−3.4'	integer	−3	3
'23'	real	23	0
'− 23'	integer	0	2
'2E2'	integer	2	2
'3E−3'	real	0.003	0
'34 '	integer	34	3

As we study the table, we can see that the Val procedure considers spaces to be invalid in any position in the string. We also see that the scientific notation symbol E is allowed for reals and not for integers. We also see that Val returns the numeric value that lies to the left of an invalid character, if any.

As an example, suppose that we want to have the user input real numbers representing profits and losses in a loop and that we don't wish to designate any particular real number as a terminating value. We can read the user input as a string, check to see if it is the terminating value ($END, in our example), and convert the string to a number using the Val procedure, if appropriate. In our example, we are to add the numbers that are input and print the total. If the total is positive, we are to print

```
                    Profit: $total
```

If the total is negative, we are to print

```
                    Loss:  ($total)
```

We could accomplish this form of output with two Writeln statements, but for the purpose of example, we will use the Str procedure to build the output line and then print it. The example program is shown as Figure 8-3.

```
program ProfitAndLoss(Input, Output);
{
       Written by:  XXXXXXXX  XX/XX/XX
          Purpose:  To read profit and loss figures for a period
                    and print the total.
   Procedures used: Instructions - to print instructions;
                    Val - to convert a string to a number;
                    Str - to convert a number to a string.
}
const
  EndOfData = '$END';                 { terminates input loop }

type
  String80 = string[80];

var
  InString   : String80;              { string read in }
  OutString  : String80;              { string to write }
  Total      : real;                  { total profit or loss }
  Amount     : real;                  { input profit or loss }
  StrTotal   : String[80];            { total in string form }
  ErrPos     : integer;               { error position for Val }

procedure Instructions; begin  {stub}  end;

begin {ProfitAndLoss}

{*** Print Instructions and initialize.}

  Instructions;
  Total := 0;

{*** Read and total profit and loss figures.}

  repeat
    Write('Enter the amount ($END to quit):');
    Readln(InString);
    if  InString <> EndOfData  then
      begin
        repeat
          Val(InString, Amount, ErrPos);
          if  ErrPos <> 0  then
            begin
              Write('*** invalid amount, redo ($END to quit): ');
              Readln(InString)
            end {if}
        until  (ErrPos = 0) or (InString = EndOfData)
      end; {if}
    if  InString <> EndOfData  then
      Total := Total + Amount
  until  InString = EndOfData;

{*** Set up output.}
```

Figure 8-3 Output of Monetary Values (Continued)

```
  if  Total < 0  then
    begin
      Str(-Total:1:2, StrTotal);
      OutString := 'Loss: ($ '+ StrTotal + ')'
    end
  else
    begin
      Str(Total:1:2, StrTotal);
      OutString := 'Profit: $ ' + StrTotal
    end; {if}

{*** Print the output.}

  Writeln;
  Writeln(OutString);

{*** Print message and terminate.}

  Writeln;
  Writeln('ProfitAndLoss program terminating.')
end.
```

SAMPLE INPUT AND OUTPUT

First run:

```
Enter the amount ($END to quit):2.34
Enter the amount ($END to quit):45..6
*** invalid amount, redo ($END to quit): 45.6
Enter the amount ($END to quit):-23.4
Enter the amount ($END to quit):$end
*** invalid amount, redo ($END to quit): $END

Profit: $ 24.54

ProfitAndLoss program terminating.
```

Second run:

```
Enter the amount ($END to quit):5.67
Enter the amount ($END to quit):/34
*** invalid amount, redo ($END to quit): -12.34
Enter the amount ($END to quit):5.6
Enter the amount ($END to quit):-99.9
Enter the amount ($END to quit):$END

Loss: ($ 100.97)

ProfitAndLoss program terminating.
```

Figure 8-3 Output of Monetary Values

1. We must be sure not to allow any string involved in a program to become longer that 255 characters. A run-time error will result for any string that has a length greater than 255.

2. Whenever we access a character of a string by indexing as in an array, we must be sure that the index is not out of range. This means it may not be less than 1 and it may not exceed the declared maximum length of the string. Conditions such as "(I = 0) or (Stg[I] = ' ')" are suspect, for example.

It will not cause a run-time error if you index to a character position past the length of a string (but not past the declared maximum size of the string), but the character at that position has no meaning for your program. Use the Length function to keep your indexes in the proper range.

3. Be careful of unwanted truncation when using string assignment statements. You can anticipate truncation by use of the Length function.

4. In Turbo Pascal, position 0 of a string contains the length of the string in character form. Usually, you should avoid the use of position 0: you can determine the length of a string by using the Length function, and you can change the length of a string by concatenation or substring extraction via the Copy function.

5. In one of the examples in this section, we used the statement

```
Writeln(' ':I, X[I])
```

in order to print the Ith character of the string in X in increasing columns. You may have noted that this prints the Ith character of X in column I + 1. It may seem obvious that we can print the Ith character of X in the Ith column with the statement

```
Writeln(' ':I-1, X[I])
```

However, note that the idea fails when I is equal to 1, because the statement

```
Writeln(' ':0)
```

prints *one* blank. These boundary value problems are a constant plague to programmers.

6. We cannot use anything but a string variable for the first parameter of the procedure Delete. We cannot use string constants or string expressions such as X + Y. Violation of this rule will be detected by the compiler.

7. Do not put quotes around the numeric expressions that you use for the Str procedure. Here is a good and a bad example:

good: `Str(-2.5, OutString)`

bad: `Str('-2.5', OutString)`

This error will be detected by the compiler.

8. When we pass a string as a value parameter, we can mix the types of the formal and actual parameters. We can produce more general purpose subprograms by using the String255 type for all value parameters. The situation is different for var parameters. In this case, the formal and actual parameters must have the same type. Thus, if we wish to produce more general-purpose subprograms, we must declare *both* formal and actual var parameters to be of type String255.

☐
TESTING When we are testing programs and subprograms that use string data, we should include the following in our test cases:

1. The null string should always be tested because it is a boundary value for string data.

2. Strings of maximum length should be tested because they are boundary values for the program's data.

3. When the program builds strings by concatenation or insertion of substrings, **stress testing** should be performed to attempt to force a string to be constructed of more than 255 characters.

▪▪▪▪▪▪ REVIEW

Terms and concepts

concatenation	Concat
string equality (=)	Copy
other string relational	Pos
operators (<>,	Delete
<, >, <=, >=)	Insert
Chr	Str
Ord	Val
Length	stress testing

Pascal syntax

General string manipulation

1. Indexing. We can refer to the Ith character of the string variable X with the char expression

```
X[I]
```

2. Concatenation. For string expressions E1 and E2, we can form the concatenation of E1 and E2 with the string expression

```
E1 + E2
```

3. Relational Operators. For string expressions E1 and E2, we can form the Boolean expression

```
E1 relational operator E2
```

where the relational operators are =, <>, <, >, <=, and >=.

4. Chr and Ord. Chr converts a character from its position in the collating sequence (ASCII code in Turbo Pascal); Ord does the opposite.

Built-in Turbo string functions

1. Length Function. For a string expression E1, we can determine the number of characters in E1 with the integer expression

```
Length(E1)
```

2. Concat Function. For string expressions E1, E2, . . . , En, we can form the concatenation of the strings with the string expression

```
Concat(E1, E2, . . . , En)
```

7. *Copy Function.* For the string expression E1, we can form the substring that begins at the Ith character of E2 and that consists of N characters with the string expression

```
Copy(E1, I, N)
```

8. *Pos Function.* For the string expressions E1 and E2, we can find the starting position of the leftmost occurrence of E1 as a substring of E2 with the integer expression

```
Pos(E1, E2)
```

The value returned is 0 if there is no occurrence of E1 as a substring of E2.

Built-in Turbo string procedures

1. *Delete Procedure.* For a string variable X, we can delete N characters from X beginning with the character in position I by use of the procedure invocation

```
Delete(X, I, N)
```

2. *Insert Procedure.* For a string variable X, we can insert the value of the string expression E1 beginning at position I by use of the procedure invocation

```
Insert(E1, X, I)
```

3. *Str Procedure.* For a real or integer numeric expression E1, we can convert E1 into the string variable X by use of the procedure invocation

```
Str(E1, X)
```

4. *Val Procedure.* For a string expression E1 that is a representation of a number, we can convert E1 into the real or integer variable X with the integer variable P indicating the first invalid position by use of the procedure invocation

```
Val(E1, X, P)
```

The integer variable P will have a value of 0 if E1 is a valid representation of a number with the same type as X.

DPT

1. Keep the lengths of all string expressions to within 255 characters.
2. Do not index beyond the length of a string.
3. Watch for unwanted truncation.
4. Avoid position 0 of a string.
5. Writeln(' ':0) prints one space.
6. The first parameter of Delete must be a string *variable.*
7. Do not use quotes around numeric expressions.
8. You cannot mix types for string var parameters.

Testing summary

1. Test the null string.
2. Test strings of maximum length.
3. Try to push against the 255- character barrier.

1. Define a string variable String1 to have maximum length 10. Assign the value 'banana' to String1 and then assign the value 'grape' to String1. Print String1[6]. Experiment some more with such meaningless activities in order to ensure that the rest of your dealing with strings will be meaningful.

2. Write careful, detailed definitions for the string comparisons '>', '<=', and '>='.

3. The purpose of this exercise is to illustrate the danger of altering position 0 of a string. Write a Pascal program to execute the following lines of code:

```
var
    X : string[80];
        . . . .
    X := 'This string is valid';
    Writeln(X);
    X := 'A mess it is in';
    Writeln(X);
    X[0] := Chr(20);
    Writeln(X);
```

*4. Suppose X has the value 'abcde' at the beginning of each of the parts of this exercise. State the value of X after the statement of each part has been executed.

```
a. X := 'yz' + X
b. if  X = 'abcde '   then
      X := 'surprise'
   else
      X := 'no surprise'
c. X := Concat('a', 'b', 'de')
d. X := Copy(X, 2, 3)
e. Delete(X, 2, 3)
f. Insert('yz', X, 3)
g. Str(Length(X), X)
h. Str(Pos('cd', X), X)
```

*5. Evaluate the following:

```
a. Length('ab' + 'cd' + ' ')
b. Pos('de', 'ad' + 'ef')
c. Pos('ce', 'abcde')
d. Copy('some' + 'where', 4, 3)
e. Copy('abcde', 4, 5)
```

*6. Suppose that X is a string variable. Is it always true that the length of Copy(X, 4, 6) is equal to 6? Explain.

7. Suppose that X is a string variable of length 4 and that Y is a string expression of length 5. Is it always true that after execution of Insert(Y, X, 2) X has a length of 9? Explain.

8. Modify the program of Figure 8-1 to allow multiple substrings between pairs of quotes on a single line.

9. Modify the program of Figure 8-2 to allow multiple instances of the word "thing" to appear on a single line.

10. Modify the program of Figure 8-2 to accept as user inputs the word to find ("thing" in the example) and the phrase to substitute ("general object" in the example).

11. Modify the program of Figure 8-3 to allow the user to input amounts using an *optional* dollar sign.

*12. Write a program that accepts as input the user's name and prints a continuous "snake" of the user's name on the screen. For example, for the user named Jane, we would begin with

```
        J
         a
          n
           e
           J
            a
           n
          e
          J
           a
            n
             e
          . . .
```

13. Write procedures or functions for the following:

    *a. Given a name and an array of names, print all the names in the array that match the given name in the first five character positions.

    b. Determine whether or not an array of strings adheres to this rule: There can be no nonempty entries after the first one that is empty.

    c. Given an array of strings, delete any duplicates by changing them to empty strings.

    *d. Given an array of strings, move all empty strings (if any) to the end of the array.

    e. Find how many blanks are in a given string.

14. Write procedures or functions for the following.

    a. Given a string containing a name such as

```
Johnson, Joseph Lawrence
```

    obtain three strings consisting of the last, first, and middle names. Assume valid input.

    *b. Create a magazine account number, given the last name, initials, city, and expiration date in the form mm/yy. The account number is in a form such as

```
CRAJW-DEC89-SP
```

    This consists of:
    (1) the first three letters of last name
    (2) the initials
    (3) a dash
    (4) the month of expiration (JAN, FEB, etc.)
    (5) the year of expiration
    (6) a dash
    (7) the first and fourth characters of city

c. Given a string Stg and an integer N, place N blanks into the string Stg beginning at position N.

*15. a. Show how to use Pos to convert a given character '0', '1', etc. to its numeric value. Hint: Consider the string '0123456789'.

b. In base 16, the "digits" are '0' through '9' and 'A' through 'F', where 'A' represents 10, 'B' represents 11, and so on. Use Pos to convert a given base 16 "digit" to its numeric value.

16. In this exercise, you will write a program to "parse" input strings. The input to the program will consist of a text file that has lines of six different types. The file should be considered as a file of commands for drawing a primitive text picture on the screen. The types of commands are identified by the first character on the line. The types are as follows:

D:
    a single character follows the D
    a positive integer follows the character
    examples:

```
Dx20
D#65
```

    meaning:
        print the specifed number of consecutive specified characters

C:
    a string follows the C
    examples:

```
CA Bar Graph
CFigure 3-4
```

    meaning:
        print the centered string on a new line, as the entire line

N:
    either a positive integer or nothing follows the N
    example:

```
N
```

    meaning:
        go to a new line
    example:

```
N2
```

    meaning:
        go to a new line twice

P:
    a string follows the P
    examples:

```
PLoss:
PMonth
```

    meaning:
        print the string without going to a new line

E:

    nothing follows the E

    example:

        `E`

    meaning:
        clear the screen

H:

    nothing follows the H

    example:

        `H`

    meaning:
        halt the program

Your program should read the file one line at a time and execute the command contained on the line. For example, suppose that your program reads the file:

```
E
CAverage Earnings
N
P1984:                 *** note: two spaces follow the colon
D$7
N
P1985:                 *** note: two spaces follow the colon
D$3
N
P1986:                 *** note: two spaces follow the colon
D$5
N2
CTable 3.1
H
```

The program should produce the output:

```
                Average Earnings

1984:   $$$$$$$
1985:   $$$
1986:   $$$$$
```

1. In some implementations of Pascal, the array of char is the only means of dealing with strings.

8-2
□□□□□□
STRING
PROCESSING

In this section, we will discuss various aspects of string processing. We will begin by developing some extensions to the basic string operations that are provided as built-in features of Turbo Pascal. We will continue with a discussion of character conversion techniques and will provide some useful illustrations of the methods. One of our examples is a conversion program that has proved to be very useful when dealing with a popular word processing program. We will complete the section with a presentation of a package for dealing with arbitrarily long string data. The ideas of this latter subsection will allow the implementation of a string data type for applications of Pascal that do not provide any built-in string processing facilities.

□
SOME ADDITIONAL STRING TOOLS

The first additional tool that we will discuss is the user-defined string function **Trim**, which deletes trailing blanks from a string. The function accepts a string of any type as a value parameter and returns the trimmed string as its value. Some examples of the behavior of the function Trim are shown in the table below, where we have used dashes to signify blanks in order to clarify the action.

InString	Trim(InString)
'abc___'	'abc'
'___abc'	'___abc'
'____'	''
'a_b'	'a_b'

We note that Trim only deletes blanks that are on the *right* of the string. It does not deal with embedded blanks or blanks on the left. If the input string consists of all blanks, then the value of Trim is the null string.

In order to be compatible with any string type, the function expects that there is a global type called String255 that has been declared in the calling program. The type of the function and of its single value parameter is String255. The function uses the built-in Length and Copy functions to produce its value. The header for the Trim function is

```
function Trim(InString : String255) : String255;
```

The function has a local integer variable I for use as a loop index and a local Boolean variable Found for loop control. The algorithm uses a standard searching loop, except that rather than searching forward, it searches backward. The first nonblank found represents the desired length of the result:

[search backwards for a nonblank character]
    set I to the length of InString, Found to false
    while no nonblank character has been found and I>=1, keep
        decrementing I
[return the trimmed string]
    set Trim to the first I characters of InString

The Trim function is shown in Figure 8-4.

The next tool that we will discuss is a function that will produce a string consisting of repetitions of a single character. The function **RunOf** is a string-valued function that has two value parameters: the number of repetitions and the character to be repeated. We show some examples of the behavior of the RunOf function in the table:

```
function Trim(InString : String255) : String255;
{
      Written by:   XXXXXXXX  XX/XX/XX
         Purpose:   To trim trailing blanks from a string.
      Parameters:   Instring - input, the string to be trimmed
   Functions used:  Length - (built-in) to get number of characters;
                    Copy - (built-in) to extract a substring.
}
const
   Blank = ' ';                      { Blank space }

var
   I       : integer;               { Loop index }
   Found   : boolean;               { Has nonblank been found? }

begin {Trim}

{*** Search backwards for a nonblank character.}

   I := Length(InString);           { Start at last position }
   Found := false;

   while (not Found) and (I >= 1)  do
      begin
        if Instring[I] <> Blank then
           Found := true
        else
           I := I - 1
      end;  {while}

{*** Return the trimmed string.}

   Trim := Copy(InString, 1, I)
end; {Trim}
```

Figure 8-4 The Trim Function

Number	Character	RunOf(Number, Character)
3	'*'	'***'
1	'#'	'#'
5	' '	' '
0	'%'	''
256	'$'	''

We note that if the number of repetitions is specified as less than 1 or greater than 255, then the value returned by RunOf is the null string.

In order to be compatible with any string type, the function expects that there is a global type called String255 that has been declared in the calling program. The type of the function is String255. The function uses the built-in Procedure **FillChar** to produce its value. The FillChar procedure accepts three parameters: a variable, the number of characters to fill, and the character to fill with. The effect of FillChar is to fill the *memory location* where the storage of the variable starts with the specified number of instances of the specified character. This is almost the same result that we want from the RunOf function. The difference is that the FillChar procedure does not work compatibly with the string types. Our approach is to let FillChar do most of the work by filling the memory with *one more* than the specified number of characters and then to fix the length of the string ourselves by modifying position 0 of the string (which will also have been filled with the character by FillChar). For a length of N, setting position 0 to Chr(N) will set the length properly.

The header for the RunOf function is

```
function RunOf(Number : integer; Character : char) : String255;
```

The function has a local String255 variable WorkString for use in creating the value to be returned. The logical steps of the algorithm for RunOf are

[check validity of Number; return the null string if invalid]
    if Number is less than 1 or greater than 255:
        set WorkString to the null string
    otherwise:
        fill Number+1 memory locations starting at the base of
            WorkString with Character
        set the length of WorkString to Number
[return the created string]
    set RunOf to WorkString

The RunOf function is shown in Figure 8-5.

Sometimes when dealing with strings, we wish they were all the same constant length. The usual character that is used to "pad" strings is the blank space. We will now introduce the function **Pad** that will pad a string to a specified length by adding spaces if necessary. Pad is a string-valued function that has two value parameters: the input string to be padded and the desired minimum length of the resulting string. Some examples that illustrate the behavior of the Pad function are shown in the table:

InString	Margin	Pad(InString, Margin)
'ab'	5	'ab '
''	3	' '
'abcd'	3	'abcd'
'abc'	0	'abc'
'abc'	256	'abc'

In order to be compatible with any string type, the function expects that there is a global type called String255 that has been declared in the calling program. The type of the function and its input string parameter is String255. The function uses the functions RunOf and Length to produce its value. The header for

```
function RunOf(Number : integer; Character : char) : string255;
{
        Written by:     XXXXXXXX  XX/XX/XX
          Purpose:      To create a string of a specified number of
                        occurrences of a specified character.
        Parameters:     Number - input, number of characters to generate
                        Character - input, character to generate
   Procedures used:     FillChar - (built-in) to fill a variable with a value.
}
const
  NullString = '';                      { Empty string }

var
  WorkString : String255;               { Variable for FillChar }

begin {RunOf}

{*** Check validity of Number; return null string if invalid.}

  if  (Number < 1) or (Number > 255)  then
    WorkString := NullString
  else
    begin
      FillChar(WorkString, Number+1, Character);
      WorkString[0] := Chr(Number)
    end; {if}

{*** Return the created string.}

  RunOf := WorkString
end; {RunOf}
```

Figure 8-5 The Runof Function

the Pad function is

```
function Pad(InString : String255; Margin : integer) : String255;
```

The logical steps of the algorithm for Pad are

[pad blanks to InString if Margin is valid]
    if Margin is greater than 255:
        set Pad to InString
    otherwise:
        set Pad to the concatenation of InString with a run of
          Margin-Length(InString) blanks

The Pad function is shown in Figure 8-6.

    The next tool is the procedure **Replace** that will replace the leftmost occur-
rence of a substring with a replacement substring. The procedure has a var parameter consisting of the string to work on and also has two value parameters: the
substring to find and the substring to replace the found string. If the substring to be
found does not exist in the input string, then the procedure does not change the

```
function Pad(InString : String255; Margin : integer) : String255;
{
         Written by:   XXXXXXXX   XX/XX/XX
            Purpose:   To add blanks to the end of InString in order
                       to extend its length to Margin.
         Parameters:  Instring - input, the string to pad
                      Margin - input, the resulting margin (if less than
                          current length, or greater than 255, answer is
                          Instring)
      Functions used: RunOf - to obtain a string of blanks;
                      Length - (built-in) to get the length of a string.
}
const
   Blank = ' ';                              { Blank space }

begin {Pad}

{*** Pad blanks to InString if Margin is valid.}

   if  (Margin > 255)  then
      Pad := InString                        { Do nothing if invalid }
   else
      Pad := Instring + RunOf(Margin-Length(InString), Blank)
end; {Pad}
```

Figure 8-6   The Pad Function

input string. Some examples of the behavior of the Replace procedure are shown in the table:

Original InString	Search	Change	After Replace(InString, Search, Change) InString
'abcd'	'bc'	'efg'	'aefgd'
'abcd'	'bd'	'efg'	'abcd'
'abcd'	''	'efg'	'efgabcd'
'abcd'	'd'	'defg'	'abcdefg'
''	''	'abcd'	'abcd'
'abcd'	'bc'	''	'ad'

In order to be compatible with any string type, the procedure expects that there is a global type called String255 that has been declared in the calling program. The type of the string to be changed is String255 for both the procedure *and for the caller.* The procedure uses the procedures Delete and Insert as well as the functions Pos and Length to produce its result. The header for the Replace procedure is

```
procedure Replace(var InString : String255; Search, Change : String255);
```

The procedure uses the local variable Start to indicate the beginning of the substring within the input string and a local variable Total to ensure that no attempt is made to produce a string of length greater than 255.

The logical steps of the algorithm for Replace are:

```
[check for existence of substring]
    set Start to Pos(Search, InString)
[check the resulting length of the replaced string]
    set Total to Length(Instring)−Length(Search)+Length(Change)
[do the replacement, if valid]
    if Start is not 0 and Total is not greater than 255:
        Delete(InString, Start, Length(Search))
        Insert(Change, InString, Start)
```

The Replace procedure is shown in Figure 8-7.

```
procedure Replace(var InString : String255; Search, Change : String255);
{
        Written by:   XXXXXXXXX   XX/XX/XX
           Purpose:   To replace the leftmost occurrence of Search in
                      InString with Change
        Parameters:   Instring − update, the string to be modified
                      Search − input, the substring to look for
                      Change − input, the substring to replace Search by
  Procedures used:    Delete − (built−in) to delete a substring;
                      Insert − (built−in) to insert a substring.
   Functions used:    Pos − (built−in) to find a substring in a string
                      Length − (built−in) to find the length of a string
}
var
   Start    : integer;              { Position of Search within InString }
   Total    : integer;              { Potential total length of result }

begin {Replace}

{*** Check for the existence of Search in InString.}

   Start := Pos(Search, InString);

{*** Check the resulting length of the replaced string.}

   Total := Length(Instring) − Length(Search) + Length(Change);

{*** Do the replacement if valid.}

   if  (Start > 0) and (Total <= 255) then
     begin
       Delete(InString, Start, Length(Search));
       Insert(Change, InString, Start)
     end {if}
end; {Replace}
```

Figure 8-7   The Replace Procedure

We will suggest a few more string-processing tools in the exercises at the end of the section.

There are a number of instances where we want to move through a string, character by character, changing the character to some other character if appropriate. Some examples of a conversion strategy are:

> Change all uppercase characters to lowercase.
> Change all lowercase characters to uppercase.
> Encode each character according to some (secret?) code.
> Decode each character according to some code.
> Change characters in graphic range to text range.

We often wish to process an entire text file using one of these schemes. A good design methodology for these tasks is to modularize according to size of data:

> Module to change an entire text file
> Module to change an entire string
> Module to change individual characters, if appropriate

The module to change an entire text file will read one line at a time into a string, call the module that changes entire strings to make the modifications, and write the line to the output file. The module to change an entire string will loop through the string one character at a time and call the module that changes individual characters, if appropriate, for each character of the string, and build the answer by replacement of the characters.

Note that one advantage of this particular modularization is that we can use essentially the same modules for the top two levels in the hierarchy. Then, by plugging in different lowest-level modules, we can change our conversion application.

Let us begin with a discussion of changing lowercase letters to uppercase. Turbo Pascal provides the built-in function **UpCase** for the third-level module. We can invoke this built-in function by providing it with a parameter of type char, and we will receive a char value in return. The function UpCase converts lowercase letters to their uppercase equivalents and leaves all other characters alone. Let us use UpCase to design a second level module to convert an entire string from lowercase to uppercase.

We will call the module **LowToUp** and will choose to implement it as a string-valued function. This will allow us to test for a terminating value in an input loop with the statement

```
until  LowToUp(String1) = '$END'
```

so that the user can enter any of the following as terminating values:

```
$END    $ENd    $EnD    $End    $eND    $eNd    $enD    $end
```

By now you have already typed '$end' instead of '$END' enough times to appreciate this more flexible way of handling user responses. The header for the function is

```
function LowToUp(InString : String255) : String255;
```

We will use the built-in functions UpCase and Length to produce the desired value. Since InString is a value parameter, we will use it as a working string inside of LowToUp with no fear of side effects. (Caution: This is a Pascal feature; some other programming languages do not provide this type of protection.) We will use a local variable I as a loop index. The basic logical steps of the algorithm are

[loop through the string, converting each character]
    loop I from 1 to the length of InString:
        set InString[I] to UpCase(InString[I])
[return the converted string]
    set LowToUp to InString

The code for the function LowToUp is shown in Figure 8-8.
    The module that deals with the text file will normally be the main program and will be responsible for the user interface and opening and closing files. We will simply list the rough steps of this module here and refer you to Figure 8-10 which,

```
function LowToUp(InString : String255) : String255;
{
        Written by:  XXXXXXXX  XX/XX/XX
          Purpose:  To convert lowercase to uppercase.
       Parameters:  Instring - the string to be converted
   Functions used:  UpCase - to convert a character;
                    Length - to get the length of a string.
}
var
  I      : integer;                { Loop index }

begin {LowToUp}

{*** Loop through the string, converting each character.}

  for I := 1 to Length(InString) do
    InString[I] := UpCase(InString[I]);

{*** Return the converted string.}

  LowToUp := InString
end; {LowToUp}
```

Figure 8-8 Converting a String To Uppercase

is a complete example of one of the applications. The rough steps of the file level module are

1. Print the instructions.
2. Ask the user for the filenames and open the files.
3. Convert the lines of input file into output file.
4. Close the files.
5. Print the terminating message and stop program.

We now turn to another application area, changing uppercase to lowercase. There is no built-in function in Turbo Pascal to perform this conversion, so we must build the lowest-level module, which we will call **LowCase**. In building LowCase, we will use the ASCII code set in which the difference between the character codes for an uppercase letter and its lowercase equivalent is 32. Because the lowercase letters have the higher values, if X contains an uppercase letter for a value, then Chr(Ord(X)+32) is the lowercase equivalent. The code for LowCase is shown in Figure 8-9.

One application that the authors often use allows the conversion of files that are used by a certain well-known word processing program into a form that is usable by other word processors and editors. This famous word processor changes characters at the end of certain words into the graphics range that renders the file unusable for certain applications such as direct display or use as program text for Turbo Pascal. The three levels of modules for this application are called:

TrashOut: the highest-level, main program
HighOff: the function that converts a string
SetLow: the lowest-level function that converts a character, if appropriate

The conversion process is fairly simple for this application: If the ASCII code of a character is greater than 127, then subtract 128 from the ASCII code of the character. The entire Trashout program is shown in Figure 8-10.

```
function LowCase(InChar : char) : char;
{
        Written by:   XXXXXXXX   XX/XX/XX
           Purpose:   To convert a character to lowercase.
    Functions used:   Ord - (built-in) to get the ASCII code;
                      Chr - (built-in) to get a character from a code.
}
begin {LowCase}
   if  (InChar >= 'A') and (InChar <= 'Z')   then
     LowCase := Chr(Ord(InChar) + 32)
   else
     LowCase := InChar
end; {LowCase}
```

Figure 8-9 Converting a Character to Lowercase

```
program TrashOut(Input, Output);
{
        Written by:   XXXXXXXX  XX/XX/XX
          Purpose:    To remove high-order bits from a text file.
   Procedures used:   Instructions - to print instructions;
                      Open Read, OpenWrite - to open files.
    Functions used:   HighOff - to remove high-order bits from strings.

}
type
  String255 = string[255];
  String80 = string[80];

var
  InFile    : text;                  { Input file }
  OutFile   : text;                  { Output file }
  Line      : String255;             { Line of file }

procedure Instructions;  begin  {stub}  end;
```

{*function Exists and procedures OpenRead and OpenWrite, as shown in Appendix E, are inserted
    here*}

```
function SetLow(InChar : char) : char;
{
        Written by:   XXXXXXXXX XX/XX/XX
          Purpose:    To turn off the high-order bit if on.
       Parameters:    InChar - input, character to be converted
    Functions used:   Ord - (built-in) to get ASCII code;
                      Chr - (built-in) to get a character from ASCII code.
}
begin {SetLow}
  if  Ord(InChar) > 127  then
    SetLow := Chr(Ord(InChar) - 128)
  else
    SetLow := InChar
end; {SetLow}

function HighOff(InString : String255) : String255;
{
        Written by:   XXXXXXXX  XX/XX/XX
          Purpose:    To remove high-order bits from a string.
       Parameters:    Instring - string to be converted
    Functions used:   SetLow - to convert a character;
                      Length - to get the length of a string.
}
var
  I       : integer;                 { Loop index }

begin {HighOff}

{*** Loop through the string, converting each character.}
```

Figure 8-10 Removing High-order Bits (Continued)

```
  for I := 1 to Length(InString) do
    InString[I] := SetLow(InString[I]);

{*** Return the converted string.}

  HighOff := InString
end; {HighOff}


begin {TrashOut}

{*** Print instructions.}

  Instructions;

{*** Ask the user for the filenames and open the files.}

  OpenRead(InFile);
  OpenWrite(OutFile);

{*** Convert lines of input file into output file.}

  while  not Eof(InFile)  do
    begin
      Readln(InFile, Line);
      Line := HighOff(Line);
      Writeln(OutFile, Line);
      Writeln(Line)
    end; {while}

{*** Close the files.}

  Close(InFile);
  Close(OutFile);

{*** Print terminating message and stop program.}

  Writeln;
  Writeln('Trashout program is terminating.')
end.
```

Figure 8-10   Removing High-order Bits

□ Although it is not usually a problem, the strings of Turbo Pascal are limited to a length of 255 characters. What if we wanted to deal with larger strings? In this subsection, we will begin to develop a package for dealing with strings of lengths longer than 255. The techniques that we employ in this package can also be used to implement string types in versions of Pascal that do not already have them.

LONGER-LENGTH STRINGS

Our basic data structure for dealing with **Big Strings** will be a type such as the following:

```
BigString = record
              Character : array[1 .. MaxLength] of char;
              Length    : integer
            end
```

MaxLength is a named constant that we are thinking of as perhaps in the range of 500. We wish to be able to perform similar activities with Big Strings as we do with the usual string types. Some of the operations that we want to perform with Big Strings are

Inputting and outputting	Searching for substrings
Determining length	Deleting substrings
Concatenating	Inserting substrings
Extracting substrings	Replacing substrings
Comparing strings	Trimming trailing blanks
Converting string to BigString	Padding with blanks
Converting BigString to string	

We will develop some of these activities and leave some of the others for the exercises. Before we move on to some development, let us agree to the following naming convention: If a string routine is called xxx, then we will call the corresponding BigString routine by the name Bigxxx. With this in mind, the names of the routines in the package are

BigReadln	BigFromStr
BigWriteln	BigPos
BigLength	BigDelete
BigConcat	BigInsert
BigCopy	BigReplace
BigEqual	BigTrim
BigLessThan	BigPad
BigToStr	

The first routines to be developed are the input and output routines because they form the interface with the user and will ultimately allow the user to check on the correctness of other elements of the package as they are developed.

The simplest routine to design is BigWriteln, so we start with it. Our version of BigWriteln will accept a single-value parameter of type BigString and will print the contents on the screen. We will use a single local variable I as a loop index. The basic logic of the algorithm is:

```
loop I from 1 to the Length of the Big String:
      Print the Ith character of the Big String
Go to a new line
```

The code for the BigWriteln procedure appears in Figure 8-11. Note that the use of the with–do construct enhances the readability of the module. The single Writeln at the end of the procedure ensures that the next data that are printed will begin on the next line.

```
    procedure BigWriteln(InString : BigString);
{
  Written by:   XXXXXXXX  XX/XX/XX
     Purpose:   To print out InString.
  Parameters:   InString - input, string to print
}
var
  I   : integer;                          { Loop index }

begin {BigWriteln}
  with InString do
    begin
      for I:=1 to Length do
        Write(Character[I])
    end; {with}
  Writeln
end; {BigWriteln}
```

Figure 8-11   Output of a Big String

The next routine that we wish to implement is BigReadln to allow us to input data to BigString-type variables. There are two details to be discussed before we look at the algorithm and code for this routine. First, we must use the compiler directive {$B−} in order for the Read procedure to allow the input of characters one at a time. This compiler directive should be at the top of your main program. Second is the use of built-in indicator **Eoln**, a Boolean system function that you may pronounce ''end of line.'' When the compiler directive {$B−} is used, Eoln will indicate when the user has hit a carriage return after entering some data. After Eoln becomes true, a Readln statement should be executed to reset the variable Eoln.[1]

Our version of BigReadln will have a single var parameter of the type Big-String, which will return the string input by the user. The basic logic of the algorithm is

set Length of the Big String to 0
while we haven't reached the end of the line:
 increment the Length of the Big String by 1
 read the next character into the Character array at the
  position Length
clear the end of line indicator with a Readln

The code for the BigReadln procedure is shown in Figure 8-12.

The next module to be developed is the integer function BigLength, which will return the length of a Big String. The function has one value parameter of the type BigString. It may surprise you that we wish to use a procedure for a ''one-line'' operation. The reason for this is to respect the principle of **information hiding**, which holds that a using program should not know the details of data structures used to represent information; instead, the using program should use higher-level operations to gain access to the information. The code for the procedure BigLength is shown in Figure 8-13.

```
procedure BigReadln(var OutString : BigString);
{
      Written by:   XXXXXXXX  XX/XX/XX
         Purpose:   To read characters into OutString.
      Parameters:   OutString - output, the string being read
   Functions used:  Eoln - (built-in) to indicate end-of-line.
}
begin {BigReadln}
  with OutString do
    begin
      Length := 0;

{*** Take characters one at a time until Eol.}

      while  not Eoln  do
        begin
          Length := Length + 1;
          Read(Character[Length])
        end {while}

    end; {with}
  Readln                             {Reset Eoln}
end; {BigReadln}
```

Figure 8-12 Input of a Big String

Next we will develop the procedure BigCopy, which extracts a substring of a Big String. Notice that the usual Copy subprogram in Turbo Pascal is a function. However, BigCopy must be a procedure because functions are unable to return a record type as an answer.

The procedure has one value input parameter and one var output parameter, both of the type BigString. The procedure also has two integer value parameters: the start position of the substring and the number of characters desired. The procedure uses the local variable I as a loop index and the local variable InLen to store the length of InString. The basic logic of the steps of the program is

set InLen to the length of InString
[see how many to copy]

```
function BigLength(InString : BigString) : integer;
{
 Written by:   XXXXXXXX  XX/XX/XX
    Purpose:   To return the length of a Big String.
 Parameters:   InString - input, the string to find the length of
}
begin {BigLength}
  BigLength := InString.Length
end; {BigLength}
```

Figure 8-13 Length of a Big String

if the number of characters to copy is less than 0, then set
   the number of characters to copy to 0
if the start position is less than one, then set the number of
   characters to copy to 0
otherwise, if the start position plus the number of characters
   is greater than InLen, then set the number of characters to
   the number that will go to the end of InString
[perform the copy]
loop I from 1 to the number of characters to copy:
   set the Ith character of OutString to the Start + (I − 1)st
      character of InString
set the length of OutString to the number of characters copied

The algorithm for BigCopy, because of our desire to remain consistent with the Turbo Pascal Copy function, contains a few subtleties due to the possibilities:

Number < 0
   in this case, we wish to set Number to 0
Start < 1
   in this case, we wish to set Number to 0
Start + Number $>$ InLen
   in this case, we wish to copy characters to the end of
   InString, so we set Number to InLen-Start+1

The code for the procedure is shown in Figure 8-14.

    The last routine that we will present is the procedure BigConcat, which concatenates two elements of the type BigString. The procedure has two value input parameters, InString1 and InString2, and one var output parameter, OutString. The procedure uses the local variable I as a loop index and two local variables InLen1 and InLen2 to store the lengths of the input Big Strings. For simplicity in the presentation, we assume that the resulting length of the answer will be less than or equal to MaxLength, the maximum length allowable. The basic logic of the steps of the procedure is

set InLen1 to the length of InString1
set InLen2 to the length of InString2
loop I from 1 to InLen1:
   set the Ith character of OutString to the Ith character of
      Instring1
loop I from InLen1 to InLen1 + InLen2:
   set the Ith character of OutString to the (I-InLen1)th
      character of InString2
set the length of OutString to InLen1 + InLen2

```
procedure BigCopy(InString: BigString; Start, Number : integer;
                  var OutString : BigString);
{
        Written by:   XXXXXXXX   XX/XX/XX
           Purpose:   Extract a substring from a string.
        Parameters:   InString - input, the string to look in
                      Start - input, where the substring should start
                      Number - input, desired length of the substring
                      OutString - output, the substring
     Functions used:  BigLength - to find the length of a Big String.
}
var
   InLen    : integer;                    { Length of InString }
   I        : integer;                    { Loop index }

begin {BigCopy}
   InLen := BigLength(InString);
   with OutString do
      begin
        if  Number < 0  then   Number := 0;
        if  Start < 1   then
          Number := 0
        else if  (Start + Number) > InLen   then
          Number := InLen - Start + 1;
        for I := 1 to Number do
          Character[I] := InString.Character[Start+I-1];
        Length := Number
      end {with}
end; {BigCopy}
```

Figure 8-14 Extracting a Substring of a Big String

There are several special cases of concatenation to consider:

InString1 is null.

InString2 is null.

Both InString1 and InString2 are null.
Resulting OutString is as large as possible.

You should hand-trace the algorithm for BigConcat to verify that these special cases cause no difficulty for the algorithm. The code for the procedure BigConcat is shown in Figure 8-15.

For testing these first routines of the package, we have written a driver program. The driver main program is shown in Figure 8-16. To run the driver, the routines of the package would have to be inserted perhaps in the order indicated.

```
procedure BigConcat(InString1, InString2 : BigString;
                    var OutString : BigString);
{
        Written by:  XXXXXXXX  XX/XX/XX
           Purpose:  To concatenate two Big Strings.
        Parameters:  InString1, InString2 - input, the strings to concatenate
                     OutString - output, the concatenated string
}
var
  InLen1   : integer;                    { End of String1 }
  InLen2   : integer;                    { End of String2 }
  I        : integer;                    { Loop index }

begin {BigConcat}
  InLen1 := BigLength(InString1);
  InLen2 := BigLength(InString2);
  with OutString do
    begin
      for I := 1 to InLen1 do
        Character[I] := InString1.Character[I];
      for I := InLen1 + 1 to InLen1 + InLen2 do
        Character[I] := InString2.Character[I-InLen1];
      Length := InLen1 + InLen2
    end {with}
end; {BigConcat}
```

Figure 8-15   Concatenating Big Strings

```
            program Driver(Input, Output);
            {
                    Written by:  XXXXXXXX  XX/XX/XX
                       Purpose:  To test the Big String Package.
            }
            type
              BigString = record
                            Character : array[1 .. 500] of char;
                            Length    : integer
                          end;

            var
              String1, String2, String3 : BigString;
              Start, Number             : integer;
```

{function BigLength inserted here}

{procedure BigConcat inserted here}

{procedure BigCopy inserted here}

{procedure BigReadln inserted here}

{procedure BigWriteln inserted here}

Figure 8-16   Testing with Big Strings (Continued)

```
      begin {Driver}

      {*** Read two big strings.}

        Write('Enter a string: ');
        BigReadln(String1);
        Write('Enter a string: ');
        BigReadln(String2);

      {*** Write out a big string.}

        BigConcat(String1, String2, String3);
        Writeln('The length of the string is: ', BigLength(String3));
        BigWriteln(String3);

      {*** Extract a substring.}

        Write('Enter start position for substring: ');
        Readln(Start);
        Write('Enter number of characters for substring: ');
        Readln(Number);
        BigCopy(String3, Start, Number, String1);
        Writeln('The length of the string is: ', BigLength(String1));
        BigWriteln(String1);

      {*** Print terminating message and stop program.}

        Writeln;
        Writeln('Driver program terminating.')
      end.
```

Figure 8-16 Testing with Big Strings

■■■■■■
REVIEW

Terms and concepts

Trim	LowCase
RunOf	Trashout
FillChar	HighOff
Pad	SetLow
Replace	Big Strings
UpCase	Eoln
LowToUp	information hiding

■■■■■■
EXERCISES

1. Write Pascal procedures or functions for the following. Use with Turbo's built-in string type:

   *a. CountSubstr, which is to count how many times a substring occurs within a given string.

   *b. IsBlank, which is to see if a given string is either null or totally blank.

   c. Equal, which is to see if two strings are equal when the shorter is padded with blanks to be as long as the longer. For 'Johnson' and 'Johnson   ', the answer would be true.

    d. InsertBlanks, which inserts a given number of blanks at a given position in a given string.

   *e. FindSubst, which locates a substring without respect to character case. For example, it would find 'Anne' in the string 'Dianne Wilson' in position 3.

    f. ReplaceAll, which will replace *all* instances of the search substring with the change substring.

2. Write the following functions:

   *a. Reverse, which will reverse the order of the characters in the input string.

    b. Repeat part (a) using a recursive function. Run the function for a string of length 255. What happens?

   *c. Use the Reverse function [of part (a)] to write a function RPos that will find the *rightmost* occurrence of a substring in a string.

    d. Use the Reverse function to write a function Clip that removes leading and trailing blanks from a string.

3. Think of a simple coding scheme that involves character exchange such as

$$A \rightarrow B$$
$$B \rightarrow C$$
$$. \quad . \quad . \quad .$$
$$Z \rightarrow A$$
$$a \rightarrow b$$
$$b \rightarrow c$$
$$. \quad . \quad . \quad .$$
$$z \rightarrow a$$
$$0 \rightarrow 1$$
$$1 \rightarrow 2$$
$$. \quad . \quad . \quad .$$
$$9 \rightarrow 0$$

all others stay the same

Write a function EnCode to encode characters according to the scheme.

4. Write the string-level function for encoding an entire string using the result of Exercise 5.

5. Write the text-file-level program for encoding a file using the results of Exercises 3 and 4.

6. Write the character, string, and text-file-level modules for decoding files produced by the results of Exercise 5.

7. Do the following for the examples of this section:

   *a. Explain why the Runof function has a local variable WorkString.

    b. Modify Concat to simply copy the first string to the output, using a record assignment, then fill in the second string. Is this better (faster, clearer)?

    c. Modify Concat to handle the situation where the sum of the lengths exceeds the maximum allowed. It should simply yield a truncated answer.

d. Rewrite Runof to build up the answer by concatenation in a count-controlled loop. Is this better (faster, clearer)?

e. Modify the BigReadln and BigWriteln procedures to handle very long strings more smoothly. For example, BigWriteln might send a carriage return every 60 characters. BigReadln should be able to get around any terminal limitations on the length of an input line. (For example, some terminals only allow 126 characters input.)

8. Write the following additions to the Big Strings package:

*a. BigChar(Str, I), a char function to return the Ith character.

*b. BigTrim(Str1, Str2), a procedure to delete trailing blanks.

c. BigRunOf(Num, Chr, Str), a procedure to produce a Big String of Num consecutive characters specified by Chr.

d. BigPos(SubStr, Str), an integer function to locate a substring.

*e. BigEqual(Str1, Str2), a Boolean function to determine equality.

f. BigLessThan(Str1, Str2), a Boolean function to determine if Str1 is less than Str2.

g. BigInsert(SubStr, Str, Start), a procedure to insert a substring.

h. BigDelete(Str, Start, Num), a procedure to delete Num characters from Str beginning with the position specified by Start.

i. BigReplace(Str, Search, Change), a procedure to replace the leftmost occurrence of Search in Str by Change.

j. BigToStr(Bstr, Lstr), a procedure to change the Big String Bstr into the regular string Lstr; Lstr should be of the type String255; truncate if the length of Bstr is more than 255.

k. BigFromStr(Bstr, Lstr), a procedure to change the regular string Lstr into the Big String Bstr; Lstr should be of the type String255.

9. Write a comprehensive test plan for the Replace procedure of Figure 8-7.

10. Write subprograms for the following:

a. Given an array of strings and a new string, add the new string to the end of the list unless it is already in the list.

*b. Extract the first word from a string. Consider a word to be any sequence of nonblank characters. The given string should not be changed.

c. Repeat part (b), but modify the original string to take the word out of it.

d. Given a string, print a list of the words in the string, one word per line.

11. Write a program to read the lines of text and to find how many times each word that appears is used. (This is a simple form of analysis of an author's style.) Hint: See Exercise 10.

*12. a. Write a function that captures the last 10 characters of a string.

b. Generalize part (a) to allow the number of characters to be captured to be a parameter.

13. Write a paragraph formatter. It should read a series of lines of text, interpreting lines that begin with a blank as the beginning of new paragraphs. The beginning of each paragraph should be indented five spaces. All strings of consecutive blanks should be converted to a single blank. As many words as possible should be placed on each line of output.

14. Add these enhancements to the paragraph formatter of Exercise 13:

a. Right-justify each line except the last line of the paragraph by inserting blanks between words and keeping the words as evenly spaced as possible on the line.

b. Do not compress blanks that immediately follow a period.

c. Handle multiple-page printed output, leaving an appropriate margin at the top and bottom.

d. Treat a line that begins with a period as a command, as outlined in the rest of this exercise. Any command immediately terminates a paragraph. After the command is processed, the next line is treated as the beginning of a new paragraph, but it is not indented unless it begins with a blank.

e. The command .C means to center the remainder of the input line on an output line by itself.

f. The command .E means to generate a top of form.

g. The command .H signifies that the rest of the line is to be treated as a header for each page of output, centered near the top of the page.

Any occurrence of the character '#' in the header line is to be replaced by the page number for each page.

h. Within the body of the text, a '^' character is to be treated as a noncompressible space. On output, it should be replaced by a blank.

15. Develop a subprogram that will create a "printable" version of a dollar-and-cents figure given as a string of up to ten digits. For example,

'1234567890'	yields	'$12,345,678.90'
'7891'		'$78.91'
'0000007891'		'$78.91'
'2'		'$0.02'
'135692'		'$1,356.92'

16. Write a conversion routine to change base 2 to base 8. Its input is a string representing a number in base 2. Its output is a string representing the same number in base 8. For example,

'101'	yields	'5'
'10101'		'25'
'111010110'		'726'

There is no limit, other than the built-in limits, on the length of the input string.

Hint: When grouped by threes from the right, the triplets of base-2 digits yield the corresponding base-8 digit. You may have to pad the leftmost triplet with 0's on the left.

17. Write a conversion routine similar to Exercise 16 for base 8 to base 2.

*18. Write a routine that converts an *integer* value to a string of binary digits. For example, the integer 26 would yield '11010'.

Hint: If you successively divide the integer by 2, each remainder is one of the digits of the base-2 string, working from right to left. For 26,

26 div 2 is 13   26 mod 2 is 0 → '0'

13 div 2 is 6   13 mod 2 is 1 → '1'

$$6 \text{ div } 2 \text{ is } 3 \qquad 6 \text{ mod } 2 \text{ is } 0 \rightarrow \text{'0'}$$
$$3 \text{ div } 2 \text{ is } 1 \qquad 3 \text{ mod } 2 \text{ is } 1 \rightarrow \text{'1'}$$
$$1 \text{ div } 2 \text{ is } 0 \qquad 1 \text{ mod } 2 \text{ is } 1 \rightarrow \text{'1'}$$

We quit when the quotient is 0.

19. Repeat Exercise 18 for base 8. Divide and mod by 8 instead of 2. For 26,

$$26 \text{ div } 8 \text{ is } 3 \qquad 26 \text{ mod } 8 \text{ is } 2 \rightarrow \text{'2'}$$
$$3 \text{ div } 8 \text{ is } 0 \qquad 3 \text{ mod } 8 \text{ is } 3 \rightarrow \text{'3'}$$

The answer is '32'.

20. Write a routine to reverse Exercise 19. That is, given a string representing a valid base-8 integer, it should calculate the integer. Assume that the integer lies between 0 and MaxInt.

□

NOTES FOR SECTION 8-2

1. The concept of using Read to deal with individual characters and the behavior of the Eoln function is an area of wide divergence among Pascal implementations, even including different versions of Turbo Pascal. Be sure to read the language manual for any particular implementation of Pascal before using the techniques of reading one character at a time. Some experimentation may also be necessary to determine exactly what is happening.

8-3
□□□□□□
INPUT/ OUTPUT TECHNIQUES

In this section, we will present some techniques for controlling the behavior of the user interface of a program. We will begin with a discussion of output formatting for both the display screen and the printer. Our next topic will be the use of a **smart screen** to control the appearance of the display during user input activities. We will then look at the much-promised "bulletproof" input techniques for integer input. Finally, we will offer a brief discussion of some specialized types of input activities.

□

FORMATTING OUTPUT TO THE DISPLAY SCREEN

We recall that the display screen is usually organized into 24 lines consisting of 80-character columns. We can clear the screen either by using the Page routine or by directly calling the built-in ClrScr procedure. An important concept is the position of the cursor on the screen. The **cursor position** determines where the next character to be output will appear. For the purpose of the discussion in this section, we will describe the cursor position in terms of a pair of coordinates (X, Y), where X denotes the horizontal position (column) in the range from 1 to 80, and Y denotes the vertical position (row) in the range from 1 to 24.[1] The top left corner of the screen (often called the **home** position) has the coordinates (1, 1).

Turbo Pascal provides a means for direct control of the cursor position by means of the built-in procedure **GotoXY**, which is used in the form

```
GotoXY(X position, Y position)
```

The procedure has no direct effect on the items that appear on the display screen. For example, the statement GotoXY(1, 1) *does not* erase the screen, it just positions the cursor in the home position.

As an example of the use of the procedure, suppose that we wish to present a "title" screen for a program that has the name of the program centered on the screen. For the purpose of this example, suppose that the program is called "Adventures in Computing." The following fragment of code will center the title on the screen:

```
Title := 'Adventures in Computing';
ClrScr;
Xpos := (80 - Length(Title)) div 2;
Ypos := 12;
GotoXY(Xpos, Ypos);
Write(Title);
```

Note that the position of the cursor after the execution of the above lines of code will be in the next position after the "g" in the word "Computing." Since a program normally does more than just display a title screen, we should provide a means for moving onward from the title screen to the main activities of the program. A common way to tell the user what to do to move from the title screen is to display a message such as "<Tap Any Key to Continue>" near the bottom of the screen and then wait for a keystroke. We can accomplish this by adding the lines of code:

```
Message := '<Tap Any Key to Continue>';
Xpos := (80 - Length(Message)) div 2;
Ypos := 24;
GotoXY(Xpos, Ypos);
Write(Message);
Read(Kbd, Keystroke);
```

In the above discussion, we have seen that the activity of centering a string on a line of the screen is a common one that deserves to be embodied as a subprogram. Therefore, we propose the procedure **Center**, which will accept a screen line and a string as input and will display the string centered on the specified line of the display. The code for the procedure Center is shown in Figure 8-17.

```
procedure Center(Ypos : integer; InString : String255);
{
          Written by:   XXXXXXXX   XX/XX/XX
             Purpose:   To display a centered string on a specified line.
          Parameters:   Ypos - input, the line to put the string on
                        InString - input, the string to display
     Procedures used:   GotoXY - (built-in) to position the cursor;
      Functions used:   Length - (built-in) to find the length of a string.
         Side effect:   The cursor is at the end of the displayed string.
}
var
   Xpos    : integer;                      { First column to use }

begin {Center}
   Xpos := (80 - Length(InString)) div 2;
   if  Xpos < 1  then  Xpos := 1;
   GotoXY(Xpos, Ypos);
   Write(InString)
end; {Center}
```

Figure 8-17 Centering a String

```
procedure Pause;
{
        Written by:  XXXXXXXX  XX/XX/XX
           Purpose:  To wait for a keystroke.
  Procedures used:  Center - to center the prompt
}
var
  Keystroke  : char;

begin {Pause}
  Center(24, '<Tap Any Key to Continue>');
  Read(Kbd, Keystroke)
end; {Pause}
```

Figure 8-18 The Pause Procedure

The activity of asking the user to tap a key to continue is also a worthy candidate for a subprogram. The procedure, which we shall call **Pause**, will display the "Tap . . ." message and wait for a keystroke. The code for the procedure Pause is shown in Figure 8-18.

If we use the two procedures, the code for producing the title screen can be changed to the following:

```
ClrScr;
Center(12, 'Adventures in Computing');
Pause;
```

Let us now look at some detailed formatting ideas. Suppose that we have an amount of money contained in the real variable Amount and we wish to produce a string in the form:

```
EXACTLY*********$4.56
```

which is precisely 21 characters in length for any (reasonable) amount of money. Let us look at some examples of the desired format of the output string:

```
    Amount          Output String
------------------------------------
       4.56      EXACTLY*********$4.56
       0         EXACTLY*********$0.00
    1024.7       EXACTLY*****$1,024.70
 2438956.25      EXACTLY*$2,438,956.25
99999999.99      EXACTLY$99,999,999.99
       4.676     EXACTLY*********$4.68
```

We want to restrict our amounts to between 0 and 99,999,999.99 for this example. For any invalid amount, we will produce a string consisting of 21 asterisks. To accomplish the task, we will design the string-valued function **Form**, which will accept a single real parameter representing the amount and which will return a 21-character string with the desired format.[2] Our first step will be to use the Str procedure to produce the numeric part of the string. We will then prefix the number with a dollar sign. Next, we will insert any necessary commas, and,

```
function Form(Amount : real) : String255;
{
        Written by:    XXXXXXXX  XX/XX/XX
           Purpose:    To create a 21-character string in the format:
                               EXACTLY*****$1,024.45
        Parameters:    Amount - input, the amount to be displayed
  Procedures used:     Str - (built-in) to covert from numeric to string;
                       Insert - (built-in) to insert a substring.
   Functions used:     Length - (built-in) to find the length of a string;
                       RunOf - to produce a run of characters.
}
var
  WorkString    : String255;          { String for building the result }

begin {Form}

{*** Produce the numeric part.}

  Str(Amount:1:2, WorkString);
  if  (Length(WorkString) < 12) and (Amount >= 0)  then
    begin

{*** Prefix with '$'.}

      WorkString := '$' + WorkString;

{*** Insert any necessary commas.}

      if  Length(WorkString) > 7  then
        Insert(',', WorkString, Length(WorkString)-5);
      if  Length(WorkString) > 11  then
        Insert(',', WorkString, Length(WorkString)-9);

{*** Prefix with the appropriate number of '*'s.}

      WorkString := RunOf(14-Length(WorkString) ,'*') + WorkString;

{*** Prefix with 'EXACTLY'.}

      Form := 'EXACTLY' + WorkString
    end
  else
    Form := RunOf(21, '*')
end; {Form}
```

Figure 8-19   Formatting Output

finally, we will add the appropriate number of asterisks and the word
"EXACTLY." In outline form, our steps are

1. Produce the numeric part.

2. Prefix with '$'.

3. Insert any necessary commas.

4. Prefix with appropriate number of '*'s.

5. Prefix with 'EXACTLY'.

We will use the Insert procedure to handle the commas and the RunOf function to build the string of asterisks. The code for the Form function is shown in Figure 8-19.

In testing the Form function, there are several boundary values that should be tested. These are

```
         Amount            Expected Output
------------------------------------------------
         -0.001        ********************
              0        EXACTLY*********$0.00
         999.99        EXACTLY*******$999.99
        1000.00        EXACTLY*****$1,000.00
      999999.99        EXACTLY***$999,999.99
     1000000.00        EXACTLY*$1,000,000.00
   999999999.99        EXACTLY$99,999,999.99
  1000000000.00        ********************
```

FORMATTING OUTPUT TO THE PRINTER □ For many printers, a printed page can be organized into 66 lines of 80-character positions each. Although we don't often refer to a cursor on the printed page, we can speak of the similar concept of **current print position**. As with the display screen, we can think of the print position as consisting of the pair of coordinates (X, Y), where X denotes the character column, and Y denotes the print line. Once again, we wish to think of the upper left corner of the paper as position (1, 1). We can set the print position to the top of the next page by use of the Page procedure or by printing the formfeed [Chr(12)] character (for most printers). For most printers, we cannot change the print position upwards, so we don't have an analogue to the GotoXY procedure for printers. However, a useful concept for printing is that of skipping *n* lines. We can use a procedure **Skip** for this activity. The procedure simply repeatedly executes Writeln(Lst) statements for the appropriate number of lines to skip. (Recall that Lst is Turbo's way of referring to the printer.) The code for the procedure Skip is shown in Figure 8-20. (Notice that it

```
procedure Skip(Lines : integer);
{
      Written by:  XXXXXXXX  XX/XX/XX
        Purpose:  To skip lines on the printer.
      Parameters:  Lines - input, number of lines to skip
}
var
  I    : integer;                      { Loop index }

begin {Skip}
  for I := 1 to Lines do
    Writeln(Lst)
end; {Skip}
```

Figure 8-20 The Skip Procedure

```
procedure PrintCentered(Lines : integer; InString : String255);
{
         Written by:   XXXXXXXX  XX/XX/XX
            Purpose:   To skip lines and print a centered string.
         Parameters:   Lines - input, number of lines to skip
                       InString - input, string to print centered
    Procedures used:   Skip - to skip lines on the printer.
     Functions used:   Length - (built-in) to find the length of a string.
}
const
  Columns = 80;                      { A common page width }

var
  Xpos   : integer;                  { Horizontal print position }

begin {PrintCentered}
  Skip(Lines);
  Xpos := (Columns - Length(InString)) div 2;
  if  Xpos < 1  then  Xpos := 1;
  if  Xpos > 1  then  Write(Lst, ' ':Xpos-1);
  Writeln(Lst, InString)
end; {PrintCentered}
```

Figure 8-21 Centering a String on the Printer

only skips the specified number of lines if the previous output was a Writeln and
not a Write.)

The idea of centering strings on a printed page is similar to that of centering
on the screen. We will use the procedure PrintCentered, which will have as its first
parameter the number of lines to skip, and as its second parameter a string to print
centered. To print a string centered on the current line, we would execute the
statement

```
PrintCentered(0, string expression)
```

The code for the PrintCentered procedure is shown in Figure 8-21.
Note that the statement

```
if Xpos > 1 then Write(Lst, ' ':Xpos-1);
```

avoids a potential bug that was discussed in Section 8-1.

Suppose that we wish to construct a title page for a report that has the
following form (in the center of the page):

THE PLIGHT OF THE TIN CAN

by Joan Smith
December 25, 1990

Assuming that we begin at the top of a page, we could accomplish this activity by
the following statements:

```
PrintCentered(31, 'THE PLIGHT OF THE TIN CAN');
PrintCentered(1, 'by Joan Smith');
PrintCentered(0, 'December 25, 1990');
```

If you execute the following two statements:

```
Writeln(RunOf(80,'*'));
Writeln('Is this on the next line?');
```

you will probably find that a line on the screen has been skipped. This occurs because the cursor has advanced to the beginning of the next line following the printing of the 80-character string. Then, when the Writeln procedure goes to the next line, a line is skipped. Try those same two lines of code on your printer. You may find that there is no skipped line. This is another of those boundary problems that continue to be troublesome for programmers. As far as the display is concerned, either of the two statement sequences below will cause no skipped lines:

```
Writeln(RunOf(79,'*'));
Writeln('Is this on the next line?');

Write(RunOf(80,'*'));
Writeln('Is this on the next line?');
```

**CONTROLLING
THE DISPLAY
DURING INPUT**

In this subsection, we will look at the problem of maintaining control when we are allowing the user to input values to our program. When we execute the statement Readln(X), the user can key in over one full line of characters.[3] A large number of keyed characters could violate your idea of how the screen should appear while the program is running. For example, you could easily be off by a line in your calculations if the user types in 126 characters when you ask for his or her name.

Our solution to the problem of control is to read each keystroke individually and deal with it according to its value. To illustrate the technique, we will develop the useful input routine **GetString** that will allow us to specify the following items when asking for user input:

A prompting message

The minimum number of characters that can be input

The maximum number of characters that can be input

The row and column on the display where the prompt will appear (the *echoed* input will appear right after the prompt)

We will design GetString as a string-valued function so that we can use it in expressions if we so desire. As we read in the keystrokes of the user, we will allow the backspace key to correct the input. We will not allow the user to terminate the input activity until the minimum number of characters has been keyed in and we will not allow the user to key in more than the maximum number of characters specified. We will require the user to tap the return key to terminate the input activity (if the minimum number of characters has been input). We will not allow the user to (effectively) key in any characters that are not in the displayable range (between the space ' ' and the tilde '~'). That is, any character not in the range will be ignored. There are two exceptions:

Backspace: the user can use the backspace to correct mistakes; the effect of a backspace keystroke will be to erase the character to the left of the cursor and to move the cursor one position to the left if there is any net amount of characters that have been keystroked. The backspace will be considered as an invalid entry if there is no positive net amount of characters that have been keyed in.

Return: The user can use the return if the minimum number of characters have been keystroked. The return will be considered as an invalid entry if the minimum number of characters has not been keystroked.

We will also treat as invalid any keystroke other than the backspace or return that is keyed in after the maximum number of characters have been attained. When the user keys an invalid character, we will cause a ''beep'' to sound, so that the user is alerted to the invalid action. It is up to the instructions of the program or the prompting message to inform the user about input requirements so that there are no surprises.

The GetString function will use the following special characters both for recognition and for their results when printed:

Character	Code	Input Considerations	Output Result
Beep	07	None	Causes an audible tone
BackSpace	08	Request for cursor to move to the left	Causes the cursor to move to the left
LineFeed	10	None	Causes the cursor to move down one line
Return	13	Request for end of input	Causes the cursor to move to the leftmost position on the line

The header line for the function is as follows:

```
function GetString(Prompt : String255;
                   Minimum, Maximum,
                   Row, Column : integer) : String255;
```

The parameters for GetString are as follows:

Prompt: [String255, input]
a message for the user indicating the nature of the input activity; may be null

Minimum: [integer, input]
the minimum number of characters that can be input; may be 0

Maximum: [integer, input]
the maximum number of characters that can be input; cannot be less than Minimum

Row: [integer, input]
the Y position of the first character of Prompt

Column: [integer, input]
the X position of the first character of Prompt

We will use the following list of local variables:

WorkString: [String255]
             used to build the result
NumChars: [integer]
             used to denote the number of characters that have been
             input
KeyStroke: [char]
             the character keyed in by the user
Done: [Boolean]
             an indicator of whether the input activity is complete

The basic steps of the algorithm for GetString are

[initialize]
    if Maximum is less than Minimum, then set Maximum equal to
        Minimum
    set Done to false
    set WorkString to null
    set NumChars to 0
[set cursor and prompt the user]
    set cursor to Column and Row
    print Prompt
[read characters and process them]
    repeat the following until Done:
        read KeyStroke
        do one of the following depending on Keystroke:
            [KeyStroke = BackSpace]
            if NumChars is greater than 0:
                set NumChars to NumChars−1
                set WorkString to its first NumChar characters
                print a BackSpace, a space, and another BackSpace
            otherwise, print a Beep
            [KeyStroke = Return]
            if NumChars is greater than or equal to Minimum:
                set Done to true
                print a Return and a LineFeed
            otherwise, print a Beep
            [KeyStroke = anything else]
            if NumChars is less than Maximum and the KeyStroke
                is valid:
                set NumChars to NumChars + 1
                set WorkString to WorkString + KeyStroke
                print KeyStroke
            otherwise, print a Beep

COMMENT You might wonder about the handling of the backspace input. Why did we not just print a BackSpace? The answer is that this would not erase the previous character. We "erase" it by overwriting it with a blank, then backspacing again.

The GetString function makes use of the Boolean function **Valid** to determine if a character is valid or not. Also used are the Ord, Chr, and Copy functions and the GotoXY procedure. The code for the GetString function is shown in Figure 8-22.

Notice that we set up the special characters Beep, BackSpace, LineFeed, and Return as integer constants in order to use the case structure.

```
function Valid(Character : char) : Boolean;
{
        Written by:   XXXXXXXX   XX/XX/XX
           Purpose:   To check a character for valid range.
        Parameters:   Character - input, character to be checked
}
const
   First = ' ';                        { First allowable character }
   Last = '~';                         { Last allowable character }

begin {Valid}
   Valid := (Character >= First) and (Character <= Last);
end; {Valid}

function GetString(Prompt : String255;
                   Minimum, Maximum,
                   Row, Column : integer) : String255;
{
        Written by:   XXXXXXXX   XX/XX/XX
           Purpose:   To put cursor in a specified location,
                      prompt the user, and read a string of
                      specified minimum and maximum lengths.
        Parameters:   Prompt - input, the string to be printed
                      Minimum, Maximum - input, allowable range of input
                                 lengths
                      Row, Column - input, place to display the prompt
                                 (assumed valid)
   Procedures used:   GotoXY - (built-in) to set the cursor.
   Functions used:    Ord - (built-in) to get the ASCII code;
                      Chr - (built-in) to make a character from a code;
                      Copy - (built-in) to extract a substring;
                      Valid - to check input characters.
}
const
   BackSpace = 08;                     { ASCII code for backspace }
   Return = 13;                        { ASCII code for return }
   LineFeed = 10;                      { ASCII code for lineFeed }
   Beep = 07;                          { ASCII code for beep }

var
   WorkString : String255;             { String read in }
   NumChars   : integer;               { Current character position
                                         in WorkString }
```

Figure 8-22 Controlling the Display During Input (Continued)

```
  KeyStroke  : char;             { Character entered by user }
  Done       : Boolean;          { Indicator for valid string input }

begin {GetString}

{*** Initialize.}

  if Maximum < Minimum then  Maximum := Minimum;
  Done := false;                 { It's only just begun }
  WorkString := '';              { Start with an empty string }
  NumChars := 0;                 { No characters read yet }

{*** Set cursor for location and prompt the user.}

  GotoXY(Column, Row);
  Write(Prompt);

{*** Read characters and process them.}

  repeat
    Read(Kbd, KeyStroke);          { Get character from user }
    case  Ord(KeyStroke)  of

      BackSpace :
        begin
          if  NumChars > 0  then
            begin
              NumChars := NumChars - 1;
              WorkString := Copy(WorkString, 1, NumChars);
              Write(Chr(BackSpace), ' ', Chr(BackSpace))
            end
          else
            Write(Chr(Beep))
        end;

      Return :
        begin
          if  NumChars >= Minimum  then
            begin
              Done := true;
              Write(Chr(Return), Chr(Linefeed))
            end
          else
            Write(Chr(Beep))
        end;

      else
        begin
          if  (NumChars < Maximum) and (Valid(KeyStroke))  then
            begin
              NumChars := NumChars + 1;
              WorkString := WorkString + KeyStroke;
              Write(KeyStroke)
            end
```

Figure 8-22   Controlling the Display During Input (Continued)

```
            else
                Write(Chr(Beep))
            end
        end; {case}
    until  Done;

{*** Return string }
```

Figure 8-22   Controlling the Display During Input

□

BULLETPROOF INTEGER INPUT

When we wish to accept integer input into a program, we can use an integer variable, say N, and the statement

```
                    Readln(N)
```

The following run-time errors can occur:

   1. A character other than a digit may be input.

   2. A value out of range may be input.

We can trap these errors in the same manner that we trap file input/output errors, but we still allow the user to ruin our screen by inputting many characters.

   We now have a better way to accept integer input:

   1. Use the GetString function to accept a string of between one and six characters.

   2. Use the Val procedure to evaluate the string and indicate any error condition.

   3. If there is an error, then keep trying to get a valid integer.

We use these ideas to produce the integer function **GetInt**, which is shown in Figure 8-23.

□

SPECIAL INPUT REQUIREMENTS

We complete our discussion of input handling with a common but difficult input situation for interactive programs: input of a telephone number. A fairly standard format for a phone number is

```
            (ddd) ddd-dddd
```

where each "d" represents a numeric digit. Our idea of a user-friendly method of phone number input is to display the following sort of prompt:

```
        Enter phone number: (    )    -
```

Part of the concept is that the user will only see the cursor positioned on the portions of the phone number format that can be filled in with digits. We also would like the user to simply type the digits of the number and not have to be concerned with skipping over the parentheses or the dash that appear in the

```
function GetInt(Prompt : String255; Row, Column : integer) : integer;
{
        Written by:    XXXXXXXX  XX/XX/XX
           Purpose:    To get a valid integer from the user.
        Parameters:    Prompt - input, string to be displayed
                       Row, Column - input, place to display prompt
                               (assumed valid)
   Procedures used:    Val - (built-in) to evaluate the input string;
                       GotoXY - (built-in) to position the cursor.
    Functions used:    GetString - to get an input string.
}
const
  Beep = 07;                                    { ASCII beep character }

var
  Error    : integer;                           { Error position from Val }
  WorkInt  : integer;                           { Working integer }
  FirstPos : integer;                           { First position of input field }

begin {GetInt}

{*** Initialize.}

   FirstPos := Column + Length(Prompt);

{*** Get a string from the user.}

   Val(GetString(Prompt, 1, 6, Row, Column), WorkInt, Error);

{*** Be persistent until the integer is good.}

   while  Error <> 0  do
     begin
       Write(Chr(Beep));
       GotoXY(FirstPos, Row);
       Write('        ');
       Val(GetString('', 1, 6, Row, FirstPos), WorkInt, Error)
     end; {while}

   GetInt := WorkInt
end; {GetInt}
```

Figure 8-23 Bulletproof Integer Input

format. We would also like the user input to be restricted to the digits 0, . . . , 9. Finally, we want the user to be able to use the backspace key.

    We have already discussed most of the ideas that will make this kind of specialized input possible, but to make this idea a generally useful one, we introduce the idea of a **template**. A template is a string that contains some blank and some nonblank characters with the understanding that the blank characters represent input positions. Thus, a template for the telephone input problem is

'(   )   -   '

A possible template for a date is

```
'  /  /  '
```

A possible template for a time is

```
'  :  :  '
```

We will develop the string-valued function called **Fetch** that allows us to supply a prompting message, a template, and cursor positions. It will return a string that consists of the template filled in with user input. Thus, if we use the phone number template and the user supplies the keystrokes 1234567890, then the value returned will be (123) 456-7890. The basic ideas of the Fetch function are

1. The cursor can only be positioned on a location that corresponds to a blank space in the template.

2. The user can neither backspace past the first blank space of the template nor enter characters past the last blank space of the template.

3. Whenever the cursor moves forward or backward, it moves from one blank space to the next. An exception to this occurs when there are no more blank spaces to be filled; in this case, the cursor will reside one location to the right of the last blank filled.

4. The user cannot tap return except after all blanks are filled.

5. Only digits are valid input characters for filling the blanks. We will use the Boolean function **IsDigit** for establishing the validity of input characters.

In order to easily implement the cursor movement, we will use the concept of a **dope vector** that will contain the positions of all of the blanks in the template string. The positions will be stored as X coordinates, so that the GotoXY procedure can be used directly on them. We shall also maintain a count of the blanks that are in the template. Suppose that we use the telephone number template and suppose that the X coordinate of the "(" in the template is to be 12. Then we have a total count of 10 blanks in the template and the dope vector contains the values:

13, 14, 15, 18, 19, 20, 22, 23, 24, 25

We will use the basic logic of the GetString function except that we will change our notion of valid character, we will use the dope vector for cursor movement, and we will set the maximum and minimum number of characters to the number of blanks in the template. The code for the Fetch function is shown in Figure 8-24.

```
function IsDigit(Character : char) : Boolean;
{
        Written by:    XXXXXXXX   XX/XX/XX
        Parameters:    Character - input, character to be checked
           Purpose:    To check a character for valid range.
}
const
  First = '0';                        { First allowable character }
  Last = '9';                         { Last allowable character }
```

Figure 8-24 Input Using a Template (Continued)

```
      begin {IsDigit}
        IsDigit := (Character >= First) and (Character <= Last);
      end; {IsDigit}

      function Fetch(Prompt, Template : string255;
                     Row, Column : integer) : string255;
      {
            Written by:   XXXXXXXX   XX/XX/XX
               Purpose:   To put cursor in a specified location,
                          prompt the user, and read a string of
                          digits in accordance with the template.
            Parameters:   Prompt - input, string to be displayed
                          Template - input, determines valid form for data
                               entered
                          Row, Column - input, location to print prompt
                               (assumed valid)
        Procedures used:  GotoXY - to set the cursor.
        Functions used:   IsDigit - to check input characters;
                          Ord - (built-in) to get the ASCII code;
                          Chr - (built-in) to get a character;
                          Length - (built-in) to find length of a string.
      }
      const
        BackSpace = 08;                  { ASCII code for backspace }
        Return = 13;                     { ASCII code for return }
        LineFeed = 10;                   { ASCII code for LineFeed }
        Beep = 07;                       { ASCII code for beep }

      var
        WorkString : string255;          { String read in }
        NumChars   : integer;            { Number of characters input }
        KeyStroke  : char;               { Character entered by user }
        FirstPos   : integer;            { X position of 1st char of template }
        I          : integer;            { Loop index }
        Done       : Boolean;            { Indicator for valid string input }
        Dope       : array [1 .. 80] of integer;
                                         { Dope vector }
        Count      : integer;            { Number of spaces in template }

      begin {Fetch}

      {*** Initialize.}

        Count := 0;
        FirstPos := Column + Length(Prompt);

        for  I := 1 to Length(Template) do
          if  Template[I] = ' '  then
            begin
              Count := Count + 1;
              Dope[Count] := FirstPos + I - 1
            end; {if}

        Dope[Count+1] := Dope[Count] + 1;    { Last cursor position }
        Done := false;                       { We've only just begun }
        WorkString := Template;              { Start with an empty template }
        NumChars := 0;                       { No characters read yet }
```

Figure 8-24 Input Using a Template (Continued)

```
{*** Set cursor for location and prompt the user.}

  GotoXY(Column, Row);
  Write(Prompt);
  Write(Template);
  GotoXY(Dope[1], Row);

{*** Read characters and process them.}

  repeat
    Read(Kbd, KeyStroke);          { Get character from user }
    case  Ord(KeyStroke)  of

      BackSpace :
        begin
          if  NumChars > 0   then
            begin
              NumChars := NumChars - 1;
              WorkString[Dope[NumChars+1]-FirstPos+1] := ' ';
              GotoXY(Dope[NumChars+1], Row);
              Write(' ');
              GotoXY(Dope[NumChars+1], Row)
            end
          else
            Write(Chr(Beep))
        end;

      Return :
        begin
          if  NumChars = Count   then
            begin
              Done := true;
              Write(Chr(Return), Chr(Linefeed))
            end
          else
            Write(Chr(Beep))
        end;
      else
        begin
          if  (NumChars < Count) and (IsDigit(KeyStroke))   then
            begin
              NumChars := NumChars + 1;
              WorkString[Dope[NumChars]-FirstPos+1] := KeyStroke;
              Write(KeyStroke);
              GotoXY(Dope[NumChars+1], Row)
            end
          else
            Write(Chr(Beep))
        end
    end; {case}
  until  Done;

{*** Return string }

  Fetch := WorkString
end; {Fetch}
```

Figure 8-24   Input Using a Template

■■■■■■ REVIEW

■■■■■■ EXERCISES

1. Write a Pascal program that displays a title screen with a title of your choice. Use the Center and Pause procedures to implement your ideas.

2. Modify the Form function so that it accepts an additional parameter for the length of the result.

3. Write a Pascal program that prints (on the printer) the following title page:

```
(skip 12 lines)
                        MY PROGRAMS
(skip 2 lines)
                (your name centered)
                 (date centered)
(skip 10 lines)
                    Copyright: (year)
(skip 1 line)
                (your name centered)
```

4. Run a Pascal program that prints an 80-character string and then prints a message intended for the next line. Check to see if the message is in fact on the next line.

5. Check your printer manual to see if you can print with other page widths, such as 96 or 132. For each of these additional widths:

   a. Write a procedure that puts your printer in the appropriate mode and another that returns it to the 80-column mode. For example, you can have four procedures: Set40, Set80, Set96, and Set132. These routines should set a global variable PageWidth to the appropriate width.

   b. Modify PrintCentered to use the global variable PageWidth so that it correctly centers text for any of the modes.

6. Modify the procedure GetString so that it only accepts uppercase and lowercase letters and blanks as valid input characters (rename it as GetAlpha). Write a program that uses this new procedure to accept a 20 character name from the user.

7. Modify the procedure GetString so that it accepts an additional parameter CharClass that can take on the following values:

   'A'   alphabetic characters and punctuation only
   'N'   numeric digits only

'X'   alphabetic and digits only (including punctuation)
'?'   any displayable characters

Use the modified procedure in a program which accepts as input:

the user's name ('A') − 1 character minimum, 20 characters maximum
street address ('X') − 5 characters minimum, 60 characters maximum
city and state ('A') − 10 characters minimum, 35 characters maximum
zip code ('N') − 5 characters minimum and maximum
password ('?') − 1 character minimum, 6 characters maximum

8. The bulletproof input routine will not accept leading or trailing spaces (the armor is a little too thick). Fix the function GetInt by using the function Clip of Section 8-2 to remove leading and trailing spaces.

9. Write a program that uses the function Fetch to input dates in the form: 00/ 00/00 .

10. Modify the program in Exercise 9 to check to see that months are in the range from 01 to 12 and days are in the range from 01 to 31.

11. Modify the program in Exercise 10 to use a dope vector to ensure that the appropriate number of days for each month is not exceeded. Use the number 29 for February.

□
NOTES FOR SECTION 8-3

1. Many microcomputers, including the IBM PC compatibles, have 25 rows on the display screen. The 25th row is often reserved for special activities, such as function key descriptions, menu options, and error messages. In this section, we will restrict our output to the first 24 rows of the screen.

2. The BCD version of Turbo Pascal has a very sophisticated built-in Form function that could be used for this example.

3. The exact number of characters that can be input in response to a Readln statement depends on the model of computer that you are using. A common value for this limit is 126 characters.

9
POINTERS

9-1
□□□□□□
**POINTER
VARIABLES**

In this chapter, we will introduce the concept of **pointers** and their use in Pascal programs. In the first section, we will discuss some reasons for using pointer variables and we will present the basic ideas of defining and using pointers. In the second section, we will look at two applications of pointers that illustrate some techniques for their effective use.

□
POINTERS

A pointer is an indirect reference to a data item. We deal with pointers often in our daily lives, although we don't often call them by that name. For example, suppose you write your name on a slip of paper and put the slip in a hat for a drawing to see who gets to wash the dishes. Would you say that you put your name in the hat? You might say that, but the statement is technically incorrect. Consider: Can you put your name in two hats at the same time? Suppose we think of your name as being similar to a variable with *you* as its content. What is the content of the slip of paper? Your name, of course. The slip of paper is an indirect reference to you. It is indirect because it leads directly to your name, and your name leads directly to you. We can maintain the indirect reference to you without mentioning your name at all by writing on the slip: "the worried-looking individual sitting on the folding chair, in the corner." Also, if a stranger enters the room and sits on the red pillow, we can enter the newcomer in the competition by writing on a slip of paper: "the confused-looking individual sitting on the red pillow." The new slip of paper is a pointer to the new individual and is certainly not the name of that individual.

We will be using pointers to data items stored in computer memory. When data items have names (in the form of variables), we will continue to use the names to directly refer to the data. But, when new data items appear, whose names we do not know, then we will use pointers to refer indirectly to the data items. We will explain later in the section where to obtain these new "nameless" data items.

□ Before we discuss using pointers in detail, we will try to supply some motivation for the learning of the details. Some of the advantages of using pointers are

Efficiency. By appropriate use of pointers, we can make our programs run faster and use less storage space. It is rare to find a technique that features both of these advantages.

Flexibility. We will find that the use of pointers will allow us more flexibility in our planning for data storage. You have already encountered some situations with arrays where you had to make some guesses for array sizes without knowing with confidence how big the arrays should be.

Higher-level programming. Pointers allows us to build data structures that are appropriate for the task at hand in a broader set of contexts. Having the appropriate data structure makes the task of programming more enjoyable and makes it easier for us to write correct programs.

□ Pointers provide us with a powerful mechanism that can be used to make our programs better or worse. Before we get carried away with our use of all of the power, let us mention some disadvantages.

Conceptual difficulty. Pointers are difficult to understand, and the context in which they are used is usually complex. There are two considerations for this difficulty: At times it may be harder to keep our algorithms and data structures under control; our programs that use pointers will usually be harder for someone other than the programmer to understand.

Reduced readability. Our programs that use pointers will be harder to read due to the notation and the indirectness of reference. We should attempt to choose names wisely and use comments to help to alleviate this problem.

Lower-level programming. If we are not careful, we may allow pointers to lead us into lower-level rather than higher-level programming. Pointers allow us to build useful data structures, but pointers also allow us to think in terms of memory addresses instead of structures. Anyone who has programmed a computer in machine or assembler languages realizes the essential harshness of a low-level programming environment.

Hidden side effects. If we use pointers unwisely, we may find hidden side effects due to complicated data dependencies in our programs. Some nasty surprises can lurk in hidden side effects.

As programmers, we cannot afford to ignore any technique that can be useful. If a technique can be misused (and most can), then we must strive to discover the circumstances in which the technique is most beneficial and let those circumstances serve as a cue as to when to use the technique. It is important to keep in mind that there are usually many alternative ways to handle a programming situation ranging from perfectly appropriate to grossly inappropriate. The hallmark of a good programmer is the ability to select the best technique for the job. In view of the possible bad effects that pointers can have on our programming, we offer some advice on their use:

Limit use of pointers. Don't overuse pointers in your programs. Make sure that you can justify every one of the pointers that you use.

Appropriate use of pointers. Be sure that you use pointers appropriately. The inappropriate use of pointers can confuse you as a programmer and can cause your programs to behave unpredictably.

Learn about data structures. To really make effective use of pointers, you should know about the important types of data structures and when and how to use them. There are several different levels of textbooks dedicated to data structures.

Every type of data can have a pointer type associated with it. We can declare named pointer types or we can declare variables as belonging to an unnamed pointer type. This is exactly the same case as for the other data types that we have dealt with. For example, if we wish to declare a variable Scores to be an integer array with at most 1000 cells, we can choose either of the alternatives:

```
type
   IntegerArray = array [1 .. 1000] of integer;

var
   Scores  : IntegerArray;
```

or

```
var
   Scores  : array [1 .. 1000] of integer;
```

The choice depends on whether it is an advantage to have the global named type available for passing as a parameter or for the declaration of other variables.

We begin with the idea of declaring pointer variables directly. Because we have suggested that pointers can hinder the readability of a program, it will be important to carefully select names for our pointer variables. Let us suppose that we have a type called ItemType and that there is some notion of "first" element for data items. If we wish to declare the variable First to be a pointer to ItemType, then we can use the declaration

```
var
   First   : ^ItemType;                 (The caret "^" specifies pointer)
```

We use the caret (^) to denote that First is to be a pointer. Note carefully where the caret is located in the declaration; it is almost "pointing to" the name of the type.

If we wish to name our pointer type, then we must choose a name first. We will select the name ItemType_Ptr,[1] which hopefully conveys the meaning that it will represent a type that points to data of type ItemType. Using the named pointer type, we can alternatively declare the variable First as

```
type
  ItemType_Ptr = ^ItemType;        { Type for pointer to ItemType }

var
  First  : ItemType_Ptr;           { Pointer variable for ItemType }
```

Note that the caret is used in exactly the same way: as a modifier of ItemType.

We can violate a principle of Pascal and declare ItemType_Ptr *before* we declare ItemType. It will always be legal to declare the pointer first, but not always valid to declare the pointer afterwards. Therefore, we will adopt the strategy of declaring the pointer first as a defensive programming measure. For example, if ItemType represents data that might appear on a shopping list, then we might have a set of declarations such as

```
type
  ItemType_Ptr = ^ItemType;
  ItemType = record
               Quantity  : integer;
               Item      : string[20]
             end;
var
  First  : ItemType_Ptr;           (First is a pointer)
```

Let us wait for a while before we discuss how we assign a data element to the pointer First that we have declared above. We will assume for now that First does point to some data of the type ItemType. We will concentrate now on how we can use the indirect referencing of a pointer variable. The general rule is that the notation

```
First^
```

provides the indirect reference to the data and *is treated as if it were a name for the data*. Therefore, if we want the item on the shopping list to be "apples," then we make the assignment

```
First^.Item := 'apples'
```

If we want to buy six apples, then we make the assignment

```
First^.Quantity := 6
```

Because the data item is of a record type, we can use the with–do construct:

```
with  First^  do
  begin
    Item := 'apples';
    Quantity := 6
  end {with}
```

If we wish to print the item, we can use the statement

```
Writeln('The item is: ', First^.Item)
```

☐
OBTAINING DATA FOR POINTER VARIABLES
Now that we have some idea of how to use a pointer once it is pointing to some data item, we will discuss how to obtain a data item to which it can point. Pascal provides us with the built-in procedure **New** to obtain a data item of any pointer type. If we wish to obtain a data item for the pointer variable First, then we execute the statement

```
New(First)
```

If we use the declarations from above, the following fragment of code will read and print a shopping list item:

declarations

. . . .

```
New(First);                    { Obtains a data item to use }
with First^ do
  begin
    Write('Enter the item: ');
    Readln(Item);
    Write('Enter the quantity: ');
    Readln(Quantity);
    Writeln('You wish ', Quantity, ' ', Item)
end; {with}
```

. . . .

Suppose that we follow the above fragment of code with the statement New(First). This statement assigns *another* data item to the pointer First and the original data item cannot be accessed because we have no way to refer to it. In a sense, we are "littering" memory with a precious storage resource. Fortunately, Pascal provides two ways for us to avoid this waste:

1. Keep the old data item. If we have available another pointer variable, Before, declared to be of the type ItemType_Ptr, then we can execute the sequence:

```
Before := First;       { Assigns old data item to Before }
New(First);            { Obtains new data item for First }
```

2. Discard the old data item. Pascal provides a mechanism for recycling old data items. If we are through with the particular data item pointed to by First, then we can execute the statement

```
Dispose(First)
```

After the statement is executed, First no longer refers to the data item and the data item is returned to available memory for potential future use.

There is a mechanism for initializing a pointer variable to a value that indicates that it is not pointing to a valid data item. This provides a convenient test for validity of data, as we shall see. Pascal provides the predefined identifier **Nil**, which conforms to all pointer types and which can be used for comparison purposes. Therefore, we can initialize First with the statement

```
First := Nil
```

and we can check if First refers to any valid data with the comparisons

```
if  First = Nil  then  . . .
if  First <> Nil  then  . . .
```

We can now look at a small example of the use of pointers. Suppose that we have two stores in which we shop, Ace Drugs and King Groceries. We may wish to buy an item at either or both stores. We shall use the two pointers AceFirst and KingFirst to refer to the items for Ace Drugs and King Groceries, respectively. The user will be asked how many items are intended for each store and will enter the items, if any. We will restrict the user to either 0 or 1 item for each store for now because we just want to become more comfortable with using pointers.

The code for the program appears in Figure 9-1. Note the manner in which we manage our use of the data items for the pointers:

1. We initialize both pointers to Nil.

2. We call New for a data item when we are sure that we are going to use it.

3. We call Dispose to return a data item when we are through with it.

4. After we call Dispose for a pointer, we set it to Nil.

```
program BuyOne(Input, Output);
{
        Written by:   XXXXXXXX  XX/XX/XX
            Purpose:  To maintain two small shopping lists.
   Procedures used:   New - (built-in) gets a data item;
                      Dispose - (built-in) returns a data item.
}
type
  ItemType_Ptr = ^ItemType;
  ItemType = record
                Quantity  : integer;    { Number to buy }
                Item      : string[20]  { Item to buy }
             end;

var
  AceFirst  : ItemType_Ptr;              { Pointer to Ace list }
  KingFirst : ItemType_Ptr;              { Pointer to King list }
  N         : integer;                   { Number of items at store }
  I         : integer;                   { Loop index }
  None      : Boolean;                   { Indicator for empty lists }

begin {BuyOne}
```

Figure 9-1 First Use of Pointers (Continued)

```
{*** Initialize.}

  AceFirst := Nil;
  KingFirst := Nil;

{*** Get and print lists in a loop.}

  repeat
    Writeln;
    None := true;
    Write('How many items for Ace Drug: ');
    Readln(N);
    if N <> 0 then N := 1;

    for I := 1 to N do
      begin
        New(AceFirst);
        with AceFirst^ do
          begin
            Write('Enter the item: ');
            Readln(Item);
            Write('Enter the quantity: ');
            Readln(Quantity)
          end {with}
      end; {for}

    Write('How many items for King Drug: ');
    Readln(N);
    if N <> 0 then N := 1;

    for I := 1 to N do
      begin
        New(KingFirst);
        with KingFirst^ do
          begin
            Write('Enter the item: ');
            Readln(Item);
            Write('Enter the quantity: ');
            Readln(Quantity)
          end {with}
      end; {for}

    Writeln;
    Writeln('Here is your shopping list: ');
    if  AceFirst <> Nil  then
      with  AceFirst^  do
        begin
          None := false;
          Writeln('  From Ace Drugs: ');
          Writeln('    You want ', Quantity, ' ', Item, '.');
          Dispose(AceFirst);
          AceFirst := Nil
        end;
    if  KingFirst <> Nil  then
      with  KingFirst^  do
```

Figure 9-1 First Use of Pointers (Continued)

```
            begin
              None := false;
              Writeln('   From King Groceries: ');
              Writeln('     You want ', Quantity, ' ', Item, '.');
              Dispose(KingFirst);
              KingFirst := Nil
            end;
        until None;

      Writeln('   *** Shopping list is empty');

   {*** Print message and terminate program.}

      Writeln;
      Writeln('BuyOne program is terminating.')
    end.
```

Figure 9-1   First Use of Pointers

MANAGING DYNAMIC MEMORY RESOURCES

□ The example of Figure 9-1 shows more disadvantages than advantages of using pointers. We will now extend the example to achieve a more realistic and useful result.

We start with one of the most important features of the pointer type: there can be fields of the pointer type within the record structure that is pointed to. That is, we can enhance our shopping list item to include a pointer to the next item on the list. Our declarations become

```
type
  ItemType_Ptr = ^ItemType;
  ItemType = record
               Quantity  : integer;     { Number to buy }
               Item      : string[20];  { Item to buy }
               Next      : ItemType_Ptr { Pointer to next item }
             end;
```

We can now organize a shopping list as a structure containing many items, each of which points to the next. To summarize the organization of the list:

A pointer First points to the first item on the list.

Within each item, a pointer Next points to the next item on the list.

For the last item on the list, Next is equal to Nil.

The above variety of data structure is called a **linked list**.

Now, we will discuss the details of enhancing the example of Figure 9-1. We will keep the logic of building the lists similar to what is already there. One addition is the requirement of a temporary pointer variable for each list. We refer to this as Temp in our algorithm, which is as follows:

get the number of elements, N, from the user
loop for I going from 1 to N:
    New(Temp)   [get a new data item]
    set Temp^.Next to First   [link new item to first on list]
    set First to Temp   [put new one first on list]
    with First^ do the following:
        get the data for the item

Before we discuss more details, let us note some points about the **dynamic** use of memory. When we must predetermine the size of our data structures, as in the case of arrays, we are making **static** use of memory. The use of pointers allows us more flexible use of memory. In our example of the two shopping lists, we can use available memory with one large list and one small list or we can have two equal-size lists. The main idea is that we *do not have to decide in advance* as to the memory needs for each list. We note a similarity with the way that disk files use the available space on a disk; each file uses as much space as it needs within the limits of the total space available.

That is the algorithm for building a list of any length. As each new **node** (that is, data item for the list) is created, its Next pointer is set to point to what was the first item on the list. For example, suppose the user enters 3 as N for the King Groceries list and that the three items are entered in this order: 12 apples, 1 newspaper, and 5 candy bars. As the items are added, the list will appear as follows.

At first, the list is empty:

Then, the node for 12 apples is added to the front:

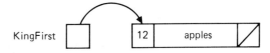

Next, the node for 1 newspaper is added to the front:

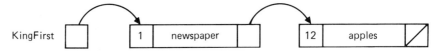

Finally, the node for 5 candy bars is added to the front:

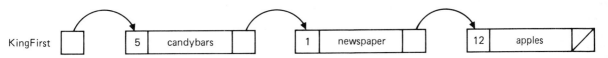

In this visual representation of the list, arrows represent pointer variables, both as named variables and as parts of records. The slash indicates Nil, that is, the pointer variable does not point to anything.

As you can see from this example, the lists we are building have the **last-in, first-out (LIFO)** property.

We also have a new algorithm for printing and disposing of each list:

> while First is not equal to Nil do the following:
>> print the item
>> set Temp to First   [hold onto for disposal]
>> set First to First^.Next   [delete the first item from list]
>> Dispose(Temp)   [dispose of the uneeded item]

This is the algorithm for printing and disposing of a list of any length. Note that we don't have any idea how long the list is before we print; we just print until the list is exhausted.

```
program BuyLots(Input, Output);
{
        Written by:   XXXXXXXX   XX/XX/XX
           Purpose:   To maintain two small shopping lists.
   Procedures used:   New - (built-in) gets a data item;
                      Dispose - (built-in) returns a data item.
}
type
  ItemType_Ptr = ^ItemType;
  ItemType = record
                 Quantity  : integer;       { Number to buy }
                 Item      : string[20];    { Item to buy }
                 Next      : ItemType_Ptr   { Pointer to list next }
             end;

var
  AceFirst  : ItemType_Ptr;              { Pointer to Ace list }
  AceTemp   : ItemType_Ptr;              { Working pointer for Ace }
  KingFirst : ItemType_Ptr;              { Pointer to King list }
  KingTemp  : ItemType_Ptr;              { Working pointer for King }
  N         : integer;                   { Number of items at store }
  I         : integer;                   { Loop index }
  None      : Boolean;                   { Indicator for empty lists }

begin {BuyLots}

{*** Initialize.}

  AceFirst := Nil;
  KingFirst := Nil;

{*** Get and print lists in a loop.}

  repeat
    Writeln;
    None := true;

{*** Build the list for Ace Drugs.}

    Write('How many items for Ace Drugs: ');
    Readln(N);
    if N < 0 then N := 0;
```

Figure 9-2   Two Linked Lists (Continued)

```
        for I := 1 to N do
          begin
            None := false;
            New(AceTemp);                  { get a data item to use }
            AceTemp^.Next := AceFirst;     { link the new item to list }
            AceFirst := AceTemp;           { new item is now first }
            with AceFirst^ do
              begin
                Write('Enter the item: ');
                Readln(Item);
                Write('Enter the quantity: ');
                Readln(Quantity)
              end {with}
          end; {for}

    {*** Build the list for King Groceries.}

        Write('How many items for King Groceries: ');
        Readln(N);
        if N < 0 then N := 0;

        for I := 1 to N do
          begin
            None := false;
            New(KingTemp);                 { get a data item to use }
            KingTemp^.Next := KingFirst;   { link the new item to list }
            KingFirst := KingTemp;         { new item is now first }
            with KingFirst^ do
              begin
                Write('Enter the item: ');
                Readln(Item);
                Write('Enter the quantity: ');
                Readln(Quantity)
              end {with}
          end; {for}

    Writeln;

    {*** Print the shopping lists.}

        Writeln('Here is your shopping list: ');

    {*** Print the list for Ace Drugs.}

        Writeln('  From Ace Drugs: ');
        while  AceFirst <> Nil  do
          begin
            with  AceFirst^  do
              begin
                Writeln('    You want ', Quantity, ' ', Item, '.');
                AceTemp := AceFirst;       { save for later disposal }
                AceFirst := Next;          { delete from list }
                Dispose(AceTemp)           { dispose of item }
              end; {with}
          end; {while}
```

Figure 9-2 Two Linked Lists (Continued)

```
{*** Print the list for King Groceries.}

    Writeln(' From King Groceries: ');
    while  KingFirst <> Nil  do
      begin
        with  KingFirst^  do
          begin
            Writeln('     You want ', Quantity, ' ', Item, '.');
            KingTemp := KingFirst;      { save for later disposal }
            KingFirst := Next;          { delete from list }
            Dispose(KingTemp)           { dispose of item }
          end; {with}
      end {while}
    until None;

  Writeln('    *** Shopping list is empty');

{*** Print message and terminate program.}

  Writeln;
  Writeln('BuyLots program is terminating.')
end.
```

Figure 9-2 Two Linked Lists

□
DPT

1. We should use pointers only when they are appropriate to the problem at hand. As with any powerful concept, we have the tendency to overuse pointers in situations where standard variables would do the task as effectively.

2. Avoid low-level programming if the nature of the task indicates that you should be operating on a higher level of abstraction. There are tasks closely related to a computer's hardware that are best done with low-level techniques, but most programs should operate as closely as possible to the context in which the problem is stated rather than in the context of a machine and its memory.

3. The use of pointers can cause a phenomenon known as **aliasing**, a situation where a single data item has two or more different references. The danger is that any of the references can modify the data item and the others will encounter a *hidden side effect*. This situation can happen in the sequence

```
New(First);
  [put some data into First^]
Temp := First;
Dispose(First);
```

The assignment Temp := First makes the pointers aliases; they both refer to the same data item. Therefore, when we execute the statement Dispose(First), we lose the data item associated with Temp also, a catastrophic side effect.

4. Never use a pointer variable until it is assigned a value by an assignment statement or by the New procedure. The results are unpredictable.

5. Never use a pointer variable after use of the procedure Dispose. The results are unpredictable.

6. Declare a pointer type *before* the type declaration for the "pointed-to" data items. This order of declaration will always be valid, whereas the other order will be illegal if the pointer type is used *within* the declaration of the other type.

7. Avoid reference to what a pointer points to when that pointer is nil. This is similar, in many ways, to avoiding references to arrays using subscripts that are out of range. For example, suppose we chose to use a repeat loop to print the list for King Groceries. We might write:

```
Writeln(' From King Groceries: ');
repeat
  with KingFirst^ do
    begin
      Writeln('     You want ', Quantity, ' ', Item, '.');
      KingTemp := KingFirst;        { save for later disposal }
      KingFirst := Next;            { delete from list }
      Dispose(KingTemp)            { dispose of item }
    end; {with}
until KingFirst = Nil
```

This will work unless the list is empty. If the list is empty, the first reference to KingFirst^.Quantity (in the Writeln statement) will cause a run-time error.

REVIEW

Terms and concepts

pointers	static
New	node
Nil	last in, first out (LIFO)
linked list	aliasing
dynamic	

Pascal syntax

1. Declare a pointer type:

```
type
   SomeType_Ptr = ^SomeType;
   SomeType = definition of the type
```

2. Declare a pointer variable:

```
var
   pointer name = SomeType_Ptr
```

3. Assign a value to a pointer:

a. To indicate that it is not pointing at any data item:

```
pointer name := Nil
```

b. To get a newly allocated data item:

```
New(pointer name)
```

c. To have it refer to an existing data item:

```
pointer name := another pointer name
```

4. Access the information of the data item:

> *pointer name*^ is used as we would use a variable name
> for the data item

5. Dispose of an unneeded data item:

$$\text{Dispose}(pointer\ name)$$

DPT
1. Use pointers only when appropriate to the problem.
2. Avoid low-level programming.
3. Be wary of aliasing.
4. Don't use a pointer until it is assigned a value.
5. Don't use a pointer after it has been disposed of.
6. Declare the pointer type before the pointed-to type.
7. Avoid reference to what a pointer points to when the pointer is Nil.

■■■■■■
EXERCISES

*1. Write declarations for:
a. A named type for strings of maximum length 30.
b. A named pointer type for the string type of part (a).
c. Two variables of the string type.
d. Two pointer variables.

*2. Suppose that we have a data structure for students set up as follows:

```
type
   StudentType_Ptr = ^StudentType;
   StudentType = record
                     Name    : string[20];
                     SSN     : string[11];
                     Roommate: StudentType_Ptr
                  end;
var
   AnyOne   : StudentType_Ptr;
   Student1 : StudentType;
```

Assume that a program has been processing some student information.
a. How could you test to find if Student1 has a roommate?
b. How could you test to find if the student referred to by AnyOne has a roommate?
c. Print the name of Student1.
d. Print the name of the student referred to by AnyOne.
e. Assign the student referred to by AnyOne as the roommate of Student1.

3. Define a data structure for members of a gourmet club that includes the following information for each member: name, favorite dessert, and spouse.

4. Suppose that we have a data structure for books defined as

```
type
   BookType_Ptr = ^BookType;
   BookType = record
                 Author  : string[20];
                 Title   : string[30];
                 Year    : string[4];
                 Comment : string[80];
                 Next    : BookType_Ptr
              end;
var
   Head : BookType_Ptr;    { Pointer to first book }
   Temp : BookType_Ptr;    { working pointer to book }
```

Suppose that a program has built a list of books so that the first book on the list is referred to by the pointer Head, the last book on the list has its pointer Next set to Nil, and each of the other books on the list has the pointer Next set to the next book on the list. (This is similar to the examples in the section.)

*a. Write a condition to test if the list is empty.

*b. Write a condition to test if there is exactly one book on the list.

*c. Suppose that the pointer Temp refers to a book not on the list. Write a Pascal code fragment that will put that book at the front of the list.

d. Suppose that the pointer Temp does not refer to any data item. Write code to obtain a data item for Temp and put that data item at the front of the list. Record the following information for the new book:

author:	Jack Fincher
title:	Lefties
year:	1977
comment:	a book about sinister people

c. Write a Pascal code fragment to delete the first book from the list if the list is not empty; if the list is empty, do nothing.

f. Assume that there are at least two books on the list. Write a Pascal fragment to delete the second book from the list.

g. Assume that there are at least two books on the list. Write a Pascal fragment to move the second book to the first position on the list.

h. Write a Pascal fragment to count the number of books on the list.

i. Write a Pascal fragment to print the information for the first book on the list. Assume that the list is not empty.

*j. Write a Pascal fragment to print the information for the last book on the list. Assume that the list is not empty.

*k. Write a Pascal fragment to delete the last book on the list. Assume that the list has at least two books.

l. Write a Pascal fragment to delete the last book on the list. Assume that the list has at least one book.

m. Write a Pascal fragment to delete the last book on the list, if any. Assume that the list might be empty.

5. Modify the shopping list data structure discussed in this section so that there are two different data types for the two different stores. Add a unit price field to the Ace Drugs record and add unit price and coupon discount fields to the King Groceries record.

a. Make all modifications that are necessary to the program of Figure 9-2 to reflect the new data structures.

b. Add code to your program of part (a) to obtain a total cost of the shopping list at each store. Assume that the coupon discount is subtracted from the price of one item only.

c. Modify your program for part (b) so that no item is added to the shopping list if the quantity is less than 1.

6. Use the data structure of the program of Figure 9-2 to write a program with the following body:

```
begin
  repeat
    New(AceFirst)
  until  false
end.
```

Predict what will happen when you run the program. Run the program and see what happens. What would happen if you added the statement "Dispose(AceFirst)" in the loop? (Don't do this unless you can interrupt the program.)

7. a. Use the data structure of the program of Figure 9-2 to write a program that creates an empty list, then tries to print the first node. Predict what will happen when you run the program. Run the program and see what happens.

   b. Modify the program to create a list with 1 node, then try to print two nodes.

8. Predict the behavior of the following program and then run it to see what happens:

```
program Aliases(Input, Output);
var
   X : ^integer;
   Y : ^integer;
begin
   New(X);
   Y := X;
   Y^ := 2;
   X^ := 5;
   Writeln(X^, Y^)
end.
```

9. Run both programs below and check the execution times with a stopwatch.

```
program Transfers(Input, Output);
type
   String255 = string[255];
var
   X, Y  : String255;
   I     : integer;
begin
   X := '************************************************';
   for I := 1 to 30000 do
      Y := X
end.
```

```
program Transfers(Input, Output);
type
   String255 = string[255];
var
   X, Y  : ^String255;
   I     : integer;
begin
   New(X);
   X^ := '************************************************';
   for I := 1 to 30000 do
      Y := X
end.
```

□

**NOTES FOR
SECTION 9-1**

1. This type name uses an underscore character, which Turbo Pascal allows as an extension to the standard. In this instance, it seems valuable because it isolates the "Ptr" part of the type identification.

9-2
□□□□□□
USING POINTER VARIABLES

In the previous section, you were introduced to the concept of pointer variables and to one frequently used application, linked lists. In this section, we indicate further some of the techniques and applications for pointer variables. In the first example, we will refine the sample program of the previous section that dealt with linked lists. The second example will give an application involving sorting that illustrates a somewhat different use of pointers. This serves only as an introduction to the topic; a second course in computer science typically goes into much more detail on the subject.

□
LINKED LISTS

The example of the previous section introduced some techniques for representing a list using pointers to link the individual items of the list. Specifically, the program in Figure 9-2 initialized two lists, read values for them, and printed them (disposing of the nodes at the same time). In this subsection, we will rewrite the program with a few changes.

As you read the program in Figure 9-2, you may have said to yourself, "This program does exactly the same things for the two lists. Wouldn't it be possible to generalize the program by using subprograms?" That is exactly what we will do in this section.

There are two "obvious" candidates for subprograms in that program:

Reading a list
Printing and deleting a list

However, we can visualize programs where printing and deleting would be totally separate activities. We will, therefore, separate those activities.

In addition to these three subprograms, which apply specifically to the program at hand, we will develop some "utility" modules. They are

A module to create an empty list
A module to see if a list is empty
A module to create a node with the values filled in

These modules can be used as they are, or modified slightly, for inclusion in almost any program that deals with linked lists. At first glance, they may seem to be too trivial to be worthy of submodules. (The first two will be one line each.) However, they do hide information about the details of the data structure from the main program. This is part of what we mean when we talk about programming at a high level rather than a low level.

Before we write the submodules, let us see what the main program declarations and body will look like using these modules. Refer to Figure 9-3. As you can see, it is much "cleaner" than the previous version. It deals with the "what" of the program, delegating the details to its submodules. Moreover, if the exact form used to represent the lists is modified in the future, we will need to make only minor changes to the main module, mostly in the declarations.

Notice the use of Empty to set the variable None used for loop control.

```
program BuyLots(Input, Output);
{
        Written by:  XXXXXXXX  XX/XX/XX
           Purpose:  To maintain two small shopping lists.
   Procedures used:  ReadList - to read a linked list
                     PrintList - to print the values of a linked list
                     DeleteList - to delete a linked list, disposing of
                        the nodes
                     NewList - to create an empty linked list
                     Empty - to see if a list is empty
}


type
  String255 = string[255];
  String20 = string[20];
  ItemType_Ptr = ^ItemType;
  ItemType = record
                Quantity  : integer;       { Number to buy }
                Item      : String20;      { Item to buy }
                Next      : ItemType_Ptr   { Pointer to list next }
             end;
var
  AceFirst  : ItemType_Ptr;               { Pointer to Ace list }
  KingFirst : ItemType_Ptr;               { Pointer to King list }
  None      : Boolean;                    { Indicator for empty lists }


{ Submodules are declared here. }

begin {BuyLots}

{*** Initialize.}

  NewList(AceFirst);
  NewList(KingFirst);

{*** Get and print lists in a loop.}

  repeat
    Writeln;

{*** Build the lists and see if both are empty.}

    ReadList('Ace Drugs', AceFirst);
    ReadList('King Groceries', KingFirst);
    None := Empty(AceFirst) and Empty(KingFirst);

{*** Print the shopping lists.}

    Writeln('Here is your shopping list: ');
    PrintList('Ace Drugs', AceFirst);
    PrintList('King Groceries', KingFirst);
```

Figure 9-3 Pointers and Procedures—First Cut (Continued)

```
{*** Delete the shopping lists. }

    DeleteList(AceFirst);
    DeleteList(KingFirst)
  until None;

  Writeln('   *** Shopping list is empty');

{*** Print message and terminate program.}

    Writeln;
    Writeln('BuyLots program is terminating.')
  end.
```

Figure 9-3 Pointers and Procedures—First Cut

Now let us write the subprograms, beginning with the utilities. The function to see if a list is empty needs one parameter: the list to check. If we call that ListHead, then the body is simply

```
Empty := (ListHead = Nil)
```

Using the same name for the parameter for the NewList procedure, we have the procedure body:

```
ListHead := Nil
```

Notice that ListHead is an output parameter and is therefore defined as a Pascal "var" parameter. Finally, the Create function will be of our pointer type. Given the values for the record that will be the new node, it will call New to create the node, then fill in the values. We choose NewQuant, NewItem, and NewNext for the three parameters and write the body as:

```
New(Temp);
with Temp^ do
  begin
    Quantity := NewQuant;
    Item := NewItem;
    Next := NewNext
  end;   {With}
Create := Temp
```

Temp is a local pointer variable used to build up the answer; the last step assigns the answer to the function name.

The ReadList procedure is generalized from the two segments of code that were used to read the two separate lists. We use an output parameter ListHead to represent the pointer to the beginning of the list that is being read. In addition, we have an input parameter that contains the list name for use in the prompt. The body of the procedure is

```
Write('How many items for ', ListName, ': ');
Readln(N);
if N < 0 then N := 0;
```

```
for I := 1 to N do
  begin
    Write('Enter the item: ');
    Readln(NewItem);
    Write('Enter the quantity: ');
    Readln(NewQuant);
    Temp := Create(NewQuant, NewItem, Nil);
    Temp^.Next := ListHead;          { link the new item to list }
    ListHead := Temp;                { new item is now first }
  end; {for}
```

The variables N, I, and Temp are local variables that play roles analogous to similar variables in the original program. Specifically, Temp is a pointer to the new node (obtained by using the Create function). This new node is placed on the front of the list by making its Next field point to what was the list head, then having the list head point to it.

PrintList is similar; we adapted it from the printing portions of the previous program. The parameters are the list name and the pointer to the first node in the list (both are input). The body is

```
Writeln('  From ', ListName, ': ');
NodeToPrint := ListHead;

while  NodeToPrint <> Nil  do
  begin
    with  NodeToPrint^  do
      Writeln('     You want ', Quantity, ' ', Item, '.');
    NodeToPrint := NodeToPrint^.Next
  end; {while}
```

Notice the use of the pointer variable NodeToPrint to "traverse" the list. The step

$$NodeToPrint := NodeToPrint^.Next$$

represents a standard way to move on to the next node in a list. It is similar in intent to the step I := I + 1 to move on to the next item in an array. (Likewise, NodeToPrint := ListHead, which starts at the front of the list, is similar in intent to I := 1, which starts at the front of the array.)

Finally, the code to delete the list is extracted from the loops that deleted and printed in the original program:

```
while  ListHead <> Nil  do
  begin
    NodeToDelete := ListHead;          { save for later disposal }
    ListHead := ListHead^.Next;        { Delete from list }
    Dispose(NodeToDelete)              { Dispose of item }
  end; {while}
```

ListHead is an update parameter that points to the first node in the list to be deleted, and NodeToDelete is a local pointer used to keep track of the node to be disposed when ListHead is advanced to the next node.

Figure 9-4 contains the complete program.

{Main program declarations, as shown in Figure 9-3, are inserted here.}

```
function Create(NewQuant : integer; NewItem : String20;
                NewNext : ItemType_Ptr) : ItemType_Ptr;
{
        Written by:   XXXXXXXX  XX/XX/XX
          Purpose:    To create a new node and fill in the values.
        Parameters:   NewQuant - input, the quantity for the new node
                      NewItem - input, the item name for the new node
                      NewNext - input, the pointer field for the new node
    Procedures used:  New - (built-in) gets a data item
}
var
  Temp     : ItemType_Ptr;                   { Temporary copy of answer }

begin   {Create}
  New(Temp);
  with Temp^ do
    begin
      Quantity := NewQuant;
      Item := NewItem;
      Next := NewNext
    end;  {With}
  Create := Temp
end;   {Create}


function Empty(ListHead : ItemType_Ptr) : boolean;
{
        Written by:   XXXXXXXX  XX/XX/XX
          Purpose:    To see if a list is empty.
        Parameters:   ListHead - input, the list to check (that is, a
                          pointer to the first item of the list)
}
begin
  Empty := (ListHead = Nil)
end;   {Empty}


procedure NewList(var ListHead : ItemType_Ptr);
}
        Written by:   XXXXXXXX  XX/XX/XX
          Purpose:    To create an empty list.
        Parameters:   ListHead - output, the list created
}
begin   {NewList}
  ListHead := Nil
end;   {NewList}


procedure ReadList(ListName : String255; var ListHead : ItemType_Ptr);
{
        Written by:   XXXXXXXX  XX/XX/XX
          Purpose:    To create a list by reading from the terminal
```

Figure 9-4   Pointers and Procedures—Refined (Continued)

```
          Parameters:  ListName - input, the ''name'' of the list
                       ListHead - update, the list created (assumed to be
                          Nil when Readlist is invoked)
     Functions used:  Create - to create one node for the list
}
var
   N          : integer;                   { Number of items for list }
   I          : integer;                   { Loop index }
   Temp       : ItemType_Ptr;              { Pointer to temporary node }
   NewItem    : String20;                  { Item to add to list }
   NewQuant   : integer;                   { Quantity to add to list }

begin  {ReadList}
   Write('How many items for ', ListName, ': ');
   Readln(N);
   if N < 0 then N := 0;

   for I := 1 to N do
     begin
       Write('Enter the item: ');
       Readln(NewItem);
       Write('Enter the quantity: ');
       Readln(NewQuant);
       Temp := Create(NewQuant, NewItem, Nil);
       Temp^.Next := ListHead;       { link the new item to list }
       ListHead := Temp;             { new item is now first }
     end; {for}

end;  {ReadList}



procedure PrintList(ListName : String255; ListHead : ItemType_Ptr);
{
        Written by:  XXXXXXXX  XX/XX/XX
           Purpose:  To print a list
        Parameters:  ListName - input, the ''name'' of the list
                     ListHead - input, the list to be printed (that is,
                        a pointer to the first node)
}
var
   NodeToPrint  : ItemType_Ptr;           { "traverses" the list }

begin  {PrintList}
   Writeln(' From ', ListName, ': ');
   NodeToPrint := ListHead;

   while  NodeToPrint <> Nil  do
     begin
       with  NodeToPrint^  do
         Writeln('    You want ', Quantity, ' ', Item, '.');
       NodeToPrint := NodeToPrint^.Next
     end; {while}

end;  {PrintList}
```

Figure 9-4 Pointers and Procedures—Refined (Continued)

```
procedure DeleteList(var ListHead : ItemType_Ptr);
{
        Written by:   XXXXXXXX   XX/XX/XX
          Purpose:   To delete a list by ''disposing'' of all its nodes
       Parameters:   ListHead - update, the list to be deleted (its value
                        is Nil when deletion is completed
   Procedures used:  Dispose - (built-in) to dispose of one node
}
var
   NodeToDelete : ItemType_Ptr;               { ''Traverses'' the list }

begin

   while  ListHead <> Nil  do
      begin
         NodeToDelete := ListHead;            { save for later disposal }
         ListHead := ListHead^.Next;          { delete from list }
         Dispose(NodeToDelete)                { dispose of item }
      end; {while}

end;   {DeleteList}
```

{*Main program body, as shown in Figure 9-3, is inserted here.*}

Figure 9-4 Pointers and Procedures—Refined

**SAVING BOTH
TIME AND
SPACE WITH
POINTERS**

In this subsection, we will present an example that shows how the use of pointers can provide dramatic savings of both space and time.

The context of the example is that we are to read a list of an unknown number of students, with the relevant information for each student including the name, section number, and grade. We wish to sort the list by name and print the list. We will organize the data for an individual student in a standard manner as shown:

```
NameType = string[20];
SectionType = integer;
GradeType = char;
StudentType = record
                 Name    : NameType;
                 Section : SectionType;
                 Grade   : GradeType
              end;
```

Now, in this example, we do not know the number of students, so it is difficult to guess an accurate size for the list of students. We do not wish to use the linked list techniques because of the requirement that we must sort the data by name, which requires fast access to the various elements of the list. An array appears to be the appropriate data structure for the student list. However, if we use an array of StudentType, then each unused array element is costing us about 24 memory locations. To play it safe, we intend to set the array size to some large number such as 10,000. We will be requiring approximately 240,000 memory locations for our student list even if we only have 25 students in the list for some particular run of the program. To save space, we will utilize an array of pointers for the student list. We declare the list as follows:

```
const
   MaxNumber = 10000;                        { Maximum size for list }

type
   NameType = string[20];
   SectionType = integer;
   GradeType = char;
   StudentType_Ptr = ^StudentType;
   StudentType = record
                   Name    : NameType;
                   Section : SectionType;
                   Grade   : GradeType;
                 end;
   StudentArray = array [1 .. MaxNumber] of StudentType_Ptr;

var
   Student     : StudentArray;              { Array of pointers }
```

If there are no students on the list, the array of pointers will occupy approximately 40,000 memory locations. If we run the program with 25 students on the list, then, using pointers, we will utilize approximately 40,600 memory locations as compared to 240,000 memory locations using a standard array.

Now that we have seen the space savings of the technique, we will look at the time savings. We intend to sort names by using a version of the quick sort discussed in Chapter 6. Computer runs have shown a time ratio of better than 3.8:1 when using assignment statements with StudentType records as compared to using assignment statements using pointers to the records. Since the quick sort uses assignment statements for swapping data items, we can expect significant time savings from the use of pointers in the example.

We will now discuss each of the modules of the example and indicate where the use of pointers has made a difference in the program.

The *main program* has the steps:

initialize the number of students to 0
get the list of students using AddStudent in a loop until done
sort the student list by name using NameSort
loop for I going from 1 to the number of students:
   print the student record for Ith student using PrintStudent

We see that the three major modules of the program are AddStudent, NameSort, and PrintStudent.

The AddStudent procedure has the single parameter Done, a Boolean type, which indicates when the user is finished. The procedure has the steps:

set number of students to number plus 1
get a new data item using New
read student name from the user
if the name is empty then:
   set Done to true
   return the data item using Dispose
   set number of students to number minus 1

otherwise:
  set Done to false
  read the section and grade from the user

We see the difference that pointers make in this module through the use of the New and Dispose procedures and in one statement that refers to the record as Student[Number]^ instead of as Student[Number], which we would use if it were not for the pointers.

The NameSort procedure is an adaptation of the quick sort procedure that was presented in Chapter 6. We have made very few changes, which are

1. We have called the sort NameSort and the partitioning procedure NamePartition.

2. We have eliminated the first parameter of both procedures.

3. We have used the global type NameType for the Pivot variable.

4. We have changed all references of the form A[*expression*] to the form Student[*expression*]^.Name.

5. We have declared the variable Temp to be a pointer for use in swapping.

6. We have replaced the use of the Swap procedure with the three-statement swapping logic.

These few changes allow the quick sort to be used in a very different context than that of Chapter 6.

The procedure PrintStudent simply prints the information for the Ith student on one line. The only evidence of the use of pointers is in the one statement that refers to the record as Student[Number]^ instead of as Student[Number], which we would use were it not for the pointers.

The example program is presented in Figure 9-5.

```
program Efficiency(Input, Output);
{
        Written by:  XXXXXXXXX  XX/XX/XX
           Purpose:  To illustrate the use of arrays of pointers.
    Procedures used: AddStudent - adds a student to the list;
                     NameSort - sorts by student name;
                     PrintStudent - prints a student record.
}
const
  MaxNumber = 10000;                          { Maximum size for list }

type
  NameType = string[20];
  SectionType = integer;
  GradeType = char;
  StudentType_Ptr = ^StudentType;
  StudentType = record
```

Figure 9-5 Array of Pointers (Continued)

```
                   Name    : NameType;
                   Section : SectionType;
                   Grade   : GradeType
                 end;
  StudentArray = array [1 .. MaxNumber] of StudentType_Ptr;

var
  Student    : StudentArray;          { Array of pointers }
  Number     : integer;               { Actual number of students }
  I          : integer;               { Loop index }
  Done       : Boolean;               { Indicator for finished }

procedure AddStudent(var Done : Boolean);
{
       Written by:    XXXXXXXX  XX/XX/XX
          Purpose:    To get student information and add to list.
       Parameters:    Done - output, indicates finished when true.
  Procedures used:    New - (built-in) gets new data item;
                      Dispose - (built-in) returns data item.
     Globals used:    Number - actual number of data items, updated;
                      MaxNumber - maximum number for list, used;

}
const
  EndOfData = '';                     { Terminating value }

begin {AddStudent}
  if  Number >= MaxNumber then
    Done := true
  else
    begin
      Number := Number + 1;
      New(Student[Number]);           { Get new data item }
      with  Student[Number]^  do
        begin
          Write('   Name (Empty to quit): ');
          Readln(Name);
          if  Name = EndOfData  then
            begin
              Done := true;
              Dispose(Student[Number]);  { Return data item }
              Number := Number - 1
            end
          else
            begin
              Done := false;
              Write('   Section: ');
              Readln(Section);
              Write('   Grade (A,B,C,D,F): ');
              Readln(Grade)
            end
        end; {with}
    end
end; {AddStudent}
```

Figure 9-5 Array of Pointers (Continued)

```
procedure NamePartition(Low, High :  integer;
                        var PivotLocation : integer);
{
        Written by:  XXXXXXXXX  XX/XX/XX
           Purpose:  To partition an array into three parts:
                        1. values less or equal to the pivotal element
                        2. the pivotal element
                        3. values greater than or equal to the pivotal
                           element
        Parameters:  Low, High – the portion of the array to partition
                     PivotLocation – the location for the pivotal element
                     (sent back to the calling module, therefore a var
                     parameter)
}
var
  I        : integer;              { used to locate large values }
  J        : integer;              { used to locate small values }
  Pivot    : NameType;             { the pivotal element }
  Temp     : StudentType_Ptr;      { for swapping }

begin   {Partition}
  I := Low;
  J := High + 1;
  Pivot := Student[Low]^.Name;

  repeat

{*** Move I to right looking for a value greater than or equal to
      the pivot.}

    repeat
      I := I + 1
    until (I = High) or (Student[I]^.Name >= Pivot);

{***  Move J to left looking for a value less than or equal to
      the pivot.}

    repeat
      J := J – 1
    until Student[J]^.Name <= Pivot;

{***  Swap if the values are out of order.}

    if I < J then
      begin
        Temp := Student[I];
        Student[I] := Student[J];
        Student[J] := Temp
      end {if}
  until I >= J;
```

Figure 9-5   Array of Pointers (Continued)

```
{*** Put the pivotal element in the proper place, and return the
     value of its subscript to the calling module.}

     Temp := Student[Low];
     Student[Low] := Student[J];
     Student[J] := Temp;
     PivotLocation := J
end;  {Partition}

procedure NameSort(Low, High :  integer);
{
     Written by:  XXXXXXXXX  XX/XX/XX
        Purpose:  To sort students by names, using the quick sort
                  technique.
     Parameters:  Low, High – the portion of the array to sort
}
var
  PivotSub : integer;                  { location of pivotal element }

begin  {NameSort]
  if Low < High then
    begin
      NamePartition(Low, High, PivotSub);
      NameSort(Low, PivotSub – 1);
      NameSort(PivotSub + 1, High)
    end  {if]
end;  {NameSort}

procedure PrintStudent(I : integer);
{
     Written by:  XXXXXXXXX  XX/XX/XX
        Purpose:  To print the student record for one student.
     Parameters:  I – input, index of student to print.
}
begin {PrintStudent}
  with  Student[I]^  do
    begin
      Writeln(Section:6, ' ':5, Name, ' ':30-Length(Name), Grade)
    end {with}
end; {PrintStudent}


begin {Efficiency}

{*** Initialize.}

  Number := 0;

{*** Get students.}

  repeat
    AddStudent(Done)
  until  Done;
```

Figure 9-5 Array of Pointers (Continued)

```
{*** Sort the data.}

  NameSort(1, Number);

{*** Print the student records.}

  Writeln;
  Writeln('            Student Records');
  Writeln('            ---------------');
  Writeln('Section       Name                    Grade');

  for I := 1 to Number do
    PrintStudent(I);

{*** Print message and terminate.}

  Writeln;
  Writeln('Efficiency program is terminating.')
end.
```

Figure 9-5 Array of Pointers

1. For the program of Figure 9-4, revise the ReadList procedure to read an unknown number of list items, terminated by an appropriate terminal value.

2. Modify the program of Figure 9-4 to create 10 lists. Use an array of list names and an array of pointers to the first item in the lists.

*3. Why does the Create function in Figure 9-4 need the Temp variable? Why not just write

```
New(Create);
with Create^ do . . .
```

*4. In the ReadList procedure of Figure 9-4, we use Create to fill in the quantity and item portion of the new record, but we fill in the Next portion ourselves. Tell how to modify the steps so that the Create call completes the entire record.

*5. The comments for the ReadList procedure in Figure 9-4 say that it assumes the list is empty when the procedure is called. By hand-tracing the procedure with a nonempty list, find what happens if the list is not empty upon entry to the procedure.

6. a. Given is a segment of code for searching in an array. By examining the intent of each step of that code, write a segment of code for searching in a linked list. (Use the linked-list structure of the program of Figure 9-4.)

```
I := 1;
Found := false;
while (not Found) and (I <= N) do
  begin
    if A[I] = Key then
      Found := true
    else
      I := I + 1
  end;   {while}
```

```
if Found then
    Locate := I
else
    Locate := 0
```

*b. Write the code of part (a) as a function that returns a pointer to the node that contains the desired value or Nil if there is no such node.

c. In linked-list applications, it is often useful to obtain a pointer to the node just before the one that contains the desired value. Assuming that there is such a node and that it is not the first node, write a segment of code to accomplish this. Hint: Modify part (b).

d. Write a procedure with these parameters. Use the linked list structure from the program of Figure 9-4.

> A pointer to the first node of a list—input
>
> A value to look for—input
>
> An indication of the result (either NotFound, First, or NotFirst—use a user defined type)—output
>
> A pointer to the node before the one with the value (only defined if NotFirst is the result)—output

e. By using the procedure of part (d), write a segment of code to insert a new node containing the entry 2 toothpaste in the list right before the entry for vegetable soup. Assume that vegetable soup is in the list.

f. Repeat part (e), but put the new entry in the front of the list if vegetable soup is not in the list.

7. Write procedures or functions for each of the parts of Exercise 4 of Section 9-1.

8. Modify the program of Figure 9-5 by using a Create procedure in the Add-Student procedure.

9. Modify the program of Figure 9-5 by using a SectionSort procedure in place of the NameSort procedure that is shown. Use the discusssion of the changes that were made to quick sort for NameSort to guide your modifications.

10. Redo the program of Figure 9-5 by using a linked list as the data structure. You will want to perform a simpler sort, such as the bubble sort or one of the selection sorts, rather than the quick sort. Compare the performance of your program with that of the program of Figure 9-5.

*11. Write a function that will return a pointer to the Nth record on the student list using the data structure of Figure 9-5.

*12. Write a function that will return a pointer to the Nth record of the data structure for your program of Exercise 10.

13. Modify the program of Figure 9-5 so that it prints the students in reverse order.

14. What would be needed to print the students in reverse order in your program of Exercise 10?

15. Modify the program of Figure 9-5 so that it prints only the students who have received a particular grade specified by the user.

16. Modify your program of Exercise 10 so that it prints only the students who have received a particular grade specified by the user.

17. Modify the program of Figure 9-5 so that instead of printing all of the students, it asks the user for a student name and prints the information for that student. Use a binary search (see Chapter 6) to locate the correct student.

18. Modify the program of Figure 9-5 so that it obtains the student information from a text file with three lines per student. Offer a menu of options for the user that includes:

Displaying all students

Printing all students on the printer

Displaying a specified student (by binary search)

Changing a grade for a specified student (by binary search)

Calculating the average grade for the students (using 4 for A, 3 for B, 2 for C, 1 for D, and 0 for F)

10
RECURSION

10-1
THINKING RECURSIVELY

In this chapter, we will take a more in-depth look at the topic of recursion. We have been introduced to recursion in Chapter 4 and have seen it used with arrays in Chapter 6. We will present a more focused discussion in this chapter. In this first section, we will deal with recursion as a problem-solving strategy without dealing with the programming aspects involved. In the second section, we will concentrate on its implementation in our Pascal programs. In the third and final section, we will consider the practical matters of choosing recursion or some other method when we are offered alternative solutions to a problem.

□
PROBLEM-SOLVING TOOLS

One way to view computer programming is in the broader context of problem solving. When we are presented with a problem in the "real world," it is not often obvious which line of attack will lead most fruitfully to a solution. Problem solvers through the ages have developed strategies and techniques that can be helpful aids for any problem-solving effort. We have already discussed some of these tools in the text; a list of some useful tools is as follows:

- **Historical Approach**. If someone has already solved the problem, why reinvent the solution? The "classical" algorithms, such as the Euclidean Algorithm for the greatest common divisor and the QuickSort, are good examples of algorithms that should not have to be reinvented.

- **Reasoning by Analogy**. Many problems are analogous to problems that have been solved by us or by others. With the proper changes, we can find that an old solution will solve a new problem.

- **Divide and Conquer**. We have continually emphasized the advantages of simplifying a problem by cutting it into "bite-size" pieces. We have used the concept of modularity to utilize this problem-solving tool.

654

- **Geometric Methodology**. When appropriate, the theory and techniques of geometry can provide leverage for solving problems.

- **Algebraic Methodology**. When appropriate, the theory and techniques of algebra provide powerful tools for dealing with problems.

- **Analytic Methodology**. When appropriate, the theory and techniques of mathematical analysis, as commonly encountered in Calculus courses, prove to be an effective tool for solving problems.

- **Statistical Methodology**. When appropriate, the methods of probability and statistics can provide quick, effective solutions to a wide class of problems.

- **Simulations**. Often the best way to solve a real-world problem is to simulate it in a simpler computerized environment. Simulating the situation allows the possibility of testing the proposed solution thousands or millions of times in order to test the behavior of the solution repeatedly.

- **Recursion**. When applicable, recursion can provide a solution that is almost "magical" in its simplicity and effectiveness.

A good problem solver will become fluent with all of the above tools. It is as important to know which tools are inappropriate as to know which tools are appropriate for a given problem. We should not remain ignorant of any area of problem-solving methodology as protection for the day when a particular method is the only one that will work. In addition, as we will see, it is better to have two solutions to a problem than just one. Paradoxically, it is more than twice as good to have two solutions rather than one because we can now choose the *better* solution for our context. Also, having two solutions to a problem means that we can use each method to test the other for correctness. There are many times when we can be confident that having two different solutions for a problem that provide the same results means that *both* solutions are correct. Thus, we see that recursion is an important problem-solving technique when it provides an alternate solution to a problem, even if the recursive solution is not the one that is finally selected as the better.

□
THE TEMPLATES OF RECURSION
Recursion is often seen in the context of problems that depend on one or more positive integers that in some way measure the *size* of the problem. A classical example is provided by the factorial function Factorial(N), which is recursively defined (and solved) by

$$\text{Factorial}(N) = \begin{cases} N * \text{Factorial } (N - 1), \text{ for } N > 0 \\ 1, \text{ for } N = 0 \end{cases}$$

An algorithm for the factorial of N is

```
if N=0 then Factorial := 1
else Factorial := N * Factorial(N − 1)
```

The simple factorial example provides evidence for the general recursive strategy:

1. Solve the given problem in terms of smaller instances of the same problem. For the above problem, Factorial(N) := N * Factorial ($N - 1$).

2. Decide what to do with the bottom level case(s) of the problem. For the above problem, Factorial(0) := 1.

Observe that "smaller" means "closer to the base case(s)."

This strategy applies for problems that deal with more than one measure of size also. For example, the coefficient of the mth term of the binomial raised to a power

$$(a + b)^n$$

is given by the **combinatorial coefficient** $C(n, m)$, which is defined by

$$C(n, m) = \begin{cases} 1, \text{ if } m = 0 \text{ or } m = n \\ C(n - 1, m) + C(n - 1, m - 1), \text{ otherwise} \end{cases}$$

These numbers are often presented via a device that bears the same name as the language that we are studying, **Pascal's Triangle**:

n											
1						1	1				
2					1	2	1				
3				1	3	3	1				
4			1	4	6	4	1				
5		1	5	10	10	5	1				
6	1	6	15	20	15	6	1				
7	1	7	21	35	35	21	7	1			
8	1	8	28	56	70	56	28	8	1		
9	1	9	36	84	126	126	84	36	9	1	
10	1	10	45	120	210	252	210	120	45	10	1

For each line of the triangle, the value of m begins with 0 on the left and moves to 1, 2 , ... Thus, the fifth row of the triangle has values of m as shown:

			m			
n	*0*	*1*	*2*	*3*	*4*	*5*
5	1	5	10	10	5	1

Thus, we can see from the table that

$$C(5, 2) = C(4, 1) + C(4, 2)$$
$$10 \ = \ \ 4 \ + \ \ 6$$

Note that our concept of a "smaller case" when we are dependent on two integers is interpreted as "either (or both) of the integers is smaller." This moves us closer to the base cases.

□

REVERSING A STRING

We turn to the problem of reversing a string, making the last character first and so on. If the given string is "Joan Smith," then the reversed string is "htimS naoJ." The main point of this example is that the measure of size of a case is not always directly available as in the previous examples. In this case, the measure of size is the number of characters in the string. Let us denote the reversed form of a string S by Reversed(S). Then our recursive formulation will be

to calculate Reversed(S):
    let x be the first character of S
    let T be S with the first character removed
    Reversed(S) is Reversed(T) + x

Thus, if S is "plum", then x is "p", T is "lum", Reversed(T) is "mul", and Reversed(T) + x is "mulp". What is the bottom case for this example? There are two choices that naturally present themselves:

    If S is null, then Reversed(S) is S.
    If S has exactly one character, then Reversed(S) is S.

We choose the former alternative to provide a slightly more general algorithm for reversing the string S. We use the built-in Copy function of Turbo Pascal to extract substrings of a string. The substring of a string S, which consists of all of S except the first character, is Copy(S, 2, Length(S)−1), where the built-in function Length provides the number of characters of S. You can refer to Chapter 8 for more details of string handling. The algorithm is as follows:

if S is null, then Reversed := S
else S := Reversed(Copy(S, 2, Length(S)−1)) + S[1]

□

RECURSIVE SORTING

We have seen an example of sorting numbers recursively in Chapter 6 with the quick sort algorithm. In this subsection, we will consider two other sorting techniques that can be done recursively. For each example, we will assume that an array X has been passed to the sorting routine Sort, along with the lower and upper limits of the array to be sorted in ascending order. For example, suppose that the first several members of the array X have values as shown:

subscript	1	2	3	4	5	6	7	8	9
value	33	10	50	−8	5	8	9	44	3

Then, after invoking Sort(X, 3, 7), X would appear as follows:

subscript	1	2	3	4	5	6	7	8	9
value	33	10	−8	5	8	9	50	44	3

The first example is a variation of the **selection sort** algorithm presented in Chapter 6 in which we repeatedly move the larger elements of the array to the right. The recursive idea is to move the largest element to the right and then call ourselves recursively to deal with all but the last element in the specified range. The algorithm for the selection sort version of Sort(X, First, Last) is as follows:

if First >= Last, then return without doing anything
else:
   interchange the largest of X[First], . . . , X[Last] into
     position X[Last]
   invoke Sort(X, First, Last−1)

The only redeeming virtue of this selection sort is that it can be so simply described. The process of exchanging the largest value to position X[Last] is accomplished via the following algorithm:

set Large to X[First] and set Place to First
loop for I going from First+1 to Last:
   if X[I] > Large, then set Large to X[I] and set Place to I
set X[Place] to X[Last] and set X[Last] to Large

The second example is called the **merge sort** and is slightly more complex than the selection sort. The basic idea is to divide the range of X to be sorted into roughly half, to sort each half, and to merge the two results. If we use the example above, then we want to sort the numbers:

$$50 \quad -8 \quad 5 \quad 8 \quad 9$$

Our procedure is to divide the numbers into two parts:

$$50 \quad -8 \quad 5 \quad \text{and} \quad 8 \quad 9$$

Then, we sort the two parts into:

$$-8 \quad 5 \quad 50 \quad \text{and} \quad 8 \quad 9$$

Finally, we merge the two parts into:

$$-8 \quad 5 \quad 8 \quad 9 \quad 50$$

Of the two basic tasks to be done, sorting the parts and merging the results, the easier of the two is the sorting because we simply call ourselves recursively to do that. If we assume for the moment that the merging of the results is already defined, then our algorithm for the merge sort invocation of Sort(X, First, Last) is as follows:

if First >= Last, then return
else:
    set Middle to (First+Last)/2 [truncate the result, if necessary]
    invoke Sort(X, First, Middle)
    invoke Sort(X, Middle+1, Last)
    merge the results

Actually, the merging process is not too difficult if we use an auxiliary array Temp to merge into. The algorithm for merging the sorted parts X[First], . . . , X[Last] with X[Middle+1], . . . , X[Last] is as follows:

    set LPlace to First
    set RPlace to Middle+1
    set I to First

[work with both halves, while neither exhausted]

    while LPlace<=Middle and RPlace<=Last do:
        if X[LPlace] <= X[RPlace], then:
            set Temp[I] to X[LPlace] and set LPlace to LPlace+1
        else:
            set Temp[I] to X[RPlace] and set RPlace to RPlace+1
        set I to I+1

[work with one half, when other exhausted]

    if LPlace > Middle, then:
        set Start to RPlace and set Finish to Last
    else:
        set Start to LPlace and set Finish to Middle
    loop for XPlace going from Start to Finish:
        set Temp[I] to X[XPlace] and set I to I+1

[copy from Temp to X]

    loop for I going from First to Last
        set X[I] to Temp[I]

The above algorithm is a bit heavy with notation, but the concept is an example of a "two-finger" algorithm: set the left finger to the first element of the first part and set the right finger to the first element of the second part; then, whichever element is smaller is moved to Temp and that finger moves; when either part is exhausted, then the other part moves to Temp one by one. We suggest that the reader try the "two-finger" version of the algorithm on a small example and then try to see that the more formal algorithm accomplishes the same task.

Note that in both sorting examples that we have discussed, the bottom level is reached when the range of the array to be sorted contains at most one element and then we do nothing but return.

In this subsection, we will consider two routines that are of the general class that is sometimes called **predicates**. In each case, the routine will simply report whether a situation is true or false.

For the first case, we are interested in whether a given string is a **subsequence** of another given string. We will consider one string to be a subsequence of another if all the characters of the first string appear in the second string and *in the same order*. It is not necessary that the characters of the first string appear consecutively in the second string. Here are some examples of subsequences of strings:

String	Subsequence of the String
abcdefghijkl	bdgl
apple	pl
banana	ann
house	house
abc	⟨empty string⟩

The recursive idea in determining if one string is a subsequence of another is to locate the first character of the first string within the second, and then ask recursively if the rest of the first string is a subsequence of the rest of the second string. The bottom cases are

1. If the first string is null, the predicate is true.

2. If the first string is not null and the second string is null, the predicate is false.

The reason that the empty string is a subsequence of any other string is that it cannot be false that "all of the characters of the empty string appear in the second string and in the same order." (Think about it.) An algorithm for determining if the string InSeq is a subsequence of the string InString is as follows:

To calculate the predicate SubSeq(InSeq, InString):
    if InSeq is null, then set SubSeq to true
    else if InString is null, then set SubSeq to false
    else:
        set Place to the leftmost location of InSeq[1] in InString
        if Place is 0 (not found), then set SubSeq to false
        else:
            set SubSeq to
                SubSeq(Right(InSeq, 2), Right(InString, Place+1))

In the above algorithm, we are assuming the existence of the string-valued function Right, which is given a string and a position and which returns all the characters of the string that come after the position.

We turn now to a related problem of recognizing whether a string is a substring of another string. We note that the built-in Turbo Pascal function Pos accomplishes this task and more because it will identify the starting location of the substring within the string. However, we will discuss this problem without using the Pos function. The recursive idea is that if the first string is not the same as the leading several characters of the second string, then we check to see if the first string is a substring of the second string from its second character onward. The bottom cases are

1. If the first string is null, the predicate is true.

2. If the length of second string is less than the length of first string, the predicate is false.

An algorithm for determining if the string InSub is a substring of the string InString is as follows:

To calculate SubString(InSub, InString):
    if InSub is null, then set SubString to true
    else if Length(InString)<Length(InSub), then set SubString to false
    else if InSub is equal to Left(InString, Length(InSub)),
       then set SubString to true
    else:
       set SubString to SubString(InSub, Right(InString, 2))

In the above algorithm, we assume the availability of the string function Right as discussed earlier and we also assume the existence of the string function Left, which is given a string and a position and which returns all the characters of the string up to and including the specified position.

□ **SOME COUNTING PROBLEMS**

In this subsection, we consider a few counting problems of varying degrees of difficulty.

For our first problem, we attempt to count the number of strings of length N that can be made by an alphabet of M letters. For example, if we use the alphabet consisting of 'a' and 'b' (M = 2) and ask for strings of length 3, then we have the following complete list:

    aaa
    bbb
    aab
    aba
    baa
    abb
    bab
    bba

The recursive idea for this problem is that we can produce all strings of length N using M letters by first producing all strings of length N − 1 using M letters and then prefixing each of them with each of the M letters. If we use the notation StringsNM(p, q) to denote the number of strings of length p using q letters, then the recursive counting formula is

$$\text{StringsNM}(n, m) = m * \text{StringsNM}(n-1, m)$$

The bottom case is that StringsNM(1, m) = m. Therefore, the algorithm for counting strings of length N using M letters is

To calculate StringsNM(n, m):
    if n is equal to 1, then set StringsNM to m
    else set StringsNM to m times StringsNM(n−1, m)

Let us turn next to the problem of counting the number of divisors of an integer N. First, we consider some examples:

N	Divisors	Number of Divisors
1	1	1
2	1, 2	2
3	1, 3	2
4	1, 2, 4	3
5	1, 5	2
6	1, 2, 3, 6	4
7	1, 7	2
8	1, 2, 4, 8	4
9	1, 3, 9	3
10	1, 2, 5, 10	4
11	1, 11	2
12	1, 2, 3, 4, 6, 12	6

How do we approach this problem recursively? An obvious choice for measuring the size of the problem is to use the magnitude of the number itself. So, to use recursion, we must decide on a method of meaningfully reducing the size of the number. When dealing with divisors of a number, it is not a good idea to reduce the size by subtracting 1 because the divisors of a number N and the number N − 1 do not relate to one another. A better choice for reducing size is to *divide* the number by one of its factors. The resulting number is smaller in magnitude and shares some of the same divisors as the original number. This observation provides the crucial insight into the problem. Our approach will be to find the smallest divisor of the number and divide by it. The question is: How do we relate the divisors of the smaller number with the divisors of the larger number? If we study the above table of divisors, we do not see an easy relationship between the divisors of 6 (12 divided by 2) and 12. However, if we look at the divisors of 3 and the divisors of 4, we see that the number of divisors of 12 is equal to the number of divisors of 3 times the number of divisors of 4. So our procedure will be

To calculate the number of divisors of N:
1. find the smallest divisor of N, S (note that S is prime)
2. let S^K be the highest power of S that divides into N evenly
3. the number of divisors of N is equal to (K + 1) times the number of divisors of N divided by S^K (note that K + 1 is the number of divisors of S^K because S is prime)

The bottom level for the process is that the number of divisors of the number 1 is 1. According to our procedure, we see that the number of divisors of 72 is 12 because, using the notation above, N is 72, S is 2, and K is 3.

Our next problem is to calculate the number of ways to express a positive integer as a sum of positive integers where we don't distinguish different orderings (that is, we consider 2 + 1 and 1 + 2 to be the same). For example, the number 6 can be expressed in the following ways:

$$6$$
$$1 + 5$$
$$2 + 4$$
$$3 + 3$$
$$1 + 1 + 4$$
$$1 + 2 + 3$$
$$2 + 2 + 2$$
$$1 + 1 + 1 + 3$$
$$1 + 1 + 2 + 2$$
$$1 + 1 + 1 + 1 + 2$$
$$1 + 1 + 1 + 1 + 1 + 1$$

Note that we include 6 itself as a degenerate form of a sum. The way we choose to organize the sums in this problem is by the *lowest factor* that appears in the sum. This organization for the number 6 appears as follows:

Lowest factor = 1: $1 + 1 + 1 + 1 + 1 + 1$
$$1 + 1 + 1 + 1 + 2$$
$$1 + 1 + 1 + 3$$
$$1 + 1 + 2 + 2$$
$$1 + 2 + 3$$
$$1 + 1 + 4$$
$$1 + 5$$

Lowest factor = 2: $2 + 2 + 2$
$$2 + 4$$

Lowest factor = 3: $3 + 3$

Lowest factor = 6: 6

Our procedure for counting the number of ways to express N as a sum is to count the number of ways to express N as a sum using I as the lowest factor for I = 1, 2, 3, . . . , N. So far, we haven't used any recursive ideas. Let us use the notation AddendsAux(N, I) to represent the number of ways to express N as a sum using I as the lowest factor. The recursive idea is to recognize that

$$\text{AddendsAux}(N, I) = \text{AddendsAux}(N-I, I) +$$
$$\text{AddendsAux}(N-I, I+1) +$$
$$\text{AddendsAux}(N-I, I+2) +$$
$$. \quad . \quad . \quad .$$
$$\text{AddendsAux}(N-I, N-I)$$

The bottom level for our procedure has two cases:

1. If N = I, then AddendsAux is 1.
2. Otherwise, if I > N div 2, then AddendsAux is 0.

Let us use the notation Addends(N) to denote the number of ways to express N as a sum of positive integers. Then our algorithms are as follows:

To calculate Addends(N):
 set Total to 0
 loop for I going from 1 to N:
  set Total to Total + AddendsAux(N, I)

To calculate AddendsAux(N, I):
 if N is equal to I, then set AddendsAux to 1
 else if I is greater than N div 2, then set AddendsAux to 0
 else:
  set Total to 0
  loop for J going from I to N−I:
   set Total to Total + AddendsAux(N−I, J)

□ THE PROBLEM OF N QUEENS

There is a classical problem that asks the solver to place eight queens on a standard 8-by-8 chessboard so that no queen can take another. This means that no two queens are in the same row, in the same column, or on the same diagonal. To get a feeling for the problem, get a chessboard and, using eight pawns pretending to be queens, try to set up eight nontaking queens. The problem generalizes to considering nonstandard chessboards with N-by-N cells and N queens. A solution to the problem for N = 4 is shown below, where 0 indicates an empty cell and 1 represents a queen:

0	1	0	0
0	0	0	1
1	0	0	0
0	0	1	0

There are only two different solutions for N = 4. Can you find the other? (Hint: Look at the chessboard from behind.)

The problem that we will consider here is to count the number of ways to place N nontaking queens (that is, none can capture any other) on an N-by-N chessboard. An obvious choice for measuring the size of the problem is to use the number N. An obvious choice for reducing the size of the problem is to use the case of N − 1 queens on an (N − 1)-by-(N − 1) chessboard. However, it is not so obvious as to how to relate the N − 1 case to the N case. To see this, note that there are 0 solutions for N = 1, 2, or 3. We have to be a bit more creative in reducing the size of the problem. A fruitful approach is to consider the number N to be a constant and to vary the number of columns that are used for placing queens. That is, we will consider the problem of placing I queens in columns 1, 2, 3, . . . , I of an N-by-N chessboard and use I as our measure of the size of the problem. Also, instead of just counting the number of ways to place the queens, we will expect to have the boards available that have queens placed on them. Our procedure will be to generate the solutions and then to count them. To illustrate the approach, the following are the four different 4-by-4 chessboards with three nontaking queens in columns 1, 2, and 3:

1 0 0 0	0 0 1 0	0 1 0 0	0 1 0 0
0 0 1 0	1 0 0 0	0 0 0 0	0 0 0 0
0 0 0 0	0 0 0 0	1 0 0 0	0 0 1 0
0 1 0 0	0 1 0 0	0 0 1 0	1 0 0 0

Now, for each of these boards, we will place a queen in an empty row and then check to see if we have any problems on the diagonals. In this case, we have the following four candidates (we have marked the possible new queen with a question mark):

1 0 0 0	0 0 1 0	0 1 0 0	0 1 0 0
0 0 1 0	1 0 0 0	0 0 0 ?	0 0 0 ?
0 0 0 ?	0 0 0 ?	1 0 0 0	0 0 1 0
0 1 0 0	0 1 0 0	0 0 1 0	1 0 0 0

We can see that the first and last candidate boards have problems with the diagonals, so they must be rejected. The two boards that we don't reject are our solutions.

We will now attempt to formulate the algorithm. We will assume the existence of a board-checking function OK that will indicate whether or not a board has nontaking queens. We will denote our procedure for placing I nontaking queens on an N-by-N chessboard by SetQueens(I, Solution), where Solution is a collection of all of the generated boards. The bottom level is when I is 1; in this case, we generate N boards with a single queen in the different possible rows. Our algorithm is as follows:

To calculate SetQueens(I, Solution):
    if I is equal to 1, then generate boards with a single queen in
      each possible row and set Solution to the collection of boards
    else:
      invoke SetQueens(I−1, Candidates) to get boards with I−1
        queens in columns 1, . . . , I−1
      loop through each of the boards in the collection of Candidates:
        loop through each row of the board which is empty:
          place a queen in the empty row and in column I
          if the board is OK, then add it to the Solution collection

To have the algorithm solve our problem of the N queens, we simply invoke SetQueens(N, Solution) and count the number of boards in the Solution collection. We encourage you to hand-trace the algorithm in order to get a feel for the way the recursion works.

□
**THE POWER
SET OF A SET**

A mathematical set is an unordered collection of distinct objects often presented as a list using notation such as:

$$\{a, b, c\}$$
$$\{1, 0\}$$
$$\{b, a, c\}$$

Since order is not important, the two sets $\{a, b, c\}$ and $\{b, a, c\}$ are the same. A set may have no elements; in this case, it is referred to as the **empty set** and we can denote it as $\{\}$. A **subset** of a set is any second set all of whose elements are members of the first set. Thus, some subsets of $\{a, b, c\}$ are

$$\{\}$$
$$\{a\}$$
$$\{b, c\}$$
$$\{a, b, c\}$$

A problem sometimes arises that involves the consideration of all subsets of a given set. Let us begin with the question: How many subsets will a given set have? A recursive solution to this counting problem can be formulated as follows (we will use $\{a, b, c\}$ as an example):

To calculate the number of subsets of S, Subs(S):	
suppose that S is the given set	[S = $\{a, b, c\}$]
let x be any member of S	[x = b, for example]
let A be S with x removed	[A = $\{a, c\}$]
note that any subset of S is either a	[$\{a\}$ is of the first
subset of A or can be derived from a	kind]
subset of A by adding x to the subset	[$\{b, a\}$ is of the
of A	second kind]
thus, Subs(S) = 2 * Subs(A)	

The basic recursive idea here is illustrated by listing all of the subsets of $\{a, c\}$:

$$\{\,\}$$
$$\{a\}$$
$$\{c\}$$
$$\{a, c\}$$

If we augment each of these by adding the element b, we get the list:

$$\{b\}$$
$$\{b, a\}$$
$$\{b, c\}$$
$$\{b, a, c\}$$

Together, these two lists of subsets contain all of the subsets of the original set $\{a, b, c\}$:

$$\{\,\}$$
$$\{a\}$$
$$\{b\}$$
$$\{c\}$$
$$\{a, b\}$$
$$\{a, c\}$$
$$\{b, c\}$$
$$\{a, b, c\}$$

What is the bottom case for counting subsets? The natural choice is the empty set, which has exactly one subset (itself). Thus, an algorithm for counting subsets of a set can be presented as follows:

To calculate the number of subsets of a set of n elements, NSubs(n):
    if n = 0 then NSubs := 1
    else NSubs := 2 * NSubs(n−1)

Our discussion has provided us with the means of solving a slightly more difficult problem: that of collecting all of the subsets of a set S. The algorithm for collecting the subsets of S is

if S is empty then just collect $\{\,\}$
else:
    choose any element x from S
    let A be S with x removed
    let C1 be the collection of all of the subsets of A
    let C2 be the collection of all of the subsets of A with x added to each
    our answer is the union of C1 with C2

An interesting exercise in recursion is to trace the above algorithm to see in what order the subsets of S will appear in the final collection. Suppose that the following scenario is followed in choosing x at each level of recursion:

Level 1: S = {a, b, c}, choose x = a
Level 2: S = {b, c}, choose x = b
Level 3: S = {c}, choose x = c
Level 4: S = { }, collection is {{ }}
Level 3: Collection is {{ }, {c}}
Level 2: Collection is {{ }, {c}, {b}, {b, c}}
Level 1: Collection is {{ }, {c}, {b}, {b, c}, {a}, {a, c}, {a, b}, {a, b, c}}

□
MUTUAL
RECURSION

We will now illustrate the idea of two **mutually recursive** subprograms, that is, each subprogram invokes the other. We will use as the context of our discussion the concept of **prefix** arithmetic expressions. When we symbolically represent the arithmetic expression for the sum of the numbers 2 and 3, we usually write

$$2 + 3$$

This form is known as the **infix** form of the expression. The prefix form of the expression is

$$+23$$

We will keep all of our numbers as single digits for simplicity in this discussion and offer extensions in the exercises. We will allow for two arithmetic operations, "+" and "*", representing addition and multiplication, respectively. One advantage of the prefix form is that parentheses are unnecessary. In the infix form, with the usual notions of precedence and associativity, we must use parentheses to denote "the product of 2 with the sum of 3 and 4", as shown:

$$2 * (3 + 4)$$

Without parentheses, the expression 2 * 3 + 4 has the value of 10, not the value of 14. However, we can represent our expression in prefix notation as

$$*2+34$$

The table shows some more examples of the prefix form:

Infix Form	Prefix Form	Value
2 * (3 + 4)	*2+34	14
2 * 3 + 4	+*234	10
(2 + 3) * (4 + 5)	*+23 + 45	45
2 + 3 + 4 + 5	+++2345	14
2 + (3 + (4 + 5))	+2+3+45	14
4	4	4

Our intention is to write an algorithm for the evaluation of prefix expressions. We will use three main routines to accomplish the evaluation process.

The first routine, called Eval, will accept a prefix expression and return its value. At first thought, this seems to be no more than the top-level routine, until we realize that there are often several prefix subexpressions to evaluate during the evaluation of the whole expression. Eval must be able to handle the simplest prefix expression that contains a single number with no operators. If we look at the second and third columns of the table, we see some examples of the behavior of Eval.

The second routine, called Apply, will accept an operator and an expression that can be split into the two operands for the operator. Apply returns the value attained by *applying* the operator to the operands. Some examples of the behavior of Apply are shown in the table:

Op	InString	Apply(Op, InString)
+	23	5
+	*234	10
*	45	20
*	2+34	14
*	+23+45	45

The third main routine, called Split, will accept an expression and split it into two operands. Let us refer to the two operands as First and Second. The behavior of Split is shown with some examples in the following table:

InString	First	Second
23	2	3
*234	*23	4
45	4	5
2+34	2	+34
+23+45	+23	+45

The Eval routine has two cases: either it is dealing with a single number or it has an expression whose first character is an operator. The algorithm for Eval is as follows:

```
if the expression is a number, then return the numeric value
else call Apply with the leading operator and the rest of the expression
```

So we see that Eval leaves the hard work for Apply.

The Apply routine must divide the expression into the two parts and then apply the operator to the two parts *after they are evaluated*. The algorithm for Apply is as follows:

```
use the Split routine to divide the expression into the two parts:
    First and Second
```

depending on the operator:
'+': return Eval(First) + Eval(Second)
'*': return Eval(First) * Eval(Second)

We shall see that the Split routine is not really very difficult, so that Apply leaves the hard work for Eval to do (it's only fair).

The Split routine must find the point at which the expression is to be divided into two operands. By studying a few examples, we see that the dividing point comes just after there is exactly one more number than operators as we view the expression from left to right. Review the previous table to see that this idea is correct. The algorithm for Split is as follows:

set the variable Count to 0
scan the expression from left to right, looking at single characters:
    if the character is an operator then set Count to Count−1
    if the character is a number then set Count to Count+1
when Count becomes equal to 1, divide the expression into two parts
    just after the current character

Let us now trace these algorithms through an example. We begin with attempting to evaluate the expression +2*34. We explicitly trace only the Eval and Apply calls, assuming that Split will work properly.

Level 1:	We invoke Eval with the parameter +2*34. Eval sees that the first character is the operation + and
Level 2:	invokes Apply with the parameters + and 2*34. Apply invokes Split with the parameter 2*34 and receives back the two parts 2 and *34. Apply
Level 3:	invokes Eval with the parameter 2. Eval sees the character '2' and returns the number 2.
Level 2:	Apply
Level 3:	invokes Eval with the parameter *34. Eval sees that the first character is the operation * and
Level 4:	invokes Apply with the parameters * and 34. Apply invokes Split with the parameter 34 and receives back the two parts 3 and 4 Apply
Level 5:	invokes Eval with the parameter 3. Eval sees the character '3' and returns the number 3.
Level 4:	Apply
Level 5:	invokes Eval with the parameter 4. Eval sees the character '4' and returns the number 4.
Level 4:	Apply applies the operation '*' to the numbers 3 and 4 and returns the number 12.
Level 3:	Eval receives the number 12 from Apply and returns the number 12.

Level 2:   Apply applies the operation '+' to the numbers 2 and 12 and returns the number 14.

Level 1:   Eval receives the number 14 from Apply and returns the number 14 to us.

The following diagram may help you follow the tracing. This diagram was constructed during the hand-tracing and represents the entire execution of the algorithm for the given input.

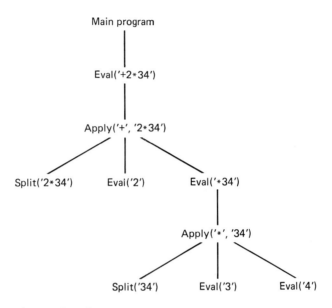

After tracing such a simple example and seeing the complexity of the behavior of the process, we may be mystified by the simplicity of the algorithms for Eval, Apply, and Split as compared to their synergistic behavior. The answer to the paradox of simplicity producing complexity is that the recursive process itself takes care of a substantial amount of bookkeeping, thus relieving the programmer of the easy but error-fraught steps of keeping track of who is invoking whom and who returns what to whom. The example presented here should dramatically illustrate the power of recursive thinking.

REVIEW

Terms and concepts

historical approach
reasoning by analogy
divide and conquer
geometric methodology
algebraic methodology
analytic methodology

Pascal's Triangle
selection sort
merge sort
predicates
subsequence
empty set

statistical methodology   subset

simulations   mutually recursive

recursion   prefix

combinatorial coefficient   infix

■■■■■■
EXERCISES

1. For each of the problem-solving strategies listed at the beginning of this section, find a problem that is best solved using the particular strategy.

*2. Evaluate each of the following:
   a. Factorial(8)
   b. Factorial(0)
   c. C(5, 3)
   d. C(1000, 0)

*3. Write the eleventh row of Pascal's Triangle.

4. Hand-trace the execution of the algorithm for Reversed on the input string "fun".

5. Hand-trace the execution of the algorithm for Merge Sort on the array 3, 5, 7, 2, 1, 8, 6, 5.

*6. Which of the following are subsequences of the string "abcdefg"?
   a. abcdefg
   b. gfedcba
   c. a
   d. ⟨empty⟩
   e. aa
   f. beg
   g. ach

*7. Which of the following are substrings of the string "abcdefg"?
   a. abcdefg
   b. a
   c. ⟨empty⟩
   d. aa
   e. beg
   f. def

*8. a. For the string InString, write an expression for Right(InString, 3) in terms of the built-in function Copy.
   b. Write an expression for Right(InString, N).

9. a. For the string InString, write an expression for Left(InString, 3) in terms of the built-in function Copy.
   b. Write an expression for Left(InString, N).

10. Write all strings of length 2 using the three-letter alphabet {a, b, c}.

11. Write all of the divisors of 72.

12. Use the algorithm for counting divisors to calculate the number of divisors of 72.

13. Write all of the ways to represent the number 7 as a sum of positive integers.

14. Hand-trace the function Addends(7).

*15. There are 12 chessboards of size 5 by 5 that have four nontaking queens in columns 1 to 4. Write the 12 boards and use them to find the 10 boards with five nontaking queens.

16. Write all of the subsets of {a, b, c, d}.

17. Hand-trace the function NSubs(3).

*18. Translate the following infix expressions into prefix form:
   a. 4 + 5 + 6
   b. 4 * 3 + 2
   c. (3 + 3) * (2 + 1)
   d. 1 + 2 * 3 + 4
   e. 1 + ((2 + 3) + 4)

*19. Evaluate the following prefix expressions:
   a. ++123
   b. +*123
   c. *+123
   d. **123
   e. +1*23
   f. *1+23
   g. +*1+2*3+456

20. Hand-trace the Eval-Apply-Split algorithms on the expressions +1*23 and +*1+2*3+456.

21. Enhance the set of valid prefix expressions by including the *unary* operator $, which means to square the biggest prefix subexpression that lies to the right. Some examples:

$+23 is equal to 25

+$23 is equal to 7

+2$3 is equal to 11

*2$+12 is equal to 18

22. Write a recursive algorithm to count the number of ways to divide a string of length N into pieces. For example, the divisions for the string "aaa" are

aaa

a aa

a a a

aa a

23. Write a recursive algorithm to generate r-digit binary sequences (strings of 0's and 1's) with no adjacent 0's. For example, the sequences for r = 4 are

1111

1110

1101

1011

0111

1010

0101

0110

24. Think of ways to represent some of the data objects that we have discussed in this section:
   a. Sets of letters a, b, c, . . .
   b. Collections of sets of letters a, b, c, . . .
   c. Prefix expressions
   d. N-by-N Chessboards
   e. N-by-N Chessboards containing at most one queen per column
   f. Collections of N-by-N chessboards

25. Another approach to the N queens problem is to use the technique of *backtracking*. In this technique, the nature of the recursion is slightly different from that given for the N queens problem in the section. The approach there was call yourself recursively to do almost all the work, then add on the last little bit. In the backtracking method, the approach is do the first little bit of the work, then call yourself to do the rest.

   At the first level, the problem can be stated as follows: Given an empty chessboard, place a queen in the first column; call yourself recursively to place the queens in columns 2 through N. When the recursive call is finished, remove the queen you placed, try to place a queen in another position in the first column, and repeat the whole process. (The term *backtracking* comes from this process of removing your previous attempt and generating another attempt.)

   At the second level of recursion, the problem will be similar. Given a chessboard with a queen in the first column, place a queen in the second column; call yourself recursively to place the queens in columns 3 through N. When the recursive call is finished, remove the queen you placed, try to place a queen in another position in the second column, and repeat the whole process.

   At each level, we begin with a partially filled chessboard and try to successfully add a queen in the next column. If we can add a queen in our column, we call ourselves recursively to finish the board.

   As always, we need a "bottom level" for the recursion. In this approach, it occurs when we have filled all the columns of the chessboard. If the column we are supposed to fill is greater than the maximum allowed, then the chessboard is added to our list of solutions.

   a. Hand-trace the method for a 3-by-3 chessboard (there are no solutions, but tracing the method will help you see why it is called backtracking). Within each column, try to place the queen in the first row, then the second, and so on.
   b. Hand-trace the method for a 4-by-4 chessboard.
   *c. Write the method in a slightly more formal algorithmic form.

26. There are three basic ingredients to a backtracking algorithm:

   • a way to order the possible actions at each stage, so you do not keep trying the same one; in the queens problem, we can attempt the rows from top to bottom for each column

   • a way to record the actions taken, and to "back up" the action after the recursive call returns; in doing the queens problem by hand, we can use marks on a paper, or place queens on a chessboard

   • a way to know when a successful solution is reached; in the queens problem, this was the condition "present column > maximum number"

Another classic group of problems amenable to solution by backtracking involves graph traversal. For example, suppose you want to list all the paths from node 1 to node 5 in the diagram below, where the arrows indicate one-way streets. You do not want to revisit any node on the way. (One possible path is 1 → 4 → 5.)

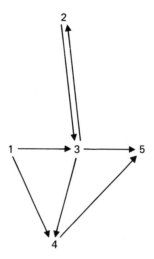

a. Describe ways to handle the three basic ingredients mentioned above for a backtracking solution.
b. Carry out a backtracking solution by hand.
c. Repeat part (b) for this graph. You want to get from node 1 to node 7.

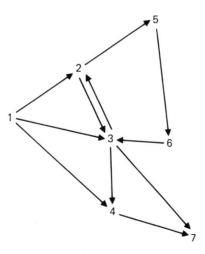

d. Describe algorithmically a general solution to the problem of traversing from node I to node J in a graph using backtracking.

10-2
□□□□□□
**RECURSIVE
PROGRAM-
MING**

We move in this section from the theory of recursive program design to the practice of using recursion in our programs. We will find that it takes more than algorithms for effective recursive programming; we will have concerns about data types and scope of variables and we will discuss some data representation ideas. We will present Pascal code for several examples discussed in the previous section. Only the most important ideas in the code will be explicitly discussed; in many cases, the code will stand on its own.

□
FACTORIAL

We expect the code for the Factorial function to be short and simple. The code that we present in Figure 10-1 is quite simple, but you may be surprised at the type that we have chosen for the Factorial function. The reason for the choice of "real" as the type is that even 8 factorial is larger than the maximum allowable integer in many versions of Pascal (Maxint). By using the real type, we extend our range of factorials to 16 (on the author's computer) before we begin to experience round-off error. We will have a suggestion in the exercises of a way to extend the range further.

```
function Factorial(N : integer) : real;
{
 Written by:  XXXXXXXXX  XX/XX/XX
    Purpose:  To calculate N factorial.
 Parameters:  N - input, number for computation.
}
begin {Factorial}
   if  N = 0  then
      Factorial := 1
   else
      Factorial := N * Factorial(N-1)
end; {Factorial}
```

Figure 10-1 Recursive Factorial Function

□
**COMBINA-
TORIAL
COEFFICIENTS**

The combinatorial coefficients can be calculated by the integer function Combinatorial, as is shown in Figure 10-2. Note that here, as in the case of the Factorial function, the use of var parameters is not only inappropriate, but also illegal because we use expressions in the recursive calls. We note also that it is legal to have both recursive calls to Combinatorial appear in the same expression.

```
function Combinatorial(N, M : integer) : integer;
{
 Written by:  XXXXXXXXX  XX/XX/XX
    Purpose:  To calculate a combinatorial coefficient, recursively.
 Parameters:  N - input, row of Pascal's triangle;
              M - input, term in the row.
}
begin {Combinatorial}
```

Figure 10-2 Recursive Combinatorial Function (Continued)

```
{*** See if we're done.}

   if  (N = M) or (M = 0) then
      Combinatorial := 1

{*** If not done, get lower-level values.}

   else
      Combinatorial := Combinatorial(N-1, M) + Combinatorial(N-1, M-1)
   end; {Combinatorial}
```

Figure 10-2   Recursive Combinatorial Function

REVERSING A STRING

□   The function Reversed, shown in Figure 10-3, depends on a global declaration of the type String255 (declared to be = string[255]). Reversed also uses the function Right, which extracts a **cofinal** substring of a string. That is, Right will return a substring that starts in some specified position and extends all the way to the end of the string.

```
function Right(InString: String255; Position : integer) : String255;
{
         Written by:   XXXXXXXX  XX/XX/XX
            Purpose:   To return a cofinal substring of InString.
         Parameters:   InString - input, string for substring extraction;
                       Position - input, position to begin substring.
      Functions used:  Copy - (built-in) to extract a substring;
                       Length - (built-in) to find the length of a string.
}
begin {Right}
   if  Position < 1  then
     Right := InString
   else if  Position > Length(InString)  then
     Right := ''
   else
     Right := Copy(InString, Position, Length(InString)-Position+1)
end; {Right}

function Reversed(InString : String255) : String255;
{
         Written by:   XXXXXXXX  XX/XX/XX
            Purpose:   To reverse a string.
         Parameters:   InString - input, string to reverse.
      Functions used:  Right - to extract a cofinal substring.
}
const
   Null = '';                                      { Empty string }

begin {Reversed}
   if  InString = Null  then
     Reversed := InString
   else
     Reversed := Reversed(Right(InString, 2)) + InString[1]
end; {Reversed}
```

Figure 10-3   Recursive String Reversing Function

□ In this subsection, we present two versions of the procedure Sort. For both, we rely on the following set of global declarations:

```
const
   MaxSize = 1000;                              { Highest subscript }

type
   BaseType = integer;
   ArrayType = array [1 .. MaxSize] of BaseType;
```

By using this set of declarations, we can utilize the Sort procedures to sort different types of data by adjusting the definition of BaseType. We can also modify the maximum size of the array to be sorted by adjusting the value of the constant MaxSize.

We show the recursive selection sort in Figure 10-4. Note that the array X is a var parameter and that the procedure would not work otherwise. Another feature worthy of note is that the procedure as presented is not **stable**. A sorting technique is stable if two elements of equal value maintain their order relative to each other. For example, if we were to use our sort of Figure 10-4 on a hypothetical array consisting of a blue 2 followed by a red 2, then the resulting array would consist of the red 2 followed by the blue 2. To remedy this situation, we could change the comparision X[I] > Large to X[I] >= Large. Alternatively, we could change the for loop to the form:

```
            for I := Last downto First do
```

For the second alternative, we would also want to initialize Large to X[Last] and Place to Last.

```
procedure Sort(var X : IntArray; First, Last : integer);
{
 Written by:   XXXXXXXX   XX/XX/XX
    Purpose:   To sort an array with a recursive selection sort.
 Parameters:   X - update, array to sort;
               First - input, left limit of portion of array;
               Last - input, right limit of portion of array.
}
var
   I        : integer;              { Loop index }
   Large    : ArrayType;           { Largest element }
   Place    : integer;             { Place largest element found }

begin {Sort}

{*** Check to see if done.}

   if  First < Last  then
      begin

{*** Find largest element.}

         Large := X[First];
         Place := First;
```

Figure 10-4 Recursive Selection Sort (Continued)

```
      for I := First+1 to Last do
         if  X[I] > Large then
            begin
              Large := X[I];
              Place := I
            end; {if}

{*** Exchange largest value with X[Last].}

         X[Place] := X[Last];
         X[Last] := Large;

{*** Call upon Sort to do the rest.}

         Sort(X, First, Last-1)
      end {if}
   end; {Sort}
```

Figure 10-4 Recursive Selection Sort

We show the recursive merge sort in Figure 10-5. Note that the merge sort procedure is stable because our merge algorithm is stable.

```
procedure Sort(var X : IntArray; First, Last : integer);
{
       Written by:  XXXXXXXX   XX/XX/XX
          Purpose:  To sort an array with a recursive merge sort.
       Parameters:  X - update, array to sort;
                    First - input, left limit on portion;
                    Last - input, right limit on portion.
}
var
   I        : integer;            { Loop index }
   Large    : ArrayType;          { Largest element }
   Place    : integer;            { Place largest element found }
   Middle   : integer;            { Midpoint of First and Last }
   LPlace   : integer;            { Place on left half of array }
   RPlace   : integer;            { Place on right half of array }
   XPlace   : integer;            { Place in X array }
   Start    : integer;            { Marks the rest of the . . . }
   Finish   : integer;            { . . . array X to copy to Temp }

begin {Sort}

{*** Check to see if done.}

   if  First < Last  then
     begin

{*** Sort the bottom and top halves, if necessary.}

        Middle := (First + Last) div 2;
        if First < Middle then
          Sort(X, First, Middle);
```

Figure 10-5 Recursive Merge Sort (Continued)

```
            if Middle+1 < Last then
                Sort(X, Middle+1, Last);

{*** Merge the two halves.}

            LPlace := First;
            RPlace := Middle + 1;
            I := First;

            while  (LPlace <= Middle) and (RPlace <= Last)   do
              begin
                if  X[LPlace] <= X[RPlace]   then
                  begin
                     Temp[I] := X[LPlace];
                     LPlace := LPlace + 1
                  end
                else
                  begin
                     Temp[I] := X[RPlace];
                     RPlace := RPlace + 1
                  end; {if}
                I := I + 1
              end; {while}

            if  LPlace > Middle   then
              begin
                Start := RPlace;
                Finish := Last
              end
            else
              begin
                Start := LPlace;
                Finish := Middle
              end; {if}

            for XPlace := Start to Finish do
              begin
                Temp[I] := X[XPlace];
                I := I + 1
              end; {for}

            for I := First to Last do
              X[I] := Temp[I]

       end {if}
     end; {Sort}
```

Figure 10-5 Recursive Merge Sort

SUBSEQUENCES AND SUBSTRINGS OF A STRING

□ Recall that a subsequence of a string consists of zero or more characters of the string in the same order as they appear in the string. It is not required that the characters be consecutive in the string. A substring of a string is a subsequence consisting of consecutive characters of the string. In Figure 10-6, we present code for the Boolean function, SubSeq, which determines if one string is a subsequence of another. Note that the function requires the declaration of the global type, String255.

```
function SubSeq(InSeq, InString : String255) : Boolean;
{
        Written by:   XXXXXXXX  XX/XX/XX
           Purpose:   To determine if InSeq is a subsequence of InString.
        Parameters:   InSeq - input, candidate for subsequence;
                      InString - input, string to check for subsequence.
    Functions used:   Right - to extract a cofinal substring;
                      Pos - (built-in) to find a substring of a string.
}
const
  Null = '';                                  { Empty string }

var
  Place   : integer;                          { Position of character }

begin {SubSeq}

{*** First, take care of empty sequence or string.}

  if  InSeq = Null  then
    SubSeq := true
  else if  InString = Null  then
    SubSeq := false

{*** Take care of nonempty sequence and string.}

  else
    begin
      Place := Pos(InSeq[1], InString);
      if  Place = 0  then
        SubSeq := false
      else
        SubSeq :=  SubSeq(Right(InSeq, 2), Right(InString, Place+1))
    end {if}
end; {SubSeq}
```

Figure 10-6   Subsequence of a String

> In Figure 10-7, we present code for the Boolean function SubString, which
> determines if one string is a substring of another. Again, note that the function
> requires the declaration of the global type String255. In addition to the function
> Right discussed above, we also use the function Left for extracting a **coinitial**
> substring of a string. That is, Left returns a substring that starts at the beginning of
> the string and extends to some specified position.

```
function Left(InString: String255; Position : integer) : String255;
{
        Written by:   XXXXXXXX  XX/XX/XX
           Purpose:   To return a coinitial substring of InString.
        Parameters:   InString - input, string for extraction of substring;
                      Position - input, last position for substring.
    Functions used:   Copy - (built-in) to extract a substring;
                      Length - (built-in) to find the length of a string.
}
```

Figure 10-7   Substring of a String (Continued)

```
begin {Left}
  if  Position < 1  then
    Left := ''
  else if  Position > Length(InString)  then
    Left := InString
  else
    Left := Copy(InString, 1, Position)
end; {Left}

function SubString(InSub, InString : String255) : Boolean;
{
        Written by:  XXXXXXXX  XX/XX/XX
           Purpose:  To determine if SubString is a substring of InString.
        Parameters:  InSub - input, candidate for substring;
                     InString - input, string to check for substring.
    Functions used:  Length - (built-in) to find length of a string;
                     Left - to extract a coinitial substring of a string;
                     Right - to extract a cofinal substring of a sting.

}
const
  Null = '';                                 { Empty string }

begin {SubString}
  if  InSub = Null  then
    SubString := true
  else if  Length(InString)<Length(InSub)  then
    SubString := false
  else if  InSub = Left(InString, Length(InSub))  then
    SubString := true
  else
    SubString := SubString(InSub, Right(InString, 2))
end; {SubString}
```

Figure 10-7 Substring of a String

□

STRINGS OF LENGTH N USING M LETTERS

We continue to discuss programs dealing with strings. We show how to count the number of possible three letter words in the English Language (including lots of non-words). We also illustrate how you might print all of those words, but we don't suggest that you try it. In Figure 10-8, we show the code for the function StringsNM(P, Q), which counts the number of strings of length P using Q letters. Because these values tend to be large, we use the type real for the function.

In the spirit of considering some interesting programming techniques, suppose that we don't just want to count all of the strings, but that we want to print a list of the strings. One way to accomplish this is to use a technique of building the recursive answers from the top to the bottom, rather than from the bottom to the top (as we do in building factorials, for example). For simplicity, suppose that we restrict the alphabet of letters to a, b, and c. We design a procedure PrintStrings to print all of the strings of length N using the letters a, b, and c by specifying the parameters:

StringSoFar—one of the strings still being formed

MoreToAdd—number of letters to be added to StringSoFar

```
function StringsNM(N, M : integer) : real;
{
        Written by:  XXXXXXXX  XX/XX/XX
           Purpose:  To count the number of strings of length N
                     using M letters.
        Parameters:  N - input, length of strings;
                     M - input, number of letters in alphabet.
}
begin {StringsNM}
  if  N = 1 then
    StringsNM := M
  else
    StringsNM := M * StringsNM(N-1,M)
end; {StringsNM}
```

Figure 10-8   Number of Strings of a Given Length

We will invoke the procedure to print all of the strings of length N by the call

PrintStrings('', N)

The algorithm is as follows:

if MoreToAdd is equal to 0, then print StringSoFar
else:
> PrintStrings('a'+StringSoFar, MoreToAdd-1)
> PrintStrings('b'+StringSoFar, MoreToAdd-1)
> PrintStrings('c'+StringSoFar, MoreToAdd-1)

We can see that the algorithm causes the strings to grow as they are passed downward by the recursive calls until there are no more characters to add to the string.

We show the code for the PrintStrings procedure in Figure 10-9.

```
procedure PrintStrings(StringSoFar : String255; MoreToAdd : integer);
{
        Written by:  XXXXXXXX  XX/XX/XX
           Purpose:  To print strings from the alphabet: a, b, c.
        Parameters:  StringSoFar - input, string building up;
                     MoreToAdd - input, number of characters left to add.
}
begin {PrintStrings}
  if  MoreToAdd = 0  then
    Writeln(StringSoFar)
  else
    begin
      PrintStrings('a'+StringSoFar, MoreToAdd-1);
      PrintStrings('b'+StringSoFar, MoreToAdd-1);
      PrintStrings('c'+StringSoFar, MoreToAdd-1)
    end {if}
end; {PrintStrings}
```

Figure 10-9   Printing Substrings (Continued)

<dialogue that supplies the value of MoreToAdd = 2>

```
aa
ba
ca
ab
bb
cb
ac
bc
cc
```

Figure 10-9 Printing Substrings

□ In order to implement the algorithm presented in the previous section, we need some help from a few small subprograms.

NUMBER OF DIVISORS OF AN INTEGER

First, we need an integer function Power for raising one integer to the power of the other. This function has been discussed earlier in the book and will simply be shown as part of Figure 10-10. For example, Power(2, 3) is 8.

Second, we need an integer function SmallDivisor that finds the smallest divisor (greater than 1) of a number. This function was discussed in Chapter 4 and is also located within Figure 10-10. For example, SmallDivisor(15) is 3.

Third, we use the integer function Degree that tells us the highest power of a factor that divides into a number. This function can also be found within Figure 10-10. For example, Degree(2, 24) is 3.

Finally, we also present our recursive function in Figure 10-10.

```
function Power(N, K : integer) : integer;
begin
  if  K = 0  then
    Power := 1
  else
    Power := Round(Exp(K * Ln(N)))
end; {Power}

function SmallDivisor(N : integer) : integer;
{
      Written by:   XXXXXXXX   XX/XX/XX
         Purpose:   To find the smallest divisor of N > 1.
      Parameters:   N - input, number for smallest divisor.
}
var
  Test     : integer;              { Used to check for divisor }

begin {SmallDivisor}
  Test := 2;

  while  (N mod Test) <> 0  do   Test := Test + 1;

  SmallDivisor := Test
end; {SmallDivisor}
```

Figure 10-10 Number of Divisors of an Integer (Continued)

```
function Degree(Factor, Number: integer) : integer;
{
        Written by:   XXXXXXXX   XX/XX/XX
          Purpose:    To find the highest power of Factor that divides Number.
        Parameters:   Factor - input;
                      Number - input.
}
var
  Total : integer;

begin {Degree}
  Total := 0;

  while  Number mod Factor = 0  do
    begin
      Total := Total + 1;
      Number := Number div Factor
    end; {while}

    Degree := Total
end; {Degree}

function NumDivisors(N : integer) : integer;
{
        Written by:   XXXXXXXX   XX/XX/XX
          Purpose:    To count the number of divisors of N, recursively.
        Parameters:   N - input.
   Functions used:   SmallDivisor - to get the smallest divisor of N;
                     Degree - to get the highest power of a factor;
                     Power - to raise an integer to an integer power.
}
var
  Factor       : integer;          { Smallest divisor of N }
  Multiplicity : integer;

begin {Numdivisors}

{*** See if we're done.}

  if  N = 1  then
    NumDivisors := 1
  else
    begin

{*** Get smallest divisor of N.}

    Factor := SmallDivisor(N);

{*** Use it for recursive call.}

    Multiplicity := Degree(Factor, N);
    NumDivisors := (Multiplicity+1) *
                   NumDivisors(N div Power(Factor, Multiplicity))
    end {if}
end; {Numdivisors}
```

Figure 10-10 Number of Divisors of an Integer

□ In this example, shown coded in Figure 10-11, we show the use of an auxiliary
function to provide a more straightforward interface to the calling program. We
are ultimately interested in the number of ways that we can sum to a specified
number. So at the top level, we want to simply call the integer function Addends,
perhaps in a write statement such as

**OBTAINING
A NUMBER
AS A SUM**

```
Writeln('The number of ways to add to ', N, ' is :',Addends(N))
```

Once inside of Addends, we set up the loop of calls to the Auxiliary function
AddendsAux.

```
function AddendsAux(N, M : integer) : integer;
{
        Written by:   XXXXXXXX  XX/XX/XX
          Purpose:    To provide the recursive calculation for Addends:
                      number of ways to add to N using M as the lowest factor.
        Parameters:   N - input, number to sum to;
                      M - input, lowest factor in sum.
}
var
  I     : integer;
  Total : integer;

begin {AddendsAux}
  if  M = N then
    AddendsAux := 1
  else if  M > N div 2 then
    AddendsAux := 0
  else
    begin
      Total := 0;

      for I := M to N-M do
        Total := Total + AddendsAux(N-M, I);

      AddendsAux := Total
    end {if}
end; {AddendsAux}

function Addends(N : integer) : integer;
{
        Written by:   XXXXXXXX  XX/XX/XX
          Purpose:    To calculate the number of ways to sum to N.
        Parameters:   N - input, number to sum to.
    Functions used:   AddendsAux - to find sums with lowest factor.
}
var
  I     : integer;
  Total : integer;

begin {Addends}
  Total := 0;
```

Figure 10-11 Obtaining Sums to a Number (Continued)

```
    for I := 1 to N  do
       Total := Total + AddendsAux(N, I);

    Addends := Total
  end; {Addends}
```

Figure 10-11   Obtaining Sums to a Number

THE N QUEENS
□   In order to transform the algorithm of the previous subsection in the program shown as Figure 10-12, we have several issues to address:

> Data representation for the chessboard containing queens
>
> Data representation for the collection of chessboards containing queens
>
> Design of the Boolean function OK to check a chessboard
>
> Design of a subprogram to print the collection of boards that have the N queens placed

```
program NQueens(Input, Output);
{
        Written by:   XXXXXXXXX  XX/XX/XX
            Purpose:  To generate all positions of N nontaking queens.
    Procedures used:  PrintBoards - to print chessboards;
                      SetQueens - to find the queen placements.
}
const
  MaxRows = 4;                       { Maximum number of rows }
  Most = 1000;                       { Most boards ever needed }

type
  String255 = string[255];
  ChessBoard = string[MaxRows];      { One chessboard }
  Boards = record
              Number   : integer;    { Number of boards on hand }
              OneBoard : array [1 .. Most] of ChessBoard
                                     { Represent one board each }
           end;

var
  Solution    : Boards;              { Final result }

function RowPosition(Board : ChessBoard; Column : integer) : integer;
{
        Written by:   XXXXXXXXX  XX/XX/XX
            Purpose:  Given a chessboard and a column number, to tell
                      what row the queen in that column is in
         Parameters:  Board - input, the chessboard
                      Column - input, the column to examine
     Functions used:  Ord - (built-in) position of character
}
begin  {RowPosition}
  RowPosition := Ord(Board[Column]) - Ord('0')
end;  {RowPosition}
```

Figure 10-12   N Non-Taking Queens (Continued)

```
function Digit(N : integer) : char;
{
        Written by:    XXXXXXXXX  XX/XX/XX
           Purpose:    To convert a numeric digit to its character form
        Parameters:    N - input, the number to convert (range 0 to 9)
    Functions used:    Chr - (built-in) ASCII-to-character converter
                       Ord - (built-in) character-to-ASCII converter
}
begin  {Digit}
  Digit := Chr(N+Ord('0'))
end;  {Digit}

procedure PlaceQueen(var Board : ChessBoard; Row, Column : integer);
{
        Written by:    XXXXXXXXX  XX/XX/XX
           Purpose:    To place a queen into the board data structure
        Parameters:    Board - update, the chessboard
                       Row, Column - input, where to place the queen
    Functions used:    Digit - to convert 0-9 to '0'-'9'
}
begin  {PlaceQueen}
  Board[Column] := Digit(Row)
end;  {PlaceQueen}

function InUse(Row : integer; Board : ChessBoard) : boolean;
{
        Written by:    XXXXXXXXX  XX/XX/XX
           Purpose:    To see if a row in a board is occupied by a queen
        Parameters:    Row - input, the row to check
                       Board - input, the board to check in
    Functions used:    Pos - (built-in) to search for a substring
                       Digit - to convert 0-9 to '0'-'9'
}
begin  {InUse}
  InUse := Pos(Digit(Row), Board) <> 0
end;  {InUse}

function OK(Candidate : ChessBoard; NewColumn : integer) : Boolean;
{
        Written by:    XXXXXXXXX  XX/XX/XX
           Purpose:    To test one chessboard with a queen in NewColumn to
                       see if it is OK.
        Parameters:    Candidate - input, a chessboard to check;
                       NewColumn - input, where a new queen is located.
    Functions used:    RowPosition - to find the row placement for a column
                       Abs - (built-in) absolute value.
}
var
  I          : integer;             { Loop index }
  NewRow     : integer;             { Row of new queen }
  CheckRow   : integer;             { Row of queen to check }
```

Figure 10-12   N Non-Taking Queens (Continued)

```
begin {OK}
  OK := true;
  NewRow := RowPosition(Candidate, NewColumn);

  for I := 1 to NewColumn-1 do
    begin
      CheckRow := RowPosition(Candidate, I);
      if Abs(NewRow - CheckRow) = NewColumn-I then
        OK := false
    end {for}

  end; {for}

procedure PrintBoards(InBoards : Boards);
{
      Written by:  XXXXXXXX  XX/XX/XX
         Purpose:  To print all of the chessboards.
      Parameters:  InBoards - input, collection of boards to print.
}
var
  I    : integer;                         { Loop index }
begin {PrintBoards}
  with InBoards do
    begin
      for  I := 1 to Number do
        Writeln(OneBoard[I])
    end {with}
end; {PrintBoards}

procedure SetQueens(Column : integer; var AllWays : Boards);
{
      Written by:  XXXXXXXX  XX/XX/XX
         Purpose:  To return all chessboards which have Column
                   nontaking queens located within columns
                   1 to Column.
      Parameters:  Column - input, last column for queens;
                   Allways - output, all chessboards with the queens.
  Functions used:  InUse - to see if a row is in use
                   OK - to check a chessboard.
  Procedures used: PlaceQueen to place one queen
}
const
  EmptyBoard = '000000000';                { string for empty chessboard }

var
  WorkBoard  : string[MaxRows];            { Working chessboard }
  Row        : integer;                    { Loop index }
  I          : integer;                    { Loop index }
  Count      : integer;                    { Count of new boards }

begin {SetQueens}
  with  AllWays  do
    begin
      if  Column = 1  then                 { We have 1 queen to place }
```

Figure 10-12   N Non-Taking Queens (Continued)

```
            begin

              for Row := 1 to MaxRows do
                begin
                  OneBoard[Row] := EmptyBoard;
                  PlaceQueen(OneBoard[Row], Row, 1)
                end;  {for}

              Number := MaxRows
            end
          else                           { We have more than 1 to place }
            begin
              Count := 0;                { Number of boards found }
              SetQueens(Column - 1, AllWays); { Set one fewer queens }

              for  I := 1 to Number do   { Use each board returned }
                begin

                  for  Row := 1 to MaxRows do
                    begin
                      if not InUse(Row, OneBoard[I]) then
                        begin
                          WorkBoard := OneBoard[I];
                          PlaceQueen(WorkBoard, Row, Column);
                          if  OK(WorkBoard, Column)  then
                            begin
                              Count := Count + 1;
                              OneBoard[Number+Count] := WorkBoard
                            end {if}
                        end {if}
                    end {for Row}

                end; {for I}

              for  I := 1 to Count do        { Rebuild the collection }
                OneBoard[I] := OneBoard[Number+I];

              Number := Count
            end {if}
      end {with}
end; {SetQueens}


begin {NQueens}
  SetQueens(MaxRows, Solution);
  PrintBoards(Solution);
  Writeln('The number of solutions is: ', Solution.Number);

{*** Print message and terminate.}

  Writeln;
  Writeln('NQueens program is terminating.')
end.
```

Figure 10-12   N Non-Taking Queens (Continued)

```
2413
3142
The number of solutions is: 2

NQueens program is terminating.
```

Figure 10-12 N Non-Taking Queens

We choose to make the simplifying assumption that we are not interested in more than a 9-by-9 chessboard. We will indicate how to generalize in the exercises. Our data structure for representing a chessboard with queens placed on it is to use a string of length N, consisting of digits from 0 to N, inclusive. The digits represent the row number that a queen resides in for the column represented by the character position. For example, the string

0246003

represents a 7-by-7 chessboard with no queen in column 1, a queen in row 2 of column 2, a queen in row 4 of column 3, a queen in row 6 of column 4, no queens in columns 5 and 6, and a queen in row 3 of column 7. In the previous section, we would have represented the same board with the notation:

0	0	0	0	0	0	0
0	1	0	0	0	0	0
0	0	0	0	0	0	1
0	0	1	0	0	0	0
0	0	0	0	0	0	0
0	0	0	1	0	0	0
0	0	0	0	0	0	0

If you look carefully at the second representation of the board, you will see that two queens can take each other: the queens in column 4, row 6 and column 7, row 3. How do the numbers for the rows and columns of the two queens show that they lie on the same diagonal? Two queens lie on the same diagonal if their vertical separation is equal to their horizontal separation. We can measure the vertical separation by the absolute value of the difference in rows (3 in our example). We can measure the horizontal separation by the absolute value of the difference in columns (also 3 in our example). This idea is the basis for our OK function.

We choose to represent a collection of chessboards by use of the record definition in the following declarations:

```
const
  MaxRows = 4;                           { Maximum number of rows }
  Most = 1000;                           { Most boards ever needed }

type
  String255 = string[255];
  ChessBoard = string[MaxRows];          { One chessboard }
```

```
Boards = record
            Number   : integer;          { Number of boards on hand }
            OneBoard : array [1 .. Most] of ChessBoard
                                          { Represent one board each }
        end;
```

Note that the constant MaxRows is the number N of the N Queens problem. We use the constant Most to allocate the maximum number of chessboards that can ever be in the collection at any stage throughout the process. The value of this kind of number is often a guess.

Note that in the recursive procedure SetQueens, the collection of boards is a var parameter. This means that all levels of the recursion have access to the same information. In this case, as in the case of sorting an array, we want all levels of recursion to work with the same information; but, in general, we must be careful about using var parameters or referring to global variables from within a recursive subprogram.

We use the procedure PrintBoards to print all the chessboards that are in the final solution. The printing is accomplished by use of a count-controlled loop because the number of boards in the collection is available in the data structure.

There are a number of procedures and functions whose job is to interface with the data structure. RowPosition shows the row of a queen in a given column. InUse checks if a row is in use. OK checks a board to see if it is legal. PlaceQueen puts a queen on the board.

Because we use strings for the data structure representing the chessboards, these utilities make heavy use of the Chr and Ord functions to translate digits from numeric to character and vice versa. If we changed the data structure, these utilities would have to change drastically, but the changes to the rest of the program would be relatively minor.

□
**THE POWER
SET OF A SET**

The data structures involved in programming the algorithm as presented in the previous section are beyond the scope of this book. However, in this subsection, we will present a procedure that performs a similar activity. The procedure, WriteSeq, prints all subsequences of a string and is shown in Figure 10-13. If we begin with the string 'abc', then the list of subsequences of the string is

(empty)
c
b
bc
a
ac
ab
abc

Compare this list of subsequences to the list of subsets of the set {a, b, c} that we discussed in the previous section. We use the basic idea of the algorithm for power sets, but we use the top-down method that we used earlier in this section for printing strings. The procedure WriteSeq has two parameters:

Prefix: a subsequence in formation

Rest: the remainder of the original string that can be used for further building of subsequences

If our original string is called InString, then at top level, we invoke WriteSeq with the command

$$\text{WriteSeq('', InString)}$$

to indicate that no work on subsequences has been done yet, and all of the original string is left to process. At bottom level, Rest is the null string; at this point, the subsequence that is contained in Prefix can be printed. To see how WriteSeq works ''in the middle,'' suppose that it has been invoked by

$$\text{WriteSeq('ac', 'efg')}$$

somewhere in the process of trying to print all the subsequences of the string 'abcdefg'. The recursion consists of making the two recursive calls:

```
WriteSeq('ac', 'fg')
WriteSeq('ace','fg')
```

The first call is for subsequences that do not involve 'e', and the second call is for subsequences that do involve 'e'. In both cases, the length of the parameter Rest is reduced by 1.

```
procedure WriteSeq(Prefix , Rest : String255);
{
        Written by:   XXXXXXXX   XX/XX/XX
          Purpose:    To print subsequences of a string.
        Parameters:   Prefix - input, building string;
                      Rest - input, rest of string.
    Functions used:   Right - extracts cofinal substring.
}
const
  Null = '';                       { Empty string }

begin {WriteSeq}
  if  Rest = Null   then
    if  Prefix = Null   then
      Writeln('(empty)')
    else
      Writeln(Prefix)
  else
    begin
      WriteSeq(Prefix, Right(Rest, 2));
      WriteSeq(Prefix + Rest[1], Right(Rest,2))
    end {if}
end; {WriteSeq}
```

Figure 10-13 All Subsequences of a String

□ The main issue of this subsection is how to reconcile the two conflicting ideas of defining procedures before using them and mutual recursion. From what we have discussed so far in the book, it seems as though we are stuck with one of the two procedures calling the other before the other has been defined, and we know how the compiler deals with that situation. The solution to the quandary is provided by a mode of declaration known as **forward reference**. The idea is that we let the compiler know about the *heading* of the subprogram in advance, and then later, we present the *body* of the subprogram. For our situation, the order in which we will present Apply and Eval to the compiler is

Declare Apply as a forward reference.
Define Eval (which uses Apply).
Define the body of Apply (which uses Eval).

This ingenious solution provided by Pascal allows us to achieve mutual recursion. A complete program for the evaluation of prefix expressions is shown in Figure 10-14. We note two points about the syntax of the forward reference:

1. After the normal heading line of any subprogram that is declared as a forward reference, use the suffix ''; forward''.

2. When the body of the subprogram is defined, we must use an abbreviated form of the heading; we cannot list parameters and we cannot specify the type of a function.

The only other issue to be discussed is the use of the Code function to help the procedure Split to divide an expression into two pieces. The Code function provides the means for generalizing the program along the lines explored in the exercises.

```
program PreFix(Input, Output);
{
      Written by:   XXXXXXXX  XX/XX/XX
         Purpose:   To evaluate prefix expressions.
   Functions used:  Eval - evaluates the expression.
}
const
  Null = '';                          { Empty string }
  EndOfData = '';                     { Terminating value }

type
  String255 = string[255];

var
  Expression    : String255;         { Input expression }

function Code(InChar : char) : integer;
```

Figure 10-14 Mutual Recursion and Forward Reference (Continued)

```
          Written by:   XXXXXXXX  XX/XX/XX
             Purpose:   To return a code depending on the character.
          Parameters:  InChar - input, character to encode.
}
begin {Code}
  if  InChar in ['0' .. '9']  then
    Code := 1
  else if  InChar in ['+', '*'] then
    Code := -1
  else
    Code := 0
end; {Code}

procedure Split(InString : String255; var Left, Right : String255);
{
          Written by:   XXXXXXXX  XX/XX/XX
             Purpose:   To split a string into two parts.
          Parameters:  InString - input, string to split up;
                       Left - output, left part of split string;
                       Right - output, right part of split string.
     Functions used:   Code - to get code for character;
                       Length - (built-in) gets length of string;
                       Copy - (built-in) extracts substring.
}
const
  Null = '';                           { Empty string }

var
  Count   : integer;                   { For operators and numbers }
  I       : integer;                   { Loop index }

begin {Split}
  Count := 0;
  I := 0;

  while  (Count <> 1) and (I < Length(InString))   do
    begin
      I := I + 1;
      Count := Count + Code(Instring[I])
    end; {while}

  if  Count = 1  then
    begin
      Left := Copy(InString, 1, I);
      Right := Copy(InString, I+1, Length(InString)-I+1)
    end
  else
    begin
      Left := Null;
      Right := Null
    end {if}
end; {Split}
```

Figure 10-14 Mutual Recursion and Forward Reference (Continued)

```
function Apply(Op : char; InString : String255) : integer; forward;

function Eval(InString : String255) : integer;
{
        Written by:  XXXXXXXX  XX/XX/XX
           Purpose:  To evaluate a prefix expression.
        Parameters:  InString - input, expression to evaluate.
    Functions used:  Apply - to apply an operator;
                     Length - (built-in) gets length of string;
                     Ord - (built-in) position of character in set;
                     Copy - (built-in) extracts substring.
}
const
  Null = '';                                  { Empty string }

var
  FirstChar    : char;                        { First character of InString }

begin {Eval}
  if  InString = Null  then
    begin
      Writeln('*** error in expression ');
      Eval := 0
    end
  else
    begin
      FirstChar := InString[1];
      if  FirstChar in ['0' .. '9']  then
        if  Length(InString) = 1  then
          Eval := Ord(FirstChar) - Ord('0')
        else
          begin
            Writeln('*** error in expression');
            Eval := 0
          end
      else
        Eval := Apply(FirstChar, Copy(InString, 2, Length(InString)-1))
    end {if}
end; {Eval}


function Apply;
{
        Written by:  XXXXXXXX  XX/XX/XX
           Purpose:  To apply an operator to two operands.
        Parameters:  Op - input, operator to apply;
                     InString - input, contains operands for operator.
    Procedures used:  Split - to split InString into operands.
    Functions used:  Eval - to evaluate operands.
}
var
  First   : String255;                  { First operand }
  Second  : String255;                  { Second operand }
```

Figure 10-14 Mutual Recursion and Forward Reference (Continued)

```
begin {Apply}
  Split(InString, First, Second);

  case  Op  of
    '+' :  Apply := Eval(First) + Eval(Second);

    '*' :  Apply := Eval(First) * Eval(Second);

    else
      Writeln('*** Invalid operator')
  end {case}
end; {Apply}


begin {PreFix}

{*** Get user input in a loop.}

  repeat
    Write('Enter the expression: ');
    Readln(Expression);
    if  Expression <> EndOfData  then
      Writeln('The answer is: ', Eval(Expression))
  until  Expression = EndOfData;

{*** Print message and terminate.}

  Writeln;
  Writeln('PreFix program is terminating.')
end.
```

Figure 10-14   Mutual Recursion and Forward Reference

□
DPT
1. Recursive algorithms have a good chance of "going off to never-never-land" during the early stages of development and testing. Good design will head off most problems, but to be safe, you should save a version of any recursive program before running any test of it. Also, it is a good idea to set the Turbo Pascal compiler directive {$U+} to allow user interrupts while testing recursive routines.

2. Be careful when using var parameters and global variables from within recursive subprograms. Quite often, you will find that lower levels of the recursion are having undesirable side effects on upper levels. For example, if you change the loop indexes, I, of Addends and AddendsAux of Figure 10-11 to a single global variable, I, you will find that the program still runs, but it provides erroneous information.

□
TESTING
1. We must always test each of the bottom-level cases in a recursive solution. Because these cases form the building blocks for all of the other cases, it is absolutely essential that they be handled correctly.

2. The next level above the bottom level should be tested to be sure that the reduction to smaller cases is functioning correctly.

3. When the reduction to smaller cases is different from the simple moving from N to N − 1, we should practice some **error guessing** tests to see if we can cause the algorithm to skip over the bottom-level cases and plunge into an inescapable abyss.

4. Recursive programs are particularly vulnerable to **stress testing**. It is a good idea to attack a recursive routine with a lot of maximum-size data.

■■■■■■ REVIEW

Terms and concepts	cofinal	forward reference
	stable	error guessing
	coinitial	stress testing

Pascal syntax

Forward reference:

```
header line for subprogram A ; forward;
other declarations
abbreviated header line for subprogram A
body of subprogram A
```

DPT

1. Save work before testing.

2. Be careful of var parameters and global variables.

Testing

1. Test each bottom-level case.

2. Test the next level up from the bottom.

3. Practice error guessing.

4. Perform stress testing.

■■■■■■ EXERCISES

1. Write a Pascal program that discovers the lowest numbered factorial that is calculated incorrectly by the function of Figure 10-1.

2. We can extend the range of the factorial function by defining a data structure for representing large integer values. One possibility is to declare the record structure:

```
const
  MaxSize = 1000;
type
  BigInteger =
    record
      Positive  : Boolean;
      NumDigits : integer;
      Digits    : array [1 .. MaxSize] of integer
    end;
```

The array Digits is intended to contain the decimal digits of a number. For example, the number 1024 would be represented in the data structure as

Positive − true

NumDigits − 4

Digits − . . . , 1, 0, 2, 4

In order to use this new data type to assist in calculating factorials, we need three subprograms:

a. `procedure Init(var BigInt : BigInteger; Value : integer);`

The task for Init is to assign an initial value to a large integer.

b.   `procedure Mult(Int : integer; BigInt : BigInteger;`
                     `var Product : BigInteger);`

The task for Mult is to allow us to multiply an integer by a large integer in order to perform the step:

$$(k \text{ factorial}) = k \text{ times } (k\text{-}1 \text{ factorial})$$

c. `procedure PrintBig(BigInt : BigInteger);`

The task for PrintBig is to display a large integer on the screen.
Use the ideas sketched above to write a factorial procedure that will allow the calculation of large factorials.

3. Suppose that we had a data structure defined as

```
Student = array [1 .. 1000] of
              record
                 Name  : string[20];
                 Major : string[15]
              end;
```

If we wanted a list of students grouped within their majors and listed alphabetically by name within each major, then we might sort the Student array first by Name and then by Major.

a. Discuss the desirability of having a *stable* sorting algorithm for accomplishing the job.

b. Write a Pascal program to read in the students and print out the students in the order suggested above.

4. Use an unstable sort for the program of Exercise 3(b) to observe the effects.

5. Enhance the PrintStrings procedure of Figure 10-9 by adding the letter "d" to the alphabet.

6. Enhance the PrintStrings procedure of Figure 10-9 by allowing the user to input the alphabet into an array.

7. Run the NQueens program with values of N between 4 and 9. Are there any surprises? Is the declared value for Most large enough? (Turbo Note: Be sure to use the {$R+} compiler directive to get range checking.)

*8. a. Write a ColumnPosition function analogous to the RowPosition function in the NQueens program.

b. Modify the PrintBoards procedure so that it prints chessboards as "squares" of 0's and 1's as in Section 10-1.

9. Use an integer array instead of a string to represent a chessboard in the NQueens program of Figure 10-12. Make all necessary modifications of the program and run a test for N = 10.

10. Modify the code of Figure 10-11 so that each of the sums is printed as in the example:

$$1 + 1 + 1$$
$$1 + 2$$
$$3$$

11. Remove the error checking from the function Right and cause it to have a run-time error.

12. Remove the error checking from the function Left and cause it to have a run-time error.

13. Change the WriteSeq procedure so that it maintains a global variable Count that can be printed after all subsequences have been printed.

14. Change the SetQueens procedure so that it maintains a "high water mark" for the array OneBoard. You should use a global variable that is initialized to 0 and that is changed whenever a level of SetQueens increases the maximum number of boards in the array.

15. Run the NQueens program for N = 8. Of the 92 solutions, find a basis set of 12 boards that generates all the other boards by rotating or flipping over the boards. Draw pictures of those 12 boards arranged on a single sheet of paper as four rows and three columns. Frame the picture and hang it on your wall.

16. Generalize the program of Figure 10-14 as suggested in Exercise 21 of Section 10-1.

17. Write a program to print 10 rows of Pascal's Triangle.

18. Write a program to perform the algorithm of Exercise 22 of Section 10-1.

19. Write a program to perform the algorithm of Exercise 23 of Section 10-1.

*20. Write a program to perform the algorithm of Exercise 25 of Section 10-1.

21. Write a program to perform the algorithm of Exercise 26 of Section 10-1.

10-3 □□□□□□ RECURSION, ITERATION, OR . . . ?

In this section, we consider questions of efficiency in the design and coding of our programs. We will present tools for measuring the space and time utilization of our programs. We will consider alternative methods for the solution of several of the examples that we have discussed in the previous two sections. We close the section (and the chapter) with a few points of summary concerning recursion.

□ PROGRAM MEASURE-MENTS

When we are comparing alternative ways to solve a problem with the computer, we should consider the following categories:

1. Use of processing time
2. Use of computer memory space
3. Time to develop the program
4. Time to debug the program
5. Time to maintain the program

As a generalization, recursive solutions tend to do well in categories 3, 4, and 5. Because recursive solutions tend to be simple and small, the time needed to develop the programs, remove their bugs, and to modify the programs later usually is less than the time needed for nonrecursive solutions of the same problems.

Again, as a generalization, recursive solutions do not tend to do very well in their use of computer processing time and the amount of computer memory space that they require. When we are writing and running programs on our own computer, we often don't care about the time that a program takes to run as long as it gets finished in "a reasonable amount of time." We usually don't care about memory utilization if the program doesn't require more than the amount of memory that we have in the computer. However, when we are programming for an environment that allows several programs to execute concurrently (**multitasking**) or that also allows several users to work concurrently (**multiuser**), we should be conservative in our use of shared processor time and computer memory resources.

There is no simple formula for obtaining the answer to the question of which one of several solutions for a problem is the best. Even if we have accurate statistics for each of the categories 1 to 5 above, it isn't obvious how to compare the sets of numbers. Factors such as the predicted life span of the program, frequency of usage, relative importance of the program, and costs of programming and processing must enter into the decision procedure. The field of **Software Engineering** attempts to address categories 3, 4, and 5. The field of **Algorithm Analysis** attempts to address the theoretical aspects of categories 1 and 2. We will attempt to address some practical aspects of categories 1 and 2 in this section.

□
MEASURING TIME AND SPACE

We will use a tool that we call "StatPack" to aid in the measurement of time and space utilization for our programs. The StatPack package consists of several subprograms that can be merged into a Pascal program. The code for StatPack is shown in Figure 10-15.[1]

```
{*** StatPack begins here.}
var
  BeginTime     : real;
  MostSpace     : real;
  LeastSpace    : real;

function StopWatch : real;
{
      Written by:  XXXXXXXX  XX/XX/XX
         Purpose:  To return the present time in seconds.
}
type
  RegPack = record
              AX,BX,CX,DX,BP,SI,DI,SE,ES,Flags  : integer
            end;
```

Figure 10-15 The StatPack Package (Continued)

```
var
  Regs    : RegPack;
  Hour    : integer;
  Min     : integer;
  Sec     : integer;
  Frac    : integer;

begin {StopWatch}
  with Regs do
    begin
      AX := $2C00;
      MSDOS(Regs);
      Hour := hi(CX);
      Min := lo(CX);
      Sec := hi(DX);
      Frac := lo(DX)
    end; {with}

  StopWatch := Hour * 3600.0 + Min * 60.0 + Sec + Frac/100.0
end; {StopWatch}

procedure InitStat;
{
      Written by:  XXXXXXXX  XX/XX/XX
         Purpose:  To initialize the run-time statistics.
  Functions used:  MemAvail - (built-in) to get available memory;
                   StopWatch - to get the system time in seconds.
}
const
  AddOn = 65536.0;

begin {InitStat}

{*** Get the available memory.}

  MostSpace := MemAvail;
  if  MostSpace < 0  then
    MostSpace := MostSpace + AddOn;
  LeastSpace := MostSpace;

{*** Get the time now in seconds.}

  BeginTime := StopWatch
end; {InitStat}

procedure DisplayStat;
{
      Written by:  XXXXXXXX  XX/XX/XX
         Purpose:  To display elapsed time and space used.
}
begin {DisplayStat}

{*** Display elapsed time.}
```

Figure 10-15   The StatPack Package (Continued)

```
      Writeln('The elapsed time is: ',
              StopWatch - BeginTime:1:2, ' seconds.');

{*** Display maximum space used.}

   Writeln('The maximum space used was: ', MostSpace - LeastSpace:1:0)
end; {DisplayStat}

procedure CheckSpace;
{
       Written by:   XXXXXXXX   XX/XX/XX
          Purpose:   To check space utilization.
}
const
  AddOn = 65536.0;

var
  WorkSpace    : real;

begin {CheckSpace}
  WorkSpace := MemAvail;
  if  WorkSpace < 0  then
    WorkSpace := WorkSpace + AddOn;
  if  WorkSpace < LeastSpace   then
    LeastSpace := WorkSpace
end; {CheckSpace}
{*** StatPack ends here.}
```

Figure 10-15 The StatPack Package

To use this tool in your own programs, insert the code for StatPack just before the declarations of your subprograms. Be sure that your program does not have any name conflicts with the global variables and subprograms of StatPack. Avoid the use of the names:

Global variables:	BeginTime
	MostSpace
	LeastSpace
Subprograms:	StopWatch
	InitStat;
	DisplayStat;
	CheckSpace;

In order to use the StatPack, do the following:

1. Place the following statement at the *beginning* of the executable part of each subprogram:

```
CheckSpace;
```

This invocation allows the program to keep track of the maximum space used at any point in the execution.

2. After any user input to the program, place the following statement in the main program:

InitStat

This procedure initializes the time- and space-measuring variables.

3. After the program has done its appointed task, place the following statement in the main program:

DisplayStat

This procedure prints the amount of time and space used by the program.

It is important for you to note that the time and space statistics that are reported by StatPack are to be used for comparisons only. The use of StatPack increases the time and space requirements for the program (this is sometimes called the **observer effect**). When using this technique to compare your programs, be sure that the numbers compared have been generated by the same computer. Differing computer memory sizes and processor speeds will influence the numbers that are reported by StatPack.[2] Also note that the StopWatch function is an adaptation from the *Turbo Pascal version 3.0 Reference Manual*. The space statistics do not include global variables, which must be considered separately.

□ **ELIMINATION OF RECURSION**

One technique for the removal of recursion from a program is to attempt to replace the recursion with **iteration** (use of loops). It is often the case that a recursive solution is the easiest to produce first; and then we wish to derive nonrecursive solutions in order to find the best solution. Subprograms that undergo recursion with a single call at the end of the code (called **tail recursion**) are the easiest to transform into iterative alternatives. To illustrate, consider the recursive algorithm for the factorial:

if N = 0 then Factorial := 1
else Factorial := N * Factorial(N − 1)

We can easily change this algorithm into one that uses a loop as follows:

Total := 1
loop for I going from 1 to N:
    Total := I * Total
Factorial := Total

Note that the nonrecursive algorithm still works for N = 0, but it is not so obvious that it does. When we gather the time and space statistics for factorial functions using the above two algorithms, we obtain the following results:

Algorithm	Maximum Space	Time
Recursive factorial (N = 16)	22	0.06
Iterative factorial (N = 16)	2	0.05

While not overwhelming, the evidence indicates that the iterative approach to the factorial problem is probably the better one. Because the time measurements are so close, we can get better evidence by calculating 16 factorial 1000 times in a loop. When we do this, we get a time of 17.25 seconds for the recursive function and a time of 9.56 seconds for the iterative one. On that basis, the iterative technique definitely is preferred.

□
THE FIBONACCI NUMBERS

The sequence of numbers introduced in the exercises of Section 4-2 provides an excellent example for comparison of solution techniques. In Figure 10-16, we show a recursive function for the generation of the Nth Fibonacci number.

```
function Fibo(N : integer) : real;
{
        Written by:  XXXXXXXX  XX/XX/XX
           Purpose:  To generate the Nth Fibonacci number.
        Parameters:  N - input, which number to calculate.
}
begin {Fibo}
  if  N < 3  then
    Fibo := 1
  else
    Fibo := Fibo(N-1) + Fibo(N-2)
end; {Fibo}
```

Figure 10-16 Fibonacci Numbers—By Recursion

The recursion used in the Fibonacci numbers is not tail recursion, but is a simple example of **tree recursion**. The transformation of the recursive algorithm into an iterative algorithm is a bit more difficult in this case. In Figure 10-17, we show an iterative version of the function.

```
function Fibo(N : integer) : real;
{
        Written by:  XXXXXXXX  XX/XX/XX
           Purpose:  To generate the Nth Fibonacci number.
        Parameters:  N - input, which number to calculate.
}
var
  First  : real;
  Second : real;
  Temp   : real;
  I      : integer;

begin {Fibo}
  First := 1;
  Second := 1;

  for I := 1 to N-2 do
```

Figure 10-17 Fibonacci Numbers—By Iteration (Continued)

```
      begin
        Temp := First;
        First := First + Second;
        Second := Temp
      end; {for}

    Fibo := First
  end; {Fibo}
```

Figure 10-17 Fibonacci Numbers—By Iteration

The iterative function has a more complicated algorithm and uses more variables than the recursive function. The time to develop and debug the iterative solution is certainly greater than for the recursive one.

In this case, there is another approach: a formula. It happens that we can calculate the Nth Fibonacci number directly by the formula:

$$\frac{(1 + \sqrt{5})^N}{\sqrt{5}}$$

The number $1 + \sqrt{5}$ is related to an old problem of geometry called the **golden section**, so we choose to call this constant by the name Golden in our third version of the Fibo function, as shown in Figure 10-18. Also included in Figure 10-18 is a version of the Power function that is needed in the calculation.

```
function Power(X : real; N : integer) : real;
{
        Written by:  XXXXXXXX  XX/XX/XX
           Purpose:  To calculate X to the N.
        Parameters:  X - input, base for the calculation;
                     N - input, exponent for the calculation.
    Functions used:  Exp - (built-in) exponential;
                     Ln - (built-in) natural logarithm.
}
begin {Power}
  Power := Exp(N * Ln(X))
end; {Power}

function Fibo(N : integer) : real;
{
        Written by:  XXXXXXXX  XX/XX/XX
           Purpose:  To generate the Nth Fibonacci number.
        Parameters:  N - input, which number to calculate.
    Functions used:  Power - exponentiation.
}
const
  Golden = 1.6180339887;
  Root5 = 2.2360679775;

begin {Fibo}
  Fibo := Power(Golden, N) / Root5
end; {Fibo}
```

Figure 10-18 Fibonacci Numbers—By Formula

We show the time and space results for the calculation of Fibo(25) in the table:

Algorithm	Maximum Space	Time
Recursive Fibo(25)	28	97.66
Iterative Fibo(25)	3	0.05
Formula Fibo(25)	2	0.11

We see a dramatic example of the potential inefficiency of a recursive function. We would certainly not choose the recursive function as the best way to produce Fibonacci numbers even though it has the easiest formulation. How do we choose between the other two possible solutions? The fact that the iterative version only uses the addition of numbers with no fractional part means that the results will be exact up to the degree of precision of the representation of real numbers (11 digits for Turbo Pascal 3.0).[3] Because the formula uses the exponential and logarithm functions, we do not have the same level of confidence in the accuracy of the values. On this basis, we choose the iterative approach for the computation of Fibonacci numbers as the best in this case.

□ **COMBINATO-RIAL COEFFICIENTS**
One way to calculate the combinatorial coefficients iteratively is to use an array to hold the rows of Pascal's Triangle. We choose to use a rectangular array with rows ranging from 1 to 21 and columns ranging from 0 to 21. (See Section 7-1 for any desired details on the syntax for dealing with these types of array.) Our strategy for calculating Combinatorial(N, M) is to fill in the triangle for rows 1, 2, . . . , N − 1, and then to use the recursive formula (once) to get our result.

We have already shown the recursive version of Combinatorial as Figure 10-2 in Section 10-2. We show the iterative version of the function as Figure 10-19.

```
function Combinatorial(N, M : integer) : integer;
{
        Written by:   XXXXXXXX   XX/XX/XX
           Purpose:   To calculate a combinatorial coefficient, iteratively.
        Parameters:   N - input, the row of Pascal's Triangle;
                      M - input, the entry in the row.
}
var
  Triangle : array [1 .. 21, 0 .. 22] of integer;
  Row : integer;
  Column : integer;

begin {Combinatorial}
  if  (M = 0) or (M = N)   then
    Combinatorial := 1
  else
```

Figure 10-19   Combinatorial Coefficients—By Iteration (Continued)

```
      begin
         Triangle[1,0] := 1;
         Triangle{1,1] := 1;

         for  Row := 2 to N-1  do
            begin
               Triangle[Row, 0] := 1;
               Triangle[Row, Row] := 1;

               for  Column := 1 to Row-1  do
                  Triangle[Row, Column] := Triangle[Row-1, Column-1]
                                         + Triangle[Row-1, Column]

            end; {for}
         Combinatorial := Triangle[N-1, M-1] + Triangle[N-1, M]
      end;
   end; {Combinatorial}
```

Figure 10-19   Combinatorial Coefficients—By Iteration

Another approach is to use the mathematical formula for the combinatorial coefficient Combinatorial(N, M) given by:

$$\frac{N!}{M!(N-M)!}$$

This formula is best not used in the above form, but should undergo some algebraic transformation to become the product (assuming that M is not greater than N − M):

$$\frac{N}{M}\frac{N-1}{M-1}\frac{N-2}{M-2}\frac{N-3}{M-3}\cdots\frac{N-M+1}{1}$$

The fact that Combinatorial(N, M) = Combinatorial(N, N − M) means that we can use the above formula in every case by changing M to N − M, if necessary.

We show the code for the formula version of the Combinatorial function in Figure 10-20.

```
function Combinatorial(N, M : integer) : integer;
{
        Written by:  XXXXXXXX   XX/XX/XX
           Purpose:  To calculate a combinatorial coefficient, by formula.
        Parameters:  N - input, row of Pascal's Triangle;
                     M - input, entry in the row.
}
var
   Num   : integer;
   Denom : integer;
   Prod  : real;
```

Figure 10-20   Combinatorial Coefficients—By Formula (Continued)

```
begin {Combinatorial}
  if  N-M < M  then
    M := N - M;
  Prod := 1;
  Denom := M;

  for  Num := N downto N-M+1  do
    begin
      Prod := Prod * (Num/Denom);
      Denom := Denom - 1
    end; {for}

  Combinatorial := Round(Prod)
end; {Combinatorial}
```

Figure 10-20 Combinatorial Coefficients—By Formula

The results of running the three different solutions for the combinatorial coefficient for the case of Combinatorial(17, 8) are shown in the table:

Algorithm	Maximum Space	Time
Recursive Combinatorial(17, 8)	14	27.02
Iterative Combinatorial(17, 8)	62	0.05
Formula Combinatorial(17, 8)	2	0.06

In this case, we can't be sure of the time comparison of the iterative and formula approaches, so we run each 1000 times. We get a time of 15.88 seconds for the iterative approach and a time of 13.24 seconds for the formula approach. Since both the time and space utilization are better, we give a slight nod to the formula approach for the combinatorial coefficients.

REVERSING A STRING

☐ The recursive form of the Reversed function has been shown in Figure 10-3 of Section 10-2. This provides another example of tail recursion that can be easily transformed into iterative form. We show the iterative form in Figure 10-21.

For the purpose of time and space comparisons, we use the string:

abcdefghijklmnopqrstuvwxyz

The time and space statistics are

Algorithm	Maximum Space	Time
Recursive Reversed	881	0.11
Iterative Reversed	49	0.05

It is evident that the iterative form is preferable because the time and space statistics are better and the algorithm is as simple.

```
function Reversed(InString : String255) : String255;
{
        Written by:   XXXXXXXX   XX/XX/XX
          Purpose:   To reverse a string iteratively.
       Parameters:   InString - input, string to reverse.
   Functions used:   Length - (built-in) gets length of a string.
}
var
  WorkString  : String255;
  I           : integer;

begin {Reversed}
  WorkString := '';

  for  I := 1 to Length(InString)  do
    WorkString := InString[I] + WorkString;

  Reversed := WorkString
end; {Reversed}
```

Figure 10-21   Reversing a String—By Iteration

Another reason for not recommending the recursive form of the function is that it can exhaust available memory, resulting in a run-time error. On one of the author's computers, memory becomes exhausted with a string of length 124.

There is another iterative algorithm that may have occurred to you as you considered the reversal problem. The alternative solution is to do a character by character replacement and avoid the concatenation. The alternative function is presented in Figure 10-22.

When the alternative iterative algorithm is run on the test string, its maximum space is 33 and its time is 0.05 seconds. Because we cannot tell which of the

```
function Reversed(InString : String255) : String255;
{
        Written by:   XXXXXXXX   XX/XX/XX
          Purpose:   To reverse a string iteratively.
       Parameters:   InString - input, string to reverse.
   Functions used:   Length - (built-in) gets length of a string.
}
var
  N           : integer;
  I           : integer;

begin {Reversed}
  Reversed := InString;
  N := Length(InString);

  for  I := 1 to N  do
    Reversed[I] := InString[N-I+1]

end; {Reversed}
```

Figure 10-22   Reversing a String—Character Replacement

iterative algorithms is better, we run both with the test string 1000 times. The algorithm that uses concatenation has a reported time of 8.57 seconds and the algorithm that uses character replacement has a reported time of 2.20 seconds.

We conclude that the best way to reverse a string is to use the character replacement form shown in Figure 10-22.

□

SORTING   We finally arrive at a problem for which we will recommend a recursive solution. We will compare the quick sort and iterative selection sort from Section 6-3 with the merge sort and recursive selection sort from Section 10-2.

We have run each sort with different sets of data. The results are shown in the series of tables:

Test Set 1: Array of 1000 randomly generated integers in the range from 1 to 10000

Algorithm	Maximum Space	Time
Quick sort	28	1.86
Iterative selection sort	3	22.80
Recursive selection sort	1251	16.65
Merge sort	21	2.04

In the context of random data, quick sort shows its superiority.

Test Set 2: Array of 500 randomly generated integers in the range from 1 to 10000

Algorithm	Maximum Space	Time
Quick sort	25	0.93
Iterative selection sort	3	5.77
Recursive selection sort	636	4.39
Merge sort	19	0.93

The tables for test sets 1 and 2 make it seem likely that the two selection sorts are $O(n^2)$, and the quick sort and the merge sort are both $O(n \log n)$. (The "O" notation was introduced in Section 6-3.)

Test Set 3: Array of 1000 distinct integers in the range from 1 to 1000 in ascending order

Algorithm	Maximum Space	Time
Quick sort	1127	15.38
Iterative selection sort	3	22.80
Recursive selection sort	1251	26.59
Merge sort	21	1.81

In this context, quick sort is at its worst. If the data are already sorted, or nearly so, then quick sort is not recommended.

Test Set 4: Array of 1000 randomly generated integers in the range from 1 to 10

Algorithm	Maximum Space	Time
Quick sort	20	1.81
Iterative selection sort	3	22.80
Recursive selection sort	1251	16.65
Merge sort	21	2.03

Once again, we see that random data (even in a small range of values) are the context in which quick sort shows its superiority.

Test Set 5: Array of 1000 integers in the range from 1 to 10 in ascending order

Algorithm	Maximum Space	Time
Quick sort	71	2.36
Iterative selection sort	3	22.80
Recursive selection sort	1251	16.65
Merge sort	21	1.82

We see that quick sort is not slowed as much by sorted data in a small numeric range.

Test Set 6: Array of 1000 integers all with the same value

Algorithm	Maximum Space	Time
Quick sort	13	1.81
Iterative selection sort	3	22.80
Recursive selection sort	1251	16.65
Merge sort	21	1.81

The context wherein all data have the same value is one of the boundary conditions of sorting. Quick sort does well in this context.

Test Set 7: Array of 1000 distinct integers in descending order

Algorithm	Maximum Space	Time
Quick sort	1127	19.94
Iterative selection sort	3	23.89
Recursive selection sort	1251	21.58
Merge sort	21	1.82

Quick sort does not do well when its data are sorted in reverse order either.

Our conclusions are as follows: If you are sure that you have nearly random data, or if the range of values of the data is small, then use the quick sort. If you think that the data are almost sorted, then use merge sort. Never use either selection sort.

□
**PREFIX
EXPRESSIONS** We will not attempt to transform our algorithms into iterative form in this case. It is certainly possible to accomplish the task, but the development and debugging time do not warrant the effort. We will analyze the performance of the program shown in Figure 10-14 of Section 10-2. The basis for our comparisons will be differing prefix expressions. The following is a table of some examples:

Expression	Maximum Space	Time
++++++++++++++++111111111111111111	995	0.22
+1+1+1+1+1+1+1+1+1+1+1+1+1+1+1+11	997	0.11
++++11+11++11+11+++11+11++11+11	279	0.16

The reason for the variation in the space requirements depends on the highest level of recursion that is attained in the running of the program. To see this, let us modify the Eval and Apply functions so that they add 1 to a global count when invoked and subtract 1 from the global count when they end. In addition, we will have both Eval and Apply check if the global count is larger than a global variable that represents the largest count so far. If we begin the process by setting the largest value and the count both to 0, then we have a strategy for checking levels of recursion. The following table shows the results of the level checking on the expressions shown above:

Expression	Highest Level of Recursion
++++++++++++++++111111111111111111	31
+1+1+1+1+1+1+1+1+1+1+1+1+1+1+1+11	31
++++11+11++11+11+++11+11++11+11	9

Another influence on the space requirements is that we used 255 as the maximum size for all strings in the program. After changing the maximum size from 255 to 80, we arrive at a new table of statistics:

Expression	Maximum Space	Time
++++++++++++++++111111111111111111	328	0.22
+1+1+1+1+1+1+1+1+1+1+1+1+1+1+1+11	330	0.11
++++11+11++11+11+++11+11++11+11	93	0.11

We note that the maximum size chosen for all strings in a program can have a significant influence on the memory requirements of the program.

☐ SOME FINAL THOUGHTS ON RECURSION

The discussion and examples of this chapter have pointed toward some conclusions that can be usefully applied to our programming efforts.

1. A recursive algorithm is often the first solution that we discover.

2. A recursive algorithm can be transformable to a nonrecursive, usually iterative, form.

3. Having more than one solution to a problem is an advantage when we want to find the "best" solution.

4. Recursive solutions may have the smallest development, debugging, and maintenance times, but they may use more computer time and memory resources than nonrecursive solutions.

5. It is more likely that a recursive solution is "best" if the problem is complex (sorting, prefix notation).

6. There are techniques for analyzing the behavior of programs that can be used for judging program efficiency.

7. Recursion is indispensable as one of the tools in our programmer's "toolbox."

■■■■■■ REVIEW

Terms and concepts

multitasking	iteration
multiuser	tail recursion
software engineering	tree recursion
algorithm analysis	golden section
observer effect	

■■■■■■ EXERCISES

1. a. Modify the Factorial function so that it works by means of a "lookup table" embodied in a case structure. Put in the factorials from 0 to 16. Measure the performance against the iterative factorial. Which method of factorials do you recommend as best?

   b. Modify the Combinatorial function so that it references a global array containing the factorials from 0 to 16. Build the array iteratively in the main program before invoking Combinatorial. Measure the performance against the other Combinatorial functions. (Be sure to include the time to build the factorial array.)

c. Repeat part (b) for 1000 calls to the combinatorial function. Only build the factorial array once. Can you draw any conclusions?

2. If you wrote the extended range Factorial procedure as suggested in the exercises of Section 10-2:
   a. Write an iterative version.
   b. Measure the performance of the two forms.

3. Show that Fibo(50) is accurately calculated by the iterative approach, but not accurately calculated by the formula approach. What is the smallest number N for which the iterative approach fails? The formula approach?

4. Use a calculator to compute Fibo(N) by the formula for N = 2, 3, and 4.

5. Draw a picture of the recursive levels of the calculation of Fibo(5) in the following manner:

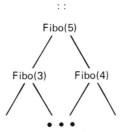

When you are done, color all of the lines brown and the expressions "Fibo(. . .)" green. Turn the picture upside down. Now you see why this kind of recursion is called *tree recursion*. (It might be insulting to call it "bush" recursion.)

6. a. Modify the Power function that is used for the calculation of Fibonacci numbers so that it calculates by iteration instead of using the exponential and logarithm functions. Measure the performance of this method of calculation for Fibo(25).
   b. Repeat part (a), but use the recursive Power function presented in Section 4-2 (page 293).

7. By hand, calculate Combinatorial(5, 3) by the first formula given.

8. Repeat the picture drawing activities of Exercise 5 for the recursive calculation of Combinatorial(5, 3).

9. Find what size of string exhausts memory in the recursive form of the Reversed function.

10. Write a nonrecursive merge sort for the special case when the number of elements in the array is a power of 2. Hint: Start at the bottom level with subarrays of size 1 and work upward to size 2, 4, . . . , merging the two subarrays on the level below. Test the performance of this sort against the recursive merge sort for 512 randomly generated numbers in the range from 1 to 10,000.
    As a simple example, we show the merge steps for an array of size 8.

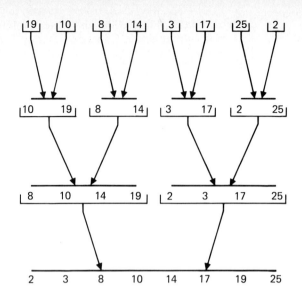

11. How might you remove the restriction to arrays of size a power of 2 in Exercise 10?

12. Write an iterative version of the SubSeq function in Figure 10-6 of Section 10-2. Measure the performance against the recursive form.

13. Write an iterative version of the SubString function in Figure 10-7 of Section 10-2. Measure the performance against the recursive form.

14. Write a simple looping version of the NumDivisors function in Figure 10-10 of Section 10-2. This example should show you the value of common sense when choosing an approach to solve a problem.

15. Write an iterative version of the Addends function in Figure 10-11 of Section 10-2. Measure the performance against the recursive form.

16. Write an iterative version of the NQueens program. Use the backtracking algorithm discussed in Exercise 25 of Section 10-1. Measure the performance against the recursive form.

17. Write an iterative version of the WriteSeq function in Figure 10-13 of Section 10-2.

18. What would be some necessary ingredients of a nonrecursive solution of the PreFix program in Figure 10-14 of Section 10-2? Formulate a *rough* algorithm.

19. Write a Pascal program for a nonrecursive solution of the PreFix program in Figure 10-14 of Section 10-2. Measure the performance against the recursive version.

20. Find the maximum levels of recursion for the sorting procedures discussed in this section for all the test sets listed. What are your conclusions about these (constant versus varying) maximum levels?

□

1. The StatPack package is specifically a Turbo Pascal tool. To do similar statistics in other versions of Pascal, one would have to invoke similar system facilities (if available).

2. The numbers reported in this section were gathered using a computer with 640K of memory and a 8-mHz clock.

3. Actually, the number 745058059690 is the largest whole number that can be represented exactly as a real on the author's computer.

11

FILE I/O

11-1
INTRODUC-
TION

In this chapter, we explore **files** in depth. Files were introduced in Chapter 5, and you have probably written some programs that used files. In this chapter, we describe two important application types with the files you have learned about. The first involves applications based on **control break** logic; the second is related to sequential file **merging** and to sequential file **update** strategies. In addition, we give a brief introduction to the concept of **random-access** files.

The presentation is not intended to be a complete discussion of file-processing techniques. Indeed, whole textbooks have been written on that subject. Nor do we give an exhaustive description of the Pascal file-processing commands. Our purpose is to indicate some methods for working with files using the Pascal language, expanding on what we learned in Chapter 5.

We begin with a brief review.

□
FILE
TERMINOLOGY

A file consists of a number of **records**. (Pascal has borrowed and generalized on the concept of record.) A record contains one or more values, frequently relating to one given entity. For example, we might have a record that contains the following **fields**:

Name
Social security number
Date of birth
Marital status
And so on

In this case, the record refers to a particular individual.

Files can appear in many forms. For many years, punched cards were an important medium for input files. Data is encoded on a punched card by a pattern

718

of holes that can be interpreted as character data by a card reader. In such a file, each data card might be a single record of the file. Another example of a file is a printed report. In this case, each line printed is considered to be one record of the file.

It is frequently desirable to store and maintain data in a more convenient form. For example, we might want to have one program put some information on a file and later use that information as input to some other program. A printed report is not appropriate in this application. We could have the first program create a set of punched cards to be read by the second program. However, this would require maintaining the deck of cards (which could be sizable) over an extended period of time.

Fortunately, today there are more convenient storage media for files available economically. Two of the most commonly used are **magnetic tape** and **magnetic disk**. (In addition, **optical disk** systems are becoming feasible, and may be increasingly important as time goes on.)

The magnetic tape used by the computer to store a data file is analogous to the tape used for sound recording. Indeed, some microcomputers use ordinary audio cassettes as a storage medium. The records of the file are placed on the tape, one after another, from first to last, as shown in Figure 11-1. In reading a file that has been written on tape, the computer will have to read the records in order (sequentially). As a result, a magnetic tape is referred to as a **sequential-access** storage medium. A file stored on tape will be accessed sequentially.

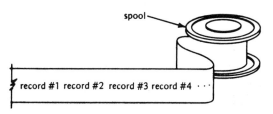

spool

record #1 record #2 record #3 record #4 · · ·

Figure 11-1 Tape File

Likewise, a magnetic disk is somewhat analogous to the phonograph records used to store sound. One form of magnetic disk you are almost certainly familiar with is the diskette, or floppy disk, commonly used by microcomputers. In addition, you may be familiar with microcomputer hard disk devices, or perhaps with the disk devices used by minicomputers or mainframe computers. These devices all have the fundamental strategy for storing data in common, as shown in Figure 11-2. The data is stored on a series of concentric rings, rather than on one continuous spiral, as is true for a phonograph record. The disk is rotated at a high rate of speed by a device called a **disk drive**. The **disk drive** mechanism includes a **read/write head** on an arm that can be moved to any of the concentric rings, or **tracks**, of the disk. Again, this is somewhat analogous to the audio record player arm, which can be moved to any groove on the record.

A magnetic disk is called a **direct-access** storage medium. In order to access a particular record (perhaps record 735), it is not necessary to read all the records up to the record. The read/write head can be moved directly to the track (concen-

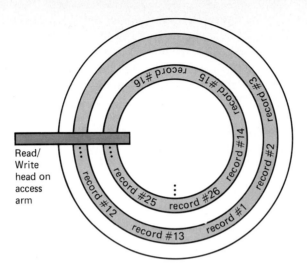

Figure 11-2 Disk File

tric ring) on which the desired record is located. Since the disk is rotated by the disk drive, the desired record will pass under the read/write head soon after the head is in place. This direct-access capability of the magnetic disk and disk drive does not, however, mean that the records of the file cannot be processed in order. If a file is stored on a disk, then it can be accessed either sequentially or directly.

□
PASCAL FILES

The standard Pascal language supports two types of files, both of which are sequential-access types. (As we shall see, Turbo Pascal supports a third type, which is a direct-access type.) These were introduced in Chapter 5. The first is the **text file**, declared as type "text" in the var section of the program. A text file is a file of characters organized into text lines. Although it is possible to read such a file one character at a time, we have preferred to read one line at a time. We have done so by making extensive use of Turbo Pascal's string data types.

Text files in which a line contains several data items can be more difficult to use when not all the data is numeric. As a simple example, suppose that two programs each contain these declarations:

```
var
    LastName : string[15];
    FirstName: string[10];
```

Suppose program 1 writes the data to a text file:

```
Writeln(FriendFile, LastName, FirstName);
```

and that later program 2 reads the data:

```
Readln(FriendFile, LastName, FirstName);
```

Will this work properly? Probably not, unless the last name that was written was 20 characters long. For example, suppose that we have assigned

```
LastName := 'Frederickson'
FirstName := 'Arthur'
```

When the record is written, it will contain the characters

```
FredericksonArthur
```

Now when the next program reads the data, there is nothing to tell it where LastName ends, so it reads the first 15 characters because LastName is string[15]. As a result, LastName becomes 'FredericksonArt' and First Name becomes 'hur'.

We could avoid this problem by padding the output of the last name with blanks to achieve a length of 15. However, the name we read in would then have the extra blanks at the end.

As another example, consider

```
Readln(Age, Sex)
```

where Age is integer and Sex is char. To enter the values 25 and 'F', what should the input line be? If we use

```
25 F
```

then Age would be 25 and Sex would be a blank. What we must do, according to standard Pascal, is use

```
25F
```

Unfortunately, Turbo Pascal has a "feature" that causes this input to create an I/O error. Turbo insists that numeric data be terminated by a blank or a return.

Again, we could get around this, perhaps, by issuing a Readln as

```
Readln(Age, Sex, Sex)
```

and using an input line

```
25 F
```

This would read 25 for Age, the blank for Sex, and then the F for Sex. However, this is not very satisfactory.

Because of these subtleties, we have tended to read one data item per record when reading from a text file or from the keyboard. This is a matter of defensive programming: avoid known pitfall areas.

The second type of file is the **binary file**. These are declared using a declaration similar to

```
type
   PersonFile = file of PersonRecord;

var
   FriendFile :  PersonFile;
```

This illustrates the most common use. However, we can declare types such as

```
file of integer
```

In this case, the file "records" are not Pascal records; rather each "record" of the file would be a single integer.

There are tradeoffs to be considered in choosing between text files and binary files:

1. A text file can be processed in a text editor. Therefore, text files are frequently used as original input to a program or set of programs.

2. A text file is readable by humans. Files meant to be printed as reports would definitely be text files.

3. As we have mentioned, there are certain subtleties to be avoided in reading text files. It may be desirable to arrange the input file with one value per line.

4. Binary files are more efficient. The data is stored on the file in precisely the form in which it is stored in the computer. No conversion routines are needed to translate back and forth to text form.

5. One disadvantage of binary files is that they can require special "protocols" so that they can be transmitted over phone lines to remote computers. Generally, transmitting text files is easier.

Before we discuss new material, let us remind you very briefly of the file-handling features we have studied. For more information, review Chapter 5.

1. Type can be: text
  or: file of *component type*

2. Assign (*file designator*, *file name*)

3. Reset (*file designator*)
  Rewrite (*file designator*): removes any previous data

4. Read (*file designator*, . . .)
  Write (*file designator*, . . .)

5. Readln (*file designator*, . . .): these are for text files
  Writeln (*file designator*, . . .): only

6. Eof (*file designator*): becomes true as the last record is read

7. Close (*file designator*)

8. Error trapping. We have used this to trap the error of a file not existing. It can, however, be used to trap an error in any I/O statement, as shown here. (See also Exercise 1.)

```
{$I-}                            {Turn off error messages}
some I/O statement               {Reset, Read, etc}
{$I+}                            {Turn on error messages}
ErrorOccurred := (IOResult <>0)  {Check for error}
```

▪▪▪▪▪▪ REVIEW

Terms and concepts

file	optical disk
control break	sequential access
merging	disk drive
update	read/write head
random access	track
record	direct access
field	text file

magnetic tape   binary file

magnetic disk

*1. To demonstrate the use of error trapping in other than a file context, write a procedure GetScore as described here. This procedure obtains a valid test score between 0 and 100. There should be three possible error messages: "too low," "too high," and "not valid integer input." Use the $I compiler directive and the IOResult function to trap this third error type.

Exercises 2 to 5 refer to a binary file that contains inventory figures for a chain of drugstores. Each record of the file contains these fields:

Description	Type	Number of Characters/Digits
Item number	Numeric	4
Item name	Character	Maximum 20
Department code	Character	3
Inventory at each of nine locations	Numeric array	4 digits each

The file is in ascending order by item number.

2. Write a program to create this file.

In order to create the file, you will read a set of input records. Each will have exactly the information that will be put on the file and an additional field that contains the total inventory for the entire chain (numeric, five digits). The input file is a text that will be created by the user with a text editor. It is up to you to describe the exact layout of the input file.

Your program is to perform the following "correctness" checks:

- The item name field must begin with a nonblank character.
- The department code must be one of the following eight codes: COS, DRU, TOY, CRD, PRE, HHG, CLO, or BKS.
- The sum of the individual inventory amounts must equal the total inventory (this helps catch data-entry errors).
- The item numbers must be in order.

In addition, perform the following "reasonableness" check:

- Each inventory amount must be between 0 and 3,000, inclusive. Records with no errors will be placed in the file; records with errors will not. All errors will be listed on a text file as illustrated below:

```
12345     BLANK ITEM NAME
12345     BAD DEPT CODE
12345     BAD INVENTORY AMT (STORE 2)
12345     BAD INVENTORY AMT (STORE 9)
12345     INCORRECT TOTAL
*********************************************************
12479     BAD INVENTORY AMT (STORE 6)
*********************************************************
13780     OUT OF ORDER (PREVIOUS ITEM = 13792)
*********************************************************
```

3. This exercise is exactly the same as Exercise 2 except for the error report form. In this case, it should be listed on a printed exception report, as illustrated below:

```
                         EXCEPTION REPORT                    PAGE 1
                         ----------------

    ITEM NUMBER                           TYPE OF ERROR
    -----------                           -------------
      12345                       BLANK ITEM NAME
                                  BAD DEPT CODE
                                  BAD INVENTORY AMT (STORE 2)
                                  BAD INVENTORY AMT (STORE 9)
                                  INCORRECT TOTAL
      12345                       BAD INVENTORY AMT (STORE 6)
      13780                       OUT OF ORDER (PREVIOUS ITEM=13792)
```

Notice that you should continue checking for further errors even after finding one error. Also, notice that the output is "group indicated" by item number. If the list for a single item spans two pages, print the item number in a form such as 19345(CONT.) on the new page.

4. Write programs to create partial files containing:

   *a. All TOY items.
   b. All items whose item number is between 10000 and 30000, inclusive.
   c. All items where any single inventory amount is less than 30. The output record should contain only the item number, name, and department.

5. Write a program to create a file where each record contains an item number and the total inventory for the entire chain.

11-2 ☐☐☐☐☐☐ SEQUENTIAL FILES— CONTROL BREAKS

In the next two sections, we will examine two classical categories of algorithms for working with sequential files. Either can be used with text files or with binary files. In fact, for the programs of this section, we could even obtain input from the terminal. The only differences would occur in the details of reading the fields of the input record. For simplicity, we assume that the input is a binary file.

The first algorithm category we consider is that of **control breaks**. While we cannot claim that this is the most exciting class of algorithm to learn, it can certainly be argued that it is one of the most widely used. In any case, it should be in every professional's "toolbox," along with other problem-solving methods.

There are many instances, especially in business applications of the computer, where the data to be processed occurs in groups. If there are special tasks to be performed when one group ends and another begins, we have the structure frequently referred to as a control-break structure. In this type of application, information contained within the data itself is generally used to determine when to move from one group to another.

An important consideration for this type of problem is that the records being processed must be prearranged into the groups involved.

☐ Each data record contains a department number (integer), a salesperson number (integer), and an expense amount (real). The records are arranged with the salespersons for each department grouped in the file.

Write a program to create a summary listing, as illustrated in Figure 11-3.

```
                           EXPENSE TOTALS
                           ------- ------

Department                 Salesperson              Expenses
----------                 -----------              --------

       100                    5000                  1000.00
       100                    5001                  1000.00

                           Department Total:        2000.00


       200                    8907                   500.00
       200                    3798                  1603.45
       200                    4359                  1000.75

                           Department Total:        3104.20


       300                    2987                   984.50

                           Department Total:         984.50


      1800                    3871                  1500.00
      1800                    8340                   390.25
      1800                    8469                    50.75
      1800                    8307                   500.00

                           Department Total:        2441.00


      2050                    3498                    35.50

                           Department Total:          35.50


                           Grand Total:             8565.20
```

Figure 11-3 Control Break—Desired Output Format

Suppose we start with the realization that a loop will be needed to process the data. We will need at least the following variables:

Input:	Department	integer	Employee department
	IDNumber	integer	Employee number
	Expense	real	Employee expense
Output:	DeptTotal	real	Total for department
	GrandTotal	real	Total for entire file

Many file-processing problems follow this general pattern:

```
initialization
while  not Eof(file-designator) do
   begin
      read a record
      process the record
      print information
   end; while
```

However, the control-break logic will require a somewhat more complex algorithm because there are special tasks to be performed when we finish one group and start another. Somewhere after the read step, we will insert a step that is something like this:

```
if this is a new department then
   perform 'change of department' steps
```

The "change of department" steps will include, among other things, printing the total for the previous department. In general, we must perform some "cleanup" steps for the old department and some "setup" steps to get ready for the new department. These general categories can overlap somewhat.

NOTE In many programs, the test to check whether we have a new group will come immediately after the read step. However, there are instances when some preliminary processing must be done prior to determining whether a new group has occurred.

If we ask, "How can we tell if this is a new department?" the answer might be to compare the department number just read with the previous department number; we might, therefore, make an addition to our variable list:

Other: OldDept   integer   Previous department number

With a little more thought, we might conclude that the first data record should be treated separately because there is no "old department number" with which to compare the first department number. We might be led to read and process that first record before we enter the loop because it will be treated differently from the rest. If so, we would come up with an algorithm something like this:

print headings
set GrandTotal to 0
read the first record
do 'setup' steps for the first department
print the first record
add the first record's expense to DeptTotal
as long as there is any data left, do these steps:
   read a record
   if Department is different from OldDept,
      perform 'change of department' steps ('cleanup'
      and 'setup')

> print the record
> add the record's expense to DeptTotal
> after the loop, perform 'cleanup' for the last department,
> and print GrandTotal

We perform the "setup" for the first department prior to the loop. This is sometimes referred to as **priming**. In addition, we must perform the "cleanup" for the last department after the loop, when we have run out of data.

To complete the algorithm, we must determine what will be involved in setting up for a new department and cleaning up after an old department. To do so, we should review the required output. If we concentrate on the "department change," we should be able to determine most of what will be required. Each step will be labeled as "cleanup" or "setup".

This step should be obvious:

1. Print DeptTotal (cleanup).

Some others are not quite as obvious:

2. Set DeptTotal back to 0 to prepare to accumulate a new total for the new department (setup).

3. Give OldDept the value of this record's department (setup).

4. Add DeptTotal to GrandTotal (before setting DeptTotal back to 0). GrandTotal represents the sum of the individual department totals (cleanup).

NOTE As "cleanup" for the last department, we must perform steps 1 and 4. The "setup" for the first department will consist of steps 2 and 3.

Adding these refinements to our algorithm, we obtain the program in Figure 11-4. This program reads its data from a text file. It also "prints" its report to a text file. The text file can then be printed (as often as needed) using the operating system's printing facilities. As we mentioned in Chapter 5, this is a handy method both for this and for the situation where several microcomputers are sharing the same printer. (Another important reason is that it reduces the development time because output to a disk file is faster than output to a printer. As it happens, this was the primary reason the method was used in this particular example.) We use the OpenRead and OpenWrite procedures discussed in Chapter 5.

```
program ControlBreak(Input, Output);
{
        Written by:   XXXXXXXX   XX/XX/XX
          Purpose:   To print a report for input data grouped
                      by department.
  Procedures used:   Header - to print headings.
}
```

Figure 11-4 Control Breaks (Continued)

```
var
  DeptFile    : text;                    { input file }
  ListFile    : text;                    { report file }
  Department  : integer;                 { department # }
  IDNumber    : integer;                 { employee # }
  Expense     : real;                    { employee expense }

  DeptTotal   : real;                    { total expense for dept. }
  GrandTotal  : real;                    { total expense for company }

  OldDept     : integer;                 { previous employee's dept. # }
```

{*function Exists, as shown in Appendix E, is inserted here.*}

{*procedure OpenRead, as shown in Appendix E, is inserted here*}

{*procedure OpenWrite, as shown in Appendix E, is inserted here*}

```
procedure Header;
{
        Written by:   XXXXXXXX   XX/XX/XX
           Purpose:   To print headings
}
begin  {Header}
  Writeln(ListFile, ' ':20, 'EXPENSE TOTALS');
  Writeln(ListFile, ' ':20, '------- ------');
  Writeln(ListFile);
  Writeln(ListFile, ' ':2, 'Department', ' ':9, 'Salesperson',
                    ' ':14, 'Expenses');
  Writeln(ListFile, ' ':2, '----------', ' ':9, '-----------',
                    ' ':14, '--------');
  Writeln(ListFile)
end;   {Header}

begin  {ControlBreak}

{*** Preliminary setup and initialization. }

  OpenRead(DeptFile);
  OpenWrite(ListFile);
  Header;
  GrandTotal := 0;

{*** Handle first employee. }

  Readln(DeptFile, Department, IDNumber, Expense);
  DeptTotal := 0;
  OldDept := Department;
  Writeln(ListFile, Department:10, ' ':14, IDNumber:5, ' ':15,
          Expense:10:2);
  DeptTotal := DeptTotal + Expense;

{*** Handle other employees in loop. }
```

Figure 11-4 Control Breaks (Continued)

```
  while not Eof(DeptFile) do
    begin
      Readln(DeptFile, Department, IDNumber, Expense);
      if OldDept <> Department then
        begin
          Writeln(ListFile);
          Writeln(ListFile, ' ':21, 'Department Total:', DeptTotal:16:2);
          Writeln(ListFile);
          Writeln(ListFile);
          Writeln(ListFile);
          GrandTotal := GrandTotal + DeptTotal;
          DeptTotal := 0;
          OldDept := Department
        end;  {if}
      Writeln(ListFile, Department:10, ' ':14, IDNumber:5, ' ':15,
              Expense:10:2);
      DeptTotal := DeptTotal + Expense;
    end;  {while}

{*** Finish last department and print grand total. }

  Writeln(ListFile);
  Writeln(ListFile, ' ':21, 'Department Total:', DeptTotal:16:2);
  Writeln(ListFile);
  Writeln(ListFile);
  Writeln(ListFile);
  GrandTotal := GrandTotal + DeptTotal;
  Writeln(ListFile, ' ':26, 'Grand Total:', GrandTotal:16:2);

{*** Close files and print terminating message. }

  Close(DeptFile);
  Close(ListFile);
  Writeln('ControlBreak program terminating');
  Writeln('Report is in file named expense.rep')
end.
```

Figure 11-4 Control Breaks

CONTROL BREAKS: GENERAL

□ The preceding example illustrates the control-break concept. There are some general comments we can make about planning this type of algorithm. The algorithm will usually involve a loop that terminates on end of file. We will discuss in some detail what types of steps will generally appear before, in the body of, and after this loop.

Keep in mind that the underlying feature of the control-break structure is that the data is arranged in groups based on some field of the individual records. In addition to the usual analysis of the steps to be performed for each individual data record, we must determine the steps required due to the grouping. As a general rule, these steps fall into two categories:

1. Those steps used in starting a new group, such as initializing (or reinitializing) counters or accumulators or printing special lines of information

2. Those steps used in finishing up an old group, such as printing summary information.

Whenever we encounter a new group, we must perform all these steps. The principal features of the algorithm will be:

1. Before the loop:
   a. Initialize for the entire file (for example, GrandTotal := 0).
   b. Read the first record.
   c. Set up for the first group.
   d. Process the first record.

2. In the loop:
   a. Read the new record.
   b. If a new group, finish the previous group and set up for the new group.
   c. Process the record.

3. After the loop:
   a. Finish the last group.
   b. Print summary information for the entire file.

Most control-break problems fit fairly well into this general outline. For some applications, steps 2(b) and 2(c) must be modified slightly because the first record of each new group is processed slightly differently from the subsequent records in that group. However, this outline should help us obtain a good algorithm for any control-break problem we may encounter.

□ **USING SUBPROGRAMS WITH CONTROL BREAKS**

In the preceding discussion, we have not indicated how subprograms fit into the control-break program logic. We have at least these four possibilities:

1. We can use a procedure for reading the data. This might be especially useful in two instances. First, we could use it to validate the input. Second, if the input file is a text file containing data for one record spread over several lines of text, it could be used to hide the details of reading the data. In either case, it would enable us always to translate the algorithm step "read a record" into a single line of Pascal code.

2. We can use a procedure for printing detail lines. In this way, we can proceed to a new page of output when we reach the bottom of each page.

It will frequently be helpful to pass, as an input parameter for this procedure, a Boolean flag indicating whether or not this is the first record in a new group. We might use a variable NewGroup for this purpose. (The first record in each group is frequently handled differently in the detail line printing routine.)

3. The processing of the record can very well involve complicated logic that will warrant one or more subprograms.

4. The "setup" and "cleanup" steps themselves can be placed in subprograms. We discuss this possibility further.

There are several possible reasons for placing the setup and the cleanup steps in subprograms. First of all, each one is generally used twice. For example, the setup steps are performed before the loop for the first record and in the loop whenever a new group is encountered. In addition, these steps could be fairly complex. The more complex they become, the more likely it becomes that we will choose to place them in subprograms. Finally, using subprograms emphasizes the similar structure of the various control-break programs we write.

We will reexamine our sample control-break algorithm to illustrate these ideas. For example, the algorithm for a SetUp subprogram is

```
set DeptTotal to 0
set OldDept equal to this record's department
```

This will require a procedure; the parameters are the department total (output), the current record's department (input), and the old department number (output).

For a CleanUp subprogram, we have

```
print DeptTotal line, plus three blank lines
add department total to grand total
```

The department total is an input parameter and the grand total is an update parameter for this procedure.

For the detail line routine, we will have input parameters for the record to print together with the Boolean variable NewGroup discussed earlier. We write

```
if this is a new group, add 5 to LineCount
if LineCount ≥ 45 print headings, set LineCount to 6
print the record
add 1 to LineCount
```

COMMENT This procedure is somewhat different from some earlier ones in its handling of the LineCount variable. This is to adjust to the fact that lines other than detail lines are being printed by this program. If we simply count detail lines, we will be unable to judge when we are near the bottom of the page. Rather than merely counting detail lines, we count all lines of output.

As a result, LineCount is set to 6 after printing headings. In addition, for a new group, we add 5 to LineCount. This counts the Department Total line we have printed and the one blank line before and three blank lines after that line.

Using these ideas, we develop the main program as shown in Figure 11-5.

```
program ControlBreak(Input, Output);
{
        Written by:  XXXXXXXX  XX/XX/XX
           Purpose:  To print a report for input data grouped
                     by department.
   Procedures used:  Header - to print headings
                     Setup - to initialize a new department
                     Cleanup - to perform final actions for a department
                          that is finished
                     GetData - to obtain data
                     DetailLine - to print detail lines, with headings
}
const
  MaxLines = 45;                        { maximum lines per page }

var
  DeptFile    : text;                   { input file }
  ListFile    : text;                   { report file }
  Department  : integer;                { department # }
  IDNumber    : integer;                { employee # }
  Expense     : real;                   { employee expense }

  DeptTotal   : real;                   { total expense for dept. }
  GrandTotal  : real;                   { total expense for company }

  OldDept     : integer;                { previous employee's dept. # }

  LineCount   : integer;                { counts report lines on page }
  NewGroup    : boolean;                { for use by detail line printer }
```

{*function Exists, as shown in Appendix E, is inserted here*}

{*procedure OpenRead, as shown in Appendix E, is inserted here*}

{*procedure OpenWrite, as shown in Appendix E, is inserted here*}

```
procedure Header;
{
        Written by:  XXXXXXXX  XX/XX/XX
           Purpose:  To print headings.
}
begin  {Header}
  Writeln(ListFile, ' ':20, 'EXPENSE TOTALS');
  Writeln(ListFile, ' ':20, '------- ------');
  Writeln(ListFile);
  Writeln(ListFile, ' ':2, 'Department', ' ':9, 'Salesperson',
                    ' ':14, 'Expenses');
  Writeln(ListFile, ' ':2, '----------', ' ':9, '-----------',
                    ' ':14, '--------');
  Writeln(ListFile)
end;   {Header}
```

Figure 11-5 Control Breaks With Procedures (Continued)

```
procedure Setup(var DeptTotal : real; Department : integer;
                var OldDept : integer);
{
        Written by:  XXXXXXXXX  XX/XX/XX
           Purpose:  To initialize a new group.
        Parameters:  DeptTotal - output, set to 0;
                     Department - input, current record's department;
                     OldDept - output, set equal to Department.
}
begin  {Setup}
  DeptTotal := 0;
  OldDept := Department
end;  {Setup}

procedure Cleanup(DeptTotal : real; var Grand : real);
{
        Written by:  XXXXXXXXX  XX/XX/XX
           Purpose:  To perform final actions for a department that
                        is finished.
        Parameters:  DeptTotal - input, total for the department;
                     Grand - update, total for the company.
     Globals used:   ListFile - the handle for the report file.
}
begin  {Cleanup}
  Writeln(ListFile);
  Writeln(ListFile, ' ':21, 'Department Total:', DeptTotal:16:2);
  Writeln(ListFile);
  Writeln(ListFile);
  Writeln(ListFile);
  Grand := Grand + DeptTotal
end;  {Cleanup}

procedure GetData(var Department, ID : integer; var Expense : real);
{
        Written by:  XXXXXXXXX  XX/XX/XX
           Purpose:  To read one person's data
        Parameters:  Department - output, the department
                     ID - output, the employee number
                     Expense - output, the expense amount
     Globals used:   DeptFile - the handle for the input file
}
begin  {GetData}
  Readln(DeptFile, Department, IDNumber, Expense)
end;  {GetData}

procedure DetailLine(Department, ID : integer;
                     Expense : real; NewGroup : boolean);
{
        Written by:  XXXXXXXXX  XX/XX/XX
           Purpose:  To print a line of data, with headings when needed.
        Parameters:  Department - input, the department
                     ID - input, the employee number
                     Expense - input, the expense amount
                     NewGroup - input, is this a new department?
```

Figure 11-5   Control Breaks With Procedures (Continued)

```
         Globals used:   ListFile - the handle for the report file
      Globals modified:   LineCount - the detail line counter
       Procedures used:   Header, to print headings
   }
   begin   {DetailLine}
     if NewGroup then
       LineCount := LineCount + 5;
     if LineCount >= MaxLines then
       begin
         Header;
         LineCount := 6
       end;   {if}
     Writeln(ListFile, Department:10, ' ':14, IDNumber:5, ' ':15,
             Expense:10:2);
     LineCount := LineCount + 1
   end;   {DetailLine}


   begin   {ControlBreak}

   {*** Preliminary setup and initialization. }

     OpenRead(DeptFile);
     OpenWrite(ListFile,);
     Header;
     LineCount := 6;
     GrandTotal := 0;

   {*** Handle first employee. }

     GetData(Department, IDNumber, Expense);
     Setup(DeptTotal, Department, OldDept);
     DetailLine(Department, IDNumber, Expense, true);
     DeptTotal := DeptTotal + Expense;

   {*** Handle other employees in loop. }

     while not Eof(DeptFile) do
       begin
         GetData(Department, IDNumber, Expense);
         NewGroup := false;
         if OldDept <> Department then
           begin
             NewGroup := true;
             Cleanup(DeptTotal, GrandTotal);
             Setup(DeptTotal, Department, OldDept)
           end;   {if}
         DetailLine(Department, IDNumber, Expense, NewGroup);
         DeptTotal := DeptTotal + Expense;
       end;   {while}

   {*** Finish last department and print grand total. }

     Cleanup(DeptTotal, GrandTotal);
     Writeln(ListFile, ' ':26, 'Grand Total:', GrandTotal:16:2);
```

Figure 11-5   Control Breaks With Procedures (Continued)

```
{*** Close files and print terminating message. }
   Close(DeptFile);
   Close(ListFile);
   Writeln('ControlBreak program terminating');
   Writeln('Report is in file named expense.rep')
end.
```

Figure 11-5 Control Breaks With Procedures

COMMENT With the use of the NewGroup parameter for the detail line procedure, it is a simple matter to **group indicate** the output. For example, this output is not group indicated:

100	5.43
100	6.17
150	0.41
150	1.23
150	0.61

The same output group indicated would be

100	5.43
	6.17
150	0.41
	1.23
	0.61

▪▪▪▪▪▪
REVIEW

Terms and concepts

control break

priming

group indicate

Program logic: control break

1. Before the loop:
   a. Initialize for the entire file (for example, GrandTotal := 0).
   b. Read the first record.
   c. Set up for the first group.
   d. Process the first record.
2. In the loop:
   a. Read the new record.
   b. If a new group, finish the previous group and set up for the new group.
   c. Process the record.
3. After the loop:
   a. Finish the last group.
   b. Print summary information for the entire file.

1. There are several possible revisions to the output indicated in Figure 11-3. In general, it should be possible to make these revisions by modifying only the detail line routine, provided the totals are still printed in the same manner. Make the necessary changes for each of the following:

   a. Group indicate the data by department.
   b. Group indicate by department; when a page break occurs in the middle of a department, the first line on the next page should look something like this:

   ```
   4157 (CONTINUED)        16141              945.30
   ```

   c. Obtain output in the format illustrated in Figure 11-6.

```
                              EXPENSE TOTALS
                              ─────── ──────

Department Number 100              SalesPerson         Expenses
                                      5000             1000.00
                                      5001             1000.00

                                Department Total:      2000.00

Department Number 200              SalesPerson         Expenses
                                      8907              500.00
                                      3798             1603.45
                                      4359             1000.75

                                Department Total:      3104.20

Department Number 300              SalesPerson         Expenses
                                      2987              984.50

                                Department Total:       984.50

Department Number 2050             SalesPerson         Expenses
                                      3498               35.50

                                Department Total:        35.50

                                    Grand Total:       6124.20
```

Figure 11-6 Report Format for Exercise 11.1

2. Write algorithms and variable lists for each of the following:

   *a. Each data record has a name, course number, and letter grade. Records are grouped by name. Output should be group indicated by name. For each person, print the number of courses taken and the number of courses failed.

   b. Each data record has a department (six characters), name, rank (four characters), and salary. Records are grouped by department. Output should be similar to that in Figure 11-3. For each department, print the number of full professors (rank = 'PROF') and the average salary. Also count the departments.

   c. Modify the algorithm of part (b) to also find the department with the highest average salary.

d. Each record contains a state abbreviation (two characters), a city name (20 characters), and a population figure to the nearest 1000. For example, 253 would denote 253,000. Records are grouped by state. Output should be similar to that of Figure 11-6. For each state, print the total population of the cities given and count the cities with population over 500,000.

e. Modify the algorithm of part (d) to also find the total number of cities listed with population over 500,000 and the average population of all the cities listed (for the entire file).

f. Each data record has a department number, employee number, and hourly wage. Use output similar to that in Figure 11-3. For each department, print the number of the person with the lowest hourly wage; also print the number of the employee in the entire company with the lowest hourly wage.

3. Write Pascal programs for each of the algorithms of Exercise 2.

4. Each record contains a numerical grade, course number, and name. The records are in ascending order based on the numerical grade.

   The letter grade is calculated by the rule: 0 to 59.99, F; 60 to 69.99, D; 70 to 79.99, C; 80 to 89.99, B; and 90 to 100, A. Write an algorithm to generate the report illustrated in Figure 11-7.

   Hint: Some preliminary processing of the data may be needed prior to determining if you have a new group.

5. Write the program for the algorithm of Exercise 4.

6. Each data record contains an ID number for a sample steel rod and the measured length of that particular sample. The records are arranged in ascending order based on the length of the samples. The report format of Figure 11-8 groups the samples; for example, the heading "1–2 inches" means "between 1 and 2 but not including 2." Give an algorithm to generate this report.

   See the hint of Exercise 4. Notice that there can be "gaps" in the groups. After "16–17 inches" might come "23–24 inches."

7. Write the program for the algorithm of Exercise 6.

8. Each data record contains a division number, department number, and employee number. The records are grouped by division and by department within each division. Give an algorithm to generate the report illustrated in Figure 11-9. This is an example of a **multiple-level control break**.

Grade	Name	Course
F	XXXX...X	XXX
	XXXX...X	XXX
	.	
	.	
	.	
D	XXXX...X	XXX
	.	
	.	
	.	
	(and so on)	

Figure 11-7   Report Format for Exercise 11.4

```
Group                        Sample #                    Length
-----                        --------                    ------

1-2 inches                     XXXX                     XXX.XXX
                               XXXX                     XXX.XXX
                                 .                          .
                                 .                          .
                                 .                          .
              XXX   Samples In This Group

2-3 inches                     XXXX                     XXX.XXX
                                 .                          .
                                 .                          .
                                 .                          .
                         (and so on)
```

Figure 11-8 Report Format for Exercise 11.6

Hint: Each new record could be the start of a new division; also, it could be the first record of a new department within the same division.

9. Each of these exercises refers to Exercise 2. State what assumptions you make on the order of the data.

   a. Modify 2(b) to print a report group indicated by department and by rank within departments.

   b. For 2(d), create a report group indicated by state, which lists cities group indicated by size, as shown here

```
              XX              0- 49        XXXXX...XXX
                             50-100        XXXXX...XXX
                    (and so on, in steps of 50,000)
```

```
Division              Department                      Employee
--------              ----------                      --------
  XXXX                  XXXX                            XXXXX
                                                        XXXXX
                                                        XXXXX
                                                        XXXXX

                              XXXXX Employees In Dept XXXX

                        XXXX                            XXXXX
                                                        XXXXX
                                                        XXXXX
                              XXXXX Employees In Dept XXXX

       XXXXX Employees in XXX Departments in Division XXXX

  XXXX                  XXXX                            XXXXX
                                                        XXXXX
                                 .
                                 .
                                 .
                         (and so on)
```

Figure 11-9 Report Format for Exercise 11.8

11-3
⬚⬚⬚⬚⬚⬚
SEQUENTIAL FILES— MERGE, UPDATE

☐
THE MERGE ALGORITHM

Sequential files are most useful for applications that require all, or most of, the records on the file. For applications that require only a small portion of the file, a direct file might be more useful. However, sequential files are frequently more efficient both in terms of the actual space occupied on the storage medium and in the time required to process the entire file.

Because of these savings, sequential files are widely used. As a result, a number of techniques have been developed for efficient modification and utilization of this type of file. The **merge** algorithm discussed here is one example. Others are indicated in the next subsection and in the exercises.

Suppose we have two nonempty binary files, each of which contains records in this format:

Identification(ID) number is the first field

Other information can be contained in other fields

Each of these files is known to be in ascending (low to high) order based on the ID number. Moreover, neither file contains any duplicates.

Our goal is to create a combined file with these same properties: in order by ID number and with no duplicates. The technique we use is called "merging" the files and is similar to the action when two lanes of traffic merge into one.

The basic idea is to repeatedly compare ID's from the two files, always placing the lower one into the output file. Here is a very rough algorithm. (Record 1, ID1 refer to the data from the first file. Record 2, ID2 refer to the second file.)

```
read a record from each file to get started
repeat these steps in a loop
      take action based on comparing ID1 to ID2:
            a. (ID1 < ID2) put record 1 on output file
                  read another record from file 1
            b. (ID1 > ID2) put record 2 on output file
                  read another record from file 2
            c. (ID1 = ID2) process a "duplicate" error
after the loop, perform ???
```

Because we have not discussed how to terminate the loop, it is not yet clear what steps may follow the loop.

There are a number of options for processing a duplicate record. For this example, we choose to place the record from the first file on the output file and print an error message. Because both records have then been processed, we will read a new record from each of the two files.

There are several ways to handle loop termination. For example, we might use a while loop with the condition.

```
while (not Eof(File1)) and (not Eof(File2)) do
```

When the loop terminates, then Eof(File1) is true, or Eof(File2) is true, or possibly both. We could write a decision structure based on these conditions.

This method is complicated by the fact that in Pascal the end-of-file condition becomes true as the last record is read. Thus, for example, the code for the case where Eof(File1) is true but Eof(File2) is not would have to do two things: process the remaining record from file 1 and then copy the rest of file 2 (if any) to the output file. To simplify matters, we might use Boolean variables File1Done and File2Done. File1Done signifies that we have attempted a read when no more records are in file 1, and similarly for File2Done. The step "read record from file 1" in the algorithm could be written similar to this:

```
if Eof(File1) then              {Previous read got last record}
  File1Done := true
else
  Read(File1, Record1)
```

A third possibility uses **sentinel records** on the input files. These are records whose ID number field is "$+\infty$". By "$+\infty$" we mean a value larger than any ID existing on either input file. For example, MaxInt would probably be appropriate for our integer ID's, because it is probably larger than any legal ID number.

NOTE If we use this "plus infinity" technique, then the **sentinel value** "$+\infty$" must be chosen carefully. It must not be possible to use this value for actual data.

How will the sentinel record help us? Suppose that we reach the end of file 1 first. Then ID1 will be MaxInt and the condition (ID1 > ID2) will be true for each record of the second file until it also reaches its sentinel record. This will cause the remaining records of file 2 to be copied to the output file. We should terminate the loop when both sentinel records are reached.

In Figure 11-10, we present a procedure to accomplish the merge using this technique. The main program is to handle the file open and close operations. The types DataRecord and DataFile are defined in the main program. For the purpose of our procedure, we need only know that the data record contains an ID field. Likewise, we use a constant "Infinity" defined in the main program. Thus, this procedure could be used in a variety of contexts.

```
procedure MergeFiles(var File1, File2, MergedFile : DataFile);
{
      Written by : xxxxxxxx, xx/xx/xx
         Purpose : To merge files
     Globals used : Infinity - a constant larger than any ID
      Parameters : File1 - the first file to merge
                   File2 - the second file to merge
                   MergedFile - the resulting merged file
}
var
  Record1        :  DataRecord;        {first file record}
  Record2        :  DataRecord;        {second file record}
begin  {MergeFiles}

  {***  Prime the loop by reading from both files.}
```

Figure 11-10 Merging Sequential Files (Continued)

```
      Read(File1, Record1);
      Read(File2, Record2);

{*** Repeatedly put the smaller on the output.}

while (Record1.ID <> Infinity) or (Record 2.ID <> Infinity) do
    begin
        if Record1.ID < Record2.ID then
          begin
            Write(MergedFile, Record1);
            Read(File1, Record1)
          end
        else if Record1.ID > Record2.ID then
          begin
            Write(MergedFile, Record2);
            Read(File2, Record2)
          end
        else
          begin
            Writeln('Duplicate ID: ', Record1.ID);
            Writeln('Tap <RETURN> to continue ');
            Readln;
            Write(MergedFile, Record1);
            Read(File1, Record1);
            Read(File2, Record2)
          end  {if}
    end;  {while}

  {*** Put a sentinel record on the output file.}

  Write(MergedFile, Record1)
end; {MergeFiles}
```

Figure 11-10 Merging Sequential Files

An important question for this procedure is: How did the sentinel record get on the input files? The answer is: Because these are binary files, they were created by a program. The program put them there. If they were text files created by a user, then that person would have had to put them there.

Observe that the procedure puts a sentinel record at the end of the output file. Thus, the output file would be suitable as input to the merge at some later date.

This raises an important point. If this technique is to be used for merging, then all the sequential files maintained by the organization must have a sentinel record. This will affect every program that accesses those files. Perhaps a better approach is *not* to use an actual sentinel record, but to write the program to simulate the existence of a sentinel record. For example, rather than Read(File1, Record1), we could use

```
  if Eof(File1) then                    {last record has been read}
    Record1.ID := Infinity
  else
    Read(File1, Record1)
```

The details of the modifications are left to the exercises.

Efficiency note. Suppose that one of the files reaches the end long before the other. For example, suppose file 2 reaches end-of-file with approximately 1000 records remaining in file 1. Then this procedure compares Record1.ID to "infinity" 1000 times in order to copy the rest of file 1. Isn't this inefficient? Couldn't we simply terminate the loop when either file is done and copy the rest of the other file?

The answer is "yes and no." It is inefficient, and we could terminate the loop as suggested. (This would make the procedure slightly more complicated.) However, in a file merge, the inefficiency is very minor. The time it takes to do the 1000 comparisons will be miniscule in comparison to the 2000 accesses to the disk (or to tape) used to copy the records.

(In an array merge, on the other hand, the inefficiency would be more significant.)

This basic merge algorithm is one of the most important in computer science. In addition to being the basis for various file-update algorithms, it appears in many contexts. For example, it is the basis for an order NlogN sort called Mergesort. It finds application in some forms of data structure used to represent polynomials. And it appears in handling "sparse matrices," matrices most of whose entries are 0.

□

SEQUENTIAL-FILE UPDATE

In this subsection, we give some indication of how the merge algorithm can be used to build procedures for **sequential-file update**. The exercises will develop the theme further.

First, consider this situation. A **master file** contains a list of employees and their year-to-date earnings. A **transaction file** contains a list of transactions to be processed against the master file. In this case, the transaction file represents a weekly payroll. The transactions records contain employee number and this week's pay. Provided both files are in increasing order, we can write an algorithm similar to our first merge algorithm:

read a record from both files to get started
repeat these steps in a loop:
    take action based on comparing master ID (MID) to transaction
    ID (TID):
        a. (MID < TID). This means that this employee had no check this week. Write the master record to the output file, and read a new master record.
        b. (MID > TID). This is an error situation—a check was issued for an employee number not on the master file. Report the error, and read another transaction record.
        c. (MID = TID). Add the week's pay to the year-to-date figure. Write the modified master record to the output file, and read a new record from both files.
after the loop, perform any necessary final steps

As for the merge algorithm itself, there are a variety of ways to accomplish the loop control. Depending on the method used, there may have to be some action taken after the loop terminates.

In this example, the resulting output file would become the input master file when the program was run the following week. Exactly how this would be handled would be up to the organization. Here are two possibilities at opposite extremes:

1. Start with a master MASTER.IN with all figures 0. Run this with a file WEEK.1, creating MASTER.OUT. Use a file copy to copy this to MASTER.IN for the second week, and so on.

2. Start as before, but call the output MASTER.1. Use this as input for the second week, creating MASTER.2. By the end of the year, you would have 52 files containing a complete record of the year.

For our final example, suppose that the transaction file contains a list of items to be deleted from the master file. A deletion is accomplished by simply not writing the record to the output. Thus, in the decision structure of the basic merge algorithm, we would have:

> a. (ID1 < ID2) same as merge
> b. (ID1 > ID2) error; read transaction file
> c. (ID1 = ID2) just read both files

REVIEW

Terms and concepts

merge
sequential-file update
sentinel record
infinity (+∞)

sentinel value
master file
transaction file

Algorithms

Basic merge algorithm:

read a record from each file to get started
repeat these steps in a loop
    take action based on comparing ID1 to ID2:
        a. (ID1 < ID2) put record 1 on output file
           read another record from file 1
        b. (ID1 > ID2) put record 2 on output file
           read another record from file 2
        c. (ID1 = ID2) process a duplicate error
after the loop, perform???

Loop control possibilities:

1. Terminate when Eof is true for either file.

2. Terminate when an attempt is made to read past end-of-file for either file.

3. Use sentinel records and terminate when both values are +∞

4. Same as item 3, but terminate when either is $+\infty$.

5. "Simulate" the sentinel record.

Sequential-file updates:

Sequential-file updates can be based on the fundamental merge algorithm; differences occur in what is done for each of the three branches in the decision structure.

1. Write a procedure similar to the one in Figure 11-10, but not using sentinel records. The loop should be terminated as soon as Eof is true for either file. Be careful to write the portion following the loop correctly.

2. Repeat Exercise 1 using Boolean variables File1Done and File2Done as suggested in this section. Terminate the loop when either is true.

3. Repeat Exercise 1 "simulating" the sentinel record as suggested in this section. Terminate when both ID values are infinity.

4. Repeat Exercise 3 terminating when either ID value is infinity.

5. Comment on the pros and cons of the approaches in Figure 11-10 and in Exercises 1 to 4.

*6. Two files containing names and other data are to be merged based on the names. What is an appropriate value for "plus infinity" in this case?

*7. Suppose files that are in order from high to low are to be merged. How would this affect the algorithm? What type of sentinel value would be appropriate?

8. Write a procedure that, for a master file as shown in Figure 11-10, accepts from the terminal a list of numbers to be deleted. It should warn the user if the number entered is lower than the previous entry.

9. a. Write a procedure to merge three files rather than two.
   b. Write a procedure to expand this to merge 10 files. Can you suggest a way to merge 10 files without writing a new program?

*10. Sometimes students try to write the decision structure of the merge algorithm using three if statements:

```
if Record1.ID < Record2.ID then
    {code for < as in Figure 11-10};
if Record1.ID > Record2.ID then
    {code for > as in Figure 11-10};
if Record1.ID = Record2.ID then
    {code for = as in Figure 11-10};
```

Criticize this by finding a pair of files for which it would not work properly.

11. Someone has suggested modifying the third branch of the merge algorithm (ID1 = ID2) to the following: print the error message, and read a new record from file 2. Will this work? Justify your answer.

12. Write procedures similar to Figure 11-10 for the following:

*a. A master file has records consisting of an item number, department, and quantity. A transaction file has records containing only an item number.

Each record in the transaction file represents a record to be removed from the master file. Both files are in order by item number and have no duplicates.

Create an output file consisting of the records in the master file with the indicated records removed. Print an error message for any faulty transaction item numbers.

b. The master file is the same as for part (a). The transaction file contains a list of changes to be made. Each transaction record contains an item number and a new quantity for that item. Both files are in order by item number and have no duplicates.

Create an output file consisting of the records in the master file with the new quantity for each of the indicated items. Print an error message for any faulty transaction item numbers.

13. Combine the merge (which adds records) with the delete and change procedures of Exercise 12. The master file is the same as for Exercise 12. Each transaction record contains:

Transaction code (A = add, D = delete, C = change)
Item number
Department (blank for codes D or C)
Quantity (blank for code D)

Both files are in order by item number and have no duplicates.

Write a procedure to create an output file consisting of the records in the master file with the indicated additions, deletions, and changes.

14. Write a program to update the drugstore inventory file created in Exercise 2, Section 11-1

You have a transaction file containing this information: an item number, an item name, a department code, an inventory of each of nine locations, and a transaction code. Except for the transaction code, the information is precisely the same as that on the master file. The transaction code has the same meaning as in Exercise 13. The transaction record can leave blank (or 0) any of the fields not actually being used in that type of transaction. You can assume that the information on the transaction record has been edited.

The following are to be done for a "change" transaction:

- If the item name on the transaction record is not blank, then change the item name.

- If the department code on the transaction record is not blank, then change the department code.

- Add each element in the inventory array to the corresponding element in the master record.

Instead of printing errors on the terminal, create an exception file. This file will have records containing all the fields of the transaction record and a code for the type of error:

- Trying to add a record already there.
- Trying to delete a record not there.
- Trying to change a record not there.

- A resulting inventory amount that is less than 0 or more than 5000. (For this error, leave the master record with the faulty inventories; assume the error will be corrected later.)

15. Update algorithms based on the file merge algorithm have one serious drawback. They do not handle multiple transactions for a single master record. Computer scientists have devised an algorithm, known as the **balance line algorithm**, which does handle multiple transactions.

     The basic idea is this: Rather than putting master records directly to the output file, put them in a new master record. Apply the transactions to this new master record. After all transactions have been applied, write the record to the output. In rough form, the algorithm can be described as follows:

     read a record from both files to get started
     repeat these four steps in a loop:
         1. ActiveKey := lower of MasterKey, TransactionKey
         2. if the MasterKey is equal to the ActiveKey:
             copy the master record to new master record
             read another master record
        else:
             set the new master record empty
         3. apply 0 or more transactions to the new master record, in a loop, as long as the Transaction Key equals the ActiveKey
         4. if the new master record is not empty, write it to the output file
     after the outer loop, do any necessary final steps

     *a. By tracing the algorithm for some sample files, determine what the phrase "apply a transaction" means for the six possible combinations:

Type of Transaction	New Master Record
Add	Empty
Add	Not empty
Delete	Empty
Delete	Not empty
Change	Empty
Change	Not empty

     b. Refine the algorithm to write a procedure to update a master file, as outlined in Exercise 13.
     c. Refine the algorithm to write a procedure to update a checking account master file. Each master record has an account number and balance. Each transaction record has an account number, type (check or deposit), and amount. The output file has an account number and the resulting balance. Record all error situations on an error file.

RANDOM-ACCESS FILE TECHNIQUES

Sequential files are convenient for the long-term storage of data. As long as a file is updated fairly infrequently, sequential access can be adequate. For example, a mailing list for an organization might be stored on a sequential file. Generally, this information will be used in its entirety to generate a set of mailing labels. Updating might occur only once a month or even less frequently.

Even when a file is updated frequently, sequential access can be appropriate. For example, the "hours worked" and other fields on a file used to generate payroll checks might change every week. However, in this case, most records in the file will be modified. An algorithm that goes through the file sequentially making the changes would be fairly efficient.

Sequential files become inadequate in situations where frequent changes occur to records scattered throughout the file. As we discussed in Section 11-3, each batch of changes to a sequential file requires going completely through the file. In addition, if we are using the file to "look up" records that are scattered at random throughout the file, we will want a **random-access file** (in which records can be accessed directly in a random order). Even in applications where a sequential file is adequate, a random-access file may be more convenient. For example, consider a conversational payroll system. Using a sequential file, a payroll clerk could enter the hours for each person on the file. However, the clerk would have to do so in the same order as the records were listed on the file. With a random-access file, the values could be entered in any desired order, perhaps by several payroll clerks, one per department.

As a result of these and similar considerations, random-access files have become more and more important in computing. As a result, Turbo Pascal has included facilities for using this type of file, even though it is not called for in standard Pascal.

COMMENTS

1. Because this type of file is nonstandard, our discussion will be totally oriented toward Turbo Pascal. Other versions of Pascal have also implemented random-access files, but with differing syntax.

2. These files go under a variety of names. The term **direct file** signifies the ability to directly access the desired record, without having had to access all the preceding records. The term **random-access file**, similarly, signifies the ability to access the records in "random" order. The term **relative file** signifies the fact that, in order to access a record, the program supplies the **relative record number** (or just **record number**).

We will generally refer to the files as random-access files, but we will feel free to use the terms interchangeably.

RANDOM-ACCESS FILE COMMANDS

We already know quite a bit about Turbo Pascal random-access files. For Turbo Pascal, a random-access file is any binary (that is, non-text) file. What we need to learn, then, is the commands (that is, procedures and functions) that will allow us to access binary files in a random fashion.

Two useful concepts in this regard are the **record number** and the **file pointer**. Each record in a binary file has a record number. The records are numbered starting at 0. As a simple example, suppose we have a file containing five records (fields of name and major):

Sue	CPS
Sam	MAT
Joe	MGT
Mary	ENG
Eileen	HIS

We will soon learn how to read record 3. If we do so, we will obtain the record (Mary, ENG) because the record numbers start at 0.

The file-management system maintains a file pointer, which is initialized to 0 by the Reset procedure. After any read or write, the file pointer will point to (contain the record number of) the next record. For example, after we read record 3, the file pointer's value would be 4. At this point, unless we do something to modify the file pointer, another Read would read record 4 (and a Write would replace the current value of record 4).

With these concepts in mind, let us describe the various capabilities provided by Turbo Pascal. The first seven are procedures and the last 3 are functions.

1. Assign(*file designator, file name*). Connects the program's name for the file (the "file designator" variable) and the file's name on the disc (the "filename" string).

2. Reset(*file designator*). Opens the file, and sets the file pointer to 0 (that is, the first record of the file).

3. Rewrite(*file designator*). Opens the file, sets the file pointer to 0, and deletes any existing data in the file.

4. Read(*file designator, variable*). Reads the record indicated by the file pointer, and advances the file pointer to the next record (adds 1 to the file pointer).

5. Write(*file designator, variable*). Writes the record indicated by the file pointer, and adds 1 to the file pointer. This replaces the previous data stored in that record.

6. Seek(*file designator*, N). Sets the file pointer to the Nth record, where N is an integer expression. The value of N should generally lie between 0 and the file size.

7. Close(*file designator*). Closes the file. This is necessary to make sure that all changes are reflected in the file on the disk. As a general principle, your program should close all the files it opens.

8. Eof(*file designator*). This Boolean function's value is true if the file pointer is positioned beyond the end-of-file, otherwise false.

9. FilePos(*file designator*). This integer function supplies the current value of the file pointer (0 for the first record, and so on).

10. FileSize(*file designator*). This integer function shows how many records the file contains.

To illustrate these ideas, we show some segments of Pascal code. In each, we will assume that the files are opened and closed by other portions of the program. We will work with the direct file described above: each record has a name and an age. We assume these declarations for the files and records involved.

```
type
  StudentRecord = record
                    Name  : String20;
                    Major : String3;
                  end;
  StudentFile   = file of StudentRecord;

var
  Person       : StudentRecord;
  ClassFile    : StudentFile;
```

We assume that a procedure GetData(Person) prompts the user for a person's name and major.

The first segment writes 25 records to the file, numbered 0 to 24. (The file was opened using Rewrite.)

```
for I := 1 to 25 do
  begin
    GetData(Person);
    Write(ClassFile, Person)
  end;  {for}
```

The second segment illustrates how we can add a record to the end of an existing file:

```
GetData(Person);
NewPosition := FileSize(ClassFile);
Seek(ClassFile, NewPosition);
Write(ClassFile, Person);
```

Suppose, for example, that the file size is 23. Then there are currently 23 records numbered 0 to 22. The Seek sets the file pointer to record 23, so that the Write puts the new record right after record 22.

Our third segment reads a series of record numbers from the user and prints the corresponding data from the file. For record numbers equal to the file size, or larger, an error message is printed.

```
repeat
  Write( 'Enter a record number (negative to quit): ');
  Readln(RecNum);
  if RecNum >= FileSize(ClassFile) then
    Writeln('Too High')
  else if RecNum >= 0 then
    begin
      Seek(ClassFile, RecNum);
      Read(ClassFile, Person);
      with Person do
        Writeln('Name: ', Name, ' Major: ', Major)
    end  {if}
until RecNum < 0;
```

Finally, we present a segment that changes all 'CPS' majors to 'CSC'. (The file has just been Reset.)

```
while not Eof(ClassFile) do
   begin
      Read(ClassFile, Person);
      if Person.Major = 'CPS' then
         begin
            Person.Major := 'CSC';
            Seek(ClassFile, FilePos(ClassFile)-1));   {go back to record}
            Write(ClassFile, Person)
         end  {if}
   end;  {while}
```

Notice that, if we did not use a Seek to "back up one," we would have overwritten the wrong record.

□
**RANDOM-
ACCESS FILE
ALGORITHMS**

The examples that follow illustrate some basic techniques for working with random-access files. The major difficulty with these files is that the program must know the proper record number. If this number is read from some other file or from the user, as in the example above, then the user must know the record numbers of the records to be processed. There are a number of techniques that have been devised for this purpose. One of the simplest is illustrated by the following example.

COMMENT   Studying the techniques for determining the desired record number in a direct file typically occupies a major portion of a course in file processing. Obviously, in our limited space, we will barely scratch the surface of this fascinating topic.

A small liberal arts college maintains a student data file. Among other things, the file contains a four-digit student number, the total number of credits attempted to date, and the number of quality points earned to date.

When the file was originally created, it was decided to use the student number itself as the record number. A file was created containing records 0 to 9999, where each record contained a flag telling whether or not that student number was active.

The student number can be viewed as a **key** to the record; given the student number, we know which student's record we wish to see. In this case, we have the record number equal to the key.

The procedure in Figure 11-11 updates this file. To do so, it reads a sequential file containing a series of student numbers, credit hours attempted during one semester, and quality points earned during that semester. Using the given student number, it retrieves the student's record, updates the record, and writes it back onto the file.

COMMENTS   *1.* It would not be necessary to include the student number on the record because this number is the same as the record number.

2. A field of the record indicates whether that record number is active. Requests to update an inactive record are logged on an error file. (The record number is, however, assumed to be valid, that is, between 0 and the file size minus 1.)

3. We assume that the main program handles opening and closing the files.

```
procedure UpdateQP(var StudentFile : Masterfile;
                   var UpdateList : TransactionFile;
                   var ErrorLog : text);
{
    Written by:   XXXXXXXX   XX/XX/XX
       Purpose:   To read a sequential transaction file, and add
                  data to the records of a master student file.
    Parameters:   StudentFile - the file of student records
                  UpdateList - the file of transactions
                  ErrorLog - a text file for error messages
}

var
  Semester : UpdateRecord;                {figures for this semester}
  Student  : StudentRecord;               {master record}
  RecNum   : integer;                     {record number}

begin

  while not Eof(UpdateList) do
    begin
      Read(UpdateList, Semester);
      RecNum := Semester.StudentNumber;
      Seek(StudentFile, RecNum);
      Read(StudentFile, Student);
      with Student do
        begin
          if not Active then
            Writeln(ErrorLog, 'Inactive record: ', RecNum)
          else
            begin
              Hours := Hours + Semester.Hours;
              QP := QP + Semester.QP;
              Seek(StudentFile, RecNum);              { "back up" }
              Write(StudentFile, Student)
            end   {if}
        end   {with}
    end   {while}

end;   {UpdateQP}
```

Figure 11-11 Updating a Random Access File

Using the record number as the key can be a problem. When the record number is the key, then we must know the key to obtain the record. Moreover, this key must be numerical, and the number of digits allowed in the key will be limited. There are many applications where it is more convenient to use an alphabetic key. For example, when students come in to check their records, they may not remember their student numbers. Either their name or social security number might be a more convenient key.

As a similar example, consider a file that lists the local tax rate for each of the various cities, towns, and so forth in a given state. For such a file, the most convenient key would be the locality name or perhaps an abbreviation of that name. If the file is set up with this alphabetical key, then some means must be provided in the program to determine the desired record number, given the locality name.

A number of techniques have been devised to handle these and other considerations when working with random-access files. These techniques are beyond the scope of this text (although we do indicate some possibilities in the exercises). However, keep in mind that once the record number is calculated, the Seek, Read or Write will be identical in form to those presented in our examples.

□ **INACTIVE RECORDS**
The example in Figure 11-11 illustrates one important aspect of working with random-access files. It is possible that there can be "gaps" in the file. In Turbo Pascal files, those gaps will be "logical" rather than "physical" gaps. That is, if a file contains record 200, it will also contain records 0 through 199. However, some of those records may not contain meaningful information.

One way to deal with this is indicated in Figure 11-11. A Boolean field of the record can indicate that the record is inactive. Another possibility is to set some field of the record to a specific "dummy" value. For example, a name field that is null might signify an inactive record.

Whatever technique is used, all programs that access the file will have to apply the technique consistently. We would, perhaps, have a program to create the original file containing nothing but inactive records. Later, other programs would change some records to active status. We might also have a procedure to delete a record. For the file used in Figure 11-11, it could do so by setting

```
Student.Active := false
```

and then writing the record. Notice that a "deleted record," as used here, is one that is "logically deleted," not "physically deleted." The record is still there; it has just been marked inactive.

■■■■■■
REVIEW

Terms and concepts

sequential file	relative record number
random-access file	record number
direct file	file pointer
relative file	key

File operations

1. Assign, Reset, Rewrite, Close, Eof: Same as for sequential-file use.

2. Read (Write): Reads (writes) the current record, then advances the file pointer to the next record.

3. Seek(*file designator*, N): Sets the file pointer to Nth record (generally use N in the range $0 \leq N \leq$ file size).

4. Function FilePos(*file designator*): Shows current value of the file pointer (record number).

5. Function FileSize(*file designator*): Shows the file size (in records).

1. Need to know desired record number.
2. Can mark records as inactive (''deleted'') in a variety of ways.

■■■■■■
EXERCISES

1. Rewrite Case Study No. 9 (Section 6-4) to use random-access files rather than arrays. Use the item number as the key for the item file and the customer number as the key for the customer file.

2. A direct file contains a list of persons and companies to whom a church typically writes checks. Write the following set of routines for the church treasurer.

   Note: Each record contains the account name (25 characters) as it is to appear on the checks. If the name is '*', the account has been deleted.

   *a. Lookup. Given an account number (record number), display the account name.
   b. Addition. Given a new account name, add it to the end of the file. (Make sure it isn't a duplicate.)
   *c. Printout. Print a list of the current contents of the file: record number and account name. Ignore deleted records.
   d. Deletion. Given a record number, mark it as deleted. (First display the name on the screen and verify that this is the one the user wanted to delete.)
   e. Compression. Remove all deleted records by copying the valid records to a temporary file, then reopening the account file and recopying the valid records.

3. A direct file keeps a list of checks written by a church. A control file contains one record with three fields: the first check number in the file, the last check number in the file, and the last check number printed and sent. For the other records, the check number is the record number, and the records contain these fields:

Description	Type
Date (yymmdd)—870407 is April 7, 1987	String
Paid to whom (three-digit code)	integer
Budget category (two-digit code)	integer
Amount (dollars, cents)—1013,45 is $1013.45	A record with two integer fields

The ''paid to whom'' code refers to the file of Exercise 2. The ''budget category'' code refers to a similar file that lists budget category names.

   Give subprograms for the following. Assume the main program has opened the files.

   a. New check. Given a date, ''paid to'' code, ''category'' code, and amount, add a check to the end of the file. First, however, make sure that the given date is after the date of the last check written and that both codes are valid. Set a Boolean output parameter OK to indicate success or failure.
   b. Check list. Create a printed list of the checks on the file with these columns: date, number, paid to (name, not code), budget category (name), and amount. As an optional extra, group indicate by date, that is, print the date only when it changes. Print the dates in the form mm/dd/yy.

c. Partial list. Modify part (b) to print only those checks whose dates lie between two given dates, inclusive.

d. Check print. Print all checks that have not yet been printed. Devise a reasonable check layout. Print the date in the form "January 16, 1988." Print the amount preceded by asterisks, as in '***35.49'. Also print the amount in the form 'EXACTLY 35 DOLLARS AND 49 CENTS'.

e. Budget summary. Create a printed report showing how much was spent in each budget category between two given dates. You can assume that the budget category file records contain a field for use as an accumulator.

*4. How would you modify the program of Exercise 3 so that the first check written in the year would be record 0, the next record 1, and so on? (For a church whose first check was 1927, this would save almost 2000 empty records.)

5. An employee file contains records 0 to 999. Among the fields is a LastName field set to '*' for unused records. For several applications, we wish to access the records in alphabetical order by last name. Write the following collection of program segments to accomplish this (see also Exercise 6).

*a. Write code to set up an array of records with fields RecNum and Name. For record I in the array, RecNum is the record number and Name is the name of the Ith active record on the file. (Skip unused records.)

b. Sort the array into alphabetical order by name.

c. Create a sequential file that contains the record number field from the sorted array, one number per file record.

6. See Exercise 5. If we are given a list of record numbers to be processed, we can easily process a direct file in that order.

Use the file created in Exercise 5(c) to display a printed list of the name, hourly rate, department, clock number, marital status, and number of dependents in alphabetical order by last name. Make reasonable assumptions about the structure of the master file.

7. See Exercise 5. Rather than creating a separate file to get an alphabetical listing, we could have each record in the master file show which record is next in alphabetical order. Each record might contain these fields:

Description	Type
Name	String
"Next"—a three-digit number showing which record number comes next in alphabetical order	integer
Other data	Miscellaneous

Suppose that a control file contains only a single number ("First") that tells which record is first in alphabetical order. Also, suppose that the "Next" field for the person who is last contains the number -1.

*a. Write a program to print the file as in Exercise 6, using the control file to get started and using the "Next" field to move through the file.

b. Write algorithms for inserting a new employee and for deleting an employee. Each will involve changing some of the "Next" fields in the file (and perhaps the "First" field on the control file).

8. In this exercise we explore simple **hashing** and **collision-handling** strategies for determining where a record should be placed in a direct-access file.

*a. Suppose we want to place some records in a file that we have set up to have 10 empty records, numbered from 0 to 9. The records have keys that are four digit numbers. Let us follow the rule: Try to place the record in the location (that is, record number) indicated by the last digit of the key. (This rule is an example of a **hashing function**.)

What record would that rule have us use for the following keys: 1403, 1695, 1138, 5689, 4122, 8904?

*b. These records ran well. There were no **collisions**; that is, no two records yielded the same output from the hashing function. (We may say, "No two records hashed to the same location.") In the more general case, we must use some **collision-handling** strategy. One approach has a number of names, including the very descriptive "consecutive spill." For example, "if the record hashes to location 4 and that is full, put it in 5; if that is full, put it in 6; and so on." Using this strategy to handle collisions and the same empty file and hashing function as in part (a), show where these records would go: 1403, 1795, 1138, 2014, 1183, 8998, and 3114. (Notice that locations can be full because of collisions or due to records that have already spilled out of their hash location.)

*c. What should you do with a record that "spills" past location 9, which is the last location in the file? The usual method is to treat the file as if it were circular, so that location 0 follows location 9. Continuing with the file in part (b), add these records: 9000, 8615, and 4029.

*d. A "probe" is the act of examining a location to see whether it is empty. For example, putting in 1403 required one probe because location 3 was empty. How many probes did each of the other records require?

e. Write a program to create a file containing 10 empty records, numbered 0 to 9. Each record contains a key and a name. Read data from the user to be placed into the file. Using the hashing function (Hint: use the mod function) and the collision-handling method described above, the program should insert the records. At the end, it should print the file in order by record number, to verify that it worked correctly.

Note: The loop that examines locations to see if they are empty should have three ways to terminate: an empty location is found, a duplicate key is found, or all 10 locations have been examined and none is empty (file is full).

f. Modify part (e) to handle more keys by setting up a file of size 100. Modify your hashing function appropriately.

g. If you placed 75 records into a file of size 100 using the program of part (f), about how many total probes would you expect it to take? [See part (d).] To answer the question, write a program that does the steps described below in a loop and reports the statistics. The steps are initialize the file to contain 100 empty records; generate random keys and place them into the file, counting the probes for nonduplicate keys; and terminate the loop when 75 different keys have been inserted.

APPENDIX

A. ADDITIONAL PASCAL TOPICS

In this Appendix, we describe a few features of the Pascal language which were not covered in the body of the text. These topics are "extra" in the sense that it is possible to get by quite adequately without them. (We have done so in all the program examples in the text.) However, there are instances in which some of these additional capabilities prove useful in designing and writing Pascal programs.

Some of the features we describe are standard Pascal. Others are extensions provided by Turbo Pascal.

□ TRANSFER STATEMENTS (LABELS, GOTO, EXIT)

Pascal permits us to define a **label** and use a **goto** statement. Labels are strings of digits between 0 and 9999, and must be declared in a label declaration of the form

```
label
   10, 100, 200;
```

for example. The label declaration precedes the constant declaration in a program or procedure. A label is attached to a statement by writing in a program or procedure. A label is attached to a statement by writing the label, followed by a colon, before the statement as in:

```
10:   if X = Y then A := B + C;
100:  Y := X + Z;
200:  ;
```

Notice in the last example that the label is attached to a null statement.

The statement

```
goto 10;
```

causes the program to start executing statements at the statement labeled 10. We say that control has transferred to the statement labeled 10. Generally, a goto can be used to transfer out of the body of a loop or the true or false part of an if–then–else, or within those same sections, but it must not be used to transfer into such a section from outside. For example, the following code would be valid:

```
      . . .
label 10;
      . . .
begin
  . . .
  while .. do
    begin
        . . .
        if .. then goto 10;
        . . .
    end;
  . . .
  10: ;
  . . .
end.
```

The following code would not be valid because the goto branches into the body of the while loop.

```
      . . .
label 10;
      . . .
begin
  . . .
  if .. then goto 10;
  . . .
  while ... do
    begin
        . . .
        10: ;
        . . .
    end;
  . . .
end.
```

The goto statement is controversial. Historically, it has been used in ways that have made programs extremely difficult to understand. As a result, some individuals (and some companies) completely forbid its use. Others use it only in a few well-defined situations. For example, some might use the goto to leave a nested loop when an error is discovered.

As an example of the controlled use of the goto, consider this procedure that does some unspecified process. During the course of this process, two error conditions could be detected. The procedure is to quit processing upon discovering an error. Here are two solutions:

```
procedure XXXX(. . .);
  label 10;
  begin
    . . .
    if error #1 exists then
      begin
        Error := 1;
        goto 10
      end;
    . . .
    if error #2 exists then
```

```
            begin
               Error := 2;
               goto 10
            end;
                . . .
        10 : end;


        procedure XXXX(. . .);
           begin
                . . .
              if error #1 exists then
                 Error := 1
              else
                 begin
                      . . .
                    if error #2 exists then
                       Error := 2
                    else
                       begin
                          . . .
                       end
                 end
           end;
```

The use of the goto avoids nesting decisions. You might want to ponder the form of the two solutions if there were, say, five possible errors instead of only two.

This particular use of a goto, to terminate the execution of a procedure, is one that is used by many programmers. However, because of the tendency to abuse the goto, those who use it in this fashion may feel uncomfortable doing so. Turbo Pascal provides an alternative that achieves the same result but without opening the Pandora's box of the unrestricted use of the goto. This alternative is the **exit** statement. "Exit" means "leave the procedure (or function)." It is equivalent to a goto that branches to the end of the procedure. Each "goto 10" in the example above could be replaced by the word "exit." We would not declare or use the label 10 in this case.

COMMENTS

1. Even the use of the exit is somewhat controversial. If you are programming for someone else, find out if it is allowed.

2. The exit statement is not available in standard Pascal.

3. In the main program, exit means "halt the program."

4. In standard Pascal, a goto in a procedure or function can branch to a label in the main program. This is not allowed in Turbo Pascal; all branches must be within the body of the module in which the goto occurs.

□
THE INCLUDE COMPILER DIRECTIVE

Turbo Pascal provides a (nonstandard) method for inserting the text of a file into the program being compiled. A comment of the form

```
{$I filename}
```

causes the file whose name appears in the directive to be inserted into the text being compiled. This can be used to insert the text of written procedures into your program. The authors, for example, each have a number of procedures that they use in many of their programs. Only a $I comment is needed to place those procedures into their programs. Because no retyping is needed, there is no possibility of making a typing error. Another use of include files is for a number of different programs that need a common variable or type definition. The definition could be placed in a file, and each program could then include that definition file. If any changes were needed in the definition, the changes would be made only in its file and not in each of the program files. This eliminates the chance of forgetting to make the changes in all the programs.

The files that are included can contain not only procedure and function definitions, but also type, variable, and other declarations. Turbo Pascal relaxes the rule in Pascal that the declarations must appear in the order: label, const, type, var, and subprograms. In Turbo, the declarations can be in any order, and a given section can be split if desired. (Each individual item must still be declared before use, except as noted earlier.) Therefore, an include file can contain type, const, and variable declarations needed by the procedures in the file.

Include files cannot be nested. In other words, a file that is to be included cannot itself contain any $I directives.

A number of companies produce add on libraries of procedures for Turbo Pascal programs. They are often supplied in the form of files to be included using the $I directive.

VARIANT RECORDS

Records are first introduced in Chapter 5 and are used extensively in the following chapters. The Pascal record structure is useful both as a way to organize our data in a program and as an implementation of the record concept for files.

The Pascal record data type includes a capability not discussed in the body of the text: the ability to contain what is called a **variant part**. (The records we have previously used contained only a **fixed part**.) As an example of a record structure with a variant part, suppose we want to store data on various people associated with a college. These people are in three categories, with the following associated data to be stored:

Faculty:
> Name
>
> Age
>
> Position (faculty)
>
> Highest earned degree
>
> University awarding this degree

Student:
> Name
>
> Age
>
> Position (student)
>
> High school graduated
>
> Combined SAT score

Staff:
> Name
>
> Age
>
> Position (staff)
>
> Job description

One approach would be to define data types as follows:

```
type
  PositionType = (Faculty, Staff, Student);
  PersonalData =
    record
      Name       : string[20];
      Age        : integer;
```

```
             Position    : Person;
             Degree      : string[8];
             University  : string[25];
             HighSchool  : string[20];
             SAT         : integer;
             Job         : string[15]
          end;
```

For each person, the data that did not apply would be left as null or zero.

The alternative is to define a record with both a fixed part and a variant part:

```
          PersonalData =
            record
              Name     : string[20];
              Age      : integer;
              case Position : PositionType of
                Faculty : ( Degree     : string[8];
                            University : string[25] );
                Student : ( HighSchool : string[20];
                            SAT        : integer );
                  Staff : ( Job        : string[15] );
            end;
```

NOTES

1. The fields Name and Age form the fixed part of the record. Every record of this type contains these fields.

2. The field Position is called the **tag field**. It determines whether the remainder of the record will consist of a degree and university, or a high school and SAT score, or a job description.

3. The remainder of the record is the variant part. It consists of a list of fields for each value of the tag field. This list is enclosed in parentheses. It can be empty, but the parentheses are required in any case.

With a variable Person of type PersonalData, we can write code similar to these examples:

```
          Person.Name := 'Joe Smith'
          Person.Position := Staff
          Readln(Person.SAT)
          with Person do Job := 'President'
          if Person.SAT > 1000 then
```

CAUTION

It is up to the programmer to maintain consistency. For example, the assignment Person.SAT := 1215 would be allowed even if Person.Position were Faculty. The results would be unpredictable.

As an example of how the variant record concept might be used, consider the program of Figure 6-10 (page 461). In that program, we used two files, a control file and a data file. The control file contained a single record that gave the number of students, tests, and programs represented in the data file. An alternate approach is to place this count as the first record in the data file. To do so, we would redefine the StudentRecord type as follows:

```
    type
      RecordType = (ControlRec, StudentRec);
      StudentRecord =
        record
          case Indicator : RecordType of
            Control : ( NStudents : integer;
                        NTests    : integer;
                        NPrograms : integer );
            Student : ( Name      : String20;
                        TestList  : TestArray;
                        Exam      : integer;
                        ProgList  : ProgramArray;
                        Average   : real;
                        Letter    : char );
        end;
```

We would do away with the control file, with the variable Control declared to be of type StudentRecord. (Control.Indicator would have the value ControlRec.)

What are the advantages and disadvantages of using variant records? They allow us to store data when the records share some types of information but have some information that is different. In doing so, they save space. In the PersonalData example, each record using the original form is about 95 bytes, but only about 56 with the variant record form. (Space is allotted for the fixed part and the longest of the alternatives in the variant part.) Another advantage is that they can remove the need for control files. On the other hand, the syntax is more difficult and can lead to confusion on the part of the programmer or the reader of the program.

As a final comment, we note that the tag field variable can be omitted. This is an advanced topic we will not pursue in this text.

☐ NESTED PROCEDURES

You have seen many examples of procedures and functions in this book. For the rest of this subsection, we will be using the word *procedure*, but what we discuss here will apply equally to *functions*. These user-defined procedures have been declared within a program unit after the global variables have been declared and before the executable statements of the program. Variables referenced within these procedures have been one of the following:

- arguments of the procedure
- local variables, accessible only within the procedure
- global variables, accessible everywhere within the program [unless the name was as in (a) or (b)]

In Pascal, we can define a procedure within another procedure. Such are called **nested procedures**. The effects are to limit access to the procedures nested within another and to create classes of variables between the local and global variables discussed above. Consider, for example, the program in Figure A-1.

```
program Nested(Input, Output);
var
  I, J, K : integer;

procedure P1(X1, X2 : integer);
var
  L, M, N : integer;
```

Figure A-1 (Continued)

```
procedure P2(Y1, Y2 : integer);
var
  O, P, Q : integer;
begin  {P2}
    . . .
end;  {P2}

procedure P3(Z1, Z2 : integer);
var
  R, S, T : integer;
begin  {P3}
    . . .
end;  {P3}

begin  {P1}
    . . .
end;  {P1}

begin  {Nested}
    . . .
end.
```

Figure A-1

In this example, the procedures P2 and P3 are defined within procedure P1. They are said to be nested within P1. This has implications concerning the scope of the various variables. For the discussion that follows, it may be helpful to refer to Figure A-2, which shows P1 and P2 defined within P1 and P1 defined within the main program Nested.

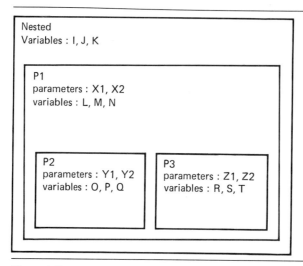

Figure A-2

The variables I, J, and K are global, as before. They can be referenced in any of the procedures P1, P2, and P3, or in the main program. The variables O, P, and Q and the parameters Y1 and Y2 are local to P2 and can only be referenced there. Likewise, R, S, T, Z1, and Z2 can be referred to only within the body of P3.

The variables L, M, and N and the parameters X1 and X2 can be referenced within the body of P1. Moreover, they can also be referenced within the bodies of P2 and P3 because P2 and P3 are declared within P1. If we visualize the boxes in Figure A-2 as one-way mirrors that allow us to look out but not in, they can help us determine what can be referenced.

The portion of a program in which a variable can be referenced is called the **scope** of the variable. Thus, the scope of the variable L in the example consists of the bodies of procedures P1, P2, and P3. In general, the scope of a variable is the procedure in which it is declared and any procedure nested within that procedure. However, declaring a variable within a procedure "masks" or "hides" variables of the same name. For example, suppose that procedure P3 declared a variable L. Then the scope of the variable L defined in P1 would no longer include P3; any reference to L within P3 would refer to the L declared in P3.

COMMENT   There is no restriction on the levels of nesting.

What are the disadvantages and advantages of nested procedure definitions? The primary disadvantage is obvious: They considerably complicate determining the scope of a variable. They also make it less likely that the compiler will detect the failure to declare a variable. As a result, nested procedures should be used with some care.

There are, however, at least two important advantages. One is found with a package of programs supplied by a developer. The person writing the package may want to place subprograms within the modules that use them. These modules will not be visible to the user of the package so that he or she will not have to avoid the module names in choosing identifiers.

A second advantage is illustrated by the QuickSort procedure of Figure A-3. This procedure is a modification of Figure 6-14 (page 484); the changes are shaded.

```
procedure QuickSort(var A : IntegerArray; N :  integer);
{
        Written by:   XXXXXXXXXX  XX/XX/XX
           Purpose:   To sort an array, using the quick sort technique.
        Parameters:   A - update, the array to sort
                      N - input, indicates the upper bound of the
                          portion of the array to sort
   Procedures used:   QSort, to perform the actual sort
}

procedure Partition(Low, High :  integer;  var PivotLocation : integer);
{
        Written by:   XXXXXXXXXX  XX/XX/XX
           Purpose:   To partition an array into three parts:
                      1. values less or equal to the pivotal element
                      2. the pivotal element
                      3. values greater than or equal to the pivotal
                         element
        Parameters:   Low, High - input, the portion of the array to partition
                      PivotLocation - output, the location for the pivotal
                          element
   Procedures used:   Swap, to swap two elements of the array
   Globals modified:  A (from QuickSort), the array being partitioned
}
var
   I       : integer;              { used to locate large values }
   J       : integer;              { used to locate small values }
   Pivot   : integer;              { the pivotal element }
```

{*procedure Swap, as shown in Figure 6-14, is inserted here*}

Figure A-3   (Continued)

```
begin  {Partition}
  I := Low;
  J := High + 1;
  Pivot := A[Low];

  repeat

{*** Move I to right looking for a value greater than or equal to
     the pivot.}

    repeat
      I := I + 1
    until (I = High) or (A[I] >= Pivot);

{*** Move J to left looking for a value less than or equal to
     the pivot.}

    repeat
      J := J - 1
    until A[J] <= Pivot;

{***  Swap if the values are out of order.}

    if I < J then
      Swap(A[I], A[J])

  until I >= J;

{*** Put the pivotal element in the proper place, and return the
     value of its subscript to the calling module.}

  Swap(A[Low], A[J]);
  PivotLocation := J
end;  {Partition}
```

```
procedure QSort(Low, High :  integer);
{
        Written by:   XXXXXXXXX  XX/XX/XX
           Purpose:   To sort an array, using the quick sort technique.
        Parameters:   Low, High - input, the portion of the array to sort
  Procedures used:    Partition, to partition the array into two subarrays
                      QSort, called recursively to sort the two subarrays
  Globals modified:   A (from QuickSort), the array being sorted
}

var
  PivotSub : integer;                     { Location of pivotal element }

begin  {QSort}
  if Low < High then
    begin
      Partition(Low, High, PivotSub);
      QSort(Low, PivotSub - 1);
      QSort(PivotSub + 1, High)
    end  {if}
end;  {QSort}

begin  {QuickSort}
  QSort(1, N)
end;  {QuickSort}
```

Figure A-3

The advantages to this arrangement are

1. The main program can invoke the quick sort using

```
QuickSort(TestArray, TestSize)
```

rather than

```
QuickSort(TestArray, 1, TestSize)
```

Having to supply the parameter 1 seemed unnatural.

2. The recursive calls do not have to pass the parameter A; Partition and QSort are defined within QuickSort, so the scope of its parameter A includes those procedures. This is slightly more efficient because A was a "var" parameter. If the array A had been a "value" parameter, the improvement would be quite significant. (For example, try writing a recursive binary search using the two approaches. If the array to be searched is passed as a value parameter, as it should be, the difference in speed will be significant.)

3. The procedure Partition is a quite specialized procedure that only seems useful within the context of the quick sort. Defining it within QuickSort thus seems reasonable.

4. The procedure Swap could be defined inside of any one of several places: Partition, QuickSort, QSort, or the main program. It has been placed inside Partition because that is where it is used. However, it is a "utility" procedure, so we might reasonably have chosen to define it in the main program. In this way, a main program that needed to do some swapping could reference the procedure.

□
TYPED CONSTANTS

Turbo Pascal provides a useful extension to the standard Pascal notion of a constant. (This extension was used in the program of Figure 7-6, page 556, to define the constant array Action.) It is called "typed constants" by the creators of Turbo Pascal. As we shall see, the name is slightly misleading.

The general form of the declaration is

```
const
  name : type = value;
```

For example,

```
const
  VLen : integer = 15;
  Test : Boolean = true;
```

The unusual thing about typed constants is that they are used like variables. In other words, we can use them as variables that are initialized to some known value. Thus, they are not really constants. In standard Pascal, there is no method of initializing variables other than by assigning values at execution time.

(Actually, there is another difference between typed constants and variables. They are stored in different parts of the memory used by the program, and this can be important in a few very specialized advanced applications.)

The major advantage of this capability, however, occurs in setting up constant arrays, records, or sets. For example, we could create an array containing the print names of the days of the week as shown below. Contrast this to the method used in several examples in Chapters 5 and 6.

```
type
  String10 = string[10];
  Days = ( Sun, Mon, Tue, Wed, Thu, Fri, Sat );
  WeekArray = array[Days] of String10;
```

```
const
   PrintDays : WeekArray =
     ( 'Sunday', 'Monday', 'Tuesday', 'Wednesday', 'Thursday',
       'Friday', 'Saturday' );
```

Notice the use of parentheseses around the values. For an example using a two-dimensional array, see Figure 7-6.

In declaring a record constant, we use the names of the fields, as in this example

```
type
   Fraction = record
                   Num : real;      {numerator}
                   Den : real       {denominator}
                end;
   const
      Zero : Fraction = (Num : 0; Den : 1);
```

Observe the semicolons between the fields of the record.

Finally, a set constant can be defined as illustrated by this example:

```
type
   Letters = set of Char;

const
   Responses : Letters = ['Y', 'y', 'N', 'n'];
```

This example illustrates an approach that would also prove useful in handling menus.

B. DOCUMENTATION

Part of the process of writing a program to solve a problem is **documenting** the program. As we shall see, this process involves a variety of different techniques. Thus, program **documentation** takes a variety of forms. However, the ultimate purpose of documentation is always the same: *to make the program understandable to those persons who must deal with the program in any way*.

The people who deal with a program usually fall into one of two groups. In the first group are those who will use the program. For a payroll program, for example, it might be a payroll clerk. For an equation-solving program, it might be an engineer. For a package of modules that provide polynomial operations, it might be a programmer whose program is to work with polynomials.

The other group contains individuals who will modify the program at some time in the future. These modifications can occur for a variety of reasons. For example, it may be necessary to fix bugs that come up as the program is used. Other modifications may add additional capabilities to the program. Another common source of change is the user, who, after working with the program, sees places where he or she would like it to behave differently. The process of modifying a program is frequently referred to as program **maintenance**.

In this appendix, we discuss documentation briefly. As with so much of the subject matter of this text, our coverage forms only an introduction to the topic. We will suggest forms for some of the documentation. They will be abbreviated forms, adapted from the types of forms frequently used in companies or departments that develop computer programs.

CATEGORIES OF DOCUMENTATION

One useful way to categorize documentation is as "internal" and "external." **Internal documentation** refers to comments within the program itself. It is not for the program user; it is useful for program maintenance. (In addition to the comments themselves, good programming techniques can enhance the documentation. For example, using consistent indentation and spacing strategies and choosing good names for variables enhance the readability of a program.)

In the examples in this text, we have used three types of internal comments: header comments, signpost comments, and in-line comments. The header comments describe each module, especially in terms of its parameters and what submodules it invokes. The signpost comments describe the purpose of major pieces of the module. The in-line comments clarify individual variable declarations or explain individual lines of code.

External documentation is generally divided into two categories: user documentation (for the program user) and system documentation (for program maintenance).

The nature of the user documentation depends on the nature of the anticipated user. For most programs, the person who will use the program is relatively "naive" about computers. He or she is not a programmer and may not have used a computer before. The purpose in using the program is to solve a problem more easily or quickly with a computer than without. The documentation for this type of user must *not* be technical. It should concentrate on issues such as what the program will do, what information will have to be supplied to run the program, what reports or other output will be generated, and the mechanics of using the program.

For a package of modules, on the other hand, the user definitely is a programmer. (Case Studies Nos. 7 and 10, pages 404 and 508, respectively, are examples of packages of modules.) She or he will invoke modules within the package to perform tasks for the program. The documentation includes such items as the module names, descriptions of the parameters, what each module does, and details on what must be done to make the modules available. The descriptions of the built-in functions of Pascal (Sqrt, Abs, etc.), as provided in this text, are examples of this type of user documentation.

System documentation is provided to assist in program maintenance. It is, therefore, much more technical than user documentation. Together with the internal documentation and the code itself, it forms the basis for understanding the program in depth. (In practice, it also serves a secondary function as a design tool. For example, an algorithm is written as part of program development to aid in the development process. After the program is finished, the algorithm becomes part of the system documentation.)

For a complicated program or set of related programs, the design process is generally divided into a number of steps. The exact division points tend to vary. One possibility is as follows:

1. Requirements. Identify what needs the planned program must meet.

2. Functional. Plan for the different capabilities to meet the identified needs. Determine inputs to the system and outputs from the system. Begin to plan the user interaction.

3. Design. Design the program (or programs). Split the task into subtasks and plan the interfaces (parameters) between the subtasks (submodules). Write algorithms for the submodules. Write detailed test plans.

4. Implementation. Write code and construct the system. Use stubs and drivers to allow for incremental development and testing.

5. System test. Testing the code as it is written is part of the development process. However, a system is usually subjected to a variety of tests after development is "complete." The purpose of this testing is to check for adherence to the requirements and capabilities laid out in steps 1 and 2, as well as to eliminate bugs that may still be present.

Each general phase can generate a document that becomes part of the system documentation. (The suggested form given below concentrates on the third and fourth steps.)

To summarize, we have described documentation in the categories listed:

Internal:
　　"Self-documenting" program style
　　Header comments

Signpost comments
In-line comments

External:
    User
       Program
       Package of modules
    System
       Requirements
       Functional
       Design
       Implementation
       System test

In the following subsections, we give possible formats for user and system documentation. These formats are adapted and simplified from the types of formats used in various companies.

FORMAT— SYSTEM DOCUMENTATION

☐ The first page of the system documentation describes the overall program. The remaining pages give details concerning the modules of the program. Each module should start on a new page. The modules should be ordered in a top-down fashion, beginning with the main module.

First page

I. *Purpose*

Describe what the program accomplishes.

II. *Hierarchy chart*

Provide a hierarchy chart of the modules used in the program. This gives a graphical representation of the relationships among the various modules that make up the program (who calls whom). For example, the chart shown indicates that the main module invokes modules A, B, and D, that module A invokes modules C and E, and that module D invokes modules C and F.

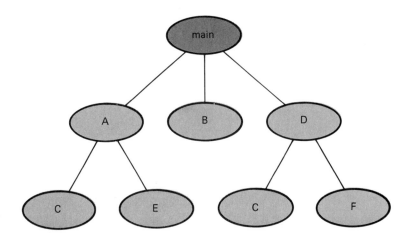

In addition, the hierarchy chart should contain a *brief* description of what each module accomplishes.

III. *Global variables.*

If global variables are used by any of the modules, describe that use here. (Global variables are discouraged due to the added complexity their usage introduces. If global variables are used, this portion of the system documentation may well be the most important part.)

As defined here, *global variable* refers to any variable that is used in any module in which it is not either declared within the module itself or defined as a parameter for the module.

For each variable that is used as a global variable, list these four items:

1. The variable name

2. The module that declares the variable

3. The other modules that use or modify the variable

4. A complete discussion of how the variable is used: the module that initializes it, how it is used and modified by other modules, etc.

Other pages *Module name*

Give the name of the module.

Discussion

Briefly describe what the module does.

Algorithm

Describe how the module works. This can be given, for example, as a (perhaps numbered) list of steps.

Test plan:

Describe the testing used to verify the correctness of the module. Organize the tests in a meaningful fashion. For example, you might list boundary tests first, then other "branch" tests, and so on.

□
SAMPLE—SYSTEM DOCUMENTA-TION

The sample given here refers to Case Study No. 3 in Section 2-8. For the most part, it records for future use portions of the planning process described in that case study.

First page I. *Purpose*

This program reads an employee's clock number, hours worked for the week, hourly pay rate, and number of dependents. It calculates the weekly pay (hours over 40 earn time and a half) and the state tax to be withheld.

The program continues until the user enters 0 or a negative number for the clock number.

II. *Hierarchy chart*

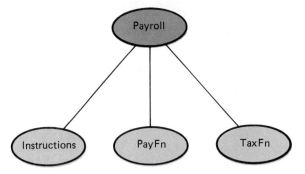

Main program (payroll):	reads data (some minor checking), calls functions, and prints answers in a loop
Instructions:	procedure that prints instructions
PayFn:	function that calculates weekly pay
TaxFn:	function that calculates state tax withholding

III. *Global variables.*

There are none.

Second page **Module name**

Payroll (main module)

Discussion

The Payroll module calls the Instructions module, then reads the data in a loop. The pay function and the tax function calculate the answers, which are printed.

Algorithm

The asterisk (*) denotes steps not performed for the terminating value of ClockNumber.

```
print instructions (use procedure Instructions)
repeat these steps until a clock number ≤ 0 is entered:
    issue prompt for clock number
    read ClockNumber
    issue prompt for hours, rate, # dependents (*)
    read HoursWorked, HourlyRate, Dependents (*)
    if HoursWorked < 0 do these two steps: (*)
        print an error message (including HoursWorked)
        set HoursWorked to 0
    calculate Pay (*)
    calculate StateTax (*)
        print ClockNumber, Pay, and StateTax (*)
print a closing message
```

Test plan

The boundary tests for the bad hours input are

−0.1	(bad)
0	(good)
0.1	(good)

Other branch tests for the bad hours input are

−5	(bad)
30	(good)

Repeat some of the tests which were done earlier for the individual functions.

Third page   Module name

Instructions

Discussion

The Instructions module prints directions for the user, if desired.

Algorithm

ask the user if instructions are desired
read Answer
if Answer is 'Y' or 'y', then print the instructions

Test plan

The branch tests for the instructions desired are

'Y'	(get instructions)
'y'	(get instructions)
'N'	(no instructions)

A test for invalid entry for the instructions desired is

'h'	(treated as 'N' by program)

Fourth page   Module name

PayFn

Discussion

The PayFn function calculates the pay based on the number of hours worked and the hourly pay rate. Overtime is paid for hours in excess of 40.

Algorithm

if Hours > 40, then do these steps:
    calculate Regular Pay (formula 40 * HourlyRate)
    calculate OvertimePay (formula (Hours − 40) * HourlyRate * 1.5
    calculate PayFn as RegularPay + OvertimePay
otherwise do this step:
    calculate PayFn as Hours * HourlyRate

Test plan:

The boundary tests for the number of hours are

39.9	(no overtime)
40.0	(no overtime)
40.1	(overtime)

The other branch tests for the number of hours are

25	(no overtime)
50	(overtime)

Fifth page   *Module name*

TaxFn

Discussion

The TaxFn function calculates the state withholding tax based on the weekly pay and the number of dependents.

Algorithm

calculate TaxableIncome (based on Pay and Dependents)
calculate TaxFn based on TaxableIncome, using this table:

TaxableIncome:	TaxFn:
<0	0
0–300	0.02 * TaxableIncome
any other	15.00 + 0.025 * (TaxableIncome − 300)

Test plan

The branch and borderline tests for number of dependents are

0
1
5

The branch and borderline tests for taxable income are

−1	(pay 23,	2 dependents)
0	(pay 12,	1 dependent)
1	(pay 1,	0 dependents)
299	(pay 299,	0 dependents)
300	(pay 360,	5 dependents)
301	(pay 337,	3 dependents)
−50	(pay 10,	5 dependents)
100	(pay 148,	4 dependents)
400	(pay 400,	0 dependents)

□

FORMAT— USER DOCUMENTA- TION (NOT A PACKAGE)

I. *Overview*

Describe, in general terms, what the program will do for the user.

II. *Data you will need to supply*

A. Data you supply when you run the program. Let the user know what the program will be asking for when it is run. This will allow the user to be prepared with the required data before running the program.

For each piece of data, describe the rules for that data. For example, if it must be a whole number between 10 and 23, say so. Also tell what happens if the rules are violated.

B. Files that must be present for the program to work. If the program reads any of its data from files, then this section supplies details about the files. Among the types of information that the user of the program must be told are:

1. Does the file require a certain prescribed name or will the program allow you to provide the name when it is run?

2. Is the file a text file created using an editor or is it the output from some program that was previously run?

3. What is the structure of the file? Describe both the overall structure of the file and the details about each line (record).

Example: "The first line is the student name, followed by any number of test scores, one score per line. Use a test score of −1 to terminate the list. Then repeat the process for the next student, then the next, and so on. The name can be up to 20 characters, and each score should be a whole number between 0 and 100, inclusive."

4. If possible, include a copy of a sample file.

III. *Information supplied by the program*

A. Information at the terminal. Describe what "answers" are supplied as the program is running.

B. Printed reports. If the program generates printed output, attach a sample. It may be helpful to put explanations with the sample.

C. Files generated by the program. If the program creates any files (or perhaps modifies one of the files listed above), describe the files here. The comments given concerning the file name, the file structure, and a listing of the file apply here as well.

IV. *Program interaction*

Describe how to use the program. A printout of a sample run is a good idea.

V. *Errors*

Describe each error situation that can occur, what it means, and what the user should do to fix the error.

The sample given here refers to Case Study No. 3 of Section 2-8. It is based on the assumptions that the Instructions procedure has been completed and that the Case Study has been modified to generate a printed report.

I. *Overview*

This program allows you to calculate part of the payroll information for employees. The current version of the program calculates gross pay for a weekly pay period and the amount of state tax to be withheld from the check. It displays the answers both at the terminal and by a printed report.

You can repeat the calculations for as many employees as you wish. Entering a negative clock number stops the program.

II. *Data you will need to supply*

A. Data you supply when you run the program. To use this program, you need to know four facts about each employee:

The employee clock number

The number of hours the employee worked this week

The employee's hourly pay rate

The number of dependents the employee claims

1. Clock Number. This is a four-digit number, but the program doesn't check to make sure that you type four digits.

2. Hours Worked. This can be any number 0 or greater. If you enter a number less than zero, the program will change it to zero. The number can have a decimal fraction (for example, 37.5 hours or 17.25 hours).

3. Hourly Rate. This should be greater than zero, but the current version of the program doesn't check. Enter it as a dollar and cents figure (for example, 7.63).

4. Number of Dependents. This is a whole number, 0 or higher. The program doesn't check it.

B. Files that must be present for the program to work. There are none. All input is from the terminal.

III. *Information supplied by the program*

A. Information at the terminal. The program shows the gross pay and state withholding for each employee.

B. Printed reports. To create a permanent record, the program generates a printed report. A sample is shown:

			Payroll		
Clock	Hours	Rate	Dependents	Pay	State Tax
1345	34.00	5.67	8	192.78	1.94
1015	44.00	6.78	3	311.88	5.52
1096	0.00	10.00	0	0.00	0.00
1096	15.00	10.00	0	150.00	3.00

C. Files generated by the program. There are none.

IV. *Program interaction*

When you first start the program, it asks if you want instructions. Answer Y or y to get instructions; any other answer is treated as no.

The program asks for the first clock number. Enter the number and hit RETURN. It then asks for the hours, hourly rate, and number of dependents. Enter the three values, separated by at least one space. (If you forget to type all three, don't panic. It will wait for the ones you forgot on the next line.)

The program then prints the answers (earnings and withholdings) and you repeat the whole process for the next employee. Entering 0 (or less) for the clock number stops the program.

Here is a sample session:

```
             PAYROLL PROGRAM

Do you want instructions (Y, N)?  n

Enter clock number for next employee: 1345
Now enter the hours, rate, and number of dependents: 34 5.67 8
1345 earned 192.78 and was taxed 1.94

Enter clock number for next employee: 1015
Now enter the hours, rate, and number of dependents: 44 6.78 3
1015 earned 311.88 and was taxed 5.52

Enter clock number for next employee: 1096
Now enter the hours, rate, and number of dependents: -5 10 0
-5 is invalid; changed to 0.
1096 earned 0.00 and was taxed 0.00

Enter clock number for next employee: 1096
Now enter the hours, rate, and number of dependents: 15 10 0
1096 earned 150.00 and was taxed 3.00

Enter clock number for next employee: 0

Payroll program terminating.
```

V. *Errors*

1. When the program asks for a number, entering invalid characters (such as letters, commas, etc.) will abort the program. The same is true for entering decimal points in the clock number or in the number of dependents. You will have to start over.

2. If you enter a negative number of hours, it will be changed to 0. This will cause an answer of 0 for the pay and the tax. You can reenter the data for the same person, if you wish.

3. No other data entry errors are checked in the current version of the program. Erroneous input will cause erroneous answers.

□

FORMAT— USER DOCUMENTA- TION (PACKAGE)

The form is similar in some ways to the system documentation form. There is a first page that describes the package as a whole. It is followed by one page describing each module that the user can invoke.

First page

I. *Overview*

Describe briefly what the package of programs is designed to do.

II. *Requirements*

If the user of the package must meet certain requirements, describe them here. For a Pascal package, this might include the requirement that certain global variable types be declared in the main program.

III. *Capabilities*

Give a quick synopsis of the capabilities available with the package. If there are any interrelationships among the modules, describe them. (For example, many packages require the using program to invoke an initialization procedure before calling any other procedures in the package.)

List the available modules by name as part of this section.

Other pages

Module name

Give the procedure or function name, and tell whether it is a procedure or function.

Purpose

Give a brief description.

Sample call

Show a sample invocation of the module. Describe the meaning of each parameter, including whether it is input, output, or update. What must its value represent on invocation? What does its value represent upon return?

Errors

If the module traps any errors, describe them and how the module handles them. (Frequently, modules in a package pass back an error code parameter. If so, describe the meaning of the error codes.)

If there are any noteworthy features of the module that are not covered in the previous discussion, list them here.

□
**SAMPLE—
USER
DOCUMENTA-
TION (PACKAGE)**

The sample refers to Case Study No. 7 of Section 5-4. We show the first page and two sample module description pages.

First page   I. *Overview*

The real variables in Pascal provide only approximations to the rational numbers. This rational number package provides facilities for working with rational numbers precisely. Capabilities include input and output, as well as various arithmetic operations.

Fractions are represented in a standard form i/j where j is positive, and i and j have no common factors. The numerator and denominator are each restricted to lie between -MaxInt and MaxInt.

II. *Requirements*

The type RationalNumber must be declared in the main module of the program that uses this package. This declaration must take the following form:

```
RationalNumber = record
                     Numerator   : integer;
                     Denominator : integer
                 end;
```

III. *Capabilities*

The package includes the following user-callable procedures or functions, with the indicated purposes:

Arithmetic
Add   Add two fractions
Subtract   Subtract two fractions
Multiply   Multiply two fractions
Divide   Divide two fractions

I/O
ReadOne   Read a fraction (and reduce it to the standard form)
WriteOne   Print a fraction on the terminal

Comparison
Equal   See if two fractions are equal
Less   See if one fraction is less than another
LessEqual   See if one fraction is less than or equal to another

Conversions
RealValue   Convert a fraction to a real number
IntegerValue   Convert a fraction to an integer (rounded)
ConvertToFraction Convert an integer to a fraction

The comparison operations are Boolean functions. RealValue and IntegerValue are real and integer functions, respectively. All other modules are procedures.

Second page   *Module name*

        Add

Purpose

        The purpose of Add is to add two fractions.

Sample call

        Add(FirstNumber, SecondNumber, Sum).

FirstNumber:	input, type RationalNumber the first fraction to be added must be a valid fraction
SecondNumber:	input, type RationalNumber the second number to be added must be a valid fraction
Sum:	output, type RationalNumber the sum of the input fractions will be in standard form

Errors

        The module does not report any errors to the calling program.

Notes

        The input fractions must have numerators and denominators of "reasonable" size, so that integer overflow does not occur. Specifically for fractions a/b and c/d, it is necessary that ad, bc, bd, and ad + bc must all lie in the range -MaxInt to MaxInt

Third page   *Module name*

        ReadOne

Purpose

        The purpose of ReadOne is to read a fraction from the user at the terminal.

Sample call

        ReadOne(Number).

Number:	output, type RationalNumber the fraction read, in standard form

Errors

        The module does not report any errors to the calling program.

Notes

  1. The user is required to enter a nonzero denominator. If not, the prompt for the denominator is repeated.

  2. Otherwise, the user is allowed to enter any fraction. The module will convert the input to standard form.

  3. The module does not trap user errors such as entering a string rather than a number for the numerator or denominator.

C.
HOW TO USE TURBO PASCAL

The body of the book is concerned with teaching program design, implementation, and testing. It does not discuss the mechanics of program creation using the Turbo Pascal editor. In this appendix, we include three sections designed to help you during program creation:

  1. A "walkthrough" that leads you through a session using Turbo Pascal. This culminates in running a simple program taken from Section 1-2.

  2. A synopsis of some useful operating system (PCDOS or MSDOS) commands.

  3. More details on using the Turbo editor.

A SAMPLE TURBO SESSION

In this section, we will lead you through some steps that will give you preliminary knowledge of how to use the editor supplied with Turbo Pascal. There are five steps:

  1. Format disks to use for your programs and other data.

  2. Use the editor to create a text file.

  3. Modify that text file.

  4. Use the editor to create a simple program with some known errors.

  5. Fix the errors in the program, and run the program.

  To get started, insert a disk containing a part of the MSDOS operating system and the Turbo Pascal system into drive A.[1] Insert your own disk into drive B. Start the computer in the usual fashion. The remainder of the discussion assumes that you have done this.

  Note. If you have a single-drive system or a hard disk system, there will be minor adjustments to make in what follows. These will involve using different disk names or swapping disks into drive A.

☐ PART I
Format disks to use for your programs and other data

CAUTION

Formatting a disk will erase its contents, so skip this part if you have already formatted your disks. This part will be used any time you want to start with a new disk, or to reformat a disk whose contents you no longer need.

At the A> prompt, type FORMAT B: and tap the return key. The computer screen will look something like this:

```
A>FORMAT B:
                    FORMAT version x.xx
Copyright(C) 19xx xxxxxxxxxxxxxxxxxxxxxxxxxxxxxxxxxxxxxx

Insert new disk in drive B:
and press RETURN when ready
```

If you have not already inserted your disk into drive B, do so now. Then press return. The computer will then prepare the disk in drive B to allow you to store your programs and other data on it. When it asks for a label, you may enter a label such as Sue1 or you may simply tap return.

It is always a good idea to maintain two copies of every disk you create, with one labeled as a backup for the other. Thus, you should answer Y to the question "Do you want to format another disk (Y/N)?" and put another new disk in drive B when asked to do so.

Unless you want to format more pairs of disks, answer N when asked the next time.

After you remove your formatted disks, label them to identify them. Suggestions: your name, an indication of the purpose of the disk, and the word *Backup* on the backup disk.

CAUTION

Never write on a label on a disk with a ballpoint or other hard writing instrument. Doing so can destroy the data stored on the disk. Either fill out the label in advance or use a felt tip pen and write lightly.

☐ **PART II**
Use the editor to create a text file

An "editor" is a program that is used to manipulate text. The editor provided with the Turbo Pascal system is patterned after the WordStar word processing program. If you are familiar with that program, much of what is described here will be similar to what you already know.

As your first exercise with the editor, you will create some text that is not a program. Later, you will use the editor to create text that represents a valid Pascal program.

1. At the A> prompt, type TURBO to invoke the Turbo system. Your screen will appear similar to the following:

```
-------------------------------------------
TURBO Pascal system        Version 3.01A
                                    PC-DOS
Copyright (C) 1983,84,85   BORLAND Inc.
-------------------------------------------

Default display mode

Include error messages (YN)?
```

2. Answer Y to the question; there will be a message saying that the error messages are being loaded, then the screen will clear and display the Turbo system's main menu:

```
Logged drive: A
Active directory: \

Work file:
Main file:

Edit      Compile   Run    Save

Dir       Quit   compiler Options

Text:       0 bytes
Free: 62024 bytes


>
```

The characters L, A, W, M, E, C, R, S, D, Q, and O are highlighted in whatever manner your terminal uses; these are the menu options. Hitting any character other than one of these causes the menu to be redisplayed.

3. Use menu option L to change the logged drive to drive B, so you can work with your disk. Hit L and the system prompts

```
                  New drive:
```

Enter B and hit return.

4. Use menu option E to edit a file. The system prompts

```
              Work file name
```

You may enter any name, followed by return. You might choose the name LETTER.

```
         Work file name: LETTER
```

The system indicates that it is loading the file and that it is a new file (you have never worked on it before). It then clears the screen, and you are in the Turbo editor, with a line at the top like this:

```
     Line 1     Col 1    Insert   Indent   B:LETTER.PAS
```

Note: The B:LETTER.PAS is the full name of your file. The Turbo system has added the extension ''.PAS'' to the file name you supplied.

5. Type the following brief letter. Hit return at the end of each line. The letter has some errors that you should imitate. Don't worry if you make other mistakes. You will correct the mistakes in Part III.

Here is the text of the letter:

```
Dear momm,

I'm writing a sample letter with my Turbo editro. School
is gong grate rite now. Hope it continues that way.

I'll see you next weekend.
```

6. Get out of the editor. This uses a ''control sequence.'' Hold down the Control key (labeled CTRL, just above the left shift key), and hit K. Then release the control key and hit D. This returns you to the menu, although it is not visible. Hitting the space bar (or any other illegal command) displays the menu.

This sequence will be described as ''control-K D.'' The sequence ''control-K control-D'' also does the same thing, so you do not have to release the control key before striking the D.

7. Save the file to disk using the option S. The computer displays a message telling that it is saving the file.

8. Save a copy of the file to your backup disk. To do so, remove your disk from drive B, insert the backup disk in drive B, use the S option, then exchange the disks in drive B again.

9. Quit the Turbo system using the option Q. This returns you to the operating system prompt B>. Change back to the A drive by typing A: and hitting return.

10. Next you want to print the file. Make sure the printer is connnected, then type this command:

```
A>type b:letter.pas >prn
```

☐ PART III
Modify that text file

In this part, you will modify the letter to appear as follows:

```
Dear Mom,

    I'm writing a sample letter with my Turbo editor. School
is going great right now. Hope it continues that way.

    I'll see you next weekend.

                        Love,
                        Sue
```

(You may wish to substitute your name in place of "Sue".)

In making the changes, you will learn only the simplest features of the Turbo editor. Later, you will want to investigate some of the more sophisticated features (see the third section of this Appendix).

1. Repeat the first four steps under Part II. The only difference you will observe is that the computer no longer says that the file LETTER.PAS is a new file, and it loads the previous version of the file for you to work on.

2. There are four control keys used to move the cursor around in the file. Their layout on the keyboard suggests the direction of movement:

$$E$$
$$S \quad D$$
$$X$$

Control-E moves up, control-S to the left, control-D to the right, and control-X down. For each key, hold down the control (CTRL) key while hitting E, S, D, or X. (Note: On some keyboards, the arrow keys can be used in place of these control keys for cursor movement.)

Experiment with these by using them to move the cursor around the file. Notice that the top line keeps track of the cursor position.

3. One easy way to correct errors is to move the cursor to the right of the error, use the backspace key to erase the error, then retype the correct value. For example, move the cursor to the comma on the first line, hit the backspace key four times, and type Mom to fix the first error.

4. Another way to correct an error is to change the "mode" of the editor from "insert" to "overwrite." This is done by hitting control-V. Hitting control-V again changes the mode back. Do this several times, and notice that the top line of the screen keeps track of the current mode.

Leaving the editor in overwrite mode, move the cursor to the r in the word "editro", and type the letters "o" and "r" to correct this error. Don't forget to use control-V to change the mode back to its default value of "insert."

5. Use either approach to fix the remaining spelling errors (gong, grate, and rite). Also fix any errors you made while entering the letter originally.

6. Now you can insert the blanks at the start of each paragraph. Make sure that the mode is insert, move the cursor to the proper spot, and hit the space bar several times.

7. Finally, let's add the ending. Move the cursor to the end of the letter, hit return to move down a couple of lines, and space over and type the word "Love,". When you hit return, notice that the cursor moves to just below the L in Love, ready for you to type your name. Do so. (This feature of the Turbo editor will prove to be very useful in writing Pascal programs.)

8. Use the sequence control-K D to exit the editor, and hit the space bar to obtain the menu.

9. Right now you should save the modified file. You might wonder what will happen if you forget. To find out, choose option Q to quit.

Fortunately, the Turbo system will warn you about your mistake and will give you a chance to recover from that mistake. You should answer Y to the question:

```
Workfile B:\LETTER.PAS not saved.   Save (Y/N)?
```

If you answer N, you will have lost all the changes made.

10. Again, return to drive A and print the new version of the file.

```
B>A:
A>type b:letter.pas >prn
```

□ PART IV
Use the editor to create a simple program with some known errors

The steps in this part are identical to those in Part II, but you should call the file something different (perhaps SAMPLE). The program you are to create follows. After you create the program, use control-K D to leave the editor, and save the program on both the original and the backup disks, but do not quit—go directly to Part V.

NOTE A useful feature of the Turbo editor is the TAB key, which tabs to a point directly under the next word on the previous line. For example, this can be used to tab over for the comments for the Price and Tax variables.

Here is the program:

```
{ $B-} { $U+} { $R+}
program NetCost(Input, Output);
{
   Written by:  Winston Crawley   8/27/87
      Purpose:  To add sales tax to price
}
const
  Rate = 0.06;                          { rate for sales tax }
```

```
var
  Cost    : real;                        { cost to customer }
  Price   : real;                        { retail price }
  Tax     : real;                        { sales tax }

begin
  Write('Enter the Price: ')
  Readln(Price);
  Tax := Rate * Priec;
  Cost := Price + Tax;
  Writeln('The cost is:  $', Cost)
end.
```

☐ **PART V**
Fix the errors in the program, and run the program

The program given has two errors. Try to run the program and see what happens.

1. Use the R option of the menu to run the program. The compiler will respond that it is compiling and indicate the lines it is working on. It will then print this message:

```
        Error 1: ';' expected. Press <ESC>
```

You should press the escape key (ESC). This returns you to the editor, with the cursor showing where the compiler was when it detected the error. In the segment of your program shown below, the cursor position is shaded.

```
        Write ('Enter The Price: ')
        Readln (Price);
```

2. The problem is that there should have been a semicolon at the end of the previous line. Insert it, leave the editor (control-K D), and save the program. (Caution: Always save a program before you run it.)

3. Run the program again (the R option). This time the error message is

```
  Error 41: Unknown identifier or syntax error. Press <ESC>
```

When you press escape, the cursor is on the "P" in "Priec", as illustrated:

```
        Tax := Rate    Priec;
```

The problem is that the identifier (the variable name) was misspelled. Change it to "Price", leave the editor, and save the program.

4. Now run the program. It should compile correctly, giving a screen that looks something like this:

```
Compiling
  21 lines

Code:        000C paragraphs (   192 bytes), 0D1C paragraphs free
Data:        0004 paragraphs (    64 bytes), 0FD8 paragraphs free
Stack/Heap:  88BD paragraphs (560080 bytes)

Running
Enter the Price:
```

The word "Running" means that your program is now running, and any output beyond this point is generated by your program.

5. Your program is waiting for you to enter the price. Try entering 1 (followed by return). The program prints the line

```
The Cost is:   $   1.0600000000E+00
```

This means 1.06 times 10 to the 0 power, or 1.06.

6. Run the program again, trying a different value for the price. Repeat this several times. You may include values such as 2.53, etc.

7. Use option E to edit the program. Change the last line of the program by replacing "Cost" by "Cost:1:2", and save and run the program again. Observe the more readable form of the answer.

8. Obtain a "hard copy" of your screen, which contains the results of several runs of the program, by using the shift-PrtSc combination.[2]

9. Save the program (original and backup copy), quit, change to drive A, and print the program in the usual way:

```
A>type b:sample.pas >prn
```

<table>
<tr><td>□
OPERATING
SYSTEM
COMMANDS</td><td>In this section, we describe a few useful operating system concepts and commands. For complete information, you should refer to the documentation that came with the operating system.</td></tr>
</table>

1. File Names. File names consist of a primary name and an optional extension. For example, in the walkthrough in the previous section, you created a file named LETTER.PAS. (The .PAS extension is automatically attached to a file when you create it in the Turbo editor, unless you specify an extension yourself.)

The primary name can be 1 to 8 characters long, consisting of letters, digits, and a few allowable special symbols such as '$' and '−'. The extension is 1 to 3 characters long. It is separated from the primary name by a period. Uppercase and lowercase letters are considered to be the same.

When you specify a file name, you can precede it by the drive letter and a colon, as in

```
b:letter.pas
```

If you omit the drive letter and colon, the current drive is used.

2. Changing the Current Drive. The system prompt always indicates the current drive. For example,

```
A>
```

indicates the current drive is A. To change to a different drive, type the new drive letter and a colon at the prompt. For example,

```
A>b:
```

changes the current drive to drive B.

3. Copying Files. The command

```
copy fromfile tofile
```

makes a copy of "fromfile" to the named "tofile". For example,

```
A>copy   b:sample.pas   a:mysample
A>copy   step2.pas   prog3.pas
A>copy   b:letter.pas   a:
```

In the third example, we omit the file name to be copied to; the computer assumes it is the same as the one being copied from, so it copies to "a:letter.pas".

4. Directory Listing. The command dir, with an optional drive, gives a complete list of all the files on the drive. The current drive is the default drive. For example,

```
A>dir
A>dir b:
```

5. Deleting Files. There are two different commands that can be used to delete a file:

```
del filename
erase filename
```

They both work the same way.

6. Renaming Files. The command

```
rename oldfilename newfilename
```

can be used to change the name of an existing file.

7. Printing files. The command

```
type filename
```

can be used to print a file on the screen. Note: Hitting control-S will stop the scrolling. Hitting control-S again restarts the scrolling.

This command can also be used to get a hard copy of files by directing the output to the printer. The form is

```
type filename > prn
```

(There is also a print program supplied with the operating system that can do a "fancier" print. See the manuals for your computer.)

8. Wildcards. Some of the commands can use an asterisk as a "wildcard." For example,

```
A>copy  *.pas  b:
A>del   *.bak
A>dir   b:samp*.*
```

The first copies every file on the current drive, whose extension is ".pas", to the B drive (as the same file name). The second deletes all files on the current drive whose extension is ".bak". The third gives a directory listing of all the files on the B drive whose name begins with "samp".

In essence, an asterisk indicates any sequence of zero or more characters.

□ The material presented earlier in the walkthrough is sufficient for creating or modifying any text file. However, after a while, you will want to learn some additional commands that will make your work easier. In this subsection, we discuss most (but not all) of these additional facilities. In the discussion, we use the character "^" to indicate the control key. For example, ^S means control-S, and ^K D means control-K D. We suggest that you "play" with the commands so as to become familiar with them.

Cursor movement

The following keys can be used for cursor movement:

^S	Moves the cursor left one character
^D	Moves the cursor right one character
^E	Moves the cursor up one line
^X	Moves the cursor down one line
^A	Moves the cursor left one word
^F	Moves the cursor right one word
^R	Moves the cursor up one screen
^C	Moves the cursor down one screen

The layout of these keys on the keyboard will help you learn what they do:

```
              E     R
       A  S      D      F
              X      C
```

E and R move up, X and C down, A and S to the left, and D and F to the right.

In addition, the tab key moves the cursor under the beginning of the next word on the previous line.

Deletion

Four control keys are used for deletion:

^G	Deletes the character under the cursor (same as delete on some keyboards)
^H	Deletes the character to the left of the cursor (same as backspace on some keyboards)
^T	Deletes the word where the cursor is located
^Y	Deletes the line where the cursor is located

Quick movement

The ^Q key, in combination with other keys, allows for rapid movement of the cursor:

^QS or ^Q^S	Moves the cursor to the left end of the line
^QD or ^Q^D	Moves the cursor to the right end of the line
^QR or ^Q^R	Moves the cursor to the top of the file
^QC or ^Q^C	Moves the cursor to the bottom of the file

Find and replace

The ^Q key is also used to locate strings within the file, or to locate and modify those strings. Generally, the search for the string starts at the current cursor position and moves toward the end of the file.

^QF or ^Q^F	The editor asks for a string to search. It then asks for options. Just hit return for a standard search. Two useful options are *b* (search backwards from the cursor) and *u* (treat uppercase the same as lowercase in doing the search). The cursor is moved to the first occurrence of the string. If none is found, an error message occurs.
^QA or ^Q^A	The editor asks for a string to search, then for what that string should be replaced by. It then asks for options. Both *b* and *u* work the same as for ^QF. Other useful options are *g* (do a global search throughout the entire file), *n* (don't ask me to verify each change, just do it), and any number (repeat the process that number of times). Without the *n* option, the editor will locate the string, then ask if you wish to replace it.
^L	Repeats the previous ^QF or ^QA.

Interrupt

The ^U can interrupt an operation. For example, you may need to interrupt a ^QA because you entered the change string wrong.

Block operations

The ^K key is used for working with "blocks" of the file. A block can be set up to contain any contiguous portion of the file.

^KB or ^K^B	Marks the beginning of the block
^KK or ^K^K	Marks the end of the block

Once the block is marked, the editor highlights it and it can be worked with (copied, deleted, etc.) using these commands:

^KV or ^K^V	Moves the block to the current cursor position
^KC or ^K^C	Copies the block to the current cursor position
^KW or ^K^W	Writes the block to a file (the editor asks you for the file name, and attaches a ".pas" extension if you don't supply your own extension)
^KR or ^K^R	Reads a file into the editor at the cursor position (the editor asks you for the file name, and attaches a ".pas" extension if you don't supply your own extension). The text read in becomes a highlighted block
^KY or ^K^Y	Deletes the block.
^KH or ^K^H	Because of the danger of accidentally deleting a block, the editor allows you to "hide" the block using ^KH or ^K^H. The block is no longer highlighted and cannot be moved, deleted, etc. (Hitting ^KH again brings back the block.)
^KD or ^K^D	Leaves the editor mode

More menu options

When you are out of the edit mode, you can use the menu options such as S (save). The option W (workfile) allows you to change the file you are working on without leaving the editor. (If you haven't saved the current file, it warns you.)

The C option compiles the program without running it. It is possible to create a permanent copy of the compiled program that can be run without entering the Turbo system. To do so:

1. Choose O (compiler Options).

2. Select C (COM file on the options submenu).

3. Select Q to leave the submenu.

4. Select C to compile the program.

This process creates a .com file. (For example, for a program sample.pas it creates sample.com.) This .com file can be run directly from the operating system just by typing its name (with or without the .com extension).

□

NOTES FOR APPENDIX C

1. This disk should be supplied by your instructor. If not, you can build the disk yourself. To do so, follow the instructions for creating bootable disks that came with your operating system. Copy the format program to this disk. Then copy your turbo editor to this disk using the copy command; see the next subsection of the Appendix.

(Caution: It is unethical and illegal to copy an operating system or Turbo system belonging to someone else.)

2. Not all keyboards have a PrtSc Key. If yours doesn't, skip this step.

D. □□□□□□ SYNTAX DIAGRAMS

In this appendix, we describe the syntax of the Pascal language through syntax diagrams. This provides a handy visual way to determine what form each construct of the language must follow in order to be syntactically correct. In reading the diagrams, take verbatim those items in ovals or circles. Items in rectangles are to be filled in by specific instances of the concept described. For example, the diagram

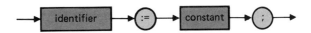

indicates "any identifier," followed by the := operator, followed by "any constant," followed by a semicolon. Valid instances of this diagram might be

```
A := 3;
CutOffPoint := 155.27;
```

(For items enclosed in rectangles, you will find the concepts further explained in other diagrams, or occasionally in the notes.)

Along with some of the diagrams, we include some semantic notes (comments about the meaning of the construct). These notes should be considered as general guidelines, rather than as an exhaustive reference. For additional information, you can refer to the index entry for the item being described.

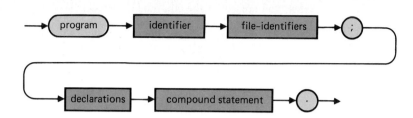

1. The *identifier* is the program name.

2. The *file-identifiers* portion is optional in Turbo Pascal. This text consistently uses the string

which denotes the standard input and output devices. In some versions of Pascal, this list must include all the files used by the program.

3. The *compound statement* is called the "body" of the program.

Comment

1. The *comment-text* can be any text not containing the character "}".

2. Comments can be placed in the program at any spot where a blank space would be allowed.

3. Comments do not affect the meaning of the program.

Declarations

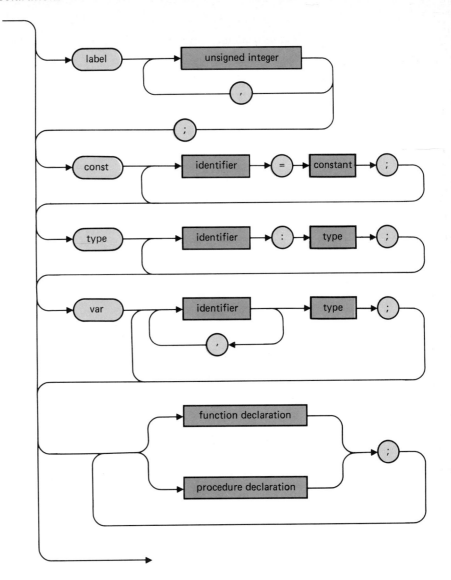

1. In standard Pascal, this order must be followed; Turbo relaxes the rule.

2. *Const* defines named constants that cannot be modified by the program.

3. *Type* gives names to user-defined types. This is frequently useful; it is mandatory if variables of that type are to be passed as parameters.

4. *Var* declares variables whose scope is the module in which this declaration occurs.

5. The function declaration and procedure declaration can be mixed. The general rule is that a submodule must be declared before it is used.

Function declaration

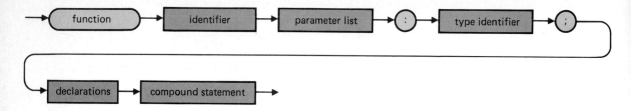

1. The *identifier* is the function name.

2. The *parameter list* is optional.

3. The function type must be a named type: either user-defined (by the "type" declaration) or built-in (integer, etc.).

4. The function type must be a built-in type (real, integer, char, Boolean), a named pointer type, or a named scalar or subrange type. In Turbo Pascal, it can also be a named string type. It cannot be a record, array, file, or set type.

5. The *compound statement* is the body of the function. It should include at least one statement assigning a value to the identifier that is the function name. (This causes the answer to be sent back to the module using the function.)

Procedure declaration

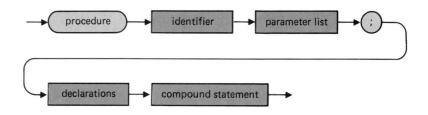

1. The *identifier* is the procedure name.

2. The *parameter list* is optional.

3. The *compound statement* is the body of the procedure. It should *not* attempt to assign a value to the procedure name identifier.

Parameter list

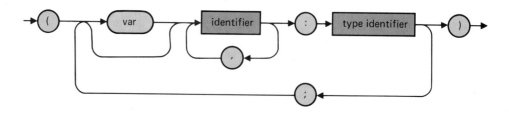

1. The parameters in the list are called "formal" parameters.

2. The effect of the *var* is to make the identifier(s) that immediately follow variable parameters. Its effect ends at the end of that list (at the colon).

3. If the *var* is omitted, the identifiers in the list (up to the colon) are value parameters.

4. For a variable parameter, the corresponding actual parameter must be a variable. Any reference to the formal parameter is directed to the corresponding actual parameter.

5. For a value parameter, the corresponding actual parameter can be any expression. Its value is passed in when the module is invoked; no value is ever passed back with a value parameter.

6. The parameters must be named types (built-in, or user-defined).

Forward declarations

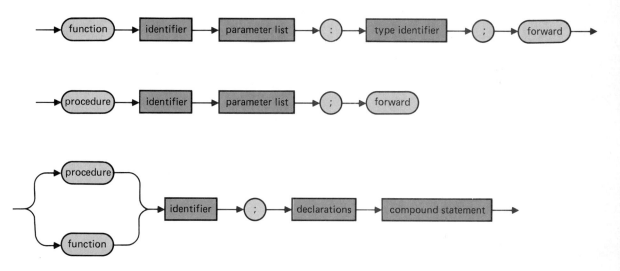

1. Forward declarations allow the body of a procedure or function to be separated from its declaration. This is useful in cases of mutual recursion.

2. The module is first declared using the directive *forward* to notify the compiler that the body is found later. This declaration includes all the usual parameter and function type information.

3. Later, the body (including local declarations) of the module is supplied. That module is identified by an abbreviated declaration of the module: just the word "procedure" or "function" followed by the module name (no parameter or function type information).

□ *Statement*

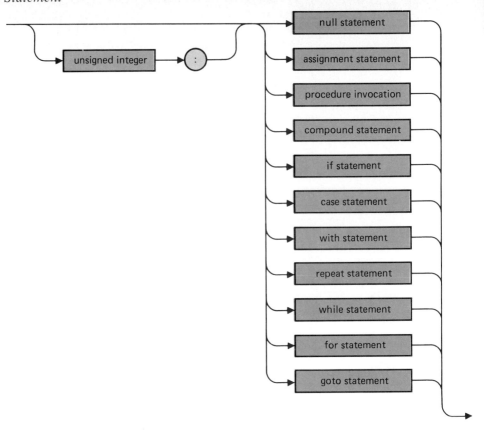

1. The *unsigned integer* is called the statement label. It must have been defined in the "label" part of the declarations of the module in which it appears (or, in standard Pascal, in a module containing that module).

2. Statement labels are needed only when a goto statement is used. This is *not* encouraged.

3. The *null statement* consists of nothing. For example, the compound statement

```
begin
   T := 5;
   X := 3;
end
```

contains two assignment statements and a null statement.

Assignment statement

1. The *identifier* is either a variable or a function name.

2. A function name is assigned a value inside the function body to pass back the answer to the calling module.

3. The specific variable referred to by the *identifier* is determined by using the scope rules. Look first for any local definition of the identifier. If there is none, look in the successive surrounding modules, going back to the main program.

4. The types of the *identifier* and of the *expression* must be the same, with some exceptions. For example:

(a) Integer values can be assigned to real variables.

(b) Any two string types in Turbo Pascal are considered compatible (truncation might occur).

(c) Subtypes are considered compatible.

5. Expressions are described in detail below.

Procedure invocation (call)

1. The *argument list* is optional.

2. The named procedure is invoked. When it terminates, execution continues at the next statement following the procedure call.

3. Among the procedures available are (* denotes a Turbo extension)

Read	*Assign	*Delete	New
Readln	Reset	Insert	Dispose
Write	Rewrite	*Str	
Writeln	Close	*Val	
*Randomize	*Seek		

Argument list

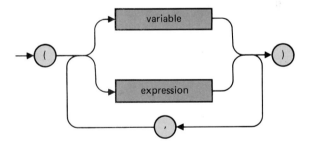

1. Arguments are also called actual parameters.

2. The argument list must match the parameter list for the module being invoked:

(a) Correct number of arguments

(b) Correct types for each argument

(c) Must be a variable for a ''var'' parameter

3. For var parameters, the subprogram will work directly with the variable in the argument list.

4. For value parameters, the value of the expression in the argument list is calculated and sent to the matching parameter in the subprogram; no value is ever returned.

Compound statement

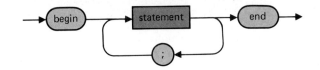

    1. This is Pascal's way of allowing multiple statements where the syntax calls for one (for example, as the body of a while loop).

    2. The statements are executed in order from first to last.

If statement

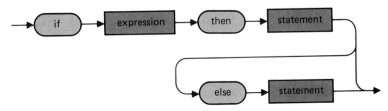

    1. The *expression* must be Boolean type.

    2. If the value of the expression is true, the statement following the "then" is executed.

    3. If the value of the expression is false, the statement following the "else" is executed. (If there is no else, nothing is done).

    4. In either case, execution continues with the statement following.

    5. In case of ambiguity, as in

```
if X > 5 then if Y > > then T := 5 else T := 10;
```

the "dangling else" goes with the closest unmatched if. The meaning of the example above is "if X > 5 then perform the if–then–else statement 'if Y > > then T := 5 else T := 10'."

Case statement

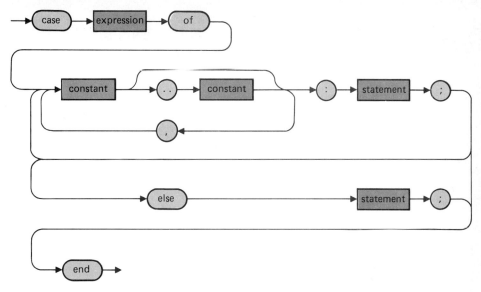

1. The semicolon just before the *else* and just before the *end* are optional.

2. The type of the *expression* must be integer, char, Boolean, or a user-defined scalar. Its type must match that of the constants in the "branches" of the case.

3. The values indicated by the constants and by the ranges *constant .. constant* must be unique. For example, having 3 and also 1 .. 4 is illegal.

4. The expression is evaluated and its value compared to the lists of constants and ranges. If a match is found, the corresponding statement is executed.

5. If no match is found, the statement following *else* is executed. (If there is no *else*, nothing is done.)

6. There are three Turbo extensions to standard Pascal:
   (a) The *constant .. constant* option is not standard.
   (b) The *else* portion is not standard.
   (c) In standard Pascal, there is an error if there is no match.

With statement

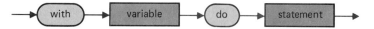

1. The *variable* must be of a record type.

2. Within the *statement* following *do,* references to fields of the indicated *variable* can be made without the prefix "variable." For example,

```
with Student do Readln(Name)
```

in place of

```
Readln(Student.Name)
```

Repeat statement

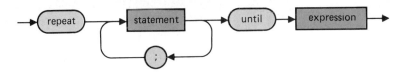

  1. The *expression* should be Boolean type (that is, a condition).

  2. The list of *statements* is called the "body" of the repeat loop.

  3. The body is executed, then the condition is evaluated. If the condition is false, the process is repeated.

  4. When the condition is true, execution proceeds to the next statement of the program.

While statement

  1. The *expression* should be Boolean type (that is, a condition).

  2. The *statement* is called the "body" of the while loop.

  3. The condition is evaluated; if it is true, the body is executed. This process is repeated.

  4. When the condition is false, execution proceeds to the next statement of the program.

For statement

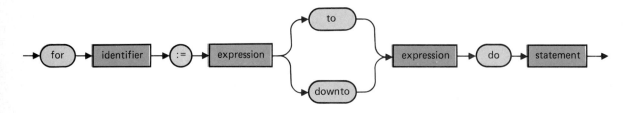

  1. The *statement* is called the "body" of the for loop.

  2. The *identifier* must be a variable of type integer, char, Boolean, or a user-defined scalar. Its type must match that of the *expressions*.

  3. The *identifier* is called the "loop-control variable."

  4. If the form expression1 *to* expression2 is used, the loop-control variable successively takes on the values in the range expression1 .. expression2. For each value, the loop body is executed.
  (If the range is empty, the body is not executed.)

  5. If the form expression1 *downto* expression2 is used, the control variable takes on the value in the range expression2 .. expression1, *in reverse order*.
  (If the range is empty, the body is not executed.)

6. The loop-control variable can be used but not modified within the loop body.

7. After the body has been executed the indicated number of times, execution proceeds to the next statement in the program. *At this point, the loop-control variable is undefined.*

Goto statement

1. The *unsigned integer* is a label. It must appear on a statement in the module containing the *goto* (or in standard Pascal, in a surrounding module). See Note 1 for the "statement" diagram.

□ *Type*

DATA STRUCTURES

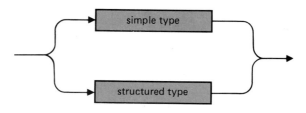

Simple type

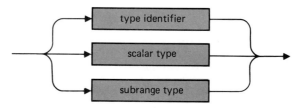

1. *Type identifier* refers to a type that has been defined in the *type* portion of the declarations. It must be an integer, real, Boolean, char, or user-defined scalar or subrange type.

Scalar type

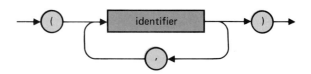

1. The *identifiers* form a list of legal values for the type.

2. The order in which they are listed is significant. (It is used by the Ord, Pred, and Succ functions and for determining the meaning of for loops. The first item in the list is number 0.)

3. The identifiers must be unique.

Subrange type

    1. The *constants* must be of the same type. That type must be integer, Boolean, char, or a user-defined scalar.

    2. The Ord value of the first constant must be less than or equal to that of the second constant.

    3. The legal values for entities of this type are values lying between and including the two constants.

Structured type

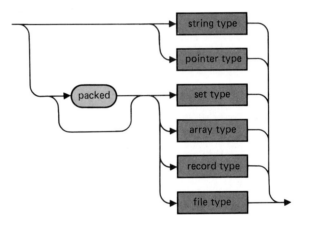

    1. The string data type is a Turbo extension to the language, although many other versions have very similar concepts.

    2. The word *packed* relates to how the data are stored in the computer memory. In some versions of Pascal, it saves on memory space. In addition, in standard Pascal, a packed array of characters is a string and has a few (but not all) of the capabilities of the Turbo Pascal string type.

    In Turbo Pascal, the word packed is meaningless.

String type (Turbo specific)

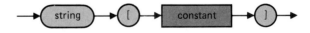

    1. The *constant* must be an integer in the range 1 to 255. It indicates the maximum length of the string.

    2. As the program is running, the current actual length of the string is automatically maintained.

Pointer type

    1. The *type identifier* can be defined after it is used to define the pointer type.

    2. There is a predefined constant *nil* that is a possible value for any variable of any pointer type.

Set type

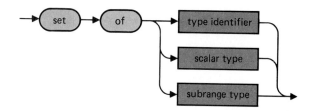

    1. The *type identifier* must indicate an integer, Boolean, char, or user-defined scalar type.

    2. In practice, there are limitations on the size of set allowed. In Turbo Pascal, the limit is 256 and the Ord values of the set elements must lie from 0 to 255.

Array type

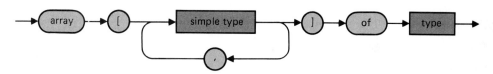

    1. The notation using several *simple types* is a shorthand notation. For example,

$$\texttt{array[1 .. 3, 5 .. 17] of integer}$$

is shorthand for

$$\texttt{array[1 .. 3] of array [5 .. 17] of integer}$$

    2. Array elements are referenced by indicating indexes (subscripts) in the given range. For example,

$$\texttt{A[2, 10] or A[2] [10]}$$

Record type

Field list

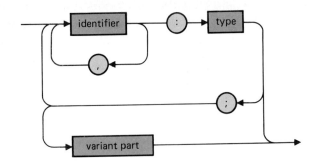

1. The *identifiers* denote "fields" of the record.

2. Field values within a variable of record type are denoted by indicating the variable name, a period, and the field name. For example,

```
Student.Name
```

(But see the *with* statement diagram.)

3. The fields of the record can in turn be structured types, including arrays and records.

Variant part

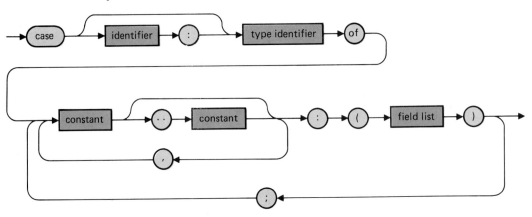

1. This allows the list of fields within the record to depend upon the value of a field within the record.

2. The responsibility for ensuring consistency is the programmer's.

3. The *identifier* determining which list of fields is to occur can be omitted. This is called a "free union."

File type

1. The predefined type identifier *text* denotes "file of char." Moreover, for this type of file, the procedures Readln and Writeln can be used.

2. For all other file types, only Read and Write can be used.

3. A common use involves having the *type* be a record type.

4. In addition to the standard I/O operations, Turbo Pascal provides facilities that allow random access to the values in the file.

□

EXPRESSIONS It is possible to give syntax diagrams for expressions. However, they are probably more useful to a compiler writer than to a person who is writing programs in Pascal. Instead, we summarize some of the important points concerning expressions.

1. Expressions can contain combinations of
  constants
  variables
  fields of records
  array elements
  pointer references
  function invocations (syntax is the same as procedure invocation)
  sets
  strings
(Any use of a function name in an expression is interpreted as an invocation of that function.)

2. Subject to rules involving compatibility, these can be combined using the following operations to form "simple expressions":
  parentheses for grouping
  +   −   *   /   div   mod
  not   and   or
There cannot be two operators in a row. For example, A * − B is illegal; use A * (−B) or −A * B.

3. Simple expressions can be combined, using
  <   =   >   <=   >=   <>   in
The result will be Boolean.

4. The precedence is
  not
  *   /   div   mod   and
  +   −   or
  <   =   >   <=   >=   <>   in
Within each list, the order is "left to right." (Parentheses can be used for grouping.)

5. The operators +, −, *, and / can be applied to integers or reals. The result is real, except that the sum, difference, or product of two integers is integer.

6. The operators div and mod can only apply to integers. The results are truncated division and remainder, respectively.

7. The operators *not, and,* and *or* apply only to Boolean values. The result is Boolean.

8. The comparisons <, <=, >, >=, =, and <> apply to any real, integer, string, char, Boolean, or user-defined scalar type. For char, Boolean, and user-defined scalars, the result is based on the Ord value of the operand. String comparisons generally yield alphabetical comparisons.

9. The operator + applied to strings (or char) denotes concatenation. This is a Turbo extension.

10. The operators +, −, and * when applied to sets are set union, difference, and intersection, respectively. The operators <=, >=, =, and <> denote set inclusion and set equality tests. The operator *in* determines if a value is an element of a set.

11. Among the functions available are (* denotes a Turbo extension)

Sqr	Round	Ord	Odd
Sqrt	Trunc	Chr	Eof
Abs	Arctan	Succ	
Exp	Cos	Pred	
Ln	Sin		

*Frac	*Copy
*Int	*Concat
*Random	*Length
*UpCase	*Pos

12. Constants can be signed or unsigned numbers, or constant identifiers and strings, or the predefined constants nil or MaxInt.

13. Identifiers begin with a letter, followed by zero or more letters or digits (Turbo allows underscores).

14. Sets can be denoted by a list of expressions enclosed in square brackets. The expressions can be ranges (for example, ['A' .. 'Z', 'a' .. 'z']) and they can be variables (for example, [0, 1, Sum]).

15. Fields of records are denoted by the record name, a period, and the field name (for example, Student.Age).

16. Array elements are denoted by the array name and a list of subscripts enclosed in square brackets (for example, A[5], B[7,2], and B[7][2]).

17. Pointer references consist of the pointer variable name followed by "^" (for example ListHead^). Very frequently, pointers point to records, whose fields can be indicated using the usual field notation (for example, ListHead^.Name).

18. Integer constants consist of sequences of digits (the value must lie between -MaxInt and MaxInt).

19. Real constants contain either a decimal point, an exponent part, or both. The syntax diagram is

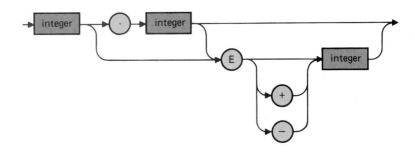

The exponent part indicates a power of 10. For example, 1.2E3 means 1.2 times 10^3.

20. String constants consist of any string enclosed in single quotes (that is, apostrophes). The character for apostrophe is represented by two consecutive apostrophes, as in 'don''t'.

Character constants have the same form as string constants of length one.

E.
UTILITIES

In this Appendix, we present some utility subprograms and we also discuss some alternative techniques that can be used in various programming environments. In particular, we will address the environments:

- Turbo Pascal with IBM PC compatible microcomputers (PC-Turbo)
- Turbo Pascal with Apple MacIntosh microcomputers (Mac-Turbo)
- Standard Pascal with any computer (Standard)

The topics covered in the Appendix are:

- Some File Utilities (PC-Turbo)
- Turbo Pascal for The MacIntosh (Mac-Turbo)
- Random Number Generator (Standard)
- Obtaining the System Time (PC-Turbo)
- A String Package (Standard)
- Page Procedure (PC-Turbo)

(PC-TURBO) SOME FILE UTILITIES

Exists. Here is a Boolean function which can be used to determine the existence of a file with a specified PC-DOS or MS-DOS filename.

```pascal
function Exists(FileName : String20) : boolean;
{ . . . comments }
var
  DummyFile    : text;                { used to check file name }

begin    {Exists}
  Assign(DummyFile, FileName);
  {$I-}                               { turn off error messages }
  Reset(DummyFile);                   { try to open for input }
  {$I+}                               { turn on error messages }
  Exists := IOResult = 0;             { call IOResult function to see if o.k. }
  Close(DummyFile)                    { don't leave files lying around open }
end;   {Exists}
```

OpenRead. Below is a general purpose procedure for obtaining the name of an existing file from the user and opening the file for reading. Note that the type of the file is specified by the global type FileType, so that the procedure can be used in different contexts.

```pascal
procedure OpenRead(var InputFile : FileType);
{ . . . comments }
var
   FileName  : String20;             { file name on disk }
   ValidName : boolean;              { name entered exists }

begin   {OpenRead}
```

```
repeat
  Write('Enter the input file name: ');
  Readln(FileName);
  ValidName := Exists(FileName);
  if not ValidName then
    Writeln('***File does not exist.')
  until ValidName;

  Assign(InputFile, FileName);      { open the file for input }
  Reset(InputFile)
end;   {OpenRead}
```

OpenWrite. We now present a procedure for obtaining the name of a file and opening the file for writing. There are two issues to deal with: does the file already exist? and is the filename valid?

```
procedure OpenWrite(var FileVar : FileType);
{  . . . comments }
var
  FileName     : String20;        { Name of the file }
  ValidName    : Boolean;         { Indicator for file name }
  Answer       : char;            { User response }

begin OpenWrite

{*** Ask the user for the filename.}

  ValidName := false;

  while  not ValidName  do
    begin
      Write('Enter the filename: ');
      Readln(FileName);
      if  Exists(FileName)  then
        begin
          Write('File already exists. Delete(Y,N)?');
          Read(Kbd, Answer);
          Writeln(Answer);
          if  Answer in ['Y', 'y']  then
            begin
              ValidName := true;
              Assign(FileVar, FileName);
              Rewrite(FileVar)
            end
        end
      else
        begin
          {$I-}
          Assign(FileVar, FileName);
          Rewrite(FileVar);
          {$I+}
          if  IOResult = 0  then
            ValidName := true
```

```
                else
                    Writeln('Invalid filename. Re-enter.')
                end
            end; {while}

        end; {OpenWrite}
```

FileBuild. When writing a program to deal with files of records, it is convenient to have an easy method of building samples for testing. Given below is a utility which can be easily customized for any such file. To customize this file building utility, you must modify the declaration of RecordType and the fields used in the ReadRecord procedure. These portions are in color in the listing.

```
program FileBuild(Input, Output);
{  . . . comments }
type
  RecordType =
    record
      ???    : ???;                    { Customize the fields }
    end;
  FileType = file of RecordType;
  String20 = string[20];              { For filename }

var
  FileVar       : FileType;           { File designator }
  RecordVar     : RecordType;         { Record variable }
  Quit          : Boolean;            { User wants to quit }

{ function Exists is inserted here. }
{ procedure OpenWrite is inserted here. }

procedure ReadRecord(var RecordOut : RecordType; var Quit : Boolean);
{  . . . comments }
const
  EndOfData = ???;                    { customize terminating value }

begin {ReadRecord}
  with RecordOut do
    begin
      Writeln;
      Writeln('Enter fields of record:');
      Write('  ???: ');
      Readln(???);
      Quit := ??? = EndOfData
    end {with}
end; {ReadRecord}


begin {FileBuild}

{*** Open the file.}

  OpenWrite(FileVar);

{*** Process the file.}
```

```
    repeat
      ReadRecord(RecordVar, Quit);
      if  not Quit  then
        Write(FileVar, Recordvar)
    until  Quit;

{*** Close the file.}

   Close(FileVar);

{*** Print message and terminate.}

   Writeln;
   Writeln('FileBuild program terminating.')
end.
```

FileList. Our last file utility is a program to display the contents of a file of records. The program asks for a keystroke after each record of the file is displayed. Once again you can easily customize this utility by modifying the declaration of RecordType and the fields used in the WriteRecord procedure. These portions are shown in color in the listing.

```
program FileList(Input, Output);
{  . . . comments }
type
  RecordType =
    record
      ???    : ???;                       { Customize the fields }
    end;
  FileType = file of RecordType;
  String20 = string[20];                  { For filename }

var
  FileVar     : FileType;                 { File designator }
  RecordVar   : RecordType;               { Record variable }

procedure Pause;
{  . . . comments }
var
  KeyStroke   : char;                     { user response }

begin {Pause}
  Writeln;
  Writeln(' ': 27,'<Tap any key to continue>');
  Read(Kbd, KeyStroke);
  ClrScr
end; {Pause}

{ function Exists is inserted here. }
{ procedure OpenRead is inserted here. }

procedure WriteRecord(RecordIn : RecordType);
{  . . . comments }
begin {WriteRecord}
  with RecordIn do
```

```
      begin
        Writeln;
        Writeln('Fields of record:');
        Write('  ???: ');
        Writeln(???);
      end; {with}
    Pause
  end; {WriteRecord}


begin {FileList}

{*** Open the file.}

  OpenRead(FileVar);

{*** Process the file.}

  while  not Eof(FileVar)  do
    begin
      Read(FileVar, RecordVar);
      WriteRecord(RecordVar)
    end; {while}

{*** Close the file.}

  Close(FileVar);

{*** Print message and terminate.}

  Writeln;
  Writeln('FileList program terminating.')
end.
```

(MAC-TURBO) TURBO PASCAL FOR THE MACINTOSH

This book is primarily about computer programming and secondarily about the Pascal programming language. All of the examples in the book have been tested using the IBM PC version of Turbo Pascal, but with minor modifications, the examples can be executed in other Pascal environments. One particular environment which is a popular choice is Turbo Pascal for the Macintosh computer. This Pascal dialect has many features that are specific to the Macintosh, including full use of the event-handling and the toolbox. However, the use of graphics, sound, and other machine-specific features of a particular version of Pascal are better left for programming courses that follow the first, introductory course. We have attempted to be 'generic' with most of the discussion in the book. As an example of the generality of our examples, we list here the changes that have to be made to enable our examples to execute under Turbo Pascal on the Macintosh.

For all interactive programs. After printing the terminating message, add the line:

```
Readln
```

This will keep the output window open until the user hits return.

Clearing the screen. Use the statement: 'ClearScreen;' in place of 'ClrScr;' in our examples.

Reading a single keystroke. Use the statement: 'KeyStroke := ReadChar;' in place of 'Read(Kbd, KeyStroke);' in our examples.

Opening a file. The 'Assign' statement is not used in this version of Pascal. To open a file for reading, use the statement:

```
Reset(FileVar, 'MYFILE');
```

in place of the two statements:

```
Assign(FileVar, 'MYFILE');
Reset(FileVar);
```

To open a file for writing, use the statement:

```
Rewrite(FileVar, 'MYFILE');
```

in place of the two statements:

```
Assign(FileVar, 'MYFILE');
Rewrite(Filevar);
```

The case statement. Use the keyword 'otherwise' in place of the keyword 'else' in our examples.

Printing. In order to use the printer, include at the top of your main program declarations the statement 'uses PasPrinter;'. In order to complete the definition, one of the first lines of the main program should be:

```
Rewrite(Printer, 'Printer:');
```

Note the ':' that follows the printer device name in the Rewrite statement. You do not declare the variable Printer, because it is predefined in the PasPrinter unit. In order to execute a printing statement, use the form 'Writeln(Printer, ...)' instead of the corresponding statement 'Writeln(Lst, ...)' that we use in our examples.

The 'Page' procedure that we have presented will not work on the Macintosh. Use our alternative technique: 'Write(Printer, Chr(12));' to advance to the next page on your printer.

The UpCase function. This function is not built-in to the Macintosh version of Turbo Pascal. The language reference manual shows how to define the function in assembly language in the chapter, 'Inside Turbo Pascal'. You may also choose to write the function in Pascal as we have done for the LowCase function in Chapter 8.

Obtaining the system time. The technique for obtaining the value of the computer's timer is different on the Macintosh than on the IBM PC. See the material on event-handling in the Turbo Pascal reference manual.

Typed constants. There are no typed constants in Turbo Pascal for the Macintosh. The identifiers must be moved from the const section to the var section and the initial values must be provided by assignment statements.

Random numbers. The Randomize procedure and the Random function are not provided with Turbo Pascal for the Macintosh. There is a random number generating function called 'RandomX' in the SANE unit, but it behaves quite differently from the Random function that we have described. The following is the definition of a random number generator which will behave as does the function Random in this book.

```
{*** Global variable for random number generator.}
var
  Seed       : integer;                {last random number}
function Random(N : integer) : integer;
{
    Written by:  XXXXXX  XX/XX/XX
       Purpose:  To generate a random number in the range 0 .. N-1
    Parameters:  N - input, determines range of random number.
  Globals used:  Seed - changed to the next 'random number'.
        Source:  This function uses the technique described in
                 Donald Knuth's classic, Art of Computer Programming,
                 Volume 2, Chapter 3.
}
const
  Addend = 6925;
  Multiplier = 3141;
  Base = 32768;
  High = 32769;

begin {Random}
  Seed := (Multiplier*Seed + Addend) mod Base;
  Random := Trunc(Abs(N * (Seed/High)))
end; {Random}
```

The Randomize procedure can be simulated in an interactive program by utilizing the user's response time as a random element. This may be accomplished by using code similar to the following within the Instructions procedure:

```
Writeln(' ':27, '<Tap any key to continue.>');

repeat
   X := Random(100)
until KeyPressed;
```

(STANDARD) RANDOM NUMBER GENERATOR

The example used for generating random numbers in Turbo Pascal for the Apple MacIntosh may be modified to produce a general purpose random number generator for those environments which do not have a built-in facility. The main program must contain the following global declaration:

```
          Seed : integer;            { last random number }
  function Random(N : integer) : integer;
  {  . . . comments }
  const
    Addend = 6925;
    Multiplier = 3141;
    Base = 32767;
    High = 32769.0;

  var
    Divisor   : integer;
```

```
begin {Random}
   Divisor := Base + 1;
   Seed := (Multiplier*Seed + Addend) mod Divisor;
   Random := Trunc(Abs(N * (Seed/High)))
end; {Random}
```

To make effective use of the random number generator, you must find a "random" way to set the initial value of the global variable, Seed. Some possibilities:

> **when the program exits, write the last random value to a file**
> **ask the user for a random seed**
> **get the system time of day and build a seed value from it**

(PC-TURBO) OBTAINING THE SYSTEM TIME

It is sometimes useful (or necessary) for a program to know the time of day maintained by the operating system. The utility below prints the time. For an alternative approach based on a similar strategy, refer to the StatPack package of Figure 10-15.

```
procedure PrintTime;
{ . . . comments }
type
  MsDosParam =
    record
      AX, BX, CX, DX, BP, SI, DI, DS, ES, Flags : integer
    end;

var
  Regs         : MsDosParam;    { Parameter for MsDos call }
  HoursTens    : integer;       { First digit of hours }
  HoursUnits   : integer;       { Second digit of hours }
  MinutesTens  : integer;       { First digit of minutes }
  MinutesUnits : integer;       { Second digit of minutes }
  SecondsTens  : integer;       { First digit of seconds }
  SecondsUnits : integer;       { Second digit of seconds }

begin {PrintTime}

{*** Invoke MsDos to get the time. }

  with Regs do
    begin
      AX := $2C00;
      MsDos(Regs);
      HoursTens := hi(CX) div 10;
      HoursUnits := hi(CX) mod 10;
      MinutesTens := lo(CX) div 10;
      MinutesUnits := lo(CX) mod 10;
      SecondsTens := hi(DX) div 10;
      SecondsUnits := hi(DX) mod 10
    end;   {with}
```

```
{*** Print the time. }

   Writeln('Time = ', HoursTens:1, HoursUnits:1, ':',
            MinutesTens:1, MinutesUnits:1, ':',
            SecondsTens:1, SecondsUnits:1)
end;  {PrintTime}
```

(STANDARD) A STRING PACKAGE

As we emphasized in Chapter 8, strings are an important class of data types. Since Standard Pascal does not have built-in string data types, you may have to implement your own string package to be used with your programs. We showed in Section 8-2 how you can build a package for handling longer length strings. The ideas presented there can also be used for dealing with strings of moderate size. The various names used in Section 8-2 for longer length strings made use of the prefix "Big" for type declarations and subprogram names. For a package of smaller strings, you should rename things by dropping the "Big" prefix.

A simpler method of creating strings data types is to use type declarations similar to the following for strings of maximum length 20:

```
           String20 = packed array [1 .. 20] of char;
```

If StringVar has been declared to be of type String20, then the following activities are legal in Standard Pascal:

```
StringVar := 'A constant value    ';  { constant assignment }
Writeln(Output, StringVar);            { output of a string }
```

Two string variables of the same type may be compared for equality or inequality using the relational operators. String assignment is also valid for strings of the same type.

We may also define string constants which may be used with a string variable of the same length for assignment or comparison purposes.

Input of strings must be done on a character-by-character basis and should be done by means of a procedure such as the following.

Global declarations:

```
   const
     MaxLength = 20;
   type
     StringType = packed array [1 .. MaxLength] of char;

procedure ReadString(var OutString : StringType);
{ . . . comments }
var
   I          : integer;              { loop index}
   J          : integer;              { loop index}

begin {ReadString}
   I := 1;
   while  (not Eoln(Input)) and (I <= MaxLength)  do
     begin
       Read(Input, OutString[I]);
       I := I + 1
     end; {while}
```

```
      Readln(Input);                    { this line may have to precede
                                          the while loop, depending on
      for  J := I to MaxLength  do       your computer system }
        OutString[J] := ' '

  end; {ReadString}
```

A reasonable notion of length for this type of string-handling is to ignore trailing spaces as in the example function below, which assumes the string is not totally blank.

```
        function Length(InString : StringType) : integer;
        { . . . comments }
        var
          I  : integer;                        { loop index }
        begin {Length}
          I := MaxLength;

          while  (InString[I] = ' ') and (I >= 1)  do
            I := I - 1;

          Length := I
        end; {Length}
```

(PC-TURBO) PAGE PROCEDURE

In a few places in the textbook, we have mentioned that the standard Page procedure is not implemented in Turbo Pascal. If you would like to use a Page procedure in your Turbo Pascal programs, the following will work for most PC-DOS and MS-DOS versions.

```
procedure Page (var Unit);
{ . . . comments }
var
  Device   : string[6] absolute Unit;   { FIB of Unit }
  Printer  : string[6] absolute Lst;    { FIB of Lst }
  Console  : string[6] absolute Con;    { FIB of Con }
  FileType : integer:                    { Pos. 6 of Unit FIB }

begin {Page}
  Filetype := Ord(Device[6]);            { Unit buffer offset }
  if  Filetype = Ord(Printer[6])  then
    Write(Lst, Chr(12))                  { for printer }
  else if  Filetype = Ord(Console[6])  then
    Clrscr                               { for screen }
end;  {Page}
```

To use the procedure to clear the screen, use the statement

Page(Con)

To use the procedure to go to the top of a new page on your printer, use the statement

Page(Lst)

F.
CHARACTER CODE SETS

□□□□□□

In a few places in the text we have used specific features of the underlying code set which represents character data in the computer. For example, we have used character codes to "beep" upon bad input, to force a printer to top of page, and to recognize backspace and return keys as tapped by the user. As examples we have consistently used one of the alternative methods of encoding character information known as the ASCII code set. ASCII is an acronym for the longer phrase "American Standard Code for Information Interchange." The code is ancient history compared with the short time line of the computer field and thus contains some codes which have lost or changed their original meanings. When the ASCII code appeared (circa 1963), the teletype terminal was a predominant input-output device; thus, some of the codes specifically relate to that artifact. There are code sets other than ASCII that are used with computers, but the major alternative is the EBCDIC code set found on mainframe computers manufactured by the IBM corporation. The name EBCDIC is an acronym for "Extended Binary Coded Decimal Interchange Code." The purpose of having standard code sets is to ease communications among various computers and devices so that, for example, an 'A' tapped on a keyboard, processed by a computer, communicated to another computer via a modem, processed by the second computer, and printed by a printer will appear as an 'A'.

There are two main ways in which the particular code set can affect Pascal programs. The first way, as evidenced in this text, has to do with the particular values of various "control characters" which produce effects such as beeping, backspace, top of form, and so on. The second, more subtle way, is the inherent order of characters enforced by the particular code set used. This so-called "collating" sequence has a direct effect on programs which sort string or character data. For example, the order of the three strings:

```
Elephant
e.e. cummings
E4
```

would be in ASCII:

```
E4
Elephant
e.e. cummings
```

and in EBCIDIC:

```
e.e. cummings
Elephant
E4
```

The behavior of an individual character code varies not only with the code set used by the computer but may also depend on a particular brand of printer, plotter, or modem which is being used. Not all printers advance to the top of a new page when an ASCII form feed character is sent (most do, however).

To be in complete control of the environment, the programmer may need to study manuals for the computer, printer, modem, etc. being used. The possible combinations are almost endless, but there is common adherence to standards (official or de facto) of either ASCII or EBCDIC code sets for computers, Hayes-compatible codes for modems, and Epson-compatible codes for printers.

Below we present the ASCII code set, giving the decimal codes, the standard mnemonic abbreviation, a typical keyboard or printer character (if any) in unshifted, shifted, and control-key mode.

The ASCII Code Set (Continued)

Dec Code	Standard Abbrev	Unshift Key	Shift Key	Cntrl Key	Comments
0	NUL			@	Rarely used
1	SOH			A	Smiley face on IBM PC
2	STX			B	Rarely used
3	ETX			C	End of text
4	EOT			D	End of transmission
5	ENQ			E	Rarely used
6	ACK			F	Acknowlegement
7	BEL			G	Beep (or bell)
8	BS	BS	BS	H	Backspace
9	HT	TAB	TAB	I	Tab
10	LF			J	Linefeed
11	VT			K	Vertical tab
12	FF			L	Form feed (top of form)
13	CR	RET	RET	M	Carriage return
14	SO			N	Rarely used
15	SI			O	Rarely used
16	DLE			P	Rarely used
17	DC1			Q	Unfreeze screen
18	DC2			R	Rarely used
19	DC3			S	Freeze screen
20	DC4			T	Rarely used
21	NAK			U	Negative acknowlegement
22	SYN			V	Communications synchronization
23	ETB			W	Rarely used
24	CAN			X	Cancel
25	EM			Y	Rarely used
26	SUB			Z	End of file
27	ESC	ESC	ESC	[	Escape
28	FS			\	Rarely used
29	GS			]	Rarely used
30	RS			^	Rarely used
31	US			—	Unit separator
32	SPC	bar	bar		Blank space
33	!		!		Exclamation point
34	,,		,,		Double quote
35	#		#		Pound sign
36	$		$		Dollar sign
37	%		%		Percent sign
38	&		&		Ampersand
39	,	,			Single quote (apostrophe)
40	(		(		Left parenthesis
41	)		)		Right parenthesis
42	*		*		Asterisk
43	+		+		Plus sign
44	,	,			Comma
45	-	-			Hyphen (minus sign)
46	.	.			Period (decimal point)
47	/	/			Slash (division sign)
48	0	0			Zero
49	1	1			One
50	2	2			Two

The ASCII Code Set (Continued)

Dec Code	Standard Abbrev	Unshift Key	Shift Key	Cntrl Key	Comments
51	3	3			Three
52	4	4			Four
53	5	5			Five
54	6	6			Six
55	7	7			Seven
56	8	8			Eight
57	9	9			Nine
58	:		:		Colon
59	;	;			Semicolon
60	<		<		Less than
61	=	=			Equal sign
62	>		>		Greater than
63	?		?		Question mark
64	@		@		"At" sign
65	A		A		First uppercase letter
66	B		B		
67	C		C		
68	D		D		
69	E		E		
70	F		F		
71	G		G		
72	H		H		
73	I		I		
74	J		J		
75	K		K		
76	L		L		
77	M		M		
78	N		N		
79	O		O		
80	P		P		
81	Q		Q		
82	R		R		
83	S		S		
84	T		T		
85	U		U		
86	V		V		
87	W		W		
88	X		X		
89	Y		Y		
90	Z		Z		Last uppercase letter
91	[	[			Left bracket
92	\	\			Back slash
93	]	]			Right bracket
94	^		^		Caret
95	_		_		Underscore
96	`	`			Back quote
97	a	a			First lowercase letter
98	b	b			
99	c	c			

The ASCII Code Set

Dec Code	Standard Abbrev	Unshift Key	Shift Key	Cntrl Key	Comments
100	d	d			
101	e	e			
102	f	f			
103	g	g			
104	h	h			
105	i	i			
106	j	j			
107	k	k			
108	l	l			
109	m	m			
110	n	n			
111	o	o			
112	p	p			
113	q	q			
114	r	r			
115	s	s			
116	t	t			
117	u	u			
118	v	v			
119	w	w			
120	x	x			
121	y	y			
122	z	z			Last lowercase letter
123	{		{		Left brace
124	|		|		Vertical bar
125	}		}		Right brace
126	~		~		Tilde
127	DEL	DEL	DEL		Delete (rubout)

128 to 255 are not official ASCII codes; these are used for various special purposes such as graphics characters, data compression codes, or to indicate word wrapping on some word processors.

The EBCDIC code set uses a broader numerical range (0 - 255) than does the ASCII code set. In addition, there are gaps within the set of upper case letters and within the set of lower case letters. Note that, for example, it is not true that Succ('I') = 'J' in the EBCDIC context. We present below only the most important of the EBCDIC codes.

The EBCDIC Code Set

Decimal Code	Character	Decimal Code	Character	Decimal Code	Character
64	space	133	e	201	I
74	cent sign (¢)	134	f	208	}
75	.	135	g	209	J
76	<	136	h	210	L
77	(	137	i	211	M
78	+	145	j	212	N
79	|	146	k	213	O
80	&	147	l	214	P
90	!	148	m	215	Q
91	$	149	n	216	R
92	*	150	o	224	\
93	)	151	p	226	S
94	;	152	q	227	T
95	logical not (¬)	153	r	228	U
96	-	161	~	229	V
97	/	162	s	230	W
98	|	163	t	231	X
99	,	164	u	232	Y
100	%	165	v	233	Z
101	—	166	w	240	0
102	>	167	x	241	1
103	?	168	y	242	2
122	:	169	z	243	3
123	#	192	{	244	4
124	@	193	A	245	5
125	'	194	B	246	6
126	=	195	C	247	7
127	"	196	D	248	8
129	a	197	E	249	9
130	b	198	F		
131	c	199	G		
132	d	200	H		

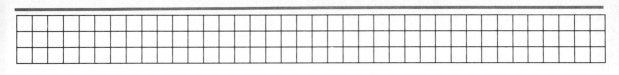

ANSWER KEY

□ CHAPTER 1

Section 1-2

1. c. Not valid; begins with a digit.
   d. Not valid; embedded space.
   f. Not valid; ";" not allowed.
   (All others valid.)

2. a. integer
   b. real
   c. Not valid; commas not allowed.
   d. string
   e. string
   f. string
   g. Not valid; one embedded quote not allowed.
   h. real
   i. Not valid; must have digit in front of decimal point.

3. a.

```
SSN       : string[11];    { Form: ddd-dd-dddd }
Age       : integer;       {In whole years}
HourlyPay : real;          {Rate of pay per hour}
Hours     : real;          {Number of hours worked}
```

Section 1-3

1. a.

```
program Squares(Input, Output);
{
  Written by:  XXXXXXXX  XX/XX/XX
    Purpose:  To calculate the areas of squares.
}
const
    EndOfData = 0;              {Used to terminate loop}
var
    Side : real;               {Length of a side, input}
    Area : real;               {Area of the square}
begin
  Writeln('This program calculates areas of squares. You');
  Writeln('supply the length of a side when asked.');
  Writeln('To stop the process, enter a length of 0,');
  repeat
    Writeln;
    Write('Enter the length of a side: ');
    Readln(Side);
    if Side <> EndOfData then
      begin
        Area := Side * Side;
        Writeln('The area is ', Area)
      end
  until Side = EndOfData
```

2. In writing the program for Exercise 1c, you probably had a statement similar to

```
Sum := Number1 + Number2;
```

You should change the variable "Sum" to "Difference," the operator "+" to "−", and any comments and messages to the user that refer to sum.

Section 1-4

5. For the programs of Exercises 1a and 1b:

10	Easy
1000	Large
5.65	Typical
12.3	Typical
1.004	Test of precision of numbers
0.001	Near the terminating value; small
−1	Bad, not detected
0	Terminating value
0.0	Terminating value

For the program of Exercise 1c:

−2	3	Easy
−12.5	12.5	Unusual pair
1000	2000	Two large values
1000	0.001	Large value and small value
0.001	1000	Small value and large value
0.001	0.0005	Near the terminating value; small values
0	0	Terminating value
0	5	Terminating value

6. c.

```
program InToCent(Input, Output);
{
  Written by:  XXXXXXXX  XX/XX/XX
    Purpose:  To convert inches to centimeters.
}
const
    EndOfData = 0;             {Value to terminate input}
    Factor = 2.54;            {Conversion factor}
var
    Inches     : real;        {Value in inches}
    Centimeters : real;       {Value in centimeters}
begin {InToCent}

{*** Before the loop print instructions.}

  Writeln('This program converts inches to centimeters.');
  Writeln('For each conversion, you will be asked for the');
  Writeln('quantity in inches. The program will print out');
  Writeln('the equivalent number of centimeters, and redo');
  Writeln('the whole process. When you wish to terminate',
```

```
{*** In loop, read quantity in inches; calculate and print
     amount of centimeters; quit when user enters 0 inches.}

repeat
  Writeln;
  Write('Enter the inches (0 to quit): ');
  Readln(Inches);
  if Inches <> EndOfData then
    begin
      Centimeters := Factor * Inches;
      Writeln('The centimeters are ', Centimeters)
    end
until Inches = EndOfData;

{*** After loop print message and stop the program.}

Writeln;
Writeln('InToCent program is terminating.')
end.
```

7. Append a ';' to the end of line 29; after line 30, insert the two lines:

```
Writeln;
Writeln('Have a nice day.')
```

5. a. var

```
Length : real;     {Length of rectangle}
Width  : real;     {Width of rectangle}
Area   : real;     {Area of rectangle}
Area := Length * Width
```

d. var

```
AgeInMonths : integer;   {Total age in months}
AgeY        : integer;   {# of years old}
AgeM        : integer;   {months since birthday}
AgeInMonths := 12 * AgeY + AgeM
```

e. var

```
Income : real;   {Person's income}
Tax    : real;   {Local tax}
Tax := (Income - 1000.0) * 0.05
```

f. var

```
LName : string[80];    {Last name}

LName := 'Professor ' + LName
```

9.

```
program TitleLine(Input, Output);
{
    Written by: xxxxxxxxxxxxxxxxxx xx/xx/xx
    Purpose: Generate a title line given a name.
}
const
  TitleHead = 'To the parents of ';
  EndOfData = '';                     {Terminating value}
var
  LName       : string[20];   {Last name, input}
  FName       : string[20];   {First name, input}
  MInitial    : char;         {Middle initial, input}
  AddressLine : string[80];   {title, output}

begin {TitleLine}

{*** Read the name (if the last name is '' then quit). Form
     title line and write it. }

  repeat
    Write('Enter last name (tap RETURN to quit):');
    Readln(LName);
    if LName <> EndOfData then
      begin
        Write('Enter rst name:');
        Readln(FName);
        Write('Enter middle initial:');
        Readln(MInitial);
        AddressLine := TitleHead + FName + ' ' +
                       MInitial + '. ' + LName;
        Writeln(AddressLine)
      end
  until LName = EndOfData
end.
```

□ CHAPTER 2

Section 2-1

1.

a. 13	**b.** 1.33 (2 places)
c. 3.25 (2 places)	**d.** 2.5 (1 place)
e. 21	**f.** −2
g. −6	**h.** 'AB'
i. 6.0 (1 place)	**j.** 6.0 (1 place)
k. 16.0 (1 place)	**l.** '4*65'

2.

a. 1.6 (1 place)	**b.** 5
c. 1.6 (1 place)	**d.** 12.3 (1 place)
d. 12.3 (1 place)	**e.** 68
f. −7.7 (1 place)	

3.

a. $Y := A * X + B$

b. $T := (1.0 / 2.0) * A + R$ or $T := 0.5 * A + R$

d. $J := K + 5$

e. $S := 5 * T$

f. $R := X / (Y + 3)$

g. $W := (X + 3 * Y) / (R + A - 3)$

h. $J := (K + 3) * J$

c. $W := (X + Y) / 2$

4.

a. bbb	**b.** bbb
c. ccc	**d.** bbb
e. bcccc	**f.** bbbbccc
g. cBc	**h.** Str
i. 'b'+c	**j.** bbb

3. (Section 1-4, Exercise 6.c.) We indicate where header comments would be placed by putting {. . . comments}

```pascal
program InToCent(Input, Output);
{. . . comments}
const
    EndOfData = 0;          {Value to terminate input}
    Factor    = 2.54;       {Conversion factor}

var
    Inches      : real;     {Value in inches, input}
    Centimeters : real;     {Value in centimeters, output}

procedure Instructions;
{. . . comments}
var
    Answer      : char;     {User's answer to question}

begin Instructions
    Write('Do you want instructions (Y, N): ');
    Readln(Answer);
    if Answer = 'Y' then
        begin
            Writeln('This program converts inches to centimeters.');
            Writeln('For each conversion, you will be asked for');
            Writeln('quantity in inches. The program will print');
            Writeln('equivalent number of centimeters, and repeat');
            Writeln('the whole process. When you wish to terminate');
            Writeln('the program, enter 0 for the quantity.')
        end
end; {Instructions}

begin {InToCent}

{*** Print instructions before the loop.}

    Instructions;

{*** In the loop, read quantity in inches, calculate and print
     the value in centimeters. Quit when 0 is entered.}

    repeat
        Writeln;
        Write('Enter inches (0 to quit): ');
        Readln(Inches);
        if Inches <> EndOfData then
            begin
                Centimeters := Factor * Inches;
                Writeln('Centimeters are ', Centimeters);
            end
    until Inches = EndOfData;

{*** After loop print message and stop.}

    Writeln;
    Writeln('InToCent program is terminating.')
end.
```

4. No instructions will be printed.
   a. Could test for 'y' as well as 'Y'.
   b. Could change the case of the answer to uppercase before checking for 'Y'.

5. We illustrate the general form to be used:

```pascal
if . . . then
    begin
        Writeln(' 1st line');
        ...........................
        Writeln(' 20th line');
        Writeln;
        Writeln('Press RETURN for rest of instructions');
        Readln;                              {Wait for RETURN}
        Writeln(' 21st line');
        ...........................
        Writeln(' 35th line')
    end;
```

2. a. var
```pascal
      Income : real;    {Person's income}
      Rate   : real;    {Tax rate}

   if Income < 8000.0 then
       Rate := 0.02
   else
       Rate := 0.045
```

b. var
```pascal
      SexCode : char;      {M for male, F for female}
      Males   : integer;   {Count the males}
      Females : integer;   {Count the females}

   if SexCode = 'M' then
       Males := Males + 1
   else
       Females := Females + 1
```

e. var
```pascal
      Tax : real;          {Person's tax}

   if Tax > 550.00 then
       Tax := Tax + 0.06 * Tax
```

Actually penalties are usually given as a percent of the amount over the specified limit. In that case the statement would be:

```pascal
   if Tax > 550.00 then
       Tax := Tax + 0.06 * (Tax - 550.00)
```

k. var
```pascal
      Hours   : integer;   {Hours portion of time}
      Minutes : integer;   {Minutes portion of time}
```

New Test Values	Improving	Exempt	Pass
70 80 75	No	No	Yes
70 80 76	Yes	No	Yes
30 40 35	No	No	No
30 40 36	Yes	No	No
100 94 97	No	Yes	Yes
100 94 98	Yes	Yes	Yes

```
Minutes := Minutes + 1;
if Minutes >= 60 then
  begin
    Hours := Hours + 1;
    Minutes := Minutes - 60
  end
```

3. a. Boundary at 8000.00, test at 7999.99, 8000.00, and 8000.01.
e. Boundary at 550.00, test at 549.99, 550.00, and 550.01.

4. a.

```
program TaxRate(Input, Output);
{. . . comments}
const
  EndOfData  = '';         {Terminating value}
  BreakPoint = 8000;       {Point where rule changes}
  LowRate    = 0.02;       {Rate for lower incomes}
  HighRate   = 0.045;      {Rate for higher incomes}

var
  Name   : string[20];     {Person's name, input}
  Income : real;           {Person's income, input}
  Rate   : real;           {Tax rate, computed}
  Tax    : real;           {Tax to be paid, computed}

procedure Instructions;
begin {Instructions}
  {Left as exercise.}
end; {Instructions}

begin {TaxRate}
  Instructions;

  repeat
    Write('Enter name (tap RETURN to quit)!');
    Readln(Name);
    if Name <> EndOfData then
      begin
        Write('Enter income:');
        Readln(Income);
        if Income < BreakPoint then
          Rate := LowRate
        else
          Rate := HighRate;
        Tax := Rate * Income;
        Writeln('Rate = ', Rate, ', Tax = ', Tax)
      end
  until Name = EndOfData;

  Writeln;
  Writeln('TaxRate program is terminating.')
end.
```

5. After the shaded statement, if Total > 290 etc., add the statement:

```
if 2 * Score3 > (Score1 + Score2) then
  Writeln('**********IMPROVING**********')
```

Note: A semicolon must be added to the shaded statement.

Section 2-4

5. a. $1 + Sqrt(X)$
b. $Sqrt(1 + X)$
c. $Abs(X - Y)$
d. $Abs(3 - 2 * X) + Y$
e. $X * X * X$ or $X * Sqr(X)$
f. $Abs((X + 2) / (Y + 3))$
g. $Sqrt(Sqr(B) - 4 * A * C)$
h. $Sqrt((Abs(R+5)-5) / (5-Y))$
i. $Sqrt((X - Y) / Abs(Z))$

6. Money := Round(Money * 100) div 100

7.

a. 1	**b.** 2
c. 5	**d.** 0
e. 5	**f.** 31
g. 5	**h.** 5
i. 2	**j.** 66
k. 25.0 (1 place)	**l.** Illegal, since Sqrt(4) is real.
m. 3	**n.** 5
o. Illegal, division by 0.	**p.** Illegal, 4/5 is real.
q. 125.0 (1 place)	**r.** 1

8. The loop for the program is

```
repeat
  Write('Enter X:');
  Readln(X);
  if X >= 0 then
    Writeln(Sqrt(X):1:5,' is the square root of ', X:1:5)
  else
    Writeln('Cannot take square root of negative number.');
    Writeln(Abs(X):1:5,' is the absolute value of ', X:1:5);
  Writeln;
  Write('Continue(Y,N)? ');
  Readln(Answer)
until Answer = 'N'
```

14. a.

```
Temp := Number div 100;
Temp := Temp mod 10;
```

16. Trace for Amount = 37.62

```
Dollars <- 37
Cents    <- Round(100 * .62)        62
Twenties <- 37 div 20                1
Dollars  <- 37 mod 20               17
   condition is true so print.
Tens     <- 17 div 10                1
Dollars  <- 17 mod 10                7
   condition is true so print
Fives    <- 7 div 5                  1
Dollars  <- 7 mod 5                  2
   condition is true so print
Ones     <- 2
   condition is true so print
Quarters <- 62 div 25                2
Cents    <- 62 mod 25               12
   condition is true so print
Dimes    <- 12 div 10                1
Cents    <- 12 mod 10                2
   condition is true so print
Nickels  <- 2 div 5                  0
Cents    <- 2 mod 5                  2
   condition is false
Pennies  <- 2
   condition is true so print
```

17. The steps to read, calculate, and print follow. These would appear in a loop similar to all the programs we have seen so far.

```
Readln(Monkeys);
Barrels  := Monkeys div 11;
Monkeys  := Monkeys mod 11;
if Barrels > 0 then
   Writeln(Barrels:10, ' Barrels');
Crates   := Monkeys div 7;
Monkeys  := Monkeys mod 7;
if Crates > 0 then
   Writeln(Crates:10, ' Crates');
Coconuts := Monkeys;
if Coconuts > 0 then
   Writeln(Coconuts:10, ' Coconuts');
```

Section 2-5

1. a. (Status = 'M') and (Sex = 'M')

b. not ((Status = 'M') and (Sex = 'M')) is one solution
(Status <> 'M') or (Sex <> 'M') is another solution

c. (Status = 'M') and (Sex <> 'M')

d. (Class = 'FR') or (Class = 'SO')

e. not ((Class = 'FR') or (Class = 'SO')) is one solution
(Class <> 'FR') and (Class <> 'SO') is another solution

f. ((Class = 'FR') and (QPA = 4.0)) or
((Class = 'SO') and (QPA >= 3.7)) or
(((Class = 'JU') or (Class = 'SR')) and (QPA >= 3.5))

h. (I mod 2 = 0) or (J mod 2 = 0) or (K mod 2 = 0)

j. (J >= 0) and (J <= 100)

m. (X > 0) and (Y > 0)

o. ((X > 0) and (Y <= 0)) or ((X <= 0) and (Y > 0))

p. (X <= 0) and (Y <= 0)

s. (Y > 5) and ((Z < 0) or (X > 5))

2.
a. false   b. true
c. true   d. true
e. false   f. true
g. true   h. true

3. a. X <> 45

d. (Y >= Z) and (Y < Z + 4.0)

e. not ((Class = 'FR') and (Sex = 'M') and (QPA < 3.2)) is one.
(Class <> 'FR') or (Sex <> 'M') or (QPA >= 3.2) is another.

h. not ((Class = 'FR') or (Class = 'SO') and (Hours < 35))

i. not (((Class = 'FR') or (Class = 'SO')) and (Hours < 35))

j. not (I in [3, 4, 5])

l. I in [3, 4, 5]

4. a.
```
Write(Name:20, Grade:10:2);
if Grade > 0.93 then
   Writeln(' excellent')
else if Grade < 0.75 then
   Writeln(' poor')
else
   Writeln;
```

d. Observe that a branch of the case statement can contain more than one value, as illustrated here:
```
Case Roll of
   7, 11 : Writeln(' You win.');
   2, 12 : Writeln(' You lose.');
   else    Writeln('  Roll again.');
end;
```

f.
```
Case Month of
   1 : Write('January ');
   2 : Write('February ');
   ..........................
   11 : Write('November  ');
   12 : Write('December  ');
end;
Writeln(Day:1, 19',Year:2);
```

5. a.
```
if CityCode = 'MUR' then
   Rate := 0.005
else if CityCode = 'MORR' then
   Rate := 0.01
else if CityCode = 'JCY' then
   Rate := 0.03
else if CityCode = 'BSTA' then
   Rate := 0.005
else
   Rate := 0.0;
Tax := Rate * Wages;
```

1. a. No

```
if (Class = 'FR') or (Class = 'SO') then
   begin
      if GPA >= 3.8 then Writeln('eligible')
   end
else
   begin
      if GPA >= 3.5 then Writeln('eligible');
   end
```

3. a. Three solutions are given, each with the same declarations.

```
var
   Number : integer;      {The number to check}
   Even   : Boolean;      {Is it even?}

Even := not Odd(Number);

Even := (Number mod 2 = 0);

if Number mod 2 = 0 then
   Even := true
else
   Even := false;
```

b.

```
var
   Valid : Boolean;           {Is the data valid?}
   Code  : char;              {Marital statis code}
   NumDependents : integer;   {Number of dependents}

Valid := ((Code = 'M') or (Code = 'S')) and
         ((NumDependents >= 0) and (NumDependents <= 12));
```

h. Two solutions are given, each with the same declarations.

```
var
   Vowel : Boolean;     {Is the letter a vowel?}
   Letter : char;       {The letter to check}

Vowel := (Letter = 'A') or (Letter = 'E') or (Letter = 'I')
         or (Letter = 'O') or (Letter = 'U');
Vowel := Letter in ['A', 'E', 'I', 'O', 'U'];
```

4. a.

```
Case Round(Grade) of
   60 .. 100 : Writeln('Passing');
    0 ..  59 : ;              {Do nothing}
   end;
```

6. b. Caution: Just being within 10 points is not the condition because that would not have 81 and 97 close, even though they are letter grades B and A. Suppose that AvgTest and AvgHomework are the two averages and that they are integers. Try this idea: First divide them by 10 to get a value between 0 and 10. Notice that 0 through 5 would be F's, 6 a D, . . . , and 9 and 10 A's. Now compare these quantities to see if they are within one of each other. Be sure to handle the special cases where there is more than one number per letter grade.

---

d. Two solutions are given:

```
if Item = 4927 then
   Price := 100.50
else if Item = 2178 then
   Price := 3000.00
else if Item = 2111 then
   Price := 100.50
else if Item = 1137 then
   Price := 100.50
else if Item = 1342 then
   Price := 25505.00;
```

```
case Item of
   4927 : Price := 100.50;
   2178 : Price := 3000.00;
   2111 : Price := 100.50;
   1137 : Price := 143.50;
   1342 : Price := 25505.00;
   end;
```

6. a. (Exercise 4a.) Grades of 0.93, 0.931, 0.80, 0.75, and 0.749.
d. (Exercise 4d.) Can be tested with all possible legal values of Roll: 2, 3, 4, 5, 6, 7, 8, 9, 10, 11, and 12.

7. (Exercise 1a.)

Status = 'M'	Sex = 'M'	Result
true	true	true
true	false	false
false	true	false
false	false	false

(Exercise 1f.) For this one, there would be seven columns, leading to 128 entries. It is not reasonable to test all combinations. It may be helpful to do a slightly different analysis, as illustrated here:

QPA	Class	Result
4.0	FR	true
3.99	FR	false
3.70	SO	true
3.69	SO	false
3.50	JU	true
3.50	SR	true
3.49	JU	false
3.49	SR	false

(Exercise 1h.)

I mod 2 = 0	J mod 2 = 0	K mod 2 = 0	Result
true	true	true	true
true	true	false	true
true	false	true	true
true	false	false	true
false	true	true	true
false	true	false	false
false	false	true	true
false	false	false	false

e. `Close := (Abs(X - Y) <= 10);`
f.
```
D1 := Number div 1000;
D2 := (Number mod 1000) div 100;
Palindrome := ((D2 * 10 + D1) = (Number mod 100));
```

11. a.
```
program LeapYear(Input, Output);
{. . . comments}
var
   Year : integer;          {Year to test}
   Done : Boolean;          {Used to control loop}

procedure Instructions; begin {left as exercise} end;

begin {LeapYear}
   Instructions;
   repeat
      Write('Enter year (1920 - 1990, other to quit): ');
      Readln(Year);
      Done := (Year < 1920) or (Year > 1990);
      if not Done then
         if Year mod 4 = 0 then
            Writeln(Year:1, ' is a leap year.')
         else
            Writeln(Year:1, ' is not a leap year.');
   until Done;
   Writeln;
   Writeln('LeapYear program is terminating')
end.
```

12. a. The program given here prints the answers on the terminal; an easy modification sends the output to the printer.

```
program CountyTax(Input, Output);
{. . . comments}
const
   EndOfData    = '';
   PembrokeCode = 'P';
   RichlandCode = 'R';
   TiogaCode    = 'T';
   PembrokeRate = 0.02;
   RichlandRate = 0.015;
   TiogaRate    = 0.03;
var
   Name       : string[20];   {Person's name, input}
   CountyCode : char;         {Code for county, input}
   Income     : real;         {Income, input}
   Tax        : real;         {County tax, computed}
   Error      : Boolean;      {Used to print error message}
   Rate       : real;         {county tax rate, computed}
   Tax        : real;         {County tax, computed}

procedure Instructions; begin {left as exercise} end;

begin {CountyTax}
   Instructions;
   repeat
      Writeln;
      Write('Enter name (tap RETURN to quit) :');
      Readln(Name);
      if Name <> EndOfData then
         begin
            Write('Enter county code:');
            Readln(CountyCode);
            Write('Enter income');
            Readln(Income);
            Error := false;
            case CountyCode of
               PembrokeCode : Rate := PembrokeRate;
               RichlandCode : Rate := RichlandRate;
               TiogaCode    : Rate := TiogaRate;
               else           Error := true
            end;
            if not error then
               begin
                  Writeln('Name :', Name);
                  Write('County code :', CountyCode);
                  Writeln(' Rate : ', Rate:7:4);
                  Write('Income : ', Income:10:2);
                  Tax := Rate * Income;
                  Writeln(' Tax : ', Tax:8:2)
               end
            else
               Writeln('County code is incorrect.')
         end
   until Name = EndOfData;
   Writeln;
   Writeln('CountyTax program is terminating.')
end.
```

13. a. Test plan for Exercise 11a: Years 1920, 1990, 1921, 1989 and some intermediate years both leap and nonleap years. Also, use 1919 to quit and 1991 to quit.

d. Test plan for Exercise 12b: There should be Sales amounts of 499.99, 500.00, 1000.00, 1000.01, 1499.99, and 1500.00, along with a few intermediate amounts. For each of the Sales figures, there should be Years figures of 7, 8, 15, and 16, along with a few intermediate values and some above 16. Probably the program would be designed to compute a commission figure from the Sales and then modify it by the Years worked. If that is the case, then one would not need each of the Sales figures repeated for all of the Years. As long as each of the Sales figures and each of the Years figures were represented in the tests, they would be reasonably adequate. Assuming there were eight Sales figures and six Years figures, this would reduce the number of tests from 48 to just 8.

Section 2-7

1. a. No type for A or for the function.
   b. No type for A or B.

4.

```
function Large3I(I1, I2, I3 : integer) : integer;
{. . . comments}
var
  Big : integer;        {Used to calculate answer}

begin  {Large3I}
  Big := I1;
  if I2 > Big then
    Big := I2;
  if I3 > Big then
    Big := I3;
  Large3I := Big
end;  {Large3I}
```

9. b.

```
function VacationDays(Type : char; Years : integer) : integer;
{. . . comments}
begin  {VacationDays}
  case Type of
    'A' :   VacationDays := 7;
    'E' :   VacationDays := 21;
    'S' :   if Years <= 6 then
              VacationDays := 10
            else
              VacationDays := 15;
    else
      VacationDays := 0
  end {case}
end;  {VacationDays}
```

10. b. Try := Large2I(M, N)

11. b. BasketsPerDay := Round2(Baskets / Days, 2)

12. c. Function for Exercise 5a of Section 2-5:

```
function Tax(CityCode : integer; Wage : real) : real;
{. . . comments}
var
  Rate : real;              {tax rate}

begin  {Tax}
  if CityCode = 395 then
    Rate := 0.005
  else if CityCode = 217 then
    Rate := 0.01
  else if CityCode = 152 then
    Rate := 0.03
  else if CityCode = 911 then
    Rate := 0.005
  else
    Rate := 0.0;
  Tax := Rate * Wages
end;  {Tax}
```

e. Function for Exercise 5d of section 2-5:

```
function Price(Item : integer) : real;
{. . . comments}
begin  {Price}
  if Item = 4927 then
    Price := 100.50
  else if Item = 2111 then
    Price := 100.50
  else if Item = 1137 then
    Price := 143.50
  else if Item = 1342 then
    Price := 25505.00
end;  {Price}
```

15.

```
function DegreeSin(X : real) : real;
{. . . comments}
const
  Pi = 3.14159265358979323846;

begin  {DegreeSin}
  DegreeSin := Sin(Pi / 180.0 * X)
end;  {DegreeSin}
```

DegreeCos is similar. The value of π is given to more figures than would be present with most versions of Pascal. Generally, using the full number of digits possible does not require any extra computation time over using some less accurate representation. The value of π could also be computed using the statement:

$$\pi := 4.0 * \text{Atan}(1.0).$$

This is because the tangent of 45 degrees, $\pi/4$ radians, is 1 exactly.

Section 2-8

3. b. Test plan for Exercise 4 of Section 2-7: This should be tested with cases where the largest value is negative, zero, and positive, where the largest value is the first, second, or third argument, and where there are repetitions in the argument values.

Test Values			Results
1	2	3	3
2	1	3	3
3	1	2	3
3	2	1	3
1	3	2	3
2	3	1	3
-1	-2	-3	-1
and rearrangements like above			
0	-1	-2	0
and rearrangements like above			
1	2	1	2
2	1	1	2
1	1	2	2
1	2	2	2
2	1	2	2
2	2	1	2

There should also be checks with numbers of larger magnitude.

e. Test plan for Exercise 9 of Section 2.7: There should be checks for each of the types A, E, and S and for a number of the other types. For type 'S', the value of Years should be tested at 6, 7, some values less than 6, and some values greater than 7.

The actual test should be carried out in a random order, not in the straightforward order listed below.

Type	Years	Results
A	6	7
A	7	7
A	10	7
E	6	21
E	7	21
E	10	21
S	4	10
S	6	10
S	7	15
S	10	15
B	6	0
B	7	0
B	10	0

6. Functions are used as follows: BuildNum to put together three digits into a single number, and GetDigit to extract either the first, second, or third digit from a three-digit number. In the next chapter, we will learn how to use a procedure to do the calculation of D1, D2, D3, D4, D5, and D6, which appears twice in the program.

```
program ModRN(Input, Output);
{. . . comments}
var
  Number    : real;        {The number to be split, input}
  ChrCode   : char;        {Code telling what to do, input}
  IntCode   : integer;     {Modifies char. code, input}
  FracPart  : integer;     {Fraction part, computed}
  IntPart   : integer;     {Integer part, computed}
  D1, D2,
  D3, D4,
  D5, D6    : integer;     {Digits of Number, computed}
  Answer    : real;        {The final answer, computed}
  Done      : Boolean;     {Used for loop control}

procedure Instructions;  begin {left as exercise} end;

function BuildNum(s1, s2, s3 : integer) : real;
{. . . comments }
begin
  BuildNum := 100 * s1 + 10 * s2 + s3
end;
```

```
function GetDigit(Num, Digit : integer) : integer;
{. . . comments}
begin
  case Digit of
    3 : GetDigit := Num mod 10;
    2 : GetDigit := (Num div 10) mod 10;
    1 : GetDigit := Num div 100;
  end;
end;

begin {ModRN}
  Instructions;

  repeat
    Write('Enter number in form ddd.ddd, (0.0 to quit):');
    Readln(Number);
    Done := not (Number > 0.0);
    if not Done then
    begin
      Write('Enter Code letter, and number: ');
      Readln(ChrCode, IntCode);
      IntPart := Trunc(Number);
      FracPart := Round(1000.0 * Frac(Number));
      case ChrCode of
        'P' : case IntCode of
                1 : Answer := IntPart;
                2 : Answer := FracPart;
                else  Answer := 0.0
              end;  {case}
        'D' : case IntCode of
                1,2,3 : Answer:=GetDigit(IntPart,IntCode);
                4,5,6 : Answer:=GetDigit(FracPart,IntCode-3);
                else  Answer:=0.0
              end;  {case}
        'R' : if IntCode <> 0 then
              begin
                D1 := GetDigit(IntPart, 1);
                D2 := GetDigit(IntPart, 2);
                D3 := GetDigit(IntPart, 3);
                D4 := GetDigit(FracPart, 1);
                D5 := GetDigit(FracPart, 2);
                D6 := GetDigit(FracPart, 3);
                case IntCode of
                  1 : Answer := BuildNum(D6, D1, D2) +
                                BuildNum(D3, D4, D5) / 1000.0;
                 -1 : Answer := BuildNum(D2, D3, D4) +
                                BuildNum(D5, D6, D1) / 1000.0;
                  else Answer := 0.0
                end
              end
              else
                Answer := Number;
        'S' : begin
                D1 := GetDigit(IntPart, 1);
                D2 := GetDigit(IntPart, 2);
```

```
D3 := GetDigit(IntPart, 3);
D4 := GetDigit(FracPart, 1);
D5 := GetDigit(FracPart, 2);
D6 := GetDigit(FracPart, 3);
case IntCode of
  1 : Answer := D1 + D2 + D3 + D4 + D5 + D6;
  2 : Answer := BuildNum(0, D1, D2) +
                BuildNum(0, D3, D4) +
                BuildNum(0, D5, D6);
  3 : Answer := BuildNum(D1, D2, D3) +
                BuildNum(D4, D5, D6);

        else Answer := 0.0
        end; {case}
      end; {if}
      Writeln('The answer is ', Answer:7:3)
end {if}
until Done;

Writeln;
Writeln('ModRN program is terminating.')
end.
```

10. Algorithm:

```
if Hours > 50 then do these steps:
  calculate RegularPay (formula 40 * HourlyRate)
  calculate OvertimePay
    (formula (Hours − 50) * 2 * HourlyRate +
      10 * 1.5 * HourlyRate)
  calculate PayFn as RegularPay + OvertimePay
else if Hours > 40 then do these steps:
  calculate RegularPay
  calculate OvertimePay
    (formula (Hours − 40) * 1.5 * HourlyRate)
  calculate PayFn as RegularPay + OvertimePay
otherwise
  calculate PayFn as Hours * HourlyRate
```

Test plan: Same as before, except add cases to test new boundary at 50, say 49.9, 50.0, and 50.1, along with some value past 50, say 60.

```
function PayFn(Hours, HourlyRate : real) : real;
{Same comments as in original inserted here.}
var
  RegularPay   : real;    {Pay for rst 40 hours}
  OvertimePay  : real;    {Pay for hours over 40}
begin {PayFn}
  if Hours > 50 then
    begin
      RegularPay := 40 * HourlyRate;
      OvertimePay := 15.0 * HourlyRate + (Hours − 50) *
        2.0 * HourlyRate;
      PayFn := RegularPay + OvertimePay
    end
  else if Hours > 40 then
    begin
      RegularPay := 40 * HourlyRate;
      OvertimePay := (Hours − 40) * 1.5 * HourlyRate;
      PayFn := RegularPay + OvertimePay
    end
  else
    PayFn := Hours * HourlyRate
end; {PayFn}
```

□ CHAPTER 3

Section 3-1

1. a.

```
Large := 0;    Small := 200;
```

2. The body of the program is

```
begin {CountPassFail}
  Instructions;
  PassCount := 0;
  FailCount := 0;
repeat
  Writeln;
  Write('Enter name (tap RETURN to quit): ');
  Readln(Name);
  if Name <> EndOfData then
    begin
      Write('Enter letter grade (A, B, C, D, F): ');
      Readln(Letter);
      if Letter = 'F' then
        FailCount := FailCount + 1
      else
        PassCount := PassCount + 1
    end
until Name = EndOfData;
Writeln;
Writeln(PassCount:1, ' passed and ', FailCount:1, ' failed');
Writeln('CountPassFail program terminating')
end.
```

4. b. The body of the program is

```
begin {CountTypeE}
  Instructions;
  Header;
  ECount := 0;
  Employees := 0;
  Total := 0.0;
repeat
  Writeln;
  Write('Enter name (tap RETURN to quit): ');
  Readln(Name);
  if Name <> EndOfData then
```

```
begin
  Employees := Employees + 1;
  Write('Enter skill level: ');
  Readln(Skill);
  Write('Enter years worked: ');
  Readln(Years);
  if Skill = 'E' then
    begin
      Bonus := Years * 15.00;
      Writeln(Lst, Name:20, ' ':10, Years:5, ' ':10,
              Bonus:10:2);
      Total := Total + Bonus;
      ECount := ECount + 1
    end
until Name = EndOfData;

Writeln(Lst);
Writeln(Lst, 'Total bonus for skill level E: ',Total:1:2);
if Employees <> 0 then
  begin
    Percent := ECount / Employees * 100;
    Writeln(Lst, Percent:1:2,
            '% of the employees are skill level E')
  end;
Writeln;
Writeln('CountTypeE program terminating')
end.
```

7. To do so, add the following in the indicated places of Figure 2-9:
In the var section, add:

```
PassCount    : integer;   {Number who passed}
FailCount    : integer;   {Number who failed}
ExemptCount  : integer;   {Number exempted}
Students     : integer;   {Number of students}
PerCent      : real;      {Percent exempt}
```

Just before the repeat, add:

```
PassCount := 0;
FailCount := 0;
ExemptCount := 0;
Students := 0;
```

Within the repeat loop, change the if-then-else to read:

```
if Total >= 210 then
  begin
    Result := 'passing';
    PassCount := PassCount + 1
  end
else
  begin
    Result := 'failing';
    FailCount := FailCount + 1
  end;
```

Within the repeat loop, change the if-then to read:

```
if Total > 290 then
```

```
begin
  Writeln('********* EXEMPT FROM FINAL **********');
  ExemptCount := ExemptCount + 1
end
```

Within the repeat loop, just before the prompt for the scores, add:

```
Students := Students + 1;
```

After the repeat loop and before the final message, add:

```
Writeln(PassCount:1, ' passed and ', FailCount:1, ' failed ');
if Students <> 0 then
  begin
    PerCent := ExemptCount / Students * 100;
    Writeln(PerCent:1:2, '% were exempt from the final')
  end;
```

9. a. Test plan for Exercise 2: The test plan involves considering boundaries on how many students there are, how many pass, and how many fail. It also includes covering all valid inputs for the letter grade. (We do not include invalid input in our test plan because the program does not detect it; however, we could if we wished.)

First run:

Inputs: immediately enter a null name to terminate program
Expected results: 0 pass, 0 fail
Reason for test: boundary on number of students (0)

Second run:

Inputs: letter grades F, F, F
Expected results: 0 pass, 3 fail
Reason for test: boundary on number of passes (0)

Third run:

Inputs: letter grades A, B, C, A, D, C, B
Expected results: 7 pass, 0 fail
Reason for test: boundary on number of failures (0)

Fourth run:

Inputs: letter grades F, F, C, A, D, B, F, B, C, F
Expected results: 6 pass, 4 fail
Reason for test: other than boundary on passes, failures, all possible letter grades.

b. Test plan for Exercise 4b: The test plan involves considering boundaries on how many employees there are and how many of these are at skill level E (anywhere from none to all). It also includes boundaries on the total bonus for skill level E. (We do not include invalid input in our test plan because the program does not detect it; however, we could if we wished.)

First run:

Inputs: immediately enter a null name to terminate program
Expected results: total bonus 0; either no percent message, or a percent of 0
Reason for test: boundary on number of employees (0)

Second run:

Inputs: skill levels A, C, R, X
Expected results: total bonus 0; percent 0
Reason for test: boundary on number who are at skill level E (0)

Third run:

Inputs: skill levels A, E (years 0), R
Expected results: total bonus 0; percent 33.33
Reason for test: boundary on total bonus (0); general case on percent at skill level E

Fourth run:

Inputs: all persons skill level E, with years 6, 4, 15, 9
Expected results: total bonus 510; percent 100.00
Reason for test: boundary on number who are at skill level E (all); general case on total bonus

Section 3-2

1.

N	printed	value of I after loop
a. 6	nothing	6
7	6	11
15	6, 11, 14	19
b. 6	6	11
7	6	11
15	6, 11, 14	19
c. 10	11	11
1	2	2
0	0	0
d. 10	2, 3, 4, 5, 6, 7, 8, 9, 10, 11	11
1	2	2
0	2	2

2. Numbers printed are 16 and 256.

3. Numbers printed are 1, 2, 3, 4, 5, 6, 7, 8, 9, 10, and 55.

5. a, b, and d are correct; (c) prints one line too many.

6. a.
```
for Feet := 1 to 30 do
  begin
    Inches := Feet * 12;
    Writeln(Feet:10, Inches:10)
  end;
```

7. a.
```
Sum := 0;
for I := 1 to 75 do
  begin
    Sum := Sum + I
  end;
Writeln(Sum:1);
```

8. a.
```
Outcome := Random(11) + 5;
```
b.
```
Outcome := Random(32) - 1;   (let -1 denote the 00 number)
```

12. a.
```
Multiple := 19;
Limit := 642;
while Multiple < Limit do
  begin
    Writeln(Multiple:10);
    Multiple := Multiple + 19
  end;
```

14. b.
```
Balance := 200;
Rate := 0.05;
Limit := 475;
repeat
  Balance := Balance + Balance * Rate;
  if Balance <= Limit then
    Writeln(Balance:10:2)
until Balance > Limit
```

15. a. 23

b. 45

c. 2

d. Ages[1]

e.
```
const
  MaxIndex = 1000;                        {or some other suitable value}
type
  IntegerArray = array[1 .. MaxIndex] of integer;
var
  Ages    : IntegerArray;
```

16. a. 28

b. 29

c.
```
for Month := 1 to 12 do
  begin
    Writeln(Days[Month]:1, ' days in month #', Month:1)
  end;
```

d. Days[2] := 29   (or Days[2] := Days[2] + 1)

17. a. Values printed are 7, 6, 5, 4, 3, 2, and 1.

b. Values printed are −2, −1, 1, 3, and 3.

c. Values printed are 3, 8; 5; 6, 11; 7, 7; and 8, 8.

Section 3-3

3. a. The following program assumes no ties for highest income and also assumes that there is at least one person. For simplicity, we show reads only for the data used in this specific program.

```
program FindHighIncome(Input, Output);
{. . . comments}
const
  EndOfData = 0;                  {Terminal ID number}
var
  ID         : integer;          {Employee ID}
  Income     : real;             {Employee yearly income}
  HighID     : integer;          {ID of person with highest income}
  HighIncome : real;             {largest income}
begin {FindHighIncome}
  HighIncome := 0;
  repeat
    Writeln;
    Write('Enter ID number (0 to quit): ');
    Readln(ID);
    if ID <> EndOfData then
      begin
        Write('Now the income: ');
        Readln(Income);
        if Income > HighIncome then
          begin
            HighIncome := Income;
            HighID := ID  {Remember who had the high income}
          end {if}
      end {if}
  until ID = EndOfData;
  Writeln;
  Writeln('Employee #', HighID:1, ' had the highest income: ',
          HighIncome:1:2);
  Writeln;
  Writeln('FindHighIncome program is terminating.')
end.
```

```
5. Readln(Number);               {Works correctly for Number = 0,
   NumDigits := 0;                if 0 is considered to have 1
                                  digit}
   repeat
     Number := Number div 10;
     NumDigits := NumDigits + 1
   until Number = 0
```

```
6. function SumOfDigits(Number : integer) : integer;
   {. . . comments}
   var
     LocalNumber : integer;   {Local variable for number}
     Sum         : integer;   {Local variable for sum of digits}
     Digit       : integer;   {Used to store one digit at a time}
   begin {SumOfDigits}
     LocalNumber := Number;
     Sum := 0;
     repeat
       Digit := LocalNumber mod 10;
       Sum := Sum + Digit;
       LocalNumber := LocalNumber div 10
     until LocalNumber = 0;
     SumOfDigits := Sum
   end; {SumOfDigits}
```

```
10. function GCD(M, N : integer) : integer;
    {. . . comments}
    var
      Test    : integer;        {Test number for divisibility}
    begin {GCD}
      if M < N then
        Test := M
      else
        Test := N;

      while (M mod Test <> 0) or (N mod Test <> 0) do
        begin
          Test := Test - 1
        end; {while}

      GCD := Test
    end; {GCD}
```

```
13. b.
    program Print(Input, Output);
    {. . . comments}
    const
      EndOfData = 0;            {Used to terminate loop}
    var
      Number : integer;         {Number whose divisor we print}

    procedure Instructions;
    begin {Instructions}
      Writeln('Stub version of Instructions called')
    end; {Instructions}

    procedure PrintDivisors(N : integer);
    begin {PrintDivisors}
      Writeln('Stub version of PrintDivisors called. N = ',N:1)
    end; {PrintDivisors}

    begin {Print}
      Instructions;
      repeat
        Writeln;
        Write('Enter a number (0 or less to quit): ');
        Readln(Number);
        if Number > EndOfData then
          begin
            PrintDivisors(Number)
          end {if}
      until Number <= EndOfData;

      Writeln;
      Writeln('Print program is terminating')
    end.
```

```
14. b.
    for I := 1 to 30 do          OR    Feet := 5;
      begin                            while Feet <= 150 do
                                         begin
```

```
Feet := I * 5;              begin
Inches := Feet * 12;          Inches := Feet * 12;
Writeln(Feet:10, Inches:10)   Writeln(Feet:10, Inches:10);
end  {for}                    Feet := Feet + 5
                            end  {while}
```

15. b. Assume that in part (a) we wrote a function CoinToss that returns a value to simulate a head and 1 to simulate a tail. Also assume a constant Head = 0 has been defined.

```
HeadCount := 0;

for I := 1 to 1000 do
  begin
    Result := CoinToss;
    if Result = Head then
      HeadCount := HeadCount + 1
  end  {for}

Writeln(HeadCount:1, ' heads occurred.')
```

d. See the assumptions of part (b).

```
LongStreak := 0;
HeadsInRow := 0;

for I := 1 to 1000 do
  begin
    Result := CoinToss;
    if Result = Head then
      HeadsInRow := HeadsInRow + 1
    else
      HeadsInRow := 0;
    if HeadsInRow > LongStreak then
      LongStreak := HeadsInRow;
  end;  {for}

Writeln(LongStreak:1, ' was the longest streak of heads.')
```

17. a. We use RollOfDice, the function defined in Section 3-2, and interpret "between" as meaning inclusive.

```
Count4To8 := 0;

for I := 1 to 12000 do
  begin
    Result := RollOfDice;       {Do we need this
                                 variable? Why?}
    if (Result >= 4 ) and (Result <= 8) then
      Count4To8 := Count4To8 + 1
  end;  {for}

Probability := Count4To8 / 12000;
Writeln("The approximate probability is ', Probability:1:2)
```

e. The function CardDraw is defined as Random(10) + 1.

```
CountBothEven := 0;
```

```
for I := 1 to 12000 do
  begin
    FirstCard := CardDraw;
    SecondCard := CardDraw;
    if (not Odd(FirstCard)) and (not Odd(SecondCard)) then
      CountBothEven := CountBothEven + 1
  end;  {for}

Probability := CountBothEven / 12000;
Writeln('The approximate probability is ', Probability:1:2)
```

19. a.

```
function Count(N, Total : integer) : integer;
{. . . comments}
var
  Counter : integer;        {Local version of answer}
  Sum     : integer;        {Sum of numbers generated}
  I       : integer;        {Loop control}
begin  {Count}
  Counter := 0;
  Sum := 0;

  while (Sum <= Total) do
    begin
      Sum := Sum + (Random(N) + 1);
      Counter := Counter + 1
    end;  {while}

  Count := Counter
end;  {Count}
```

21. If we made the function real, we could get bigger answers.

```
function Factorial(N : integer) : integer;
{. . . comments}
var
  I       : integer;        {Loop control}
  Product : integer;        {Local version of answer}
begin  {Factorial}
  Product := 1;

  for I := 2 to N do
    begin
      Product := Product * I
    end;  {for}

  Factorial := Product
end;  {Factorial}
```

23.

```
function Exp(X : real; N : integer) : real;
{. . . comments}
var
  Sum  : real;        {Local version of answer}
  Term : real;        {Individual term to add to sum}
  I    : integer;     {Loop control}
```

```
begin   {Exp}
  Term := 1;
  Sum := 0;

  for I := 1 to N do
    begin
      Sum := Sum + Term;
      Term := Term * (X / I)
    end;  {for}

  Exp := Sum
end;   {Exp}
```

25. a. Test plan for Exercise 3a: Section 3-3 (page 218) lists four important tests: largest first (no ties), largest last (no ties), largest in middle (no ties), and all the same.

First run:

Inputs: (ID, income are listed): 100, 26000; 350, 19654; 99, 25397
Expected results: ID 100 earned most: 26000
Reasons for test: first largest (no ties)

Second run:

Inputs: 254, 29001; 315, 16876; 123, 29002; 867, 17000
Expected results: ID 123 earned most: 29002
Reasons for test: largest in middle (no ties); also, borderline on comparison (29001 to 29002)

Third run:

Inputs: 165, 19000; 278, 20000
Expected results: ID 278 earned most: 20000
Reasons for test: largest last

Fourth run:

Inputs: 178, 20000; 987, 20000; 145, 20000; 443, 20000
Expected results: largest income 20000, with one of the four ID's (more than likely the first one or the last one)
Reasons for test: all the same

b. Test plan for Exercise 3c: Again the plan is based on the discussion in Section 3-1 (page 173): no data at all; count 0; all are counted.

First run:

Inputs: (years, department are listed): 10, WHSE; 14, PURC; 9, PURC; 1, DRIV
Expected results: either the message 'no one in department' or 0 average
Reasons for test: count 0

Second run:

Inputs: none (use terminal value to quit right away)
Expected results: either the message 'no one in department' or 0 average
Reasons for test: no data

Third run:

Inputs: 15, TRNG; 9, TRNG; 4, TRNG; 15, TRNG
Expected results: average 10.75
Reasons for test: all input in category being accumulated (also, input was chosen so answer is easy to check)

Fourth run:

Inputs: 11, WHSE; 14, TRNG; 7, TRNG; 10, PROC; 9, PROC; 8, PURC
Expected results: average 10.50
Reasons for test: some in category being accumulated, some not

g. Test plan for Exercise 10: The test plan involves checking numbers that have only one factor in common; numbers with more than one factor in common; numbers that are very different in size; prime numbers; numbers where the answer is 1 but neither is prime; both numbers the same; and one number a divisor of the other.

Inputs		Expected results	Reason for test
30	27	3	One common factor
30	42	6	More than one common factor
75	10765	5	Different in size, second larger
10765	75	5	Different in size, first larger
542	542	542	Same number
17	105	1	First number prime
255	29	1	Second number prime
40	693	1	Neither prime, but no common factors
17	51	17	First number divides second
350	7	7	Second number divides first

h. Test plan for Exercise 21: Factorial is defined for integers starting at 0. The most important tests are the boundary tests. Several other relatively small values for *n* are tested (with *n*! less than 32767, the value of Maxint on many microcomputers).

Inputs	Expected results	Reason for test
0	1	Boundary test
1	1	Boundary test
2	2	Still near boundary
5	120	General test
7	5040	Largest one less than 32767
8	40320 (perhaps)	With an integer function, this is the first one that will fail

26.

```
function ArraySum(A : IntegerArray; N : integer) : integer;
  var
```

Input	Expected results	Reason for test
3, 2, 1, 4, −Maxint	4	Last possible position
−Maxint, 1, 5, 4, 7	0	First possible position
4, 17, −Maxint, −Maxint, 3	2	Position in middle; also, More than one delimiter as an "Error-guessing" test

b. Hint: See Exercise 30a.

d. Test plan for Exercise 29b: Tests should be performed that fall in the following categories (based on the discussion in Section 3-1 (page 173): size of array is 0; size of array is > 0, but no numbers are even; size of array is > 0, and all numbers are even; size of array is > 0, and some are even but some are odd. At least one test should be done with the array as large as is allowed.

Section 3-4

1. a. Three lines: 10, 10, 10

b. Three lines: 10, 20, 30

c. Seven lines: 1, 1, 4, 1, 4, 7, 10

2. b. Add to declarations:

```
CountSales : integer;
```

Just before the inner (while) loop:

```
CountSales := 0;
```

In the inner loop:

```
CountSales := CountSales + 1;
```

Just after the inner loop:

```
Writeln('There were ', CountSales:1, ' sales.');
```

c. Add to declarations:

```
GrandTotal : real;
```

Just before the outer (repeat) loop:

```
GrandTotal := 0;
```

In the inner loop:

```
GrandTotal := GrandTotal + Sales;
```

(or else, just after the inner loop:

```
GrandTotal := GrandTotal + Total;)
```

Just after the outer loop:

```
Writeln('The total for the company was ',
        GrandTotal:1:2);
```

```
Sum   : integer;     {Array sum}
I     : integer;     {Subscript and loop control}
begin  {ArraySum}
Sum := 0;

for I := 1 to N do
  begin
  Sum := Sum + A[I]
  end;  {for}

ArraySum := Sum
end;  {ArraySum}
```

27. The segment assumes that −Maxint is present in the array.

```
I := 1;

while Arr[I] <> −Maxint do
  begin
  I := I + 1
  end;

N := I − 1
```

28. The segment assumes that N is less than the declared size of the array.

```
Arr[N+1] := −Maxint
```

29. a. Both solutions assume the array contains some values. They could be modified to print a message if this is not so.

```
Largest := Arr[1];        OR   Largest := Arr[1];
                               I := 2;
for I := 2 to N do
  begin                        while Arr[I] <> −Maxint do
  if Arr[I] > Largest then       begin
    Largest := Arr[I]            if Arr[I] > Largest then
  end  {for}                       Largest := Arr[I];
                                   I := I + 1
                                 end  {while}
```

b.

```
EvenCount := 0;

for I := 1 to N do
  begin
  if not Odd(Arr[I]) then
    EvenCount := EvenCount+1
  end;  {for}

Writeln(EvenCount)
```

```
EvenCount := 0;
I := 1;

while Arr[I] <> −Maxint do
  begin
  if not Odd(Arr[I]) then
    EvenCount := EvenCount+1;
  I := I + 1
  end;  {while}

Writeln(EvenCount)
```

30. a. Test plan for Exercise 27: Boundary tests are the most important. The boundaries for the position of the delimiter are at position 1 and at the last allowable position. We will also test with the delimiter somewhere in between. (The tests will be carried out with MaxIndex fairly small, say 5.)

e. Add to declarations:
```
LargeSale : real;
LargeName : string[20];
```
Just before the outer (repeat) loop:
```
LargeSale := 0;
```
In the inner loop:
```
if Sales > LargeSale then
  begin
    LargeSale := Sales;
    LargeName := Name
  end; {if}
```
Just after the outer loop:
```
Writeln(LargeName, ' had the largest sale: ', LargeSale:1:2);
```

4.
```
program PrintClassList(Input, Output);
{. . . comments}
var
  Row  : integer;          {Row number}
  Seat : integer;          {Seat number}
begin {PrintClassList}

for Row := 1 to 5 do
  begin

    for Seat := 1 to 7 do
      begin
        if Seat = 1 then
          Write(' Row ', Row:1, ' ')
        else
          Write('     ');
        Writeln('Seat ', Seat:1, '  ------------')
      end; {for Seat}

    Writeln;                {Blank line between rows}
  end  {for Row}

end.
```

5. The program body, with abbreviated prints, follows:
```
begin
  Randomize;
  NumberTies := 0;
  LastTie := 0;
  LargeLead := 0;
  ACount := 0;
  BCount := 0;

  for I := 1 to 30000 do
    begin
      if Vote <= 6 then      {Vote is a function: Random(10)+1}
        ACount := ACount + 1
      else
        BCount := BCount + 1;
      if ACount = BCount then
```

```
        begin
          NumberTies := NumberTies + 1;
          LastTie := I
        end; {if}
        if ACount - BCount > LargeLead then
          begin
            LargeLead := ACount - BCount;
            LargeBallot := I
          end {if}
      end; {for}

  Writeln(NumberTies, LastTie, LargeBallot, LargeLead)
end.
```

6. a. The body of the program follows, with abbreviated reads and prints. It is assumed that the first balance that exceeds the ending balance is also to be printed.
```
begin
  Readln(BeginBalance, Rate, EndingBalance);
  Balance := BeginBalance;

  repeat
    Interest := Rate * Balance;
    Balance := Balance + Interest;
    Writeln(Balance)
  until Balance > EndingBalance

end.
```

7. b.
```
Wins := 0;
Losses := 0;

for I := 1 to 100 do
  begin
    RollCount := 0;

    repeat
      Result := DiceRoll;
      RollCount := RollCount + 1
    until Result in [5, 6, 7];

    if (RollCount mod 2 = 0) and (Result in [5, 7]) then
      Wins := Wins + 1
    else
      Losses := Losses + 1
  end; {for}

Writeln(Wins:1, ' ', Losses:1)
```

9. b.
```
function GoodScore(Score : integer) : Boolean;
{. . . comments}
begin {GoodScore}
  GoodScore := (Score >= 0) and (Score <= 100)
end; {GoodScore}

procedure GetTests(var Test1,Test2,Test3,Test4 : integer);
{. . . comments}
```

```
var
  Valid : Boolean;                          {All four scores o.k.}
begin {GetTests}
  Write('Enter four test scores separated by blanks: ');
  Readln(Test1, Test2, Test3, Test4);
  Valid := GoodScore(Test1) and GoodScore(Test2) and
           GoodScore(Test3) and GoodScore(Test4);

  while not Valid do
    begin
      Write('At least one test was not in the proper');
      Writeln('range (0 to 100). Please try again.');
      Write('Enter four test scores separated by blanks: ');
      Readln(Test1, Test2, Test3, Test4);
      Valid := GoodScore(Test1) and GoodScore(Test2) and
               GoodScore(Test3) and GoodScore(Test4)
    end  {while}

end;  {GetTests}
```

10. b. There are many approaches. One is to add a procedure to get one score and change the body of GetTests, as shown.

```
procedure GetOneScore(Prompt: String24; var Score: integer);
{. . . comments}
begin {GetOneScore}
  Writeln;
  Write(Prompt);
  Readln(Score);

  while (Score < 0) or (Score > 100) do
    begin
      Writeln('Must be from 0 to 100. Please try again.');
      Readln(Score)
    end  {while}

end;  {GetOneScore}
```

```
begin {GetTests - revised body}
  GetOneScore('Enter the first score:   ', Test1);
  GetOneScore('Enter the second score:  ', Test2);
  GetOneScore('Enter the third score:   ', Test3);
  GetOneScore('Enter the fourth score:  ', Test4)
end;  {GetTests}
```

12. Hint: Use two variables, Low and High, set up so that you know the answer is strictly between the two. Initialize Low to 0 and High to 1001. Make the average of Low and High the computer's guess. If it is wrong, adjust either Low or High based on what the user tells the computer: either the guess is too high or too low. (Note: This is the basic idea of the "binary search" that will be covered in Chapter 6.)

15. See the solution to Exercise 7b. Rather than counting wins and losses, keep track of the money you have won or lost.

18. The modified program body, with abbreviated prints, follows:

```
begin {MatchRoll}
  Randomize;

  repeat
    Goal := RollOfDice
  until Goal <> 7;

  Writeln(Goal:1);

  repeat
    Roll := RollOfDice;
    Writeln(Roll:1);
  until (Roll = Goal) or (Roll = 7);

  if Roll = Goal then
    Writeln('You win.')
  else
    Writeln('You lose.')
end;  {MatchRoll}
```

22. a. The body of the program, with abbreviated I/O, follows:

```
begin
  repeat
    Readln(BeginBalance, Rate);
    if BeginBalance <> EndOfData then     {EndOfData is 0}
      begin
        Balance := BeginBalance;
        Years := 0;
        repeat
          Interest := Balance * Rate;
          Balance := Balance + Interest;
          Years := Years + 1
        until Balance > 2 * BeginBalance;

        Writeln(Years:1)
      end {if}
  until BeginBalance = EndOfData

end.
```

25. a. The program body, with abbreviated I/O, follows:

```
begin
  Randomize;
  FirstRoll := RollOfDice;
  Writeln(FirstRoll);
  RollCount := 0;

  repeat
    RollCount := RollCount + 1;
    Roll := RollOfDice;
    Writeln(Roll);
  until (Roll = FirstRoll) or (RollCount = 5);

  if Roll = FirstRoll then      Caution: Don't test RollCount = 5!
    Writeln('Match on roll #', RollCount:1)
  else
    Writeln('No match')
end.
```

27. b. Test plan for Exercise 6a: There are boundary situations: the balance goes over the ending balance in the first year; the balance after one of the years exceeds the ending balance by exactly 1 cent; and the balance after one of the years is exactly equal to the ending balance.

Beginning balance	Rate	Ending balance	Expected output	Reason for test
100.00	0.05	105.00	105.00	
			110.25	Balance = ending balance after 1 year
200.00	0.03	203.00	206.00	Over after 1 year
100.00	0.10	121.00	110.00	
			121.00	
			132.10	Balance = ending balance after 2 years
100.00	0.10	120.99	110.00	
			121.00	Over by 1 cent after 2 years

d. Test plan for Exercise 9b: There are boundaries that should be hit for *each* test score: 0, −1, 100, and 101. Also, there should be some variation on how many are bad; the most important are probably these: none, just the first, just the second, just the third, just the fourth, and all.

g. Test plan for Exercise 24 (without modifications): The testing should include: an account with no transactions; an account with only deposits; an account with only checks; invalid transaction codes; invalid transaction amounts (including the boundaries of 0.00, illegal, and 0.01, legal); and bad checks (including the boundaries of over by 1 cent and exactly equal to the current balance).

28. The program body given assumes (among others) declarations of the type IntegerArray and the array A as an IntegerArray. Notice that the first two loops could be combined to find the sum as we read the numbers. This would be more "efficient" (it would run faster) but less "cohesive" ("cohesive" refers to each module or segment of code ideally accomplishing one task).

```
begin

{*** Read the array.}

for I := 1 to 10 do
  begin
    Write('Enter value #',' I:1, ': ');
    Readln(A[I])
  end; {for}

{*** Find the average.}

Sum := 0;

for I := 1 to 10 do
  begin
    Sum := Sum + A[I]
  end; {for}

Average := Sum / 10;
```

```
{*** Look for the first one bigger or equal to the average.}

I := 0;

repeat
  I := I + 1
until A[I] >= Average;

Writeln('The first one bigger or equal to the average is ',
        A[I]);
Writeln('It occurred in position ', I:1)
end.
```

□ CHAPTER 4

Section 4-1

1. a. Illegal; parameters must match in number.
  b. Legal.
  c. Illegal; must use a named type for array parameters.
  d. Illegal; procedures don't have types.
  e. Illegal; a function must be invoked as an expression.
  f. Illegal; parameters must match in type.
  g. Legal.
  h. Illegal; expression cannot be passed to a var parameter.
  i. Illegal; must use a named type for string parameters.

2. a. 16 5
  b. 5 16
  c. Compiler error if T not declared as an integer in the main program; otherwise, the value of T in the main program would be changed to 5.

3. a. Yes. −3 2 6 17 5 4 9 −2 15 −53
  c. −53 15 −2 9 4 −3 17 6 2 5

4. b. Number is not needed.
  c. The actual parameter in the main program would be changed to 0.

5. a.
```
const
  MaxIndex = 1000;
type
  IntegerArray = array [1 .. MaxIndex] of integer;

procedure Shift(var Scores : IntegerArray);
```
  b.
```
type
  String2 = string[2];
  String20 = string[20];

procedure Print(Name : String20; Initials : String2;
                Score : integer);
```

7. a.
```
function CommissionFn(Sales, Rate : real) : real;
```
  b.
```
procedure BuildDate(Julian : integer; var Month : String9;
                    var Day : integer);
```

1.

```
procedure SphereStats(Radius : real;
                      var Volume, SurfaceArea : real);
{. . . comments}
const
  Pi = 3.14159265b;                    {Mathematical constant}
var
  RSquared    : real;                  {Radius squared}
  RCubed      : real;                  {Radius cubed}
begin {SphereStats}
  RSquared := Sqr(Radius);
  RCubed := Radius * RSquared;
  Volume := (4/3) * Pi * RCubed;
  SurfaceArea := 4 * Pi * RSquared
end; {SphereStats}
```

3.

```
function StateTax(Income : real; Dependents : integer) : real;
{. . . comments}
const
  PerDependent = 500;                  {Dollars per dependent}
  Percentage = 0.10;                   {Percent for deduction}
var
  StdDeduct   : real;                  {Standard deduction}
  TaxIncome   : real;                  {Taxable income}
begin {StateTax}
  TaxIncome := Income - (Dependents * PerDependent);
  StdDeduct := Percentage * Income;
  TaxIncome := TaxIncome - StdDeduct;
  if TaxIncome < 0 then
    StateTax := 0
  else if TaxIncome <= 10000 then
    StateTax := 0.02 * TaxIncome
  else
    StateTax := 200 + 0.025*(TaxIncome - 10000)
end; {StateTax}
```

4. a.

```
procedure MaxMin(Num1,Num2: integer; var Max,Min: integer);
{. . . comments}
begin {MaxMin}
  if Num1 <= Num2 then
    begin
      Min := Num1;
      Max := Num2
    end
  else
    begin
      Min := Num2;
      Max := Num1
    end
end; {MaxMin}
```

6. {procedure MaxMin . . . was given in section.}

7.

```
function Range(Num1, Num2, Num3 : integer) : integer;
{. . . comments}
var
  Maximum   : integer;                 {Largest of Num1, Num2, Num3}
  Minimum   : integer;                 {Smallest of Num1, Num2, Num3}
begin {Range}
  MaxMin(Num1, Num2, Num3, Maximum, Minimum);
  Range := Maximum - Minimum
end; {Range}
```

10. b.

```
function AlmostEqual(Num1, Num2 : real) : Boolean;
{. . . comments}
const
  FivePlaces = 0.00001;                {Measure of closeness}
begin {AlmostEqual}
  AlmostEqual := Abs(Num1 - Num2) < FivePlaces
end; {AlmostEqual}
```

e. The solution below uses an array in a similar manner to what we have already done.

```
function Passing(Quizzes : IntegerArray) : Boolean;
{. . . comments}
const
  CutOff = 12;                         {Lowest passing average}
  NumQuizzes = 14;                     {Number of weekly quizzes}
var
  Total     : integer;                 {Total of quizzes}
  I         : integer;                 {Loop index}
  Average   : real;                    {Average of quizzes}
begin {Passing}
  Total := 0;

  for I := 1 to NumQuizzes do
    begin
      Total := Total + Quizzes[I]
    end; {for}

  Average := Total  NumQuizzes;
  Passing := Average >= CutOff
end; {Passing}
```

```
function Palindrome(Num : integer) : Boolean;
{. . . comments}
const
  MaxSize = 4;                         {Digits of Num}
type
  SmallArray = array [1 .. MaxSize] of integer;
var
  WorkNumber  : integer;               {Working copy of Num}
  Digits      : SmallArray;            {Digits of Num}
  I           : integer;               {Loop index}
begin {Palindrome}
  WorkNumber := Num;

  for I := 1 to MaxSize do
    begin
      Digits[I] := WorkNumber mod 10;
      WorkNumber := WorkNumber div 10
    end; {for}
```

```
Palindrome := true;

for I := 1 to MaxSize div 2 do
  begin
    if Digits[I] <> Digits[MaxSize - I + 1] then
      Palindrome := false
  end {for}

end; {Palindrome}
```

11. a. Two alternative solutions are presented. The first solution uses an array; the second solution uses another procedure.

First alternative solution:
```
function Between(Value, Low, High : integer) : Boolean;
{. . . comments}
begin {Between}
  Between := (Value >= Low) and (Value <= High)
end; {Between}

procedure GetScores(var Score1, Score2, Score3 : integer);
{. . . comments}
const
  MaxSize = 3;       {Number of scores to read}
  Maximum = 100;     {Highest possible score}
  Minimum = 0;       {Lowest possible score}
type
  SmallArray = array [1 .. MaxSize] of integer;
var
  Scores : SmallArray;    {To get scores}
  I      : integer;       {Loop index}
begin {GetScores}

for I := 1 to 3 do
  begin
    Write(' Enter score', I, ': ');
    Readln(Scores[I]);

    while not Between(Scores[I], Minimum, Maximum) do
      begin
        Writeln('*** score must be between ', Minimum,
                ' and ', Maximum);
        Write(' Please reenter score: ');
        Readln(Scores[I])
      end {while}

  end; {for}

Score1 := Scores[1];
Score2 := Scores[2];
Score3 := Scores[3]
end; {GetScores}
```

Second alternative solution:
{function Between . . . as given above.}
```
procedure GetOneScore(var Score : integer);
{. . . comments}
const
  Maximum = 100;     {Highest score}
  Minimum = 0;       {Lowest score}
begin {GetOneScore}
  Write(' Enter score: ');
  Readln(Score);

  while not Between(Score, Minimum, Maximum) do
    begin
      Writeln('*** score must be between ', Minimum,
              ' and ', Maximum);
      Write(' Please reenter score: ');
      Readln(Score)
    end {while}

end; {GetOneScore}

procedure GetScores(var Score1, Score2, Score3 : integer);
{. . . comments}
begin {GetScores}
  GetOneScore(Score1);
  GetOneScore(Score2);
  GetOneScore(Score3)
end; {GetScores}
```

13. a.
```
procedure Vertical(InString : String255);
{. . . comments}
var
  I : integer;       {Loop index}
begin {Vertical}
  for I := 1 to Length(InString) do
    Writeln(' ':39, InString[I])
end; {Vertical}
```

b.
```
function Blanks(InString : String255) : integer;
{. . . comments}
var
  I     : integer;   {Loop index}
  Count : integer;   {For counting blanks}
begin {Blanks}
  Count := 0;

  for I := 1 to Length(InString) do
    if InString[I] = ' ' then Count := Count + 1
  end; {for}

  Blanks := Count
end; {Blanks}
```

c.
```
procedure Split(InString : String255; var First : String255;
                var Rest : String255);
{. . . comments}
const
  Null = '';         {Empty string}
```

```
begin {Split}
  if InString = Null then
    begin
      First := '';
      Rest := ''
    end
  else
    begin
      First := InString[1];
      Rest := Copy(InString, 2, Length(InString) - 1)
    end
end; {Split}
```

e.
```
procedure SplitLast(InString: String255; var Last: String255;
                    var Rest : String255);
{. . . comments}
const
  Null = '';                    {Empty string}
begin {SplitLast}
  if InString = Null then
    begin
      Last := '';
      Rest := ''
    end
  else
    begin
      Last := InString[Length(InString)];
      Rest := Copy(InString, 1, Length(InString) - 1)
    end
end; {SplitLast}
```

15.
```
procedure SmallLarge(InArray : IntegerArray; InSize : integer;
                     var Smallest, Largest : integer);
{. . . comments}
var
  I    : integer;                  {Loop index}
begin {SmallLarge}
  if InSize <= 0 then
    begin
      Smallest := MaxInt;          {Largest integer}
      Largest := -MaxInt           {Smallest integer}
    end
  else
    begin
      Smallest := InArray[1];
      Largest := InArray[1];
      for I := 2 to InSize do
        begin
          if InArray[I] < Smallest then Smallest := InArray[I];
          if InArray[I] > Largest then Largest := InArray[I]
        end {for}
    end
end; {SmallLarge}
```

16.
```
procedure MoneyTalk(Amount : real);
{. . . comments}
var
  Dollars : integer;              {Dollars in amount}
  Cents   : integer;              {Cents in amount}
begin {MoneyTalk}
  Dollars := Trunc(Amount);
  Cents := Round(100 * Frac(Amount));
  if Cents > 9 then
    Writeln('EXACTLY ', Dollars:1, ' DOLLARS AND ',
                         Cents:1, ' CENTS')
  else
    Writeln('EXACTLY ', Dollars:1, ' DOLLARS AND 0',
                         Cents:1, ' CENTS')
end; {MoneyTalk}
```

19. In the solution below, the type of the function is chosen real to extend the range of integers for which a factorial can be computed without overflowing the permissible range of possible integer values.

```
function Factorial(N : integer) : real;
{. . . comments}
begin {Factorial}
  if N < 2 then
    Factorial := 1
  else
    Factorial := N * Factorial(N-1)
end; {Factorial}
```

20.
```
function Gcd(N, M : integer) : integer;
{. . . comments}
begin {Gcd}
  if N mod M = 0 then
    Gcd := M
  else
    Gcd := Gcd(M, N mod M)
end; {Gcd}
```

23. b.
{procedure Split . . . as shown in solution to Exercise 13c.}

```
function Element(InChar: char; InString: String255): Boolean;
{. . . comments}
const
  Null = '';                    {Empty string}
var
  FirstChar : String255;        {First character}
  Remainder : String255;        {Remainder of string}
begin {Element}
  if InString = Null then
    Element := false
  else
    begin
      Split(InString, FirstChar, Remainder);
      if FirstChar = InChar then
```

```
        Element := true
    else
        Element := Element(InChar, Remainder)
    end
end; {Element}
```

Test data for Exercise 4b: The test plan involves checking when the numbers are all the same; when all are different; when two are the same; when three are the same; when four are the same; when extreme values; zero; some typical values; in order; in reverse order; smallest first; smallest last; largest first; and largest last.

Inputs	Expected Results		Reason for Test
Five Input Numbers	Largest	Smallest	
0, 0, 0, 0, 0	0	0	All the same, zero
−1, 0, 2, 32767, −5	32767	−5	Extreme
−1, −2, −1, −3, −2	−1	−3	Two are the same
1, 32767, 32767, 3, 32767	32767	1	Three are the same, extreme
12, −32767, 12, 32767, 12	32767	−32767	Three are the same, extreme
3, 5, 3, 3, 3	5	3	Four are the same
3, 2, 3, 3, 3	3	2	Four are the same
1, 2, 3, 4, 5	5	1	Typical, in order
5, 4, 3, 2, 1	5	1	Typical, in reversed order
1, 10, 20, 30, 40	40	1	Smallest first
10, 20, 30, 40, 1	40	1	Smallest last
100, 1, 2, 3, 4	100	1	Largest first
4, 3, 2, 1, 100	100	1	Largest last

c. Test data for Exercise 5: The test plan involves checking zero; extreme values; boundary values; and typical values.

Inputs	Expected Results	Reason for Test:
Number	Letter	
0	F	Zero
−32767	F	Extreme
32767	H	Extreme
90	H	Boundary
91	H	Typical
89.999	C	Boundary
89	C	Typical
75	C	Boundary
74.999	F	Boundary
74	F	Typical
95	H	Typical
85	C	Typical
75	C	Typical
100	H	Typical

25. b. Test data for Exercise 4a: The test plan involves checking when the two numbers are the same; when the first is smaller; when the first is larger; when one or both are zero; extreme values; and typical values.

Inputs		Expected Results		Reason for Test
First Number	Second Number	Largest	Smallest	
0	0	0	0	Both the same, zero
1	1	1	1	Both the same, positive
−1	−1	−1	−1	Both the same, negative
5	0	5	0	One is zero
0	5	5	0	One is zero
−5	0	0	−5	One is zero
0	−5	0	−5	One is zero
−1	2	2	−1	Negative and positive
2	−1	2	−1	Positive and negative
1	32767	32767	1	Small, large
100	55	100	55	Typical values
55	100	100	55	Check both ways
−200	−15	−15	−200	Typical values
−15	−200	−15	−200	Check both ways
32767	1	32767	1	Large, small
32767	32767	32767	32767	Large, large
−32767	32767	32767	−32767	Extremes
32767	−32767	32767	−32767	Extremes
−32767	32767	32767	−32767	Extremes
32767	−32767	32767	−32767	Extremes

n. Test data for Exercise 16: The test plan involves checking zero; bad data; single-digit dollar amounts; double-digit dollar amounts; single-digit cent amounts; double-digit cent amounts; multiple of 10 dollars; multiple of 10 cents; typical data; and boundaries.

Inputs	Expected Results	Reason for Text
0.00	EXACTLY 0 DOLLARS AND 00 CENTS	Zero
−1.12	???	Bad data
100.00	???	Bad data
1.15	EXACTLY 1 DOLLARS AND 15 CENTS	Single-digit dollar
43.23	EXACTLY 43 DOLLARS AND 23 CENTS	Double-digit dollar
55.04	EXACTLY 55 DOLLARS AND 04 CENTS	Single-digit cent
9.99	EXACTLY 9 DOLLARS AND 99 CENTS	Double-digit cent
80.72	EXACTLY 80 DOLLARS AND 72 CENTS	Multiple of 10 dollars
21.30	EXACTLY 21 DOLLARS AND 30 CENTS	Multiple of 10 cents
1.25	EXACTLY 1 DOLLARS AND 25 CENTS	Typical
99.99	EXACTLY 99 DOLLARS AND 99 CENTS	Boundary

p. Test data for Exercise 20: The test plan involves checking numbers the same; first larger; second larger; one a multiple of the other; common factor smaller than both; first number 1; second number 1; no common factor, neither number 1; typical values; and bad data.

Inputs		Expected Results	Reason for Test
First	Second	Greatest Common Divisor	
3	3	3	Numbers the same
35	7	7	First larger
7	35	7	Second larger
12	24	12	One a multiple of the other
4	6	2	Common factor smaller
1	12	1	First number 1
12	1	1	Second number 1
35	32	1	No common factor
1011	111	3	Typical
8	12	4	Typical
12	8	4	Typical
0	0	???	Bad data

r. Test data for Exercise 23b: The test plan involves checking character there, last; character there, first; character there, middle; character not there, close; character not there, not close; character in different case there; typical size string; one character string, character there; one character string, character not there; more than one instance there; and null string.

Inputs		Expected Results	
String	Character	True or False	Reason for Test
'AAAAB'	B	True	Character there, last
'BAAAA'	B	True	Character there, first
'AABAA'	B	True	Character there, middle
'AABAA'	C	False	Character not there, close
'AABAA'	Z	False	Character not there, far
'AABAA'	b	False	Different case there
'AAbAA'	B	False	Different case there
'B'	B	True	One character string
'B'	b	False	One character string
'AABB'	A	True	More than one instance
Null	B	False	Null string

Section 4-3

1.

```
program FirstNPrimes(Input, Output);
{. . . comments}
var
  Number   : integer;                 {Primes to print}
  N        : integer;                 {Primes printed}
  Candidate: integer;                 {tested for primality}

function Divisor(Num : integer) : integer;
{. . . as shown in section}

function Prime(Number : integer) : Boolean;
{. . . as shown in section}

begin {FirstNPrimes}
{Instructions;}
  Write('Enter the number of primes: ');
  Readln(Number);
  Candidate := 2;
  N := 0;

  while N < Number do
    begin
      if Prime(Candidate) then
        begin
          Writeln(Candidate);
          N := N + 1
        end; {if}
      Candidate := Candidate + 1
    end; {while}
```

```
{*** Print message and terminate.}

  Writeln;
  Writeln('FirstNPrimes program terminating.');
end.
```

Test Plan: In designing the test plan, we want to test bad data, boundary values, some typical values, and some large values.

Input Value	Output Values	Reason for Test
−1	None	Bad data
0	None	Boundary value
1	2	Boundary value
7	2, 3, 5, 7, 11, 13, 17	Typical
100	2, 3, 5, . . . , 541	Large value

4. a. Suppose that $N = ab$ and that both a and b are greater than $\sqrt{N}$. Since $a > \sqrt{N}$ and $b > \sqrt{N}$, a basic rule for inequalities allows us to deduce that

$$ab > \sqrt{N} \sqrt{N} = N.$$

By virtue of the contradiction, we know that one of a or b is less than or equal to $\sqrt{N}$.

b.

```
function Divisor(Num : integer) : integer;
{. . . comments}
var
PotentialDivisor  : integer;    {Takes on values 2, 3, etc.}

begin {Divisor}
PotentialDivisor := 2;

while (PotentialDivisor <= Sqrt(Num)) and
      (Num mod PotentialDivisor <> 0) do
  begin
    PotentialDivisor := PotentialDivisor + 1
  end; {while}

if Num mod PotentialDivisor = 0  then
  Divisor := PotentialDivisor
else
  Divisor := Num
end; {Divisor}
```

11. a.
```
function RelativelyPrime(A, B : integer) : Boolean;
{. . . comments}
begin
  RelativelyPrime := (GCD(A, B) = 1)
end; {RelativelyPrime}
```

20. a.
```
procedure PrintCard(CardNumber : integer);
{. . . comments}
```

```
begin {PrintCard}
case CardNumber mod 13 of
   0: Write('ace');
   1: Write('2');
   2: Write('3');
   3: Write('4');
   4: Write('5');
   5: Write('6');
   6: Write('7');
   7: Write('8');
   8: Write('9');
   9: Write('10');
  10: Write('jack');
  11: Write('queen');
  12: Write('king')
end; {case}
Write(' of ');
case CardNumber div 13 of
   0: Writeln('clubs');
   1: Writeln('diamonds');
   2: Writeln('hearts');
   3: Writeln('spades')
end {case}
end; {PrintCard}
```

c. The global array is declared as

```
var
Dealt    : array[0 .. 51] of Boolean;   {Global array, used}
```

The function is

```
function Card : integer;
{. . . comments}
var
  Try  : integer;
begin
  repeat
    Try := Random(52);              {Attempt to draw}
  until not Dealt[Try];

  Card := Try;
  Dealt[Try] := true               {Dealt[Try] = false}
end; {Card}
```

☐ CHAPTER 5

Section 5-1

1.
```
program Shopping(Input, Output);
{. . . comments}
var
  FileVar  : text;                 {File designator}
```

```
begin {Shopping}
  Assign(FileVar, 'SHOPPING.LST');
  Rewrite(FileVar);
  Writeln(FileVar, ' ':32, 'A Shopping List');
  Writeln(FileVar, ' ':32, '---------------');
  Writeln(FileVar);
  Writeln(FileVar, ' ':26, '2 Frozen Pizzas');
  Writeln(FileVar, ' ':26, '10 Bags of chips');
  Writeln(FileVar, ' ':26, '4 Cans of soup (assorted)');
  Writeln(FileVar, ' ':26, '1 Case of cola');
  Close(FileVar);
  Writeln;
  Writeln('Shopping program terminating.')
end.
```

3. a.
```
program Shopping(Input, Output);
{. . . comments}
type
  String50 = string[50];

const
  EndOfData = '';                    {Terminating value}

var
  FileVar : text;                    {File designator}
  Line    : String50;                {One line of file}

begin {Shopping}
  Assign(FileVar, 'SHOPPING.LST');
  Rewrite(FileVar);
  Writeln(FileVar, ' ':32, 'A Shopping List');
  Writeln(FileVar, ' ':32, '---------------');
  Writeln(FileVar);

  repeat
    Write('Enter a line (tap RETURN to quit): ');
    Readln(Line);
    if Line <> EndOfData then
      Writeln(FileVar, ' ':26, Line)
  until Line = EndOfData;

  Close(FileVar);
  Writeln;
  Writeln('Shopping program terminating.')
end.
```

8.
```
program Change(Input, Output);
{. . . comments}
var
  InFile   : text;                   {File designator for source}
  Outfile  : text;                   {File designator for target}
  FileName : string[14];             {Name of the file}
  Line     : string[80];             {Line of file}
  Response : string[80];             {User input}
{. . . procedure Copy from Figure 5-4 is inserted here.}

begin {Change}
  Write('Enter the filename: ');
  Readln(FileName);
  Assign(InFile, FileName);
  Assign(OutFile, 'TEMP.FIL');
  Reset(InFile);
  Rewrite(OutFile);
  Copy(InFile, Outfile);
  Close(InFile);
  Close(Outfile);
  Assign(InFile, 'TEMP.FIL');
  Assign(Outfile, FileName);
  Reset(InFile);
  Rewrite(OutFile);

{*** Process the file while copying back.}

  while not eof(InFile) do
    begin
      Readln(InFile, Line);
      Writeln('Line: ', Line);
      Writeln('type $DELETE to delete line, tap return for',
              ' no change, or type a new line.');
      Write(': ');
      Readln(Response);
      if Response = '$DELETE' then
        Writeln(' Line deleted.')
      else if Response = '' then
        Writeln(OutFile, Line)
      else
        Writeln(OutFile, Response)
    end; {while}

{*** Close the files.}

  Close(InFile);
  Close(OutFile);

{*** Print terminating message and stop program.}

  Writeln;
  Writeln('Change program is terminating.')
end.
```

11.
```
program Scores(Input, Output);
const
  EndOfData = -1;                    {Terminating value}
{. . . declarations}
begin {Scores}
  repeat
    Writeln;
    Write('Enter a score: ');
    Readln(ScoreToFind);
    if ScoreToFind <> EndOfData then
```

```
begin
    Writeln;
    Writeln('Students with score of ', ScoreToFind, ':');
    Reset(FileVar);                {start at beginning of file}

    while not eof(FileVar) do
        begin
            Readln(FileVar, StudentName);
            Readln(FileVar, StudentID);
            Readln(FileVar, ExamScore);
            if ExamScore = ScoreToFind then
                Writeln(' ':5, StudentName,
                    ' ':(21 - Length(StudentName)),
                    StudentID:13)

        end; {while}

    Writeln('    *** list complete')
    end {if}
until ScoreToFind = EndOfData;
{. . .code to print message and terminate is inserted here}
end.
```

19. a.

```
Joan Smith
32
qq
CPS
121
3
A
MAT
444
3
B
XXX
Bill E. Goat
78
123
   . . .
XXX
```

b. We just show the portion of the program that illustrates the file processing.

```
program Students(Input, Output);
const
    EndOfData = 'XXX';              {Terminating value}
{. . . comments}
{. . . declarations}
begin {Students}
{. . . get the file name and open the file}

while not eof(FileVar) do
    begin
        Readln(FileVar, StudentName);
        Readln(FileVar, TotalHours);
        Readln(FileVar, QualPoints);
        Writeln;
        Writeln('Student Information:');
        Writeln('           Name: ', StudentName);
        Writeln('    Total Hours: ', TotalHours);
        Writeln('  Quality Points: ', QualPoints);
        Writeln('  Course Information:');

    repeat
        Readln(FileVar, Department);
        if Department <> EndOfData then
            begin
                Readln(FileVar, CourseNumber);
                Readln(FileVar, CreditHours);
                Readln(FileVar, Grade);
                Writeln('   Course: ', Department, ' ',
                    CourseNumber);
                Writeln('   Credits: ', CreditHours);
                Writeln('   Grade: ', Grade);
                Writeln
            end
        else
            begin
                Writeln;
                Writeln(' ':26, '<Tap return to continue.>');
                Readln;
                Writeln
            end

    until Department = EndOfData

end; {while}
```

21. We just show the portion of the program that illustrates the file processing.

```
program Departments(Input, Output);
{. . . comments}
{. . . declarations}
begin {Departments}
{. . . code to get filename and open the file}

Readln(FileVar, TotalDepts);
Writeln('Department',' ':15,'Professor',' ':15,'Salary');
Writeln('----------',' ':15,'---------',' ':15,'------');

for I := 1 to TotalDepts do
    begin
        Readln(FileVar, Department);
        Readln(FileVar, TotalProfs);
        Prefix := ' ' + Department;

        for J := 1 to TotalProfs do
            begin
                Readln(FileVar, ProfName);
                Readln(FileVar, Salary);
                Writeln(Prefix, ' ':16, ProfName,
                    ' ':(28-Length(ProfName)), Salary:5);

                Prefix := ' '                  {Blank out dept}
            end {for J}

    end; {for I}
```

a. Just prior to the for J loop, set DeptSum to 0. Inside of the for J loop, set DeptSum to DeptSum + Salary. After the for J loop, calculate and print the

Average for the department (DeptSum/TotalProfs). We assume that each department has at least one professor.

b. In addition to the changes described in part a, add the following lines: Just prior to the for I loop, set Total and ProfCount to 0. Just prior to the for J loop, set ProfCount to ProfCount + TotalProfs. After the for J loop, set Total to Total + DeptSum. After the for I loop, calculate and print the SchoolAverage (Total/ProfCount).

c. Just prior to the for I loop, set NumOver to 0. Inside of the for J loop, set NumOver to NumOver + 1 for each Salary greater than 28000.

d. Just prior to the for J loop, set HiSalary to −1 and set HiName to 'NoOne'. Inside of the for J loop, set HiSalary to Salary and HiName to ProfName if Salary is greater than HiSalary. Just after the for J loop, print HiName.

e. Put in the changes from part a, except for printing each average. Just prior to the for I loop, set AboveAve to 0. After the for J loop, where the departmental average is calculated, set AboveAve to AboveAve + 1 if Average is greater than 20000. Just after the for I loop, print AboveAve.

f. Put in the changes from part a, except for printing each average. Just prior to the for I loop, set HiAve to −1 and set HiDept to '???'. After the for J loop, where the departmental average is calculated, set HiAve to Average and set HiDept to Department if Average is greater than HiAve. Just after the for I loop, print HiDept and HiAve.

Section 5-2

1. a. `Friend.Phone := '555-1212'`

b.
```
Complex =
  record
    RealPart      : real;   {Real part of number}
    ImaginaryPart : real    {Imaginary part of number}
  end;
```

c. `Number : Complex;`   {complex number variable}

d.
```
if Friend.Name = 'Joan Smith' then
  Writeln('Found')
```

e. `[1, 2, 3]`   (or `[1 .. 3]`)

f. `['1', '2', '3']` (or `['1' .. '3']`)

g.
```
if N in [3 .. 9] then
  Writeln('Yes')
```

h. `A : set of char;`   {Set variable}

2. a.
```
procedure Detail(PersonVar : PersonalData);
{. . . comments}
begin {Detail}
  Writeln(PersonVar.Phone, ':', PersonVar.Name)
end; {Detail}
```

c.
```
function SumOfSquares(InNumber : Complex) : real;
{. . . comments}
begin {SumOfSquares}
  with InNumber do
    SumOfSquares := Sqr(RealPart) + Sqr(ImaginaryPart)
end; {SumOfSquares}
```

3.
```
PersonalData =
  record
    Name       : string[20];
    Phone      : string[8];
    Address    : string[80];
    BirthMonth : integer
  end;
```

6. a. For simplicity, We will not be concerned with the number of lines per page.

```
program PrintFile(Input, Output);
{. . . comments}
type
  CompanyType =
    record
      Name    : string[40];
      Address : string[80];
      City    : string[20];
      State   : string[2];
      ZipCode : string[5];
      NumEmp  : integer
    end;
  FileType = file of CompanyType;

var
  CompanyVar : CompanyType;
  FileVar    : FileType;
  FileName   : string[14];

begin {PrintFile}
  Write('Enter the filename: ');
  Readln(FileName);
  Assign(FileVar, FileName);
  Reset(FileVar);
  {. . . print headings}

  while not eof(FileVar) do
    begin
      Read(FileVar, CompanyVar);
      with CompanyVar do
        begin
          {. . . print each field as in:
            Writeln(Lst, 'Name: ', Name);}
        end; {with}
    end; {while}

  close(FileVar);

  {*** Print message and terminate.}
  .
  .
  Writeln;
  Writeln('PrintFile program terminating.')
end.
```

6. b. We show only the code around the main loop of the program for i and ii.
i.
```
  NumCompanies := 0;

  while not eof(FileVar) do
```

repeat
  Write('Enter a number to find (', EndOfData, ' to quit): ');
  Readln(NumberToFind);
  if NumberToFind <> EndOfData then
    if not (NumberToFind in [50 .. 100]) then
      Writeln('*** invalid element, redo.')
    else if NumberToFind in A then
      Writeln('The number is in the set.')
    else
      Writeln('The number is not in the set.')
  until NumberToFind = EndOfData;

{*** Print message and terminate.}

  Writeln;
  Writeln('SetRead program terminating.')
end.

13. a. Test plan for Exercise 2: We wish to test positive and negative values, large and small values, integer and real. For the testing, we will print values rounded to two decimal places, except for very small values, which will be reported in exponential notation.

Test cases:

Real Part	Imaginary Part	Expected	Reason for Test
0	0	0.00	Always test with 0
1	1	2.00	Easy to check
1	-1	2.00	Positive, negative
-1	1	2.00	Negative, positive
-1	-1	2.00	Negative, negative
0.1	0.1	0.02	Small, small
10.1	10.1	204.02	Large, large
10.1	0.1	102.02	Large, small
0.1	10.1	102.02	Small, large
0.01	0.01	2.000000000E-4	Very small, very small

c. Test Plan for Exercise 5: We will test with an empty file, a file of one record, and files with many records. We will test with an existing company in the first record, the last record, and the middle of the file. We will test with two records for the same company and with no records for the specified company. If the program is to test queries in a loop, then we will ask first for a company toward the end of the file and then ask for a company toward the beginning of the file.

Test cases: (general)

1. Empty file: We expect a report that the file is empty or that none of the requested companies exist in the file.

2. File with one record: We expect to get the information for the one existing company and reports that other companies do not exist in the file.

3. Company in first record: We expect the company to be found.

4. Company in last record: We expect the company to be found.

5. Two records for the same company: We expect to receive information from the first of the two records

---

```
begin
  Read(FileVar, CompanyVar);
  NumCompanies := NumCompanies + 1;
  with CompanyVar do
    begin
      {. . . print each field as in:
      Writeln(Lst, 'Name: ', Name);}
    end {with}
end; {while}

Close(FileVar);
Writeln(Lst, 'The number of companies: ', NumCompanies);
```

ii.
```
NumCompanies := 0;
NumLarge := 0;

while not eof(FileVar) do
  begin
    Read(FileVar, CompanyVar);
    NumCompanies := NumCompanies + 1;
    with CompanyVar do
      begin
        if NumEmp > 700 then
          NumLarge := NumLarge + 1;
        {...print each field as in:
        Writeln(Lst, 'Name: ', Name);}
      end {with}
  end; {while}

close(FileVar);
Write(Lst, 'The percentage of large companies is: ');
if NumCompanies > 0 then
  Writeln(Lst, NumLarge / NumCompanies * 100:1:2)
else
  Writeln(Lst, 0.0:1:2);
```

8.
```
program SetRead(Input, Output);
{. . . comments}
const
  EndOfData = 0;                          {Terminating value}

var
  A            : set of 50 .. 100;        {Set for numbers}
  Element      : integer;                 {User input}
  NumberToFind : integer;                 {User input}

begin {SetRead}
  A := [];
  Writeln('Enter the set of numbers from 50 thru 100:');

repeat
  Write(' element (', EndOfData, ' to quit): ');
  Readln(Element);
  if Element <> EndOfData then
    if Element in [50 .. 100] then
      A := A + [Element]
    else
      Writeln('*** invalid element, redo.')
  until Element = EndOfData;
```

6. Query for company in last record, then query for company in first record: We expect to receive information about both companies.

7. Query for nonexistent company, then query for existent company: We expect to receive information for the existing company.

h. Test plan for Exercise 8: We wish to test with an empty set, a one element set, and a set of several elements. We wish to test entering elements out of range. We wish to test elements entered in different orderings. We wish to enter the same element more than once. We wish to test the boundary values. We wish to query with data out of range, and on the boundaries of the range. We wish to query in different orders. We wish to query for both existing and nonexisting elements.

Test cases:

1. Boundaries for out-of-range data:
   49 should get error message
   50 should be accepted
   100 should be accepted
   101 should get error message
2. Empty set:
   query for 49 should get error message
   query for 50 should get 'not in' message
3. One-element set, 50:
   query for 50 should get 'in' message
   query for 51 should get 'not in' message
4. Three elements, entered: 78, 51, 99:
   query for 51 should get 'in' message
   following query for 51 should get 'in' message
5. Elements entered: 70, 50, 70, 99:
   query for 99 should get 'in' message
   query for 70 should get 'in' message

Section 5-3

2. a. 0   b. Draw
   c. Win   d. True
   e. False

3.
```pascal
function Roll : integer;
{. . . comments}

begin {Roll}
   Roll := Random(13) + 6
end; {Roll}
```

6.
```pascal
function ClassFun(Name : String09) : Classes;
{. . . comments}
var
   Index : Classes;      {Subscript}
   Found : Boolean;      {Indicator of found}

begin {ClassFun}
   Index := Dwarf;
   Found := false;
```

```pascal
   while (Index <= MagicUser) and (not Found) do
      begin
         if Name = PrintName[Index] then
            Found := true
         else
            Index := Succ(Index)
      end; {while}

   if Found then
      ClassFun := Index
   else
      Writeln('*** Error in ClassFun - invalid name')
end; {ClassFun}
```

8. a.
```pascal
function TwoThrows : Outcomes;
{. . . comments}
var
   Throw1 : integer;     {First roll of dice}
   Throw2 : integer;     {Second roll of dice}

begin {TwoThrows}
   Throw1 := (Random(6) + 1) + (Random(6) + 1);
   Throw2 := (Random(6) + 1) + (Random(6) + 1);
   if Throw1 > Throw2 then
      TwoThrows := Win
   else if Throw1 < Throw2 then
      TwoThrows := Lose
   else
      TwoThrows := Draw
end; {TwoThrows}
```

b.
```pascal
program Game(Input, Output);
{. . . comments}
const
   Start1 = 20;          {Stake for player one}
   Start2 = 14;          {Stake for player two}

type
   Outcomes = (Lose, Draw, Win);

var
   Total1 : integer;     {Dollars of player one}
   Total2 : integer;     {Dollars of player two}
   I      : integer;     {Loop index}
   Broke  : Boolean;     {Indicates someone broke}
   Result : Outcomes;    {Holds the throw result}

{function TwoThrows as above inserted here.}

begin {Game}
   Randomize;
   Total1 := Start1;
   Total2 := Start2;
   I := 0;
```

13. a.

```
procedure TimeAdd(Time1, Time2 : Times; var Sum : Times);
{. . . comments}

begin {TimeAdd}
with Sum do
  begin
    Minutes := Time1.Minutes + Time2.Minutes +
               (Time1.Seconds + Time2.Seconds) div 60;
    Seconds := (Time1.Seconds + Time2.Seconds) mod 60
  end {with}
end; {TimeAdd}
```

b.

```
procedure TimeSub(Time1,Time2: Times;var Difference: Times);
{. . . comments}

begin {TimeSub}
with Difference do
  begin
    Minutes := Time1.Minutes - Time2.Minutes;
    Seconds := (Time1.Seconds - Time2.Seconds);
    if Seconds < 0 then
      begin
        Seconds := Seconds + 60;
        Minutes := Minutes - 1
      end {if}
  end {with}
end; {TimeSub}
```

15. b. Test plan for Exercise 6: We want to test both good and bad data. Because the range of valid names is so small, we will test all valid names. We will also test invalid values that differ from a valid name by case or a single character position. We will test various boundary conditions and the empty string.

Test cases:

Name	Expected Value	Reason for Test
'Dwarf'	Dwarf	Good data, boundary
'Elf'	Elf	Good data, typical
'Halfling'	Halfling	Good data, typical
'Human'	Human	Good data, typical
'Cleric'	Cleric	Good data, typical
'MagicUser'	MagicUser	Good data, boundary
''	Error	Bad data, extreme
'Dwarf '	Error	Bad data, boundary
'Ele'	Error	Bad data, boundary
'human'	Error	Bad data, boundary

c. Test plan for Exercise 9: We want to test both good and bad data. Because the range of valid values is so small, we will test all valid values. We will test various boundary conditions.

Test cases:

9. a.

```
function DayValue(N : integer) : Day;
{. . . comments}

begin {DayValue}
case N of
  0 : DayValue := Sun;
  1 : DayValue := Mon;
  2 : DayValue := Tue;
  3 : DayValue := Wed;
  4 : DayValue := Thur;
  5 : DayValue := Fri;
  6 : DayValue := Sat;
else
  Writeln('*** Error in DayValue - invalid input.')
end {case}
end; {DayValue}
```

```
repeat
  Result := TwoThrows;
  if Result = Win then
    begin
      Total1 := Total1 + 1;
      Total2 := Total2 - 1
    end
  else if Result = Lose then
    begin
      Total2 := Total2 + 1;
      Total1 := Total1 - 1
    end;
  Broke := (Total1 = 0) or (Total2 = 0);
  I := I + 1
until (I = 100) or Broke;

Writeln('There were ', I, ' throws.');
Writeln('First player has ', Total1, ' dollars.');
Writeln('Second player has ', Total2, ' dollars.');

{*** Print message and terminate.}

Writeln;
Writeln('Game program terminating.')
end.
```

c. A run of 1000 games produced an average of $19.63 for player one and an average of $14.36 for player two. Note that each player tends to end up with the starting stake. Warning: The program of this part takes a few minutes to execute.

11.

```
type
  Fruits = (Strawberries, Raspberries, Plums, Bananas);
  Flavors = (Vanilla, Chocolate, TinRoof, TuttiFruit);
  Toppings = (ChocolateChips, Nuts, CandyBars, HardCandy);
  Sundaes =
    record
      Name          : string[30];              {Name of the creation}
      FlavorChoice  : array [1 .. 3] of Flavors;   {Flavors}
      FruitChoice   : Fruits;                      {Fruits}
      ToppingChoice : array [1 .. 3] of Toppings   {Toppings}
    end;
```

Name	Expected Value	Reason for Test
0	Sun	Good data, boundary
1	Mon	Good data, typical
2	Tue	Good data, typical
3	Wed	Good data, typical
4	Thur	Good data, typical
5	Fri	Good data, typical
6	Sat	Good data, boundary
7	Error	Bad data, boundary
-1	Error	Bad data, boundary

e. Test plan for Exercise 13a: We will only test good data because checking for valid data should occur when the data is input. We will test for values that cause a carry to minutes from seconds and also values that do not cause a carry. We will test boundary values.

Test cases:

Time1		Time2		Expected Sum		
Minutes	Seconds	Minutes	Seconds	Minutes	Seconds	Reasons for Test
0	1	0	59	1	0	Good data, boundary
0	59	0	0	1	0	Good data, boundary
0	0	0	0	0	0	Good data, zeros
1	34	3	45	5	19	Good data, carry
12	10	9	40	21	50	Good data, no carry
0	58	0	1	0	59	Good data, boundary

□ CHAPTER 6

Section 6-1

```
1. a. const
     MaxIndex = 100;
   type
     IntArray = array[0 .. MaxIndex] of integer;
   var
     A : IntArray;
   b. const
     LoIndex = -50;
     HIndex = 75;
   type
     RealArray = array[LoIndex .. HIndex] of real;
```

```
   var
     A : RealArray;
   c. const
     LoIndex = 22;
     HIndex = 53;
   type
     BooleanArray = array[LoIndex .. HIndex] of Boolean;
   var
     A : BooleanArray;
2. b. type
     DigitList = array[0 .. 15] of char;
   var
     Digits : DigitList;
       .
       .
     Digits[0] := '0';
     Digits[1] := '1';
       .
       .
     Digits[14] := 'E';
     Digits[15] := 'F';
3. a.
function Smallest(A : IntegerArray; N : integer) : integer;
{. . . comments}
var
  I          : integer;             {Loop index}
  SmallValue : integer;             {Copy of answer}
begin {Smallest}
  SmallValue := A[1];

  for I := 2 to N do
    begin
      if A[I] < SmallValue then
        SmallValue := A[I]
    end; {for}

  Smallest := SmallValue
end; {Smallest}

b.
function SmallPosition(A : IntegerArray; N: integer): integer;
{. . . comments}
var
  I             : integer;             {Loop index}
  SmallValue    : integer;             {Smallest value found}
  SmallPosition : integer;
begin {SmallPosition}
  SmallValue := A[1];
  SmallPosition := 1;

  for I := 2 to N do
    begin
      if A[I] < SmallValue then
        begin
          SmallValue := A[I];
          SmallPosition := I
        end {if}
    end; {for}

end; {SmallPosition}
```

6.

The text's solution goes through the array of children once; for each child, it decides which counter to increment, then increments that counter.

The student's solution goes through the array of children once for each of the six groups, looking for children in that group. It will be approximately six times slower.

7. b.

```
function PctPositive(A : IntegerArray; N : integer) : real;
{. . . comments}
var
  I       : integer;          {Loop index}
  Count   : integer;          {Count of pos. values}
begin {PctPositive}
  Count := 0;

  for I := 1 to N do
    begin
      if A[I] > 0 then
        Count := Count + 1
    end;  {for}

  if N <> 0 then
    PctPositive := Count / N
  else
    PctPositive := 0.0
end;  {PctPositive}
```

c.

```
function Location(A : IntegerArray; N : integer) : integer;
{. . . comments}
var
  I       : integer;          {Loop index}
  Found   : boolean;          {Negative found}
begin {Location}
  I := 1;
  Found := false;

  while (not Found) and (I <= N) do
    begin
      if A[I] < 0 then
        Found := true
    end;  {while}

  if Found then
    Location := I
  else
    Location := 0
end;  {Location}
```

10.

The idea of the solution is to go forward through the array looking for zeros. The first zero found is swapped with A[1], the next one with A[2], and so on. We will use a procedure Swap, which swaps two integers.

```
      LastZero := 0;

      for I := 1 to N do
        begin
          if A[I] = 0 then
```

```
            begin
              Swap(A[LastZero+1], A[I]);
              LastZero := LastZero + 1
            end  {if}
        end;  {for}
```

14. a.

```
function CharValue(I : integer) : char;
{. . . comments, with reference to the use of the global
                 Digits array}
begin {CharValue}
  CharValue := Digits[I]
end;  {CharValue}
```

16. a.

```
procedure CopyAll(var A : RealArray; B : RealArray);
{. . . comments}
begin {CopyAll}
  A := B
end;  {CopyAll}
```

b.

```
procedure CopyPart(var A : RealArray; B : RealArray);
{. . . comments}
var
  I       : integer;          {Loop control}
begin {CopyPart}

  for I := 1 to 50 do
    begin
      A[50+I] := B[I]
    end;  {for}

end;  {CopyPart}
```

c.

This could be very similar to part b; instead, we present a slightly different solution.

```
procedure CopyPart(var A : RealArray; B : RealArray);
{. . . comments}
var
  I       : integer;          {Loop control}
  BSub    : integer;          {Subscript for B array}
begin {CopyPart}
  BSub := 17;

  for I := 1 to 7 do
    begin
      A[I] := B[BSub];
      BSub := BSub + 1
    end;  {for}

end;  {CopyPart}
```

20.

Compare this to the solution for Exercise 7c.

```
function Equal(A, B : IntegerArray; N : integer) : Boolean;
{. . . comments}
var
  I       : integer;          {Loop index}
  Same    : boolean;          {False when difference found}
```

```
begin {Equal}
I := 1;
Same := true;

while Same and (I <= N) do
    begin
        if A[I] <> B[I] then
            Same := false
    end; {while}

Equal := Same
end; {Equal}
```

24. a. Add the following function:

```
function TotalPay(Pay : PayArray) : real;
{. . . comments}
var
I     : integer;      {Loop control}
Total : real;         {Local copy of answer}
begin {TotalPay}
    Total := 0.0;

    for I := 1 to 12 do
        begin
            Total := Total + Pay[I]
        end; {for}
    TotalPay := Total
end; {TotalPay}
```

Then modify the detail line procedure to also print the total pay, and change the main loop body to

```
while not eof(InputFile) do
    begin
        GetInput(InputFile, Name, Pay);
        YearsPay := TotalPay(Pay);
        DetailLine(Name, Pay, YearsPay)
    end; {while}
```

Section 6-2

1. c. type
```
String20 = string[20];
RainArray = array[1 .. 12] of real;
StateRainType =
    record
        Name : String20;
        RainList : RainArray
    end;
var
State : StateRainType;
```
access by:
```
State.Name        for the state name
State.RainList[I]  for the rainfall in month I
```

d. add to the above the type
```
StateArrayType = array[1 .. 50] of StateRainType;
```
and declare the array
```
StateList : StateArrayType;
```
access by:
```
StateList[I].Name        for the Ith state's name
StateList[I].RainList[J]  for the Ith state's rainfall in month J
```

g. type
```
Term =
    record
        Coefficient : real;
        Exponent : integer
    end;
Polynomial =
    record
        NTerms : integer;
        TermList : array [1 .. 20] of Term
    end;
var
Poly : Polynomial;
```
access by:
```
Poly.NTerms                   for the number of terms
Poly.TermList[I].Coefficient  for the coefficient of the Ith term
Poly.TermList[I].Exponent     for the exponent of the Ith term
```

h. type
```
AnswerType = (a, b, c, d, e);
QuestionType =
    record
        Value : integer;
        Answer : AnswerType
    end;
KeyType =
    record
        NQuestions : integer;
        QuestionList = array[1 .. 100] of QuestionType
    end;
var
Key : KeyType;
```
access by:
```
Key.NQuestions              for the number of questions
Key.QuestionList[I].Value   for the value of the Ith question
Key.QuestionList[I].Answer  for the answer for the Ith question
```

j. type
```
DigitArray = array [0 .. 9] of char;
var
Digits : DigitArray;
```
initialize by:
```
for I := 0 to 9 do                OR   Digits[0] := '0';
    Digits[I] := Chr(Ord('0')+I)       Digits[1] := '1';   etc.
```

k. type
```
VowelArrayType = array['A' .. 'Z'] of boolean;
```

```
var
    Vowel : VowelArrayType;
initialize by
    for Ch := 'A' to 'Z' do
        Vowel[Ch] := false;
    Vowel['A'] := true;
    Vowel['E'] := true; etc.
2. a. for I := 1 to N do
    begin
        Average[I] := (Test1[I] + Test2[I] + Test3[I] +
                       Test4[I] + Test5[I] + Test6[I]) / 6
    end; {for};
b. Large := -1;
   for I := 1 to N do
   begin
       if Average[I] > Large then
           Large := Average[I]
   end; {for}
   for I := 1 to N do
   begin
       if Average[I] = Large then
           Writeln(Name[I])
   end; {for}
3. e. CountW := 0;
   for I := 1 to N do
   begin
       if Letter[I] = 'W' then
           CountW := CountW + 1
   end; [for]
   PercentW := CountW / N * 100;
   Writeln(PercentW:1:2, ' have withdrawn.');
4. a. for I := 1 to N do
   begin
       Total := 0;
       for J := 1 to 6 do
       begin
           Total := Total + Student[I].Test[J]
       end; {for J}
       Student[I].Average := Total / 6
   end; {for I}
b. Large := -1;
   for I := 1 to N do
   begin
       if Student[I].Average > Large then
           Large := Student[I].Average
   end; {for}
   for I := 1 to N do
   begin
       if Student[I].Average = Large then
           Writeln(Student[I].Name)
   end; {for}
```

```
8. a. type
      String25 = string[25];
      String4 = string[4];
      EmployeeRecordType =
        record
            EmpNumber : integer;
            Name : String25;
            Sales : real;
            Age : integer;
            Sex : char;
            Department : String4;
            Group : integer
        end;
      EmployeeArray = array[1 .. 100] of EmployeeRecordType;
   var
      Employee : EmployeeArray;

b. for I := 1 to 10 do
   begin
       GroupTotal[I] := 0
   end; {for}

   for I := 1 to NEmpl do
   begin
       Subsc := Employee[I].Group;
       GroupTotal[Subsc] := GroupTotal[Subsc]+Employee[I].Sales
   end; {for}

   {For the second part, assume that Lookup looks up employee
   number in list of employee numbers for the employee array}

   Readln(EmployeeNum, Amount);
   I := Lookup(EmployeeNum, Employee, NEmpl);
   if I = 0 then
       Writeln('No such employee')
   else
   begin
       Employee[I].Sales := Employee[I].Sales + Amount;
       Subsc := Employee[I].Group;
       GroupTotal[Subsc] := GroupTotal[Subsc]+Employee[I].Sales
   end; {if}

12. a. procedure CreateEmpty(var S : Stack);
    {. . . comments}
    begin {CreateEmpty}
        S.Top := 0
    end; {CreateEmpty}

b. function IsEmpty(S : Stack) : Boolean;
    {. . . comments}
    begin {IsEmpty}
        IsEmpty := (S.Top = 0)
    end; {IsEmpty}

c. procedure Push(var S : Stack; Item : integer;
                  var Overflow : Boolean);
    {. . . comments}
    begin {Push}
        with S do
```

856 □ ANSWER KEY

```
begin
  if Top = MaxIndex then
    Overflow := true
  else
    begin
      Overflow := false;
      Top := Top + 1;
      Values[Top] := Item
    end {with}
  end {if}
end; {Push}

d. procedure Pop(var S : Stack; var Item : integer;
                 var Underflow : Boolean);
{. . . comments}
begin {Pop}
  with S do
    begin
      if S.Top = 0       {Note: Could call IsEmpty instead}
        Underflow := true
      else
        begin
          Underflow := false;
          Item := Values[Top];
          Top := Top - 1
        end {if}
    end {with}
end; {Pop}
```

13. In the program that follows, we assume that overflow never occurs; you should consider how to remove this restriction.

```
program Reverse(Input, Output);
{. . . comments}
const
  EndOfData = 0;              {Terminal data value}
{. . . type declarations for stack type}
var
  Number : integer;          {Number entered and printed}
  S      : Stack;            {Stack to hold the inputs}
  Error  : Boolean;          {Underflow or overflow}
{. . . subprograms for stack operations, and instructions}
begin {Reverse}
  Instructions;
  CreateEmpty(S);            {Set stack empty}

  repeat
    Write('Enter an integer (0 to stop): ');
    Readln(Number);
    if Number <> EndOfData then
      begin
        Push(S, Number, Error)
      end {if}
  until Number = EndOfData;

  Writeln('The input in reverse order:');

  while not IsEmpty(S) do
    begin
      Pop(S, Number, Error);
      Writeln(' ', Number:5)
    end; {while}

  Writeln;
  Writeln('Reverse program is terminating.')
end.
```

14. b. Note: Consider how using "with" would modify the code.

```
procedure PrintList(List : Integerlist);
{. . . comments}
var
  I : integer;                      {Loop index}
begin {PrintList}
  for I := 1 to List.Length do
    begin
      Write(List.Values[I]:9);
      if (I mod 8 = 0) or         (I = List.Length) then
        Writeln               {Carriage return every 8}
    end {for}
end; {PrintList}
```

d.
```
procedure Concatenate(List1, List : Integerlist;
                      var Answer : Integerlist);
{. . . comments}
var
  I : integer;                      {Loop index}
  J : integer;                      {Supplementary subscript}
begin {Concatenate}
  Answer := List1;            {Copy the first list in}

  J := List1.Length;

  for I := 1 to List2.Length do    {Then the second list}
    begin
      J := J + 1;
      Answer.Values[J] := List2.Values[I]
    end {for}

  Answer.Length := J
end; {Concatenate}
```

15. a.
```
type
  String20 = string[20];
  VoicePartType = (soprano, alto, tenor, bass);
  RangeType = (high, low);
  ChoirRecordType =
    record
      Name  : String20;
      Voice : VoicePartType;
      Range : RangeType
    end;
  ChoirArrayType = array[1 .. 75] of ChoirRecordType;
var
  ChoirMember : ChoirArrayType;
```

b.
```
type
  String10 = string[10];
var
  VoiceName = array[VoicePartType] of String10;
  RangeName = array[RangeType] of String10;

VoiceName[soprano] := 'soprano';  etc.
RangeName[high] := 'first';  {Or you may prefer 'high'}
RangeName[low] := 'second';
```

17. a.
```
function UniqueRandom(Range : integer;
                      Previous : integer) : integer;

{. . . comments}
var
  Number : integer;         {Number generated}
begin {UniqueRandom}

  repeat
    Number := Random(Range) + 1;
  until Number <> Previous;

  UniqueRandom := Number
end; {UniqueRandom}
```

b. This is an easy extension to part a.

c. Hint: Follow parts a and b, but use a lookup function to see whether the Number is a new one or not.

Section 6-3

2. 20 ms

3. 8 sec; 32 sec; 2 min; 8 min; 2 hr

4. $5(2 + 2/\log 60)$ is about $5(2 + 2/6)$, or about 11 sec.
$11(2 + 2/\log 120)$ is about $11(2 + 2/7)$, or about 25 sec.
$25(2 + 2/\log 250)$ is about $25(2 + 2/8)$, or about 56 sec.
$56(2 + 2/\log 500)$ is about $56(2 + 2/9)$, or about 125 sec.
$125(2 + 2/\log 1000)$ is about $125(2 + 2/10)$, or about 275 sec.
$275(2 + 2/\log 2000)$ is about $275(2 + 2/11)$, or about 600 sec.
notice this is 10 minutes compared to 2 hrs. in #3, even though we started out being slower for the small arrays

10. The function below would be originally invoked with a call similar to

    Location := BinarySearch(A, Key, 0, N+1);

where N is the size of the array. How would you modify it to allow the first call to be

    Location := BinarySearch(A, Key, 1, N);

Hint: See exercise 9.
```
function BinarySearch(var A : IntegerArray;
                      Key, Low, High : integer) : integer;
{. . . comments}
var
  Middle : integer;         {Middle of subarray}
begin {BinarySearch}
  if High - Low <= 1 then
    BinarySearch := 0
  else
    begin
      Middle := (Low + High) div 2;
      if A[Middle] = Key then
        BinarySearch := Middle
      else if A[Middle] > Key then
        BinarySearch := BinarySearch(A, Key, Low, Middle)
      else
        BinarySearch := BinarySearch(A, Key, Middle, High)
    end; {if}
end; {BinarySearch}
```

11. 6; 7; 7

14. These can be done as simple adaptations of one of the sorts in the section. For example, we can do part a as follows, using the QuickSort of Figure 6-14.
First, modify the Partition procedure by replacing all reference to A[subscript] by Student[subscript].Average. Second, modify Swap to swap two student records rather than two integers. Third, replace all references to the type IntegerArray by a reference to the student array type.

17. a.
```
procedure Insert(var A : IntegerArray;  Value, N : integer);
{. . . comments}
var
  I : integer;              {Subscript of array}
  SpotFound : Boolean;      {Loop control variable}
begin {Insert}
  SpotFound := false;
  I := N;

  while (not SpotFound) and (I > 0) do
    begin
      if Value > A[I] then
        SpotFound := true
      else
        begin
          A[I+1] := A[I];
          I := I - 1
        end {if}
    end; {while}

  A[I+1] := Value
end; {Insert}
```

b. The number of passes through the while loop will be anywhere from 0 (if the new value is larger than the last element) to N (if the new value is smaller than the first element). On average, we expect it to be about one-half N, which is O(N).

c. Since QuickSort is at best O(NlogN), this solution is not a good one. In fact, we might expect that it would be worse than this because QuickSort is at its worst when the array is already sorted or close to already sorted.

21. b.
```
LastSmall := 1;

for I := 2 to N do
```

```
begin
  if A[I] < A[1] then
    begin
      Swap(A[LastSmall+1], A[I]);
      LastSmall := LastSmall + 1
    end {if}
  end; {for}
```

23. procedure Merge(A, B : IntegerArray; ASize, BSize : integer;
                    var C : IntegerArray; var CSize : integer);
```
{. . . comments}
var
  ASub    : integer;          {Pointer for A array}
  BSub    : integer;          {Pointer for B array}
  CSub    : integer;          {Pointer for C array}
begin {Merge}
  ASub := 1;
  BSub := 1;
  CSub := 1;

while (ASub <= ASize) or (BSub <= BSize) do
  begin
    if ASub > ASize then
      begin
        C[CSub] := B[BSub];
        BSub := BSub + 1;
        CSub := CSub + 1
      end
    else if BSub > BSize then
      begin
        C[CSub] := A[ASub];
        ASub := ASub + 1;
        CSub := CSub + 1
      end
    else if A[ASub] <= B[BSub] then
      begin
        C[CSub] := A[ASub];
        ASub := ASub + 1;
        CSub := CSub + 1
      end
    else
      begin
        C[CSub] := B[BSub];
        BSub := BSub + 1;
        CSub := CSub + 1
      end {if}
  end; {while}

  CSize := CSub - 1
end; {Merge}
```

Section 6-4

11. a. For example, we do the PolyAdd procedure and the PolyDegree function.
```
procedure PolyAdd(P, Q : Polynomial;
                  var Result : Polynomial);
{. . . comments}
var
  I       : integer;          {Loop control}
begin {PolyAdd}
  if P.Degree >= Q.Degree then
    begin
      Result := P;

      for I := 1 to Q.Degree do
        Result.Coeff[I] := Result.Coeff[I] + Q.Coeff[I]

    end
  else
    begin
      Result := Q;

      for I := 1 to P.Degree do
        Result.Coeff[I] := Result.Coeff[I] + P.Coeff[I]

    end
end; {PolyAdd}

function PolyDegree(P : Polynomial) : integer;
{. . . comments}
begin {PolyDegree}
  PolyDegree := P.Degree
end; {PolyDegree}
```

c. Ideally, it should make no difference. The exercise should have been written without any explicit reference to the details of how the polynomials were implemented.

12. Again, we write PolyAdd and PolyDegree.
```
procedure PolyAdd(P, Q : Polynomial;
                  var Result : Polynomial);

{. . . comments}
var
  PSub    : integer;          {Pointer for P}
  QSub    : integer;          {Pointer for Q}
  RSub    : integer;          {Pointer for Result}
  Sum     : real;             {Sum of coefficients}
begin {PolyAdd}
  PSub := 1;
  QSub := 1;
  RSub := 1;

while (PSub <= P.NTerms) or (QSub <= Q.NTerms: do
  begin
    if PSub > P.NTerms then
      begin
        Result.Terms[RSub] := Q.Terms[QSub];
        QSub := QSub + 1;
        RSub := RSub + 1
      end
    else if QSub > Q.NTerms then
      begin
        Result.Terms[RSub] := P.Terms[PSub];
        PSub := PSub + 1;
        RSub := RSub + 1
      end
```

14. a. We assume that NDigits is a global constant for the array size. We also assume that the numbers are small enough not to exceed MaxInt.

```
function Value(Number: DigitArray; Base: integer) : integer;
{. . . comments}
var
    Sum    : integer;    {Sum of digit values}
    I      : integer;    {Loop control}
    Power  : integer;    {Base to current power}
begin {Value}
    Power := 1;
    Sum := 0;
    for I := NDigits downto 1 do
        begin
            Sum := Sum + Number[I] * Power;
            if I > 1 then
                Power := Power * Base
        end; {for}
    Value := Sum
end; {Value}
```

17. a. We assume a Search function with three parameters: the array of records; the ID number to look for; and the current array size. It returns 0 if the ID is not found, otherwise the subscript where it was found.

The code for the procedure body is

```
Subsc := Search(Employees, InquireID, NEmployees);
if Subsc = 0 then
    Writeln('Not found')
else
    with Employees[Subsc] do
        Writeln('Amount = ', Amount:1:2, ', rate = ', Rate)
```

□ CHAPTER 7

Section 7-1

1. X is a 3-by-4 array; X[3][2] is 0; X[2, 4] is 7; X[4, 2] is an illegal reference.

5. a. Suppose that the city name is contained in the variable City of type Cities; Total and Month are of type integer.

```
Total := 0;
for Month := 1 to 12 do
    Total := Total + RainFall[City, Month];
```

6. a.

```
Largest := X[1, 1];
for I := 1 to 21 do
    begin
```

```
else if P.Terms[PSub].Power < Q.Terms[QSub].Power then
    begin
        Result.Terms[RSub] := Q.Terms[QSub];
        QSub := QSub + 1;
        RSub := RSub + 1
    end
else if P.Terms[PSub].Power > Q.Terms[QSub].Power then
    begin
        Result.Terms[RSub] := P.Terms[QSub];
        PSub := PSub + 1;
        RSub := RSub + 1
    end
else {exponents are the same}
    begin
        Sum := P.Terms[PSub].Coeff + Q.Terms[QSub].Coeff;
        if Sum <> 0 then
            begin
                Result.Terms[RSub].Power := P.Terms[PSub].Power;
                Result.Terms[RSub].Coeff := Sum;
                PSub := PSub + 1;
                QSub := QSub + 1;
                RSub := RSub + 1
            end {if}
    end {if}
end; {while}

Result.NTerms := RSub - 1
end; {PolyAdd}

function PolyDegree(P : Polynomial) : integer;
{. . . comments}
begin {PolyDegree}
    if P.NTerms = 0 then
        PolyDegree := 0
    else
        PolyDegree := P.Terms[1].Power
end; {PolyDegree}
```

13. a. procedure Add(A, B : LongInteger; var C : LongInteger;
                        var Overflow : Boolean);

```
{. . . comments}
var
    I      : integer;    {Loop control}
    Sum    : integer;    {Sum of two digits}
    Carry  : integer;    {carry from add}
begin {Add}
    Carry := 0;
    for I := 15 downto 1 do
        begin
            Sum := A[I] + B[I] + Carry;
            C[I] := Sum mod 10;
            Carry := Sum div 10    {There is a carry if sum >= 10}
        end; {for}
    Overflow := (Carry = 1)
end; {Add}
```

```
        for J := 1 to 28 do
          begin
            if X[I, J] > Largest then
              Largest := X[I, J]
          end; {for J}

    end; {for I}
```

d. Assume that the array Large has been declared as a 21-element real array with subscripts running from 1 to 21.

```
for I := 1 to 21 do
  begin
    Large[I] := X[I, 1];

    for J := 1 to 28 do
      begin
        if X[I, J] > Large[I] then
          Large[I] := X[I, J]
      end; {for J}
  end; {for I}
```

g. This can be done without a loop; assume the declarations:

```
type
  RealArray = array [1 .. 28] of real;
var
  X : array [1 .. 21] of RealArray;
  Temp : RealArray;

Temp := X[14];
X[14] := X[19];
X[19] := Temp;
```

h. Assume that we have a Swap procedure for real variables.

```
for I := 1 to 21 do
  begin
    Swap(X[I, 14], X[I, 19])
  end; {for}
```

8. b.

```
procedure MatrixAdd(A, B : MatrixType; var C : MatrixType;
                    var Valid : Boolean);
{. . . comments}
var
  Row : integer;            {Loop index}
  Col : integer;            {Loop index}
begin
  if (A.NumberRows = B.NumberRows) and
     (A.NumberCols = B.NumberCols) then
    begin
      Valid := true.
      C.NumberRows := A.NumberRows;
      C.NumberCols := A.NumberCols;

      for Row := 1 to C.NumberRows do
        begin
          for Col := 1 to C.NumberCols do
            begin
              C[Row, Col] := A[Row, Col] + B[Row, Col]
            end {for Col}
        end {for Row}

    end
  else
    Valid := false
end; {MatrixAdd}
```

13.

```
program Sparse(Input, Output);
{. . . comments}
const
  NumberRows = 10;          {Number of rows of matrices}
  NumberCols = 10;          {Number of cols of matrices}
  EndOfData  = 0;           {Terminating value for rows}
type
  ElementType = integer;
  MatrixType = array [1 .. NumberRows, 1 .. NumberCols]
               of ElementType;
var
  Matrix1  : MatrixType;    {Matrix to read and print}

{procedure Zero—sets an entire matrix to 0}

procedure MatrixRead(var MatrixOut : MatrixType);
{. . . comments}
var
  I : integer;              {Index for rows}
  J : integer;              {Index for cols}
begin {MatrixRead}
  Zero(MatrixOut);          {Set all values to 0}

  repeat
    Write('Enter the row (0 to quit): ');
    Readln(I);
    if I <> EndOfData  then
      begin
        if (I < 1) or (I > NumberRows)  then
          Writeln('*** invalid row, reenter')
        else
          begin
            Write('Enter the column: ');
            Readln(J);
            if (J < 1) or (J > NumberCols)  then
              Writeln('*** invalid column, reenter.')
            else
              MatrixOut[I, J] := 1
          end {if}
      end {if}
  until I = EndOfData
end; {MatrixRead}
```

```
{procedure MatrixPrint, as shown in text, is inserted here.}

begin {Sparse}
   MatrixRead(Matrix1);
   MatrixPrint(Matrix1)
end.
```

16. a. Assume that the square matrix is declared via the global declarations of Number-Rows, NumberCols, ElementType, and MatrixType.

```
function Trace(MatrixIn : MatrixType) : ElementType;
{. . . comments}
var
   I   : integer;               {Loop index}
   Sum : ElementType;           {Accumulator of diagonal}
begin {Trace}
   Sum := 0;

   for I := 1 to NumberRows do
      Sum := Sum + MatrixIn[I, I];

   Trace := Sum
end; {Trace}
```

18.

```
program RandomMatrix(Input, Output);
{. . . comments}
const
   NumberRows = 4;
   NumberCols = 5;
type
   ElementType = integer;
   MatrixType = array[1 .. 4, 1 .. 5] of ElementType;
var
   ThreeDMatrix : array[1 .. 3] of MatrixType;
var
   I, J, K : integer;           {Loop indices}

{procedure MatrixPrint, as shown in text, is inserted here.}

begin {RandomMatrix}
   Randomize;

   for I := 1 to 3 do
      for J := 1 to 4 do
         for K := 1 to 5 do
            ThreeDMatrix[I, J, K] := Random(11) - 5;

   for I := 1 to 3 do
      MatrixPrint(ThreeDMatrix[I])
end.
```

19. a.

```
type
   Months = (January, February, March, April, May, June, July,
             August, September, October, November, December);
   Cities = (Philadelphia, New_York, Washington_DC,
             LosAngeles, Chicago);
```

```
var
   MonthlyRain : array [Years, Cities, Months] of real;
```

b. Assume the above declarations to be global; also assume that the names of the Months and Cities are established in the arrays MonthName and CityName, as in the text.

```
procedure PrintRain(Year : Years; City : Cities);
{. . . comments}
var
   Month : Months;              {Loop index}
begin {PrintRain}
   Writeln('The Rainfall figures for ', Year, ' for ',
             CityName[City], ':');

   Writeln;
   Writeln('   Month', ' ':15, 'Amount');
   Writeln('   -----', ' ':15, '------');

   for Month := January to December do
      begin
         Writeln(MonthName[Month],
                 ' ':20-Length(MonthName[Month]),
                 MonthlyRain[Year, City, Month]:10:2)

      end; {for}

   Writeln
end; {PrintRain}
```

20. a. Two procedures are assumed: Zero to zero the array and GetDate to read a valid date.

```
program Birthdays(Input, Output);
{. . . comments}
const
   EndOfData = 0;               {Terminating value}
var
   Counter : array[1 .. 12, 1 .. 31] of integer;
   Month   : integer;           {Month number}
   Day     : integer;           {Day number}
   None    : Boolean;           {Indicator for no duplicates}
begin {Birthdays}
   Zero(Counter);

   repeat
      GetDate(Month, Day);
      if Month <> EndOfData then
         Counter[Month, Day] := Counter[Month, Day] + 1
   until Month = EndOfData;

   Writeln;
   Writeln('Duplicate birthdays: ');
   None := true;

   for Month := 1 to 12 do
      for Day := 1 to 31 do
         begin
            if Counter[Month, Day] > 1 then
               begin
                  None := false;
                  Writeln('Month: ', Month, '; Day: ', Day)
               end {if}
```

```
  Writeln;
  if None then
    Writeln('No duplicate birthdays.')
  else
    Writeln('All duplicates printed.')
end.
```

Section 7-2

2. a.

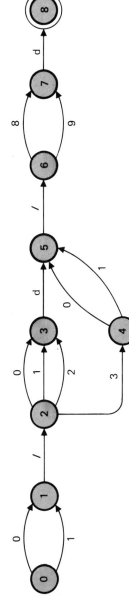

```
function ClassOf(InChar : char) : CharClasses;
{. . . comments}
begin {ClassOf}
  case InChar of
    '0' :  ClassOf := Zero;
    '1' :  ClassOf := One
    else if InChar = Chr(0) then
           ClassOf := EOS
         else
           ClassOf := Invalid;
    end {case}
end; {ClassOf}
```

4. b. In order to use the typed constant concept of Turbo Pascal, we could make the following declarations:
```
const
  PrintName : array [January .. December] of string[10]
    = ('January', 'February', 'March', 'April', 'May',
       'June', 'July', 'August', 'September', 'October',
       'November', 'December');
```

5. a.

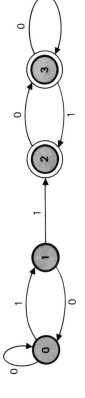

for the state diagram.

```
program Driver(Input, Output);
{. . . comments}
type
  CharClasses = (Zero, One, EOS, Invalid);
  String255 = string[255];

var
  String1  : String255;     {String to check}
  ErrorPos : integer;       {Position of error}
```

```
function Recognizer(InString : String255) : Boolean;
{. . . comments}
type
  LegalStates = (Start, First1, Two1s, MarkTime);
  ActionList = (Stay, BackStart, GoFirst1, GoTwo1s,
                GoMarkTime, Done, Error);
const
  Action : array [LegalStates, CharClasses] of ActionList =
    ((Stay, GoFirst1, Error, Error),
     (BackStart, GoTwo1s, Error, Error),
     (GoMarkTime, Error, Done, Error),
     (Stay, GoTwo1s, Done, Error));

var
  Marker       : integer;       {Current position}
  Finished     : Boolean;       {Termination indicator}
  State        : LegalStates;   {Current state}
  CurrentChar  : char;          {Current character}
  CurrentClass : CharClasses;   {Class of character}

begin {Recognizer}
  InString := InString + Chr(0);   {Append end-of-string}
  Marker := 1;
  Finished := false;
  State := Start;

  repeat
    CurrentChar := InString[Marker];
    CurrentClass := ClassOf(CurrentChar);
```

5. a. 5   **d.** 'ewh'
  b. 2   **e.** 'de'
  c. 0

6. No, not always. If there are not at least nine characters in the string X, then Copy(X, 4, 6) will have fewer than six characters.

12.
```
program Snake(Input, Output);
{. . . comments}
var
Name : string[20];    {User name}
I    : integer;       {Loop index}

begin {Snake}
Write('Enter your name: ');
Readln(Name);

while true do
begin

for I := 1 to Length(Name) do
Writeln(Name[I]:I);

for I := 1 to Length(Name) do
Writeln(Name[I]:(Length(Name)-I+1))

end {while}

end.
```

13. a. The following global declarations are assumed:
```
const
MaxIndex = 100;       {Maximum index of array}
EndOfNames = '';      {Terminating value}

type
String20 = string[20];
NameArrayType = array [1 .. MaxIndex] of String20;
```
Note the use of a special value (EndOfNames, in this case) to indicate the end of the actual data in an array. This special terminating value is assumed to be there.
```
procedure FindNames(Names : NameArrayType;
                    NameToFind : String20);
{. . . comments}
var
I         : integer;    {Array index}
FirstFive : string[5];  {First 5 chars}
FoundNone : Boolean;    {Indicates names found}

begin {FindNames}
FirstFive := NameToFind;
Writeln('Names which match first 5 characters:');
I := 1;
FoundNone := true;

while Names[I] <> EndOfNames do
begin
if FirstFive = Copy(Names[I], 1, 5) then
```

```
case Action[State, CurrentClass] of
Stay :
begin
end;
BackStart :
begin
State := Start;
end;
GoFirst1 :
begin
State := First1;
end;
GoTwo1s:
begin
State := Two1s;
end;
GoMarkTime:
begin
State := MarkTime;
end;
Done :
begin
Finished := true;
ErrorPos := 0
end;
Error :
begin
Finished := true;
ErrorPos := Marker
end;
else
Writeln('System error');
end; {case}

Marker := Marker + 1;
until Finished;

Recognizer := (ErrorPos = 0)
end; {Recognizer}

begin {Driver}
Write('Enter a string: ');
Readln(String1);
if Recognizer(String1) then
Writeln('The string is valid.')
else
Writeln('Invalid at position ', ErrorPos);
end.
```

□ CHAPTER 8

Section 8-1

4. a. 'yzabcde'   **e.** 'ae'
  b. 'no surprise' **f.** 'abyzcde'
  c. 'abde'   **g.** '5'
  d. 'bcd'   **h.** '3'

```
      Writeln(' ':5, Names[I]);
      FoundNone := false
    end; {if}
    I := I + 1
  end; {while}

if FoundNone then
  Writeln('*** no names found which match.')
end; {FindNames}
```

d. Once again, we use a special terminating value to indicate the end of the actual data in an array. The following global declarations are assumed:

```
const
  MaxIndex = 100;                  {Maximum index for array}
  EndOfstrings = '$END';           {Terminating value}

type
  String80 = string[80];
  StringArrayType = array [1 .. MaxIndex] of String80;

procedure MoveEmpty(var Strings : StringArrayType);
{. . . comments}
var
  Bottom : integer;                {Position for next}
  Top    : integer;                {Position of current}
  I      : integer;                {Loop index}

begin {MoveEmpty}
  Bottom := 1;
  Top := 1;

  while Strings[Top] <> Endofstrings do
    begin
      if Strings[Top] <> '' then
        begin
          Strings[Bottom] := Strings[Top];
          Bottom := Bottom + 1
        end; {if}
      Top := Top + 1;
    end; {while}

  for I := Bottom to Top - 1 do
    Strings[I] := ''

end; {MoveEmpty}
```

14. b. In the function below, we use the typed constant feature of Turbo Pascal to initialize the month strings. See Chapter 7 for more information and alternative approaches to the initialization.

```
function Month(NumString : String255) : String255;
{. . . comments}
const
  MonthStrings : array [1 .. 12] of string[3] =
    ('JAN', 'FEB', 'MAR', 'APR', 'MAY', 'JUN',
     'JUL', 'AUG', 'SEP', 'OCT', 'NOV', 'DEC');
var
  Index    : integer;              {Index of array}
  Position : integer;              {Position of invalid}

  Val(NumString, Index, Position);   {Convert to integer}
  if Position <> 0 then
    begin
      Writeln('**** ERROR - bad character in month string');
      Month := '****'
    end
  else
    Month := MonthStrings[Index]
end; {Month}
```

```
function CreateAccount(Name, Initials, City,
                       ExpDate : String255)
                       : String255;
{. . . comments}
begin {CreateAccount}
  Name := Name + ' ';                {3 char must be valid}
  City := City + ' ';                {4th char must be valid}
  CreateAccount := Copy(Name, 1, 3) + Initials + '-' +
                   Month(Copy(ExpDate, 1, 2)) +
                   Copy(ExpDate, 4, 2) +
                   '-' + City[1] + City[4]
end; {CreateAccount}
```

15. a. Suppose that the character variable Ch contains one of the digit characters '0' . . . '9'. Then the numerical equivalent of the digit can be obtained as:

Pos(Ch, '123456789')

If you think this is too "clever," then we could also use the expression:

Pos(Ch, '0123456789') - 1

Section 8-2

1. a.

```
function CountSubstr(Substring, Instring : String255)
                     : integer;
{. . . comments}
begin {CountSubstr}
  if (Substring = '') or (Instring = '') then
    CountSubstr := 0
  else if Pos(Substring, Instring) = 0 then
    CountSubstr := 0
  else
    CountSubstr := 1 + CountSubstr(Substring,
                   Copy(Instring, Pos(Substring, Instring)+1, 255))
end; {CountSubstr}
```

b.

```
function IsBlank(Instring : String255) : Boolean;
{. . . comments}
const
  Blank = ' ';                     {Blank space}
var
  I     : integer;                 {Loop index}
  Found : Boolean;                 {Indicates nonblank found}
```

```
begin {IsBlank}
  Found := false;
  I := 1;
  while (I <= Length(InString)) and (not Found) do
    begin
      if InString[I] <> Blank then
        Found := true
      else
        I := I + 1
    end; {while}
  IsBlank := not Found
end; {IsBlank}
```

e. The function below uses the function LowToUp, which was described in the text.

```
function FindSubst(SubString,InString : String255) : integer;
{. . . comments}
begin {FindSubst}
  FindSubst := Pos(LowToUp(SubString), LowToUp(InString))
end; {FindSubst}
```

2. a.
```
function Reverse(InString : String255) : String255;
{. . . comments}
var
  WorkString : String255;          {Local working string}
  I          : integer;            {Loop index}
begin {Reverse}
  WorkString := '';

  for I := Length(InString) downto 1 do
    WorkString := WorkString + InString[I];

  Reverse := WorkString
end; {Reverse}
```

c. In the function below, there are two chances to be "off by one."
```
function Rpos(SubString, InString : String255) : integer;
{. . . comments}
var
  MirrorPos : integer;             {Position of mirror image}
begin {Rpos}
  MirrorPos := Pos(Reverse(SubString), Reverse(InString));
  if MirrorPos = 0 then
    Rpos := 0
  else
    Rpos := Length(InString) -
            (MirrorPos + Length(SubString) - 1) + 1
end; {Rpos}
```

7. a. We need the local variable for the FilChar procedure to use. The FilChar procedure would not accept Runof in place of WorkString (it would appear as a recursive call to Runof).

8. a.
```
function BigChar(InString : BigString; I : integer) : char;
{. . . comments}
```

```
begin {BigChar}
  if (I > BigLength(InString)) or (I < 1) then
    BigChar := Chr(7)              { beep! }
  else
    BigChar := InString.Character[I]
end; {BigChar}
```

b.
```
procedure BigTrim(InString : BigString; var OutString
                                      : BigString);
{. . . comments}
const
  Blank = ' ';                     {Blank space}
var
  I   : integer;                   {Loop index}
begin {BigTrim}
  I := BigLength(InString);

  while (BigChar(InString,I) = Blank) and (I >= 1) do   {Start at last pos}
    I := I - 1;

  BigCopy(InString, 1, I, OutString)
end; {BigTrim}
```

e.
```
function BigEqual(String1, String2 : BigString) : Boolean;
{. . . comments}
var
  I     : integer;                 {Loop index}
  Found : Boolean;                 {Indicates unequal chars}
begin {BigEqual}
  if BigLength(String1) <> BigLength(String2) then
    BigEqual := false
  else
    begin
      Found := false;
      I := 1;

      while (I <= BigLength(String1)) and (not Found) do
        begin
          if BigChar(String1, I) <> BigChar(String2, I) then
            Found := true
          else
            I := I + 1
        end; {while}

      BigEqual := not Found
    end
end; {BigEqual}
```

10. b.
```
function FirstWord(InString : String255) : String255;
{. . . comments}
const
  Blank = ' ';                     {Blank space}
```

```
var
  BlankPos    : integer;         {Position of blank}
  WorkString  : String255;       {Local working string}

begin {FirstWord}
  WorkString := Reverse(Trim(Reverse(InString)));   { !!! }
  BlankPos := Pos(Blank, WorkString);
  if BlankPos = 0 then
    FirstWord := WorkString
  else
    FirstWord := Copy(WorkString, 1, BlankPos-1)
end; {FirstWord}
```

12. **a.** We assume that if the string has less than 10 characters, then the entire string is to be returned.

```
function Last10(InString : String255) : String255;
{. . . comments}
begin {Last10}
  Last10 := Reverse(Copy(Reverse(InString), 1, 10))
end; {Last10}
```

18. In the function below, we use the typed constant feature of Turbo Pascal. See Chapter 7 for more details or alternative forms of initialization.

```
function Int2Bin(Number : integer) : String255;
{. . . comments}
const
  Digits : array [0 .. 1] of char = ('0', '1');
var
  Quotient   : integer;          {Quotients of Number}
  Remainder  : integer;          {Remainders of Number}
  WorkString : String255;        {Local working string}
  Sign       : char;             {Blank or '-'}

begin {Int2Bin}
  WorkString := '';
  if Number < 0 then
    Sign := '-'
  else
    Sign := ' ';
  Quotient := Abs(Number);

  repeat
    Remainder := Quotient mod 2;
    Quotient := Quotient div 2;
    WorkString := Digits[Remainder] + WorkString
  until Quotient = 0;

  Int2Bin := Sign + WorkString
end; {Int2Bin}
```

□ CHAPTER 9

Section 9-1

1.
```
type
  String30_Ptr = ^String30;
```

```
var
  Name, Address : String30;
  Ptr1, First   : String_30Ptr;
```

2. **a.** if Student1.Roommate = Nil then   {No roommate}
   b. if AnyOne^.Roommate = Nil then   {No roommate}
   c. Writeln(Student1.Name)
   d. Writeln(AnyOne^.Name)
   e. Student1.Roommate := AnyOne

4. **a.** if Head = Nil then   {List is empty}
   b. if Head^.Next = Nil then   {Exactly one - assumes that
                                        Head is not Nil!!}
   c. Temp^.Next := Head;
       Head := Temp;
   j. Temp := Head;

```
while Temp^.Next <> Nil do
  begin
    Temp := Temp^.Next
  end; {while}

with Temp^ do
  begin
    Writeln(Author, ' ', Title, ' ', Year, ' ');
    Writeln(Comment)
  end; {with}
```

k. Assume that Previous and Temp are both pointer variables:

```
Previous := Head;
Temp := Previous^.Next;

while Temp^.Next <> Nil do
  begin
    Previous := Previous^.Next;
    Temp := Temp^.Next
  end; {while}

Previous^.Next := Nil;
Dispose(Temp);.op
```

Section 9-2

3. If we used "New(Create)" and "with Create^ do", the references to Create would be interpreted as recursive calls to the function.

4. Replace the last three lines of the procedure by

```
ListHead := Create(NewQuant, NewItem, ListHead)
```

5. The items read would be added to the front of the existing list.

6. **b.**
```
Ptr := ListHead;
Found := false;

while (not Found) and (Ptr <> Nil) do
  begin
    if Ptr^.Item = Key then
      Found := true
```

```
        else
            Ptr := Ptr^.Next
        end; {while}

    if Found then
        Locate := Ptr
    else
        Locate := Nil
```

11. Assumption: list has at least N elements.
```
function NthItem(Student : StudentArray) : StudentType_Ptr;
{. . . comments}
begin {NthItem}
    NthItem := Student[N]
end; {NthItem}
```

12. Same assumption as Exercise 11.
```
function NthItem(StudentHead: StudentTypePtr): StudentTypePtr;
{. . . comments}
var
    Ptr  : StudentType_Ptr;        {Temporary pointer}
    I    : integer;                {Loop control}
begin {NthItem}
    Ptr := StudentHead;

    for I := 1 to N-1 do
        begin
            Ptr := Ptr^.Next
        end; {for}

    NthItem := Ptr
end; {NthItem}
```

CHAPTER 10

Section 10-1

2. a. 40,320   **b.** 1
   c. 10   **d.** 1

3. 1 11 55 165 330 462 462 330 165 55 11 1

6. a. Yes   **b.** No
   c. Yes   **d.** Yes
   e. No   **f.** Yes
   g. No

7. a. Yes   **b.** Yes
   c. Yes   **d.** No
   e. No   **f.** Yes

8. a. Copy(InString, 3 Length(InString)-2)

15. Twelve chessboards of size 5 by 5 with four nontaking queens in columns 1 to 4:

Ten chessboards of size 5 by 5 with five nontaking queens:

```
10000  00100  10000  00100  00010  00010  01000  01000  00010  01000
00010  10000  00100  10000  00100  00010  00010  10000  10000  00010
01000  01000  00000  00000  00000  00000  00000  00100  00100  10000
00000  00000  00010  00010  00001  01000  01000  00010  00010  00100
00100  00000  01000  01000  10000  10000  10000  00000  00000  00000
```

```
10000  10000  01000  00100  00100  00010  00001  01000  00010  01000
00010  00100  00010  10000  00100  00100  01000  00010  01000  00010
01000  00001  00001  01000  00010  00010  00010  10000  00001  00100
00001  01000  00100  00001  10000  10000  00100  00001  00100  10000
00100  00010  10000  00010  00001  01000  10000  00100  10000  00001
```

18. a. ++456   **b.** +*432
    c. *+33+21   **d.** ++1*234
    e. +1++234

19. a. 6   **b.** 5
    c. 9   **d.** 6
    e. 7   **f.** 5
    g. 35

25. c. The procedure would be invoked with parameters consisting of the present board (OneBoard), the column number in which a queen is to be placed (Column), and the highest column number (MaxRows)

```
if Column > MaxRows then do this:
    print the board (or add it to the solution collection)
otherwise do this:
    for each Row from 1 to MaxRows do these steps:
        see if a queen can be legally placed in that Row for the
            current Column
    if so, then do this:
        place the queen on the present board OneBoard
        invoke SetQueens recursively with parameters:
            OneBoard
            Column + 1
            MaxRows
        remove the queen
```

8. a.

```
function ColumnPosition(Board : ChessBoard; Row : integer)
                        :integer;
{. . . comments}
begin {ColumnPosition}
  ColumnPosition := Pos(Chr(Row), Board)
end; {ColumnPosition}
```

20.

```
program NQueens(Input, Output);
{
  Written by:  XXXXXXXX  XX/XX/XX
  Purpose:     To generate all positions of N nontaking
               queens.

  Procedures used:  PrintBoards - to print chessboards;
                    SetQueens - to find the queen placements.
}
const
  MaxRows = 8;        {Maximum number rows}
  Most = 1000;        {Maximum number solutions}

type
  String255 = string[255];
  ChessBoard = string[MaxRows];        {One chessboard}
  Boards = record
             Number   : integer;
             OneBoard : array [1 .. Most] of ChessBoard
           end;

var
  Solution     : ChessBoard;        {Used to build results}
  AllSolutions : Boards;            {Final result}

{Insert function RowPosition, as given in Figure 10-12}
{Insert function Digit, as given in Figure 10-12}
{Insert function InUse, as given in Figure 10-12}
{Insert function OK, as given in Figure 10-12}
{Insert procedure PrintBoards, as given in Figure 10-12}

procedure SetQueens(Column : integer; var Board
                    : ChessBoard;
                    var AllSolutions : Boards);
{
  Written by:  XXXXXXXX  XX/XX/XX
  Purpose:     To set nontaking queens in cols Column
               through MaxRows of a chessboard that
               has queens in cols 1 through Column-1

  Parameters:  Column - input, column to start with
               Solution - update, chessboard with queens
               AllSolutions - update, set of solutions
  Functions used:  Digit - to convert a number 0 through q
                           to a character '0' through 'q'
                   InUse - to see if a row is in use
                   OK - to check a chessboard
}
var
  Row : integer;            {Loop index}

begin {SetQueens}
  if Column > MaxRows then
    with AllSolutions do
      begin
        Number := Number + 1;
        OneBoard[Number] := Board
      end
  else
    for Row := 1 to MaxRows do
      begin
        if not InUse(Row, Board) then
          begin
            Board[Column] := Digit(Row);
            if OK(Board, Column) then
              SetQueens(Column+1, Board, AllSolutions);
            Board[Column] := '0'
          end {if}
      end {for}
end;  {SetQueens}

begin {NQueens}
  Solution := Copy('00000000', 1, MaxRows);
  AllSolutions.Number := 0;
  SetQueens(1, Solution, AllSolutions);
  PrintBoards(AllSolutions);
  Writeln;
  Writeln('There are ',AllSolutions.Number:1,' solutions.');
  Writeln;
  Writeln('NQueens program is terminating.')
end.
```

□ CHAPTER 11

Section 11-1

1.

```
procedure GetScore(var Score : integer);
{. . . comments}
  const
    High = 100;      {Highest valid value}
    Low = 0;         {Lowest valid value}
  var
    Valid : Boolean;

  begin {GetScore}
    Write('Enter a score (0 - 100):');
    {$I-}                        {Turn off error msg}
    Readln(Score);
    {$I+}                        {Turn on error msg}
    Valid := false;              {Valid value}
```

```
while not Valid do
  begin
    if IOResult <> 0 then
      Write('Not valid integer input.')
    else if Score < Low then
      Write('Score is too low.')
    else if Score > High then
      Write('Score is too high.')
    else
      Valid := true;
    if not Valid then
      begin
        Write(' Re-enter:');        {Turn off error msg}
        {$I-}
        Readln(Score);
        {$I+}                        {Turn on error msg}
      end {if}
  end {while}

end; {GetScore}
```

4. a. In the following program we assume that we have procedures OpenRead and OpenWrite for opening files for reading and writing, respectively.

```
program Toy(Input, Output);
{. . . comments}
type
  String3 = string[3];
  String14 = string[14];
  String20 = string[20];
  IntArrayType = array [1 .. 9] of integer;
  RecordType =
    record
      ItemNumber  : integer;       {4-digit item number}
      ItemName    : String20;      {Name for the item}
      Department  : String3;       {Department code}
      Inventory   : IntArrayType   {Inventories}
    end;
  FileType = file of RecordType;

var
  FileVar1    : FileType;     {File designator}
  FileVar2    : FileType;     {File designator}
  RecordVar   : RecordType;   {Record from file}

{procedure Instructions inserted here.}
{function Exists inserted here.}
{procedure OpenRead inserted here.}
{procedure OpenWrite inserted here.}

begin {Toy}
  Instructions;               {Print instructions}

{*** Open the inventory file.}
  Writeln('Please specify the Inventory file.');
  OpenRead(FileVar1);
```

```
{*** Check for empty file.}
  if eof(FileVar1) then
    Writeln('The file is empty.')
  else

{*** Open the output file.}
    begin
      Writeln('Please specify the Toys file.');
      OpenWrite(FileVar2);

{*** Read input file and write the TOY dept records to
     output file.}
      repeat
        Read(FileVar1, RecordVar);
        if RecordVar.Department = 'TOY'  then
          Write(FileVar2, RecordVar)
      until eof(FileVar1);

{*** Close the output file.}
      Close(FileVar2);
    end;

{*** Close the input file.}
  Close(FileVar1);

{*** Print message and terminate.}
  Writeln;
  Writeln('Toy program terminating.')
end.
```

Section 11-2

1. c. Below are shown the necessary changes in the procedures: Header, Setup, Cleanup, and DetailLine:

```
procedure Header;
{. . . comments}
begin {Header}
  Writeln(ListFile, ' ':26, 'EXPENSE TOTALS');
  Writeln(ListFile, ' ':26, '------- ------');
  Writeln(ListFile)
end; {Header}

procedure Setup(var DeptTotal : real; Department : integer;
                var OldDept : integer);
{. . . comments}
begin {Setup}
  Writeln(ListFile, 'Department Number ', Department, ' ':12,
          'SalesPerson', ' ':7, 'Expenses');
```

```
  DeptTotal := 0;
  OldDept := Department
end;  {Setup}

procedure Cleanup(DeptTotal : real; var Grand : real);
{. . . comments}
begin  {Cleanup}
  Writeln(ListFile);
  Writeln(ListFile,' ':31,'Department Total:',DeptTotal:10:2);
  Writeln(ListFile);
  Grand := Grand + DeptTotal
end;  {Cleanup}

procedure DetailLine(Department, ID : integer;
                     Expense : real; NewGroup : boolean);
{. . . comments}
begin  {DetailLine}
  if NewGroup then
    LineCount := LineCount + 5;
  if LineCount >= MaxLines then
    begin
      Header;
      LineCount := 3
    end;  {if}
  Writeln(ListFile, ' ':35, IDNumber:5, ' ':8, Expense:10:2);
  LineCount := LineCount + 1
end;  {DetailLine}
```

In addition, in the main program, the following two lines should replace the single statement that writes the grand total:

```
Writeln(ListFile);
Writeln(ListFile, ' ':36, 'Grand Total:', GrandTotal:10:2);
```

2. a.

Variable List:

Input:	StudentName	String	Name of Student
	CourseCode	Integer	Course Number
	Grade	Char	Letter grade
Output:	Taken	Integer	Number of courses taken
	Failed	Integer	Number of courses failed
Working:	OldName	String	Name of current student

Algorithm:
print headings
read the first record
do 'setup' steps for first name (includes setting Taken and
   Failed to 0 and setting OldName to first name)
add 1 to Taken
if Grade is 'F', add 1 to Failed
as long as there is any data left do these steps:
  read a record
  if StudentName is different from OldName,
    perform 'change of name' steps ('cleanup', including
           printing Taken and Failed, and 'setup')

add 1 to Taken
if Grade is 'F', add 1 to Failed
after the loop, perform 'cleanup' for the last name

Section 11-3

6. zzzzzzzzzzzzzzzzzzzzz

7. Interchange '<' with '>'. The sentinel value should be 'minus infinity'; for example, −Maxint for integers, AAAAAAAAAAAAAAAAAAAA for names.

10. The problem is that the values for Record1.ID or Record2.ID change as the three if statements are processed in sequence. The following files would not be processed correctly.

File1	*File2*
Infinity	00001
	Infinity

In this case, there would be an attempt to read File1 after the sentinel record had been read. This attempt would likely lead to a run-time error or "garbage" being read. In addition, even without this problem, it would put three "Infinity" records on the output file.

12. a.

```
procedure MergeFiles(var File1,File2,MergedFile : DataFile);
{. . . comments}
var
  Record1  :  DataRecord;    {First file record}
  Record2  :  DataRecord;    {Second file record}

begin  {MergeFiles}

  {*** Prime the loop by reading from both files.}

  Read(File1, Record1);
  Read(File2, Record2);

  {*** Repeatedly compare the keys, process accordingly. }

  while (Record1.ItemNumber <> Infinity) or
        (Record 2.ItemNumber <> Infinity) do
    begin
      if Record1.ItemNumber < Record 2.ID then
        begin
          Write(MergedFile, Record1);
          Read(File1, Record1)
        end
      else if Record1.ItemNumber > Record2.ItemNumber then
```

```
begin
  Writeln('*** bad transaction: ',
          Record2.ItemNumber);
  Writeln('Tap <RETURN> to continue ');
  Readln;
  Read(File2, Record2)
end                              {Delete by not writing}
else
  begin
    Read(File1, Record1);
    Read(File2, Record2)
  end {if}
end; {while}
{*** Put a sentinel record on the output file.}
Write(MergedFile, Record1)
end; {MergeFiles}
```

15. a. copy the transaction record to the new master record
print an error message (adding a duplicate)
print an error message (attempting to delete a record which doesn't exist)
set the new master record empty
print an error message (attempting to change a record which doesn't exist)
perform the change on the new master record

Section 11-4

2. a. The program will use the following procedure in a loop. Deleted is a global constant set to '*' and LastRecord is a global variable set to the last record number of the file.

```
procedure Lookup(var FileVar : FileType;
                 AccountNumber : integer);
{. . . comments}
var
  RecordVar  : RecordType;          {Record from the file}

begin {Lookup}
  if (AccountNumber < 0) or (AccountNumber > LastRecord) then
    Writeln('*** Invalid account number.')
  else
    begin
      Seek(FileVar, AccountNumber);
      Read(FileVar, RecordVar);
      if RecordVar.Name = Deleted  then
        Writeln('*** Account has been deleted.')
      else
        WriteRecord(RecordVar)
    end
end; {Lookup}
```

c.
```
procedure Display(var FileVar : FileType);
{. . . comments}
var
  I         : integer;              {Loop index}
  RecordVar : RecordType;           {Record from file}
```

```
begin {Display}

  for I := 0 to FileSize(FileVar)-1 do
    begin
      Read(FileVar, RecordVar);
      if RecordVar.Name <> '*'  then
        Writeln('Record number: ', I:3, ' - Account name: ',
                RecordVar.Name)

    end; {for}

end; {Display}
```

4. Use the first check number on file (in the control file) to provide an adjusted record number for the seek statement as follows:

Seek(FileVar, current check number − first check number)

5. a.
```
type
  String14 = string[20];
  RecordType =
    record
      LastName : String20;
    end;                             {Employee's name}
  IndexRecordType =
    record
      RecNum : integer;              {Record number}
      Name   : String20              {Name record}
    end;
  FileType = file of RecordType;

var
  FileVar   : FileType;              {File designator}
  Index     : array[1 .. 1000] of IndexRecordType;
  RecordVar : RecordType;

OpenRead(FileVar);
J := 0;

for I := 0 to FileSize(FileVar)-1 do
  begin
    Read(FileVar, RecordVar);
    if LastName <> '*'  then
      begin
        J := J + 1;
        Index[J].RecNum := I;
        Index[J].Name := RecordVar.LastName;
      end {if}
  end; {for}

NumberActive := J;
```

7. a. The program uses the following procedure after the two files are opened. After the procedure terminates, the two files are closed.

```
procedure Display(var ControlVar : text;
                  var FileVar : FileType);
{. . . comments}
var
  First     : integer;              {First record number}
  RecordVar : RecordType;           {Record from the file}
```

```
begin {Display}

{*** Get the first record number.}

   Read(ControlVar, First);

{*** Check for empty file.}

   if First = -1 then
      Writeln('*** The file is empty.')
   else

{*** Read and display the file in alphabetical order.}

      begin
         Seek(FileVar, First);
         Read(FileVar, RecordVar);
         WriteRecord(RecordVar);

         while RecordVar.Next <> -1 do
            begin
               Seek(FileVar, RecordVar.Next);
               Read(FileVar, RecordVar);
               WriteRecord(RecordVar)
            end {while}

      end
end; {Display}
```

8. a.

Key	Record number used
1403	3
1695	5
1138	8
5689	9
4122	2
8904	4

b.

Key	Record number used	
1403	3	
1795	5	
1138	8	
2014	4	
1183	6	(tried to spill to 4 and 5)
8998	9	(spilled from 8)
3114	7	(tried 4, 5, and 6)

c.

Key	Record number used	
1403	3	
1795	5	
1138	8	
2014	4	
1183	6	(tried to spill to 4 and 5)
8998	9	(spilled from 8)
3114	7	(tried 4, 5, and 6)
9000	0	
8615	1	(tried 5, 6, 7, 8, 9, and 0)
4029	2	(tried 9, 0, and 1)

d.

Key	Record number used	Number of probes
1403	3	1
1795	5	1
1138	8	1
2014	4	1
1183	6	4
8998	9	2
3114	7	4
9000	0	1
8615	1	7
4029	2	4

INDEX

* (as wildcard, MS-DOS), 786
* (set intersection), 370, 804
* (multiplication), 13, 38, 803
+ (concatenation), 43, 803
+ (set union), 370, 803
+ (addition), 13, 38, 803
− (set difference), 370, 803
− (subtraction), 13, 38, 803
/ (division), 13, 38, 803
:= operator, 13, 36, 794
< operator, 64, 384, 803
<= operator, 64, 384, 803
<> operator, 22, 64, 384, 803
= operator, 64, 384, 803
> operator, 64, 384, 803
>= operator, 64, 384, 803
^ symbol (pointer), 625, 801

A

Abs function, 84
Absolute value, 84
Access:
   direct, 719
   sequential, 719
Accumulation, 159
   testing, 174, 254
Accumulator, 159
Action statement, 12
Action table (FSA), 545, 552
Actual parameter, 259, 795. *See also*
      Parameter; Argument
Actual size (of an array), 194, 215

Addition, 13, 38, 803
   matrix, 533
Algebraic methodology, 655
Algorithm, 3, 17
   array, 429, 434
   random-access file, 750
Algorithm analysis, 701
Aliasing, 634
Analogy, 654
Analytic methodology, 655
And, 101, 803
Antibugging, 27, 248
Apostrophe:
   as a char value, 42
   within the string literal, 43
ArcTan function, 95
Argument, 85, 133, 259. *See also*
      Parameter
Argument list:
   syntax diagram, 795
Arithmetic operator, 38, 86
Array, 191, 425, 526, 801
   algorithm, 429, 434
   of arrays, 526
   assignment, 437
   declaration, 195, 427, 449
   element, 804
   as a list, 191
   more than two dimensions, 538
   the need for, 425
   parallel, 450, 452
   as parameter, 216, 263
   potential size, 215
   of records, 368, 450

109H